Origin and Progress of Seventh-day Adventists

AMS PRESS
NEW YORK

THE THREEFOLD MESSAGE OF REVELATION 14

"I saw another angel fly in the midst of heaven, having the everlasting gospel to preach unto them that dwell on the earth, and to every nation, and kindred, and tongue, and people." Rev. 14: 6.

A HISTORY OF THE

ORIGIN AND PROGRESS

OF SEVENTH-DAY ADVENTISTS

BY M. ELLSWORTH OLSEN

"Looking for that blessed hope, and the glorious appearing of the great God and our Saviour Jesus Christ." Titus 2: 13.

"Unto them that look for Him shall He appear the second time without sin unto salvation." Heb. 9: 28.

REVIEW AND HERALD PUBLISHING ASSOCIATION

TAKOMA PARK, WASHINGTON, D. C.

South Bend, Indiana   Peekskill, New York

Printed in the U. S. A.

125355

Reprinted from the edition of 1925, Washington D.C.

First AMS edition published in 1972

Manufactured in the United States of America

International Standard Book Number : 0-404-08423-0

Library of Congress Catalog Card Number: 76-134375

AMS PRESS INC.
NEW YORK, N.Y, 10003

To All Those Who Love His
Appearing

THE WORD OF GOD

"Sanctify them through Thy truth: Thy word is truth." John 17:17.

Contents

INTRODUCTION

CONTENTS 7

FAITH AND OBEDIENCE
"The commandments of God, and the faith of Jesus." Rev. 14 : 12.

Preface

THE plan of this book will be clear to the reader who takes up the various chapters in their order. While writing the history of Seventh-day Adventists, the author has tried to see the denomination in its proper setting, as intimately associated with, and indeed having its origin in, a reform movement which from feeble beginnings has attained widespread development, and is encircling the world. With the end in view of recording the growth of a religious movement rather than that of a denomination as such, emphasis has been placed on the work in its various phases and developments rather than upon the men and women by whom it has been carried on. Moreover, it is with the work in its pioneer stages rather than as a finished product that the narrative is chiefly concerned.

The early chapters recount the first feeble beginnings in the Eastern States, followed by the move to the Middle West, and the subsequent expansion farther west and south. Thereafter chapters are inserted from time to time, telling of the plan of organization and the rise and growth of institutions connected with the movement. Otherwise the work in America receives but little further attention; the narrative moves on to other lands, these being taken up in the order in which they are entered. Here, again, the narrative does not tarry long at any one point. When the work is well under way in a given country, it passes on to other countries.

Following this general plan has involved some omissions. Men carrying large responsibilities in countries where the work is in its more advanced stages may not be dealt with, while others of even less experience may receive mention as pioneers in a new field. This plan has been followed, however, because it most nearly gives the sense of life and motion which belongs to the onward march of a great religious movement. It has seemed wise to forego completeness in the matter of names to make possible a more life-like and adequate account of the movement.

The materials for the book have been gathered from the official records, and from a variety of contemporary publications, including the back volumes of the *Review and Herald*. The writer has some first-hand acquaintance with the work in this country and in various parts of Europe. For his knowledge of the mission fields he has depended largely on interviews with our leading missionaries at the sessions of the General Conference and a considerable correspondence with others in the field. The materials received in this way, and in some cases through other missionary publications, have been freely used, with only slight adaptations as to language, the aim being to present the life of the missionaries with as much vividness as possible.

It is a privilege to mention by name some of the friends and coworkers but for whose assistance this book could not have attained even its present stage of completeness. The first name shall be that of A. G. Daniells, at whose suggestion the work was undertaken in the first place, and from whom much valuable counsel has been received. W. A. Spicer has not only placed at the disposal of the writer his own extensive reports and other writings on the missionary enterprises of the denomination, from which much material has been drawn for that portion of the book; but he also took time to read the entire manuscript, and to offer valuable criticisms. F. M. Wilcox and E. R. Palmer have given freely of their time and energies to forward the interests of the book, the latter having personally supervised the selection and preparation of the illustrations. While they were alive, S. N. Haskell and J. N. Loughborough did everything in their power to assist the writer in his researches. W. E. Howell, C. W. Irwin, and Frederick Griggs have given timely help in educational matters, and have taken an interest in the progress of the work as a whole. W. W. Prescott and M. E. Kern have offered valuable suggestions based on a reading of the first draft of the manuscript. L. R. Conradi has given welcome aid in gathering materials for the chapters on the beginnings in Europe. W. C. White, Clarence C. Crisler, and J. Vuilleumier have furnished first-hand materials of value. C. Sorenson and J. N. Anderson have offered practical suggestions from the point of view of the use of the book in the classroom. C. P. Bollman has given a critical reading to the manuscript, and has offered many helpful suggestions. H. E. Rogers has aided materially in the statistical portions of the book. Dr. H. E. Thompson, of the Advent Christian Publication Society, has kindly read the chapters dealing with he work of William Miller and his associates. Miss Mary A. Steward supervised the literary editing and proof-reading, and prepared the index.

There are many others who have furnished information, contributed letters and photographs, and in other ways given of their best that the history might attain to some measure of success. To all these, hearty thanks are rendered, both for their actual help and for the willing spirit which prompted it.

Let it be said in closing that the author is deeply sensible of the incompleteness necessarily associated with a work of this kind, and enhanced in the present instance by his own obvious limitations. He asks the kind forbearance of the reader for any mistakes that may have crept in unawares, and invites the co-operation of all friends and well-wishers in the effort to improve later editions.   M. E. OLSEN.

PETER PREACHING AT PENTECOST

"Repent, and be baptized every one of you in the name of Jesus Christ for the remission of sins, and ye shall receive the gift of the Holy Ghost." Acts 2 : 38.

THE GIFT OF THE HOLY GHOST

" Ye shall receive power, after that the Holy Ghost is come upon you: and ye shall be witnesses unto Me . . . unto the uttermost part of the earth." Acts 1 : 8.

Introduction

Section I — The Apostolic Church

THE history of a denomination is best understood when viewed in its relation to church history as a whole, and especially to that history in its earlier stages. It will be helpful, then, before considering in detail the events which make up the history of the advent movement, to take a brief survey of the apostolic church. This will enable us to get our bearings, as it were, and be qualified to pass intelligent judgment upon the various questions of doctrine and belief that will come before us. Such a course of action is the more necessary because Adventists are in no true sense of the word innovators. The truths they stand for are old and fundamental, taught by all the holy apostles and prophets, and their aim has been to free themselves from later accretions and attain as far as possible to the simplicity and purity of apostolic times.

An outstanding characteristic of the apostolic church, as we view it in the light of the brief record given in the book of Acts, is the extreme simplicity of its doctrines, its organization,

11

and its manner of work. The doctrines were Christ-centered. The members believed in Jesus for the forgiveness of sin and acceptance with God. They were justified by faith in His vicarious death on the cross; they were saved by His life. The law of God as revealed in the Old Testament Scriptures was not set aside. It was holy, just, and good, and could convince of sin; but it could not save the sinner. There was only one name under heaven whereby men could be saved.

THE GOSPEL COMMISSION
"Go ye into all the world, and preach the gospel to every creature." Mark 16:15.

The simple message preached by the early church, and adapted to the needs alike of Greek and Jew, was the message of the everlasting gospel, and was based on Scripture. In manifesting this loyalty to the written word, the apostles but followed the Master's own example, for of Him it is recorded that "beginning at Moses and all the prophets, He expounded unto them in all the Scriptures the things concerning Himself."

The Scriptures were held in the highest esteem by all Christians, and were final authority. Peter and Paul and the other apostles offered no new doctrines; they based their teaching on the Scriptures of that day, namely, the Old Testament. Of course, they viewed the Sacred Writings of old in the light of Christ's life and teaching; which was but letting the light of an inspired life shine upon an inspired book. Christ came to fulfil, not to destroy; and His disciples followed in His footsteps. The Levitical priesthood and its ordinances passed away with the arrival of that higher reality to which they had pointed forward; but God's great moral law, which lies at the foundation of His government of the universe, could not pass away, being in its nature unchangeable and eternal.

The organization of the apostolic church was both simple and effective. There were two kinds of officers,— elders (or

THE BAPTISM OF CHRIST
He that believeth and is baptized shall be saved." Mark 16 : 16.

bishops) and deacons, the former having the spiritual oversight of the church, and the latter taking charge of its temporal affairs, such as the distribution of funds to the poor.

Church government was on the democratic order. When it seemed desirable to select a successor to fill the place of Judas, the apostles called for an assembly of the believers, and in their presence and with the help, no doubt, of their counsel, two were put forward, one of whom was to be selected by lot. Again, when it became necessary to appoint officers to take the oversight of caring for the poor, we read that "the twelve called the multitude of the disciples unto them," and laid the matter before them. Of a spiritual hierarchy, such as was developed

THE CROSS OF CHRIST

" And I, if I be lifted up from the earth, will draw all men unto Me." John 12:32.

14

later, there is no hint in these records of the church in its pristine purity. The elders of the local churches and the evangelists who traveled from place to place while laboring in word and doctrine, formed a spiritual brotherhood in harmony with the divine instruction, "All ye are brethren;" "one is your Master, even Christ."

But while there was equality of rank among those who ministered the word in the early church, this did not lead to independent action. The records that have been handed down are

THE RESURRECTION OF CHRIST

"I am the resurrection, and the life: he that believeth in Me, though he were dead, yet shall he live." John 11 : 25.

extremely brief; but enough is said to show that the Christians of that day had a conception of the church as being one body in Christ, and realized from the beginning the value of mutual co-operation in the work of giving the gospel to the world.

The spirit of unity was very marked in the early days at Jerusalem. "When the day of Pentecost was fully come, they were all with one accord in one place." Of the waiting time it is recorded: "These all continued with one accord in prayer and supplication, with the women, and Mary the mother of Jesus, and with His brethren." Nor did this unity continue only while the believers were confined to a few. After the original number had been greatly increased, and thousands had been

THE ASCENSION OF CHRIST

" This same Jesus, which is taken up from you into heaven, shall so come in like manner as ye have seen Him go into heaven." Acts 1 : 11.

gathered into the church, we read: "The multitude of them that believed were of one heart and of one soul."

As the work grew, and churches were organized in various parts, the same spirit of unity which prevailed among the individual members of a church, bound the several churches together in one common brotherhood. The work was felt to be one the world over, and counsel was taken together that there might be unanimity of plan and intelligent co-operation throughout the great harvest field.

Thus it was that questions of general policy were decided only after some general consensus of opinion had been arrived at. When Gentile converts began to be made, the question naturally arose, "Shall they be required to observe the Mosaic law?" The church at Antioch did not attempt to decide the matter independently, but sent Paul and Barnabas to Jerusalem to confer with the leaders in the work, who appear to have made that city their headquarters. When the question had been presented and fully discussed, a conclusion was arrived at, which was then communicated to the Gentile churches, and by them accepted.

Later experiences recorded by Paul show him in the midst of his arduous labors in behalf of the Gentiles of various nationalities, always retaining a fervent love for his brethren in Jerusalem, and putting himself at times to considerable trouble in order to cement the bonds of friendship between the Gentile churches that he had raised up and the large body of believing Jews in Palestine. To his success in these efforts to maintain essential unity of spirit on the part of the two leading branches of the Christian church, must be attributed, in large measure, the magnificent growth and world-wide missionary activity of the church of his day.

That this unity was spontaneous, growing out of belief in a common faith and loyalty to a common Master, is evident both from the Scripture records and from the writings of the earliest of the church Fathers. It was not till the church had lost its essentially spiritual mold that its officers began to assume powers and prerogatives belonging properly to the great invisible Head, and to act arbitrarily on their own authority instead of counseling with the body of the believers, as in the early days.

This brings us naturally to the consideration of a third outstanding feature of the apostolic church; namely, its essential separation from the world. Not only were its doctrines based on Scripture, and its polity a direct outgrowth of the teaching

2

EVER PRESENT
" Lo, I am with you alway, even unto the end of the world."   Matt. 28 : 20.

of Christ, but its whole character was such as to place it in strong contrast with institutions of human origin. The eyes of its members were essentially upward, their " conversation " (i. e., their whole manner of life) was in heaven, whence they expected shortly to receive their blessed Saviour.

The church of those early days was wholly a spiritual institution; it was in no sense political or secular. Its sole weapon was the Word of God, its propaganda being the preaching of that Word. Its apostles went forth as sheep among wolves. They sought not the aid of princes, but trusted alone in the power of an Almighty God.

The members of the church were mostly from the so-called lower classes. In the words of Paul, " Not many wise men after the flesh, not many mighty, not many noble, are called." And James asks: " Hath not God chosen the poor of this world rich in faith, and heirs of the kingdom which He hath promised to them that love Him? " There was nothing in the new faith to commend it to the mere man of the world. Christians were, in the eyes of such, an obscure, despised sect, followers of a humble Nazarene who had been executed as a malefactor.

Moreover, the early Christians did not in any way attempt to court the smiles of the world. They were uncompromising in their denunciation of idolatry in every form, and they refused to join in the popular amusements. " Haters of mankind," they were called, because of their unwillingness to indulge in the diversions which were affected by the populace of that day; but they showed their fervent love for mankind by excelling in all manner of works of mercy.

While the early Christians were hated of the world, they loved one another with a fervid devotion. Not seldom did they suffer death rather than inform against one another. Their meetings for prayer and worship were well attended, though the believers often came at the risk of their lives. They could not refrain from coming together to testify to their joy in the service of their Lord, and to cheer and encourage one another to be firm even unto death.

These meetings were held in private houses, and were of a social character, the various members contributing to the edification of one another. " When ye come together," writes Paul, " every one of you hath a psalm, hath a doctrine, hath a tongue, hath a revelation, hath an interpretation. Let all things be done unto edifying."

Spiritual gifts were a prominent feature of these gatherings. The sick were often healed through the prayer of faith. The gift of tongues was manifested at different times, and likewise the prophetic gift. These miraculous manifestations were for the edification of the church, and also for a sign to unbelievers.

The family life of the early Christians was full of beauty. The wife, no longer the slave of her husband, took her rightful place by his side, as his life companion, and a colaborer in the responsible work of training their children for the kingdom. The teaching of the Scriptures, that the relation of the husband to the wife is that of Christ to the church, invested marriage with new beauty and mystery, and withal gave it a sacred character.

The instruction of the children was carefully attended to. At first this could be carried on only in the individual Christian home. Somewhat later schools were conducted in connection with the various churches. The result of this care and solicitude was seen in the firm attitude of the children when confronted with the command to offer incense to the emperor or be thrown to the wild beasts. The calm fortitude of these child martyrs was a source of wonder and amazement to pagan rulers; but their parents saw in it the answer to their prayers.

The members of the apostolic church loved their departed Lord with an intensity of devotion which words fail to express. Their religion in a very real sense centered in His person, and it was accounted apostasy not to sigh for His return. Their life was one of constant expectation. Their sacred rites pointed forward to the great consummation. Baptism was symbolic of death to sin, and resurrection to a new life. The Lord's supper, celebrated in remembrance of their Lord, reminded the believers of His temporary absence; but it also pointed forward to His return in glory, for it was to " show the Lord's death *till He come*."

The intense missionary zeal of the early church grew out of its personal devotion to the Saviour. The preaching was clearcut and definite, and as a result the heathen turned from their idols " to serve the living and true God; and to wait for His Son from heaven." The believers of those days had their affections set on things above. They did all things with a view to the near return of their Lord, and the setting up of His kingdom. Their life was full of joyous expectancy; and in place of the worldly pleasures which they had cheerfully foregone, they had a peace and a joy passing knowledge, which the world could not take away.

Section II — The Great Apostasy

"THE theologian may indulge the pleasing task," writes Gibbon, "of describing Religion as she descended from heaven, arrayed in her native purity. A more melancholy duty is imposed on the historian. He must discover the inevitable mixture of error and corruption which she contracted in a long residence upon earth, among a weak and degenerate race of beings."—"*Decline and Fall of the Roman Empire,*" *Vol. I, chap. 15, par. 2.*

An outstanding fact confronts us as we enter upon an investigation of the later history of the Christian church: the changes introduced into the doctrines and polity of the church were largely in the nature of compromise. The Christians of apostolic times were not at all inclined to pander to worldly interests, or to yield one jot of the system of truth committed to them. They regarded their life upon earth as a pilgrimage; all their thoughts and desires were heavenward, and their crowning ambition was to reign with Christ above. Later Christians lost sight of these pure, unworldly aims and high spiritual ambitions, and came to look on the church chiefly in its external aspect. They coveted power and influence in the world, and were willing to purchase them at the loss of purity and holiness. They saw that by yielding some points they could gain the adherence of large numbers of the most influential people, and they yielded the points.

The spirit of compromise first revealed itself in corrupting the doctrines of the Christian church. These had in early days been marked by great simplicity, in which they differed alike from the highly elaborated teachings of the rabbis and from the fine-spun theories of heathen philosophers. They gradually underwent a process of elaboration, intended to make them more acceptable to the philosophically inclined among the new converts.

The fundamental conception of salvation by faith gave way by degrees to the old erroneous idea that man could be saved by his own good works. To begin with, there was a classification of sins, some of which were to be regarded as venial, and thus easily forgivable; others as mortal, not to be forgiven at all, or only by special divine favor. It followed that persons who were guilty of what had been classified as mortal sins must needs do something very extraordinary to show that they were truly repentant. Hence the introduction in its earliest forms of the idea of penance.

Corresponding closely with the classification of sins, there was a classification of good works. Some were required of all Christians; others were not required, but if attained to, were evidence of special piety. Thus it was possible for a man to attain to a higher degree of holiness than was necessary for

THE GREAT COMPROMISER

"It is probable that he [Constantine] embraced Christianity, not entirely from conviction, but partly from political motives. As the historian Hodgkin puts it, 'He was half convinced of the truth of Christianity, and wholly convinced of the policy of embracing it.'"— *Myers.*

salvation. By doing a certain amount of praying, fasting, and almsgiving, he would be entitled to a place in heaven; what he did more than this would be regarded as works of supererogation, that is, works that went beyond the divine requirements.

The belief in this doctrine of supermeritorious works led in time to the notion that these works were the property of the church, and could by her be dispensed for the benefit of such of her children as stood in need of them. Still later it came to be considered proper for the church to dispense such favors to any one she pleased, and for a monetary consideration. Thus was gradually built up, as a superstructure on this foundation of salvation by works, the whole system of indulgences,[1] that fruitful source of so many and monstrous evils in the medieval church.

The notion of supermeritorious works depended for its full development and exploitation on another error that early crept

THE ARCH OF CONSTANTINE

into the Christian church; namely, the doctrine that the soul is an entity entirely apart from the body, and that when the body dies, the soul enters upon a separate state of existence, in which it continues until the time of the resurrection. The belief in natural immortality had prevailed more or less widely in the heathen world for centuries. It received its full development as a philosophic tenet at the hands of Plato, whose main teachings, in a modified form and under the name of the Neoplatonic

---

[1] "An indulgence is the extra-sacramental remission of the temporal punishment due, in God's justice, to sin that has been forgiven, which remission is granted by the church in the exercise of the power of the keys, through the application of the superabundant merits of Christ and of the saints."—" *The Catholic Encyclopedia,*" art. " *Indulgences,*" *Vol. VII, p. 783,*

philosophy, were largely introduced into the teachings of the church in the third century.

THE SACRED STAIRWAY IN ROME

When ascending this stairway on his knees, Luther heard, as it were, the words which later became the rallying call of the Reformation, "The just shall live by faith."

The conception of an intermediate state opened the way, humanly speaking, for a satisfactory solution of another problem which had confronted the theorists. Origen, meditating on the greatness of sin and the feebleness of man's attempts to free himself from it, came to the conclusion that no human being at the time of death was so entirely free from sin as to be fit for immediate entrance into heaven. He accordingly taught that the disembodied souls, even of the best men, must undergo purification by fire. At first it was believed that this purification took place at the resurrection; later it was referred to the intermediate state, or purgatory.

Along with the belief that the dead were in this intermediate state, undergoing necessary purification from sin, there naturally followed prayers for the dead. And from praying for the dead the custom arose of beseeching their prayers in behalf of the living. Thus entered the doctrine of the invocation of saints, which in time came largely to supersede prayer to God.

The falling away of the church from apostolic simplicity in the matter of government and discipline was simultaneous with the decline of spirituality, and the progressive changes in doctrines and worship that have just been mentioned. The primitive order, as recorded in the previous section, provided for only two classes of church officers,— bishops, or elders (presbyters), to whom the spiritual interests of the churches were especially intrusted; and deacons, to whom pertained the temporal affairs. Besides these officers, there were persons endowed with special gifts, as the gift of tongues, of healing, of prophecy, and these had a share in the spiritual upbuilding of the churches.

As time went on, and the tendency grew to regard the church chiefly in its external aspect,— as a human institution calculated to achieve certain ends, and officered with men who possessed the requisite talents for leadership,— these gifts disappeared, and simultaneously with their withdrawal increased emphasis came to be placed upon the office of bishop, which in the absence of the aforementioned gifts seemed to sum up in itself all that was most sacred and holy in ecclesiastical relationships.

As the cause continued to grow, and the administrative cares of the bishops increased, it became necessary to select for the office men of pronounced executive ability, and spiritual attainments came to figure less and less as requisite to the holding of important office in the church. Especially was this true in the case of the men selected to fill the office of bishop in the large cities. Moreover, the prestige of these men as leaders naturally led their brother bishops of outlying districts to look to them for advice and counsel, and in time it became a custom, and then a duty, for them to do this.

Another element that tended to magnify the office of bishop was the outbreak, in very early times, of heresies. Jerome mentions this as a chief reason for the change in church polity. "With the ancients," he says, "presbyters were the same as bishops, but gradually all the responsibility was deferred to a single person, that the thickets of heresies might be rooted out."

The outbreak of heresies had as another of its results the shaping of a hard-and-fast theological creed for the church, and this likewise tended to increase the responsibility of the episcopal office, for it fell to the bishops, as the superior officers of the church, to formulate the creed, and enforce adherence to it. Christianity as a living, vitalizing power, entering into and transforming the lives of its converts, was losing its hold on the heart, and its advocates sought to strengthen it by stating with theological exactness those transcendent truths which could be adequately expressed only in the language of inspiration. They did not rest content with this, however, but added doctrines and conceptions of human origin. Thus while the shaping of a theological creed had for one of its objects to guard against certain heresies, the actual result was to perpetuate other errors of an equally serious character by incorporating them into the authoritative teachings of the church.

The conception of the minister of the gospel as a priest, which made its first appearance at the close of the second century, and gradually became a part of the accepted theology of the day, was a powerful aid in the building up of the hierarchy. It was derived partly from heathen sources, and partly from the old Mosaic economy; but its effect was to draw a plain line of demarcation between the clergy and the laity, and to make of no effect the New Testament teaching that all the believers are priests and kings before God.

Only one thing was lacking to make complete the powers and prerogatives of a hierarchy already so powerful; namely, recognition by the state. This final step was taken during the reign of Constantine, early in the fourth century. Already in the year 313 that famous prince had issued an edict tolerating Christianity as one of the approved religions. Ten years later, in 323, he made it the established faith of the empire. At the same time he took over its bishops, for all practical purposes, as officers of the crown, and thenceforward they bore the honors and were subjected to the limitations which belong to such a relation.

That these ecclesiastics speedily learned subservience to the earthly ruler who had chosen them to be his representatives, and plied him with the most fulsome flattery, is a well-known fact; but it need not be dwelt upon in this connection. Neither need we inquire into the sincerity of Constantine's profession of religion. What is important to note is that the relationship thus established between Christianity and the state was in itself radically wrong. The Christian church, as set forth in the New Testament, is essentially a spiritual institution; its membership is composed of those who are spiritually alive, and its true and only head is the Lord Jesus Christ. Not only does the church not need state patronage; it cannot receive such patronage without denying the relation which it properly sustains to its divine Head.

One of the immediate results of making Christianity the religion of the state, was the influx of a large number of converts who became Christians, not because of any real assent to the doctrines, but because it was the popular thing to do. They took the outward form of Christianity, but remained at heart idolaters. Naturally they demanded means of satisfying the cravings of their unregenerate hearts, and the bishops, themselves influenced greatly by the new conditions which had grown out of a connection with the state, yielded to the demand. The conclusion was reasonable that if Christianity was to be the official religion, it must supply something in the way of substitutes for the extremely popular and very numerous festivals devoted to the worship of false gods, in which free rein was given to the indulgence of appetite and passion. Such substitutes were found in the martyrs' birthdays, which had already become occasions of considerable pomp and circumstance, and in response to the new demand, soon partook, in all essentials, of the character of heathen festivals.

The observance of Christmas as a Christian festival had its origin in the Roman Church about the middle of the fourth century. Of the reasons for its institution and the date finally adopted, Neander has the following to say:

"Precisely in this season of the year, a series of heathen festivals occurred, the celebration of which among the Romans was, in many ways, closely interwoven with the whole civil and social life. The Christians on this very account were often exposed to be led astray into many of the customs and solemnities peculiar to these festivals. Besides, these festivals had an import which easily admitted of being spiritualized, and with some slight change transformed into a Christian sense. . . .

"That Christian festival which could be so easily connected with the feelings and presentiments lying at the ground of the whole series of pagan festivals belonging to this season, was now, therefore, to be opposed to these latter; and hence the celebration of Christmas was transferred to the 25th of December, for the purpose of drawing away the Christian people

THE POPE OF ROME

SAINT PETER'S AND THE VATICAN PALACE

from all participation in the heathen festivals, and of gradually drawing over the pagans themselves from their heathen customs to the Christian celebration. This view of the matter seems to be particularly favored in a New Year's Discourse by Maximus, bishop of Turin, near the close of the fourth century, where he recognizes a special divine providence in appointing the birth of Christ to take place in the midst of the pagan festivals; so that men might be led to feel ashamed of pagan superstition and pagan excesses."
—" *General History of the Christian Religion and Church*," *Augustus Neander, Vol. III, pp. 441-443.*

Another institution of pagan origin which grew up about the same time and under similar conditions, is the observance of Sunday as a day of worship, rest, and recreation. Apart from the popularity of the day as more or less connected with the ancient sun worship, there was this added advantage that its adoption afforded a point of departure from the custom of the Jews, against whom there existed considerable prejudice on the part of the early Christians. Moreover, the day was the more acceptable as being associated with the resurrection.

The adoption of heathen festivals, though in itself a wide departure from apostolic usage, has its chief significance as being symptomatic of a generally prevailing worldliness in the church, a turning away from the path of self-denial and loyalty to Scriptural truth which the Saviour had plainly marked out for His followers. It was in part due to this prevailing worldliness in the church that conscientious but misguided men withdrew into the wilderness in the hope that they might there serve God more acceptably, and follow a higher ideal of personal holiness than was considered necessary for the average Christian. Such persons in time congregated together, and bound themselves by vows of honesty, chastity, and obedience to superiors. Thus were originated the numerous and powerful monastic institutions which were too often hotbeds of fanaticism, and promoters of those abuses which have so marred the history of the church.

The writings of Augustine, who was the most widely known and influential of all the Fathers of the Western church, were a powerful factor in laying the foundations of what was to become the medieval church. He had entered the church after devious wanderings in the mazes of philosophy, and some of his philosophical ideas, among them the Platonic notion that matter is in itself evil, and necessarily opposed to spirit, had considerable influence in shaping his theology. It led him very naturally into spiritualizing away the definite promises concerning the second coming of Christ and the setting up of His kingdom. On the other hand, with strange inconsistency, but in harmony with his alert, practical Roman mind, he expatiated freely over the powers and prerogatives of the church upon earth.

His notable work, " The City of God," contains the first full
setting forth of the idea of the Christian church as a great external institution fit to be compared in its organization and manner of working with the imperial city itself.   The book includes
a noble defense of Christianity, and abounds in passages of great
eloquence and beauty; but its conception of the Christian church
is fundamentally different from that of the New Testament.   It
appeared shortly after the city of Rome had been sacked by the
Visigoths under Alaric, and seemed to foreshadow a career for

THE DAYS OF PERSECUTION

the Christian church which was to outshine in power and splen-
dor the glories of ancient Rome.

Needless to say, such a conception largely ignored the supreme spiritual character of the church, and substituted a human theory of the advent hope.   It deprived the church of the
upward look which had been so characteristic of the early disciples.   The Christian's citizenship thereafter was upon earth,
not in heaven.   The bride no longer waited for her returning
Lord.   The fires of joyful expectation, that had shone so
brightly during the dark hours of persecution, burned low and
went out.   The advent hope, so far as the visible church was
concerned, well-nigh perished from the earth.

It is unnecessary to continue the history of the church as it
plunged deeper and deeper into apostasy.   All the elements that

contributed to its downfall were at work already in the fourth
century, and even the crying abuses that precipitated the Reformation of the sixteenth century were established in principle
a thousand years before they aroused the righteous indignation
of a Luther.

The development of the papacy is sometimes accused of being the chief cause of the downfall of the Christian church; but
rightly understood the papacy itself must be regarded as a symp-
tom rather than as a cause. The growth of that remarkable
institution may be traced in the various steps by which the
Bishop of Rome attained the chief place among the bishops; but
it had its beginning in the false conception of the church which
calls for a visible head.

As long as the advent hope was cherished in every Christian
heart, as long as it was considered apostasy not to sigh for the
return of the Lord, such a thing as a papacy was inconceivable.
The primacy of Christ leaves no room for the primacy of Peter.
But when the church comes to be regarded as a human organization, one which may fitly succeed to the powers and privileges
of the great seven-hilled city, and rule over the world, then it
no doubt requires a human head, and then it can also use any
number of ambitious, designing underheads. Once grant the
validity of the conception held forth in Augustine's memorable
work, and all the rest follows as a matter of course.

Yet the medieval church was not wholly bad; it was a mixture of good and evil. Had it not retained in some measure its
original power to satisfy the longings of the human heart, it
would have ceased to be. Men arose now and then from the
bosom of a corrupt church who showed a rare degree of spirituality and of devotion to the highest ends. But the very power-
lessness of these men to achieve lasting reforms grew out of the
fact that the fundamentals were wrong. In fact, their efforts
to do good resulted in some cases in aggravating the evil.

The origin of the friars is an interesting one. Francis of
Assisi, the founder of the Brothers Minor, later known as Fran-
ciscans, was undoubtedly a man of high aims and noble character. His immediate followers partook largely of his spirit;
they supported themselves by working with their hands, they
ministered to the needs of the poor, waited on the sick, including the despised and forsaken lepers, and they carried the gospel message to heathen lands. But even before the death of
Francis changes had been effected in government and discipline
which led the way to rapid deterioration. Another century, and
the Franciscan friars had become the curse of Europe. Domi-

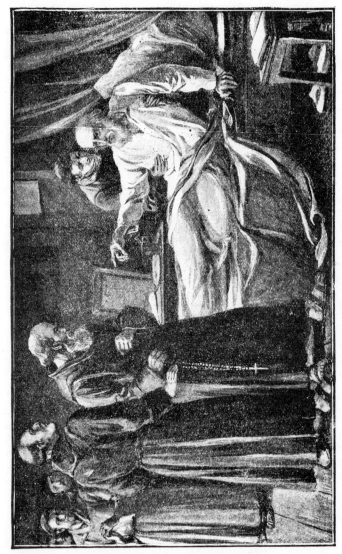

WYCLIFFE AND THE FRIARS

"I shall not die, but live, and again declare the evil deeds of the friars."

nic, the founder of the other order, started out with the intention of supplying preachers for the untaught masses; but his followers in time became chiefly known as the founders and supporters of that most cruel and oppressive of all persecuting agencies, the Inquisition.

The stream could not rise higher than its source. As long as the church stood for doctrines and ideals largely of pagan origin, and emphasized outward conformity to ritual and creed to the neglect of personal holiness, it mattered not how many of its children sought to reform it, or to hold up a higher standard of living for its professed members. Real reform had to come from a return to the Holy Scriptures as the one perfect guide to faith and morals, and it could mean nothing less than the utter overthrow of an apostate church.

Section III — Luther and His Forerunners

THE Reformation of the sixteenth century was a movement of large dimensions, including a number of more or less diverse elements; but it was at heart a reaffirming of the fundamental truths of Christianity, primarily the doctrine of righteousness by faith. It took issue with the medieval church on the great question, " How shall a man be just before God? " For centuries the answer had been: " Man must earn his salvation by his good works." Luther announced in trumpet tones, " The just shall live by his faith."

The Reformation, moreover, was not only a restatement of the fundamental Christian doctrines, but it was a restatement of those doctrines based on the teaching of Scripture. Moved by the new impulse, men turned away from the Fathers, the councils, the church, and the pope, and acknowledged adherence alone to the inspired Word.

These general characteristics belonged not only to the Reformation of the sixteenth century, but also to the movements of less widespread power and influence which may be called its forerunners. Among the most remarkable of these was the Celtic church. This had its home in Ireland, one of the earliest countries of Northern Europe to come under the influence of Christianity; but it had a very full development also in Scotland, and we know most of its doctrines and organization as seen in the little isle of Iona under the leadership of the saintly Columba. This Celtic church, in part, at least, as we find in

3

later times, observed the seventh day of the week as the Sabbath; it reckoned the time for Easter according to the method of the primitive church, and not as ordained by Rome; and it claimed for itself the spiritual independence that belongs to every Christian church, and the right to send out its missionaries everywhere, regardless of papal authority.

The leaders of the Celtic church did not lord it over the people, nor assume the rights and prerogatives claimed by the members of the Roman priesthood. The whole spirit of the early British Christianity was contrary to the spirit of Roman Catholicism. History tells us that the ministers of the Celtic church in Britain were surprised and amazed at the domineering spirit manifested by Augustine and his associates when they came over from Rome near the close of the sixth century, and began their work on the island.

Premature Protestants, these Celtic Christians have been called; but as a writer in the Schaff-Herzog Encyclopedia observes, it would be nearer the truth to connect them directly with the primitive church, and say that " as the twilight lasts so much longer in these northern regions, so also the afterglow of the primitive day was lengthened out there, when darkness was coming on apace elsewhere." The teachers of the Celtic church, the same writer continues, " retained a singularly living hold of the central doctrines of the gospel, and above all, of the evangelistic commission given by the Great Head to His church." — *Schaff-Herzog Encyclopedia, Vol. II, art. " Keltic Church," p. 1236, edition 1891.* Indeed, the missionaries sent out by these early Britons penetrated to many parts of Europe, and were everywhere distinguished alike by the purity of their doctrines and the warmth of their apostolic zeal.

It is, however, to the English Lollards of the fourteenth century, under the leadership of Wycliffe, that we are to look for complete and far-reaching reforms in the doctrines and polity of the church previous to the Reformation of the sixteenth century. John Wycliffe was master of Balliol College, Oxford, and rector of Lutterworth. He came into prominence first as the defender of the rights of England against the attempted encroachments of the papacy. He was then about forty years of age, and had spent a quarter of a century as student and teacher at Oxford University. His learning was varied and profound, and included a thorough knowledge of Roman law as well as of English jurisprudence, and in dialectical skill he was second to none. The forceful way in which he argued against the papal encroachments won him the hearty support of the king and

Parliament, and increased his already great prestige at the university.

Had Wycliffe rested content with opposing the payment of tribute money to Rome, he might have retained the almost unanimous support of Englishmen of that day; but a larger work lay before him. God was leading him onward by a path he himself knew not. As he studied more deeply into the character of the papacy and its claims to universal rule, he was led to see how far it had departed in spirit and methods from the apostolic church, and he began to speak out boldly against the cor-

MEETING IN THE FIELDS

ruption that was everywhere manifest. The greed and avarice of the clergy he unsparingly denounced, as well as the idle, useless lives of the friars.

The doctrines of the Roman Church he also came to see were largely of human origin. He utterly rejected the papal teaching concerning the way to become righteous. He pointed out the needlessness of invoking the aid of the saints. " Christ," said he, " ever lives near the Father, and is the most ready to intercede for us." The doctrine known as transubstantiation,— the teaching that the priest has the power to change the bread and wine of the communion into the real body and blood of the Lord, — he opposed with all the power of his keen intellect. His bold stand against this fundamental error lost him some of his friends among the nobility and in the university, and brought on him

THE BURNING OF HUSS

MEMORIAL MARKING THE PLACE AT CONSTANCE WHERE
HUSS AND JEROME WERE BURNED

the denunciation of the pope. Being forbidden to preach at the university, he withdrew to the living of Lutterworth, where he continued to write and to preach against the corruption in the church.

While Wycliffe sought to destroy what was false, he labored to build up the true, and he was indefatigable in his efforts to teach the gospel to the people. He was called the evangelical doctor. The standard of faith with him was the Holy Scriptures. He refused to accept any other authority for religious doctrine.

With the withdrawal of the support of the nobility, Wycliffe was led to make his appeal more and more to the people. In order to instruct them in the principles of the gospel, he organized bands of itinerant preachers, who addressed the crowds at market places, in the fields, or wherever they could get a hearing, teaching the saving truths of the gospel as set forth in the Word of God.

To instruct these preachers, and to assist them in their work of unfolding the gospel principles to the common people, Wycliffe, with the help of a learned friend, translated the entire Bible into the English of his day. This great achievement was accomplished only a few years before a stroke of paralysis put an end to the busy activities of the great scholar. It did more than anything else to spread abroad in Great Britain the light of primitive Christianity. And although a few years later, in the early part of the fifteenth century, the Word of God was put under the ban, being forbidden to the people under pain of death, and the very bones of Wycliffe were exhumed and burned and scattered on the waters of the Swift, yet the work thus nobly begun never could be stopped; the Bible, once rendered into the mother tongue, continued secretly to circulate among the people till by the labors of Tyndale in the sixteenth century, with the aid of the printing press, the Word of God was literally sown throughout the land.

Wycliffe's work reached farther than England. His Oxford pupils carried his doctrines back to the Continent. His writings also circulated outside of Great Britain, and in course of time there grew up at the University of Prague, in Bohemia, a group of earnest men who adopted the Wycliffe reforms in their entirety. The foremost men in this movement were Huss and Jerome, both of whom were faithful unto death, laying down their lives for the gospel.

While the rest of Europe was in darkness, the Waldenses, living in the fruitful valleys of the Italian Alps, maintained for many years a church polity and system of doctrines based on the Scriptures. Their colporteurs carried portions of the Scriptures to various parts of Europe, and thus they were gradually preparing the way for the Reformation of the sixteenth century.

Martin Luther, the leader in the great Reformation, was the son of a miner of Eisleben, in Saxony. He received his preparatory training in the schools of Magdeburg and Eisenach, entering Erfurt University, then one of Germany's leading centers of learning, at the age of eighteen. At the university he applied

GATEWAY TO THE WALDENSIAN VALLEYS

himself especially to the study of literature and philosophy. One day, while looking over the books of the library, he came across a Latin Bible. It was the first time he had seen the book, his previous knowledge of the Scriptures having been confined to the meager portions read at public worship. He had then been at the university for two years. The book proved wondrously attractive to his eager mind, and again and again he left his assigned work in the classic authors to turn its sacred pages, and muse over the sublime truths therein contained.

Meanwhile he continued his regular university studies with great success, receiving the degree of Bachelor of Arts in 1502, and three years later the degrees of Master of Arts and Doctor of Philosophy. It was his father's intention that he should take up the study of law, but Luther's mind was drawn toward the church. Ever since he made the acquaintance of that Latin Bible he had yearned for a deeper religious experience. The thirst for knowledge had given way, in large part, to the thirst for holiness. He was prepared to sacrifice all earthly prospects in order to be right with God. To do this in those days meant to be a monk. Luther accordingly entered the Augustinian monastery at Erfurt.

LUTHER IN THE LIBRARY AT ERFURT

The time he could claim as his own was devoted to a diligent study of theology. Especially fruitful were the hours spent in poring over a Latin Bible chained in the library of the monastery. But though he read the divine Word, it was for a time with eyes strangely holden by preconceived notions, so that it did not yield him, to begin with, the peace and comfort which he so earnestly sought. Oppressed with a feeling of his unworthiness, and of his inability to attain to that perfect holiness demanded by the law, he went to confession daily, and practised the severest mortifications, so that he seriously undermined his health. But it availed nothing. He was obliged to acknowledge to himself that entering the monastery and performing punctiliously all the duties incumbent upon a monk had not in the least degree changed his nature, nor had it rendered him one whit less guilty in the sight of a perfectly holy God.

In this time of crisis, God raised up a friend for Luther in the person of the vicar-general of the Augustinian order, John Staupitz, one of the remarkable men, sometimes called mystics, who remained connected with the Roman Church at the same time that they held and taught distinctly evangelical views. Staupitz encouraged Luther by telling him that the severe trials and conflicts through which he was passing were probably intended as a preparation for some future work God would intrust to his hands. He advised him, moreover, to put away the philosophy of the schools, and derive all his theology from the Holy Scriptures. Little did the pious mystic realize how implicitly his advice would be followed, or what tremendous consequences would ensue.

After Luther had been two years in the monastery, he was ordained to the priesthood. A year later he was called to teach at the new University of Wittenberg. He first lectured on philosophy, which was not particularly to his taste, but early in 1509 he took the degree of Bachelor of Theology, and began to lecture on the Holy Scriptures.

In the year 1511 Luther had the privilege of visiting Rome, being sent thither to attend to some matters connected with the order. He journeyed on foot, as the custom was, lodging by night at the various monasteries on the way, and as he neared the " eternal city," he was surprised and shocked at the dissolute conduct that prevailed in the Italian establishments. At Rome he piously sought out all the objects of reverence, believing every marvelous tale. But his conscience was greatly disturbed over the unblushing worldliness of priests and monks.

On returning to Wittenberg, Luther was made Doctor of Theology, and began to preach, first in the chapel attached to the monastery, and later in the city church. His preaching was founded on the Word of God; it was intensely practical, and bore fruit in a general quickening of the religious life of the community.

The atmosphere of the university underwent a great change. The philosophy of the Schoolmen, which had helped to hold Europe in intellectual bondage for so many generations, gave way to the quickening influence of an enlightened evangelism. The Word of God was magnified. The psalms of David, the Gospels, and the epistles of Paul once more imparted to men their life-giving message. The whole region round about Wittenberg was permeated with the teaching, and conditions approaching the simplicity and fervor of the early church began to prevail.

Then came the inevitable break with Rome. The immediate occasion was a particularly shameless application of the doctrine of indulgences. Leo X was desirous of completing the cathedral of St. Peter's on a magnificent scale, and resolved to obtain the necessary means by a sale of indulgences in Germany. He appointed a commission of three men to have charge of the work, Albrecht, archbishop of Magdeburg and Mayence, being chief. Albrecht in turn appointed, as the man to push the business for him, John Tetzel, a Dominican monk, who was thoroughly unscrupulous, but possessed of all the secrets of popular oratory. His entry into a city was marked by the official ringing of bells, and by a procession of the populace led by priests and magistrates, who came out to welcome him with pomp and ceremony.

Marching into the cathedral to the sound of music, Tetzel would set up a great red cross before the altar, and over it display a banner with the papal arms. In front of this banner his men would then place the capacious iron money chest. Thereupon ascending the pulpit, the wily demagogue would commend his wares with all the extravagance of an auctioneer. His claims were preposterous, blasphemous. The red indulgence cross, with the pope's armorial bearing, was equally efficacious, he said, with the cross of Christ. He would not be willing to exchange places in heaven with St. Peter himself, for he had saved more souls with his indulgences than the apostle had saved by his preaching. When any one cast money into the box for a soul in purgatory, the soul would fly up to heaven as soon as the coin tinkled at the bottom.

Already in the year 1516 Luther had had his attention called to this infamous traffic, and had preached a sermon against it. But when, in the autumn of 1517, Tetzel began to sell his wares at Jüterbock, in the near vicinity of Wittenberg, and Luther's own parishioners were induced to buy them, then the iniquity of the whole thing was very forcibly brought home to the heart of the faithful pastor, and he lifted his voice in warning and protest. In a series of stirring sermons he expounded the fundamental principles of the divine forgiveness of sin. He showed that without true repentance indulgences could avail nothing; that a money payment could not open the doors of purgatory to a single soul; and that the other claims put forth by the unscrupulous venders were unscriptural and actually blasphemous.

LUTHER'S PROTEST AGAINST INDULGENCES

He followed these sermons by posting on the door of the castle church in Wittenberg ninety-five Latin theses in which he gave formal expression to his protest against the iniquitous traffic, and the wrong principles which underlay it.

With the posting of the theses the Reformation began. Written in Latin, and intended primarily for scholars, they were quickly translated into German, and in a few weeks were being read and discussed throughout the country. Events moved rapidly for Luther after that. Tetzel brought forth counter theses, which he defended before a body of admiring monks. Sylvester de Prierio, also a Dominican, and a man of far greater learning than Tetzel, entered the lists in behalf of the indulgences. Both men based their arguments on the unique authority of the pope. He had authorized the sale; therefore it was right.

Luther, in defending his position, was thus led to consider the powers and prerogatives of the head of the papacy. He came to the conclusion that the pope might err; that he was really subject to the church councils; therefore his approval could not justify the traffic. In the debate with John Eck, which was held at Leipzig, Luther took his stand finally on the Holy Scriptures as the sole authority in all questions of faith. From that time he stood as a rock for the great fundamental principles of the gospel.

Meanwhile his enemies were active. Pope Leo X, a scholar and a man of liberal instincts, was at first inclined to make light of the matter. But when the cause of reform began to show its strength, he became alarmed for the future of the church, and determined to crush the monk who had dared to question his authority. Luther was accordingly ordered to present himself at Rome within sixty days to meet the charge of heresy, and Frederick, the elector of Saxony, Luther's friend and sovereign, was commanded to hand over this " child of the devil " to the papal legate. A hearing in Rome would necessarily lead to the condemnation and probably to the death of the Reformer. Frederick knew this; he accordingly secured, by diplomatic means, the concession that the monk should be tried on German soil.

As time went on, the conflict took a broader scope. Luther very well knew that his life was at stake, but his courage never failed, and his literary activity was tremendous. The year 1520 saw no less than fifteen books and pamphlets from his pen. Three of these, sometimes known as his " Primary Works," are deserving of special mention. The first is addressed " To the Christian Nobility of the German Nation," and is a searching arraignment of the papacy, first, in view of the errors upon

LUTHER BEFORE THE DIET AT WORMS

which it is founded, and secondly, in view of the robbery and oppression that marked its career in Germany.

In his second important work of this year, entitled, "Concerning Christian Liberty," Luther makes a clear statement of fundamental evangelical principles. He asserts the supreme authority of the Scriptures, and teaches that justification is by faith alone, and that good works are not a means of securing pardon, but a fruit of the new life.

LUTHER BURNING THE POPE'S BULL

The third important work of the year, entitled, "On the Babylonish Captivity of the Church," is perhaps the most radical of the three. In it he utterly rejects the fundamental claims of Rome, and declares the papacy to be none other than the kingdom of Babylon. He denies that there are seven sacraments. Moreover, he points out that the true sacraments, such as baptism and the Lord's supper, require faith on the part of those who are to benefit by them.

About the middle of the year 1520 the pope issued a bull against Luther, citing forty-one alleged errors of doctrine selected from his printed works. The Reformer replied with a tract entitled, "Against the Bull of Antichrist," and on December 20 he publicly burned the bull in the presence of a great

TRANSLATING THE BIBLE

LUTHER'S MONUMENT AT WORMS

crowd of professors and students. He also committed to the flames a copy of the canon law, a body of laws upholding the power of the pope. On the day following the burning of this bull, Luther solemnly warned his students against the errors of Roman Catholicism, telling them that if they did not earnestly oppose the wicked government of the papacy, they could not be saved.

By this time all Germany was astir, and indeed Luther's teachings were the theme of discussion outside of Germany. The

LUTHER'S ROOM IN THE WARTBURG CASTLE

Reformer was finally commanded to appear before the Imperial Diet at Worms to give an account of his teaching. He was in poor health at the time, but he determined to obey the summons. At the gate of Worms he encountered a greater crowd than had welcomed the emperor. The scene in the diet chamber, with one lone monk confronting that imposing array of kings and princes and dignitaries of the church, has been pictured many times. It was the beginning of modern history, especially of modern freedom of thought. In fact, it marked a new era in the annals of the human race.

Luther's brief but memorable address is worthy of careful study, for it is fundamental to an understanding of what the

Reformation really was. He was asked if he would retract. He replied that he would retract such parts of his writings as could be shown to be contrary to God's Word; otherwise he could retract nothing. Thus in a moment were brushed aside tradition, the teachings of the Fathers, the canon law, the decisions of popes and councils, while the Word of God was magnified.

The rest of the chapter may be told in few words. As he journeyed away from Worms, Luther was captured by loyal

BIRD'S-EYE VIEW OF THE CITY OF SPIRES

friends, and carried to the castle of Wartburg, where he was kept for nearly a year following the Diet of Worms. For some months neither friends nor enemies knew his whereabouts, and some mourned him as dead. The words of Albrecht Dürer, the great artist, are significant of the impression that the Reformer had made upon his countrymen. "O God," he exclaimed, "if Luther is dead, who else can expound the holy gospel to us?" Very fruitful were the quiet months at the Wartburg. They witnessed the completion of Luther's translation of the New Testament into German. The precious volume was published shortly after the Reformer's return to Wittenberg.

He then applied himself diligently to the preparation of a German rendering of the Old Testament. It, too, had been completed by 1534. When the Bible was in the hands of the German people, Luther had done his work; every one knew then that the Reformation had come to stay. The Protest of the Princes, the Confession of Augsburg, the Religious Peace of 1555, which left the princes free to choose between Lutheranism and the papacy,— these were events of importance, but they do not in real significance compare with Luther's act in giving the German people the Bible in their own tongue. The Reformation of the sixteenth century began in the heart of a young university student when he first made regular visits to the Latin Bible in the library of the University of Erfurt. It was brought to triumphant completion when that Bible was placed within the reach of every German who was able to read.

Section IV — Later Reformers

LUTHER was the chosen instrument for the accomplishment of a great reform in the Christian church. He had qualities of leadership that made him eminently fitted to head a movement away from Rome. But he did not finish the work. It was too much to expect of one man. In the providence of God, other men were called to carry to fuller development the work that he had so nobly begun.

In England the most noteworthy Reformers of the sixteenth and seventeenth centuries were the Puritans. Their leaders were largely men who had been on the Continent, and were familiar with the views of Luther. There were various branches of the sect, but they may be roughly divided into two main classes,— the Puritans proper and the Independents. The former, while holding views in advance of their time, did not distinctly dissociate themselves from the Church of England; the latter had convictions that made it impossible for them to yield allegiance to a state-imposed religion.

Both branches had much in common. Thus Puritans and Independents alike objected to the ritual and the prayer book, holding that they presented features which were unscriptural, and in fact remnants of Romanism. They held that compelling ministers of the gospel to officiate in vestments was contrary to Christian liberty. The English church seemed to them a nondescript body, consisting for the most part of persons whose Christianity was merely nominal. They pleaded for apostolic simplicity and apostolic zeal, and they exemplified both in their lives.

4

THE "MAYFLOWER"

A PURITAN SERVICE ON DECK BEFORE LANDING

The Independents had the conviction that reform would be impossible while religion continued to be an affair of state patronage. They accordingly withdrew, and formed companies of their own. The so-called Brownists,[1] who received the designation from having a pastor of that name, first went to Holland, but afterward chartered the ship " Mayflower " and sailed to America. Others followed them. A great many remained in England and endured persecution. In 1662, when the Act of Uniformity was passed, requiring every minister, and also every head master of a school, to declare publicly his adherence to the " Book of Common Prayer," two thousand ministers gave up their positions rather than obey the law.

The general spirit and attitude of the Puritans is well illustrated in the life of the poet John Milton. A man of the broadest culture, a finished scholar, a profound theologian, he yet stands out most prominently as the stanch defender of liberty, political and religious, and of the Bible as the Christian's sole rule in matters of faith. Loyalty to the Word of God is a marked characteristic of all the writings of Milton, even those not dealing directly with religion. In a controversy with the learned Usher, he summarily swept aside all his opponent's arguments drawn from the Fathers. The archbishop, he said, is not " contented with the plentiful and wholesome fountains of the gospel, as if the divine Scriptures wanted a supplement, and were to be eked out . . . by that indigested heap and fry of authors called antiquity." He then affirmed " that neither traditions, councils, nor canons of any visible church, much less edicts of any magistrate or civil session, but the Scripture only, can be the final judge or rule in matters of religion, and that only in the conscience of every Christian to himself."— *Quoted in " History of the Baptists," by Thomas Armitage, pp. 544, 545.*

· It will be noticed that on the question of infant baptism Milton occupied ground in advance of the generality of Puritans; in fact, he seems to have held precisely the same convictions as the Baptists.

Let us consider briefly the origin and development of this much-derided sect, formerly known by the name Anabaptists, and try to ascertain what part it was called to act in carrying to further completion the great reforms inaugurated by Luther.

The Baptists were opposed to a state church, and to religious doctrines and rites prescribed by law. Religion was to them

---

[1] All Pilgrims were Brownists, but only a few of the Brownists became Pilgrims. The Brownists were those Puritans who, espousing the views of Robert Browne, refused all compromise with the Established Church, and went into voluntary exile in Holland for the double purpose of securing freedom of worship and escaping wearing persecution. They were those of whom King James said, " I will make them conform, or will harry them out of the kingdom."

essentially a spiritual thing, consisting not so much in outward ceremonies as in having the heart right with God, and enjoying daily fellowship with Him.   In harmony with this opposition to external churchism, was the Baptist view of justification,— that it really involved sanctification; that is, that the sinner does not profit by the justifying blood of Christ unless his attitude to sin is such that it can be seen that the Holy Spirit is having His sanctifying influence on the life.   Baptists were essentially pleading for a church not dependent on the support of the elector of Saxony or the landgrave of Hesse, and not containing within its fold all persons, young and old, who happened to live within the dominions of that particular prince.   Their conception of the church was of a company of persons who had experienced conversion, and were living daily in the power of a new life. Moreover, like the Puritans, the Baptists objected to ceremonies performed and doctrines taught by the Lutheran Church which they deemed not in harmony with the Scriptures.

Luther, on the other hand, though in parts of his numerous writings he enunciates great spiritual truths and seems even to teach some of the fundamentals the Baptists endeavored to proclaim, never did attain to a complete and consistent view of the church and its activities as a thing apart from the state.   He left Rome, but he did not wholly dissociate himself from papal principles.   He dispensed with the pope, but practically put in the place of the pope the reigning sovereign.   His ideas in this respect were those of his time.   He saw that measure of truth which could be understood by the generality of the people of that day, and he obtained a large following and did a great and good work.

The Baptists saw beyond their time, and suffered severe persecution at the hands of both Lutherans and Romanists.   Their message was rejected by the masses of the people, but it was joyfully received by those whose hearts God had prepared. There was no German state or principality that adopted the Baptist belief, and no German prince stood up at Spires and said, " I and my people will be Baptists; " but it may be truly said of this people, as of the Christians of apostolic times, that in their hands the word grew and multiplied, and God " added to the church daily such as should be saved."

If it be asked, " What spirit did the Baptists manifest toward their persecutors? " the answer must be, " The spirit of Christ." The Baptists of those days, even as judged by their enemies, are admitted to have been simple, inoffensive people, adorning by their lives the great Scriptural truths for which they stood so firmly. The words of John Denk, pastor of the Baptist church of Augsburg, well represent the attitude of the whole denomination toward its persecutors:

"Love forgets itself, and the possessor of it minds no injury which he receives for the sake of the object of his love. The less love is recognized, the more it is pained, and yet it does not cease. Pure love stretches out to all, and seeks to be at one with all. But even if men and all things are withdrawn from her, she is so deep and rich she can get along without them, and would willingly perish herself if she could thereby make others happy." — *Id., p. 405.*

There was also a notable reform movement within the Lutheran Church, known as Pietism. Philipp Jakob Spener, the founder and chief exponent of the movement, was born at Rappoltsweiler, upper Alsace, in 1635. His early university training was chiefly at Strassburg, where he took his master's degree in 1653. After some years spent in travel and study at other centers of learning, he accepted the position of assistant preacher at the cathedral in Strassburg. Here he continued his studies, taking the doctor's degree in theology in 1664.

Spener's real life-work began when he was called in 1666 to the pastorate of a large Lutheran church in Frankfort. Here his heart was deeply stirred as he saw the low spiritual condition of the great majority of his parishioners, and he set about preaching in a direct, simple style, expounding the practical truths of the Bible, and applying its precepts to the daily lives of his people. In the summer of 1669 he preached a notable sermon on " The Vain Righteousness of the Pharisees," in which he showed that a person could attend church regularly, receive the sacraments, profess belief in all the articles of the creed, and yet not be in a saved condition.

The sermon brought about a division in the church. From that time on the awakened ones, those who wished to walk in all the light of God's Word, met Spener at regular times in his home, and were there instructed more fully in the principles of the consecrated life. These meetings, called by Spener the *collegia pietatis,* and conducted in a very free and informal manner, were the parent of the class meeting of Methodist times and of the prayer and social meeting of today. They proved so helpful in building up the spiritual life of the community that they were started in other places, and in time were being held in many different parts of Germany.

In the year 1675 Spener published his epoch-making book, " Pia Desideria," which, with the *collegia pietatis,* may be said to have laid the foundations of Pietism. The book first passes in review the Christianity of the time, showing how far short it comes of the divine standard. Then it presents the Scripture promises for a better condition of things in the church, and offers definite suggestions as to how they may be brought about:

First, the Word of God should be more widely circulated among the people, and interest in its truths should be stimulated by informal study and discussion carried on under the direction of the pastor.

Second, the fact should be recognized that there is a spiritual priesthood including every true child of God; hence the members of the laity should be taught to recognize this responsibility, and to feel under obligation to exhort, warn, and encourage their fellow Christians, that all may be kept from straying into the paths of sin, and that the church as a whole may be a pure church.

Third, the important fact must be recognized that mere knowledge is a small part of Christian living; it is doing the will of God that counts.

Fourth, the university training of candidates for the ministry should be so changed as to develop personal piety in those preparing for the sacred office; and to this end they should be required to read, not only theological and controversial works, but also books calculated to build up the spiritual life.

Fifth, sermons should be practical and devotional rather than rhetorical, and should aim to convict sinners rather than to make a display of learning.

Most of these truths would seem, in the light of today, to be self-evident, but in Spener's time they awakened intense opposition. From this time on the Frankfort pastor was a marked man. While he had friends and supporters all over Germany, he also had bitter enemies, who did what they could to oppose him personally and hinder the reform work which he was trying to bring about in the Lutheran Church. When conditions at Frankfort seemed to be such that his work there was finished, Spener accepted a call to Dresden, to serve as chaplain and court preacher to Elector John George III. Here still greater difficulties awaited him, but he continued quietly to carry on his work.

From Dresden he went to Berlin as provost of Nikolaikirche. Here, under the protection of Elector Frederick III, he was able to prosecute his labors with less local opposition; but by this time all Germany was astir over Pietism, and the Lutherans were divided into two camps. The universities took an active part in the controversy. In 1689 August Hermann Francke and Paul Anton, enthusiastic disciples of Spener, organized, among the students of the University of Leipsic, a gathering for the devotional study of the Bible on the same lines as the one organized by Spener. Francke also lectured on the Bible, expounding its practical truths with rare simplicity and fervor, to the great edification of the students and citizens of Leipsic; but the opposition was so intense that an electoral edict was issued forbidding "doubtful conventicles and private assemblies," and Francke was compelled to leave Leipsic.

When Leipsic University closed its doors to Pietism, the newly founded university at Halle became the rallying point of the new movement, and for a generation or more exerted a powerful influence throughout Germany. Francke was appointed professor of Hebrew and Greek; but he immediately began to lecture on Biblical exegesis, and under his guidance and that of his equally enthusiastic colleagues on the faculty, Joachim Breithaupt, Paul Anton, and others, the school attained a position of high eminence as a training place for ministers of the gospel of the spiritual type and for missionaries to foreign lands.

Francke also opened, in 1695, with the aid of a poor student, his school for pauper children, and shortly afterward his orphanage. Then followed in quick succession a school for boys, a Latin school, a publishing establishment, and other enterprises. All these institutions grew with almost incredible rapidity. The teachers were mostly university students who received free board in return for their services. Francke, in addition to great learning and a faculty for imparting knowledge, had organizing ability of a high order; but it was his humble trust in God that insured the success of the extensive enterprises for which he carried the chief responsibility. In response to believing prayer, voluntary contributions continued to flow in from all Germany and other parts of Europe, so that the large family of orphans and the still larger family of pupils in the various institutions never lacked the necessaries of life.

In Halle the fundamental principles of Pietism, which consisted largely in emphasizing practical Christianity, and giving a strong religious mold to education, had their fullest development. In knowledge for its own sake Francke saw little to desire. He believed the chief aim in education was to lead the child to a saving knowledge of God. Nor did he confine religious teaching to the child. In all his classes in the university, he held up the same ideal of a learning based on the principles of Holy Writ, and existing for the purpose of glorifying God, and benefiting one's fellow men. Under his leadership the university became the center alike of broad, comprehensive learning and of ardent piety, and the young men who were his enthusiastic students went out from Halle to lead Europe in philanthropic and missionary enterprises, whose widespread beneficial results may be seen even today.

The other two important centers of Pietism were in Würtemberg and at Herrnhut, the latter place being the headquarters of the Moravians, who thrived greatly under the strong spiritual leadership of Count Zinzendorf. At each of these centers certain local variations developed, but in general type they were the same. Owing to the large educational interests at Halle, and the printing press which was established there at an early date, its influence was the predominant one, at least during the first half of the eighteenth century.

We will close this section with a consideration of the religious situation in England in the eighteenth century, and the great evangelical reform movement headed by John Wesley. To appreciate fully what Methodism accomplished, one needs to recall the spiritual condition of the country when the movement began. The eighteenth century has been rightly called an age of spiritual paralysis. Rampant skepticism was fashionable among the upper classes of Europe, and seems to have flourished especially in Great Britain.

Bishop Butler, in his well-known work on " The Analogy of Religion," in which he attempts to prove the truth of the Christian religion by drawing an analogy between it and the works of nature, sadly says in his opening chapter:

" It is come, I know not how, to be taken for granted by many persons that Christianity is not so much a subject of inquiry, but that it is now at langth discovered to be fictitious. And accordingly they treat it as if in the present age this were an agreed point among all people of discernment, and nothing remained but to set it up as a principal subject of mirth and ridicule, as it were, by way of reprisals for its having so long interrupted the pleasures of the world."—" *The Analogy of Religion,*" *by Joseph Butler, Advertisement to first edition, 1736.*

Among the lower classes, immorality and amusements of the lower type, such as cockfighting, bull and bear baiting, and licentious plays, generally prevailed. Drunkenness was almost universal. Gin had been first introduced in the latter part of the seventeenth century, but it was in the eighteenth century that its use began to be general. Signs hung over the gin shops offering to give customers enough gin to make them " drunk for a penny, dead drunk for twopence, and straw to lie upon." Hogarth's horrible delineations of Gin Lane and Beer Street hardly exaggerate the facts.

The established Church of England was powerless to deal with such a desperate situation. The most earnest and God-fearing of its preachers sadly recognized that it was not beginning to hold its own. Archbishop Leighton called it "a fair carcass without a spirit." Bishop Burnet said he could not look on without the deepest concern when he saw the imminent ruin hanging over the establishment. He deplored the ignorance and indifference of the clergy. Not only the Church of England but the various independent bodies seemed to have lost their hold on the gospel as a living, vitalizing power to change men's lives, and the whole situation called loudly for a leader,— a man strong and resourceful, but with a heart full of pity for the hungering multitudes.

Such a leader was John Wesley. His parents dedicated him to God in early childhood. After completing his preparatory work, he entered Lincoln College at Oxford University, where he distinguished himself as a student and as an earnest, consistent Christian. He associated with himself for prayer and study of the Word a. group of young men whose aims in life were the same as his. The system and regularity with which these young men maintained their daily devotions, led to the term " Methodist " being applied, first to them, afterward to all who followed their example.

But while this band of young men exemplifies one important phase of Methodism, it by no means accounts for the singular power that accompanied that reform movement. The young leader of the Holy Club, as it was also called in sport by the university students, had yet very much to learn before he could be fitted to fill the responsible place for which God was preparing him. His visit to America, while it resulted in apparent failure, was an important step in the work of preparation. It brought him in touch with the Moravians, who, he was quick to see, had attained a simple trust in God to which he was a stranger. On his return to England, he sought out the Moravians in London, and learned from them the fundamental principles underlying Scriptural sanctification, of which his theological training in the Church of England had left him in complete ignorance. He also paid a visit to Herrnhut to acquaint himself more fully with this remarkable people.

Not only did Wesley obtain a knowledge of Bible teaching in reference to this great truth, but he underwent an experience in the course of which he appropriated it to his own life. Now he had indeed a message from God, and he began to give that message with power. When the churches were closed against him, he took to field preaching, and while his fellow ministers denounced him, the common people heard him gladly. His aim was very definite,— it was not to raise up a new denomination; it was not primarily to teach a new theology, nor to teach any theory as such. The aim was practical — it was to inculcate Scriptural holiness throughout the land.

To this one aim Wesley dedicated his life, and that with a whole-heartedness almost unequaled. His industry was boundless. Already in young manhood he had written: " Leisure and I have taken leave of one another. I propose to be busy as long as I live, if my health is so long indulged me." He never once

WESLEY'S CHAPEL IN LONDON

swerved from the path of arduous labor marked out for himself. Fond as he was of books and keenly interested in the questions of the day, he did nearly all his reading in the saddle. He was continually making his rounds, preaching at five in the morning, and again in the afternoon and evening. Thus it went on from week to week, year in and year out. The books and tracts that came from his pen were written in odd moments. His business always was preaching the gospel.

The preachers that Wesley trained followed in his footsteps. With few exceptions they were men who had not the advantage of a college course; but their great leader taught them habits of industry, and most of them by careful use of their spare moments added greatly to their educational acquirements. At times he would meet a company of them together, and read with them some work on theology or philosophy, pointing out its merits and its mistakes.

It was Wesley's example, however, rather than his instruction, that strongly influenced the character of his preachers. Had he, as some one has well said, " when his cause was somewhat established, retired from his self-sacrificing labors, and acted the dignified, well-endowed prelate in City Road Parsonage, his whole system would soon have fallen through." But " by traveling more, laboring more, and suffering more than any of his preachers, he kept them all traveling, laboring, suffering."

The doctrines of Methodism were not widely different from those of the Church of England. They are contained in Wesley's " Notes on the New Testament," avowedly based on Bengel's " Gnomon " and in the official collection of Wesley's sermons. If these works are carefully examined, it will be seen. that where Methodism departs from Anglicanism, it is in the direction of a closer following of the Scriptures.

It was chiefly in its discipline, however, that Methodism occupied advanced ground. Here its masterly organization proved a great help. The individual Baptist churches, for the most part, maintained good discipline, but there being no strong central organization to hold them together, it naturally followed that each was in many things a law unto itself, and the denomination as a whole could not wield the influence it might have wielded had there been stronger bonds of union. The movement headed by Wesley was organized from the start as a unit, and in it we have the first example since apostolic times of a church fully and efficiently manned and supported, and yet wholly independent of the state.

The discipline of the Methodist Church centered in the class meeting. The members of a class were voluntary adherents of a system of belief and a manner of life plainly described in the book of discipline and in the sermons of Wesley, and it was the duty of the class leader to keep careful watch over those intrusted to his care. The instructions were sufficiently explicit. Theater going, horse racing, dancing, and card playing were forbidden. The women were expected to refrain from the wearing of jewelry and superfluous ornaments of all kinds, and to clothe themselves plainly and in quiet colors.

Yet the Methodists were not harsh or censorious, and their efforts in the direction of the utmost simplicity are to be regarded, not in the light of burdensome restrictions on personal liberty, but rather as a natural outgrowth of the desire to make the life bear witness to the supreme importance of spiritual things. That the Methodists were a cheerful people, is evidenced by their love of song. In some classes the meetings, to begin with, consisted wholly of singing. Wesley encouraged sacred song in every way, and the hymns written by his brother Charles had their part in making the Methodist services the brightest and most joyful religious services of that day.

Such were the Methodists of those early days, a people whose love and zeal for the Master bore fruit in a reform which had a quickening effect upon Christian people throughout the world, and which probably did more than any other one movement to prepare for the great work in missions and other philanthropic efforts of the nineteenth century. Yet these people and their leader were in their own day despised and set at naught by their fellow Christians.

"Wesley died in 1791 [writes R. E. Tefft], generally respected in Great Britain as a sincere Christian, but as the founder of a sect of fanatics, who, ignorant and presumptuous, were supposed to arrogate all earnest Christianity to themselves. This was the general judgment of the intelligent classes, with only occasional individual exceptions, till the opening of the present century. In the halls of the English universities, even those of Oxford, where John Wesley had been a noted fellow of his college, and in those of every literary institution of the country, Methodism was always spoken of as a sorry delusion of a well-read and well-meaning man. This was its established reputation at court, in Parliament, in episcopal palaces, in the manses of charitable clergymen, in every commercial circle, among all the guilds of tradesmen and mechanics, and so down to the common level of the laboring multitude."—"*Methodism Successful*," *chap. 5, p. 236.*

The attitude of the better classes in America was not greatly different. When Jesse Lee, after three months of hard labor and continued rebuff, was able to organize his first company in the New World, he says it consisted of three women who " appeared willing to bear the cross, and have their names cast out as evil, for the Lord's sake." Books and pamphlets written in opposition to the Methodists run up into the hundreds. A catalogue containing the names of 384 was issued in Philadelphia in 1846, and it was probably far from complete.

But when we remember that Wesley was essentially a reformer, we are prepared to understand the reception given him and his followers by their fellow Christians. It was none other than that accorded Spener and Francke and Zinzendorf on the Continent. All these men were unpopular in their own day because they held and taught unpopular truth. And the measure of their unpopularity with the nominal church goers of that day was the measure of their worth as leaders of Christian thought. But they had a following. Humble men and women whose hearts God had touched, gladly listened to their life-giving words, and of these lowly ones God made mighty instruments to usher in a new era of zeal and activity in the Christian church.

Section V — Modern Missions

THE Saviour, in enumerating the signs that should precede His return, made the definite statement:

" This gospel of the kingdom shall be preached in all the world for a witness unto all nations; and then shall the end come." Matt. 24: 14.

We should accordingly expect, in harmony with this promise, that as the time of the end drew near, there would be a great world missionary movement, and facilities would be set on foot for giving the gospel to all the nations of the world. This is precisely what has happened.

For centuries the church militant had lain upon its arms. The heathen nations were known to exist; Christian nations traded with them, they even made slaves of the hapless Africans, but they did little or nothing to give them the gospel. They did not sense their responsibility toward this largest portion of the population of the globe lying in heathen darkness. Then, with all the suddenness of a revolution, public sentiment changed, and very soon all Europe was alive with missionary zeal.

More than one writer has referred to the rapidity with which the missionary spirit took hold of the people of England at the close of the eighteenth century. Doctor Sherring, in his " History of Protestant Missions in India," calls it " a curious phenomenon in the history of mankind." He says:

" The apathy of England concerning the spiritual condition of heathen countries, and the rigid, exclusive selfishness which characterized its religion, continued almost unchanged until the eighteenth century was dying out, when suddenly the Christian church awoke to the conviction of its gross neglect of duty. That it should have been so long heedless of the fact that more than one half of the human race were worshipers of idols, and slaves of the most debasing superstitions, and then should have been so thoroughly transformed, as, in the course of a few short years, to be found devising practical schemes for the spiritual regeneration of pagan races of every country on the face of the earth, is a curious phenomenon in the history of mankind.

" The burden of the world's errors and sins, no doubt, has become heavier from year to year; but why Christian people should have been able to gaze upon the increasing burden with comparative calmness, and even cheerfulness, for many generations, and in the fading years of a worn-out century should have with strange abruptness set themselves to the gigantic task of removing it from the earth, is a question not easy of solution."

It is indeed a remarkable fact that the idea of world-wide missions should first have dawned upon the mind of Christian people at the close of the eighteenth century; but it is a fact readily understood in the light of other developments. In the providence of God the time had come for the advent hope to be

WILLIAM CAREY IN INDIA TRANSLATING THE BIBLE

revived, and for the gospel message to be preached in all the world for a witness to the nations prior to the glorious second advent of Christ. Thus it was another instance where the times were " before appointed," and the contemplation of the movement in its entirety should furnish reason for renewed faith in God and His all-governing providence.

To be sure, the missions movement had its isolated pioneers and forerunners. Denmark founded a lone mission at Tranquebar on the east coast of India, and the Moravians sent some noble pioneers to the West Indies; but modern missions as a great world movement began with William Carey. He was born in 1761, and was chiefly notable in early days for his hunger for knowledge and an indomitable spirit. A shoemaker's apprentice at seventeen, he was already initiated into the rudiments of Latin, Hebrew, Greek, and French. He had been brought up in the Church of England, but hearing a sermon on the text, " Let us go forth unto Him without the camp, bearing His reproach," he made a personal application of the exhortation, and forthwith joined himself to a company of Baptists, because they were a despised sect. He began presently to do some preaching, and in 1887 he was ordained pastor of the Moulton church, a few miles from Northampton, with a salary of £15 a year, which he eked out by school teaching and shoemaking.

It was reading the voyages of Captain Cook that first led Carey's mind out to a contemplation of the needs of the heathen world. He prepared and hung up in his shoemaker's shop a rough map of the world, setting forth briefly the condition of the great harvest field. He talked about it to every one who would listen to him. He was encouraged by a sermon of Fuller's on " The Gospel Worthy of All Acceptance," and by a pamphlet by Jonathan Edwards, just then reprinted in England, in which God's people were exhorted to unite in " extraordinary prayer for the revival of religion and advancement of Christ's kingdom upon earth."

Presently Carey was called to a charge in Leicester. While there it was that, having been asked by the moderator to suggest a subject for consideration of the association, he propounded the momentous question, " Whether the command given to the apostles to teach all nations was not obligatory on all ministers to the end of the world." The curt reply of Ryland well expressed what was even at that late time the general attitude of professed Christians: " Sit down, young man. You are a miserable enthusiast to ask such a question. When God wants to convert the world, He can do it without your help; and at least nothing can be done until a second Pentecost shall bring a return of the miraculous gifts."

But Carey was irrepressible. The time had come for a world-wide missions movement to be inaugurated, and the chosen instrument was adequate to the task. He sat down for the time being, but it was to " put on paper with remarkable clearness, fulness, and cogency, a tabular statement of the size, population, religious condition, etc., of the various countries of the Old World and the New." He then went on to prove that the Lord's command to preach the gospel in all the world was perpetual; he told what had been done, and urged further efforts. The appeal, the first of its kind, closed with a request for united prayer, and suggested the gift of a penny a week. But it remained unprinted and unread for six years, the author not having the money with which to publish it.

On May 31, 1792, came the first great opportunity to present the subject of missions. The Baptist ministers were again assembled at Nottingham, and Carey was asked to preach. He spoke from Isaiah 54 : 2, 3, the two main divisions of the text being: " Expect great things from God," and " Attempt great things for God." It was an eloquent address; it came forth from the heart of a man, and it reached hearts. And yet the association was about to break up without taking action, when Carey seized Fuller by the arm and asked, " Are you going to again do nothing? " Then it was decided, " to pacify him and also to gain time," that a meeting should be held five months later to consider the matter further, and Carey was invited to publish his pamphlet. He did so. The ministers met again, and in the course of a few months there was formed in a widow's back parlor in Kettering the " Particular Baptist Society for Propagating the Gospel Among the Heathen." It included twelve members of a despised sect, and they took up a subscription for the evangelization of the world amounting to £12, 2s., 6d.

When the question was raised as to who should be sent, Carey offered himself as a candidate on the sole condition that some one be found to go with him. He had set his mind on the South Sea Islands; but a surgeon by the name of Thomas, in the employ of the East India Company, had recently returned from India, where he had done a little evangelistic work. He was accordingly invited to be Carey's associate, and accepted the call. The field fixed upon was India. After fruitless attempts to obtain the necessary license from the East India Company, passage was at length obtained on a Danish East Indiaman, and Carey and his wife and Thomas set out on their momentous voyage June 13, 1793.

While yet in mid-ocean, the brave, farseeing man wrote these remarkable words:

" I hope the society will go on and increase, and that the multitudes of heathen in the world may hear the glorious words of truth. Africa is but a little way from England, Madagascar is but a little farther. South America and all the numerous and large islands in the Indian and China Seas, I hope will not be passed over."—" *A Hundred Years of Missions*," *by Delavan L. Leonard, p. 83.*

Arriving in India, these men who desired only to preach the gospel, escaped arrest and deportation only because, landing from a ship which had cleared from a foreign port, their presence and mission were unknown. They struggled for months with all manner of difficulties, often lacking the necessaries of life; but Carey never lost heart. When things looked the darkest, he penned these immortal words:

"Well, I have God, and His word is sure; and though the superstitions of the heathen were a million times worse than they are, if I were deserted by all, persecuted by all, yet my hope, fixed on that word, will rise superior to all obstructions, and triumph over all trials. God's cause will triumph, and I shall come out of all trials as gold purified by fire."—*Ibid.*

Leaving Carey cheerfully overcoming Herculean obstacles in India, let us return to England to note the further development of the missionary campaign so nobly begun. When, after fourteen months, the first report came to the Baptists from their missionaries in India, it made them so happy that they called in some clergymen and friends of other denominations, and these too rejoiced. Moreover it occurred to them that the Baptists ought not to be the only denomination to put forth practical efforts to extend the kingdom of God upon earth. An agitation was accordingly set on foot to organize a missionary enterprise on a broad scale, independent of denominational lines, and in September the London Missionary Society was brought into being. The news spread quickly to all parts of the country, and offerings came in so rapidly that on the first of November the society had £3,000 in hand, and by the following June this sum had increased to £10,000.

It was decided to begin work at once in Otaheite (Tahiti), the Friendly Islands, and the Marquesas, with the intent later of entering Madagascar and the West Indies. And already the hope was expressed that the effort for the evangelization of the world would " spread to every Christian bosom, to the Dutch, German, American, and all Protestant churches, till the whole professing world " should " burn with fervent love, and labor to spread in every heathen land the sweet savor of the Redeemer's name."

A ship, the " Duff," was purchased and fitted out at a cost of £12,000. On the 28th of July, 1796, the twenty-nine persons who had been chosen to go as missionaries, were solemnly set apart for the work. After some weeks' delay in waiting for convoy, the vessel finally hoisted her anchors on September 23.

Measures were next taken to send four missionaries to the Foulah country, 250 miles from Sierra Leone. After that, Cape Colony was remembered. Meanwhile the promoters did not neglect to seek divine help. " Christians in every corner of the land are meeting in a regular manner, and pouring out their souls for God's blessing on the world." Moreover, a spirit of unity was coming in.

"The efforts most successfully made to introduce the gospel to the South Seas have had a most powerful tendency to unite the devoted servants of Christ of every denomination in the bonds of brotherly love, and to awaken

5

zeal to help the perishing multitudes in our own country, and also the Jews."
— *Id., p. 89.*

The missionary spirit was making itself felt in other countries. From Basel, which had for some years been a center of
evangelical earnestness on the Continent, came these words of
enthusiastic appreciation from devout German brethren:

"It is like the dawn promising the beautiful day after the dark night.
It is the beginning of a new epoch for the kingdom of God on earth. Your
undertaking and its success fills our hearts with joy and our eyes with
tears. The history of Great Britain is sanctified by this unparalleled mission.
What harmony among different persuasions! You call on the wise and good
of every nation to take interest in the work and bear a part. Such a call
was never heard of before. It was reserved for the close of the eighteenth
century to be distinguished by it."— *Id., p. 91.*

Missionary recruits were offering themselves in other lands.
In Holland the noble Vanderkemp gave himself and his fortune.
In due time he was at work teaching the gospel to the Hotten-
tots in Cape Colony. Missionary funds were being raised not
only in all parts of Great Britain, but on the Continent and in
America, by various organizations formed for the purpose, and
money was flowing in steadily.

It was nearly two years before any tidings came from the
missionary ship "Duff." In May, 1798, the long-looked-for letters arrived, and in the following July the ship lay at anchor off
the English coast. The report was most cheering. The good
ship had traversed 51,000 miles without material loss or damage. The missionaries had been kindly received, and a fruitful
work was under way in the islands.

But the members of the missionary board did not rest upon
their arms. After a day of special thanksgiving for the pros-
pering hand of God, they made arrangements for opening communication with the workers already sent out, and began to plan
an evangelistic campaign including "Hindustan, the Sandwich
Islands, and other parts of the Pacific; the Creek Indians, Canada, the Bermudas, and any West Indian islands, and any coasts
of America or Asia." To the churches they wrote:

"We must have an enlarged supply of money and men. We expect a body
of German missionaries, and we plan to engage a great company and teach
them both theological knowledge and also occupations adapted to the islands."
— *Id., p. 92.*

Plans were immediately on foot for a second voyage of the
"Duff." About the middle of November forty-six new missionaries were set apart for the work, and a few days later the
ship dropped down the Thames, although, on account of fogs
and head winds, she did not finally sail till in December.

Hitherto uninterrupted success had attended the efforts of the London Missionary Society. Now there was to be a change, with disaster following disaster. Soon after the " Duff " started on its second trip, it was captured by a French privateer and sold as a prize. Then word came that the missionaries in Tahiti had been obliged to flee for their lives. It was also learned that trouble had arisen among the missionaries sent to the Foulah country, and the work there was sadly broken up. Yet no one was discouraged. The spirit of world evangelism had taken hold of the people, and no obstacles were too great to be overcome.

THE ART OF PRINTING

Gutenberg, the Inventor of Modern Printing, Examining His First Proofs

The missionary societies resolutely set themselves to make good the losses. More funds were raised and more missionaries sent out, and in spite of many setbacks the good work, supported by well-organized home boards, went forward encouragingly.

Meanwhile, other powerful organizations were coming into being, and the work was growing apace. In the year 1799 the Church of England formed what is known as the Church Missionary Society. The American Board was organized in 1810, the Baptist Missionary Union in 1814, the Basel Society in 1815, the Wesleyan Society in 1816, the Paris Society in 1822, the Berlin Society in 1824, the Church of Scotland Society in 1829. And all these societies entered heartily upon work to which, until a few short years before, the generality of Christians had not given a thought. The time had come for the work to be done, and the Spirit of God was impelling men to take up the long-neglected task.

Not least important in the development of foreign missions was the organization of the British and Foreign Bible Society in the year 1804. Thomas Charles, of Bala, Wales, organized the Calvinistic Methodist Church in Wales, and distinguished himself not only as a preacher, but as an organizer of Sunday schools.

OFFICE OF THE BRITISH AND FOREIGN BIBLE SOCIETY

He sought the aid of the Religious Tract Society in forming an organization for the distribution of Bibles in Wales. The secretary of the society, Joseph Hughes, thought, "If for Wales, why not also for the empire, and the world!" And so the British and Foreign Bible Society was organized and began its work.

An eyewitness has given us a description of the reception of the New Testaments when the first cartload was brought into the town of Bala:

"The Welsh peasants went out in crowds to meet it, welcomed it as the Israelites did the ark of old, drew it into the town, and eagerly bore off every copy as rapidly as they could be dispersed. The young people were to be seen consuming the whole night in reading it. Laborers carried it with them to the fields, that they might enjoy it during the intervals of their labor,

and lose no opportunity of becoming acquainted with its sacred truths."—
" *The Christian Observer,*" *July, 1810. Quoted in " History of the British and Foreign Bible Society," by George Browne, Vol. I, p. 30.*

As time went on, the desire for the Word of God and for religious teaching began to be manifested in many quarters, and became one of the evidences of the timeliness of the great world movement in behalf of Christian missions. In America, missions to the Indians received an impetus as a result of a visit to St. Louis in the winter of 1832, of a deputation from the Flathead Indians, pleading for a copy of the " White Man's Book of Heaven," and for Christian teachers to explain it. They had

© S. M. Arthurs, Courtesy N. Y. Central R. R.

NINETY YEARS AGO

traveled the entire summer and autumn. In response to this call, the Methodist Mission to the Flathead Indians was organized.

Similar calls came in increasing numbers from widely separated fields, and the hearts of the missionaries were deeply stirred by the multiplying evidences that a power from above had gone before them and was opening doors that had been closed for centuries. Before the nineteenth century, the greater part of the world was practically unknown. Of Africa nothing was known except a portion of the coast line. Its interior was in fact almost a blank until Livingstone, about the middle of the nineteenth century, began his remarkable series of travels and explorations. China, Japan, and Korea excluded foreigners upon pain of death, and did not allow their own inhabitants to leave their countries. Today in all these and many other countries the doors are wide open, and urgent calls for help are coming from many quarters.

The providence of God was manifest also in supplying facilities for travel and communication between the nations, as it were, just in time to forward the great missions movement. For many long centuries men had traveled in the same old way; but the nineteenth century, by giving us steam power, revolutionized travel by land and also by sea.

MODERN TRAVEL

The earliest missionaries were subject to many inconveniences that are unknown today. Thus the first missionary ship, " Duff," after trying in vain to round Cape Horn, turned back on its course, and passing around the coast of Africa, at length made haven on the island of Tahiti. On her second voyage, as previously mentioned, she was captured by a privateer. Vanderkemp, sailing for Africa, used five months in reaching Cape Colony. Morrison found it necessary to journey to China by way of New York. He was tossed about for three months on the Atlantic; after that he was four months in getting to China. Duff on his way to the mission field suffered shipwreck three times, and was eight months in making his haven.

The work was necessarily slow at the beginning, and delays in transportation then did not hinder it as much as they would have done later. The first missionaries had to make grammars and dictionaries, translate the Bible, write tracts, and in general lay the foundation. As the work grew, and it became possible to have schools on a large scale, and the way opened for the preaching of the gospel, the improved methods of transportation were brought into use, and it was possible to send large

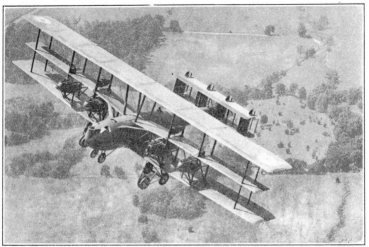

" International "
LITERALLY FLYING " IN THE MIDST OF HEAVEN "

companies of missionaries to occupy posts all over the heathen world.

Thus divine Providence in a wonderful way has gone before the missionary. When the facilities were most needed, they were provided. And no enlightened Christian can look on the marvelous intellectual advancement of the nineteenth century in any other light than as a means of bringing the gospel to every nation and kindred and tongue and people, and of preparing the world for the coming of Christ.

THE SURE WORD OF PROPHECY

" The prophecy came not in old time by the will of man: but holy men of God spake as they were moved by the Holy Ghost." 2 Peter 1 : 21.

THE WATCHMAN

"Son of man, I have made thee a watchman unto the house of Israel." Eze. 3 : 17.

CHAPTER I

A Revival of Interest in the Prophecies

PROPHECY is a characteristic feature of the Christian religion. It constitutes more than one third of the Scriptures, and may be said to form the vital framework of the whole Bible. But prophecy is more than a framework. It is everywhere mingled with the substance of the Bible as a quickening spirit, giving beauty and far-reaching significance to the most ordinary subjects therein treated, and lighting up the things of time with glimpses of the eternal.

Prophecy has been called the mold of history. It marks out the divine plan of the ages. A knowledge of it is necessary to a large view of the scheme of redemption. Mortal man, struggling onward amid darkness, oppressed mayhap by doubt and discouragement, is often led to ask, "What of the night?" Prophecy gives him the answer,—"The morning cometh, and also the night."

Prophecy was the glory of Old Testament times. By its light Abraham saw the day of the Messiah; henceforth his life was no longer bounded by the narrow limits of the earthly Canaan: "he looked for a city which hath foundations, whose

73

builder and maker is God." David was a seer, and his psalms are instinct with the very essence and glory of prophecy. God's people of old were strongly marked by the expectant spirit. Their hearts were cheered in the Babylonian captivity by the prophetic promises. When galled by the Roman yoke, they encouraged themselves by glad anticipations of a King who should rule in righteousness. And although the Jews as a nation had

THE CONFIDENCE OF ABRAHAM

" He looked for a city which hath foundations, whose builder and maker is God."
Heb. 11 : 10.

fallen from their high estate when the Saviour appeared, yet there were not wanting some faithful souls who, through their knowledge of prophecy, were looking for the Consolation of Israel.

When the Saviour came to this earth, He walked in the path marked out for Him in prophecy. And when, after His crucifixion and resurrection, He accompanied the two disciples to Emmaus, He chided them, not because they had neglected His instruction, but because of their ignorance of the prophetic word. Yet the prophecies concerning the first advent of our Saviour are really few and obscure compared with those which speak of His second coming in glory.

In the early church, prophecy was a vital part of the teaching. Those devout followers of the Lamb who are said to have coveted the crown of martyrdom, looked beyond the present life. Their hearts were cheered by the expectation of a coming

JESUS TEACHING FROM THE PROPHECIES

"Beginning at Moses and all the prophets, He expounded unto them in all the Scriptures the things concerning Himself." Luke 24 : 27.

Saviour. They pondered the words of Paul concerning the falling away which must intervene before the glorious appearing of their Master. To them, engaged in a death grapple with paganism, the world about them almost wholly given to idolatry, their own earthly lives hanging as it were by a slender thread, prophecy was indeed a light shining in a dark place, until the day of the kingdom should dawn, and the day-star arise in their hearts.

But other times followed,— years of worldly favor, but of spiritual drouth and famine. The Christian church was at ease

THE PROMISE TO DAVID (A prophecy of Christ)

"I will raise up thy Seed after thee, . . . and I will establish His kingdom. He shall build Me a house, and I will stablish His throne forever." 1 Chron. 17: 11, 12.

in Zion. She enjoyed the emoluments of the state, and her authority was recognized throughout the civilized world. No longer did she await her absent Lord, for she had formed unholy alliances with the kings of the earth, and the spirit of traffic and gain had taken possession of her.

The Reformation changed all this. With it the Christian church entered upon a new career of widespread service. And with the return to apostolic aims came a renewal of interest in the prophecies. It was in the light of the prophetic word that Luther came at length to apprehend the full import of the papacy, and to see how great is the gulf that separates it from the religion of the Bible.

Following the period of the Reformation, there was another period of spiritual deadness that prevailed more or less generally throughout Europe; and then at the close of the eighteenth century, there sprang up quite generally on the Continent and in Great Britain, as well as in some other parts of the world, a remarkable interest in the study of the prophecies. Books were written in large numbers, sermons were preached, and people's minds were drawn out to know the meaning of such books as Daniel and the Revelation, which until that time had been very generally neglected.

If the question is raised, Why did the interest spring up at just that time? the answer must be that it was in the providence of the God who " hath determined the times before appointed." The Scriptures themselves contain the key to the situation, and they alone. When the prophet Daniel sought to know the meaning of what he had seen, the word was given him, " At the time of the end shall be the vision." " Shut thou up the vision; for it shall be for many days."

Later the angel revealed to the prophet in barest outline the experiences through which the people of God were to pass, closing with the words:

" At that time shall Michael stand up, the great Prince which standeth for the children of thy people: and there shall be a time of trouble, such as never was' since there was a nation even to that same time: and at that time thy people shall be delivered, every one that shall be found written in the book. . . . But thou, O Daniel, shut up the words, and seal the book, even to the time of the end: many shall run to and fro, and knowledge shall be. increased." Dan. 12:1-4.

And so at the opening of the nineteenth century, the century in which, above all previous ones, men have run to and fro over the face of the earth and knowledge has been marvelously increased,— at this time, according to the word of prophecy, men applied themselves zealously to study the books of Daniel and the Revelation.

In this movement, however, there were forerunners, men who were in advance of their time, and by their early studies pioneered the way for those who came later. Among these men a place of special honor must be given to the English scholar, Joseph Mede, B. D., a professor of Christ's College, Cambridge, who probably did more than any other writer of the seventeenth

THE ANGEL GABRIEL RESPONDS TO DANIEL'S PRAYER

"I am now come forth to give thee skill and understanding: . . . therefore understand the matter, and consider the vision." Dan. 9 : 22, 23.

century to throw light on the book of Revelation. Says the " Dictionary of National Biography: "

"He has the merit of perceiving that a thorough determination of the structural character of the Apocalypse must be preliminary to any sound interpretation of it."

In the course of his scholarly researches, Mede discovered that a number of the prophecies are synchronous. He adopted what is called the continuistic view of the prophecies, namely, that they are predictive of progressive history, being partly fulfilled and partly unfulfilled.

Mede was widely recognized for his learning.   During his long residence at Cambridge, he gave much time and thought to the study of history and sacred chronology.   His biographer tells us that when foreigners traveling in England came to visit the University of Cambridge, they would carefully seek him out, and endeavor to make his acquaintance.   He was in correspondence with a number of learned men both in England and on the Continent.   His open-mindedness was an outstanding charac-

JOHN ON THE ISLE OF PATMOS

" Write the things which thou hast seen, and the things which are, and the things which shall be hereafter." Rev. 1 : 19.

teristic. " I cannot believe," he used to say, " that truth can be prejudiced by the discovery of truth."   His pupils, who were greatly devoted to him, he encouraged to do independent work, and get at the heart of a subject.

Mede's classic work on the Apocalypse, entitled, " Clavis Apocalyptica " [Key of the Apocalypse], was written in Latin, but was soon translated into the leading languages of Europe. The first edition appeared in England in 1627.   He also issued several other Apocalyptic studies, including a " Commentary on the Apocalypse," which came out in 1632.   He has been called the father of modern prophetic interpretation, and his faithful and conscientious labors undoubtedly helped to prepare the way for the advent movement of the early nineteenth century.   The devout spirit in which he labored is well set forth in a prayer which Doctor Worthington has left on record at the close of the general preface to Mede's published works:

" He who is the Father of mercies and the God of all grace, that giveth power to the faint, and reneweth their strength who wait upon Him, who worketh both to will and to do, and to continue patiently in so doing unto the end; to His name alone (not unto me, not unto me) be the glory and praise for His mercy and for His power's sake. The same Father of lights who commanded the light to shine out of darkness, shine into our hearts, unveil our eyes, that we may behold wondrous things out of His law; purify our souls from prejudice and passion, from every false principle and corrupt affection, that we may receive the love of the truth, and know the mysteries of the kingdom of God; that being filled with all wisdom and spiritual understanding, we may walk worthy of the Lord unto all pleasing: to whom be blessing, and glory, and wisdom, and thanksgiving, and honor, and power, forever and ever. Amen."

Mede's epoch-making work was anticipated a few years by a book coming from the pen of Patrick Forbes, bishop of Aberdeen. It was entitled, " An Exquisite. Commentary upon the Revelation of St. John," and was first published in London in the year 1613, being followed by a second English edition in the next year, and by a Latin translation for circulation on the Continent in 1646. Forbes gives special emphasis to the prophecies dealing with the Roman Catholic Church.

Another prophetic work that had a considerable circulation in the seventeenth century was written by Vitringa, a professor at the Franeker University in Holland. It bore the title, " Anakrisis Apocalypsios Joannis Apostoli " [An Exposition of the Apocalypse of the Apostle John], and like the work of Forbes, dwells largely on the prophetic symbols that are believed to refer to the papacy.

Johann Wilhelm Petersen, a German theologian born at Osnabrück, seventy-four miles southwest of Hanover, about the middle of the seventeenth century, wrote and preached extensively on the subject of fulfilling prophecy and the approach of the second advent. He received his academic training at the universities of Giessen and Rostock, and later visited the universities of Leipsic, Jena, and Wittenberg. About this time he came under the influence of Spener and other leaders among the Pietists, as a result of which he renounced the academic career he had marked out for himself, and gave himself to preaching.

Petersen held a pastorate in Hanover, but left it to become superintendent of the diocese of Lübeck and court chaplain at Eutin, where he remained for ten years. In 1688 he became superintendent at Lüneburg. Strong opposition was aroused against his views on the second advent. The consistory first forbade all preaching on the subject, then in 1692 deposed Petersen on account of this feature of his teaching, and had him expelled from the principality of Lüneburg. His remaining years were spent on a country estate near Magdeburg, where he gave himself to study and writing.

In the same year in which he was expelled from Lüneburg, Petersen brought out in two parts a work entitled, " Die Wahrheit des herrlichen Reiches Jesu Christi, welches in der siebenten Posaunen noch zu erwarten ist " (The Truth of the Glorious Kingdom of Jesus Christ, which is to be expected at [the sounding of] the seventh trumpet). He also wrote commentaries on the Psalms, on Daniel, and on the minor prophets, in all of which his convictions concerning the coming kingdom find clear expression. When he died, in Zerbst, Jan. 31, 1727, he left behind him seventy printed books and pamphlets, besides over a hundred works in manuscript. Among the latter were a large number of hymns. Petersen was one of the foremost religious teachers of his time, and a powerful advocate of the claims of prophetic study to occupy a large place in the Christian church.

The writer of greatest prominence among the German theologians of the seventeenth century who gave special attention to the prophecies, was Johann Albrecht Bengel, born at Winnenden, a village near Stuttgart, Würtemberg, on the 24th of June, 1687. Early in life he became an ardent student, giving special attention to philosophy and mathematics. At the University of Tübingen he devoted himself chiefly to the study of theology.

Like many other thoughtful students, young Bengel was troubled with religious doubts. He himself alludes to the " many arrows which pierced his poor heart, and made his youth hard to bear." But as he applied himself to the prayerful study of the Scriptures, his faith grew firm, and he rapidly advanced in the knowledge of divine things. After spending a year as vicar at Metzingen, he became a tutor at the University of Tübingen in 1708. Five years later he was made professor in the cloister school at Denkendorf, which was a seminary for the training of candidates for the ministry. After receiving this appointment, he traveled in different parts of Germany for a year, visiting various schools, including those of the Jesuits, in order to learn their methods.

It was in the course of this tour that Bengel had his attention especially attracted to the prophetic portions of Scripture. At Halle he became deeply interested in Doctor Anton's series of lectures on the Apocalypse. Professor Lang, another member of the faculty of that university, drew his attention to Vitringa's

"Anakrisis." Also while at Halle, which was becoming an important center of the Pietist movement, he found congenial society in a group of men, leaders in the movement, teachers in the university, who believed that the time was drawing near for the second advent.

Returning from his travels, Bengel took up his work at the school in Denkendorf with great enthusiasm, and for twenty-eight years devoted his best energies to the training of young

CHRIST WALKING AMONG THE CANDLESTICKS
"The seven candlesticks which thou sawest are the seven churches." Rev. 1 : 20.

men for the ministry. He was a successful teacher, and also possessed great power as a writer. His most widely known single work, entitled, "Gnomon," is a commentary on the entire New Testament, and a monument of good judgment and ripe scholarship. It furnished a large amount of the matter for Wesley's "Annotatory Notes upon the New Testament," and has been freely drawn upon for numerous other commentaries and helps. Another famous work was his "Ordo Temporum," in which he endeavored to cover the whole field of sacred chronology.

Bengel's special interest centered, however, in the prophecies of the Revelation, and it was his earnest desire to expound these important portions of the Word in such a simple way that even the common people could understand them. Following his " Exposition of the Revelation of St. John," he issued " Sixty Practical Addresses on the Apocalypse," which were a development of lectures given at the Sunday evening prayer meetings. These addresses are free from technicalities, and largely form the details of historical chronology. Their aim is to dwell on the practical help to be derived from the book of Revelation. The addresses were translated into English, and widely circulated in Great Britain under the patronage of John Wesley. There have also been a number of editions of the " Gnomon."

TYRE A WITNESS TO FULFILLED PROPHECY
" They shall destroy the walls of Tyrus, and break down her towers." Eze. 26 : 4.

Bengel's influence as a teacher of young men who entered the ministry in different parts of Germany, was very great; but his influence has extended far beyond Germany through the numerous books that he wrote. Probably no other continental theologian did so much as he to call attention to the importance of the prophetic portions of the Word, and to set forth clearly and simply their meaning, especially as relates to the second coming of Christ.

Turning again to prophetic study in England, we see the renowned Sir Isaac Newton devoting a good portion of his time during the latter part of his life to a systematic study of the books of Daniel and the Revelation, and embodying the results of his investigations in a book entitled, " Observations upon the Prophecies of Daniel and the Apocalypse of St. John," which was published posthumously in the year 1733. Newton was not the first Englishman widely celebrated for his scientific attainments, to interest himself in prophecy. Early in the seventeenth century Sir Francis Bacon, founder of the inductive method in philosophy, expressed the desire that a book might be written containing the prophecies of Holy Writ, and an account of how they had been historically fulfilled. Newton's work covers this ground in part. He gives an interpretation of Daniel's dreams, and considers the relation of the Apocalypse to the writings of Moses and to the prophecies of Daniel.

Newton, like Bengel, well understood that he was writing of some things in advance of the time. Referring to the statement in Daniel concerning the closing up of the book till the time of the end, he writes:

" 'Tis therefore a part of this prophecy, that it should not be understood before the last age of the world; and therefore it makes for the credit of the prophecy, that it is not yet understood. But if the last age, the age of opening these things, be now approaching, as by the great successes of late interpreters it seems to be, we have more encouragement than ever to look into these things. If the general preaching of the gospel be approaching, it is to us and our posterity that those words mainly belong: ' In the time of the end the wise shall understand, but none of the wicked shall understand.' Dan. 12:4, 10. ' Blessed is he that readeth, and they that hear the words of this prophecy, and keep those things which are written therein.' "— *" Observations upon the Prophecies of Daniel and the Apocalypse of St. John," pp. 250, 251, edition 1733.*

Newton was deeply impressed with the value of prophetic studies as a means of strengthening faith in God's providence, and he confidently looked forward to a future time when difficulties would be cleared away, and the full meaning of the prophecies should shine forth. The event of things predicted many ages before would then " be a convincing argument that the world is governed by Providence."

He goes on to say:

" As the few and obscure prophecies concerning Christ's first coming were for setting up the Christian religion, which all nations have since corrupted; so the many and clear prophecies concerning the things to be done at Christ's second coming, are not only for predicting but also for effecting a recovery and re-establishment of the long-lost truth, and setting up a kingdom wherein dwells righteousness. The event will prove the Apocalypse; and this prophecy, thus proved and understood, will open the old prophets, and all together will make known the true religion, and establish it. For he that will understand the old prophets, must begin with this; but the time is not yet come for understanding them perfectly, because the main revolution predicted in them is not yet come to pass. ' In the days of the voice of the seventh angel, when he shall begin to sound, the mystery of God shall be finished, as He hath declared to His servants the prophets: ' and then ' the kingdoms of this world shall become the kingdoms of our Lord and His Christ, and He shall reign forever.' Rev. 10:7; 11:15. There is already so much of the prophecy fulfilled, that as many as will take pains in this study, may see sufficient instances of God's providence; but then the signal revolutions predicted by all the holy prophets, will at once both turn men's eyes upon considering the predictions, and plainly interpret them. Till then we must content ourselves with interpreting what hath been already fulfilled.

"Among the interpreters of the last age, there is scarce one of note who hath not made some discovery worth knowing; and thence I seem to gather that God is about opening these mysteries. The success of others put me upon considering it; and if I have done anything which may be useful to following writers, I have my design."— *Id., pp. 252, 253.*

In the course of his exposition of these prophecies, Newton referred to the rapidity with which events must be brought to pass in order to prepare the way for the universal spread of the gospel at the time predicted, and he avowed his belief that men would discover the means of passing from place to place with unwonted speed, perhaps at the rate of fifty miles an hour. Voltaire scoffed at the suggestion, saying that it not only contradicted the principles of common sense and sound philosophy, but was proof of the bewildering and entangling influence of Christianity on the mind of a great man. While recognizing the services Newton had rendered to the cause of philosophy, he expressed deep regret to see the great philosopher rendered a dotard by applying his mind to the study of Holy Writ!

A longer and more elaborate work on the prophecies was written by Thomas Newton, bishop of Bristol. Appearing first in 1782 in connection with other works by this author, it was soon issued separately, and so great was the demand that eighteen editions appeared in the course of the next half century.

Another Englishman of the eighteenth century, who showed a deep interest in prophetic studies, was William Warburton, bishop of Gloucester. It was his belief that "on the right determination of the prophecies relating to Antichrist one might rest the whole truth of the Christian religion." A vigorous defender of the prophecies throughout his life, one of his last acts was to found, in 1768, the Warburtonian lecture at Lincoln's Inn, "to prove the truth of revealed religion . . . from the completion of the prophecies of the Old and New Testaments which relate to the Christian church, especially to the apostasy of papal Rome."

The first series of lectures on this foundation were delivered by Warburton's friend, Richard Hurd, D. D., bishop of Worcester. Published in 1772 under the title, "An Introduction to the Study of the Prophecies Concerning the Christian Church, and in Particular Concerning the Church of Papal Rome," they met with instant recognition as an able treatment of a subject of great timeliness, and went into a number of editions.

PROPHETIC HISTORY OF EMPIRES

"There is a God in heaven that revealeth secrets, and maketh known . . . what shall be in the latter days." Dan. 2 : 28.

As we near the close of the eighteenth century, the works dealing with prophecy become more numerous; moreover, the tone of the writers grows more confident, the books take on a more popular air, and it is easy to see that the number of persons interested in such reading is steadily increasing. One of the most scholarly works of the time bears as its title, " The Divine Origin of Prophecy Illustrated and Defended," being the Bampton Lectures of the year 1800, delivered by George Richards, M. A., D. D., vicar of Rainham, Kent. In his introductory remarks the author dwells at some length on the unique character of prophecy, and the definiteness with which it deals with individual cities and nations:

" In predicting the fate of the great cities of the East, the prophets foretold, not only the general overthrow of all, but the particular and characteristic ruin of each. Of Tyre it was predicted that the solitary fisherman should spread his nets over the rocks, on which her towers and palaces were raised; of Babylon, that her ruins should bear the appearance of a desolation occasioned by the overflow of waters; that the sea should come up upon her, and that she should be covered with the multitude of the waves thereof; that she should be made a possession for the bittern, and for pools of water: and of Nineveh, that she should entirely disappear from the earth, and that her situation should nowhere be found.

" Again, in anticipating the great empires of the world, the prophets did not simply enumerate their regular succession; they marked also their distinct and appropriate features. The Macedonian was portrayed by rapidity of conquest, and by the quadruple partition. The Roman was distinguished by a peculiarity of government, a tremendous and irresistible power, universality of dominion, and a final division into ten independent kingdoms." — *Pages 61, 62.*

" But the clearest proof [he continues] of a preternatural foreknowledge displaying itself in the discovery of minute circumstances, may be derived from the precision with which the prophets frequently fixed a particular time for the accomplishment of events, even when no human motive could be assigned for their preference of that to any other period. . . . Thus a period of four hundred years was named for the sojourning of the people of Israel in Egypt; seventy for the temporary punishment of Tyre; seventy for the captivity of the Jews in Babylon; and four hundred and ninety for the interval between their return to Jerusalem and the appearance of their expected Messiah.

" The time fixed for the continuance of the papal usurpation is still more extraordinary, because it is much more extended. The most able interpreters of the Sacred Scriptures have limited it to twelve hundred and sixty years, upon the concurring testimony of Daniel and St. John. The severe shocks which it has received, and the weakened condition in which we now behold it, justify the supposition that the period of its duration, no less than the characteristics by which it has been distinguished, will be found faithfully to coincide with the descriptions of the prophets."— *Pages 65-68.*

Of prophecy in general he says:

" It carries us back into past ages, and interests us in the most important transactions which are recorded in the history of the human race. By the absolute certainty which it affords of the interposition of the Supreme Being in the affairs of the world, it is calculated to fill the mind with astonishment, and a kind of sacred delight. And when, in addition to these powerful considerations, we reflect that it is one of the most effectual means of bringing the creature to a more perfect knowledge of the Creator, and of strengthening the confidence of mankind in divine revelation, we need not hesitate to pronounce it the most interesting and the most momentous which can occupy the attention of a being endued, like man, with reason, and formed for immortal life."— *Pages 343, 344.*

Like other writers of the time, Richards refers repeatedly to the deepening interest in prophetic studies, growing out of political and social developments then taking place in Europe.

" In seasons like the present [he says], the argument from prophecy in particular is likely to attract a more than ordinary attention, and to make a very strong impression upon the public mind."— *Page 9.*

And again:

" It appears that the wonderful scenes which have of late been presented to the view of the Christian world, are particularly favorable to the enforcement of the argument from prophecy, and that they seem to render it more peculiarly incumbent upon us to place it in that high rank among the evidences of Christianity to which, from its impressive nature, it is justly entitled, but from which, for a considerable length of time, it appears to have been undeservedly degraded."— *Page 11.*

References to current events which throw light on the prophecies become increasingly frequent in the books on prophecy that were published in the early years of the nineteenth century. George Faber, in putting out a second edition of one of his works in the year 1808, expresses his firm conviction " that the hand of God is stretched forth over the earth in a peculiar and remarkable manner; and that all things will assuredly work together to fulfil those prophecies which yet remain unaccomplished, and to prepare a way for the last tremendous manifestations of God's wrath."

Some years later, in a new edition of Sir Isaac Newton's work on Daniel, the editor speaks of the time as one " when the dark forebodings of judgment rise in thickening gloom over Christendom; when every state feels in its own feverish agitation the sympathetic echo to the rumors of war which reach it from every other; nay, when the events of the day so fulfil the predictions that they are described by the politician in language unwittingly borrowed from the page of the seer, and the burdens of judgment have become ' familiar in our mouths as household words.' "

The widespread interest in the subject of fulfilled and fulfilling prophecy, and the demand for popular instruction on the subject, is well illustrated in a work of fifty pages entitled, " The

Elements of Prophetic Interpretation, or Easy Lessons Introductory to the Study of Prophecy," which was published in London in 1828. Reference is made in the introduction to "the present day when a new interest in the prophetic parts of the Sacred Scriptures is rapidly spreading, publications on the subject are successively appearing," etc. The author goes on to say that most of these books assume a knowledge of the elements of prophetic interpretation. He proposes in his little work to give some necessary information, in order that the other books that are coming out on prophetic subjects may be read more intelligently.

He also refers to the timeliness of prophetic study in view of things then taking place in the world, asserting that the movements of Providence in reference to certain events particularized, "may well lead the most cautious and sober Christian to conclude that we are actually in a great crisis of the world."

In the foregoing pages we have mentioned a few, a very few, of the representative works dealing with prophecy, which may be said to have prepared the way for the advent movement of the nineteenth century. Lack of space makes it necessary to omit scores of vitally interesting and profitable works. It also hinders our giving even a very general summary of the contents of the few that have been mentioned. But this much may be said: Allowing for differences of opinion on various matters, mostly of a comparatively unimportant character, they agree in the large essentials. They breathe a spirit of open-mindedness, pure devotion, and firm trust in God; they are instinct with the hope of a coming Saviour, and the ushering in of His kingdom of universal peace; their authors wrote from conviction, not with any desire for human applause. Moreover, while the works of the seventeenth and eighteenth centuries laid a broad foundation of scholarship, which was exceedingly helpful to those who came after them, their authors seemed to realize that the crisis was yet some years ahead, while those written in the early nineteenth century give evidence that their authors felt that they themselves were in the crisis and a part of it, and wrote from that standpoint.

COMING IN GLORY

"I looked, and behold a white cloud, and upon the cloud one sat like unto the Son of man, having on His head a golden crown, and in His hand a sharp sickle."   Rev. 14 : 14.

JESUS' PROMISE

"I will come again, and receive you unto Myself; that where I am, there ye may be also." John 14 : 3.

CHAPTER II

The Advent Message Proclaimed in the Old World

THE widespread interest in prophetic study that prevailed in England, Germany, and other parts of Europe toward the close of the eighteenth century, was further intensified in the early part of the nineteenth century, and in connection with it various groups of believers were formed, which did much to spread a knowledge of the Scriptures, and to teach in a new setting the vital truths of Christianity. In many places also there was definite preaching in which the second coming of Christ was strongly emphasized, and little bands of faithful watchers were raised up who looked with eager eyes for their returning Lord.

Next to America, the proclamation of the second advent had its fullest development in Great Britain. Edward Irving, a prominent leader in the advent movement in that country, was born at Annan, Dumfriesshire, Aug. 4, 1792, and distinguished himself at an early age by his studious habits. Entering the

University of Edinburgh at the age of thirteen, he was graduated
M. A. at seventeen, and after some years of teaching became
assistant to Doctor Chalmers in the new people's church the
latter was building up in one of the poorer districts of Glasgow.

Irving remained with Chalmers for three years. Then he
was called to the pulpit of Caledonian Chapel, in Hatton Garden,
London, and having been ordained there, entered upon his duties
in the great metropolis. He was then twenty-nine years of age,
and of a striking physical appearance. Nearly six feet four
inches in height and of fine proportions, with dark locks hanging almost to his shoulders, framing a countenance of great dignity and beauty, he united in himself all the physical qualities
which go to make the great orator. Moreover, he had been
passing through a deep spiritual experience, in the course of
which he had burned up all his old sermons, and his face was
set resolutely forward.

Thus endowed, the young preacher took London by storm.
He drew all classes, but his preaching made a special appeal to
persons moving in high society. Sir James Mackintosh heard
him offer prayer for a family of children who had lost their
parents and their means of support. He was deeply impressed,
and the next day meeting Canning, then Prime Minister, he told
him of it. The following Sunday Canning himself was in the
audience at Hatton Garden. Other members of Parliament, with
their wives, went to hear the celebrated preacher, and it was
not long till the little Caledonian church was thronged with the
best society of London. So great was the press that strangers
wishing to obtain admission to the regular services had to secure
tickets six weeks in advance.

The membership of the Caledonian church grew so rapidly
that it became possible in two years to erect a large and commodious edifice in Regent Square, one of the finest residential
sections of London. This church in turn became crowded to its
full capacity, and the influence of the young pastor continued to
grow. He was often called upon to preach, and wherever he
went, even on the shortest notice, the meeting place would be
sure to be filled to overflowing; yet such was the strength and
compass of his admirably trained voice that persons standing
on the outer edge even of a crowd of eight or ten thousand people, could hear him distinctly.

Meanwhile Irving had become acquainted with a little band
of earnest students of prophecy, chief among whom were Henry
Drummond, who served a number of years in Parliament, and
Hatley Frere. These men, both well educated and of deep spirit-

uality, were studying prophecy in the light of the developments of their own time. As they considered the prophetical periods in the light shed upon them by Mede, Newton, and other earlier writers, it became increasingly clear to them that they were living in the closing years of the world's history, and that the kingdom for which Christendom had been praying so many hundreds of years, was soon to be set up.

Irving's intense interest in the Bible, and his growing sense of the lack of earnestness and vitality in the churches, drew him to these devoted men, and they prayed and studied together. His belief in the soon coming of Christ was further strengthened by perusing a work on the subject written in South America by a Jesuit priest, named Lacunza,[1] who used the assumed Jewish name, Juan Josafat Ben Ezra. The work was entitled, " The Second Coming of the Messiah in Glory and Majesty," and was written in Spanish; but Irving's interest in the subject was such that he soon mastered the language sufficiently, not only to peruse the book for himself, but to get out an English translation of it, to which he prefixed a copious introduction.

While he was putting the finishing touches to his translation of Lacunza, Irving joined other students of prophecy in a conference, the first of the kind, held at the residence of Drummond in Albury Park, Surrey. The Rev. Hugh M'Niel, rector of the Parish of Albury, was the chosen moderator of this gathering, and among the twenty men of every rank and church and orthodox communion who took part in it was Joseph Wolff, the well-known traveler and Orientalist. The conference lasted six full days, taking up in succession the following subjects:

" First, the doctrine of Holy Scripture concerning the time of the Gentiles. Second, the duties of Christian ministers and people, growing out thereof toward the Gentile churches. Third, the doctrine concerning the present and future condition of the Jews. Fourth, the duties growing out of the same toward the Jews. Fifth, the system of the prophetic visions and num-

---

[1] Lacunza, the son of noble though not wealthy parents, was a native of Chile, South America, and was educated in the college of the Jesuits, becoming a member of the order in 1747. Later he came to Europe and resided in Italy. Some idea of the spirit and purport of his only literary product may be gathered from the following extract: " Be it far from me to fear the coming of the Lord in glory and majesty, for I yearn for it with the greatest longing, and pray for it with all the earnestness of which I am capable. . . . The glorious advent of the Lord Jesus is a divine truth, which is as essential and fundamental to Christianity, as His first advent to suffer in the flesh. . . . When that great day has come which heaven and earth await with earnest desire, then will ' the Lord Himself descend from heaven with a shout, with the voice of the Archangel, and with the trump of God.' Then, in that moment (as I conceive it), at the Lord's contact with the atmosphere of our earth, this will occur first, the resurrection from the dead, of whom Paul says, ' And the dead in Christ shall rise first.' In a moment when this first resurrection of the saints of the first order has taken place, then will those few among the living who will be counted worthy of this designation of saints, on account of their wonderful faith and of their righteousness, be caught up together with the sleeping saints who have been resuscitated, and will ascend with them to meet the Lord in the air. All this is very clear, and very comprehensible." —" *The Church's Forgotten Hope*," *by Rev. William Bramley-Moore, M. A., p. 328.*

bers of Daniel and the Apocalypse. Sixth, the Scripture doctrine concerning the future advent of the Lord. And last, the duties to the church and the world arising out of the same."—" *The Second Coming of Messiah in Glory and Majesty,*" *by Juan Josafat Ben Ezra, The Translator's Preliminary Discourse, p. 189.*

Though the members of the conference were for the most part strangers to one another, coming from various countries, and from different churches in those countries, yet in the words of Irving, " we were so overruled by the one Spirit of truth and love, as to have found our way to harmony and coincidence in the main points of all these questions."

This conference, held in the autumn of 1826, was the first of a series of five such gatherings, held yearly, which came to be known as the Albury Conferences, and were a strong factor in the development of the second advent movement in Great Britain.

The increased emphasis on the prophecies concerning the second advent resulted in a quickening of the spiritual life in the church over which Irving presided. The young men began to devote themselves to evangelistic labor on the streets and in the homes of the poor. The church prayer meetings were fully attended, and were seasons of great spiritual refreshment. Irving was putting out pamphlets and books instinct with warning and admonition in view of the unpreparedness of professed Christians for the impending advent. " For the Oracles of God " and " For Judgment to Come " appeared in 1823, and three years later one of his most striking and eloquent works, " Babylon and Infidelity Foredoomed," which was a searching arraignment of the easy-going Christianity of the time. There followed in 1828 three volumes of sermons largely on prophetic subjects, and in 1831 an " Exposition of the Book of Revelation."

Meanwhile he continued to preach with increasing unction and power, and wherever he went, the people flocked to hear him. On a trip to Scotland in 1828, he gave a series of early morning lectures on the prophecies, which crowded the largest churches in Edinburgh. In Ireland, where he had gone for a few days' rest, he preached thirteen times in the week to enormous audiences, composed alike of Catholics and Protestants, the churches crowded to suffocation, and the people standing outside and hearing him through the open windows.

The closing years of the great preacher's life were very trying ones. A division arose in his church over certain manifestations of alleged speaking with tongues and prophesyings. Irving was unable to cope with the situation. Fanaticism was bringing reproach upon the preacher and his work. Complaint was made to the London Presbytery, and adverse judgment rendered. Irving's congregation was divided, and it was necessary for him to leave the beautiful church edifice built as a result of the blessing of God upon his ministry. He was followed by a portion of his congregation, but the incessant labor incident to such a situation told severely upon his strength, and he was brought into a condition of physical collapse. The end came peacefully at the house of a friend in Glasgow, whither he had

EDWARD IRVING

GEORGE MÜLLER

gone on one of his evangelistic tours. His last words were characteristic: "If I die, I die unto the Lord."

Among the men who were associated with Irving or who followed him in the proclamation of the advent truth, mention should be made of James Haldane Stewart, a clergyman of the Establishment, whose parish ministry was greatly blessed to the saving of souls. His heart was drawn out in prayer for a spiritual revival in view of the approaching return of the Saviour. He put out thousands of copies of a pamphlet calling upon Christians to unite in earnest prayer to this end, and after some years he resigned his charge in order to give his whole time to this work, in which God abundantly blessed him.

George Stanley Faber, another faithful worker in the advent cause, was educated at University College, Oxford, graduating

M. A. in 1796 and B. D. in 1803, after which he held a fellow-ship for ten years. He filled various positions in the church, but his voluminous writings, dealing largely with prophetic subjects, are his chief claim to notice. They were widely circulated, and helped to awaken an intelligent interest in the books of Daniel and the Revelation.

Edward Bickersteth in early life practised as a lawyer in Norwich; but his deep interest in religion led him later to enter the ministry. After a trip to Africa in the interests of the Church Missionary Society, he became in 1816 one of the society's secretaries, and traveled in its interests. In 1830 he became rector of Watton. He was one of the founders of the Evangelical Alliance, and wielded a strong influence over the religious life of his time. His numerous works breathe a deep devotional spirit. His " Guide to the Prophecies," one of the best works of its kind, went through many editions, as did also his book, " A Help to the Study of the Scriptures."

Alexander Keith, a clergyman of the Free Church of Scotland, educated at the University of Aberdeen, wrote several important works on prophecy. One of them, " Evidence of the Truth of the Christian Religion, Derived From the Literal Fulfilment of Prophecy," published first in 1828, went through no less than forty editions. Among his other works were " The Signs of the Times " and " The Harmony of Prophecy."

Archibald Mason, also of Scotland, issued about 1829 a book entitled, " Two Essays on Daniel's Prophetic Numbers of 2300 Days, and a Christian's Duty to Inquire into the Church's Deliverance." In this work the author acknowledges having seen a pamphlet on the same prophecies written by a Rev. W. E. Davis of South Carolina. Both works take the position that the 2300 days began with the seventy weeks, and would end with the Jewish year 1843.

Another devoted Scotch clergyman, whose work in behalf of the prophetic revival came a little later, was Horatius Bonar. Educated in Edinburgh, he became minister at Kelso in 1837, and with his congregation joined the Free Church in 1843. He was an ardent believer in the premillennial advent, and did much to spread right views of the prophecies in his book, " Prophetical Waymarks," and in the *Quarterly Journal of Prophecy,* founded by him in 1849. The hymn, " What a Friend We Have in Jesus," is one of a large number he has given us.

Among other men of wide spiritual influence who about this time learned to look for a soon-coming Saviour, was George Müller, the founder of the Bristol Orphanages, whom God used in a signal manner in demonstrating to the world the power of believing prayer. He himself has told how this truth came to him. After referring to other points of faith, he goes on to say:

" Another truth, into which, in a measure, I was led, respected the Lord's coming. My views concerning this point, up to that time, had been completely vague and unscriptural. I had believed what others told me, without trying it by the Word. I thought that things were getting better and better, and that soon the whole world would be converted. But now I found in the Word that we have not the least Scriptural warrant to look for the conversion of the world before the return of our Lord. I found in the Scriptures that that which will usher in the glory of the church, and uninterrupted joy to the saints, is the return of the Lord Jesus, and that, till then, things will be more or less in confusion. I found in the Word that the return of Jesus, and not death, was the hope of the apostolic Christians; and that it became me, therefore, to look for His appearing.

" And this truth entered so into my heart that, though I went into Devonshire exceedingly weak, scarcely expecting that I should return again to London, yet I was immediately, on seeing this truth, brought off from looking for death, and was made to look for the return of the Lord. Having seen this truth, the Lord also graciously enabled me to apply it, in some measure at least, to my own heart, and to put the solemn question to myself, What may I do for the Lord, before He returns, as He may soon come? "—" *George Müller of Bristol*," *by Arthur T. Pierson, pp. 388, 389.*

These are a few of the men who were active in forwarding the second advent movement in Great Britain. A number of them founded and wrote for the *Morning Watch,* a quarterly journal of high literary merit, devoted to the exposition of the prophecies, which was published regularly from 1829 to 1833.

Space does not permit mention of the many other equally zealous workers in the advent cause. It would be easy to occupy pages with the names of such men and the titles of their published works. If the reader has any doubt, let him go into any second-hand bookstore dealing largely with religious books, and he cannot help noting the large number of works on prophecy that came out in the thirties and forties, many of which went through edition after edition and had a very wide circulation. Whatever the reason assigned, it must be a generally recognized fact that the study of the prophetic portions of the Bible had a remarkable vogue in the first thirty or forty years of the nineteenth century, and during these same years the evangelical preaching of England was very generally concerned with prophetic subjects.

If we turn to the Continent, we see the same movement on foot there, but assuming in places a somewhat different form. In Holland the advent message had a distinguished exponent in Hentzepeter, keeper of the Royal Museum at The Hague. His attention was first attracted to the subject of Christ's second coming by an impressive dream. After a period of study and investigation, he put forth his first pamphlet in 1830. He published a larger pamphlet on the end of the world in 1841. In a letter to the *Midnight Cry*, he says that he had no knowledge of William Miller and others proclaiming the near approach of the advent till 1842.

In Germany the advent movement clearly had its roots in Pietism. From such centers as Halle and Tübingen and Herrnhut there have come books and also living preachers of the word that have largely dominated evangelical religion in Germany. It is a revived Pietism that is today effectively fighting rationalism in that country, holding up the standard of an all-sufficient gospel, and working for the evangelization of the world in this generation. Germany has not put out such a large number of books on prophecy as England; but in point of quality her prophetic literature ranks very high as regards both scholarship and spiritual appeal. Among the older writers, Bengel's name is easily supreme. His writings circulated all over the Continent, and kindled in thousands of honest hearts a love for the Saviour's return. Other students of prophecy whose minds were stimulated by perusing his books, wrote even more fully on certain phases of prophecy, and the public interest widened.

As a result of such writings, there was a marked revival of vital religion in Würtemberg. The awakened ones confidently looked for the coming of Christ about the year 1843, and they earnestly sought such a preparation of heart as would enable them to receive their Lord with joy. Special meetings were held, and the country was greatly stirred. Some of these waiting ones were led to see the claims of the fourth commandment, thus becoming Seventh-day Adventists purely as a result of the prayerful study of the Scriptures.

When persecution arose, many of the believers removed to southern Russia, where they spread their doctrines among other Germans who had preceded them. Denied the use of the churches, they held meetings in private homes. This was the beginning of the Stundist Movement, which rapidly spread through Russia.

Leonard Heinrich Kelber, a Bavarian schoolmaster, put out a pamphlet in 1824 entitled, " The End Near," containing an exposition of Matthew 24 and 25. A larger pamphlet from his pen appeared eleven years later in Stuttgart. A translation of the title page runs:

" The End Comes, proved in a thorough and convincing manner from the Word of God and the latest events; invalidating totally all prejudice against waiting for the coming of our Lord, or reckoning of the time; showing plainly how prelate Bengel erred seven years in reference to the great decisive year; for not 1836, but the year 1843, is the terminus, at which the great struggle between light and darkness will be finished, and the long-expected reign of peace of our Lord Jesus will commence on earth."—" *The Great Second Advent Movement," pp. 88, 89.*

Other editions were published, and the book had a wide circulation in Germany.

In later years Hengstenberg, Tholuck, and Lange occupied positions of honor among prophetic students in Germany. The writings of these men combine ripe scholarship with a devout reverence for the living Word, and their influence for good may be said to be world-wide.

While in Germany as a whole the advent movement has manifested itself chiefly in the shape of a well-developed prophetic literature, and a very general study of these portions of Holy Writ on the part of awakened persons, yet here and there in that country also the Spirit has worked in other channels, seeking to arouse the people to a sense of the nearness of Christ's coming. We have space to record only one of these. It concerns a very humble people living along the lower stretches of the Danube in Bavaria. The settlement known as Karlshuld contained, at the time of which we are writing, a population of about nine hundred. The inhabitants lived in small wooden houses consisting of two narrow rooms, and slept upon straw. For some years the village had been without regular church services or a pastor, and the moral depravity was great. The money earned during the week would be squandered in drink on Sundays, and men would lie around in the gutters.

Such was the condition when Johann Georg Lutz, a devout Roman Catholic priest, entered upon his work in the district in August, 1826. His heart was drawn out to the people in their sin, poverty, and misery, and he instructed them out of the Scriptures. The divine blessing accompanied his ministrations, and many hopeful conversions resulted. The demand was great for copies of the Word of God, and instead of giving their leisure time to card playing, dancing, and other unseemly things, the people read the Scriptures with eagerness, and found in them food for their souls.

Toward Lent, a great spirit of prayer prevailed. Young and old were earnest in their supplications, and would spend whole nights in the exercise. Combined with this there was quietness of spirit and great joy in the Lord. About the end of February occurred the first manifestation of the spirit of prophecy, two women and a man beginning to speak under the special influ-

A CHILD PREACHING IN SWEDEN

ence of the Spirit. The persons thus affected were earnest, consistent Christians, and they would be exercised in this way both in church and in private houses. When asked to explain their condition, they replied that they knew nothing of that which they uttered until they began to speak; the power came over them, and the words were put in their mouth.

The messages thus given were mostly short, the main burden of them being that the coming of Christ was near at hand, and men should prepare to meet Him. It was said that the Lord would pour out His Spirit as at the beginning, that a church would be gathered out of the different denominations, in which He would fulfil all the good pleasure of His will, and they were to be quiet and watchful. There were also some who had visions and dreams, and the general purport of these was in harmony with the prophetic utterances. There were no excesses of any kind in connection with the manifestation of these gifts, and it was the unanimous feeling that they were a gracious revival of the gifts that were such a striking characteristic of the apostolic church.

It is hardly necessary to add that the great majority of these people, including the priest Lutz, found before long that they were really Protestants, and not Catholics; and they followed the light. Lutz himself, some years later, after having passed through severe trials, came in contact with members of the church which grew out of Irving's preaching, and joined himself to it.

In the three Scandinavian countries, Sweden, Denmark, and Norway, the quickening of the spiritual life in the early nineteenth century came chiefly from Pietistic sources. In Sweden, however, chiefly in the country districts, there was a remarkable work done by the children and young people in the late thirties and early forties. Little boys and girls who had never learned to read, under the power of the Spirit gave expositions of lines of prophecy, and exhorted to repentance in view of a soon-coming Saviour. This work, so evidently of divine origin, mightily moved the country. Men and women came for miles to hear one of these little ones, mounted on a table in order to be seen and heard, expound the mysteries of God's Word, and warn of impending judgment.

The laws of the country were very strict, and some of the young people were severely punished; but they did not give up preaching. They said they were moved by a power they themselves could not explain, and when it came over them, they could not help urging people to prepare for the judgment.

JOSEPH WOLFF PREACHING THE ADVENT MESSAGE
TO THE ARABS

O. Boqvist, one of the survivors, gave in 1890 a circumstantial account of the revival as it developed in the parish of Karlskoga in Orebro.   He writes:

" In the fall of the same year [1843], I, O. Boqvist, then fifteen years of age, with another young man, Erik Walbom, eighteen years of age, became so influenced by this unseen power that we could in no wise resist it.   As soon as we were seized by this heavenly power, we commenced to speak to the people, and to proclaim with loud voice that the judgment hour had come, referring them to Joel 2:28-32 and Revelation 14:6, 7."— *Review and Herald, Oct. 7, 1890, p. 612.*

In prison the young men were cruelly whipped to make them promise not to preach any more; but they told their persecutors that when the power came over them, they could not resist it. When the harsh treatment inflicted upon the young men and children identified with this movement was brought to the attention of the king, Oscar I, he interested himself on their behalf, with the result that the persecution ceased.   The people who were roused by the child preaching in the thirties and forties form today a branch of the state church.

In Australia, in those times, the message of a soon-coming Saviour was preached in great power by Mr. Thomas Playford, of Adelaide, who was listened to by large audiences wherever he spoke.   The churches not being able to accommodate the people who wished to hear him, his friends united and built a church on Bentham Street, where he was joined by Pastor Abbott, of the Methodist New Connection Church, who was for a time associated with him in the work.

The advent message was also to be carried into parts of Asia. Joseph Wolff, the chosen instrument for this work, was in various ways a remarkable character. A close friend called him —

" A man . . . who passes his days in disputation, and his nights in digging in the Talmud; to whom a floor of brick is a feather bed, and a box a bolster; who finds or makes a friend alike in the persecutor of his former or present faith; who can conciliate a pasha, or confute a patriarch; who travels without a guide, speaks without an interpreter, can live without food and pay without money; forgiving all the insults he meets with, and forgetting all the flattery he receives; who knows little of worldly conduct, and yet accommodates himself to all men, without giving offense to any."—" *History of the Second Advent Message and Mission, Doctrine and People,*" *by Isaac C. Wellcome, p. 148.*

Wolff was born in the village of Weilersbach, in Bavaria, in 1796, the son of a Jewish rabbi.   In early life he joined the Roman Catholic Church; but while studying theology in the city of Rome, he saw many things against which his conscience revolted, and when he openly protested, he was banished from the city by decree of the pope. Some time later he went to London, where the Society for Promoting Christianity among the Jews provided for him a course of training, and received him into its employ.

He left England for his first missionary tour in 1821. For the next twelve or thirteen years he traveled incessantly among the people of the Orient, meeting hardships and dangers innumerable, but never for a moment slackening his efforts to achieve his main purpose,—" to proclaim the gospel of the kingdom." With him this included the exposition of the prophecies, and the showing by the prophetic periods that the second coming of Christ was near at hand.

Isaac Taylor, in summing up Wolff's work, says:

"He proclaimed the Lord's speedy advent in Palestine, Egypt, on the shores of the Red Sea, Mesopotamia, the Crimea, Persia, Georgia, throughout the Ottoman Empire, in Greece, Arabia, Turkey, Bokhara, Afghanistan, Cashmere, Hindustan, Tibet, in Holland, Scotland, Ireland, at Constantinople, Jerusalem, St. Helena, also on shipboard in the Mediterranean, and in New York City, to all denominations. He declares that he has preached among Jews, Turks, Mohammedans, Parsees, Hindus, Chaldeans, Yesedes, Syrians, Sabeans, to pashas, sheiks, shahs, the kings of Organtsh and Bokhara, the queen of Greece, etc."—" *The Great Second Advent Movement*," *p. 101.*

Wolff said of himself:

"I have proved by experience that a missionary, under the protection of the Highest, may have grace to persevere in preaching the gospel of Christ, through good report and evil report, under afflictions, illness, poverty, and persecution."—" *Researches and Missionary Labors Among the Jews, Mohammedans, and Other Sects*," by the Rev. Joseph Wolff, pp. 524, 525.

He was a member of the first Prophetic Conference held in Albury, and for a time taught that Christ would come about the year 1846; later he confined himself to proving by the Scriptures and the signs of the times " that the time of the coming of Jesus is at hand." He was not only a singularly forcible expounder of prophecy. He preached from the depths of a genuine Christian experience; and it was his love of the Saviour and his fervent desire to make Him known to heathen, Jew, and Mohammedan, that took him over so many perilous journeys. The inner spirit of the man is revealed in the following extract from his journals:

"There is a moment, after which we can no longer serve the Lord; a night cometh in which no man can work. Blessed are those who have the Lord always with them, in every object, on every occasion; who perceive Him in the melodious voice of the nightingale, at the recollection of a beloved departed wife, or a brother in affliction. In every event, in every object, He ought to be recognized; for the Lord reveals His wisdom, goodness, and power at all seasons: in the nocturnal sky, with its innumerable suns, no less than in the glorious light of day. The moon proclaims His grace, and the sun His glory. On every page of His revelation, He has made known His goodness. . . . Our destined portion, the portion of all redeemed souls, is to be partakers of His glory, to sit in heavenly places with Christ Jesus! "— — *Id., p. 467.*

Like other men of the time who were engaged in calling attention to fulfilling prophecy, Wolff had a deep-seated antipathy to the rationalistic spirit which was undermining the faith of so many in his day.

" Every attempt [he asserted] to bring the mysteries of our redemption within the limits of human understanding lowers the standard of Christianity, and destroys the harmony of the whole, considered as a demonstration of the infinite wisdom, glory, and goodness of the ineffable Jehovah. . . . I have met many learned men, who from being infidels became afterward believers in Christ Jesus; but not one of those who were so converted, ascribed their conversion to the result of their own researches, but acknowledged it as an effect of the grace of God, which made them sensible of their ignorance. Would to God that this might soon be the case with Doctor Channing, with the Neologists in Germany, and with infidels in France and England! "— *Id., pp. 524, 525.*

Wolff was a man of striking personality, bold and fearless in the presence of danger, and absolutely indefatigable in labor. He distributed Bibles and Testaments wherever he went, thus co-operating efficiently in the work of the Bible Society, and he did much to rouse England to renewed exertions in behalf of the evangelization of the Orient. His most characteristic note as a preacher was the emphasis he placed on the second coming in glory of the Lord Jesus Christ. Probably no other person has preached this soul-stirring truth over a wider area.

WILLIAM MILLER

RESIDENCE OF WILLIAM MILLER
The old farmhouse in Low Hampton, N. Y., as it appeared in 1895

CHAPTER III

Beginnings in America

THE outstanding pioneer in America of the doctrine of Christ's approaching second advent, was William Miller, a Baptist layman. The early life of this man throws so much light on his public career that it seems desirable to reproduce it in some detail.

Born at Pittsfield, Mass., Feb. 15, 1782, William was the eldest of sixteen children. Even in early childhood he gave promise of more than ordinary intellectual vigor, and as he advanced in years, his fondness for books and study asserted itself more and more. The district school was in operation only three months in the year; but the winter nights were long, and a pile of blazing pine knots in the spacious fireplace was no mean substitute for candles.

The father's circumstances improved in time, a good farmhouse took the place of the log cabin, and the eldest son had a room he could call his own, where he could read his favorite books by candlelight; but he failed to obtain the education that his heart longed for. In 1803 he was married, and settled on a farm in Poultney, Vt., where his constant and assiduous use of the books in the village library soon brought him to the attention of the intellectually inclined citizens, his home also becoming a favorite resort of the young people.

Like other young men, William Miller had grown up in the midst of religious influences, but he had not experienced conversion. Nevertheless he continued, while in the home town, to associate with people of a religious turn of mind, and apparently felt himself in sympathy with their main beliefs. On taking up his residence at Poultney, Mr. Miller was thrown in with a different class of associates. They were considered men of good moral character, but lacked religious principle. They fed their minds with the writings of Voltaire and other authors of that class, and their finer spiritual sensibilities were blunted. Deists, they called themselves, and Mr. Miller, having no definite church connections and no personal experience in divine things, joined them.

Mr. Miller entered the army at the outbreak of the war of 1812. Army life is not calculated in most cases to draw a man nearer to God. With him, however, it meant taking him away from the intimate society of men steeped in skepticism, and throwing him among strangers, with the natural result of making him more thoughtful and introspective. In his " Apology and Defense," published in 1845, he has this to say of his feelings:

" In 1813 I received a captain's commission in the United States service, and continued in the army until peace was declared. While there, many occurrences served to weaken my confidence in the correctness of deistical principles. I was led frequently to compare this country to that of the children of Israel, before whom God drove out the inhabitants of their land. It seemed to me that the Supreme Being must have watched over the interests of this country in an especial manner, and delivered us from the hands of our enemies.

" I was particularly impressed with this view when I was in the battle of Plattsburg, when, with 1,500 regulars and about 4,000 volunteers, we defeated the British, who were 15,000 strong; we being also successful at the same time in an engagement with the British fleet on the lake. At the commencement of the battle we looked upon our own defeat as almost certain, and yet we were victorious. So surprising a result against such odds did seem to me like the work of a mightier power than man."— " Sketches of the Christian Life and Public Labors of William Miller," by James White, p. 38.

On retiring from the army, Mr. Miller removed to Low Hampton, N. Y., the home of his boyhood days, where he bought a farm of two hundred acres, built a comfortable house, and settled down to country life. His leisure time he continued to devote to reading of a serious character. He had arrived at an age when ultimate things demand some attention. His deistic views gave him no real peace of mind, and no hope for the future. All was dark and uncertain before him.

Meanwhile he was outwardly cheerful, and his home in Low Hampton, as previously at Poultney, was a popular resort for the young people of the place, as well as the regular stopping place of the ministers who officiated in the little Baptist meeting house near by. In the absence of a regular minister, it was the custom to read a sermon, and on these occasions, Mr. Miller, at the request of the deacons, did the reading, they making the selection.

On a certain Sunday in September, 1816, it thus fell to Mr. Miller's lot to read a sermon on " The Importance of Parental Duties." He had been in an unusually serious frame of mind for the few days preceding this meeting, and there was deep feeling in the community, a stirring sermon having been preached during the week by a traveling evangelist. Soon after he had begun to read the sermon, he was overwhelmed with a flood of conflicting emotions, and had to take his seat.

" Suddenly [he afterward wrote] the character of a Saviour was vividly impressed upon my mind. It seemed that there might be a Being so good and compassionate as to himself atone for our transgressions, and thereby save us from suffering the penalty of sin. I immediately felt how lovely such a Being must be, and imagined that I could cast myself into the arms and trust in the mercy of such a One. But the question arose, How can it be proved that such a Being does exist? Aside from the Bible, I found that I could get no evidence of the existence of such a Saviour, or even of a future state. . . .

" I saw that the Bible did bring to view just such a Saviour as I needed; and I was perplexed to find how an uninspired book should develop principles so perfectly adapted to the wants of a fallen world. I was constrained to admit that the Scriptures must be a revelation from God. They became my delight; and in Jesus I found a friend. The Saviour became to me the chiefest among ten thousand; and the Scriptures, which before were dark and contradictory, now became the lamp to my feet and light to my path." — *Id., pp. 43, 44.*

Following this change of heart, Mr. Miller naturally made a corresponding outward change. He began to conduct family prayers in his home, made a public profession of his faith, and joined the little company of believers which had formerly been the object of his good-natured ridicule. He also began to consider what he could do to help his deist friends.

Shortly after he had taken his stand as a Christian, while telling a friend of his hope and belief in the merits of the Saviour, he was asked how he could even be sure of the existence of such a Being, and made the reply:

"It is revealed in the Bible."

"How do you know the Bible is true?" asked the friend, and went on to speak of apparent inconsistencies and contradictions in that book.

Mr. Miller felt the force of his friend's remarks, and was perplexed. He concluded, however, on reflection, that the Bible as a revelation of God must be consistent with itself, and having been given to man for his guidance and instruction, it must be intelligible to him.

He now gave himself to the study of the Bible with all the enthusiasm of a keen intellectual nature. He devoted whole nights as well as days to his investigations, being baffled now and then, only in time to rejoice over new victories, while the plan of salvation gradually assumed clearer outlines, and the love of God to man became more and more manifest. He says:

"I determined to lay aside all my prepossessions, to thoroughly compare scripture with scripture, and to pursue its study in a regular and methodical manner. I commenced with Genesis, and read verse by verse, proceeding no faster than the meaning of the several passages should be so unfolded as to leave me free from embarrassment respecting any mysticisms or contradictions. Whenever I found anything obscure, my practice was to compare it with all collateral passages; and by the help of Cruden, I examined all the texts of Scripture in which were found any of the prominent words contained in any obscure portion. Then, by letting every word have its proper bearing on the subject of the text, if my view of it harmonized with every collateral passage in the Bible, it ceased to be a difficulty."— *Id., pp. 47, 48.*

Mr. Miller followed this method of studying the Scriptures for a period of two years, by which time he had come to some fairly definite conclusions. He was led to reject, for instance, the then popular belief in a temporal millennium, and the return of the Jews to Palestine. He had adopted the belief in the premillennial advent of Christ.

"I found it plainly taught in the Scriptures that Jesus Christ will again descend to this earth, coming in the clouds of heaven, in all the glory of His Father; that at His coming the kingdom and dominion under the whole heaven will be given unto Him and the saints of the Most High, who will possess it forever, even forever and ever; that as the old world perished by the deluge, so the earth that now is, is reserved unto fire, to be melted with fervent heat at Christ's coming; after which, according to the promise, it is to become the new earth, wherein the righteous will forever dwell; that at His coming the bodies of all the righteous dead will be raised, and all the righteous living be changed from a corruptible to an incorruptible, from a mortal to an immortal state; that they will be caught up together to meet the Lord in the air, and will reign with Him forever in the regenerated earth."— *Id., pp. 51, 52.*

The chronological portions of Sacred Writ strongly appealed to Mr. Miller. He found that predicted events fulfilled in the past often occurred within a given time; such as the one hundred and twenty years to the flood, the four hundred years of Abraham's sojourn, the forty years in the wilderness, the seventy years' captivity, etc. This led him on to earnest study of the prophetic periods in Daniel and the Revelation. He said:

"I could but regard them as 'the times before appointed,' which God had revealed 'unto His servants the prophets.' As I was fully convinced that 'all Scripture given by inspiration of God is profitable,'—that it came not at any time by the will of man, but was written as holy men were moved by the Holy Ghost, and was written for our learning, that we, through patience and comfort of the Scriptures, might have hope,— I could not but regard the chronological portions of the Bible as being as much a portion of the Word of God, and as much entitled to our serious consideration, as any other portion of the Scriptures."— *Id., p. 56.*

Along with various other Bible students, Mr. Miller considered that a day is, in the language of prophecy, a symbol for a year. He saw that the seventy weeks of Daniel 9, which were to reach to the Messiah, had been fulfilled in 490 years, and the 1260 days of the papal supremacy in that number of years. This led him on to the conclusion, startling to him, that the 2300 days of the prophecy of Daniel 8: 14, as well as other periods of prophecy, would end in the year 1843. Assuming that the cleansing of the sanctuary, marked by this prophecy of the 2300 days, meant the purging of the earth by the glory of Christ's second coming, he was convinced that the year 1843 would bring the end of all things.

"I was thus brought, in 1818, at the close of my two years' study of the Scriptures, to the solemn conclusion that in about twenty-five years from that time all the affairs of our present state would be wound up; that all its pride and power, pomp and vanity, wickedness and oppression, would come to an end; and that, in the place of the kingdoms of this world, the peaceful and long-desired kingdom of the Messiah would be established under the whole heaven."— *Id., pp. 57, 58.*

For five more years (1818-23) he continued to study the subject, giving careful consideration to all difficulties and suggestions that occurred to him from time to time, and endeavoring to the best of his ability to test the correctness of his views.

"During that time [he tells us], more objections arose in my mind than have been advanced by my opponents since; and I know of no objection that has been since advanced which did not then occur to me."— *Id., pp. 67, 68.*

Having at length become fully convinced of the soundness of his views, Mr. Miller began to feel a sense of responsibility toward others, and communicated his convictions somewhat freely to his neighbors, in the hope that some who were better fitted for the work than himself would feel the burden to proclaim the message to a careless world. There were few of his acquaintances, however, who listened with any interest.

" Occasionally one would see the force of the evidence; but the great majority passed it by as an idle tale. I was therefore disappointed in finding any who would declare this doctrine as I felt it should be, for the comfort of saints, and as a warning to sinners."— *Id., p. 68.*

THE MILLER CHAPEL

The original meeting place, Low Hampton, N. Y., built by William Miller in 1828

Mr. Miller's correspondence at this time shows a heart full of zeal for God, and an earnest, prayerful interest in the spiritual welfare of his friends and relatives. In the winter of 1828 there was a revival in the Baptist church at Low Hampton, and Mr. Miller was one of the active workers. Two of his own children were among those converted. About the same time the meeting house was destroyed by fire, and it became necessary to build a new house of worship,— a considerable enterprise in view of the small membership of the church and its limited resources. Mr. Miller bent his whole energies to this task, and he was successful.

Meanwhile the conviction grew in strength and in intensity that he ought to warn the world of the coming of the Saviour. The text was constantly ringing in his ears: " If thou dost not speak to warn the wicked from his way, that wicked man shall die in his iniquity; but his blood will I require at thine hand." Thus the poor man struggled on for nine more years. He studied his Bible; he talked with the people with whom he was associated, of the nearness of Christ's coming; but he steadily resisted the conviction that he should present his views in public. Now he had nearly reached the age of fifty, and was unknown to the world, and indeed to his countrymen also, beyond those of his own town and neighborhood.

Mr. Miller began to lecture on the second advent in the late summer of 1831. His conviction of duty had grown stronger and stronger till he was in real distress of mind. Finally he decided with himself, and promised the Lord, that if he should receive an invitation to speak publicly in any place, he would respond to it. Within half an hour from the time he made this decision, a call came from the village of Dresden, about sixteen miles from Low Hampton. There was to be no preaching in the church that Sunday, and Mr. Guilford wished him to come over and speak to the people on the second advent.

The next day, which Mr. Miller remembers as about the first Sunday in August, 1831, he delivered in Mr. Guilford's kitchen his " first public lecture on the second advent." At the close of the service he was requested to remain and give some lectures during the week, and he complied. The outcome of these quiet talks on the prophecies was a genuine revival reaching throughout that sparsely settled neighborhood, in the course of which the members of thirteen families were brought to a saving knowledge of the gospel.

Returning home on the following Monday, Mr. Miller found a letter from a pastor of Poultney, Vt., requesting him to lecture there on the coming of Christ. Thence he went by invitation to Pawlet and other towns in the vicinity, churches of various denominations opening wide doors to him. To quote his own words:

" The most pressing invitations from the ministry and the leading members of the churches poured in continually from that time, during the whole period of my public labors. . . . Churches were thrown open everywhere, and I lectured to crowded houses through the western part of Vermont, the northern part of New York, and in Canada East; and powerful reformations were the result of my labor."— *Id., p. 81.*

Early in 1832, William Miller, at the request of friends, wrote a series of sixteen articles on " The Coming of Christ and the Final Destruction of the Beast," which appeared in the Vermont *Telegraph*, beginning with the issue of May 15. They attracted

8

a good deal of attention, and stimulated the desire to hear more on the subject. They also brought the author numerous letters from ministers and Bible students.

The views of Mr. Miller were quietly spreading. In a letter to Mr. T. Hendryx, a Baptist clergyman, dated Feb. 8, 1833, he writes:

"The Lord is scattering the seed. I can now reckon eight ministers who preach this doctrine, more or less, besides yourself. I know of more than one hundred private brethren who say that they have adopted my views."— *Id., p. 90.*

THE METEORIC SHOWER OF NOV. 13, 1833

On Nov. 13, 1833, occurred the memorable falling of the stars, which, as one of the signs of Christ's second coming, had its effect in turning men's minds to thoughts of higher things. Especially in New England did the awful spectacle produce a deep impression. The feeling prevailed generally that it was in the nature of a divine warning, and it made the people more willing to listen to the evidences from prophecy of the soon-coming Saviour.

From this time on Mr. Miller's life was a strenuous one. He had more calls to lecture than he could possibly fill, and a large correspondence. Wherever he went, his labors produced a deep spiritual quickening, which resulted in permanent additions to the various churches, as well as in the awakening of nominal believers. New York and Vermont received the greatest share of his attention during the years 1834 and 1835. He also entered Lower Canada.

Public engagements were interrupted for a short time in 1836, while he prepared his sixteen lectures for use in book form, the first edition coming out in the spring of that year. He was soon in the field again, however, lecturing in succession at Stillwater, N. Y.; New Haven and Weybridge, Vt.; and Monkton and Lansingburg, N. Y. At the latter place he received $4 to pay his stage fare. This sum, together with two half dollars that a woman handed him during his trip to Lower Canada, constituted, his biographer tells us, "all the remuneration he had thus far received for his expenses." For five years he had been traveling extensively and lecturing to crowded houses, wholly at his own expense. Subsequent to this time, as he says in his "Apology and Defense," he never received enough to meet the expenses involved in traveling to the places whither he had been invited. His labors, instead of being of pecuniary benefit to him, were a considerable drain on his resources.

Nor was Mr. Miller accorded any great recognition in the denomination to which he belonged. In the autumn of 1833 he received a license to preach from the Baptist church of which he was a member. About a year and a half later he received a certificate signed by four Baptist ministers, testifying to his character and standing as a licentiate, and commending him to the confidence of Baptists wherever he might go. Other recognition he received none, nor did he seek it.

The year 1836 closed for Mr. Miller with a number of courses of lectures delivered at various points in New York and Vermont, and he labored in the same States throughout 1837. On the first of January, 1838, he again went to Lansingburg, and gave a course of lectures lasting nine days.

It was during this year that prominent ministers of the gospel first began to join Mr. Miller in the work. One of these was Charles Fitch, pastor of the Marlboro Street chapel of Boston. Another, Josiah Litch, member of the New England Methodist Episcopal Conference, became a very active supporter of the movement. First he issued a pamphlet of forty-eight pages entitled, "The Midnight Cry, or a Review of Mr. Miller's Lectures on the Second Coming of Christ, About A. D. 1843," which had a considerable circulation in New England, and awakened an interest in many minds. In June of the same year, 1838, this pamphlet was followed by a volume of 204 pages, entitled, "The Probability of the Second Advent of Christ, About A. D. 1843," etc. In this work the calculation concerning the fall of the Ottoman supremacy as likely to take place in August, 1840, was first published. This book served greatly to increase public interest in the whole advent movement.

The editor of the Lynn *Record* wrote a notice of Mr. Miller's work in that city, which is interesting as recording the impressions of a fair-minded outsider:

" We took a prejudice against this good man when he first came among us, on account of what we supposed a glaring error in interpreting the Scripture prophecies so that the world would come to an end in 1843. We

JOSIAH LITCH

JOSHUA V. HIMES

are still inclined to believe this an error or miscalculation. At the same time we have overcome our prejudice against him by attending his lectures, and learning more of the excellent character of the man, and of the great good he has done and is doing. Mr. Miller is a plain farmer, and pretends to nothing except that he has made the Scripture prophecies an intense study for many years, understands some of them differently from most other people, and wishes, for the good of others, to spread his views before the public. No one can hear him five minutes without being convinced of his sincerity, and instructed by his reasoning and information. All acknowledge his lectures to be replete with useful and interesting matter. His knowledge of Scripture is very extensive and minute; that of the prophecies, especially, surprisingly familiar. His application of the prophecies to the great events which have taken place in the natural and moral world, is such, generally, as to produce conviction of their truth, and gain the ready assent of his hearers. We have reason to believe that the preaching, or lecturing, of Mr. Miller has been productive of great and extensive good. Revivals have followed in his train. He has been heard with attention wherever he has been."— *Id., pp. 124, 125.*

Of Mr. Miller's appearance and mode of presenting his subject, the editor has this to say:

"There is nothing very peculiar in the manner or appearance of Mr. Miller. Both are at least equal to the style and appearance of ministers in general. His gestures are easy and expressive, and his personal appearance every way decorous. His Scripture explanations and illustrations are strikingly simple, natural, and forcible, and the great eagerness of the people to hear him has been manifested wherever he has preached."— *Id., p. 125.*

Beginning with his ministry in Massachusetts, William Miller was entering upon a broader and more influential career of activity as a lecturer on the prophecies. Especially fruitful was

GRAVE OF JOSHUA V. HIMES
He died at Elk Point, S. Dak., July 27, 1895.

his association with Joshua V. Himes, whom he met in November, 1839, at a conference of the Christian Connection held at Exeter, N. H. Mr. Himes was then pastor of the Chardon Street church in Boston, and he arranged for Mr. Miller to give a course of lectures there, beginning December 8. The meetings drew large crowds, and were, as usual, accompanied by the deep movings of the Spirit of God.

Mr. Miller lodged at the house of Mr. Himes, and the two had many earnest conversations together. As a result of these talks and of the lectures, the younger man became an enthusiastic convert. He said:

"When Mr. Miller had closed his lectures, I found myself in a new position. I could not believe or preach as I had done. Light on this subject was blazing on my conscience day and night."— *Id., p. 128.*

It was in response to an earnest appeal that the Boston minister determined, as he says, to lay himself, his family, and his reputation upon the altar of God in order to help Mr. Miller to the extent of his ability, even to the end.

Joshua Vaughn Himes, the man thus providentially brought into close association with William Miller, was born at Wickford, R. I., May 19, 1805. He was converted at the age of eighteen, uniting with the First Christian church of New Bedford, Mass. Beginning as an exhorter, he soon entered upon evangelistic work in the neighboring schoolhouses, where revivals followed his efforts. In 1827 he entered the ministry of the Christian church, and was appointed to evangelistic labor in

THE FIRST AND MOST IMPORTANT PERIODICAL OF THE MILLER MOVEMENT

southern Massachusetts. After raising up a church of 125 members at Fall River, he was in 1830 called to the pastorate of the First Christian church in Boston, a position he resigned seven years later, to organize the Second Christian church, with a chapel on Chardon Street, where the advent message found him.

Mr. Himes was possessed of qualities which made him peculiarly adapted to the work upon which he was now to enter. In his character were combined deep spirituality and perfect integrity, with a winsome personality and a true instinct for popular presentation. A power in the pulpit, he was perhaps a greater power in the editor's chair. He also possessed business talents of no mean order. Under his guidance the publishing interests of the movement took on rapid growth and development, and it was not long before the best facilities the country could afford were being used to sound the advent warning.

Mr. Miller had long felt the need of a periodical devoted to the proclamation of the message; but no man had been found who could incur the financial risk of such a venture. On returning to Boston for his third course of lectures, in the winter of 1840, the matter of such a publication was broached. In the words of Mr. Miller:

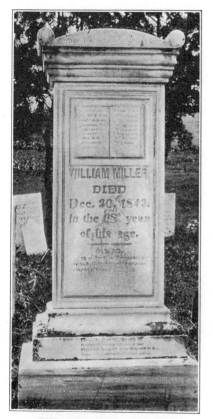

THE RESTING-PLACE OF
WILLIAM MILLER

Low Hampton, N. Y.

"I mentioned to Brother Himes my wishes respecting a paper, and the difficulties I had experienced in the establishment of one. He promptly offered to commence a paper which should be devoted to this question, if I thought the cause of truth would be thereby advanced. The next week, without a subscriber or any promise of assistance, he issued the first number of the *Signs of the Times*."— *Id., pp. 134, 135.*

The first number of this paper (dated Feb. 28, 1840) having come out, Messrs. Dow and Jackson, a well-known publishing firm, offered to issue the paper semimonthly for one year, provided Mr. Himes would furnish the editorial matter gratuitously. This he agreed to do, and the number already printed was reissued under the auspices of this firm, and dated March 20, 1840. Thus it went on for a year, after which the sole responsibility reverted to Mr. Himes, who also took over the publication of the lectures and other works on the prophecies, building up in time a very considerable publishing business.

THE END OF PROPHETIC TIME

"The angel which I saw stand upon the sea and upon the earth lifted up his hand to heaven, and sware by Him that liveth forever and ever . . . that there should be time no longer." Rev. 10 : 5, 6.

"THEY ALL SLUMBERED AND SLEPT"

CHAPTER IV

The Great Advent Awakening

IN the late spring of 1840, William Miller, after conducting meetings in Watertown, Mass., and Portland, Me., gave his first course of lectures in New York City, the audiences being large and attentive. During the summer, Josiah Litch was very active on the lecture platform.

An important event of the autumn was the holding of the first General Conference of Adventist believers. This meeting convened in Boston, at the Chardon Street chapel, on October 14, and lasted two days. At the opening session on Wednesday morning, Joshua V. Himes, the officiating pastor of the church, read the call of the conference as follows:

"The undersigned, believers in the second coming and kingdom of the Messiah 'at hand,' cordially unite in the call of a General Conference of our brethren of the United States and elsewhere, who are also looking for the advent near, to meet at Boston, Mass. [Wednesday], Oct. 14, 1840, at 10 o'clock A. M., to continue two days, or as long as may then be found best.

"The object of the conference will not be to form a new organization in the faith of Christ, nor to assail others of our brethren who differ from us in regard to the period and manner of the advent; but to discuss the whole subject faithfully and fairly, in the exercise of that spirit of Christ in which it will be safe immediately to meet Him at the judgment seat.

" By so doing we may accomplish much in the rapid, general, and powerful spread of ' the everlasting gospel of the kingdom ' at hand, that the way of the Lord may be speedily prepared, whatever may be the precise period of His coming."—" *History of the Second Advent Message and Mission, Doctrine and People*," *by Isaac C. Wellcome, p. 177.*

Henry Dana Ward, of New York City, was chosen chairman *pro tempore,* and delivered a brief address, in which he called attention to the fundamental character of the advent hope as an element in apostolic teaching and preaching. After a committee on nominations had been appointed, Josiah Litch occupied the remainder of the forenoon with an address on " Christ's Coming in Glory." The early part of the afternoon was given to a prayer and social service. The committee on nominations then made its report. Henry Dana Ward was elected chairman; Henry Jones, secretary; and J. V. Himes, Josiah Litch, and Joseph Bates were members of the committee on arrangements.

In the evening, Henry Jones presented extracts from various " Confessions of Faith," sustaining the essential views of the advent believers. The exercises of the day closed with the reading of a circular address to the churches, setting forth the position and work of the advent believers. The address is directed to " all that in every place call upon the name of Jesus Christ our Lord, both theirs and ours." It first passes in review the New Testament teaching concerning the importance of a watchful, waiting attitude on the part of the Christian church. It goes on to set forth quite explicitly the purpose of the conference and the activities of the believers generally:

" Our object in assembling at this time, our object in addressing you, and our object in other efforts, separate and combined, on the subject of ' the kingdom of heaven at hand,' is to revive and restore this ancient faith, to renew the ancient landmarks, to ' stand in the ways, and see, and ask for the old paths, where is the good way ' in which our fathers walked and the martyrs ' found rest for their souls.' . . .

"As believers in this glorious and yet ' terrible day of the Lord ' ' at hand,' it does not become us to judge, censure, or condemn others who see not as we do in regard to this subject, nor to show our zeal for the faith by personally denouncing scoffers and gainsayers. . . . We seek not the honor of this world, nor do we fear its frown; but in the meek and quiet spirit of the gospel, we would walk in all the ordinances of our respective churches blameless, and exhibit in the purity of our lives the holiness and power of the doctrine we profess, in the hope of the appearing of our Lord in His heavenly kingdom.

" Though in some of the less important views of this momentous subject we are not ourselves agreed, particularly in regard to fixing the year of Christ's second advent, yet we are unanimously agreed and established in this all-absorbing point, that the coming of the Lord to judge the world is now specially ' nigh at hand.' . . .

" We are also agreed that at the very commencement of the millennium the Lord will come in the glory of His Father, and all the saints with Him, and that the sinners then remaining alive and ungodly will be slain by the sword of the Lord, or ' taken ' and ' cast alive, with the beast and the false prophet, into a lake of fire burning with brimstone,' [1] instead of being all converted to the obedience of the gospel.

" Again, we are agreed and harmonize with the published creed of the Episcopal, Dutch Reformed, Presbyterian, and Methodist Churches, together with the Cambridge Platform of the Congregational Church, and the Lutheran and Roman Catholic Churches, in maintaining that Christ's second and only coming now will be ' to judge the world at the last day.' "— *Id., pp. 179, 180.*

On Thursday morning there was first a devotional service, then the conference continued:

" The conference heard from different members very interesting reports of the introduction and progress of the doctrine of the kingdom of heaven at hand in the various places of their abode. . . . After which the communion of the Lord's supper was administered by Messrs. Russell and Litch to some two hundred or more communicants of different evangelical denominations, many of whom were from remote distances."

Thursday evening J. V. Himes read a discourse on " The Judgment," sent by William Miller, who was detained at home by illness. The conference was brought to a close with a resolution heartily approving the establishment of *The Signs of the Times,* and calling upon Adventist believers everywhere to rally to its support.

A full report of the conference and of the lectures was issued in pamphlet form and circulated widely. Besides giving publicity to the principles and work of the Adventists, it helped to establish the sense of unity of effort, and to secure a larger degree of co-operation in spreading the message.

As soon as his health permitted, Mr. Miller was again in the field. After filling several engagements in the State of New York, he returned to Boston to give his fourth course of lectures in that city. When these meetings, held in the Chardon Street chapel, were well under way, an invitation was accepted to conduct a course also at the Baptist church in South Boston. This work completed, Mr. Miller next delivered lectures at various points in Massachusetts, and at Providence, R. I., in the latter place the use of the town hall being granted for the purpose by the city council.

During the summer of 1841, several talented men were sounding the message, each in his own sphere: Josiah Litch at the annual conferences of the Methodist Episcopal Church, Henry Dana Ward and Henry Jones in New York City, where the latter was conducting a periodical known as *The Second Advent Wit-*

[1] Rev. 19 : 11-20.

ness. Charles Fitch, who had severed his connection with the movement, rejoined the advent body about this time, and labored earnestly and efficiently. David Millard, Joseph Bates, P. R. Russell, and Calvin French were other leading workers.

Several conferences like the Boston meeting of 1840 were held during the year, the first of these being in Lowell, Mass., June 15-17. D. E. Robinson presided, Joseph Bates was one of the vice-presidents, and Joshua V. Himes and Henry Jones were secretaries. At this meeting it was voted to raise $1,000 for the work, and $649.04 in cash was collected. This action was taken:

"*Resolved,* That we solicit the co-operation of all who heartily love the appearing of Christ in the clouds of heaven, as being near at hand, whatever may be their views of the prophetic numbers, on which some of us found our argument that the advent will take place about the year A. D. 1843.

"*Resolved,* That we will, as ministers and individuals, by the help of God, exert what influence we can, by the consecration of our all to the work of spreading far and wide the great Scriptural doctrine of Christ's coming and kingdom now in all respects especially nigh at hand."—"*History of the Second Advent Message and Mission, Doctrine and People," by Isaac C. Wellcome, p. 212.*

The second conference of the year was held Oct. 12-14, 1841, in Portland, Me., and was a source of great encouragement to the large number of Adventists in attendance. It had a considerable effect also upon the people of Portland, many of whom were converted by the stirring sermons and Bible studies, and joined the number of those who were looking for the near advent of the Saviour.

The third conference was convened in Broadway Tabernacle, New York City, Oct. 25, 1841, the Rev. John Lindsey, of the Methodist Episcopal Church, presiding. The chairman announced as the topic for consideration, "The Kingdom of Heaven, as Preached in the Gospel. Is a Future Dispensation Near at Hand?" Addresses were given by Josiah Litch, Henry Dana Ward, Joshua V. Himes, and others. The following notice appeared in the New York *Tribune* of Wednesday, October 27:

"*The Millennium.*— A convention of Christians who feel a special interest in the subject of the second coming of Christ assembled on Monday in this city, and has since held three sessions daily in the Tabernacle. They are fairly attended. There is little or no discussion, but the members give their views on the subject in succession, sometimes from treatises prepared beforehand, sometimes direct from the heart. The members appear thoughtful, earnest men, and generally impressed with the conviction that some special manifestation of divine power is near at hand. The sessions will be continued, and we presume the attendance increased, today."

Another newspaper report, after commenting on the general harmony that prevailed in the meeting, mentions some divergence of opinion in reference to " fixing a time " for the advent. This point may be worthy of notice. People of today, looking back upon the advent movement of the thirties and forties, are apt to emphasize the time element at the expense of other elements equally important, and perhaps even more characteristic. It is an interesting and significant fact that prominent supporters of Mr. Miller were opposed to the setting of any definite time. Among these were Henry Dana Ward and Henry Jones, of New York City, both of whom took part in the first advent conference in Boston. They subscribed to the general teaching of the Adventists, and were themselves a part of the movement, but they could not agree to fix a date for the advent. Their attitude on this point was made clear at the first conference.

Mr. Ward wrote an article, which was published in the *Signs of the Times* of December, 1841, setting forth his view concerning time-setting, and giving reasons. He based his position chiefly on such texts as these :

" Of that day and hour knoweth no man."

" Take ye heed, watch and pray: for ye know not when the time is."

" It is not for you to know the times or the seasons, which the Father hath put in His own power."

" The Father [urged Mr. Ward] did not intend we should know them, and for this cause He ' hath put ' them ' in His own power,' that men may be constantly on the watch, and never at liberty to say, ' The Lord will not come this day, this year, these thousand years, but He will come at such a time.' "

The question may arise, " How could a man with such views associate himself with Mr. Miller? " A further quotation from the same article will help to clear up this difficulty. The writer goes on to point out the fact that the most active opponents of Mr. Miller were advocates of a temporary millennium to precede the coming of Christ. He says :

" We observe that the people, above all others, vexed at certain men for fixing dates to future events, are the same who have favorite dates of their own to watch for, and therefore their true vexation arises, not so much against the foretelling of times, which they themselves practise, as against the particular time foretold, which conflicts with some favorite view of their own. . . .

" Those who limit the times to two years, are no more transgressors for this, than those who extend them to a thousand or more. They are alike dealers in prophetic times, but the larger class on much the larger scale. Men think it good to calculate that this world will continue yet a thousand years at least, but to calculate that it will continue only two years, is the height of presumption, and it ever excites the ridicule and contempt of the larger prophets. We have nothing to do with either of these but to moderate the assurances with which one calculates this, and another that fixed time;

besides, we like to see fair play, and to defend a small minority for taking the liberty which the great majority freely use, to discuss and predetermine the times."

Mr. Jones, who is said to have been a Presbyterian minister, conducted a friendly discussion over the question of time-setting with Josiah Litch in the columns of the *Signs of the Times*. His sentiments are expressed in a letter to the General Conference held at Portland in October, 1841. He says:

" Some of us think differently as to the 'times and the seasons,' and of course, thus far, we naturally think differently as to the expediency of certain measures of each other in laboring in the common cause. But let us thank God and take courage, that so soon after our long slumbering over this subject, we are already so well agreed as we are in the most important and awakening points of the great doctrine; and let us co-operate with our whole hearts in things wherein we are entirely 'agreed,' remembering that it will not necessarily make us responsible for any mistakes we may suppose to be made by each other, while not ourselves sustaining them, and while allowed freely to disclaim them, when we think it needful."

Both Mr. Ward and Mr. Jones were consistent believers in the doctrine of the personal, premillennial coming of Christ; and although they saw danger in the preaching of even a definite year for that great event, they felt drawn in spirit to the Adventists as Christians who, like themselves, cherished the blessed hope, and were preaching it to a cold and unbelieving world. And the fact that they and others who shared their views co-operated so heartily with Mr. Miller and Mr. Himes, is eloquent testimony to the Christian charity and broad-mindedness of both parties, as well as to the unifying and consolidating influence of the belief in Christ's soon coming.

Owing to ill health, Mr. Miller did not enter the field again until about the middle of September, 1841. He then devoted a month to lecturing to crowded houses in various parts of New York State. The 18th of October saw him back again in Low Hampton, where he presided over a conference of advent believers, the fourth and last of these gatherings held in the year 1841, which assembled in the Low Hampton Baptist church early in November. This meeting was a source of special pleasure to Mr. Miller, being the first one of the kind he had been able to attend. It rejoiced his heart to be surrounded by so many able men whose hearts were on fire with the message that he had been trying, almost alone, to give to the world.

Immediately after this meeting, Josiah Litch conducted a three weeks' course of lectures at Newark, N. J., and then, at the invitation of J. J. Porter, went to Philadelphia, where he spent three weeks, and saw fruit of his labors in the raising up of a little band of believers. This was the first introduction of the advent message south of New York.

Meanwhile Mr. Miller was lecturing in various parts of New Hampshire and Massachusetts. In Boston he delivered, at Boylston Hall, his sixth course of lectures. After leaving that city, he labored in New Hampshire and New York, ending his tour in the latter State with a course of lectures at Sandy Hill, Jan. 27 to Feb. 3, 1842, in the Presbyterian church, where, during the closing days, a conference of advent believers was held. On the last evening the services were held at the courthouse, and about one hundred arose for prayer.

An impressive testimony was borne at this meeting by H. B. Northop, a prominent lawyer of the place. He had attended the lectures, he said, with a mind strongly predisposed against the doctrine taught. He had noted carefully all that was said, and had tried to make a breach at every point where he thought one could be made, but had been unable to make it; and now after studying the history, sacred and profane, and the prophetic periods, he would frankly confess that he had never found anything that would compare with Mr. Miller's position for strength of evidence.

The early spring of 1842 found Mr. Miller addressing crowded audiences in the town hall at Worcester, Mass., after which he lectured for a week in the city hall of Hartford, Conn., but could not complete the course, owing to a severe attack of catarrh and influenza. The Hartford *Christian Secretary*, a Baptist periodical, remarked upon the "immense crowd which attended the whole course of lectures," and said:

"Probably not less than from fifteen hundred to two thousand persons were in attendance every evening. This large mass of hearers was made up from nearly or quite every congregation in the city. How many of them have become converts to this new doctrine we have no means of judging, but presume the number is not very small. Of one thing we are satisfied, and that is this: unless the clergy generally present a better theory than the one offered by Mr. Miller, the doctrine will prevail to a very general extent."

It was at these meetings that Mr. Sylvester Bliss, author of "Sacred Chronology" and a "Life of William Miller," became, in his own words, "convinced that the second advent is to be premillennial; and the first resurrection, a 'resurrection out from among the dead.'"

Later in the spring, it was decided to present the advent message more fully in New York City. Apollo Hall on Broadway was rented at heavy expense, and lectures were begun by Miller and Himes in the month of May. The work went slowly

THE 1843 CHART

Made by Charles Fitch, and adopted by the Adventist Conference held in Boston in 1842

at first; but the prejudice gradually wore away, and the attendance increased, so that before the meetings were brought to a close, the house was nightly filled with attentive listeners, and the speakers felt assured that a permanent interest had been created in the great metropolis.

While these meetings were proceeding in New York, the Adventist believers in Boston decided to have a general rally in that city. The Melodeon, a large and centrally located hall, was secured for the purpose, and the meetings were fully attended and very enthusiastic. At the conference held in connection with this rally two important steps were taken, which were to exert a wide and deep influence upon the future work of the Adventists. The first was the adoption of the prophetic chart. It was at this meeting that Charles Fitch exhibited a chart which he had made to illustrate the prophecies of Daniel and the Revelation, and showed its use in giving an audience a clear understanding of the subject. The idea met with instant acceptance. A resolution was passed, authorizing the printing of three hundred lithographed copies of Elder Fitch's chart for use in lectures. The charts were soon in general use, and contributed much to the clearness and force with which the prophecies were presented.

CHARLES FITCH

The other step taken was the decision to enter upon the holding of camp-meetings as a means of building up the spiritual life of the believers, and of spreading abroad the tidings of a soon-coming Saviour. It was expected that the first such meeting would be held in the States, but as circumstances turned out, it was held in Canada. Immediately after the Boston conference, Josiah Litch, who had severed his connection with the Methodist ministry, and had labored successfully in Philadelphia and other cities, visited Canada East. We find this account in the *Advent Shield:*

"Before two weeks were passed, the country for thirty or forty miles around was awake to the subject of the Lord's coming. Immense concourses assembled, both in Canada and in Derby, Vt., where a course of lectures was given. Such was the interest to hear, and the awakening among the people, that it was determined at once to hold a camp-meeting in Canada. . . . A place was selected, the ground prepared, and the meeting held in the township of Hatley, Canada East. Such was the good effect of this first meeting, that the people of Bolton wished one to be held in their town. This was begun the next week after the Hatley meeting closed, and ended on the third of July. During that month's labor, as near as could be estimated, five of six hundred souls were converted to God."—"*The Advent Shield and Review*," *Vol. I, p. 68.*

On June 29, 1842, the advent believers assembled for their first camp-meeting in the States. Concerning this meeting, which was the precursor of larger and more important gatherings, the Boston *Post* had the following to say:

"The second advent camp-meeting, which commenced at East Kingston, N. H., on Tuesday, June 29, and continued from day to day until Tuesday noon, July 5, was attended by an immense concourse of people, variously estimated at from seven to ten thousand. . . .

"The meeting was conducted with great regularity and good order from beginning to end. The ladies were seated on one side, and the gentlemen on the other, of the speaker; meals were served uniformly and punctually at the times appointed, and the same punctuality was observed as to the hours appointed for the services.

"The preachers were twelve or fifteen. Mr. Miller gave the only regular course of lectures, the others speaking occasionally. Many of the people, without doubt, assembled from motives of curiosity merely; but the great body of them, from their solemn looks and close attention to the subject, were evidently actuated by higher and more important motives. Each tent was under the supervision of a tent-master, who was responsible for the good order within the same. . . . The meeting broke up with harmony and good feeling."

Among the casual visitors to this camp-meeting was the poet, J. G. Whittier, who a few years later referred to it in the following words:

"Three or four years ago, on my way eastward, I spent an hour or two at a camp-ground of the second advent in East Kingston. The spot was well chosen. A tall growth of pine and hemlock threw its melancholy shadow over the multitude, who were arranged on rough seats of boards and logs. Several hundred — perhaps a thousand — people were present, and more were rapidly coming. Drawn about in a circle, forming a background of snowy whiteness to the dark masses of men and foliage, were the white tents, and back of them the provision stalls and cook shops.

"When I reached the ground, a hymn, the words of which I could not distinguish, was pealing through the dim aisles of the forest. I know nothing of music, having neither ear nor taste for it; but I could readily see that it had its effect upon the multitude before me, kindling to higher intensity their already excited enthusiasm. The preachers were placed in a rude pulpit of rough boards, carpeted only by the dead forest leaves and flowers, and tasseled, not with silk and velvet, but with the green boughs of the somber hemlocks around it. One of them followed the music in an earnest exhortation on the duty of preparing for the great event. Occasionally he was really eloquent, and his description of the last day had all the terrible distinctness of Anelli's painting of 'The End of the World.'

"Suspended from the front of the rude pulpit were two broad sheets of canvas, upon one of which was the figure of a man — the head of gold, the breast and arms of silver, the belly of brass, the legs of iron, and feet of clay — the dream of Nebuchadnezzar! On the other were depicted the wonders of the Apocalyptic vision — the beasts, the dragons, the scarlet woman — seen by the seer of Patmos. . . .

"To an imaginative mind the scene was full of novel interest. The white circle of tents, the dim wood arches, the upturned, earnest faces, the loud voices of the speakers, burdened with the awful symbolic language of the Bible — the smoke from the fires rising like incense from forest altars, carried one back to the days of primitive worship, when

"'The groves were god's first temples.'"

— *Quoted on p. 438 of "Our First Century," by R. M. Devens.*

The success of this camp-meeting, and the rapidly growing interest to hear on the part of the public, coupled with the fact that the churches were somewhat generally closing their doors against the advent preaching, suggested the advisability of constructing a mammoth tent for the accommodation of the crowds who flocked to hear. The project was soon under way, and within a few weeks a canvas " Tabernacle " capable of seating four thousand people was at the disposal of the lecturers. It was used for the first time at Concord, N. H., where it was pitched to excellent advantage on an eminence in the rear of the Statehouse. Following this meeting, which was held at the close of July, the big tent was used in succession in Albany, N. Y.; at Chicopee Falls and Salem, Mass.; at Benson, Vt.; and in Newark, N. J. In all these places enormous crowds gathered to hear the message proclaimed from the pulpit, and to provide themselves with advent books and papers.

The meeting at Chicopee Falls, about four miles from Springfield, was held immediately at the close of a big Methodist camp-meeting, and on the same grounds. Hiram Munger, a Methodist whom the Adventists employed as superintendent of the grounds, has recorded his impressions of the gathering. The Methodists, he tells us, had just closed the best meeting they ever held in New England, over one hundred conversions being reported. When the Adventists came with their canvas tabernacle, he was astonished at its great size.

"I never saw half so large a tent before. I and others thought and said, 'Where are all the people coming from to fill it?' for it was estimated to hold from three thousand to four thousand."—"*History of the Second Advent Message and Mission, Doctrine and People,*" *by Isaac C. Wellcome, p. 245.*

The people kept coming, however, and finally, he says:

" A great multitude came, and many of my Methodist brethren came back and took possession of their tents, which they had left in my care.

" Sunday they began to come very early, and continued to come until the whole tent was filled, and they came till the whole circle of the tents was full, and the whole grove literally filled with people, while the preaching was listened to with great attention. . . .

" The first time Brother Himes attempted to call on sinners to come forward to the altar for prayers, I truly thought him beside himself, for our meeting had been crowned with such success that I did not think any would come forward, and I kept watch while the first three verses were being sung, when there was such a rush to the altar for prayers as I had never seen. . . . I was so astonished to see those forward who had stood through *our* meeting, that I did not speak for some time; truly, I thought, God was in the place, and I knew it not; and when prayer was offered, such a work ensued as had not been seen on that ground before. Some of my friends were forward, and some church members, all pleading for mercy. I recollect asking Brother Hawks (a Methodist minister) what he thought of it. He answered, ' It is the work of God in good earnest.' "— *Id., pp. 245, 246.*

Among the preachers who took a leading part in this meeting were Charles Fitch, J. V. Himes, P. T. Kenney, and L. C. Collins. The latter wrote a report for the *Signs of the Times,* from which a few extracts may be taken:

" There were present some fifteen ministers of the gospel, who officiated in the meetings, and were firm believers in the doctrine advocated. The friends of the cause were there assembled with their tents, from different parts of the country, some from a distance of more than two hundred miles. The tents were arranged in a circular form about the ground, and the great Tabernacle [was] pitched in the center. . . .

" The tide of feeling was overwhelming, yet it was but the result of a rational conviction that humbles the soul at the foot of the cross, and pleads for mercy in the name of Jesus."

Early in November, Mr. Himes erected the big tent in Newark, N. J., Mr. Miller joining him for seven days, during which he gave fourteen lectures. Owing to the inclemency of the weather, it was necessary to hold the meetings the last four days in the Presbyterian church. On Sunday the people assembled in the large Mechanics' Hall, and even this was too small for them. In the afternoon Mr. Miller addressed a crowd of nearly five thousand from the steps of the courthouse.

From Newark he went to New York City, where he gave a third course of lectures on the second advent. He spoke on this occasion in a church on the corner of Catherine and Madison Streets, where George Storrs had been conducting services for some weeks. While the meetings were going on, a request was made that a series of lectures might be given also in the Meth-

odist Protestant church, which was under the pastoral care of
E. Jacobs. The invitation was accepted by Apollos Hale, whose
preaching resulted in winning many earnest converts to the
advent teaching.

So great was the interest in New York that Mr. Himes
decided to publish a daily paper for at least four weeks, with
a view to getting the advent views before the public in cheap,

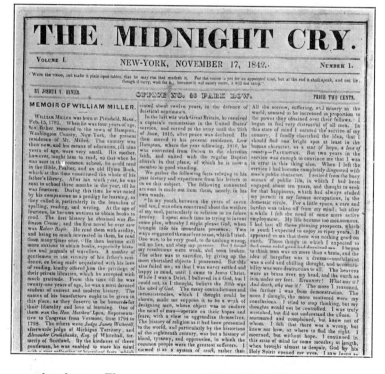

popular form. The paper was entitled *The Midnight Cry*, and
appeared in a daily edition of 10,000 copies for four weeks,
after which it was issued weekly. The editorial work was done
chiefly by N. Southard. The paper had a wide circulation outside of New York City, and did much to enlighten the public
in reference to the advent movement.

William Miller gave his next course of lectures in the Methodist Episcopal church at New Haven, Conn. Of the interest

manifested in these meetings the *Fountain,* a local temperance paper, says:

> " It is estimated that not less than three thousand persons were in attendance at the church on each evening for a week; and if the almost breathless silence which reigned throughout the immense throng for two or three hours at a time is any evidence of interest in the subject of the lectures, it cannot be said that our community are devoid of feeling on this momentous question."—" *Sketches of the Christian Life and Public Labors of William Miller,*" *by James White, p. 167.*

Referring to the speaker, the paper said further:

> " In justice to Mr. Miller we are constrained to say that he is one of the most interesting lecturers we have any recollection of ever having heard."
> — *Id., p. 168.*

The autumn and winter of 1842-43 witnessed a steady growth in the number of advent lecturers. Not only did experienced preachers join the movement in increasing numbers, but young men who had intended to devote their lives to other pursuits were brought under deep conviction, and after very short preparation, went out to sound the warning. Prominent among these was James White, of Palmyra, Maine. The advent preaching found him planning to complete his course at the Academy at St. Albans, Maine, and then go through college; but the Spirit did not permit him to return to his books. After struggling for months against the conviction that God had called him to preach, he finally yielded, and was soon in the field.

After doing some preaching in the vicinity of Palmyra, he received an urgent invitation to visit Brunswick, where he was told the Freewill Baptists would gladly hear lectures on the second advent. " So, in January, 1843," he says, " I left on horseback, thinly clad, and without money, to go more than a hundred miles among strangers." He spent the first night at a small place near Augusta, the capital, where he was invited to lecture. This opened the way for other invitations, and it was some days before he could proceed farther. The Freewill Baptists received him cordially. He first lectured in the church of Andrew Rollins, known as the Reed meeting house, and then went on to meet other engagements, coming back two weeks later to attend the general meeting of Freewill Baptists for that section.

At this meeting the young preacher received invitations from nearly all the ministers present to speak in their churches, and a series of appointments was planned for him in twelve of the more important places. It was necessary to cover the ground rapidly because only six weeks of firm sleighing remained.

He was accordingly to give on the average twenty lectures a week, which allowed him only a half day each week in which to travel often fifteen or twenty miles to the next meeting place. At the next quarterly meeting it was stated publicly that no less than one thousand souls dated their Christian experience from the lectures given during those six weeks. Such were the mighty results of the advent message, even when it came from the lips of a mere youth.

About the same time Charles Fitch had encouraging success in giving the message in Ohio. Especially cordial was the reception he met in Cleveland. Soon after he began to lecture in that city, Mr. Smead, a printer, began to publish a paper in the interests of the work, which, with the aid of voluntary donations from friends of the movement, he was able to issue regularly for some months. Another convert bought a hundred dollars' worth of Adventist literature, which he distributed free to spread the principles. Mr. Fitch also visited Oberlin Institute, where he lectured before the students and faculty on the fulfilling prophecies, and was encouraged by the deep interest manifested.

Time was passing rapidly, the looked-for year was just ahead, and there was a general demand for a brief but definite statement of Adventist views, especially in reference to the time when the great event should take place. Mr. Miller accordingly issued, at the close of the year 1842, the following synopsis of his views, which may be taken as embodying the teaching of Adventists at the time of which we are writing:

" 1. I believe Jesus Christ will come again to this earth. Proof: John 14:3; Acts 1:11; 1 Thess. 4:16; Rev. 1:7.

" 2. I believe He will come in all the glory of His Father. Proof: Matt. 16:27; Mark 8:38.

" 3. I believe He will come in the clouds of heaven. Proof: Matt. 24:30; Mark 13:26; Dan. 7:13.

" 4. I believe He will then receive His kingdom, which will be eternal. Proof: Dan. 7:14; Luke 19:12, 15; 2 Tim. 4:1.

" 5. I believe the saints will then possess the kingdom forever. Proof: Dan. 7:18, 22, 27; Matt. 24:34; Luke 12:22, 29; 1 Cor. 9:25; 2 Tim. 4:8; James 1:12; 1 Peter 5:4.

" 6. I believe at Christ's second coming the body of every departed saint will be raised, like Christ's glorious body. Proof: 1 Cor. 15:20-29; 1 John 3:2.

" 7. I believe that the righteous who are living on the earth when He comes, will be changed from mortal to immortal bodies, and with them who are raised from the dead, will be caught up to meet the Lord in the air, and so be forever with the Lord. Proof: 1 Cor. 15:51-53; Phil. 3:20, 21; 1 Thess. 4: 14-17.

" 8. I believe the saints will then be presented to God blameless, without spot or wrinkle, in love. Proof: 1 Cor. 4:14; Eph. 5:27; Col. 1:22; Jude 24; 1 Thess. 3:13; 1 Cor. 1:7, 8.

" 9. I believe, when Christ comes the second time, He will come to finish the controversy of Zion, to deliver His children from all bondage, to conquer their last enemy, and to deliver them from the power of the tempter, which is the devil. Proof: Deut. 24:1; Isa. 34:8; 40:2, 5; 41:10-12; Rom. 8: 21-23; Heb. 2:13-15; 1 Cor. 15:54, 56; Rev. 20:1-6.

" 10. I believe that when Christ comes, He will destroy the bodies of the living wicked by fire, as those of the old world were destroyed by water, and shut up their souls in the pit of woe, until their resurrection unto damnation. Proof: Ps. 50:3; 97:3; Isa. 66:15, 16; Dan. 7:10; Mal. 4:1; Matt. 3:12; 1 Cor. 3:13; 1 Thess. 5:2, 3; 2 Thess. 1:7-9; 1 Peter 1:7; 2 Peter 3:7, 10; Isa. 24:21, 22; Jude 6-15; Rev. 20:3-15; John 5:29; Acts 24:15.

" 11. I believe, when the earth is cleansed by fire, that Christ and His saints will then take possession of the earth, and dwell therein forever. Then the kingdom will be given to the saints. Proof: Ps. 37:9-11, 22-34; Prov. 2:21, 22; 10:30; Isa. 60:21; Matt. 5:5; Rev. 5:10.

" 12. I believe the time is appointed of God when these things shall be accomplished. Proof: Acts 17:31; Job 7:1; 14:14; Ps. 81:3; Isa. 40:2; Dan. 8:19; 10:1; 11:35; Hab. 2:3; Acts 17:26.

" 13. I believe God has revealed the time. Proof: Isa. 44:7, 8; 45:20, 21; Dan. 12:10; Amos 3:7; 1 Thess. 5:4.

" 14. I believe many who are professors and preachers will never believe or know the time until it comes upon them. Proof: Jer. 8:7; Matt. 24:50; Jer. 25:34-37.

" 15. I believe the wise, they who are to shine as the brightness of the firmament (Dan. 12:3), will understand the time. Proof: Eccl. 8:5; Dan. 12:10; Matt. 24:43-45; 25:6-10; 1 Thess. 5:4; 1 Peter 1:9-13.

" 16. I believe the time can be known by all who desire to understand and to be ready for His coming. And I am fully convinced that sometime between March 21, 1843, and March 21, 1844, according to the Jewish mode of computation of time, Christ will come, and bring all His saints with Him; and that then He will reward every man as his works shall be. Proof: Matt. 16:27; Rev. 22: 12."—" *Sketches of the Christian Life and Public Labors of William Miller,*" *pp. 170-173.*

Mr. Miller also, at the opening of the year 1843, addressed a letter to the believers, which sheds so much light upon both the character of the revered leader himself and the nature of the Adventist teaching at that time, that we reproduce it in part (see idem., pp. 173-176) :

" DEAR BRETHREN: This year, according to our faith, is the last year that Satan will reign in our earth. Jesus Christ will come and bruise his head. . . . Let us then put forth our best energies in this cause; let every one of us try, by persuasion, by the help and grace of God, to get one, at least, of our friends to come to Christ in this last year of redemption; and if we succeed, what an army of regenerated souls may we not hail in the new heavens and new earth! I pray God, my brethren, that nothing may deter you from this work. . . .

" The world will watch for our halting. They cannot think we believe what we speak, for they count our faith a strange faith; and now beware, and not give them any vantage ground over us. They will, perhaps, look for the halting and falling away of many. But I hope none who are looking for the glorious appearing will let their faith waver. Keep cool; let patience have its perfect work; that, after ye have done the will of God, ye may receive the promise. . . .

"Then let me advise to a continual searching for truth, both for faith and practice; and wherever we have wandered from the Word of God, let us come back to the primitive simplicity of the gospel once delivered to the saints. Thus we shall be found ready at His coming to give an account of our stewardship, and hear our blessed Master say, 'Well done, thou good and faithful servant; enter thou into the joy of thy Lord.' . . .

"May you be patient in all tribulation, and endure unto the end. May you this year be crowned with immortality and glory. And finally, my brethren, pray God, your whole body, soul, and spirit be preserved blameless unto the coming of the Lord Jesus Christ.

(Signed) "WILLIAM MILLER.

"*Low Hampton, Jan. 1, 1843.*"

Meanwhile Mr. Miller did not in the least abate his labors. After addressing the usually large audiences in Waterford and Utica, N. Y., and in Bennington, Vt., he went to Philadelphia, and entered upon one of the most important of his engagements. The city had listened to one series of lectures given by Josiah Litch, and there was a general desire to hear more. The meetings were held in the large hall of the Chinese Museum, and the interest deepened till the close. Something like a thousand persons testified to their faith in the doctrines taught.

These meetings, says the *Advent Shield,* placed the cause in Philadelphia on a firm foundation, and prepared the way for extensions to the south and west. A book-room was opened early in January, and thirteen numbers of a penny paper, *The Philadelphia Alarm,* were issued in editions of 4,000 each. This paper was succeeded by *The Trumpet of Alarm,* an illustrated paper giving a connected view of the advent doctrines, and intended especially for circulation in the West.

About this time Josiah Litch paid a short visit to Washington, D. C., and obtained a hearing in the Methodist Protestant church at the Navy Yard. Later, accompanied by E. Hale, Jr., he proceeded west as far as Pittsburgh, finding everywhere an eager interest in the advent views. Work was also carried on in Cincinnati, and thence spread rapidly over the West, little bands of believers beginning to form in Illinois, Michigan, and other States, and sending urgent messages for the living preacher.

In the East a number of able men, such as N. N. Whiting, J. B. Cook, and F. G. Brown, were taking their stand with the Adventists, and devoting their whole energies to the proclamation of the message. In Canada on the north, H. B. Skinner and L. Caldwell, in the winter and spring of 1843, were putting out many thousands of copies of a weekly paper entitled, *The*

Faithful Watchman, as well as scattering other literature and giving lectures as the way opened.

EVIDENCE

FROM

SCRIPTURE AND HISTORY

OF THE

SECOND COMING OF CHRIST,

ABOUT

THE YEAR 1843;

EXHIBITED

IN A COURSE OF LECTURES.

By WILLIAM MILLER.

BOSTON:
PUBLISHED BY JOSHUA V. HIMES,
14 Devonshire Street.
1842.

ONE OF MANY SUCH PUBLICATIONS

The large use made of the printing press has from the first been a characteristic feature of the advent movement. Periodicals were conducted for a time at all the important centers. Books were published and sold from house to house, and in many cases given away by friends of the movement. Tracts and pamphlets dealing with a large variety of subjects and written by many different authors, among them Miller, Himes, Litch, Jones, Ward, Fitch, and Hale, were continually coming out, and were being circulated by thousands.

From Philadelphia, Mr. Miller went to Trenton, N. J., to spend Sunday, but remained at the invitation of the mayor, and lectured three days to crowded houses. Then followed engagements at various points in New York State, occupying the time till after the middle of March, when Mr. Miller was incapacitated for labor by an attack of erysipelas, which, with complications, kept him very low for a time. Early in September he had recovered his usual health, and entered upon a course of engagements in New Hampshire and Massachusetts.

About this time the advent cause in Boston suffered a slight backset, from which it quickly recovered. John Starkweather, a graduate of Andover Theological Seminary, and an accepted minister among the orthodox Congregationalists, joined the Adventists in the autumn of 1842, and was installed assistant pastor of the Chardon Street chapel, Mr. Himes, the pastor, being at this time compelled to do considerable preaching and lecturing in other places, besides being burdened heavily with editorial work. The new incumbent was of fine presence, possessed a powerful voice, and had a reputation for sanctity. But he had peculiar views on the subject of sanctification, and endeavored to make them a test of Christian fellowship.

Mr. Himes bore with his assistant for a time; but when it became manifest that his course was greatly injuring the cause of God, he called the people together and told them plainly what was the nature of the teaching which they were receiving, and to what it would lead. Mr. Starkweather, after a vehement reply, withdrew with his sympathizers. Thereafter he and his few followers had no connection with the body of Adventists, who were loyal to the principles taught by Messrs. Miller and Himes. He professed, however, to be a part of the movement, and enemies of Mr. Miller were eager to blame him and his followers for the unwise course of this ill-balanced and self-seeking enthusiast.

Starting from Rochester, N. Y., on Nov. 9, 1843, William Miller spoke to the passengers on the canal boat on the way, finding them attentive. At Rochester he addressed large audiences in the afternoon and evening of each day from the 12th to the 19th. His work here was the more effective because Mr. Himes and others had done some preliminary work in the early summer, publishing thirteen numbers of a paper entitled *Glad Tidings,* which had been widely circulated.

After filling other appointments, Mr. Miller began early in December to hold meetings in the theater at Buffalo, N. Y. Writing to a friend on the third day after his arrival, he said: "Yesterday I saw the tears of some in the congregation, who, I am informed, were old, hardened infidels." Nothing gave Mr. Miller greater joy than to see the hearts of unbelievers melt under the subduing influences of God's love.

Toward the close of January, 1844, Mr. Miller began his seventh course of lectures in Boston. In this city, at that time the cultural center of the United States, the interest in the advent movement had grown steadily ever since the giving of the first series of lectures in the Chardon Street chapel. That house of worship proving wholly inadequate to accommodate the rapidly growing number of believers, there had been erected on Howard Street, in the spring of 1843, at comparatively small expense, a large assembly hall known as the Tabernacle, which could seat an audience of 3,500; but even the Tabernacle was too small to accommodate the crowds that came to hear on this occasion.

Mr. Miller and Mr. Himes arrived in New York on February 6, and found an Adventist conference in session in Franklin Hall. Mr. Miller began lecturing there, but the seating capacity being inadequate, the meetings were taken to Broadway chapel, where the large audience was "solemn and attentive."

The nation's capital was now to have a good opportunity to hear the advent message under the labors of Miller, Himes, and Litch. The meetings began on February 20, in a Baptist church near the Navy Yard; but this place becoming greatly crowded, the evangelist moved on the 26th to Apollo Hall, close by the White House, where they continued till the 2d of March, numbers of Representatives and Senators attending.

Mr. Miller was deeply impressed with the hearty response given the message in Washington. Writing to Sylvester Bliss, he said:

"This place is being shaken. The common-sense people who hear, go away convinced of the truth of our exposition of God's blessed Book, and we have some advocates in every public place, even in the halls of justice. and some in the legislative councils. . . . I must say, although I am astonished while I say it, never have I been listened to with so deep a feeling, with such intense interest for hours; and never have the lectures done apparently so much in convincing the hearers of the truth of the doctrine we advocate, as on this tour."

Two numbers of an advent periodical, *The Southern Midnight Cry,* were issued in connection with the lectures in Washington. Later numbers were issued at Baltimore. Urgent calls came from Charleston, Savannah, Mobile, and other large cities in the South, but it was not possible to respond to them, owing to previous engagements.

The lecturers held meetings in Baltimore, March 3-8. Mr. Miller lectured in Philadelphia on the 10th, in Newark, N. J., on the 11th, in New York on the 12th, and in Brooklyn and Williamsburg, N. Y., on the 13th, after which he returned to his home at Low Hampton.

From this on, his biographer tells us, he seems to have kept no account of his labors, his notebook closing at the end of this tour with the words: " Now I have given, since 1832, three thousand two hundred lectures." The tired workman thought he was laying down his tools; for his exposition of the prophecy had led him to expect the Lord to appear in glory during that year from March 21, 1843, to March 21, 1844. He expected soon to hear the " Well done, good and faithful servant; " but he was to be disappointed. The Lord had yet larger things in view for the advent people. The command had gone forth: " Thou must prophesy again before many peoples, and nations, and tongues, and kings." But before this larger sphere of usefulness could be entered upon, there must come a period of bitter trial and disappointment, which would test to the utmost the patience and endurance of the advent believers.

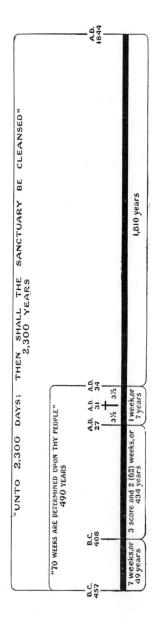

"UNTO 2,300 DAYS; THEN SHALL THE SANCTUARY BE CLEANSED"
2,300 YEARS

"70 WEEKS ARE DETERMINED UPON THY PEOPLE"
490 YEARS

| B.C. 457 | B.C. 408 | A.D. 27 | A.D. 31 | A.D. 34 | | A.D. 1844 |

7 weeks,or 49 years

3 score and 2 (62) weeks,or 434 years

3½ 3½

1 week,or 7 years

1,810 years

THE 2300 DAYS

The heavy line represents the full 2300 year-day period, the longest prophetic period in the Bible. Beginning in B. C. 457 when the decree was given to restore and build Jerusalem (Ezra 7:11-26; Dan. 9:25), seven weeks (49 years) are measured off to indicate the time occupied in this work of restoration. These, however, are a part of the sixty-nine weeks (483 years) that were to reach to Messiah, the Anointed One. Christ was anointed in 27 A. D., at His baptism. Matt. 3:13-17; Acts 10:38. In the midst of the seventieth week (31 A. D.), Christ was crucified, or "cut off," which marked the time when the sacrifices and oblations of the earthly sanctuary were to cease. Dan. 9: 26, 27. The remaining three and one-half years of this week reach to 34 A. D., or to the stoning of Stephen, and the great persecution of the church at Jerusalem which followed. Acts 7:59; 8:1. This marked the close of the seventy weeks, or 490 years, allotted to the Jewish people.

But the seventy weeks are a part of the 2300 days; and as they (the seventy weeks) reach to 34 A. D., the remaining 1810 years of the 2300-day period must reach to 1844, when the work of judgment, or cleansing of the heavenly sanctuary, was to begin. Rev. 14:6, 7. Then special light began to shine upon the whole sanctuary subject, and Christ's mediatorial or priestly work in it.

Four great events, therefore, are located by this great prophetic period,— the first advent, the crucifixion, the rejection of the Jewish people as a nation, and the beginning of the work of final judgment.

142

THE MIDNIGHT CRY

"At midnight there was a cry made, Behold, the bridegroom cometh ; go yet out to meet him." Matt. 25 : 6.

CHAPTER V

The Summer and Autumn of 1844

IT was in the summer of 1844 that the followers of William Miller first became a separate body. In tracing the steps leading up to this consummation, it will be necessary to go back a few years in the history of the movement. When Mr. Miller first began to lecture on the second advent, he was cordially welcomed by the ministers and laymen of all evangelical denominations. In fact, he expounded his views only where he was invited to do so, and the hearers, if they did not wholly agree with the lectures, manifested a friendly interest in the subject.

As an example of this open-minded attitude, the Rockingham Christian Conference, held at Newton, N. H., in the summer of 1840, passed the following resolutions:

"*1. Resolved,* That the doctrine of Christ's second coming to judge the world, is, in our view, one of great importance to be taught, and very generally found in the Bible; and although we are not prepared to decide in regard to the particular period of the event, we consider it perfectly safe and Scriptural for all to be looking out and prepared for it as being, now, specially '*at hand.*'

143

"2. *Resolved*, That it be recommended to all, so far as our influence may extend, to give the subject a ready and faithful examination, as found in the Scriptures; and to avail themselves of such help in doing it, as in their views shall be most safe and scriptural.

"3. *Resolved*, That the *Signs of the Times of Christ's Second Coming*, published at Boston, so far as we have had opportunity to learn, bids fair as being a useful help on the subject.

"4. *Resolved*, That we approve of the doings of our appointed council for conducting the *Christian Herald* (published at Exeter), in regard to their opening its columns, as they have done, for a fair and judicious discussion of the subject of Christ's coming and kingdom 'at hand.'"— *Signs of the Times, 1840, Vol. I, p. 95.*

This generally friendly attitude, with some exceptions, lasted well through the year 1840. But as the work went on, and papers, tracts, and books were issued, and Himes, Litch, and other practised speakers began to do aggressive work on the platform, the ministers who had not accepted Mr. Miller's views, nor perhaps even investigated them, began to find themselves in an embarrassing position. Some of them favored Whitby's theory of a millennial age upon this earth previous to the second advent. This teaching the Adventist preachers very strongly opposed, believing it to be contrary to the plain declaration of Scripture, and calculated to produce spiritual apathy and worldliness.

Thus there developed gradually on the part of many a feeling of dislike and suspicion toward the " Miller " movement, as it was sometimes called. It began to assume in their eyes the semblance of fanaticism, or at least of unwise emphasis upon portions of the Bible not susceptible of being understood. Yet for a time there was little active opposition; for the results of the lectures in producing deep spiritual awakenings, could not be gainsaid.

Perhaps this intermediate position of the clergy is well exemplified in the attitude of some of the Methodist ministers toward Josiah Litch when he attended the annual gathering of ministers of the Providence Conference in the summer of 1841, after having been for two or three years more or less connected with Mr. Miller. The presiding elder, under whose supervision he labored during the last year, said he had nothing against Brother Litch, but he believed he preached the Miller doctrine, and he felt it his duty to bring up the matter.

Various questions were then asked by the bishop and others, embracing nearly every point in the advent doctrine. After due deliberation, the conference came to the conclusion that Mr. Litch held to nothing contrary to Methodism, although he went in some points beyond it.

This second period, in which the advent movement was under suspicion, but was not to any great extent opposed by the evangelical clergy, lasted a little more than two years, from the end of 1840 to the early part of 1843. From that time on the opposition was general, and grew more intense from month to month.

When the Methodists held their annual meeting in Bath, Maine, in 1843, resolutions were passed condemning the advent teaching as having " an immediate, and more particularly an ultimate, disastrous tendency." Methodist ministers " who persist in disseminating these peculiarities," were to be " admonished by the chair, and all be hereby required to refrain entirely from disseminating them in the future."

The resolutions were rigidly carried out, and created a very painful situation for the members of the conference who had adopted Mr. Miller's views. One of these, L. F. Stockman, who was laboring in Portland, continued to preach as he had done, and was, after due admonishment, brought to trial for heresy. The general charge was " disseminating doctrines contrary to our articles of religion, as explained by our standard authors." Stockman was expelled, and a few months later was laid away to rest. The obituary notice in *Zion's Herald* gave him a noble Christian and ministerial career, " with the exception of this one dark blot upon his character," referring to his belief in Christ's soon coming.

With official action being taken to expel ministers who taught the advent views, it was not to be expected that the churches would long retain Adventist believers in their membership. The crisis was precipitated by the presence in the various congregations of a number who had imbibed a violent prejudice against the Adventists and their doctrines, and objected strongly to their expressing in class or prayer meeting their hope in the near advent of the Saviour. In some cases they were advised to withdraw quietly, and did so; in others they were publicly disfellowshiped.

To Mr. Miller this growing opposition on the part of church members was a source of pain and anxiety. He was a man of peace, and one who valued the friendship of his fellow Christians. It cut him to the quick to have the churches take a hostile attitude toward him and his associates, and he wrote a letter of protest, addressed to " believers in Christ of all denominations." The letter was published in the *Advent Herald and Signs of the Times* of Feb. 14, 1844, and possibly in some of the church papers; but in general little notice was taken of it.

10

By the early summer of 1844 it had become evident to all concerned that the preaching of Miller and his associates had been rejected by the great majority of their fellow Christians, and their followers could not remain in fellowship with the churches as then constituted. There could be no unity of spirit, with some members rejoicing in the hope of Christ's coming and others feeling a spirit of irritation, if not of downright animosity, when the matter was mentioned. The Adventists were by this time practically a church by themselves, only they were not so organized.

It was not wholly the setting of a definite time for the coming of Christ that separated between the followers of Miller and the popular churches. There were those within the Adventist ranks, some of them prominent in the movement, who did not subscribe to the definite time idea, but simply believed the great event to be near at hand. The real cause of separation seems to have been the fact that the Adventists loved the doctrine of the second coming, and longed for the return of their absent Lord. Many of their fellow members in the churches did not love the doctrine, and did not long for their Lord's return.

As this fact gradually dawned upon the Adventists, and they saw clearly the gulf that lay between them and their former associates in the various churches, they recognized it in many cases by voluntarily withdrawing from the associations that they felt were not a help but a hindrance to their spiritual upbuilding and growth. They believed, moreover, that the unwillingness of their fellow members in these churches to study the Scripture evidence concerning the imminent second advent, and their feelings of irritation when the subject was mentioned, gave evidence of a falling away from the first love, a spiritual deadness, a preoccupation with the things of this world, entirely out of keeping with the essential genius of New Testament Christianity. In short, they believed that the Protestant churches were following the example of papal Rome, and that the prophetic message of Revelation 14: 8 and 18: 4: "Babylon is fallen, is fallen;" "Come out of her, My people, that ye be not partakers of her sins, and that ye receive not of her plagues," applied to their own time, and made their duty of complete separation from such churches very clear. It is only fair to say that they proclaimed this message in no spirit of self-righteousness, nor of harsh condemnation of their fellow Christians.

In this movement the rank and file of the members were in advance of their leaders, Mr. Miller and Mr. Himes, who were very slow to separate from the churches. Like Wesley in England, a century earlier, they hated separation, and they worked for union as long as there was any possible hope of achieving it. But when the fact was brought irresistibly home to them that the Adventists were already in spirit widely separated from the churches, they had to acknowledge it and act accordingly.

Mr. Himes expressed his own and doubtless Mr. Miller's feelings in a letter published in the *Midnight Cry* of Sept. 2, 1844. After pointing out that Mr. Miller and his associates had from the beginning sought most earnestly to avoid separatism of every kind, and had labored faithfully to build up the churches, the letter went on to show that further co-operation was impossible because of the attitude taken by the churches toward the movement and its representatives. It closed with a ringing appeal to all believers to cut loose from a connection which had become impossible:

"It is death to remain connected with those bodies that speak lightly of, or oppose, the coming of the Lord. It is life to come out from all human tradition, and stand upon the word of God, and look daily for the appearing of the Lord."

Meanwhile the Adventists had been going through an experience on their own account, first of disappointment and then of renewed hope, which had its influence in separating them from their fellow members in the churches. This experience grew out of their having set a definite time within which, as they believed, the advent must occur. The second coming of Christ, according to Mr. Miller's teaching, was to take place some time during the Jewish year running from March 21, 1843, to March 21, 1844. In all his public utterances he held to this general statement, though to an intimate friend he expressed his belief that the event would not take place early in 1843, but that the believers' faith would be tested.

When, however, the Jewish year had fully passed, Mr. Miller was in every sense of the word a disappointed man. Nevertheless he was not dismayed. His feelings at this trying time may be judged from these paragraphs taken from a letter he wrote to Mr. Himes, under date of March 25, 1844:

"The time, as I have calculated it, is now filled up; and I expect every moment to see the Saviour descend from heaven. I have now nothing to look for but this glorious hope. I am full in the faith that all prophetic chronology except the 1000 years in the 20th of Revelation is now about full. Whether God designs for me to warn the people of this earth any more, or not, I am at a loss to know; yet I mean to be governed, if time should continue any longer than I have expected, by the word and providence of Him who will never err, and in whom I think I have trusted, and been supported during my twelve years' arduous labors, in trying to awaken the churches of God, and the Christian community, and to warn my fellow men of the necessity of an immediate preparation to meet our Judge in the day of His appearing. . . .

" I feel almost confident that my labors are about done, and I am, with a deep interest of soul, looking for my blessed and glorious Redeemer, who will then be King over all the earth, and God with us forevermore."— *" Sketches of the Christian Life and Public Labors of William Miller," by James White, pp. 279-281.*

Some weeks later he addressed a brief message " to second advent believers," in which he said among other things:

"Were I to live my life over again, with the same evidence that I then had, to be honest with God and man I should have to do as I have done. Although opposers said it would not come, they produced no weighty arguments. It was evidently guesswork with them; and I then thought, and do now, that their denial was based more on an unwillingness for the Lord to come than on any arguments leading to such a conclusion.

" I confess my error and acknowledge my disappointment; yet I still believe that the day of the Lord is near, even at the door; and I exhort you, my brethren, to be watchful, and not let that day come upon you unawares. The wicked, the proud, and the bigot will exult over us. I will try to be patient. God will deliver the godly out of temptation, and will reserve the unjust to be punished at Christ's appearing.

" I want you, my brethren, not to be drawn away from the truth. Do not, I pray you, neglect the Scriptures. They are able to make you wise unto eternal life. Let us be careful not to be drawn away from the manner and object of Christ's coming; for the next attack of the adversary will be to induce unbelief respecting these. The manner of Christ's coming has been well discussed."— *Id., pp. 282, 283.*

The Adventists held their annual conference in the Tabernacle at Boston in the last week of May. Mr. Miller attended, and made a statement at the close of one of the meetings, confessing his mistake as to the coming of the Saviour within the appointed time, yet humbly affirming his belief in the general correctness of the position taken and his firm confidence in the truth of the divine promises. A writer in the Boston *Post* expressed himself as feeling " well paid " for his time and trouble in attending. He continued:

" I should judge also by the appearance of the audience, and the remarks I heard from one or two gentlemen not of Mr. Miller's faith, that a general satisfaction was felt. I never heard him when he was more eloquent or animated, or more happy in communicating his feelings and sentiments to others."— *Id., p. 284.*

The summer of 1844 was a trying one for the Adventists. They had staked their all on the issue, and were sorely disappointed when the time passed without any outward sign or manifestation. That which sustained them in this hour of deep sorrow, was a sense, in the first place, of the reality of the experience they had been passing through, combined with a humble trust in God. They knew what the advent hope had done for them in purifying their lives. They felt that they could not be wrong in the belief that the signs of Christ's second coming had been fulfilled, and that they were living in the last days of this world's history. For the rest, they trusted in God, and continued in the attitude of waiting, meanwhile earnestly studying the Bible, in the hope that it might shed some fresh light upon the situation. The reproaches and ridicule of their unbelieving neighbors they suffered in silence and as a matter of course.

Meanwhile the advent movement did not suffer the collapse its enemies had confidently predicted. It could not, for it was built on the Word of God. Adventism had never been for Mr. Miller and his associates a mere matter of dates. It was rather the concrete expression of a great Christian doctrine. The Saviour had bidden His church to await His return. He had said, " Be ye also ready," adding the warning word, " for in such an hour as ye think not, the Son of man cometh." This was the burden of Mr. Miller's preaching. He placed the doctrine of Christ's second advent where it belonged in the galaxy of the great and important truths of the Bible. He taught men, as did Paul in the apostolic days, to turn from their idols to serve the living God, and to wait for His Son from heaven.

That the general public chose to regard Mr. Miller chiefly in the light of one who had figured out the time when the earth would come to an end, is a common illustration of the popular tendency to seize on certain striking features of any message that may be given, and from them to construct a message which is a caricature of the original.

But if Mr. Miller threw chief emphasis upon the broad facts concerning a coming Saviour, and the need of a preparation of mind and heart to receive Him, he was not negligent in respect of the minute facts in prophetic study. He took his hearers back over the whole ground involved, rehearsing to them the historical facts concerning the fulfilment of those promises, and leading them step by step to the conclusions to which his investigations had brought him. Thus the faith of those who joined the Adventists rested not merely upon the statements of William Miller, but upon the reasons which had led him in the beginning to embrace the advent views; and the fact that confirmed infidels by scores were influenced by these reasons to embrace similar views and to give up at one and the same time their objections to the Bible as faulty, and to Christianity as a mere man-made religion, speaks eloquently for the strong intellectual appeal made by Mr. Miller's presentation of the advent doctrine.

To the strength and security which came from the general teaching of the Word concerning the second advent, and from the good results attendant upon the preaching, might be added a conviction on the part of many intelligent men that some great change was imminent. Said George Bush, professor of Hebrew and Oriental Literature in the University of the City of New York:

" If we take the ground of right reason, we must believe that the present age is one expressly foretold in prophecy, and that it is just opening upon the crowning consummation of all prophetic declarations."

Continuing in a letter to Mr. Miller, Professor Bush said:

" Neither is it to be objected, as I conceive, to yourself or your friends, that you have devoted much time and attention to the study of the *chronology* of prophecy, and have labored much to determine the commencing and closing dates of its great periods. If these periods are actually given by the Holy Ghost in the prophetic books, it was doubtless with the design that they *should* be studied, and *probably*, in the end, fully understood; and no man is to be charged with presumptuous folly who reverently makes the attempt to do this. On this point, I have myself no charges to bring against you. Nay, I am even ready to go so far as to say that I do not conceive your errors on the subject of chronology to be at all of a serious nature, or in fact to be very wide of the truth. In taking a day as the prophetical term for a *year*, I believe you are sustained by the soundest exegesis, as well as fortified by the high names of Mede, Sir I. Newton, Bishop Newton, Kirby, Scott, Keith, and a host of others who have long since come to substantially your conclusions on this head. They all agree that the leading periods mentioned by Daniel and John, do actually expire *about this age of the world*, and it would be a strange logic that would convict you of heresy for holding in effect the same views which stand forth so prominent in the notices of these eminent divines. Your error, as I apprehend, lies in another direction than your *chronology;* not, however, that I am prepared to admit all the details of your calculations, but, in general, your results in this field of inquiry do not strike me so far out of the way as to affect any of the great interests of truth or duty."— *Advent Herald and Signs of the Times, March 6, 1844.*

Professor Bush went on to give philosophic reasons why the close of the 2300 days would usher in, not the end of the world, but the beginning of a new order of things which would result in the conversion of the world. He did not attempt to prove this statement from the Bible. Nor indeed was his letter on the whole based on the teaching of the Bible, and while he was able to point out some weaknesses in the argument of Mr. Miller, his own position was from the standpoint of Scripture untenable.

Other men, especially those whose minds had been drawn to the study of the situation in the light of prophecy, gave expression to similar views. On the other hand, so far as we are able to discover, none had given the teaching of Mr. Miller the thoughtful, impartial hearing that it deserved, and then proceeded to point out its deficiencies from the Bible viewpoint. Thus the Adventists, when their hopes were disappointed, could not look to their fellow men for comfort and help. They could only wait on their God, and through prayerful study of His Word seek for further light.

Thus the situation continued till, in the late summer of 1844, the camp-meeting at Exeter, N. H., brought together a large assemblage of believers, chiefly from different parts of New England and from the Canadas. The meeting opened August 12, in an atmosphere of doubt and uncertainty. The people looked to their leaders, but these were not able to lead. The ministers went over the old ground, and showed from the prophecies that the coming of Christ must be near; but the sense of disappointment hung heavy over preachers and people, and clear knowledge of where they were and what they ought to teach, was wanting.

When the situation was at its worst, and the majority looked upon the meeting as perhaps already a failure, there came to the front an element which had not been prominent before, namely, those members of the Adventist body who were fully convinced that the 2300 days would end on the tenth day of the seventh Jewish month. They had kept themselves in the background, not from lack of courage of their convictions, but wishing rather to let the Spirit speak to others. But when it became evident that the meeting would break up in utter gloom and disappointment unless some one spoke out, they came forward.

In the midst of a somewhat dull, prosy sermon rehearsing what everybody already knew, one of these, a middle-aged woman, rose to her feet with the words:

" It is too late, Brother ———. It is too late to spend our time upon these truths, with which we are familiar, and which have been blessed to us in the past, and have served their purpose and their time."—" *Life Incidents in Connection with the Great Advent Movement,*" *by James White, pp. 159, 160.*

The preacher sat down, and his interrupter continued:

" The Lord has servants here who have meat in due season for His household. Let them speak, and let the people hear them. " Behold, the Bridegroom cometh; go ye out to meet Him! ' "—*Id., p. 160.*

The testimony thus borne, while in the nature of an interruption, was characterized by perfect calmness, and was so evidently actuated by the Spirit of God that it met with a hearty response. There were fervent cries of "Amen" from every part of the large audience. The request became general that the arguments in favor of the tenth day of the seventh month as marking the close of the 2300 days should be given on the morrow from the stand. This was accordingly done, and with telling effect.

The speaker, John Couch, one of the less prominent of the Adventist leaders, first showed that in order to make up the full 2300 days, it would be necessary to have 457 full years before Christ and 1843 full years after Christ, this bringing us up to the beginning of the Jewish year 1844 as the earliest possible time for the advent to take place according to prophecy. He then gave his reasons for believing that this prophetic period began, not in the spring, but in the autumn of the year. These arguments, as reported by one who was present and heard them, are as follows:

"That as the seventy prophetic weeks are the first 490 years of the 2300, and as the first seven weeks of the seventy mark the time of the work of restoring and building Jerusalem in troublous times, the great period must commence with the commencement of the work of restoring and building, which did not commence in the spring, on the first month, when Ezra started from Babylon, but after he had reached Jerusalem, in the autumn, *probably on the seventh month.* 'For upon the first day of the first month began he to go up from Babylon, and on the *first day* of the fifth month came he to Jerusalem,' Ezra 7: 9. This would give more than two months for necessary preparations for the work of restoring and building to commence on the seventh month, immediately after the great day of atonement.

"That as the words of the angel to the prophet Daniel — 'In the midst of the week He shall cause the sacrifice and the oblation to cease' — mean that in the middle of the last week of the seventy, Christ should be crucified; and as He was crucified in the spring, that prophetic week of seven years must commence and close in the fall. Consequently the seventy weeks commenced and closed in the fall, and therefore the 2300 days terminate in the fall."— *Id., pp. 161, 162.*

The speaker gave evidence drawn from the Old Testament types why the second advent of our High Priest should take place on the tenth day of the seventh month. The spring types, pointing to the great events connected with the first advent of the Saviour, were fulfilled, not only in respect to their nature and order, but also as to time. Then why should not the autumnal types pointing to the second advent, be fulfilled as to time?

"Therefore, as the High Priest on the tenth day of the seventh month, on the great day of atonement, came out of the sanctuary and blessed the people, so Christ, our great High Priest, would upon the same day of the same month come from heaven to bless His waiting people with immortality."— *Id., p. 163.*

These arguments, and others like them, were not wholly unfamiliar to the Adventists. For some months previously, earnest Bible students among the believers had had their minds drawn to the seventh month of the current Jewish year as marking the termination of some important prophetic period.

William Miller himself had referred to it in an article in the *Signs* as far back as May 17, 1843. S. S. Snow had been preaching in New York, Philadelphia, and other places during the spring and summer, that the 2300 days would expire on Oct. 22, 1844; but though a number were led to accept this view, there was no general response till in July.

Moreover, there had been other tokens that the Holy Spirit was at work, preparing the Adventists for a general forward movement. Joshua V. Himes wrote:

"In the early part of the season, some of our brethren in the north of New Hampshire had been so impressed with the belief that the Lord would come before another winter, that they did not cultivate their fields. About the middle of July . . . others, who had sown and planted their fields, were so impressed with a sense of the Lord's immediate appearing, that they could not, consistently with their faith, harvest their crops. Some, on going into their fields to cut grass, found themselves entirely unable to proceed, and conforming to their sense of duty, left their crops standing in the field. . . . This feeling rapidly extended through the north of New England. . . .

"About the middle of July, the blessing of God in reclaiming backsliders, began to attend the proclamation of the *time*. . . . As was predicted, 'at midnight there was a cry made, Behold, the Bridegroom cometh; go ye out to meet Him. Then all those virgins arose and trimmed their lamps.' From July these movements were in different parts of New England, and were distinct from each other; but they were all attended by the blessing of God in reclaiming many whose lamps had well-nigh gone out, and in the sanctification of His saints. At the Exeter camp-meeting all these influences met, mingled into one great movement, and rapidly spread through all the advent bands in the land."— *Signs of the Times, Oct. 30, 1844, p. 93.*

Adventists had accordingly been prepared for the seventh-month doctrine, and its presentation at this camp-meeting met with general favor. On the following day the same speaker, by unanimous request, went over the ground once more, with equal clearness and force, and after him other ministers who had come to the same conclusion gave stirring discourses, confirming the minds of the people in the doctrine, and exhorting them to a holy life, in preparation for the soon-coming Bridegroom.

The parable of the ten virgins was much dwelt upon in the advent preaching of those days. It seemed to throw light upon the experience Adventists were passing through. The ten virgins were believed to represent those who accepted the belief of Christ's soon coming, and the lamps to signify the prophetic

THE ADVENT HERALD,

AND SIGNS OF THE TIMES REPORTER.

BEHOLD! THE BRIDEGROOM COMETH!! GO YE OUT TO MEET HIM!!!

VOL. VIII. NO. 10. Boston, Wednesday, October 9, 1845. WHOLE NO. 180.

THE ADVENT HERALD
IS PUBLISHED EVERY WEDNESDAY BY
J. V. HIMES,
AT NO. 14 DEVONSHIRE STREET, BOSTON.

J. V. Himes, S. Bliss, & A. Hale, Editors.

TERMS.—One Dollar per Volume, of 26 Numbers. Five Dollars for 6 Copies, Ten Dollars for 13 Copies.

All communications for the Advent Herald, or orders for Books or remittances, should be directed to "J. V. Himes, Boston, Mass." post paid.

Post Masters are authorized by the Post Office Department to forward free of expense orders for, or to discontinue publications, and also money to pay for the same.

Subscribers' names with the State and Post Office should be distinctly given when money is forwarded. Where the Post Office is not given, we are liable to misdirect the paper, or credit to the wrong person, as there are often several of the same name, or several Post Offices in the same town.

Dow & Jackson, Printers.

"Go ye out to meet Him."

THE TENTH DAY OF THE SEVENTH MONTH.

I take up my pen with feelings such as I never before experienced. Beyond a doubt, in my mind, the tenth day of the seventh month will witness the revelation of our Lord Jesus Christ in the clouds of heaven. We are then within a few days of that event. Awful moment to those who are unprepared —but glorious to those who are ready. I feel that I am making the last appeal thus, I will ever make through the press. My heart is full. I see the ungodly and the sinner disappearing from my view, and there now stands before my mind the professed believers in the Lord's near approach. But what shall I say to them! Alas! we have all been slumbering and sleeping—both the wise and the foolish; but so our Savior told us it would be; and " thus the Scriptures are fulfilled," and it is the last prophecy relating to the events to precede the personal advent of our Lord; now comes the True Midnight Cry. The previous was but the alarm. Now the cry one is sounding; and Oh, how solemn the hour. The "virgins" have been asleep or slumbering; yes, all of us. Asleep on the time: that is the point. Some have indeed preached the seventh month, but it has with doubt whether it is this year or some other; and that doubt is now removed from my mind. " Behold, the Bridegroom cometh," This Year, " Go ye out to meet him." We have done with the nominal churches and all the wicked, except so far as this cry may affect them; our work is now to wake up the " virgins" who " took their lamps and went forth to meet the Bridegroom." Where are we now! " If the vision tarry, wait for it." Is not that our answer now. Just March and April. Yes. What happened while the bridegroom tarried!— The virgins all slumbered and slept, did they not! Christ's word's have not failed; and " the Scriptures cannot be broken," and it is of no use for us to pretend that we have been awake: we have been slumbering; not on the fact of Christ's coming, but on the time. We came into the tarrying time—we did not know " how long" it would tarry, and on that point we have slumbered—some of us have said, in our sleep, " Don't fix another time;" so we slept. Now the trouble is to wake us up. Lord help, for vain is the help of man. Speak thyself, Lord. O, that the " Father" may now " make known" the time.

Peter, 1st Epistle, chap. i. 11, positively declares that the Spirit of Christ, in the prophets, did testify the time for the sufferings of Christ and the glory that should follow, and gives us to understand, in the 12th verse, that that glory was to be " at the revelation of Jesus Christ." Speaking of the prophets, Peter says—" Searching what, or what manner of time the Spirit of Christ, which was in them did signify, when it testified beforehand the sufferings of Christ, and the glory that should follow. . . . Wherefore gird up the loins of your mind, be sober, and hope to the end for the grace that is to be brought unto you at the revelation of Jesus Christ." Here we have the fact stated, that the Spirit of Christ did reveal to the prophets the time not only of Christ's sufferings, but of his glory, or " revelation." Peter tells us the time revealed was but literal but symbolical. " What manner of time!?!. He also says that " the angels desire to look into?" these " things." By turning to the 12th chapter of Daniel, we find, that after the angel had finished the detailed explanation of the visions, and wound up with the small ing up of Michael, (one like God—the Son of God,) the resurrection of the saints, and those that had turned many to righteousness shine as the stars, &c., that Daniel here, verse 5, two angels, " and one said to the man clothed in linen, which was upon the waters of the river—how long shall it be to the end of these wonders?" Here is an inquiry about time, by the angels. Well, Peter said the angels desired to look into it. Did they get an answer! See Dan. xii. 7.—"And I heard the man clothed in linen, which was upon the waters of the river, when he held up his right hand and his left hand unto heaven, and sware by him that liveth for ever, and it shall be for a time, times, and an half and when he shall have accomplished to scatter the power of the holy people, all these things shall be finished." The person who swear was no other other than the Lord Jesus Christ; and he says to time. Yea, to time connected with the second advent, the resurrection, and the glorification of his people. The time, however, is symbolical. But will any man deny with the blasphemous position that the Lord Jesus sware " a time that meant nothing ; or, which is the same thing, sware, with the most solemn oath, to time that is intended should never be understood! Such a notion, one would suppose, is blasphemous enough to make a devil tremble ; for, it is virtually charging the Lord of Glory with meaning a lie!! Beware, O vain man, how you thus charge the Son of God. This is revealed. But it cannot be understood without obeying Christ, and " inquiring and searching diligently what, and what manner of time." Those who are too indolent to search, or who are afraid to follow truth when they find it, for fear of man, whose breath is in his nostrils, will of course remain in ignorance of time, and that day, most likely, will come upon them unawares.

I will now present a brief argument from the types to show that the tenth day of the seventh month is the time in the year to look for our coming Lord.

Matt. v. 17, 18.—Our Lord says, " Think not that I am come to destroy the law or the prophets ; I am not come to destroy, but to fulfil. For verily I say unto you, Till heaven and earth pass, one jot or one tittle shall in no wise pass from the law, till all be fulfilled." This must relate to the law of types as well as the moral law. Let us now inquire how the types have been fulfilled. The first we will notice is the slaying of the pascal lamb, Exodus xii. 6.—" And ye shall keep it up until the fourteenth day of the same month : and the whole assembly of the congregation of Israel shall kill it in the evening." " Between the two evenings," is the marginal reading. The Jews divided their afternoon into two evenings, viz., from the sixth to the ninth hour, and from the ninth hour to sundown ; this is, from mid-day to our three o'clock, and from three o'clock to the setting of the sun setting. The lamb, which was a type of Christ, was killed in the point at the day we call three o'clock in the afternoon, on the fourteenth of the first month. Was this type exactly fulfilled to our Lord's death? Yes. He was put to death as the Passover, and died at three o'clock, or the ninth hour. See Mark xv. 33—37. Then the type had an exact fulfilment on the day, and at the very hour ; so exact is God about time.

Leviticus xxiii. 9—11.—We read thus, "And the Lord spake unto Moses, saying, Speak unto the children of Israel, and say unto them, When ye be come into the land which I give unto you, and shall reap the harvest thereof, then ye shall bring a sheaf of the first fruits of your harvest unto the priest ; and he shall wave the sheaf before the Lord, to be accepted for you : on the morrow after the Sabbath the priest shall wave it." Here is a type of Christ's resurrection, and Paul tells us, 1st Cor. 15 : 20.— " But now is Christ risen from the dead, and become the first-fruits of them that slept." On what day of the week, or the " morrow after the Sabbath." The apostle fulfilling the type, not only in the thing signified, but in the time. Lev. xxiii. 15, 16—we have the time of the feast of weeks, or, as it is called, the Pentecost, which signifies the fiftieth day. This was the anniversary of the giving of the Law, and the descent of the Lord upon Mount Sinai. Exactly on that day did the Holy Spirit descend on the Apostles. Acts ii. 1—4.

If the types have been fulfilled exact, as to time, even to the hour, where that is known, will those that remain to be fulfilled, be less exact! I think not. God always has kept time in the fulfilment of the prophecies; and thus far, as we have seen, in the types. He will not fail us as now. No, no!—" not one or one tittle shall pass from the law till all be fulfilled." Let us then look at those types that remain to be accomplished. Lev. xxiii. 26, 27.— " And this shall be a statute for ever unto you, that in the seventh month, on the tenth day of the month, ye shall afflict your souls, and do no work at all, whether it be one of your own country, or a stranger that sojourneth among you ; For on that day shall the priest make an atonement for you, to cleanse you, that ye may be clean from all your sins before the Lord. It shall be a Sabbath of rest unto you, and ye shall afflict your souls, by a statute forever. And the priest, whom he shall anoint, and whom he shall consecrate to minister in the priest's office in his father's stead, shall make the atonement, and shall put on the linen clothes, even the holy garments : and he shall make an atonement for the holy sanctuary, and he shall make an atonement for the tabernacle of the congregation, and for the altar ; and he shall make an atonement for the priests, and for all the people of the congregation. And this shall be an everlasting statue unto you, to make an atonement for the children of Israel, for all their sins, once a year." In the 9th chap. we have an account of what was to be done on that day, and at the closing part it of we are told, Lev. ix. 22, 23—" And Aaron lifted up his hand towards the people and blessed them, and came down from offering of the sin-offering, and the burnt offering, and peace-offerings. And Moses and Aaron went into the tabernacle of the congregation, and came out, and blessed the people : and the glory of the Lord appeared unto all the people." Christ, our great High Priest, has gone into the Holy of Holies for us, with his own blood, and " to them that look for him shall appear the second time without sin unto salvation." Heb. ix. 28. When he comes out of the Holy of Holies, will it not be on the day typified ? Beyond a doubt in my mind it will be. Look at this type as set forth in Lev. xxiii. 26, 27, 29, 32 — " And the Lord spake unto Moses saying, Also on the tenth day of the seventh month there shall be a day of atonement : it shall be an holy convocation unto you ; and ye shall afflict your souls, and offer an offering made by fire unto the Lord. . . . For whatsoever soul it be that shall be not afflicted in that same day, he shall be cut off from among

NEARING THE TIME

word.   The wise virgins, who provided oil in their vessels, were those who obtained a genuine experience, through the operation of divine grace, and who clung to this experience, even though puzzled and temporarily silenced by the disappointment.   The foolish virgins represented those for whom a deep heart-searching work had not been done, who had given assent to the doctrines preached, but had not made them a part of their lives. The tarrying time was believed to represent the period of darkness and discouragement that followed the disappointment at the end of the Jewish year 1843.   And the midnight cry, " Behold, the Bridegroom cometh; go ye out to meet Him," was the definite message that Christ would come on the tenth day of the seventh month, which began to be taught in July, but first became the general belief of the Adventist people as a result of the preaching at the Exeter camp-meeting and at various gatherings immediately following.

Indeed, the application seemed an obvious one, and it came home with force to the great body of the Adventists.   From the Exeter camp-meeting, earnest, zealous men and women went out in all directions, preaching the message of the Lord's return on the 22d of October, and enjoying in their work a power which was clearly from above.   In a few short weeks the Adventists had arisen as one man, and were giving the cry with united voice.   The burden of the work was not carried by a few; it rested upon all.   Means with which to carry on the publishing work flowed in freely from many quarters, and the spirit of personal labor for souls was marked.   We quote again from Mr. Himes:

" At first the definite time was generally opposed; but there seemed to be an irresistible power attending its proclamation, which prostrated all before it.   It swept over the land with the velocity of a tornado, and it reached hearts in different and distant places almost simultaneously, and in a manner which can be accounted for only on the supposition that God was in it.   It produced everywhere the most deep searching of hearts and humiliation of souls before the God of high heaven.   It caused a weaning of affections from the things of the world, a healing of controversies and animosities, a confession of wrongs, a breaking down before God, and penitent, broken-hearted supplications to Him for pardon and acceptance. It caused self-abasement and prostration of soul, such as we never before witnessed. . . .

" The lecturers among the Adventists were the last to embrace the views of the time, and the more prominent ones came into it last of all.   It seemed not to be the work of men, but to be brought about in spite of men.   The several advent papers came into the view only at a late hour; and this paper [the *Signs*] was the last to raise its voice in the spread of the cry.   For a long time we were determined to take no part in the movement, either in opposition or in the advocacy of it.   We afterward endeavored to point out what we considered to be a few inaccuracies in the arguments used, but which did not materially affect the result. It was not until within about two weeks of the commencement of the seventh month, that we were particularly impressed with the progress of the movement, when we had such a view of it that to oppose it, or even to remain silent longer, seemed to us to be opposing the work of the Holy Spirit; and in entering upon the work with all our souls, we could but exclaim, What were we, that we should resist God? It seemed to us to have been so independent of human agency that we could but regard it as a fulfilment of the ' midnight cry,' after the tarrying of the Bridegroom, and the slumbering and sleeping of the virgins, when they were all to arise and trim their lamps. And this last work seems to have been done; for there has never been a time before when the respective advent bands were in so good a state of preparedness for the Lord's coming."— *Ibid.*

Quietness of outward demeanor, combined with depth of feeling and great solemnity, characterized the believers. In the words of an eyewitness:

" The time for shouting, and display of talent in speaking, singing, and praying, seemed to be past. The brethren and sisters calmly consecrated themselves and their all to the Lord and His cause, and with humble prayers and tears sought His pardon and His favor. All those unhappy divisions and extravagances which had threatened the prosperity of the advent cause, were lost sight of, and the watchmen, and the people also, were beginning to lift up one united voice with strength and heartfelt solemnity, ' Behold, the Bridegroom cometh; go ye out to meet Him.' "—" *Life Incidents,*" *p. 166.*

Means flowed in freely with which to print and supply, free of charge, thousands of copies of the Adventist papers and tracts. Some who had been backward in supporting the cause came to the various publishing offices, and pleaded with the editors to accept their money. They were told: " You are too late! We don't want your money now! We can't use it! " When they asked, " Cannot it be given to the poor? " the answer was, " We have made provision for the immediate wants of all such that we can reach," and the belated givers, thus turned away, went home with a keen sense of disappointment in having lost an opportunity to do good and " to communicate."

William Miller, at first inclined to view with distrust the preaching of so definite a date, was deeply impressed with the unanimity and zeal of the brethren, and joined heartily in the movement. Writing under date of October 11, he said:

" I think I have never seen among our brethren such faith as is manifested in the seventh month. ' He will come,' is the common expression. ' He will not tarry the second time,' is their general reply. There is a forsaking of the world, an unconcern for the wants of life, a general searching of heart, confession of sin, and a deep feeling in prayer for Christ to come. . . . No arguments are used or needed; all seem convinced that they have the truth. There is no clashing of sentiments; all are of one heart and of one mind.

Our meetings are all occupied with prayer, and exhortation to love and obedience. The general expression is, 'Behold, the Bridegroom cometh; go ye out to meet Him.'"—*Id., pp. 177, 178.*

As the fateful day drew near, all preparations were made. Men dismissed their employees, settled their accounts, and set their houses in order. Those who had the least ground for

THAT "LAST" COPY OF THE *SIGNS*

Note that marked paragraph advertising this number "without money, and without price."

thinking any person bore them ill will, went to such, and sought a complete reconciliation. They were looking for their coming King, and it was their ardent desire that they might be at peace with all men. Thus the work of preparation went on, increasing in power and influence from day to day, while what was believed to be the time of the great consummation drew on apace.

But the expected Saviour did not come. His waiting people were doomed to bitter disappointment. God's ways are not always our ways, nor His thoughts our thoughts. Not even those who enjoy the most loving and intimate fellowship with their Lord can always understand His doings.

TO OUR READERS.

Dear Brethren and Sisters:—We find that we have arrived at a most solemn and momentous crisis; and from the light we have, we are shut up to the conviction that the 10th day of the seventh month, must usher in the glorious appearing of the great God and our Saviour Jesus Christ.

We therefore find our work is now finished, and that all we have to do, is to go out to meet the Bridegroom, and to trim our lamps accordingly. In looking back upon our past labors, we can see the workings of God's providence. At first the message of the coming Saviour was given, and its evidence presented in all kindness and love. The effect was by the blessing of God efficacious in the conversion of many souls. But when men arose on every hand, to overthrow the truth, it became necessary to fight the battles of the Lord, and to finish the controversies of Zion. We seemed then to be moved to enter the arena of debate, and contended earnestly for the faith once delivered to the saints. But now we find that our controversies are all over—that the battle has been fought, and our warfare ended. And now we wish to humble ourselves under the mighty hand of God, that we may be accepted at his coming.

We desire to be truly grateful to God, for all his assistance, without which, our labors would have been in vain; and we would also be thankful to all of you, dear readers and patrons, for the many prayers you have offered in our behalf; and for all the kindness, hospitality and assistance, by which, with God's blessing, we have been greatly cheered, encouraged and strengthened, and enabled to continue to the present time, in the work, to which we trust God has called us.

We feel sensible of our many imperfections. Whilst we have contended for what we believe to be truth, we can see that pride of opinion and self, have arisen. When new truths have been presented, we have been slow to receive them; we have been asleep during the tarrying of the vision, and we have not labored with that ardour we should have done, had we so fully realized the nearness of the Judgment. We have been slow of heart to believe all that Moses and the prophets have spoken, and all our labors and toils appear to us as nothing; and that at best we have been but unprofitable servants. We can therefore only offer the prayer of the publican,—God be merciful to us sinners.

We feel that we are now making our last, appeal that we are addressing you through these columns for the last time. In this crisis we must stand alone. If any are hanging upon our skirts, we shake them off.—Your blood be upon your own heads. We ask forgiveness of God and all men, for every thing which may have been inconsistent with his honor and glory; and we desire to lay ourselves upon his altar. Here we lay our friends and worldly interests, and trust alone in the merits of Christ's atoning blood, through the efficacious and sanctifying influence of God's Holy Spirit, for pardon and forgiveness and acceptance at the Father's mercy seat. May the blessing of God rest upon all of us; and that we may all meet in God's everlasting Kingdom, is the prayer of your unworthy servant.   J. V. HIMES.

The above was written in Boston, with the expectation that this would be the last paper. I heartily join in the prayer and confession expressed by Bro. H.   N. S.

every Christian has had opportunity to observe that Christians before their death, like their great representative Moses, have been apprised of it by the pre-monitions of the Spirit: accidental death has not even been an exception from this, as previously written letters and papers have frequently shown. "The secret of the Lord is with them that fear him."

So it was with Elias, as representative of those that are alive and remain, ("We shall not all sleep,") when the Lord would take him up, by a whirlwind, sent him from Gilgal to Bethel, and the sons of the prophets at Bethel came forth and said to Elisha, "Knowest thou the Lord will take away thy master from thy head *to-day?*" What was Elisha's answer? Yea, I *know it.* Here the Lord saw fit to try yet farther the faith and patience of the aged prophet: he could not go up from Bethel, the Lord sent him to Jericho, there the sons of the prophets came forth and asked the same question, and received the same answer. Is it not for our instruction that Elijah *knew the day* he was to be taken up? Elisha KNEW IT— the sons of the prophets KNEW IT, in Bethel, and Jericho too! The "Lord will do nothing but he revealeth his secret to his servants the prophets."

Here again Elijah was tried by being sent yet further, even to Jordan. Elijah might, with *seeming* propriety, have said: I am an old man, and am weary with traveling, the Lord has promised to take me to-day, and he can as well take me from this place as from Jordan. I will not go to Jordan. But did he reason thus? O! no. The Lord said *go* to Jordan, and that was enough for him. They journey on, and now they stand beside the stream; the sons of the prophets view afar off;—but he cannot yet ascend;—he must go *over* Jordan. He takes his mantle, shutes the waters,—they part,—he passes over, —yes, glory to God, on dry ground;—and now as they still go on and commune together, (Heb. 10 : 28,) behold, there appeared a chariot of fire, and horses of fire, and they were parted asunder, and Elijah went up by whirlwind into heaven. O! praise the Lord, glory, glory to God, for victory over death! The chariot of *Israel* and the horsemen thereof, and praise—forever, praise the Lord, for the instruction thus given, by our brother who has gone before us. Then, brethren and sisters, although the Lord has led us from one point of prophecy to another, and now we stand before the dark waters of Jordan, yet faith says, pass over. Yes, pass over, the similitude of death, even a voluntary death, for he that seeks to save his life shall lose it. Yours, in this glorious hope of seeing the king on the 10th day, 7th month.
                                                        s. s. b.

New York City, Oct. 11, 1844.

We believe this to be our LAST paper.

THE LAST NUMBER OF *THE MIDNIGHT CRY*

The reader should not overlook that last significant line, "We believe this to be our LAST paper."

October 22 came and went, to all appearance just as other days. The world was as busy as ever with its concerns. The tradesman plied his business, the carpenter and mechanic their trades, the crowds came and went the same as usual, and no one heeded, unless to scoff at them, the little companies of earnest watchers for their returning Lord.

It was indeed a heartbreaking disappointment. These loyal souls had given their all in order to embrace an unpopular doctrine. They had braved the reproaches of their friends, the taunts and sneers of a pleasure-loving world. They had given up all worldly prospects; and had left farms and places of business in order to sound the warning message. They had lived for weeks on the very borders of the eternal world, their eyes continually turned upward, their ears attuned to the heavenly harmonies. And now they were rudely thrust out of this world of sweet expectation into the hard, actual world of facts. They faced a severe winter, for which many of them had made no proper provision. They faced what was harder to bear,— a cruel, sneering world. How should they ever be able to look people in the face again? How were they to account for the failure of their fondest hopes?

The prospect looked sufficiently dark to discourage the stoutest heart; but once more the Adventists showed their true character. Like David of old, they turned to the Lord in their need, and He did not forsake them. The promises of the Bible were precious in those days, especially that noble passage in Hebrews:

"Cast not away therefore your confidence, which hath great recompense of reward. For ye have need of patience, that, after ye have done the will of God, ye might receive the promise. For yet a little while, and He that shall come, will come, and will not tarry. Now the just shall live by faith: but if any man draw back, My soul shall have no pleasure in him." Heb. 10:35-38.

The application was apt. The Adventists had to the best of their knowledge done the will of God; their motives had been pure; they had taken their stand upon the word of prophecy, not impulsively or presumptuously, but with the calmness born of knowledge; and in this second and greatest crisis they patiently waited on the Lord. They had learned to trust God in the darkness as well as in the light, and they never gave finer proof of the essential nobility of their character and the purity of their faith, than when they quietly and unobtrusively returned to their daily tasks, still confidently looking for the longed-for Deliverer, and saying with Job, "Though He slay me, yet will I trust in Him."

Provision was speedily made by means of a fund for the benefit of those members who might otherwise suffer want during the on-coming winter, and ministers and people alike continued to cherish the hope that their fond expectations might soon be realized. They were deeply disappointed, but they had the conviction that God was leading out a people who loved His appearing, and they continued to believe that the main facts relating to the prophetic periods could be depended upon.

To be sure, this attitude of humble faith in God and steadfast continuance in the faith that had been taught them, characterized only a part of the fifty thousand persons who had made a profession of belief in the advent doctrines. As in other great reform movements, there were in the advent body elements of weakness as well as of strength. Some persons will take up quickly with a doctrine when it seems to be winning widespread assent, and then as quickly drop it when the circumstances become unfavorable. Adventists of this type, who in the time of prosperity were upborne and carried by their more conscientious and persevering brethren, naturally fell away at this second disappointment, and some of them became bitter opponents. In the doubt and uncertainty that reigned in the Adventist ranks for a time, even those whose experience had been of the deeper kind were not free from the attacks of the enemy, and some fell away. All told, a great many left the ranks of Adventist believers at this time, some to join the popular churches, and some, no doubt, to assume a position of religious indifference.

One reason for the great losses was the lack of a thorough organization to hold the believers together. The people were as sheep without a shepherd. This was a weakness inherent in the early advent movement. It lacked plan, system, organization. It had good preaching and a fairly efficient publishing bureau; but its various elements had never been fully welded into an organic whole.

There were various reasons for this lack. Men with a talent for sustained leadership are always scarce. Some of the believers, moreover, seeing the abuse of ecclesiastical power in other churches, were unwilling that it should exist in any form among themselves, and regarded even church organization as evil. Again, the movement had grown with great rapidity, and many of those connected with it had only recently begun to feel that they were unwelcome in their respective churches. The fact that the advent was believed to be immediately at hand, would also tend to make organization seem unnecessary. Thus the whole situation made for the looseness of structure which was a large cause of the rapid falling away as a result of the disappointment.

But not all fell away; there were many who remained steadfast. William Miller and Joshua V. Himes, the foremost of the leaders, stood nobly in their place, and were never greater than in the hour of disappointment and apparent defeat. They frankly acknowledged the facts, but they did not lose faith in God, nor rashly give up their main position. They counseled believers to hold fast. Other cheering voices were heard. F. G. Brown wrote a stirring letter to the Adventist believers. It was published in the *Advent Herald* of Nov. 11, 1844, from which a few representative extracts are given:

" The great God has dealt wonderfully with us. When we were in a state of alarming blindness in relation to the coming of the great and terrible day of the Lord, He saw fit to awaken us from our deathlike slumbers to a knowledge of these things. How little of our own or man's agency was employed in this work, you know. Our prejudices, education, tastes, both intellectual and moral, were all opposed to the doctrine of the Lord's coming. We know that it was the Almighty's arm that disposed us to receive this grace. The Holy Ghost wrought it in our inmost souls, yea, incorporated it into our very being, so that it is now a part of us, and no man can take it from us. It is our hope, our joy, our all. The Bible reads it, every page is full of the Lord's immediate coming, and much from without strengthens us in the belief that the Judge standeth at the door! At present everything tries us. Well, we have heretofore had almost uninterrupted peace and exceeding great joy. . . . We know that God has been with us. Perhaps never before this has He for a moment seemed to depart from us. Shall we now begin, like the children of Israel, to doubt, and to fear and repine, after He has so frequently and signally shown us His hand in effecting for us one deliverance after another? . . . Let us pause, and wait, and read, and pray, before we act rashly, or pronounce a hasty judgment upon the ways and works of God. If we are in darkness, and see not as clearly as heretofore, let us not be impatient. We shall have light just as soon as God sees it will be for our good. . . .

" It was necessary that our faith and patience should be tried before our work could be completed. We closed up our work with the world some time ago. This is my conviction. And now God has given us a little season of self-preparation, to prove us before the world. Who now will abide the test? "—" *Life Incidents*," *pp. 195-197.*

Joseph Marsh, editor of the *Voice of Truth,* expressed the feelings of the main body of Adventists at this time in an editorial appearing in the issue of Nov. 7, 1844:

" We did believe that He would come at that time; and now, though we sorrow on account of our disappointment, yet we rejoice that we have acted according to our faith. We have had, and still have, a conscience void of offense in this matter, toward God and man. God has blessed us abundantly, and we have not a doubt but that all will soon be made to work together for the good of His dear people, and His glory.

11

" We cheerfully admit that we have been mistaken in the nature of the event we expected would occur on the tenth day of the seventh month; but we cannot yet admit that our great High Priest did not on that very day accomplish all that the type would justify us to expect. We now believe He did." — *Id., p. 198.*

It was but natural that the Adventists, in the first hurried view of the situation, should conclude that their work upon earth was finished. They had given the message, and now they waited patiently for God to do His part. The general attitude of the public seemed to bear out this idea. Scoffers were so hardened, and the members of the popular churches seemed so firmly set against the advent preaching, so averse apparently to the mere thought of Christ's returning to this earth, that the believers in the near advent felt they could do nothing for them.

But the Adventists did not long remain passive. Indeed, the most earnest, aggressive ones had immediately begun to study their Bibles for further light, and in due time it came. As many times previously in the history of the church, the humble seekers after truth were being led step by step. Not all were of this type, however. Some of the members most willing to spread their views lacked balance and good sense. William Miller was deeply pained as he observed in some quarters a prevailing tendency to extreme views and fanciful interpretations of Scripture. He said:

" The truth is not responsible for such devices of Satan to destroy it. I have never taught a neglect of any of the duties of life which make us good parents, children, neighbors, or citizens. I have ever inculcated a faithful performance of all those duties, enjoining good works with faith and repentance. Those who have taught the neglect of these, instead of acting with me, or being my followers, as they are called, have departed from my counsels, and acted in opposition to my uniform teachings."—*"History of the Second Advent Message and Mission, Doctrine and People," by Isaac C. Wellcome, page 412.*

Considerable confusion arose as a result of the numerous advent publications. Mr. Miller tells of receiving in one week sixteen different publications advocating doctrines and sentiments more or less in conflict with one another.

It was with a view to arriving at some degree of unity in faith and practice that a mutual conference of Adventists was assembled at Albany on the 29th of April, 1845. Mr. Miller attended, and served as chairman of a committee which drafted a statement of the belief and working plans of the large majority of the faithful. The doctrines set forth are in essentials those which have already been given as Miller's belief. The church organization agreed to was congregational:

"We regard any congregation of believers, who habitually assemble for the worship of God and the due observance of the gospel ordinances, as a church of Christ. As such, it is an independent body, accountable only to the great Head of the church. To all such we recommend a careful examination of the Scriptures, and the adoption of such principles of association and order as are in accordance therewith, that they may enjoy the advantages of that church relation which Christ has instituted."—*Id., p. 419.*

The plans suggested were not the most aggressive, but they seemed feasible. Camp-meetings were thought impracticable.

"What we now do must be done more by dint of persevering and determined effort than by moving the masses of [the] community.

"We would, therefore, advise that our mode of operation, in this respect, be varied so as to meet the exigencies of the times, and are of the opinion that our camp-meetings, except in particular cases where the brethren deem it will advance the cause, should be dispensed with for the present, and our energies expended by visiting the towns and villages, and in some convenient place giving courses of lectures and holding series of conferences. By this we think our means could be better husbanded, and fewer laborers could carry on the meetings, and thus a wider field be occupied."—*Id., p. 420.*

Sabbath schools and Bible class instruction were to be encouraged, and the circulation of advent literature was enjoined. The congregations were warned against accepting the views of irresponsible persons.

The conference was productive of good in emphasizing the fundamental principles of the movement. In connection with the report of this meeting, William Miller issued an address full of wise counsel, and well adapted to direct the activities of the believers in their relations with one another and with the world. It begins:

"The present state of our faith and hope, with the severe trials which many of us experience, call for much brotherly love, forbearance, patience, and prayer. No cause, be it ever so holy, can exist in this present world without its attendant evils. Therefore it becomes necessary for all who are connected with this cause to exercise great charity, for charity covers a multitude of sins."—*Id., p. 424.*

The address goes on to urge patient waiting on God combined with prayerful study of the Word:

"How did we receive this doctrine at first? Was it not by searching the Word of God and a careful comparison of scripture with scripture? Yes; our faith did not rest on the word of man. We then required chapter and verse, or we would not believe. Why should we leave our former rule of faith to follow the vain and changing opinions of men? Some are neglecting the lamp, and seeking to walk by sparks of their own kindling. . . .

"When minds are contracted by selfishness and bigotry, they lose sight of the glory of God and His word, and seek only their own glory. On the other hand, they neglect, if they do not actually reject, such parts of the oracles of God as militate against their views, and rush headlong into error.

If we are thus liable to be deceived by the cunning craftiness of men, we ought to be cautious how we are led by every fanciful interpretation of Scripture. Let us then be more wary, and, like the noble Bereans, search the Scriptures daily, to see whether these things are so. Then, if we err, we shall have the consolation that we have made a careful examination of the subject, and that the error was one of the head, and not of the heart. Christians should receive no evidence but the testimony of God as a ground of faith. . . .

"We would, therefore, recommend more study of the Scriptures, and less writing, and that we be careful not to submit to public inspection mere speculations until they are closely scrutinized by some judicious friend. Thus we shall avoid many errors. We should always be more jealous of ourselves than of others. Self-love is the strongest, most dangerous and deceitful foe that we meet in our Christian warfare. We have arrived at a period of deep interest and peril. It is interesting because the evidence of the Saviour being at the door is plain, so that no sincere student of prophecy can be at a loss to know that that day, for which all other days were made, is near.

"How interesting to live in expectation of the day which patriarchs, prophets, and apostles desired to see, but died without the sight! Persecution and death lose their sting in prospect of the coming Conqueror, who hath all power, and who hath engaged to put all enemies under His feet. We need not murmur, for in this our day, God will bring to pass this act, this (to the worldly man) strange act, for which all the weary saints, for six thousand years, have lived and prayed.

"We entreat you to hold fast the confidence which you have had in the word of God until the end. 'Yet a little while, and He that shall come will come, and will not tarry.' 'Here is the patience and the faith of the saints.' 'Be ye also patient; stablish your hearts: for the coming of the Lord draweth nigh.'"—*Id., pp. 425-427.*

Mr. Miller was in feeble health during the rest of his life, and took little part in the advent activities, though his interest never slackened. He passed away quietly at his home, Dec. 20, 1849, in his sixty-eighth year, his faith unshaken in the movement in which he had acted so prominent a part, and his hope firmly fixed on the coming Saviour. The inscription on his tomb in Low Hampton cemetery is an appropriate one, beautifully expressive of his resignation and faith:

"But go thy way till the end, for thou shalt rest, and stand in thy lot at the end of the days."

Already, in the autumn of 1844, the Adventists who continued to look for the return of their Lord had begun to form two groups. One of these believed that some mistake had been made in the figures, that the 2300 years perhaps did not close in 1844. The members of this group naturally began to set other dates, and in time split up into several bodies, each of which, however, continued to emphasize the Bible teaching concerning the soon-coming Saviour.

The others, much the smaller number at the time, held to the belief that the 2300 days closed in 1844, and prayed and studied chiefly to know the true nature of the event which took place at that time; for that some important event did take place then they felt convinced on at least two grounds: First, the period of 2300 prophetic days, according to the best available light from the Bible and from history, ended at that time, and must mark an important era in God's work; second, the marked manifestations of the Spirit of God in connection with the giving of the midnight cry, and the freedom of that movement on the whole from fanatical elements, together with its thoroughly Scriptural character, forbade their allowing themselves to doubt for one moment that it was of divine origin.

It is with this branch of the Adventists that the present history has to do. Small to begin with, the fixed belief of its members that God had led them hitherto, and that the prophetic periods were correct, saved them from disastrous attempts to set other dates, and thus gave them from the beginning a certain unity of faith and spirit that made for steady growth. It was in connection with this branch, too, that the spirit of prophecy was manifested, as we shall see in the following chapter, and the spiritual leadership thus provided was a further source of unity and strength.

MRS. ELLEN GOULD WHITE

THE BIRTHPLACE OF ELLEN G. WHITE, GORHAM, MAINE

CHAPTER VI

Spiritual Gifts

THERE is, perhaps, no phase of the Christian church more peculiar to it, nor one that more triumphantly demonstrates its perfect adaptation to human needs, than its possession of what are known as " spiritual gifts." The presence of these gifts in the church of apostolic times is universally conceded. They were not only recognized when they appeared, but they were expected. The leaders both instructed the churches as to the reception of these tokens of the divine presence and guidance, and gave needed advice as to the order and decorum that were to govern their manifestation.

The exercise of the miraculous gifts was not intended in any way to supplant or even supersede the regular church officers. On the contrary, the gifts were designed to strengthen the hands of such officers, and to quicken the spiritual life of the church as a whole. They were gracious manifestations of the divine care, evidences that the Spirit was doing His office work in the church, and in times of doubt and uncertainty, or of impending crisis, a means for the direct communication of the divine will to the church.

Various gifts are named by Paul, such as healing, teaching, speaking in tongues, working miracles, etc., but special emphasis is placed upon the prophetic gift as a means for the edification of the members of the church. In the history also of ancient Israel the gift of prophecy is seen to occupy a large and important place.

The prophet was God's special messenger. He reproved sin in the individual, especially if he occupied a position of responsibility; as Nathan carried the divine message to David when the king had so grievously sinned in the matter of Uriah the Hittite. The prophet also spoke words of encouragement to kings and people in times of crisis; as Isaiah reassured Hezekiah, and confirmed him in his stand against the threats and revilings of the leader of the Assyrian host. The prophet gave messages of reproof when the people neglected their duty to God; as Haggai to the returned Israelites who dwelt at ease in their "ceiled houses," while the house of the Lord lay in ruins. He not only reproved, but he stirred them to action; and then, when they heeded the reproof, and set about to build the house of God, the prophet was the channel for messages of encouragement and commendation.

In the New Testament there are various recorded cases of the exercise of the prophetic gift, from which it is to be inferred that its character had not materially changed. It was a means of imparting instruction and encouragement for the spiritual edification of the faithful. It was especially likely to be manifested when there was greatest need of that sense of the divine presence and guidance which it was able to impart.

The band of waiting Adventists who had within a few months passed through two severe disappointments, and were patiently praying for light, were in a situation peculiarly trying. They had given the message intrusted to them, they had realized the power of the Spirit in so doing, and had continually enjoyed by faith the sweet presence and fellowship of their Redeemer. But He had not come in person as they fondly expected; the set time had passed, and they were sad and perplexed. It was for a little season their hour of darkness,—almost as if their Lord had hid His face from them.

But God had not forsaken His people. He was permitting them to be tested and tried almost beyond measure, in order to fit them for the special work that lay before them. When the right time came, He sent through a chosen instrument the special guidance and encouragement needed by His people, both collectively and individually. In doing this, He was but following the plan adopted in the case of his ancient people Israel. There is a phase of this guidance that belongs especially to the individual, and there is one that pertains peculiarly to a people as a body, called out to perform a work that is a part of the divine purpose. This guidance, whether of individuals or of a movement, is usually given through divine inspiration.

The instrument used among the Adventists was a young woman named Ellen G. Harmon, born at Gorham, Maine, Nov. 26, 1827, the daughter of Robert and Eunice Harmon. When she was yet a child, her parents moved to Portland. In her early years Ellen showed no unusual development of the spiritual faculties. She was of a bright, vivacious temperament, fond of books, and forward in her school studies, but also fond of innocent merriment. When she was nine years old, she met with an accident which was to affect her whole after-life. Returning from school one day, she was struck on the nose by a stone flung in a sudden fit of anger by an older playmate. The injury proved to be a severe one, and only after a long and painful illness, in the course of which she was reduced to a mere shadow of her former self, did she recover even a reasonable degree of health. The resulting deformity, though not greatly noticeable (the bridge of the nose had been broken), was a severe trial to the young girl.

During the first part of her illness, life seemed to have lost all its attractions. Happiness there could be none for her; she was rebellious, and wanted to die. But these feelings did not long continue. She sought and found divine help in her trouble, and became a radiant Christian.

The physical consequences of the accident were, however, far-reaching. For two years she could not breathe through her nose. Her nervous system had suffered a general breakdown. Her hand trembled if she tried to write, and when she bent her mind to her studies, the letters on the page ran together, and she became faint and dizzy. She also suffered from a bad cough. After fruitless attempts, she was finally obliged, though very reluctantly, to give up her cherished ambition of getting a good education. It was hard for the active girl to look forward to a life of confirmed invalidism, and she felt disposed to murmur at her lot. The joyous confidence in the Saviour's love which had once been her comfort, departed, and God and heaven seemed very far off.

Such was the young girl's frame of mind when, in the early spring of 1840, William Miller visited Portland, and gave a course of lectures on the second advent. The meetings were

AN OLD LANDMARK

This old church, now a carriage factory, is the place where Ellen G. Harmon (Mrs. White) accepted the advent doctrine under the preaching of William Miller, held in the Christian church on Casco Street, and a large number of persons attended from the town and country around, among them Ellen and her parents. The solemn announcement that in three short years the Saviour would come in His glory, took instant effect.

"Terror and conviction spread through the entire city. Prayer meetings were established, and there was a general awakening among the various denominations."—"*Testimonies for the Church,*" *Vol. I, p. 14.*

Ellen Harmon was deeply affected. She writes:

"When sinners were invited forward to the anxious seat, hundreds responded to the call, and I, among the rest, pressed through the crowd and took my place with the seekers. But there was in my heart a feeling that I could never become worthy to be called a child of God. A lack of confidence in myself, and a conviction that it would be impossible to make any one understand my feelings, prevented me from seeking advice and aid from my Christian friends. Thus I wandered needlessly in darkness and despair, while they, not penetrating my reserve, were entirely ignorant of my true state."— *Id., pp. 14, 15.*

This condition of despondency continued, with short intermissions, for more than two years. In one of her bright intervals Miss Harmon was baptized, and became a member of the Methodist Church. In the summer of 1842 she attended a second course of lectures given by William Miller, but failed to attain to the longed-for peace. She also attended the advent meetings conducted by Elder Stockman, and sought his advice. She writes:

"Upon hearing my story, he placed his hand affectionately upon my head, saying with tears in his eyes, 'Ellen, you are only a child. Yours is a most singular experience for one of your tender age. Jesus must be preparing you for some special work.' . . .

"He spoke of my early misfortune, and said it was indeed a grievous affliction, but he bade me believe that the hand of a loving Father had not been withdrawn from me; that in the future life, when the mist that then darkened my mind had vanished, I would discern the wisdom of the providence which had seemed so cruel and mysterious. . . .

"I returned home and again went before the Lord, promising to do and suffer anything He might require of me, if only the smiles of Jesus might cheer my heart. The same duty was presented to me that had troubled my mind before,— to take up my cross among the assembled people of God. An opportunity was not long wanting; there was a prayer meeting that evening, which I attended.

"I bowed trembling during the prayers that were offered. After a few had prayed, I lifted up my voice in prayer before I was aware of it. The promises of God appeared to me like so many precious pearls that were to be received only for the asking. As I prayed, the burden and agony of soul that I had so long endured, left me, and the blessing of the Lord descended upon me like the gentle dew. I praised God from the depths of my heart. Everything seemed shut out from me but Jesus and His glory, and I lost consciousness of what was passing around me.

"The Spirit of God rested upon me with such power that I was unable to go home that night. When I did return, on the following day, a great change had taken place in my mind. It seemed to me that I could hardly be the same person that left my father's house the previous evening. This passage was continually in my thoughts: 'The Lord is my shepherd; I shall not want.' My heart was full of happiness as I softly repeated these words. . . .

"The night after receiving so great a blessing, I attended the advent meeting. When the time came for the followers of Christ to speak in His favor, I could not remain silent, but rose and related my experience. Not a thought had entered my mind of what I should say; but the simple story of Jesus' love to me fell from my lips with perfect freedom, and my heart was so happy to be liberated from its bondage of dark despair that I lost sight of the people about me and seemed to be alone with God. I found no difficulty in expressing my peace and happiness, except for the tears of gratitude that choked my utterance as I told of the wondrous love that Jesus had shown for me."— *Id., pp. 29-32.*

Miss Harmon had no sooner obtained peace for herself than she began to work untiringly for others. Young as she was, and physically feeble, she displayed a zeal and a knowledge of spiritual things which attracted wide attention. She arranged meetings with some of her unconverted friends, many of them older than herself, and some of them married. She followed up the meetings with personal labor, exhorting and praying with each person separately till the blessing was obtained. Indeed, the days were not long enough for the ardent young worker. She says:

"Night after night in my dreams I seemed to be laboring for the salvation of souls. At such times special cases were presented to my mind; these I afterward sought out and prayed with. In every instance but one these persons yielded themselves to the Lord. Some of our more formal brethren feared that I was too zealous for the conversion of souls, but time seemed to me so short that it behooved all who had a hope of a blessed immortality, and looked for the soon coming of Christ, to labor without ceasing for those who were still in their sins and standing on the awful brink of ruin."— *Id., p. 34.*

Not long after this, Miss Harmon, with her parents, brother, and sisters, was expelled from the local Methodist church. Like other believers in the advent near, they had been accustomed at class meetings and on other suitable occasions to give expression to their joy in the hope of a soon-coming Saviour; but they felt that this testimony was displeasing to their fellow Christians, and often the leader would advance in opposition his firm confidence in the doctrine of a temporal millennium to precede the second advent. Meanwhile the members generally were manifesting a growing antagonism to the advent teaching, and it was becoming evident that a wide gulf separated the Adventists from those who did not share their convictions.

As the time first set for the advent drew near, the meetings of the believers in Portland were marked by an ever-deepening interest, and the crowds increased. High and low, rich and poor, flocked to Beethoven Hall, where night after night the teachings concerning a soon-coming Saviour were clearly set forth. Meetings were also held in private houses in different parts of the city, and the conversions were many.

But the expected time passed; the waiting Adventists were sorely disappointed, and the scoffers triumphed. Many, as we have seen in a previous chapter, gave up their faith, but the large majority held fast their confidence in God and in the movement, and these were soon able to discover the mistake in the reckoning, and to look for the fulfilment of their hopes in the autumn of 1844.

Again the set time passed, and the Saviour did not appear. The grief and disappointment of Ellen Harmon were indeed great. Life in this world had lost all its charms for her, and even her hope in God was no substitute for the expectation of soon-coming translation. Her Christian experience was too deep, however, to allow of long-continued discouragement, and with other faithful ones she patiently waited for the Lord's will to be made known, earnestly praying for more light.

While in this eager, watchful, yet resigned condition, a few weeks after the passing of the time she received a definite token of her call to be a special messenger of encouragement and reproof to God's waiting people. While at morning worship in the house of Mrs. Haines, in Portland, Maine, where she was then staying, she was taken off in vision, and given a view of the Adventist people and of the work that lay before them. There were five persons present, all women, and members of the Adventist body. Miss Harmon, following others, was praying in a whisper, being unable to speak aloud, when the power of God came upon her as she had never felt it before, and in a moment she was lost to all about her.

" I seemed to be surrounded with light [she writes], and to be rising higher and higher from the earth. I turned to look for the advent people in the world, but could not find them, when a voice said to me, ' Look again, and look a little higher.' At this I raised my eyes, and saw a straight and narrow path, cast up high above the world. On this path the advent people were traveling toward the city."— *Id., pp. 58, 59.*

Consideration of space prevents quoting further from this view of the advent experience, which may be found complete in the book " Early Writings." Suffice it to say that the vision was of a character to encourage and strengthen the faithful believers, and to give them a sense of the divine presence in the experience through which they were passing.

When the believers in Portland next came together, Miss Harmon related to them what she had seen in vision, and the hearts of all were greatly cheered and comforted. The known character of the young woman, and the circumstances under which the vision was given her, as well as the nature of the communication itself, all testified to its genuineness as a work of God. Her personal attitude, so free from anything that savored of pride or self-exaltation, corroborated this impression. In the words of a contemporary:

" A solemn sense of eternal interests was constantly upon her, and she seemed to be filled with an unspeakable awe, that one so young and feeble as she should be chosen as an instrument through whom the Lord would communicate light to His people."—" *Rise and Progress of Seventh-day Adventists,*" *p. 92.*

The Adventist believers, however, did not depend upon their impressions in determining the character of the manifestations of which Miss Harmon was the subject. In this matter, as in all others, they looked to the Scriptures for guidance. As they made themselves familiar with what the Bible has to say, and learned that the manifestations they had witnessed were such as characterized the apostolic church, they felt deeply grateful to God for this manifest token of His presence.

About a week after the first vision, Miss Harmon had a second one, in which she was bidden to tell others what had been revealed to her. This was a responsibility from which she naturally shrank. She was but seventeen years of age. Her health was not good; in fact, she was in pain much of the time, and people thought she had not long to live. Moreover, she was timid and retiring to a degree, so that it was painful for her to meet people. She besought the Lord earnestly that this burden might be laid on some one else, but in vain. The word came again and again: " Make known to others what I have revealed to you."

While thus troubled and perplexed in spirit, Miss Harmon attended a meeting held in her father's house, where special prayer was offered for her, and she consecrated herself to God, and felt willing to do His bidding. While praying, the darkness scattered, and she was once more taken off in vision. Again the burden was laid upon her, and this time she did not refuse, but pleaded that she might be kept from spiritual exaltation.

It had been shown to Miss Harmon that she must go to Poland, Maine, and tell her vision. The day after she received this instruction, her brother-in-law unexpectedly drove up to the door of her father's house, and proposed to take her in his sleigh to Poland. Although in a feeble condition of health, she resolved to obey the summons, and rode thirty miles to her sister's house.

Shortly after her arrival, she attended a meeting at Mc-Guire's Hill, ten miles distant. Of her experience at this meeting J. N. Loughborough writes:

"At this meeting she had an opportunity to bear her testimony. For three months her throat and lungs had been so diseased that she could talk but little, and then only in a low, husky tone. On this occasion she arose in meeting and began speaking in a whisper. She continued thus for about five minutes, when the soreness and obstruction left her throat and lungs. Her voice became clear and strong, and she spoke with perfect ease and freedom for nearly two hours. When her message was ended, her voice was gone until she stood before the people again, when the same singular restoration was repeated."— *Id.*, *pp. 104, 105.*

From this time on, Miss Harmon gave herself largely to public work. She went from place to place in New England, delivering the messages that had been given to her. She had reproof for some and encouraging words for others. Everywhere her influence tended to bring together scattered elements, to unify and build up.

Her lot was not an easy one. Some had refrained from labor, and had disfellowshiped those who did not do likewise. These erring ones had their mistake pointed out to them; but some of them rejected the message, and asserted that the messenger herself was worldly. Others accused her of the very practices that she was trying so hard to put down.

The work of a messenger of God has never in the past been an easy one, and hers was no exception. It must suffice that her labors were highly appreciated by many, and that her influence grew from year to year as the people saw with what untiring industry she devoted herself to the work, as well as with what holy boldness and courage, combined with womanly tenderness, she discharged her delicate mission.

THE SANCTUARY

"Christ is not entered into the holy places made with hands, which are the figures of the true; but into heaven itself, now to appear in the presence of God for us." Heb. 9 : 24.

CHRIST THE ANTITYPE

"So Christ was once offered to bear the sins of many." Heb. 9 : 28.

CHAPTER VII

The Sanctuary and the Sabbath

THE little band of Adventists who had taken their stand upon the prophetic periods and the seventh-month movement, continued to study their Bibles in order to understand the nature of the event that took place on the 22d of October, 1844. That Christ did not in any sense come to this earth on that date, they frankly acknowledged. The question then became, "What did mark the end of the 2300 days?" The prophecy said the sanctuary was to be cleansed, and William Miller believed that the sanctuary was this earth. On this latter point he was evidently in error. What, then, did the cleansing of the sanctuary signify? The final answer to this question was found by a systematic study of the Old Testament types and of the whole sanctuary service.

Meanwhile there was much praying, the believers feeling that the subject was one that the Holy Spirit alone could elucidate, but confident that light would come in due time. One day, the account goes, a brother was crossing a cornfield, and seeing it was a retired place, knelt behind one of the shocks of corn

12

OUR ADVOCATE

"We have such a High Priest, who is set on the right hand of the throne of the Majesty in the heavens; a minister of the sanctuary, and of the true tabernacle, which the Lord pitched, and not man." Heb. 8 : 1, 2.

and pleaded for light on this perplexing question. While thus engaged, the Spirit came upon him powerfully, and seemed to give him the impression very distinctly: "The sanctuary to be cleansed is in heaven." He made known his experience to another brother, O. R. L. Crosier, and they made a thorough study of the subject in the light of this hypothesis.

They found that Moses built the tabernacle according to a pattern shown him in the mount, and that the priests of the Aaronic order served "unto the example and shadow of heav-

A PATTERN OF THINGS IN HEAVEN

"The temple of God was opened in heaven, and there was seen in His temple the ark of His testament." Rev. 11 : 19.

enly things." Our Saviour, moreover, is said to be a priest after the order of Melchizedek. John the revelator saw the temple of God opened in heaven, and in the temple the ark of the testament. These passages and other similar ones all seemed to harmonize with the conception of a sanctuary in heaven and a service connected with it, where Christ ministers as priest in behalf of His people.

Now the cleansing of the earthly sanctuary occurred once a year, when the high priest put on his "holy garments," and entered the most holy place to make reconciliation for the sins of the people. (See Leviticus 16.) But Christ, because He made His offering once for all, enters the most holy place in heaven, not yearly, but once for all at the close of His priestly ministry, just prior to His return to this earth to take the kingdom. This, then, would be the beginning of the cleansing of the heavenly sanctuary, the solemn event which really began on Oct. 22, 1844. And as the blotting out of sin presupposes an investigation of the lives and characters of those concerned,

THE INVESTIGATIVE JUDGMENT
"The judgment was set, and the books were opened." Dan. 7 : 10.

this entrance of Christ upon His duties in the most holy, clearly marks the beginning of the investigative judgment, which is indicated in the words, " Fear God, and give glory to Him; *for the hour of His judgment is come.*" Rev. 14: 7.

Such seemed to be the import of the scriptures examined, and such the general line of thought followed by the two men in their study of the question. At length there appeared in the *Day Star* of Canandaigua, N. Y., a lengthy article by Mr. Crosier, in which it was set forth that the cleansing of the sanctuary is a work which Christ accomplishes in heaven just before returning to this world to take the kingdom. This view of the subject gradually prevailed among that portion of the believers who held that the prophetic periods were correctly calculated, and the only question was as to the event.

About this time these Adventists also saw their mistake in supposing, as they had done in the period of darkness and uncertainty immediately following the disappointment, that probationary time had ended. With the entrance of light on the subject of the heavenly sanctuary, it was seen that the advent message had a breadth of meaning which had not been divined before, and to receive the new light was but a preparation for giving it to the world.

Meanwhile the Bible continued to be studied for any further light it might afford as to the position and work of the Adventists. The minds of a number were especially drawn out on the subject of the law of God, which was so intimately bound up with that of the sanctuary. Their prayers for help were answered through an unexpected agency. The Adventists had been teaching the members of other denominations concerning the prophetic periods and the second coming of Christ. They were now themselves to take the place of learners. There was a denomination which had advanced light on the subject of the divine law, especially on the fourth commandment. This denomination was accordingly, in the providence of God, called upon to act the part of instructor to the truth-seeking Adventists.

For centuries the Seventh Day Baptists had been keeping alive the observance of the Bible Sabbath. There have always been in the Christian church observers of the Sabbath of creation, and not a few laid down their lives for their faith in the days of persecution. The first Sabbath keeper came to America in 1664, just forty-four years after the landing of the Pilgrims. One or two others followed from England, and some embraced their views in this country, so that in 1668 Dr. E. Stennet, a member of the struggling Sabbatarian church in London, which had just seen its pastor dragged from the pulpit and executed, was able to send greetings " to the remnant in Rhode Island who keep the commandments of God and the testimonies of Jesus."

The first American Seventh Day Baptist church was organized in 1671, after which thirty-six years elapsed before a second was organized with seventeen members. When the Seventh Day Baptist General Conference was organized in 1802, it included eight churches, nine ordained ministers, and 1,130 members. Thus the work developed slowly; but in the early forties there was an awakening among the witnesses to the Bible Sabbath, and they were led to plead earnestly with God in behalf of the truth especially committed to them, that by His divine grace the message might go with greater power to the world. At their General Conference of 1843 the following action was taken:

MRS. RACHEL PRESTON

"*Resolved*, That in view of the necessity of the influence of the Holy Spirit to incline men to the love of truth, it is our solemn duty to connect with all our efforts to enlighten them in reference to the Sabbath, earnest prayer to God for His blessing; therefore,

"*Resolved*, That it be recommended to the churches of this denomination to observe the first day of November next (fourth day of the week), as a day of fasting and praying, humbly imploring Almighty God to arise and plead for His holy Sabbath."

Again at the Conference of 1844 the subject came up, and this further action was taken:

"*Resolved*, That inasmuch as the first day of November, 1843, was observed, in accordance with the recommendation of this General Conference, as a day of humiliation before God, and earnest entreaty to Him to arise and plead for His holy Sabbath; since which time a deeper and wider-spread interest upon the subject has sprung up than has ever before been known in our country; therefore,

"*Resolved*, That the fourth day of the first week in January [1] next, be observed as a day of fasting, devout acknowledgment for blessings bestowed, and earnest prayer that God would continue to plead for His holy Sabbath, and also prepare us by His Holy Spirit for the labor thus devolved upon us.

"*Resolved*, That we invite all who love the Sabbath, and desire its better observance, to unite with us in presenting its interests at the throne of grace."—"*History of the Seventh Day Baptist General Conference from Its Origin, September, 1802, to Its Fifty-third Session, September, 1856,*" *by Rev. James Bailey, pp. 243, 244.*

---

[1] The first line of this resolution was taken from a printed copy so old and indistinct as to be scarcely readable. We cannot vouch for the exact wording.

Thus while the Adventists were praying for more light, and had their minds especially directed to the law of God, the Seventh Day Baptists were praying that God would arise and plead for His holy Sabbath. The prayers of both were speedily answered.

It was in the spring of 1844 that the truth concerning the seventh-day Sabbath was first brought to the attention of the Adventist church at Washington, N. H. At that time Mrs. Rachel Preston, a Seventh Day Baptist, went to Washington on a visit to her daughter, the wife of Cyrus Farnsworth, of the Adventist church. She was an ardent believer in the claims of the Bible Sabbath, and brought with her a supply of Seventh Day Baptist literature.

WILLIAM FARNSWORTH

These Sabbath tracts were duly distributed and read, and they produced results. At the service on a certain Sunday in the spring a member of the congregation rose to his feet and said he had been studying the subject, and was convinced that the seventh, and not the first, day of the week was the true Sabbath according to the Bible, and had decided to observe it. He was followed by another, and another, till a considerable number had signified their determination to walk in the new light.

Mrs. Preston, seeing the seed she had sown thus quickly spring up and bear fruit, sat weeping for joy. Within a few days practically the whole church of forty members had taken their stand for the Sabbath of the Bible.

Thus was brought into being the first Seventh-day Adventist church. The original church building, standing three miles south of Washington Center, is still in good repair. Mrs. Preston herself joined the church, being as willing to accept the good news of a soon-coming Saviour as the Adventist company were to accept the Bible teaching concerning the Sabbath. The first Adventist minister to accept the Sabbath was Frederick

Wheeler, of this Washington church, formerly a Methodist minister, and an associate of William Miller. It was in March, 1844, he says, that he began to keep the Sabbath.

Among the first of the Adventist ministers to accept the Sabbath was T. M. Preble, who issued a pamphlet on the subject early in February, 1845, in which, after setting forth the claims of the Bible Sabbath, and giving proof that the change had been made by the papacy, he added:

> "Thus we see Daniel 7:25 fulfilled, the little horn changing times and laws. Wherefore it appears to me that all who keep the first day for the Sabbath are the pope's Sunday keepers and God's Sabbath breakers."

With Mr. Preble, however, it was apparently a matter merely for academic discussion, for he continued his connection with non-Sabbath keeping churches, and presently lost interest in the question, even joining with those who opposed the Bible Sabbath. He had sown the seed, however, and in due time the harvest appeared. From this time on, the Sabbath truth continued to be a definite part of the belief of a small but steadily growing band of Adventists.

FREDERICK WHEELER

Another, and more consistent, advocate of the Sabbath arose in Capt. Joseph Bates, to whom reference has already been made in a previous chapter. Mr. Bates was in many ways a remarkable man, and one destined to have no small part in giving the mold to the Seventh-day Adventist Church. He was born at Rochester, Plymouth Co., Mass., July 8, 1792, and was brought up in the town of Fair Haven, seven miles distant. His father, a descendant of an old New England family, fought under Lafayette in the Revolutionary War. The son had an unconquerable longing for the sea, and after winning his parents' reluctant consent, embarked as cabin boy in the summer of 1807. After some years of adventurous sea life, he was impressed into the English navy shortly before the outbreak of the war of 1812, and remained a prisoner during the conflict, confined for most of the time in Dartmouth prison. After his release, he again took to the seas, and rose rapidly to the post of captain, the ships he commanded sailing chiefly between New York and various points in South America. At the age of thirty-five he retired with a reasonable competence. He had learned a number of things while at sea, and being a man of decision, had acted on his knowledge. He saw that

FIRST SEVENTH-DAY ADVENTIST CHURCH, WASHINGTON, N. H.

spirituous liquors were deleterious, and forthwith gave them up. Later he gave up wine and beer, and finally tobacco.

Mr. Bates had formed the habit of keeping an open mind for truth, and when the advent doctrine was preached in New England, he gave it a thorough investigation, and ended by accepting it. His means were used freely for its promulgation, and when the great disappointment came in 1844, he was at the end of his resources.

The Sabbath truth received his enthusiastic support. He saw the fourth commandment as a part, and an important part, of God's moral law. He believed that this venerable institution, handed down from creation, had in it a blessing, not merely for the Jews, but for all mankind. As a result of his active labors, Adventists here and there began to observe the Sabbath.

With most of these new believers the light shed upon the Sabbath question by the prophetic word was a large determining factor. They came to feel that it was not merely a question of days, but rather of institutions. The Sabbath of Jehovah stood for loyalty to God; the other sabbath represented a rival power.

In this connection they studied anew the three messages of the fourteenth chapter of the Revelation. The first of these messages, it will be remembered, reads: " Fear God, and give glory to Him; for the hour of His judgment is come: and worship Him that made heaven, and earth, and the sea, and the fountains of waters."

This message began to be given to the world, as we have seen, in the advent preaching of 1831-44.

The second message, " Babylon is fallen, is fallen, that great city, because she made all nations drink of the wine of the wrath of her fornication," was first sounded in the summer and early autumn of 1844, when it finally became clear to the Adventists that they must separate from the popular churches.

The message of the third angel, which is a warning against the worship of the beast and his image, closes with, or is followed by, the significant words: " Here is the patience [R. V., " patient endurance "] of the saints: here are they that keep the commandments of God, and the faith of Jesus."

The passage taken as a whole enjoins on the one hand loyalty to the commandments of God and the faith of Jesus, and on the other utters strong denunciation against the worship of a rival power. The position of this message in close proximity to the two already given, naturally made it of special interest to the Adventist believers. But while all their energies were absorbed in warning the world that the Saviour would appear in judgment within a few months, they had little time or inclination to break new ground in prophetic study. Now, in the opening months of 1845, when the Sabbath truth had dawned upon a goodly number of Adventists, and the unchangeable character of God's great moral law was beginning to be understood, the way was open for a true understanding of the message of the third angel.

Further light was shed upon the matter by a view given Miss Ellen G. Harmon, who did not, to begin with, share Captain Bates' convictions concerning the importance of the Sabbath commandment. She saw in vision the heavenly sanctuary, with the ark of God and the mercy-seat, over which two angels bent with covering wings. This, she was told by her accompanying angel, represented the heavenly host looking with reverential awe upon the law written with the finger of God. The cover of the ark was then raised, and she saw the tables of stone, the fourth commandment in the center encircled by a soft halo of light. Said the angel:

" It is the only one of the ten which defines the living God who created the heavens and the earth and all things that are therein."—" *Life Sketches*," *p. 96.*

" When the foundations of the earth were laid," said Miss Harmon, " then was also laid the foundation of the Sabbath."

When the waiting Adventists caught the larger vision of a commandment-loving people gathered out from every country of the world, who should stand on Mount Zion, having the Father's name written in their foreheads; when they perceived the fuller meaning of the significant verse: " Here is the patient endurance of the saints: here are they that keep the commandments of God, and the faith of Jesus; " when they came to look on the Sabbath as the sign of loyalty to God, and saw that the great conflict with the beast and with the image of the beast involved this neglected and misunderstood but very vital part of the great moral law,— when this broader conception had fully dawned upon their consciousness, then there was revealed to them a meaning and a consistency in the advent movement which they had never before seen. In the glory of this light, their hearts cheered by the larger vision, the believing ones dedicated themselves to the great work that lay before them.

The message, to be sure, advanced slowly and amid great difficulties in those pioneering days; but the workers trusted God, and found in Him a present help in every time of need. Joseph Bates, who was the first to lead out in giving the Sabbath reform message, traveled all over New England and New York. and also entered Michigan, Indiana, Ohio, and other of the Middle Western States: yet he had no money except what came to him in freewill offerings from the believers, most of whom were in humble circumstances. He was often in severe straits financially, but he never suffered want, nor was he hindered in the accomplishment of what he believed to be his duty. It was a habit with him to say, " The Lord will provide."

On one occasion, feeling impressed that he ought to give the Sabbath message in New Hampshire, Captain Bates was about to make the journey on foot when the necessary money came unexpectedly from a young sister in the faith. She had hired herself out at a dollar a week in order to earn some money with which to help the cause; but after working a week she felt strongly impressed that Captain Bates needed money immediately. She accordingly went to her employer and obtained $5 in advance, which came to hand just in time to enable the contemplated trip to be made by train instead of on foot, as he had thought of doing.

On another occasion Captain Bates was under conviction to go to a certain place, and actually took his seat in the train, having neither money nor ticket. He had been in his seat only a few moments when a man who was a perfect stranger to him came and handed him $5 to assist him in his work. Such providences were common in the life of this devoted pioneer, and he was always so sure of the divine help just when it was needed that he was never known to hold back from any enterprise that promised to help forward the cause he loved.

The story of how he wrote and published his tract on the Sabbath is a good example of his customary habit of going forward step by step as the Lord opened the way, and never for one moment ceasing to advance because he could not see more than a day ahead.

When he sat down to begin the writing of this tract, he had just one York shilling (12½ cents) in his pocket. He had been thus occupied about an hour when Mrs. Bates came into the room and said she had not enough flour to make out the baking. He asked how much she lacked. She replied: "About four pounds," and then mentioned one or two other articles that were needed. He went to a near-by store, purchased the flour and other things, and returned with them. He then resumed his writing. His wife came in presently, and seeing the flour and the other articles, asked, "Where did you get the flour?" He replied, "I bought it. Isn't that the amount you needed to complete the baking?" "Yes," was the reply; "but have *you*, Captain Bates, a man who has sailed vessels out of New Bedford to all parts of the world, been out and bought *four pounds* of flour?"

It was necessary now to tell her the real situation, and the captain did not hold back or falter. "Wife," he said, with perfect calmness, "for those articles on the table I have paid out the last money I have on earth." It was a severe blow to the faithful companion, who, while well aware that her husband had used his means very freely in forwarding the advent movement, had no idea that he was actually at the end of his financial resources, so that a condition of real want confronted the family.

"What are we going to do?" she asked amid sobs.

The captain arose, and with all the dignity of a commander directing his ship at sea, he said: "I am going to write a book

on the Sabbath question; I'm going to get it printed, and spread
the Sabbath truth before the world."

" But what are we going to live on? "

" The Lord will provide for that," was the smiling rejoinder.

" Yes, that is what you always say," was the wife's reply,
and she went back to her work with a heavy heart.

When the captain had continued his writing for another half
hour, a voice seemed to say to him, " Go to the post office; there
is a letter there for you." He did so, and received the letter;
but in those days prepayment of postage was optional, and this
letter had not been paid for. Captain Bates was obliged to tell
the postmaster that he could not pay the postage, being entirely
without money; but he added, " Will you let me see where it is
from? "

" Take it along," said the postmaster, " and pay some other
time."

" No," said Bates, " I will not take the letter out of the office
until the postage is paid." Holding the letter in his hand, he
said, " I am of the opinion that there is money in this letter.
Will you please open it? If there is money in it, you can take
the postage out; if not, I will not read it."

The postmaster opened the letter and found $10. The writer
stated that he was impressed that Captain Bates needed money,
and in the haste of dispatching the letter he had evidently forgotten to pay the postage.

On receiving this money, Captain Bates went to a provision
store, where he bought a barrel of flour for $4, as well as sup-
plies of potatoes, sugar, and other household necessities. In
giving the order for the delivery of the goods, he said that his
wife would probably say they didn't belong there, but no attention was to be paid to her protests; the goods were to be un-
loaded on the porch.

He then went to a printing office and arranged for publishing
a thousand copies of his contemplated pamphlet, with the understanding that the manuscript was to be set up as copy was
received, and proofs supplied to the writer, who was to pay in
money from time to time as he was able, the books to remain
in the office till all bills had been paid.

After attending to this matter and purchasing paper, quills,
etc., Captain Bates returned to his house, going in by a back
entrance and seating himself at his desk, saying nothing to
Mrs. Bates.

Presently his wife came in excitedly, " Joseph, just look out
on the front porch! Where did that stuff come from? A dray-

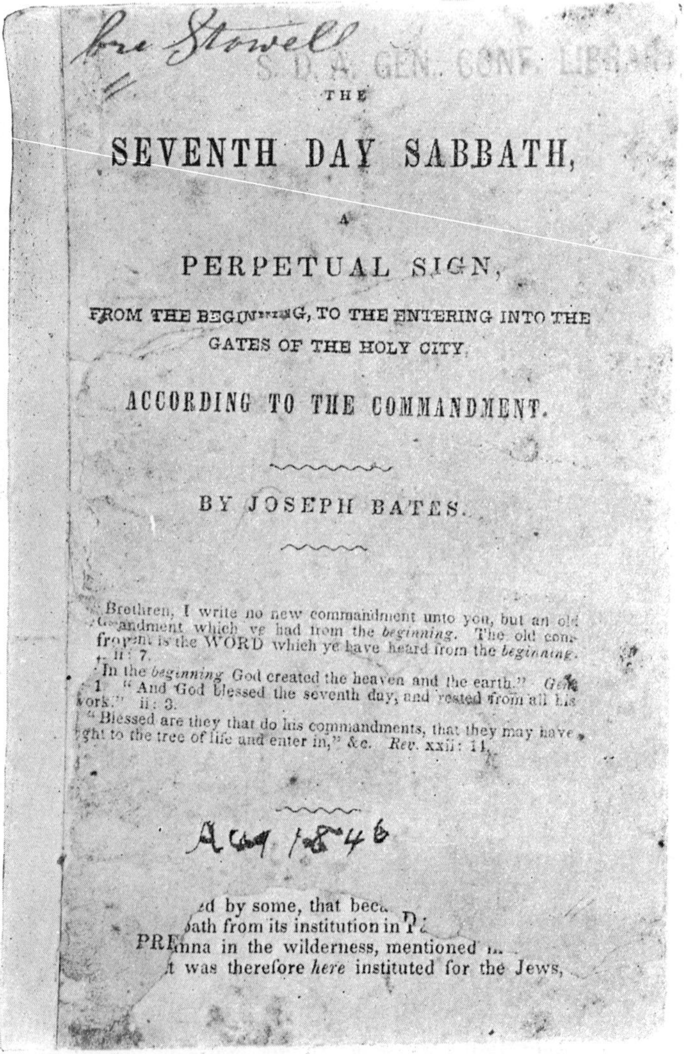

THE

SEVENTH DAY SABBATH,

A

PERPETUAL SIGN,

FROM THE BEGINNING, TO THE ENTERING INTO THE
GATES OF THE HOLY CITY,

ACCORDING TO THE COMMANDMENT.

~~~~~

BY JOSEPH BATES.

~~~~~

"Brethren, I write no new commandment unto you, but an old
Commandment which ye had from the *beginning*. The old commandment is the WORD which ye have heard from the *beginning*."
— ii: 7.

"In the *beginning* God created the heaven and the earth." *Gen.*
1. "And God blessed the seventh day, and rested from all his
work." ii: 3.

"Blessed are they that do his commandments, that they may have
right to the tree of life and enter in," &c. *Rev.* xxii: 14.

Aug 1846

...ed by some, that beca...
...bath from its institution in P...
PR...nna in the wilderness, mentioned ...
...t was therefore *here* instituted for the Jews,

OUR FIRST SABBATH TRACT

This is a facsimile of the much-worn title page of this interesting publication.

man came here and would unload it. I told him it didn't belong here, but he would unload it."

" Well," said the captain, " I guess it's all right."

" But," persisted his wife, " where did it come from? "

" The Lord sent it," was the reply, and then she was given the letter to read.

The work of writing and printing went on, and money was paid in from time to time, coming from friends of the cause in various parts of New England who felt impressed that it was needed. The tract was to be delivered in large sheets, the captain doing his own folding and stitching. When all the proofs had been read, and the day arrived for the delivery of the sheets, there was still a portion of the bill unpaid. Captain Bates went to the printer, and was beginning to apologize for being behind in his payments, when he was told that he might have the sheets at once, as the bill had been settled in full. Said the printer: " A man came in this morning, an entire stranger to me, and paid the remainder of the bill. He did not give me his name, so I cannot tell you who he is. But the bill is paid and the sheets are yours."

With a glad heart Captain Bates took the sheets home, where he and Mrs. Bates were soon hard at work folding and stitching and sending out to various addresses the little messengers of truth. The tract was set solid in small type, and contained forty-eight pages. The full title reads: " The Seventh-day Sabbath, a Perpetual Sign, from the Beginning to the Entering into the Gates of the Holy City, According to the Commandment." It was published in August, 1846, and proved to be an effective means of spreading a knowledge of the Bible Sabbath.

Associated with Joseph Bates in these early years of the movement was a much younger man, James White, whose activities as a lecturer in the 1844 movement have been recorded in part in an earlier chapter. He was a thoroughly consecrated man, and one who manifested great energy and perseverance in seeking out and ministering to the spiritual needs of those members of the advent movement whose minds were open to truth. Indeed, his leadership seems to have been a well-nigh indispensable element in the early history of the Seventh-day Adventist denomination.

James White was born in Palmyra, Somerset Co., Maine, Aug. 4, 1821, the son of John White, a direct descendant of one of the Pilgrims who came over in the " Mayflower." His mother was a granddaughter of Dr. Samuel Shepard, a Baptist minister well known in New England.

There were nine children in the family, James being the fifth. Feeble in health and suffering from weak eyes, he was behind boys of his age in school advantages. He made good progress, however, after entering the academy at St. Albans, Maine. At the end of the term of twelve weeks, he received a certificate in the common branches, and the following winter taught school. His health was better now, he had grown rapidly, and was in size and strength in advance of his years.

At the close of his first term of teaching, he attended school at St. Albans for five weeks, then shouldered his pack and walked forty miles to the Penobscot River, where he obtained employment as a raw hand in a sawmill. After four months he returned to his home. He had been unfortunate in suffering a severe cut in the ankle·joint, which had involved loss of time. After settling bills, he found he had but $30 and a scanty supply of worn clothing. He now started for the school at Reedfield, Maine, where, in addition to courses in the common branches, he took up natural philosophy, algebra, and Latin. He says of himself at this time:

" My thirst for education increased, and my plans were laid to take a college course, and pay my way, if labor, economy, and study would accomplish it. . . . At Reedfield I wore old clothes, while my classmates wore new, and lived three months on cornmeal pudding prepared by myself, and a few raw apples, while they enjoyed the conveniences and luxuries of the 'boarding house."—" *Life Incidents,*" *p. 14.*

The following winter, 1840-41, he taught school and gave lessons in penmanship in two districts, and returned home with his winter's earnings, fully resolved to continue his studies.

His religious experience had been much like that of other young men of the time. At the age of fifteen he had been baptized, and had joined the Christian Church, but five years later found him engrossed with his studies, and quite indifferent to spiritual matters. Adventism in particular he held in aversion as a piece of wild fanaticism, which could in no way concern him. When, however, he returned to his home for the summer vacation, and found his mother and a number of his young friends, formerly indifferent, deeply interested in the advent doctrines, he studied the subject himself, and was convinced.

Along with the belief that Christ would soon return to judge the world, there came to the young man a strong conviction that he ought to give up his worldly plans, and devote himself to the work of warning the world of a soon-coming Saviour. Especially did the burden rest upon him to labor for the pupils whom he had taught the previous winter. It was as if a voice said to him: " Visit your scholars from house to house and pray with them." He tried to shake off the impression, saying to himself that he would not go; so he packed his books and clothes, and started for Newport Academy; but he could not study, for he had no peace of mind. Finally he resolved to do what he believed to be his duty, and went from the schoolroom directly to Troy, where he had taught school. He had gone, he tells us, but a few rods on the way, when sweet peace flowed into his heart.

The account he gives of the first homes he visited, is interesting, as showing the need of such work. When he informed one family that he wished to pray with them, the mother burst into tears, and asked the privilege first of sending word to her neighbors. He says:

"In less than half an hour I had before me a congregation of about twenty-five. In conversing with them, I learned that not one of that company professed Christianity. Lectures on the second advent had been given near them, and a general conviction that the doctrine might be true rested upon the people. And as I related my experience of the few weeks in the past, stating my convictions relative to the soon coming of Christ, all were interested. I then bowed to pray, and was astonished to find that these twenty-five sinners all bowed with me. I could but weep. They all wept with me. And after pointing them to Christ as best I could with my limited experience and knowledge of the Scriptures, I shook their hands, said farewell, and joyfully pursued my journey."—" *Life Incidents*," pp. 21, 22.

This work occupied only a few days, after which Mr. White returned to his home feeling he had done his duty. He was rather unsettled during the summer. He dared not go back to his books, the Spirit had once already driven him away from school; and yet he feared that he would not be able to make a success of preaching. He heard Elders J. V. Himes and A. Hale speak several times in Bangor, Maine, and began to feel more and more impressed with the advent teaching, especially as he studied publications of the movement in connection with the Bible. He also preached occasionally on these themes, and with acceptance.

After attending the Adventist camp-meeting in eastern Maine, and hearing stirring lectures from such men as William Miller, J. V. Himes, and T. M. Preble, he fully decided to give his life to the proclamation of the advent message, and soon afterward entered upon the work. The blessing that attended his labors among the Freewill Baptists during the winter and spring of 1843 gave further evidence of his call to the sacred work of the ministry. In the following summer he was ordained by the Christian denomination to which he then belonged. He

13

continued to lecture during the autumn and winter of 1843-44, and entered very heartily into the movement in the late summer and autumn of 1844, known as the " midnight cry." The disappointment was a bitter one to him. He says:

" When Elder Himes visited Portland, Maine, a few days after the passing of the time, and stated that the brethren should prepare for another cold winter, my feelings were almost uncontrollable. I left the place of meeting and wept like a child."—" *Rise and Progress of Seventh-day Adventists,*" *p. 79.*

On the 26th of August, 1846, James White was married to Ellen G. Harmon, whose early life has been narrated in a previous chapter, and a little later they both began to observe the Sabbath. There were at that time about twenty-five Sabbath-keeping Adventists scattered through the State of Maine, and a somewhat larger number in other parts of New England. Among these persons Elder and Mrs. White began to labor with gratifying results in spiritual quickening and clear apprehension of Scriptural truths, but under circumstances outwardly unfavorable. Financial support there was none, and the devoted couple gladly labored with their hands to supply the bare necessities of life.

" We entered upon our work penniless [writes Mrs. White of this time], with few friends, and broken health. . . . We had no houses of worship at that time. And the idea of using a tent had not then occurred to us. Most of our meetings were held in private houses. Our congregations were small. It was seldom that any came into our meetings excepting Adventists, unless they were attracted by curiosity to hear a woman speak.

" At first I moved out timidly in the work of public speaking. If I had confidence, it was given me by the Holy Spirit. If I spoke with freedom and power, it was given me of God. Our meetings were usually conducted in such a manner that both of us took part. My husband would give a doctrinal discourse, then I would follow with an exhortation of considerable length, melting my way into the feelings of the congregation. Thus my husband sowed and I watered the seed of truth, and God did give the increase."— " *Testimonies for the Church, with a Biographical Sketch of the Author,*" *by Mrs. E. G. White, Vol. I, p. 75.*

In the autumn of 1847, their first-born son being then about two months old, they began housekeeping with borrowed furniture in a part of the home of Stockbridge Howland at Gorham, Maine.

" We were poor, and saw close times. We had resolved not to be dependent, but to support ourselves, and have something with which to help others. But we were not prospered. My husband worked very hard hauling stone on the railroad, but could not get what was due him for his labor."—*Id., p. 82.*

Later the young preacher left the railroad, his wife tells us, and went into the woods to chop cordwood.

" With a continual pain in his side, he worked from early morning till dark to earn about fifty cents a day. He was prevented from sleeping nights by severe pain. We endeavored to keep up good courage, and trust in the Lord. I did not murmur. In the morning I felt grateful to God that He had preserved us through another night, and at night I was thankful that He had kept us through another day."— *Ibid.*

Calls came from believers in various parts, inviting Mr. and Mrs. White to labor among them; but there being no money to pay traveling expenses, their child also being at such a tender age, it was necessary to reply that the way was not open.

" We did not wish to be dependent, and were careful to live within our means. We were resolved to suffer rather than get in debt. I allowed myself and child one pint of milk each day. One morning before my husband went to his work, he left me nine cents to buy milk for three mornings. It was a study with me whether to buy the milk for myself and babe or get an apron for him. I gave up the milk, and purchased the cloth for an apron to cover the bare arms of my child."— *Id., p. 83.*

About this time it was revealed to Mrs. White that the trials through which she and her husband had been passing were for their good, being intended to prepare them to labor for souls. God had been stirring up their nest, lest they should settle down at ease. A severer trial came upon them when their darling babe was suddenly taken very sick, and his recovery was pronounced doubtful. The stricken parents felt condemned. They had made the child an excuse for not traveling, and they feared he was to be taken from them.

" Once more we went before the Lord, praying that He would have compassion upon us, and spare the life of the child, and solemnly pledging ourselves to go forth, trusting in God, wherever He might send us. . . . Our prayers were graciously answered. From that hour the child began to recover."— *Id., p. 84.*

Just then a letter came from Connecticut, urging Elder and Mrs. White to attend a conference of the believers in that State in April, 1848. Mrs. White writes:

" We decided to go, if we could obtain means. My husband settled with his employer, and found that there was $10 due him. With five of this I purchased articles of clothing which we much needed, and then patched my husband's overcoat, even piecing the patches, making it difficult to tell the original cloth in the sleeves. We had five dollars left to take us to Dorchester, Mass. Our trunk contained nearly everything we possessed on earth; but we enjoyed peace of mind and a clear conscience, and this we prized above earthly comforts.

" In Dorchester we called at the house of Brother Nichols, and as we left, Sister Nichols handed my husband $5, which paid our fare to Middletown, Conn. We were strangers in that city, and had never seen one of the brethren in the State. We had but 50 cents left. My husband did not dare to use that to hire a carriage, so he threw the trunk upon a pile of boards, and we walked on in search of some one of like faith. We soon found Brother Chamberlain, who took us to his house."— *Id., pp. 84, 85.*

The conference was held at Rocky Hill in a large, unfinished room in the house of Stephen Belden. There were about fifty in attendance, only a part of whom had accepted the Sabbath and the advent faith. Captain Bates enjoyed much freedom in presenting the binding claims of God's law, and personal testimonies were given which cheered and encouraged many longing hearts.

Elder and Mrs. White were next invited to labor in Oswego County, New York. Hiram Edson, who sent the invitation, said that the brethren were poor, and he could not promise much toward expenses. Elder White met this need by earning $40 in the hayfield. This money paid their traveling expenses, and provided much-needed clothing.

About thirty-five persons were in attendance at this meeting, which was held in the carriage house of one of the brethren. Great difference of opinion prevailed, and each believer was anxious to advance his own views. For instance, as the emblems of our Saviour were about to be distributed, one brother arose and said that he had no faith in what they were about to do — that the Lord's supper should be observed but once a year, being a continuation of the Passover.

Mrs. White was under great burden of soul during the meeting; her spirit was oppressed, for she felt that God was dishonored by these wide differences of opinion. Prayer was offered in her behalf, she revived, and was taken off in vision, and shown the errors that were pulling Adventists apart. In the course of the vision she took in her left hand the family Bible, and while holding it aloft, turned from text to text, and placing her finger on the scripture, would repeat it, all the while looking upward. The scriptures thus read had a direct bearing on the things that were bringing divisions into the little company of believers, and they threw such light on the matters at issue that the meeting ended in triumph for the truth. Those who had been drawn aside by matters of little importance, now united with their brethren in adopting as fundamentals the Sabbath and the second coming of Christ.

Meetings were also held in Madison County, at Port Gibson and Port Byron, and in New York City. In these gatherings the labors of Elder White and his wife were in the interests of unity and harmony. To fix on fundamental truths of Holy Scripture and hold to them, was the aim set before the believers.

The year 1848 was one of great commotion and unrest among European nations. France suddenly arose against its king, Louis Philippe, and Russia, Sardinia, Naples, and Rome caught the same spirit of unrest. Revolutions seemed brewing in many countries, and not a few crowned heads were uneasy.

In the midst of this time of confusion, those Adventists who had not embraced the third angel's message quite naturally believed the nations were rallying for " the battle of the great day of God Almighty." To the Seventh-day Adventists, who were beginning to teach that the Sabbath is the sign, or seal, of the living God, and were laying plans to give the sealing message of Revelation 10: 1-4 to the world, they were saying: " You are too late with your sealing message, for the battle of the great day is just upon us."

But the European situation quieted down again almost as suddenly as it had been stirred up. Horace Greeley, writing of it in the New York *Tribune,* said:

" It was a wonder to us all what started so suddenly that confusion among the nations; but it is a greater wonder still what stopped it."

The little struggling company of Seventh-day Adventists felt that it was their opportunity to work, and they took hold with a will.

A MAIL CARRIER MAKING HISTORY

Elder James White, editor and publisher, carrying the first edition of *Present Truth* in a carpetbag from Middletown, Conn., to Rocky Hill and back, a distance of sixteen miles.

HOME OF S. HOWLAND, TOPSHAM, MAINE
At this place the first conference was held to consider the publishing work.

CHAPTER VIII

Beginning to Publish

THE circumstances under which Joseph Bates' tract on the Sabbath came out, have been related in the previous chapter. In point of time that important publication had been preceded by two others. The first of these was a leaflet containing Mrs. White's first vision. The printed matter occupied the front page and half of the back page of a sheet of foolscap paper, and appended to the narrative was a note inviting the reader to write out his impressions in the blank space, and return the sheet to the author, Ellen G. Harmon. The leaflet was addressed " To the Remnant Scattered Abroad," and the expense of printing the edition of two hundred fifty copies was borne by H. S. Gurney and James White.

Another publication of 1846 was a tract of forty pages, entitled, " The Opening Heavens." It was written by Joseph Bates, and is indicative of his enthusiastic interest in matters astronomical. Its chief purpose, however, was to emphasize the fact of the literal, personal coming of Christ as opposed to the view that He had already come spiritually, which some were adopting.

TO THE REMNANT SCATTERED ABROAD.

As God has shown me in holy vision the travels of the Advent people to the Holy City, and the rich reward to be given those who wait the return of their Lord from the wedding, it may be my duty to give you a short sketch of what God has revealed to me. The dear saints have got many trials to pass through. But our light afflictions, which are but for a moment, worketh for us a far more exceeding and eternal weight of glory—while we look not at the things which are seen, for the things which are seen are temporal, but the things which are not seen are eternal. I have tried to bring back a good report, and a few grapes from the heavenly Canaan, for which many would stone me, as the congregation bade stone Caleb and Joshua for their report, (Num. 14 : 10.) But I declare to you, my brethren and sisters in the Lord, it is a goodly land, and we are well able to go up and possess it.

While praying at the family altar, the Holy Ghost fell on me, and I seemed to be rising higher and, higher, far above the dark world. I turned to look for the Advent people in the world, but could not find them—when a voice said to me, "Look again, and look a little higher." At this I raised my eyes and saw a straight and narrow path, (a) cast up high above the world. On this path the Advent people were travelling to the City, which was at the farther end of the path. They had a bright light set up behind them at the first end of the path, which an angel told me was the Midnight Cry. (b) This light shone all along the path, and gave light for their feet so they might not stumble. And if they kept their eyes fixed on Jesus, who was just before them, leading them to the City, they were safe. But soon some grew weary, and they said the City was a great way off, and they expected to have entered it before. Then Jesus would encourage them by raising his glorious right arm, and from his arm came a glorious light which waved over the Advent band, and they shouted Hallelujah! Others rashly denied the light behind them, and said that it was not God that had led them out so far. The light behind them went out leaving their feet in perfect darkness, and they stumbled and got their eyes off the mark and lost sight of Jesus, and fell off the path down in the dark and wicked world below. It was just as impossible for them to get on the path again and go to the City, as all the wicked world which God had rejected. They fell all the way along the path one after another, until we heard the voice of God like many waters, (c) which gave us the day and hour of Jesus' coming. (d) The living saints, 144,000 in number, knew and understood the voice, while the wicked thought it was thunder and an earthquake. (e) When God spake the time, he poured on us the Holy Ghost, and our faces began to light up and shine with the glory of God as Moses' did when he came down from Mount Sinai. (f)

By this time the 144,000 were all sealed and perfectly united. On their foreheads was written, God, New Jerusalem, and a glorious Star containing Jesus' new name. (g) At our happy, holy state the wicked

a Mat, 7 : 14. b Mat. 25 : 6. c Eze. 43 : 2. Joel, 3 : 16. Rev. 16 : 17.
d Eze. 12 : 25. Mark, 13 : 32. e John, 12 : 29. f Isa. 10 : 27.
g Rev. 3 : 12.

So far as known, there is no copy preserved of that first leaflet, "To the Remnant Scattered Abroad," mentioned in the first paragraph of this chapter. The above is a facsimile of the first page of the reprint of that vision in "A Word to the Little Flock," published by James White in 1847.

In the spring of 1847 James White put out a small pamphlet entitled, " A Word to the Little Flock," which contained Mrs. White's first vision, already published, as well as further writings by her and by others relating to the advent work. In a letter to Mrs. Hastings, written a few weeks after the printing of this pamphlet, Mr. White wrote:

" God has abundantly blessed me with health to labor with my hands. My lameness has troubled me but little this summer. I have been able to earn about $25 the past six weeks, and my health is very much improved. When we have no special work to do in visiting the scattered saints, I feel it my duty to labor with my hands, so as not to be chargeable to others. This is a privilege to me."

The next publication put out by the Adventists was a pamphlet of eighty pages, by Captain Bates. It was addressed " to the little flock," and came out in 1848, bearing the title, " Second Advent Waymarks and High Heaps, or a Connected View of the Fulfilment of Prophecy of God's Peculiar People from the Year 1840 to 1844." Its design, as indicated by the title, was to show the guiding hand of Providence all through the advent movement, and to make it clear that God was leading out a people to do a work of reform in the world.

The publication of this little book was made possible by the self-sacrificing act of a young widow, who sold her cottage, and was thus able to place in the hands of Captain Bates a sum of money sufficient to defray the cost of publishing. She said she could easily do without the house and lot, and go out to service. This generous giver was spared for many years of usefulness, and her descendants today rejoice in the message that she helped to publish.

In the following January, 1849, Captain Bates put out his fourth work, a seventy-two-page pamphlet entitled, " A Seal of the Living God," in which was set forth what Mrs. White had been shown in reference to the sealing work. The money to publish this work was supplied by a woman whose heart the Lord had touched.

The Adventists were now shortly to enter upon a publishing enterprise of greater moment than any yet undertaken, namely, the getting out of a regular periodical devoted to the advocacy of the truths they believed. Already in the autumn of 1848 the believers had begun to pray for light in reference to this matter. There were then possibly a hundred scattered members. A conference was called to meet at the home of S. Howland, in Topsham, Maine, beginning the 20th of October, 1848. At this meeting the question of a paper was considered, but the way not being entirely clear, it was resolved to give it further thought and prayer at a conference to be held at the home of Otis Nichols, in Dorchester, Mass. It was at this conference that Mrs. White was given the view of the sealing work referred to in the previous chapter.

When Mrs. White had come out of that vision, she said to her husband:

"I have a message for you. You must begin to print a little paper, and send it out to the people. Let it be small at first; but as the people read, they will send you means with which to print, and it will be a success from the first. From this small beginning it was shown to me to be like streams of light that went clear round the world."—"*Life Sketches,*" *p. 125.*

THE BELDEN HOME, ROCKY HILL, CONN.

The prediction could not have arisen from anything particularly encouraging in the situation that then obtained among the scattered believers. Humanly speaking, it seemed absurd. What could be done by three penniless preachers, and less than one hundred Adventists supplied with a few little tracts and pamphlets? Surely a humbler beginning of a reform movement could hardly be conceived. But the little band of believers continued to pray and to work.

The first number of the much-desired journal came out in the month of July, 1849. The printing was done at Middletown, Conn., eight miles from Rocky Hill where Elder White was then living. Mrs. White wrote:

"When he brought the first number from the printing office, we all bowed around it, asking the Lord, with humble hearts and many tears, to let His blessing rest upon the feeble efforts of His servant. He then directed the papers to all he thought would read them, and carried them to the post office in a carpetbag. Every number was taken from Middletown to Rocky Hill, and always, before preparing them for the post office, we spread them before the Lord, and with earnest prayers mingled with tears, entreated that His blessing might attend the silent messengers. Very soon letters came bringing means to publish the paper, and the good news of many souls embracing the truth."—" *Testimonies for the Church,*" *by Mrs. E. G. White, Vol. I, p. 88.*

THE MIDDLETOWN PRINTING OFFICE

The paper was called *Present Truth,* and the editorial on the front page opened with the quotation: " Wherefore I will not be negligent to put you always in remembrance of these things, though ye know them, and be established in the PRESENT TRUTH." 2 Peter 1: 12. The theme of the editorial is in the opening sentence: " It is through the truth that souls are sanctified, and made ready to enter the everlasting kingdom,"—

THE PRESENT TRUTH.

PUBLISHED SEMI-MONTHLY—BY JAMES WHITE.

Vol.1.   MIDDLETOWN, CONN, JULY, 1849.   **No. 1.**

" The secret of the Lord is with them that fear him; and he will shew them his covenant."—Ps. xxv. 14.

" WHEREFORE, I will not be negligent to put you always in remembrance of these things, though ye know them, and be established in the **PRESENT TRUTH**." 2 Pet. i : 12.

It is through the truth that souls are sanctified, and made ready to enter the everlasting kingdom. Obedience to the truth will kill us to this world, that we may be made alive, by faith in Jesus. " Sanctify them through thy truth ; thy word is truth;" John xvii: 17. This was the prayer of Jesus. " I have no greater joy than to hear that my children walk in truth," 3 John iv.

Error, darkens and fetters the mind, but the truth brings with it freedom, and gives light and life. True charity, or LOVE, "rejoiceth in the truth;" Cor. xiii: 6. " Thy law is the truth." Ps. cxix: 142.

David describing the day of slaughter, when the pestilence shall walk in darkness, and destruction waste at noon-day, so that, "a thousand shall fall at thy side and ten thousand at thy right hand," says—

" He shall cover thee with his feathers, and under his wings shalt thou trust; his TRUTH shall be thy SHIELD and BUCKLER." Ps. xci : 4.

The storm is coming. War, famine and pestilence are already in the field of slaughter. Now is the time, the only time to seek a shelter in the truth of the living God.

In Peter's time there was present truth, or truth applicable to that present time. The Church have ever had a present truth. The present truth now, is that which shows present duty, and the right position for us who are about to witness the time of trouble, such as never was. Present truth must be oft repeated, even to those who are established in it. This was needful in the apostles day, and it certainly is no less important for us, who are living just before the close of time.

For months I have felt burdened with the duty of writing, and publishing the present truth for the scattered flock ; but the way has not been opened for me to commence the work until now. I tremble at the word of the Lord, and the importance of this time. What is done to spread the truth must be done quickly. The four Angels are holding the angry nations in check but a few days, until the saints are sealed ; then the nations will rush, like the rushing of many waters. Then it will be too late to spread before precious souls, the present saving, living truths of the Holy Bible. My spirit is drawn out after the scattered remnant. May God help them to receive the truth, and he established in it. May they haste to take shelter beneath the "covering of the Almighty God," is my prayer.

The Weekly Sabbath Instituted at Creation, and not at Sinai.

" And on the seventh day GOD ended his work which he had made ; and he rested on the seventh day from all his work which he had made. And GOD blessed the seventh day, and sanctified it: because that in it he had rested from all his work which GOD created and made." Gen ii: 2, 3.

Here GOD instituted the weekly rest or Sabbath. It was the seventh day. He BLESSED and SANCTIFIED that day of the week, and no other ; therefore the seventh day, and no other day of the week is holy, sanctified time.

GOD has given the reason why he blessed and sanctified the seventh day. " Because that in it he had rested from all his work which GOD had created and made." He rested, and set the example for man. He blessed and set apart the seventh day for man to rest from his labor, and follow the example of his Creator. The Lord of the Sabbath said, Mark ii: 27, " The Sabbath was made for man." Not for the Jew only, but for MAN, in its broadest sense ; meaning all mankind. The word man in this text, means the same as it does in the following texts. " Man that is born of woman is of few days and full of trouble." Job xiv : 1. " Man lieth down and riseth not, till the heavens be no more." Job xiv : 12.

No one will say that man here means

words that may almost be said to give the key to the faith of Seventh-day Adventists.

It was not a narrow, one-sided view of the Christian life that animated this first number of the Adventists' paper.

" The keeping of the fourth commandment is all-important present truth [wrote the editor]; but this alone will not save us. We must keep all ten of the commandments, and strictly follow all the directions of the New Testament, and have living, active faith in Jesus."

In his address to the " dear brethren and sisters," the editor said:

" I hope this little sheet will afford you comfort and strength. Love and duty have compelled me to send it out to you. I know you must be rooted and built up in the present truth, or you will not be able to stand in the battle in the day of the Lord. Eze. 13: 5."

Eleven numbers of the paper were printed, the first four being issued from Middletown, Conn., in the months of July, August, and September, 1849. Numbers five and six were printed at Oswego, N. Y., and are both dated the following December. Numbers 7 to 10 inclusive were issued in March, April, and May, 1850, being printed at the same place. Number 11, the last of the series, came out in November, at Paris, Maine. The paper was an eight-page sheet, the reading matter on each page measuring eight by four and five-eighths inches. One thousand copies of each number were printed.

In the issue of December, 1849, the editor says:

" When I commenced the *Present Truth*, I did not expect to issue more than two or three numbers; but as the way opened before me, and as the cause of truth seemed to demand something of the kind, I have continued thus far. While publishing the first four numbers in Connecticut, the brethren sent in more means than was necessary to sustain the paper."

The policy and plan of *Present Truth* grew with the work which it represented. In the fourth issue appeared the first letter from the field. The letter is from J. C. Bowles, of Jackson, Mich., and reads as follows:

" Your first and second numbers of the *Present Truth* are received, and we are thankful to our heavenly Father for the light of the truth. I would say for your encouragement, that the little band here have received the truth on the Sabbath, without exception. And we thank the Lord for ever inclining Brother Bates' mind to come to Jackson. We herein send you $10 for the spread of the truth. If you need it all, use it; if not, let Brother Bates have a part of it to travel with."— *The Present Truth, Vol. I, No. 4, p. 32.*

In the following number appears a letter from Hiram Edson, of Port Byron, N. Y.:

"God is reviving His people, and building up His cause in western New York. . . . During the scattering time we have passed through many heart-rending trials, while we have seen the precious flock scattered, torn, and driven; but, thank God, the time has come for the flock to be gathered into the 'unity of the faith.' Divisions are being thoroughly healed, and strong union and fervent Christian love increase among us. The 'commandments of God, and the testimony of Christ' are to us the present truth — the meat in due season. The little flock here in this region are established on the Sabbath, and our past advent experience. Our number is constantly increasing. Honest souls are seeking for the truth, and are taking their stand with us. . . . Our general meetings have been rising in interest and power for some time past; but very recently they have been exceedingly interesting and powerful."— *Id., p. 34.*

HIRAM EDSON

The writer goes on to tell of a successful effort put forth by himself and another brother to seek out S. W. Rhodes, of New York State, one of the lecturers in the 1844 movement, and encourage him once more to return to the ministry. About the same time G. W. Holt began to labor. An editorial note in the seventh number of *Present Truth* has this to say of them:

"Brethren Holt and Rhodes returned to this city last week, in good health, and strong in faith. Their labors for a few weeks past have been effectual in bringing out the precious jewels, and establishing them in the present truth. About forty have embraced the Sabbath within a few weeks where they have labored. They feel that they cannot rest; but must go as fast as possible, and hunt up the scattered 'sheep' who are perishing for want of spiritual food. Brethren, let them have your prayers; also, be careful to see that their temporal wants are supplied."— *Id., p. 56.*

Very deep in human interest is the little sheet, reflecting as it does the varied activities of James White, its editor:

"We now expect to leave this State in a few days, to spend some weeks visiting the dear brethren in the East; therefore the brethren may not expect to receive *Present Truth* for a short time, at least."— *Ibid.*

The last number closes with a report from Joseph Bates, in which he gives an account of his labors in Vermont and New Hampshire, ending with these words addressed to Brother White:

" So you see, dear brother, that in places where all was dark and dreary a few weeks since, light is now springing up. Then let all the swift messengers that God has called, and still is calling, into the field, to give the loud cry of the third angel, move forward."—*Ibid.*

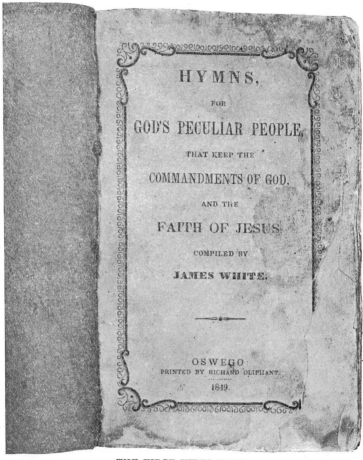

HYMNS,

FOR

GOD'S PECULIAR PEOPLE,

THAT KEEP THE

COMMANDMENTS OF GOD,

AND THE

FAITH OF JESUS

COMPILED BY

JAMES WHITE.

OSWEGO:
PRINTED BY RICHARD OLIPHANT.
1849.

THE FIRST HYMN BOOK

In the same year, 1849, in which *Present Truth* began to be published, the first Seventh-day Adventist hymn book was issued. It was a diminutive volume, measuring about three and one-half by five inches, and contained forty-eight pages filled with stirring advent hymns. The tunes were omitted, the believers being familiar with them. The title page reads, " Hymns for God's Peculiar People That Keep the Commandments of God and the Faith of Jesus." James White appears as the compiler.

Meanwhile Mr. and Mrs. White were doing considerable evangelistic work in addition to getting out the paper. When it was decided to issue *Present Truth* from Oswego, N. Y., they

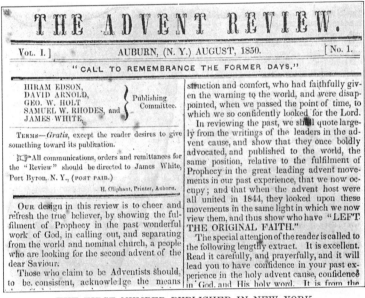

THE ADVENT REVIEW.

Vol. I.] AUBURN, (N. Y.) AUGUST, 1850. [No. 1.

" CALL TO REMEMBRANCE THE FORMER DAYS."

HIRAM EDSON,
DAVID ARNOLD,
GEO. W. HOLT, } Publishing
SAMUEL W. RHODES, and } Committee.
JAMES WHITE,

TERMS—*Gratis*, except the reader desires to give something toward its publication.

☞ All communications, orders and remittances for the "Review" should be directed to James White, Port Byron, N. Y., (POST PAID.)

H. Oliphant, Printer, Auburn.

OUR design in this review is to cheer and refresh the true believer, by showing the fulfilment of Prophecy in the past wonderful work of God, in calling out, and separating from the world and nominal church, a people who are looking for the second advent of the dear Saviour.

Those who claim to be Adventists should, to be consistent, acknowledge the means

struction and comfort, who had faithfully given the warning to the world, and were disappointed, when we passed the point of time, to which we so confidently looked for the Lord.

In reviewing the past, we shall quote largely from the writings of the leaders in the advent cause, and show that they once boldly advocated, and published to the world, the same position, relative to the fulfilment of Prophecy in the great leading advent movements in our past experience, that we now occupy; and that when the advent host were all united in 1844, they looked upon these movements in the same light in which we now view them, and thus show who have "LEFT THE ORIGINAL FAITH."

The special attention of the reader is called to the following lengthy extract. It is excellent. Read it carefully, and prayerfully, and it will lead you to have confidence in your past experience in the holy advent cause, confidence in God, and His holy word. It is from the

THE FIRST NUMBER PUBLISHED IN NEW YORK

removed thither from Rocky Hill, rented a house, and began housekeeping with borrowed furniture. There also was convened, on Nov. 3, 1849, a conference of the believers which further helped to establish them in a knowledge of the message.

In the summer of 1850 Elder White published six numbers of a series entitled, *The Advent Review,* which was made up of selections from the advent writers connected with the 1844 movement. These articles, largely from the *Advent Shield,* gave a review of the prophetic periods, and seemed well calculated to cheer and encourage the hearts of the little companies of Sabbath keepers. There were also published in tract form some of the articles that had appeared in *Present Truth.*

One of the first tracts thus put out was entitled, " The Seventh-day Sabbath Not Abolished." It was written by James White, and was a review of an article by Joseph Marsh in the *Advent Harbinger,* entitled, " Seventh-day Sabbath Abolished." *The Third Angel's Message* was another publication that appeared about the same time. Among the tracts issued in the following year was one entitled, " Thoughts on the Sabbath and the Perpetuity of the Law of God," by J. N. Andrews, then

THE FIRST NUMBER PUBLISHED IN MAINE

This was the beginning of the church paper, *The Review and Herald,* the successor of *The Present Truth. The Advent Review,* published in Auburn, N. Y., was only a special series of six numbers.

twenty-one years of age. So far as is known, this was his first tract.

In the autumn of 1850 the interests of the advent cause in Maine seemed to require the labors of Mr. and Mrs. White. They accordingly moved to Paris, in the near vicinity of Portland, and there printed the eleventh and last number of the *Present Truth.* It was shortly to be followed by a successor bearing the title, *The Second Advent Review and Sabbath Herald.* This new paper was of somewhat larger size, the printed page of two columns measuring seven and one-eighth by ten and one-fourth inches. It was issued semimonthly, the first

14

number being dated November, 1850; the thirteenth and last of the volume, June, 1851. The responsibility of publishing this periodical rested upon a committee consisting of Joseph Bates, S. W. Rhodes, J. N. Andrews, and James White. It had for its motto the text: " Here is the patience of the saints: here are they that keep the commandments of God, and the faith of Jesus."

During the eight months in which the first volume of the *Review* was issued, further additions were made to the list of men who gave themselves more or less to the ministry of the word in connection with the movement. Among these were Hiram Edson, of Port Byron, N. Y.; F. Wheeler, of Washington, N. H.; E. P. Butler, of Waterbury, Vt.; and J. N. Andrews, of Paris, Maine. The last soon came to occupy a position of prominence as a writer for the paper. In the number for May, 1851, he had an article occupying five pages, in which he gave what is believed to be the first detailed exposition of the thirteenth chapter of Revelation, interpreting the two-horned beast as a symbol of the United States.

In the spring of 1851 Mr. and Mrs. White moved to Saratoga Springs, N. Y., a believing farmer in that place having invited them to make their home with him. From this place was issued the second volume of the *Review,* consisting of fourteen numbers, the last being dated March 23, 1852. The name of the paper, as issued from Saratoga Springs, was changed to *The Advent Review and Sabbath Herald,* and this name it has continued to bear to the present time.

In the first number of this second volume, Joseph Bates refers to the rapid growth of the work:

" Within two years the true Sabbath keepers have increased fourfold in Vermont and New Hampshire. Within one year we believe they have more than doubled their number; and they are daily increasing as the papers and the messengers go forth."

During the publication of this second volume, eight more ministers began to labor in behalf of the Adventist views, among these being R. F. Cottrell, W. S. Ingraham, and Joseph Baker. The last-named took the place of S. W. Rhodes on the publishing committee, which otherwise remained the same. This volume of the *Review* contains numerous reports of labor and letters from interested persons in various parts of the field.

Toward the close of the second volume of the *Review* the movement had developed sufficient strength to cause the believers to plan for a printing equipment of their own. The decision to take this step was made at a conference of the believers held

March 12-15, 1852, at the house of J. Thompson, in Ballston, N. Y. Among the workers present at this conference were Joseph Bates, J. N. Andrews, who had just returned from his tour in Michigan, W. S. Ingraham, Joseph Baker, Hiram Edson, Washington Morse, F. Wheeler, and S. W. Rhodes. Great unanimity prevailed, and the proposition to have a printing press of their own met with a favorable response. The report in the *Review* runs thus:

" It was decided by a unanimous vote (1) that a press, type, etc., should be purchased immediately; (2) that the paper should be published at Rochester, N. Y.; (3) that Brethren E. A. Pool, Lebbeus Drew, and Hiram Edson compose a committee to receive donations from the friends of the cause. . . . It was thought that $600 would be sufficient to establish the press at Rochester."— *Review and Herald, March 23, 1852; Vol. II, No. 14, p. 108.*

The decision of the conference was reported in the *Review*, and as the brethren learned of the need, their gifts began to come in. One woman sold her only cow, and sent the money to help pay for the press. Others made similar sacrifices, and the enterprise was an assured success when Hiram Edson sold his farm in order to have some ready money to use for the work. He made a personal donation, and then advanced for an indefinite time enough money to purchase the needed equipment.

It was decided to locate the office in Rochester, N. Y. One of the first needs was the securing of a good foreman, none of the Adventists having a practical knowledge of printing. The problem was solved when Luman Masten, a young man who had worked on the paper at Saratoga, volunteered his services. He was not a Christian, but he had a praying mother, was not addicted to tobacco using, and desired to work for the Adventists. He was willing to accept a comparatively small wage, and to refrain from labor on the Sabbath. The other workers in the office at Rochester were Stephen Belden, an apprentice in typesetting; Warren Bacheller, roller boy; Oswald Stowell, of Maine, who was to work the hand press; and Annie R. Smith, literary assistant.

A home for the family of workers, over whom Mr. and Mrs. White presided, was found in a house at 124 Mount Hope Ave., which was also to serve as printing office and meeting hall. Here for the first time Elder and Mrs. White set up housekeeping with articles of furniture purchased instead of borrowed.

Thus the first number of the third volume of the *Review* came out, the type having been set up and the paper printed on a Washington hand press owned by Seventh-day Adventists.

James White wrote an editorial for this number, in which he briefly reviewed the history of the publishing enterprise, comparing the earlier situation with that which prevailed in 1852:

"In the summer of 1849 we issued the first number of the little sheet entitled, *The Present Truth*. We commenced the work under circumstances the most unfavorable, being destitute of means, and the very few friends of the Sabbath being generally very poor. . . .

THE ORIGINAL WASHINGTON HAND PRESS

"Since that time the cause has advanced far beyond the expectations of its warmest friends. Where there was but about a score of advent brethren in the State of New York that observed the Sabbath three years since, there are now probably near one thousand, and several hundred in the Western States, where there were none, to our knowledge. The increase in some portions of New England has been greater than in this State; and in the Canadas, where there were none in 1849, there are a goodly number that 'delight' in the whole 'law of God.' . . .

"It is true that there are but few laborers in the wide harvest. Three years since there was not one that labored constantly in the field. Now there are a few, and the Lord is constantly raising up and sending out others. They must go in the name of the Lord, and bear reproach and learn how sweet it is to suffer for Jesus in this cause. And as they go they must carry with them publications containing the reasons of our faith and hope to hand to those who are perishing for spiritual food."— *Review and Herald, May 6, 1852; Vol. III, No. 1, p. 5.*

Meanwhile, with doors opening on every side, the enemy was at work. Masten, the faithful though unbelieving printer, was smitten with cholera, and the doctor gave no hope; but prayer was offered for him, and he was raised up to health, and experienced conversion. Oswald Stowell, prostrated with a severe attack of pleurisy, was likewise healed by prayer. The little son of James and Ellen White was attacked by the cholera just as they were about to enter upon a series of important appointments. The disease was prevalent in the city, and all night long the carriages bearing the dead were heard rumbling through the streets to Mount Hope Cemetery. The child's case was taken to God in prayer, and the disease was stayed, but he continued very weak, not taking food for three days. Appointments were out for two months, reaching from Rochester, N. Y., to Bangor, Maine, and the journey was to be made with horse and carriage. Mrs. White writes:

" We hardly dared to leave the child in so critical a state, but decided to go unless there was a change for the worse. In two days we must commence our journey in order to reach our first appointment. We presented the case before the Lord, taking it as an evidence that if the child had appetite to eat, we would venture. The first day there was no change for the better. He could not take the least food. The next day about noon he called for broth, and it nourished him.

" We began our journey that afternoon. About four o'clock I took my sick child upon a pillow, and we rode twenty miles. He seemed very nervous that night. He could not sleep, and I held him in my arms nearly the whole night. The next morning we consulted together as to whether to return to Rochester or go on. The family who had entertained us said that if we went on, we would bury the child on the road; and to all appearance it would be so. But I dared not go back to Rochester. We believed the affliction of the child was the work of Satan, to hinder us from traveling; and we dared not yield to him. I said to my husband, ' If we go back, I shall expect the child to die. He can but die if we go forward. Let us proceed on our journey, trusting in the Lord.'

" We had before us a journey of about one hundred miles, to perform in two days, yet we believed that the Lord would work for us in this time of extremity. I was much exhausted, and feared I should fall asleep and let the child fall from my arms; so I laid him upon my lap, and tied him to my waist, and we both slept that day over much of the distance. The child revived, and continued to gain strength the whole journey, and we brought him home quite rugged."—" *Life Sketches*," *pp. 144, 145.*

In the summer of 1852 another forward step was taken in the publishing work, in the founding of a paper for the children and youth. *The Youth's Instructor* was the name of this new monthly, and the first number came out in August, 1852.

Vol. I.   ROCHESTER, AUGUST, 1852.   **No. 1.**

AN ADDRESS

TO THOSE WHO ARE INTERESTED IN THE YOUTH'S INSTRUCTOR.

WE are happy to send you the first number of this little paper. For some time we have been impressed that we had a more special work to do for the youth, but have not been able to commence it until the present time. We now cheerfully engage in this work, praying the Lord to help; and we feel sure of success.

The young, at this day, are exposed to many evils and dangers, and they must have right instruction to enable them to know how to shun them. And although the world never was so full of books and papers as at the present time, yet there is but very little written that is calculated to lead the youth to feel the need of the Saviour, and to impress them with the importance of shunning vice, and living a virtuous, sober and holy life.

The young are receiving impressions, and forming characters for Eternal Life or for Death, in an unfortunate age of the world, when spiritual darkness, like the pall of death, is spread over the earth. Pride is fostered; self-will, anger and malice are not timely and faithfully rebuked. Many parents who profess religion have become so worldly and careless, that they do not instruct their children in the way to heaven. In fact, not living devoted and holy lives themselves, they do not set good examples before their children, therefore they are unprepared to instruct them. Thus the light of Heaven is obscured, or entirely shut out from their youthful minds, and they are left to their own thoughts and the temptations of Satan, to move on in the broad way to destruction.

The Apostle, in pointing out some of the sins of the perilous times of the last days, states that children would be disobedient to their parents. Their lamentable condition was to be so much worse than in former times as to constitute a sign of the last days.

And it is a fact that many who profess to be looking for Christ and the judgment, have greatly neglected their duty to their children. Some have thought that because Christ was so soon coming, they need not bestow much labor on their children. This is a grievous error, sufficient to call down the frown of Heaven. We do not say that parents should bestow labor on their children that can be of no real benefit to them, which would only lead them into the spirit of the world; but we do say, that no pains should be spared to impart to them right instruction, calculated to elevate the mind, and guide in the way to the kingdom of God.

As we have seen children growing up at this corrupt age of the world, without an experimental knowledge of the religion of Christ, yet tender, and sometimes seen to weep when brought under a good influence, and then have seen their parents, professing to be looking for Christ, yet careless about their salvation, our heart has yearned over their children.

Parents must feel that they are training souls for heaven or hell, and act their part in giving good instruction to their children, in the fear and strength of God, without delay. And the children must give their hearts to the dear Saviour who died to save them.

We now feel like taking hold of this work in good earnest. And we expect that God will add his blessing, and a good and glorious work will be seen among the youth.

Parents and guardians, in order for this to be accomplished, we must have your help. We do not speak of means to publish the INSTRUCTOR, for we know that if we labor faithfully, in the fear of God, for the salvation of children intrusted to your care, it will be in your heart to sustain us. But you must take hold of this work in love and faith in your own families, and in your closets before God in prayer. The good seed of truth may be planted and watered, but God alone can give the increase. After you have placed good reading in the hands of your children, have taught them their duty, with a heart filled with love—after you have done all in your power—then you can consistently go to God with their case in prayer, and believe without a

FIRST COPY OF THE *INSTRUCTOR*

It contained, among other interesting features, the first of a series of Sabbath school lessons prepared by James White, which represented the first attempt of that kind among the Adventists.

In the autumn of 1852, about half way through the third volume of the *Review,* the work had grown to such dimensions that it became necessary to rent an office near the business center of the city. No. 21, Stone's Block, South St. Paul Street, was the location selected. The editions of the *Review* in this volume were not less than two thousand, and considerable quantities of tracts were also put out.

At the close of the third volume, in the spring of 1853, a very important addition was made to the office force in the person of Uriah Smith, of West Wilton, N. H. He first heard the message presented at a conference held in Washington, N. H., Sept. 10-12, 1852. On returning to his home, he made a careful study of the Adventist views, with the result that he kept his first Sabbath in the following December. He began his work in the Rochester office May 3, 1853, at the same time rejecting an attractive position as teacher in an academy. For his work at the Review office he received for some time little more than board and room.

His sister Annie had embraced the Adventist faith and begun her work about a year earlier. Her experience in doing so was a remarkable one. She was at the time attending a boarding school, and had ambitions in quite another direction. But her mother embraced the views taught by the Adventists, and she continually kept her son and her daughter before the Lord in prayer.

The daughter, on attending for the first time one of the meetings conducted by Captain Bates, recognized him and the whole gathering as exactly coinciding with a dream she had had the night before. Moreover, Captain Bates had also seen the gathering in a dream, and when Miss Smith entered, a little late, just as it occurred in the dream, he recognized her at once, though he had never before seen her. The young woman saw the hand of God in this coincidence, and embraced the Adventist views. Learning that help was needed in the editorial office at Saratoga Springs, she offered her services, and was accepted.

She labored faithfully and efficiently for three years, reading proof and doing other literary work, and receiving in return only her room and board. She died of quick consumption on the 26th of July, 1855. Her term of service was brief, but full of the beauty and power of a surrendered life. It pleased God

to take her away in the freshness and bloom of young womanhood, but not till by her deeply spiritual writings and her consecrated life she had endeared herself to all the believers.

She wrote a number of short poems and hymns, but one
especially endeared her to the Adventists of those early days.
It embodies as does no other hymn the spirit and attitude of
the early leaders in the movement.   These are the words: [1]

> " I saw one weary, sad, and torn,
>   With eager steps press on the way,
> Who long the hallowed cross had borne,
>   Still looking for the promised day;
> While many a line of grief and care,
> Upon his brow was furrowed there:
> I asked what buoyed his spirits up,
> ' O this! ' said he —' the blessed hope.'

> " And one I saw, with sword and shield,
>   Who boldly braved the world's cold frown,
> And fought, unyielding, on the field
>   To win an everlasting crown.
> Though worn with toil, oppressed by foes,
> No murmur from his heart arose:
> I asked what buoyed his spirits up,
> ' O this! ' said he —' the blessed hope.'

> " And there was one who left behind
>   The cherished friends of early years,
> And honor, pleasure, wealth resigned,
>   To tread the path bedewed with tears.
> Through trials deep and conflicts sore,
> Yet still a smile of joy he wore:
> I asked what buoyed his spirits up,
> ' O this! ' said he —' the blessed hope.'

> " While pilgrims here we journey on
>   In this dark vale of sin and gloom,
> Through tribulation, hate, and scorn,
>   Or through the portals of the tomb,
> Till our returning King shall come
> To take His exile captives home.
> O! what can buoy the spirits up?
> 'Tis this alone —' the blessed hope.' "

Miss Smith's quiet, retiring, self-effacing character is illustrated by the fact that when an effort was made to secure a
picture of her to appear in connection with this biographical
notice, it was impossible to find one, and inquiry among old

---

[1] It adds to the interest in this poem, which reflects the spirit of many a pioneer of
the time, to know that in those early days it was well understood that the writer had in
mind James White in the first stanza, J. N. Andrews in the second, and Uriah Smith in
the third.

friends and relatives elicited the information that she was not known to have had a picture taken.

Among the important tracts published at Rochester were: " The Twenty-three Hundred Days and the Sanctuary; " one on the Sabbath by James Clark, a Seventh Day Baptist, known later as " Elihu on the Sabbath; " and a pamphlet of 124 pages, by James White, entitled, " The Signs of the Times." These and most other publications of the time appeared first in the columns of the *Review*.

Hitherto tracts had been furnished free, donations being made to cover the cost of publishing. There were some disadvantages in carrying forward the rapidly growing work on this plan. It was accordingly decided at a conference held in Rochester in July, 1853, to recommend that all tracts and pamphlets be put on a price basis.

The conference also recommended that the *Review* be issued weekly, and the recommendation was forthwith carried out, the paper appearing once a week beginning with the first issue in August. Later, owing to lack of means, it dropped back for a time to a semimonthly issue.

At the conference held a year later it was decided to place a price on the *Review*. The announcement was made in the issue of July 4, 1854:

" By advice of the friends of the cause in Wisconsin and Michigan, and agreeable to the action of the Conference recently assembled in this city, we state the terms of the *Review* weekly, at One Dollar a year in advance, to commence with Volume VI."

The publishing work was now established on a firm basis. It had its own printing equipment, and its products, *The Advent Review, The Youth's Instructor*, and tracts and pamphlets, had created for themselves a sufficient demand to enable a regular price to be put on them. The next advanced step was the erection of a suitable building to accommodate the growing work. To understand the circumstances leading up to this important development, we shall need to turn our attention for a while to the evangelistic work, which was fully keeping pace with the growth of the publishing interests.

Elder and Mrs. White, while active in writing and publishing, were traveling much of the time, and were doing their best to stir up the gift in others. In the course of a visit to various points in Vermont and New Hampshire, Frederick Wheeler, who had been active in the 1844 movement, was encouraged to enter the field once more, and some months later we see him fully engaged in the work. " My future course," he writes to the *Review,* " I leave with God to direct. I have started out to labor when and where He shall open the way."

About the same time J. N. Andrews, who, while still a mere youth, had had a deep spiritual experience, wrote a report of labor in Oswego, Cleveland, Cincinnati, and other places in Ohio, being then on the point of starting for Indiana. " In the midst of tribulation and affliction," he writes, " my soul is joyful in God. I was never more deeply impressed with the importance of the work in which we are engaged, than at the present time. My heart is bound up in it, and in a work so sacred I would cheerfully spend and be spent."

Joseph Bates was almost continually in the field, laboring in New England and Canada East and West, as well as in New York, Michigan, and farther west. He usually stayed but a short time in each place. He writes:

" June 11 and 12 [1853], Sabbath and first day, we enjoyed interesting seasons with our dear brethren in Boston. The Lord is strengthening and encouraging them, and they are showing their faith by their works. Their new place of meeting in West Castle Street, No. 25, is commodious and pleasant. Four were buried in baptism on first day, and were strengthened in the Lord."— *Review and Herald, July 7, 1853; Vol. IV, No. 4, p. 31.*

In the previous year he reported a Western tour. After mentioning various places visited in New York, he continues:

" Brother Edson met me at Auburn, N. Y. We crossed the St. Lawrence for Canada West the last week in November, and have been working our way to the west along the shore of Lake Ontario, and wherever we have learned that there were scattered sheep in the back settlements north of us, we have waded through the deep snow from two to forty miles to find them, and give the present truth; so that in five weeks we have traveled hundreds of miles, and gained on the direct road westward one hundred eighty miles.— *Id., Jan. 13, 1852; Vol. III, No. 10, p. 80.*

S. W. Rhodes returned from a tour of six or seven hundred miles through the south and west of New York, and then started for Jackson, Mich. He says:

" I had liberty in explaining to the church much of the prophecies of the book of Revelation, while the blessing of the Lord rested upon us, and greatly refreshed, strengthened, and united in love the saints of God."— *Id., Dec. 23, 1851; Vol. II, No. 9, p. 69.*

Speaking of his own spiritual experience, he says:

" The Lord has of late ravished my soul, while I have been traveling, and reading and committing to memory the prophecies in Revelation, from the tenth chapter to the end of the book, and in comparing one portion of the book with the other. I now see a light, a beauty, a glory, and a harmony in this book, that I never could have seen had I not committed it to memory. I feel, as I once expressed myself in 1843, that my faith is eternally fixed, and that nothing shall be able to separate me from the love of God,᾽ His truth, and His people."— *Ibid.*

Not only the ministers, but the rank and file of the believers were having deep experiences in putting away sin and laying hold of a personal Saviour. Joseph Jackson wrote from Corunna, Mich.:

" We are striving to be ready to meet our blessed Lord when He shall come from heaven in like manner as He ascended. O what a glorious scene that will be for those that are ready! We are striving to have our hearts in order, that we may share largely of the refreshing when it shall come from the presence of the Lord."— *Id., Feb. 17, 1853; Vol. III, No. 20, p. 159.*

E. L. Barr wrote from Johnson, Vt.:

" Our conference of two days at this place has been one of thrilling interest to the saints who came together from a large number of towns in this vicinity. Our heavenly Father presided over it, from its commencement to its close. The Spirit of the Lord filled the hearts of His waiting people, causing them to rejoice with joy unspeakable and full of glory. God's power to preserve soul, body, and spirit blameless unto the coming of the Lord Jesus, was made known. The power of the enemy is mighty; but the power of our God is almighty. Many never saw it on this wise before. It was truly a time of the Lord's power. A number for the first time confessed the truth, with a determination to be purified by obeying it, and to go with the remnant that keep the commandments of God."— *Ibid.*

During the issuance of the third volume of the *Review*, running from May 6, 1852, to May 12, 1853, great advancement was made in the evangelistic work, and the list of ministers who devoted a considerable share of their time to preaching the word was increased by some fifteen names, among whom were A. S. Hutchins, of New England; M. E. Cornell, of Michigan; J. H. Waggoner, J. M. Stephenson, and D. P. Hall, of Wisconsin; and J. N. Loughborough, of Rochester, N. Y.

The last-named minister was for some years very intimately associated in the work with Elder and Mrs. White. He heard the Adventist views presented for the first time when J. N. Andrews held a series of meetings in Rochester in the autumn of 1852. Aside from the convincing logic of Elder Andrews' presentation, Elder Loughborough, who was at the time a preacher among the First-day Adventists, was deeply impressed by the cases of healing by prayer that occurred among the employees of the publishing house in Rochester. He had had his mind drawn out on the subject of divine healing as one of the gifts of the church, and the instances that came under his observation among the Sabbath-keeping Adventists were so manifestly the work of God that they had no little influence in leading him to cast in his lot with this people.

Along with the conviction that he should keep the Sabbath of the Bible, came the call to give himself to the proclamation of the message. For a time he held back, feeling his lack of fitness. At the general meeting held in Rochester that December he resolved to move out as Providence should direct. The brethren united with him in prayer that God would open the way. Their prayers were answered.

G. W. AMADON, L. O. STOWELL, WARREN BACHELLER, URIAH SMITH

The " First Press " as it stood in the Review office, Battle Creek, Mich., with the same men who, when young, worked in the office at Rochester, N. Y.

Hiram Edson, living about forty miles from Rochester, had not expected to attend the general meeting, but on Sabbath morning, while conducting family worship, the impression came to him very distinctly that he must go to Rochester. He accordingly took the train at the close of the Sabbath, told Elder White that same evening the exercises of his mind, and asked what was wanted of him. The reply was: " We want you to take J. N. Loughborough, and with my horse and carriage take him over your field in southwestern New York and Pennsylvania." In a day or two the men were off for a six weeks' trip.

In May, 1853, Elder Loughborough visited Michigan, holding meetings at Tyrone, Jackson, Battle Creek, and Hastings. Later in the month Elder and Mrs. White also went to Michigan, Mrs. White bearing her testimony before some of the little companies in that State, as a result of which discord was eliminated, and unity and harmony were established. At a meeting held in Jackson to plan for the prosecution of evangelistic work, it was decided that J. N. Loughborough and M. E. Cornell should travel together through the States of Illinois, Wisconsin, and Indiana, holding meetings with the scattered companies of believers, the members of the company at Jackson bearing the expense of the trip.

In the spring of 1855, Elder and Mrs. White being again in Michigan, a conference was held in Battle Creek on the 29th of April, in the course of which the members in Michigan extended an invitation to Elder White to move the printing office from Rochester to Battle Creek. J. P. Kellogg, of Tyrone; Henry Lyon, who lived near Plymouth; and Cyrenius Smith, of Jackson, had all sold their farms in order to have money to spend for the cause they loved. These three, with Dan R. Palmer, of Jackson, now agreed to furnish $300 each, without interest, with which to purchase a lot and erect a publishing office. A lot was secured on the southeast corner of West Main and Washington Streets, and a two-story wooden building, 20 x 30 feet, was erected. About the same time the members of the company of believers in Battle Creek built a little meeting house, 18 x 20 feet, boarded up and down, and battened to keep out the wind and rain.

The first number of the *Review* published in a home of its own was dated Dec. 4, 1855, being the tenth number of Volume VII. The personnel was as follows:

Publishing Committee: Henry Lyon, Cyrenius Smith, D. R. Palmer.

Resident Editor: Uriah Smith.

Corresponding Editors: J. N. Andrews, James White, J. H. Waggoner, R. F. Cottrell, and Stephen Pierce.

JOSEPH BATES

A TENT-MEETING OF PIONEER DAYS

CHAPTER IX

Pioneer Work in the Middle West

WE will go back a little in this chapter in order to trace the beginnings of the growing interest in the Middle West, which resulted in the removal of the Seventh-day Adventist publishing work to Battle Creek, Mich.

It was in the summer of 1849 that Joseph Bates first went to Michigan. He was devoting himself in those days chiefly to seeking out isolated believers in the advent movement of 1844, and acquainting them with the additional light which had sprung from the study of the Bible. It had been reported to him that in the village of Jackson, in southern Michigan, there was a company of about twenty such persons who held regular weekly meetings. To Jackson he accordingly went, and by making inquiries, found his way to the shop of one of the members, D. R. Palmer, who was a blacksmith. Standing in the door of the shop, he talked Bible truth as well as he could between the blows of the hammer, and that day and the next visited among the other members of the company. When he was able to get them together on Sunday, they all sat down with open Bibles and studied the views of Seventh-day Adventists.

Captain Bates left the following day at noon; but before he did so, Mr. Palmer took him with his horse and buggy three miles out into the country to the home of Cyrenius Smith, who had not attended the meeting on Sunday. The ground was gone over with him, and then the messenger went on his way to seek out other members of the scattered flock. Probably he little realized how much he had accomplished in the few days spent at Jackson. The members of the advent band there all accepted the Sabbath truth within the next three weeks, and some of them rendered valuable aid in the financial support of the cause while in its infancy. D. R. Palmer, the man who had had the Sabbath presented to him while working at his forge, was the first to take his stand.

During his stay in Jackson, Elder Bates heard of a family at Kingsbury, Ind., and one at Salem, Steuben Co., Ind., whom he determined to visit; but on praying over the matter, he felt strongly impressed that before leaving Michigan, he ought also to call at Battle Creek. This he accordingly did, and not knowing any one in the town, he went to the post office and asked to be directed to the home of the most honest man in Battle Creek. The postmaster directed him to David Hewitt, a Presbyterian, living on Van Buren Street in the West End.

Captain Bates walked at once to the home of Mr. Hewitt, to whom he said with characteristic directness: " I have been directed to you as the most honest man in Battle Creek; if this is so, I have some important truth to present to you."

The reply was, " Come in; I will hear it." Brother Bates entered the house, hung up his chart, and gave a brief but comprehensive survey of the principles of Seventh-day Adventism, dwelling especially on the Sabbath and the prophecies. Mr. Hewitt kept the next Sabbath.

In the spring of the following year, Elder and Mrs. White and J. N. Loughborough held a meeting at the house of Mr. Hewitt, attended by several Sabbath keepers from Bedford and the neighboring districts, as well as the few who had accepted the Adventist views in Battle Creek, numbering, with one unbeliever, fifteen. Elder White expressed himself as pleased with the little gathering, and added: " Brethren, if you are faithful to the work, God will yet raise up quite a company to observe the truth in Battle Creek." Little did any one then realize that within a few years Seventh-day Adventists to the number of twenty-five hundred would be living in the city, running the largest publishing house in the State, a well-equipped sanitarium, and a college.

Among those who listened to Joseph Bates' exposition of the prophecies and the Sabbath given on that memorable Sunday in Jackson, was M. E. Cornell, who was then visiting in the place. As soon as he had received the message himself, he started with his wife for Tyrone, where Henry Lyon, his father-in-law, lived. Arriving in the neighborhood, he saw John P. Kellogg out in his field raking hay, and immediately alighted from his buggy, and went up to him and told him of the truth he had accepted. Others were approached in a similar way, and were favorably impressed, so that on the following Sabbath quite a company of believers gathered for divine worship.

During the next few years the seed planted by Joseph Bates continued to grow. Some of the most cheering letters in *Present Truth* and the early volumes of the *Review and Herald* are from Michigan. Among the early workers, aside from M. E. Cornell, were H. S. Case and C. P. Russell.

It was a great boon to the work in Michigan when Elder and Mrs. White visited the State in the summer of 1853, and labored in behalf of the believers. The meeting held at Jackson resulted, as we have seen in a previous chapter, in that church's sending J. N. Loughborough and M. E. Cornell on a mission to Illinois, Wisconsin, and Indiana. These first laborers to be sent out at the expense of a Seventh-day Adventist church, drove in a private conveyance along the Grand River to Grand Haven, intending to take the steamer to Milwaukee. The vessel they boarded, however, took them to Chicago; they accordingly decided first to visit the believers in Illinois.

From Chicago they drove across the prairie to Alden, McHenry Co., Ill., holding meetings there for several days. Thence they traveled to Beloit, Janesville, Madison, and Koshkonong, Wis., finding a company of believers in the latter place. From there they went on to Packwaukee, Marquette County, the home of J. H. Waggoner, a pioneer in the Seventh-day Adventist work in Wisconsin. He was just then in another part of the State, however, and T. M. Steward, who had recently begun to labor, undertook to find him. Later other points farther south in Wisconsin were visited, Elders Loughborough and Cornell returning to Michigan the last of September, after an absence of three months.

It does not appear that they visited Indiana on this trip. Elder Loughborough soon afterward returned to Rochester, N. Y., leaving that city some weeks later for Ohio, where he labored in Huron and Seneca Counties till the month of May, 1854. He closed his labors in Ohio with a general meeting of

15

the believers held at Milan on the 5th and 6th of May, 1854, Elder and Mrs. White being present. The meeting was attended by between thirty and forty representative believers.

From Milan Elder and Mrs. White and Elder Loughborough journeyed to Michigan, " riding over log ways and through mud sloughs," in order to visit the scattered companies of believers, who gave them a warm reception. At Sylvan they found M. E. Cornell with others holding a three days' meeting. Here light was given Mrs. White in regard to the work in the West, and the duty was laid upon her and her husband to visit Wisconsin.

After spending two days at Jackson, Mich., the whole party journeyed by wagon to Locke, Ingham County, where meetings were held in a schoolhouse May 20 and 21. The crowd that gathered was too great to be accommodated in the schoolhouse. The speaker accordingly stood by an open window, the larger part of the audience being on the outside. It was this meeting that suggested to Elder White the advisability of resorting to tents. He broached the matter to M. E. Cornell, saying that perhaps in another year the use of a tent might be ventured. Elder Cornell asked, " Why not have one at once? "

" The more the subject was considered," writes Elder Loughborough, " the more our minds were impressed with the importance of immediate action in the matter."

The decision was delayed, however, until they could learn the mind of the brethren at Sylvan and Jackson, Mich. On arriving at C. S. Glover's on the 22d of May, Elder White told him what they were thinking of doing. He asked what the tent would cost, and was told that $200 would probably deliver it in Jackson, ready for use. Taking out $35, and handing it to Elder White, Mr. Glover said, " There is what I think of it." Elder Loughborough says:

"Before night we were at Jackson, and saw Brethren Smith, Palmer, and J. P. Kellogg. Each of these expressed his opinion respecting the tent in the same manner as had Brother Glover, with the exception of Brother Kellogg, who proposed to lend us all that was lacking to purchase it, and wait until the brethren in the State were disposed to make it up.

"Having met with such favorable responses from our brethren, we wanted a double assurance that the enterprise was right, and this we had. Near sunset of that day, Elders White, Cornell, and myself retired to a grove near Cyrenius Smith's, in West Jackson, and there laid the matter before the Lord in earnest prayer. When we arose from our knees, we all felt fully satisfied that purchasing a tent would be a move in the right direction. At noon of May 23, 1854, Elder Cornell started for Rochester, N. Y., to purchase of E. C. Williams the first meeting tent ever used by Seventh-day Adventists."—"*Rise and Progress of Seventh-day Adventists,*" *by J. N. Loughborough, p. 200.*

M. E. Cornell returned to Battle Creek from Rochester June 8, bringing with him a 60-foot circular tent, which was soon erected on a piece of ground lying on the southeast corner of Van Buren and Tompkins Streets. There, on June 10, J. N. Loughborough opened the first Seventh-day Adventist tent-meeting, with a discourse on the second chapter of Daniel. The meetings in Battle Creek lasted only two days, after which the tent was moved to Grand Rapids, Mich., where meetings were held June 16-18, James White returning from Wisconsin in time to take part in the preaching.

THE FIRST TENT

The Adventists in Vermont were the first to follow Michigan in purchasing a tent, which was pitched in Whitefield, July 11, 1854. In the spring of the following year, the believers in New York held their first tent-meeting in Mill Grove, June 2 and 3. Wisconsin had a tent in the field the same summer. From this time on, tents were used very extensively in the proclamation of the advent message, and being something of a novelty for the first few years, they usually attracted good audiences.

Tent-meetings in the early days were held mostly in villages or small towns, often right out in the country, where the attendants were nearly all of the farming class. During the day, the preacher would usually visit around, and very likely go out in the field and help the farmer gather in his hay or other crops. While they were thus working together, the minister would lead the conversation along Bible lines, and would judiciously amplify and make clear the sermon of the night before. Many of the early preachers thought nothing of spending the whole day in hard work under a burning harvest sun, then at evening going to the tent and preaching a vigorous sermon on some phase of the message.

The tent used was of a circular form, about sixty feet in diameter. When it had been brought to the place arranged for, which might very likely be a pasture adjoining a public road, the first thing to do was to select a suitable tree for the center pole. Often this would be a pine or an oak. After it had been cut down and trimmed, the neighbors' help would be obtained in bringing it to the perpendicular position, after which the canvas was duly raised, the side poles put in place, and the platform, pulpit, and seats added. The seats consisted of boards laid across other boards set edgewise, and fastened by stakes. To begin with, there were no backs; but later it was customary, at least in the case of seats near the front, to furnish backs formed of boards nailed to upright stakes. The platform was about two feet high, and built up at the front about four feet high and eight or ten feet long, to serve as a desk. This was often covered with cloth. Behind this the speaker stood. Along the entire front of the platform ran a table consisting usually of one long wide board, properly supported, on which was displayed a variety of books, tracts, and pamphlets. These were always well advertised at the close of the meeting, and as soon as the benediction had been pronounced, the people would come forward, curious to examine the publications.

In some of the more important efforts, it was quite customary for the work to be carried on by two preachers, speaking on alternate nights; but laborers were scarce, and a great many excellent tent-meetings were carried on by only one preacher with the aid of a tent-master.

Evangelistic work by means of tents in the summer and schoolhouses in the winter went on briskly during the years 1854 and 1855, and the number of believers steadily increased. One great drawback was the lack of a definite organization. This was keenly felt when H. S. Case and C. P. Russell, already referred to in connection with the work in Michigan, drew off from the main body, and began to publish a rival sheet called *The Messenger of Truth*. The first number came out early in 1854, and it, as well as succeeding numbers, contained so much that was false and misleading that the Adventists might well have been tempted to devote their efforts, in Michigan at least, to answering the charges and clearing away the misrepresentations. But Mrs. White, who was one of the chief objects of attack, advised the believers to go on with their work of warning the world of a coming Saviour, and leave the rest with God. This course was taken in general, and with the happiest results.

The lack of systematic support brought a measure of temporary discouragement to some of the faithful ministers. Elder and Mrs. White felt the situation keenly, and about the middle of the year 1856 began to sound an alarm. They felt that there was great danger of lukewarmness, even among the Adventists, and emphasized the warning given to the Laodicean church. In the early winter of 1856, while laboring at Round Grove, Ill., Mrs. White's mind was especially drawn out in behalf of certain brethren in Iowa who seemed to have lost their interest in the message. She felt that she and her husband must somehow get to them before it was too late.

They accordingly started out to travel the two hundred miles by sleigh. Arriving at Greenvale, Ill., they were detained there nearly a week by a severe snowstorm, meanwhile holding meetings with the believers. Mrs. White writes:

" At length we ventured to pursue our journey, and weary, cold, and hungry, we stopped at a hotel a few miles from the Mississippi River. The next morning about four o'clock, it commenced raining. We felt urged to go on, and rode through the rain, while the horses broke through the crusted snow at almost every step. We made many inquiries about crossing the river, but no one gave us encouragement that we could cross it. The ice was mostly composed of snow, and there lay upon the top of it about a foot of water. We ventured upon the ice, praying as we went, and were carried safely across. As we ascended the bank on the Iowa side of the river, we united in praising the Lord."—" *Life Sketches of James White and Ellen G. White,*" *pp. 330, 331.*

The party drove on six miles beyond Dubuque that afternoon, and put up at a hotel to rest over the Sabbath, resuming the journey Sunday, in bitterly cold weather. Wednesday night they reached Waukon, Iowa. The situation was discouraging enough to begin with; but the Spirit of God came into the meetings, and there was a general renewal of courage and a laying hold of the divine promises. J. N. Loughborough, who had for a time been working as a carpenter, resolved to give himself once more unreservedly to the preaching of the word. J. N. Andrews received a great blessing, and returned with new courage to his work. The other believers were all helped to a clearer vision, and dedicated themselves anew to the unfinished work.

Altogether, this meeting at Waukon was one of the decisive points in the development of the work in the Middle West. It marked the beginning of a higher tide of spirituality which was to sweep over the country, giving new life and vitality to the preaching of the message.

The spirit of the Waukon gathering was carried to the Conference held at Battle Creek in the autumn of 1857. The meeting was held in the new meeting house which had just been completed, the first one, built only two years before, having already become too small to accommodate the believers there. About 250 Sabbath keepers were in attendance.

Special attention was given at this meeting to the gifts in the church, a number of the brethren expressing their warm appreciation of the light received through the spirit of prophecy. In the course of the meeting, Mrs. White read a testimony given her for the church, and the congregation requested by rising vote that it be issued in printed form.

The publishing work received due consideration. Elder White's action in purchasing an engine and a power press was ratified. It was further decided henceforth to conduct the paper and the book publishing interests as one business instead of keeping the two separate, as had been done. In order to relieve the financial embarrassments of the ministers, a committee of seven men was appointed to look after the financial interests of the cause in Michigan. Dr. H. S. Lay, of Allegan, was elected chairman of this committee, which proposed to raise the sum of $2,000 for the advancement of the work in the State during the coming year. Another action of the Conference was to appoint an editorial committee, consisting of J. H. Waggoner, James White, and J. B. Frisbie, through whose hands should pass all matter intended for publication in book form.

Meantime the cause had been advancing steadily in other parts of the Middle West. Wisconsin was very little behind Michigan in furnishing pioneer believers in the third angel's message. H. S. Case, who has been mentioned in connection with the work in Michigan, was the first to preach the advent doctrines. Reaching Wisconsin in the spring of 1851, he labored extensively, chiefly in the southern and western portions of the State. Among his first converts was Waterman Phelps, of southern Wisconsin, who began to travel and lecture in the winter following. The friends of the movement were then few and far between. He traveled on foot till so worn with walking and preaching that he could do it no longer. Then through the kind assistance of friends he obtained a horse and carriage, with which he continued his work till obliged to give it up because of hemorrhage of the lungs.

In the same year in which Waterman Phelps began to preach, J. H. Waggoner, of Baraboo County, accepted the advent doctrines, and soon he also entered the field. Brother Waggoner had first heard the message presented in December, 1851. He was then living in Sauk County, a member of the Baptist church, and joint publisher and editor of a political paper. A friend invited him to hear two strangers who were to talk on the prophecies. These men reviewed the prophetic periods, called attention to the message of the third angel of Revelation 14, and to the work of the two-horned beast, and presented arguments in favor of the Bible Sabbath. They covered all this ground in about an hour, and very cursorily; but the interest of the young editor was awakened. He applied himself earnestly to the study of his Bible, using every available hour, night and day.

The Bible settled the question for him, as for many others. He knew that he would have to go out of business, would lose his standing in the Baptist church, and probably be considered to have lost his mind. But on the other side were the claims of conscience. The decision was soon made to walk in the path of obedience. The immediate results, he tells us, were a peace, a fulness of the divine presence, which he had never reached during his previous nine years' experience as a Christian.

At the time Mr. Waggoner embraced the Sabbath truth, he took reform ground in another matter. He had used tobacco for eleven years, though sometimes under conviction that the habit was inconsistent with Christian living; but on the day he resolved to keep the Sabbath, he put his tobacco in the stove, " resolved," he said, " that the Lord at His coming should not find me a slave to such a filthy habit." When, a little later, he learned that Seventh-day Adventists as a body were of the same mind, it rejoiced him greatly. He soon began to preach the message, and among his earliest converts were J. M. Stephenson and D. P. Hall, who also began to preach.

The first of the old pioneers to visit Wisconsin was Joseph Bates, who met the believers at a conference held in Albion in the year 1852. At a later conference held at Rosendale and Metomen, at the end of March, 1852, and attended by M. E. Cornell of Michigan, J. H. Waggoner, Waterman Phelps, D. P. Hall, and J. M. Stephenson were ordained to the work of the gospel ministry.

Stephenson and Hall, however, never fully identified themselves with the Adventist view of the millennium, and they began to teach, first in private and then publicly, divergent views of prophecy, thus bringing serious confusion into the ranks of the believers in Wisconsin, and threatening for a time to make havoc of the work which had had so promising a beginning.

In the course of his Western tour of 1854, James White attended two conferences in Wisconsin, one at Koshkonong in May and one at Rosendale in June. About this time Brethren Stephenson and Hall agreed to drop their advocacy of erroneous views, and to devote their energies to preaching the fundamental doctrines of the Seventh-day Adventists. The promise was not kept. Not long after the departure of Elder White, the two men began once more publicly to teach their theories, to the grief and confusion of many of the believers in Wisconsin and the serious retarding of the work.

J. H. Waggoner continued to teach the true doctrines, and he was presently joined by Isaac Sanborn. The latter embraced the Adventist views in 1852, and shortly afterward began to preach, beginning in Green County. He said of his call to the work: " The Lord told me to go and teach the people what He had taught me." For five years he traveled about the country with his own horse and carriage, preaching the message in new places, exhorting and building up the companies of believers, and holding up a high standard of Christian living. He labored likewise in adjacent States, especially in Illinois, and spent three years in New England. Good work was done in Wisconsin also by W. S. Ingraham, from the East, who traveled and labored with Brother Sanborn for a time.

Thus the work continued to grow steadily till the autumn of 1862, when the Illinois and Wisconsin Conference was organized at a meeting held at Avon, Wis., W. S. Ingraham being chosen president and J. G. Wood secretary. There were at that time six churches in Illinois and eight in Wisconsin. The first annual session of the newly formed conference was held at Avon in the following year, beginning October 3. At this meeting Isaac Sanborn was elected president, T. M. Steward secretary, and H. W. Decker was made a member of the executive committee. The membership reported at this meeting was 390.

Iowa

A knowledge of the Adventist views was brought to Iowa by members who moved into the State from the East at the invitation of James White. Among the first of these was J. N. Andrews, who left Maine with his father and family, and settled at Waukon, in the northeast corner of the State, late in 1855. Among others who followed and helped to make up the membership of this, the first Adventist church in the State, were E. P. Butler and his son, George I. Butler, J. N. Loughborough, Asa Hazelton, and Calvin Washburn.

The first lecturing tour in the interests of the message was made by Jesse Dorcas in the summer of 1856. In the southern part of the State he lodged with a David Christopher and another man by the name of Westbrook, these being among the very few Sabbath keepers in the State at that time. Toward the end of the year 1857, Moses Hull made the first sustained effort to preach the Adventist views in Iowa, his labors resulting in the bringing out of about twenty Sabbath keepers. In the following summer a tent was secured, and J. H. Waggoner, of Wisconsin, lent a helping hand, with the result that little companies of believers were raised up in several towns in the southeast portion of the State. These were gathered together at a general meeting in Iowa City in the autumn. The interests of the work demanding it, a tent was secured for the exclusive use of Iowa, and thenceforward the number of successful tent and hall efforts steadily increased. Somewhat later, M. E. Cornell joined the work, and had good success in arousing the public to a sense of spiritual realities. The season of 1859 was an especially favorable one, a considerable number of new converts being made in that summer.

In the autumn of 1859 a company of 100 was organized at Knoxville, Iowa, this company starting a Sabbath school of seventy members. About a year later the members put up a church building, the first Seventh-day Adventist meeting house in Iowa.

There was rapid growth again in the summer of 1860, when the number of believers is said to have increased nearly fourfold. The members of the churches organized in the early days banded themselves together on the basis of a covenant, in which they referred to themselves as the Church of Jesus Christ. The company at Richmond, Iowa, was the first to be organized as a Seventh-day Adventist church. It had a membership of thirty-one when its organization was effected.

In the spring of 1862 Elder and Mrs. White visited Iowa, and their labors were especially helpful in building up and unifying the work. There was also an eagerness to hear on the part of the public. When they spoke in the courthouse at Knoxville, the building was crowded. At this meeting B. F. Snook, a former Methodist minister, and William H. Brinkerhoff, a lawyer, were set apart to the ministry, and soon became prominent among the leaders of the work in Iowa.

The question of organizing the denomination on a legal basis was discussed in Iowa more or less in the early sixties, but there were some who opposed the idea. There was also some opposition to the work of Elder and Mrs. White, partly due to lack of knowledge of the Adventist faith and of the Bible teaching on the subject of the gifts in the church, and partly to the desire of some persons least fitted for it to make leaders of themselves. In January, 1863, a meeting was held at Fairview, Iowa, which was attended by delegates from nine companies and churches favoring organization. These formed themselves into the Iowa State Conference of Seventh-day Adventists, J. F.

M. E. CORNELL

Mitchell being elected chairman of a committee of four to supervise the work. To this nucleus other churches were added as they were organized.

The work in Iowa sustained a severe blow in the year 1865, owing to the unfortunate course taken by Snook and Brinkerhoff. They returned from the General Conference held in Battle Creek, Mich., in the spring of that year, with feelings of deep distrust toward Elder and Mrs. White and the other leaders in the work, and they began at once to spread disaffection among the Iowa churches. At the State conference held in Pilot Grove in the following autumn, the opposition came to a head, but after Elder and Mrs. White had laid the situation fully before the brethren, the objections raised were seen to have no weight, and Snook and Brinkerhoff, as well as their sympathizers, repudiated their former course of action, and wrote letters of confession to the members of the Battle Creek church whom they had wronged.

The leaven of discontent was still at work, however, and six months later the two men reaffirmed their objections, and did their utmost to draw after them all the Seventh-day Adventist churches and companies in the State. The nature of their objections is not very clear. They found fault with the teachings of the denomination in reference to certain passages in Revelation; but they seemed to have no definite views of these scriptures themselves, on which they could agree. Their objections to the work and writings of Mrs. White had no sound scriptural ground. They criticized certain passages in " Early Writings," which were easily susceptible of explanation. They troubled themselves over the fact that during the Civil War the light which had come through Mrs. White had been chiefly on such matters as healthful food and dress reform, whereas they had desired help on the subject of war, the draft, etc. They had a good deal to say, too, about the independence of the individual churches. But these were really minor matters. The chief difficulty the two men labored under seems to have been an unwillingness to join heartily in a work the complete direction of which was not committed to them. Their names were finally dropped from the roll of Iowa Seventh-day Adventist members in 1866. The headquarters of their movement was at Marion, more than half of the members of the Seventh-day Adventist church in that place identifying themselves with them.

The influence of the controversy was distracting, but it led many to seek divine help as never before, and to win definite personal victories. At the time of the crisis, in May, 1866, a

ISAAC SANBORN

WILLIAM INGRAHAM

R. J. LAWRENCE

T. M. STEWARD

236

general period of fasting and prayer was appointed for the believers throughout the country, the time being May 9-13. The work in Iowa, further strengthened at this time by the faithful labors of D. T. and A. C. Bourdeau, J. H. Waggoner, and W. S. Ingraham, was soon in a flourishing condition, and on a sounder footing than before. The labors of George I. Butler, who succeeded Snook as president of the Iowa Conference in 1865, were of great value in building up the work throughout the State on a good foundation, and in carrying the message into new fields.

Missouri

Sabbath keepers began to be raised up in Missouri before 1860. L. Morrison, of Daviess County, formerly a minister of the Disciple Church, wrote in the *Review* of July 3, 1860, that he had accepted the Adventist views two years before that time, as a result of hearing sermons preached by Moses Hull. He called himself the first Sabbath keeper in the State, and asked that a tent-meeting be held in his neighborhood. In the *Review* of Oct. 30, 1860, Elder White wrote: " Brother Hull has gone to Missouri with Brother Boltin, who came more than one hundred miles for him." From later references we learn that Moses Hull baptized fourteen persons on this trip. In the *Review* of Oct. 17, 1865, there was a note from J. H. Rogers, writing from Altavista, Mo., in which he spoke of himself and others as interested in the cause of present truth, and expressed the desire that a " messenger " might visit them. D. T. Bourdeau wrote in the *Review* of Nov. 13, 1866: " At Sandyville we found Brother J. H. Rogers prepared to take us to Altavista, Mo., a distance of 130 miles." He held six meetings in Civil Bend, Mo., and organized a church of nine members. It seems from other information that these nine members were only a part of the company of believers at Civil Bend. James White, visiting the place in the fall of 1870, held meetings for more than a week, and had the pleasure of seeing all the believers united in one Seventh-day Adventist church. The combined Missouri and Kansas Conference was organized at a meeting held at Pleasanton, Kans., Oct. 16, 1870. Three churches in Missouri and two in Kansas were at that time voted into the conference.

For some time laborers from various outlying conferences made preaching tours into these States where the work was yet in its initial stages. In the summer of 1870 the Michigan Conference sent R. J. Lawrence into Missouri. He traveled by train to Kingsville, near Kansas City, and from there walked six miles, carrying a heavy bag, to the home of a member of the

Disciple Church, to whom he announced that he would speak that evening in the schoolhouse. The word was passed around, and the house was filled with Disciples. Elder Lawrence hung up his chart, and gave such an interesting lecture on the prophecies that the same people came every night for six weeks. On Sunday morning the Presbyterian minister preached a sermon against the views of Elder Lawrence. The latter was present, and at the close of the service asked the privilege of reviewing it at once. The majority of the people remained, and these, with few exceptions, accepted the Adventist views, and formed the first Seventh-day Adventist church in Missouri.

Elder Lawrence preached every night, but he spent his days visiting from farm to farm, where he made himself very agreeable to the farmers, young and old. The roughs of the neighborhood took kindly to the Adventist preacher, and if those of other communities threatened to give him any trouble, they were warned to desist, which they did.

One Sunday evening, after Elder Lawrence had gone away, one of the ministers who had not attempted to refute the Adventist views while he was on the ground, was orating quite vigorously against him and the doctrines he taught. Outside the church on the grass lay about twenty cowboys, some of Brother Lawrence's friends, who always went to church with two or three revolvers tucked in their belts. As they lay there on the grass, they heard the preacher say some rather severe things against Elder Lawrence, whom they had affectionately dubbed the " Old Horn." Presently one of them, a great burly fellow, arose and went to the open window, the weather being warm, and called out to the minister: " Parson, you wouldn't dare talk like that if the Old Horn were present, and inasmuch as some of his friends are here, the less you say against him, the better it will be for you." The preacher made an apology, and immediately changed the tone of his sermon.

Among those who embraced the Adventist views in the course of, or very soon after, this preaching tour of R. J. Lawrence, were Dan T. Jones and Andrew Flowers, both of whom became prominent workers. One of the men who followed up Elder Lawrence's work in Missouri was Smith Sharp. He, too, preached in the schoolhouse at night, and made a regular hand in the fields of different farmers during the day.

Ohio

The message was first preached in Ohio in the early fifties, H. S. Case being the pioneer worker. From that time on that

State had labor bestowed upon it occasionally, the most sustained effort being the series of meetings held by J. N. Loughborough in Huron and Seneca Counties in the winter and spring of 1854.

In February, 1858, G. W. Holt gave a course of lectures on the Adventist views in a schoolhouse about two miles north of Bowling Green, Wood County. The meetings lasted only about a fortnight, but no less than thirty people began to keep the Sabbath. Early in June of the same year J. N. Loughborough and T. J. Butler held a tent-meeting in the neighborhood, during which the believers were more fully instructed. Two years later they were further established in the faith by a series of meetings held in a tent by Elder and Mrs. White. On Feb. 8, 1862, this company was organized into the first Seventh-day Adventist church in Ohio, being known as the Lovett's Grove church. A church building, the first one in the State, was erected in 1864 at that place, about two miles north of Bowling Green, and stood there till the spring of 1911, when it was moved into the city of Bowling Green.

Oliver Mears, the organizer of the Lovett's Grove church, was for a number of years at the head of the work in Ohio. He traveled all over the State in his lumber wagon, preaching, organizing, reproving backsliding members, and raising money for the prosecution of the work. He kept his modest little farm, and did some work on it; but he spent most of his time in soul-winning efforts. When a tent was needed for Ohio, he started the subscription with $100.

The period of the Civil War was a trying one for the struggling companies of Adventists. People's minds were so engrossed in the terrible struggle that they did not seem able to give proper consideration to the truths of the Bible. Not a great amount of aggressive evangelistic work could be done during the most critical period of the great conflict; but the time was profitably spent in effecting a more efficient organization, and in instructing the believers in the principles of hygienic reform.

In the troublous times preceding the war, when many were making light of the danger, Adventists were given an impressive warning. It was on the 12th of January, 1861, just three months before the first shot was fired at Fort Sumter, when dedicatory services were being celebrated at the Seventh-day Adventist meeting house in Parkville, Mich. At the close of the dedicatory address, delivered by James White, Mrs. White arose and gave a stirring exhortation, thereupon resuming her seat.

While in this position, and in the presence of a crowded house, she was taken off in vision, on coming out of which she arose, and looking over the audience said:

"There is not a person in this house who has even dreamed of the trouble that is coming upon this land. People are making sport of the secession ordinance of South Carolina, but I have just been shown that a large number of States are going to join that State, and there will be a most terrible war. In this vision I have seen large armies of both sides gathered on the field in battle. I heard the booming of the cannon, and saw the dead and dying on every hand. Then I saw them rushing up engaged in hand-to-hand fighting. Then I saw the field after the battle, all covered with the dead and dying. Then I was carried to prisons, and saw the sufferings of those in want, who were wasting away. Then I was taken to the homes of those who had lost husbands, sons, or brothers in the war. I saw there distress and anguish."—"*Rise and Progress of Seventh-day Adventists,*" *pp. 236, 237.*

After saying these words, she paused a moment, then added: "There are those in this house who will lose sons in that war."

One year later, J. N. Loughborough was preaching in the same house of worship, and sitting before him in the audience were two men who were present at the dedication and had expressed to him their disbelief in what Mrs. White had said. In the course of his address, he referred to what had been said in the house just one year before, and as he did so, those two men buried their faces in their hands, and one began to sob aloud. Six weeks before, his only son had been brought home dead from the front; the man beside him had lost one son in the war, and had another in a Southern prison.

The Adventists as a body were naturally Northern in sentiment, the pioneers of the movement being mostly from New England. But while their sympathies were with the North, the Adventists did not feel that to take up arms was in keeping with their profession as Christians. However, some who were drafted entered the army. It shortly became possible for a person who was conscripted to commute by paying $300, and most of the Adventists who were drafted availed themselves of this privilege. This they did, not from lack of sympathy with the Union cause or from cowardice, but because of unwillingness to shed blood even in support of a righteous cause.

Meanwhile, in every Adventist home earnest prayers were being offered on the nation's behalf, that right principles might prevail. As the conflict dragged on, and the situation of the country became more and more critical, days were set apart by the Adventists for fasting and prayer, to the end that right might prevail, and the great conflict might speedily be brought to a successful close. Feb. 11, 1865, and the first four days of

March were appointed by the General Conference to be thus observed. James White said of the season in Battle Creek:

" Never have we realized such intensity of feeling, such drawing of the spirit to the very throne of heaven, such confidence in the answer of fervent prayers, as during these days of humiliation and prayer."— *Review and Herald, April 25, 1865.*

In a very few weeks after the March appointment came the welcome news that the war was over and bloodshed at an end.

Throughout their history, Seventh-day Adventists have had conscientious scruples against engaging in war. They have felt that their mission was not to destroy men, but to save them; not to take life, but to preserve it. Whether in America or in other lands, under other flags, their attitude has ever been one of loyalty to existing governments, not as partisans, but as law-abiding sojourners, wherever their lot was cast.

The war over, the work began once more to make rapid advancement. Evangelistic efforts were multiplied, a number of new men were called to the ministry, and the improvements in denominational organization enabled them to receive some measure of support. Especially encouraging was the steady growth and development in the Middle West. The wisdom of the steps taken in moving the publishing work to Battle Creek became more and more apparent. It placed the headquarters of the cause, then in its infancy, in a section of the country populated largely by intelligent, progressive farmers and tradesmen, men who had a hold on the realities of life, and who were not spoiled by over-refinement and the spirit of religious indifference that is so liable to prevail in older and more wealthy communities. It gave the best of scope to the Adventist preachers, who were of much the same mold as the circuit riders of early Methodist days,— men of large build physically, of great endurance, of limited education in the schools, but well versed in the Scriptures and in human nature, and above all else, men with a message,— a definite, clear-cut evangel that came home to men's hearts, moving many to obedience.

With poor traveling facilities and extensive journeys to make, it was often necessary for the preachers to be absent from their families months at a time. Captain Bates wrote in the spring of 1858:

" On the 14th inst., I came to my family in safety after an absence of nearly six months. I thank and praise the Lord for preserving them and unworthy me, and permitting us to meet again. I thank the dear brethren where I have passed on from Michigan to Massachusetts for assisting me with means to defray my necessary expenses."— *Review and Herald, May 6, 1858; Vol. XI, No. 25, p. 198.*

Long absences were especially trying in the case of the younger men, whose slender means made it impossible for them to make proper provision for the comfort of their loved ones. One young licentiate returned home in the midst of a northern winter to find his wife and child living in a summer kitchen built of a single layer of rough boards, with open floor, and with no provisions on hand except a little cornmeal and some frosted potatoes. The situation was unavoidable, for there was no money with which to pay rent, and this shed could be had rent free. And yet that faithful wife had not a word of blame to offer, but only continued to offer up importunate prayers that her husband might be successful in saving souls.

There were noble women in those days as well as noble men, and they wrought as earnestly and faithfully as their husbands. Some of them have long since passed away, but their faithfulness and self-sacrifice still linger in the memory of all who knew them. Their children, well along in years themselves, rise up and call them blessed.

Not all the credit for the work done in the early days is due to the ministers and their wives. The lay members were remarkably active, often going out alone and single-handed, and by their simple testimony, backed up by earnest Christian living, winning converts to the faith. At a social meeting held in La Porte, Ind., in the late fifties, different members told of how they were brought to a knowledge of the truth. Said one member:

" When Brother [George] Smith came here, some little while ago, and wanted some one to go with him, he found me and showed me the truth, and then he found another, and still others."

A sister then told her experience:

" Sister Place came after me again and again. She would come and read the books and the papers and the Bible to me, and I was unwilling to believe. But now I bless God she ever came to give me the light."— *Review and Herald, Jan. 21, 1858.*

Not only were the churches often raised up with very little ministerial help, but they learned to sustain themselves spiritually by frequently uniting with neighboring companies in grove meetings and monthly gatherings and convocations of various kinds. The following is a typical report of one of these gatherings:

" The monthly meeting for Tuscola County, Mich., was held at Vassar according to appointment. A goodly number of friends came from Watrousville and Tuscola, and we were glad to meet with them. We hoped to have the presence of a messenger to teach us, but as Providence had otherwise ordered, we did the very best we could by ourselves. Our elder read for our benefit several texts out of the Word, and gave his mind on the same, after which we had a social meeting, nearly every one taking part. We believe that all were satisfied, and felt that it was good to wait before the Lord. . . . We feel more than ever to thank God for the light of present truth, and it is our determination by His assisting grace to be more faithful in the future, and live nearer to Him."— *Id., Feb. 19, 1867.*

Many of the churches carried on vigorous evangelistic work of various kinds, resulting in a steady growth in membership. In the village of Avon, Wis., the message was first preached in the late fifties by Isaac Sanborn. A little company embraced the Sabbath; and during the next few years, with scarcely any ministerial help, but by means of systematic work with papers, tracts, and pamphlets, the company grew to a substantial church of nearly a hundred believers. In due time a meeting house was erected, the first one of the kind west of Battle Creek, and the third church building erected by the denomination. Preachers seldom visited the church, but when they came, there were always new converts awaiting baptism.

The older churches would adopt resolutions from time to time, with a view to giving definite shape to their ideals and aspirations toward higher living. The church at Allegan, Mich., passed the following at a special meeting held early in 1867:

"WHEREAS, We hold the advancement of the cause of present truth to be paramount in importance to everything else; and,

"WHEREAS, This is rapid or slow, according as those who are engaged in presenting it to the people are consistent or inconsistent in their lives; therefore,

"*Resolved, First,* That we will make an earnest, persistent, and prayerful effort to the end that our daily walk shall at all times and under all circumstances be characterized by that meekness in deportment, that patience and forbearance under difficulties and annoyances, that integrity in matters of deal, that sobriety, sincerity, and chastity in conversation, which are always essential qualities of the Christian character, but which are peculiarly so at the present time. . . .

"*Fifth,* That in our opinion, prayer and conference meetings, both on the Sabbath and on week-day evenings, are essential helps to growth in grace. And that it is a duty which we owe to the Lord, to ourselves, and to the cause, to see to it that we are not prevented from attending them by obstacles which we have it in our power to remove.

"*Sixth,* That as the perils of the last days thicken around us, and the attacks of the enemy upon the remnant become more fierce, frequent, and protracted than ever before, we can find security only in a corresponding increase of efforts on our part for higher attainments in godliness. And that, as a means for the accomplishment of this end, we, the church in Allegan, deem it advisable to hold two evening prayer meetings a week instead of one as heretofore."— *Ibid.*

It was such ministers and such churches that laid firm and deep the foundations of the work in the Middle West.

JOHN BYINGTON
First President of the General Conference, May 21, 1863, to May 17 1865

"Let all things be done decently and in order." 1 Cor. 14 : 40.

CHAPTER X

The Organization of Churches and Conferences

In taking up the subject assigned to this chapter, we shall need to retrace our steps a little in order to obtain a clear understanding of the development from the beginning, in the Adventist denomination, of the principle of gospel order. It is necessary first to remember the conditions under which the Adventists under Mr. Miller's preaching were separated from the churches of which they had been members. They were in many cases expelled in a very summary manner. No opportunity was given them for defense, nor was any account taken of the teachings of the Bible.

This arbitrary action on the part of the churches created in many Adventists a strong feeling against church organization as such, which they were inclined to regard as a form of ecclesiastical despotism. George Storrs wrote:

"Take care that you do not seek to organize another church. No church can be organized by man's invention but what it becomes Babylon *the moment it is organized.* The Lord organized His own church by the strong bond of love. Stronger than that cannot be made; and when such bonds will not hold together the professed followers of Christ, they cease to be His followers, and drop off from the body as a matter of course."

This attitude was the prevailing one with the Adventists for some years following the separation. During this time there were no regular church records of any kind, not so much as a bare list of members. If a person sincerely believed and was baptized, his name was entered in the Lamb's book of life. What need of other record? There was no regular election of church officers, and with one or two exceptions, no ordaining of preachers.

Those who felt disposed to do so, gave what they could spare directly to the ministers, there being no system of denominational finance. On this plan, naturally, some ministers were fairly well paid; others received practically nothing.

This loose condition of things existing among the Adventists as a class, it was only natural that Seventh-day Adventists should be affected by it, and share the prejudices against gospel order entertained by their brethren. But the inconvenience of such anarchy became obvious, and the leaders in the work early set about seeking a remedy.

A beginning was made with the ministry. It seemed no more than proper for the church to look carefully into the lives of the men engaged more or less in public labor, consider their qualifications, and then designate in some way those who gave manifest evidence of having received a divine call. It was decided to issue to such, a card stating that they had been approved in the work of the gospel ministry, and recommending them to the fellowship of the Adventist believers everywhere. The cards were dated, and were signed by two of the leading ministers, usually James White and Joseph Bates.

This plan began to be carried out in January, 1853. Naturally, cards were not issued to some who were opposed to the principles of gospel order, and wished to go and come as they pleased, regardless of the wishes of their brethren. These withdrew, and for a time formed an opposition party. But the effect, on the whole, was good. James White, writing retrospectively at the close of the year 1854, said:

"There never has been such a strong union as seems to exist with the remnant at the present time, and there seems to be a general waking up to the work of the Lord."

The next move was in the direction of proper support for the gospel messengers who had been duly approved. With the renewed confidence springing from unity of effort, the number of ministers was increasing. In the summer of 1854 tents began to be used for holding meetings, and being somewhat new, they attracted large crowds of people. The situation demanded a considerable number of ministers who could give practically all their time to the work. Obviously, they could not do this to the best advantage without regular support for their families.

This lack of definite support was seriously interfering with aggressive evangelistic work. In a note appearing in the *Review* about this time, Elder White suggested that no more tents be put in the field than could be well manned and sustained. Then he added the significant words:

"Is it not too late to talk about working on the farm part of the time, and going as a preacher with a tent the rest of the time? Should not every tent company be free from worldly care and embarrassment? Brethren, think of these things, and may the Lord direct His people."

The brethren did think it over, and the conviction became general that some feasible plan for financing evangelistic effort would be necessary in order to put the cause on vantage ground. The liberality of the people must somehow take a more systematic and definite form, but what that form should be was a difficult question.

Recourse was had, as in other times of perplexity, to a prayerful study of the Bible. In the month of April, 1858, a little company of interested ones formed themselves into a Bible class under the direction of J. N. Andrews, for the purpose of ascertaining the teaching of the Scriptures concerning the support of the gospel ministry. The outcome of that Bible class was the recommendation of what was called "systematic benevolence on the tithing principle."

The plan was adopted by vote by the Battle Creek church Jan. 26, 1859, and was published in full, with reasons for its adoption, in the *Review* of February 6. An address on the same subject was presented at a general gathering of Sabbath keepers in Battle Creek, June 3-6, 1859, and the plan adopted. A majority of believers began to carry out the plan at once. Some held back, but it was not long till the principle was thoroughly established. The liberally inclined felt that a tithe was too little, the penurious, that it was too much; but the plan prevailed in the end.

The next forward step to be taken in the matter of conducting the affairs of the denomination in a safe and orderly manner, was the creation of a legal organization for holding church property. Here opposition appeared. Those who led out in this much-needed reform, were charged with desiring to make a name so as to be like the churches around them. They were also said to be going back to Babylon. These and other objections were duly published in the *Review*, and were followed by

REVIEW AND HERALD PUBLISHING ASSOCIATION
Showing Its Development in Battle Creek, Mich., from 1855 to 1887

a common-sense reply by James White, in the course of which he pointed out that the Lord's goods could be managed in the present state of things only according to the laws of the country; and further, that it is vain to talk of church property if the church is not in a position to hold it legally.

By the autumn of 1860 it seemed that the time had come to act. At a general meeting held September 26 to October 1,

THE REVIEW AND HERALD AT THE TIME OF ITS INCORPORATION
IN 1861
This was the first legal organization of the Seventh-day Adventist body.

the question of organization was thoroughly discussed in all its various phases. The outcome was a unanimous vote to organize legally a publishing association, and a committee of five was appointed to create such a corporation as soon as practicable.

Organizing the publishing house, which was at the time the chief denominational institution, virtually meant finding a name for the denomination. Various suggestions were made, among others the "Church of God," which was rejected as not at all distinctive. It seemed desirable that a name should be found which would embody the outstanding features of the denominational belief. The name "Seventh-day Adventist" accordingly won increasing favor, and when the matter was put to a vote, only one person voted in opposition, and that one afterward changed his mind.

The Seventh-day Adventist Publishing Association was accordingly organized May 3, 1861, and it formed the first of the corporations identified with the work of the denomination.

The one institution of the denomination thus provided for, it was next in order to organize the evangelistic affairs of the denomination. The writings of Mrs. White had been urging the value of mature plans, and of counseling frequently together. In 1855 came the word:

" There is too much of an independence of spirit indulged in among the messengers. This must be laid aside, and there must be a drawing together of the servants of the Lord. . . . ' Press together, press together.' "—" *Testimonies for the Church,*" *Vol. I, pp. 113, 114.*

Again:

" God is leading out a people, not a few separate individuals, here and there, one believing this thing, another that."— *Id., p. 207.*

And again:

" The people of God should move understandingly, and should be united in their efforts. They should be of the same mind, of the same judgment; then their efforts will not be scattered, but will tell forcibly in the upbuilding of the cause of present truth. Order must be observed, and there must be union in maintaining order, or Satan will take the advantage."—*Id., p. 210.*

The situation called loudly for something to be done. Ministers had no specified fields of labor, and though they tried to keep in touch with one another, their efforts were not always successful. There might be three ministers at one church at one time; while other churches equally needing labor might not be visited for many months. Moreover, the labor was all of a scattered character, there being no way of following it up systematically.

Under a sense of the pressing need of some orderly way of securing unity of action and an effective organization, James White suggested, in an article in the *Review* of July 21, 1859, that it might be well for the believers in each State to hold a yearly meeting, at which plans could be laid for the evangelistic work in that State during the ensuing year. The suggestion met with favor, and beginning with the year 1860, such meetings were held in the States where there were sufficient believers.

These somewhat informal gatherings for counsel grew into regularly elected bodies of delegates. Before they could become such, however, it was necessary that the churches should be properly organized. Elder White accordingly addressed the Conference assembled in Battle Creek in the spring of 1861, calling for a more complete and effective organization of the churches. Recommendations were passed favoring such a course of action, and a committee of nine ministers was selected to study the Bible on the subject of church order and officers. About the same time the suggestion was made that churches appoint delegates to the State conferences, and also that State conferences elect delegates to a General Conference. Both ideas met with general favor.

At a Conference of the leading workers held in the spring of 1861, as already recorded, the Publishing Association had been incorporated. During the summer the discussion of effective conference organization went on, and in the autumn seven of the leading ministers met again in Battle Creek, October 6, the first business presented being the organization of churches. The Conference recommended the following church covenant:

"We, the undersigned, hereby associate ourselves together as a church, taking the name of Seventh-day Adventists, covenanting to keep the commandments of God and the faith of Jesus Christ."

A committee was appointed to prepare an address setting forth in detail plans for organizing churches, and this address was published in the *Review* of Oct. 15, 1861.

At the general meeting just mentioned, it was decided to issue certificates of ordination to ministers, and annual credentials. A resolution was also passed, recommending that the churches in the State of Michigan unite in one conference, bearing the name of the Michigan Conference of Seventh-day Adventists. A chairman, secretary, and advisory committee of three were appointed, and it was decided that the first session of the conference should be held in Monterey in the autumn of the following year.

The Michigan Conference convened in September, 1862. It adopted the plan of receiving churches into the conference by vote, just as members are taken into churches. Seventeen churches had been organized in the State, and these were taken into the conference, all members present being accepted by vote as delegates. At this conference it was decided to pay ministers a stated sum weekly for services rendered, the rate to be fixed by an auditing committee selected at the annual meeting; and to require ministers to report their time and expenses to the conference.

From the State conference to the General Conference there was but a step, and that an inevitable one. At the Monterey meeting of the Michigan Conference this resolution was passed:

"That we invite the several State conferences to meet with us, by delegate, in General Conference, at our next annual Conference."

It was intended at first to hold this Conference in the autumn of 1863; but the spring proved to be a more favorable time. A call was accordingly made by James White, J. N. Loughborough, and John Byington, for a meeting to be held in Battle Creek, May 20-23. This meeting, the first general gathering of delegates representing the work as a whole throughout the country, was attended by the following elected delegates:

New York: J. N. Andrews, N. Fuller, C. O. Taylor, J. M. Aldrich.

Ohio: I. N. Van Gorder, H. F. Baker.

Michigan: James White, Joseph Bates, J. H. Waggoner, John Byington, J. N. Loughborough, Moses Hull, M. E. Cornell, R. J. Lawrence, James Harvey, W. S. Higley, Jr.

Wisconsin: Isaac Sanborn.

Iowa: B. F. Snook, W. H. Brinkerhoff.

Minnesota: Washington Morse.

Committees were appointed as follows:

On General Conference Constitution: J. N. Andrews, N. Fuller, I. Sanborn, W. Morse, H. F. Baker, B. F. Snook, J. H. Waggoner, J. N. Loughborough.

On State Conference Constitution: J. N. Loughborough, I. Sanborn, W. H. Brinkerhoff, J. M. Aldrich, and W. Morse.

A constitution was adopted for the General Conference, consisting of nine articles. The duty of the executive committee is thus defined:

" They shall take the special supervision of all missionary labor, and as a missionary board shall have the power to decide where such labor is needed, and who shall go as missionaries to perform the same."

The basis of representation was made as follows:

" Each State conference shall be entitled to one delegate in the General Conference, and one additional delegate for every twenty delegates in the State conference."— *Quoted in the Year Book for 1913, p. 245.*

A constitution was also adopted for State conferences, with delegate representation providing that each church to the number of twenty members or under shall be entitled to one delegate, and one additional delegate for each additional fifteen members.

The committee on nominations reported the following officers: *President,* James White; *Secretary,* Uriah Smith; *Treasurer,* E. S. Walker; *Executive Committee,* James White, John Byington, J. N. Loughborough.

The report was unanimously adopted, but Elder White declined to serve as president, feeling that in view of his prominent advocacy of a definite organization, it would be better for the place of chief responsibility to be filled, for the first year at least, by another man.   John Byington was accordingly elected in his stead.

Thus was adopted a representative form of organization which, in principle, has continued ever since, the organization being extended from time to time to meet the needs of a rapidly growing work.   At every step there was free discussion through the columns of the *Review,* in which many took part.   The form finally agreed upon commended itself as allowing the fullest degree of individual liberty consistent with effective action on the part of the body as a whole.   It has proved such in practice.

Looking back on the agitation leading up to the adoption of this organization, Elder White, in an article in the *Review* of Jan. 4, 1881, only a few months before his death, effectively reviewed the situation:

"Organization was designed to secure unity of action, and as a protection from imposture.   It was never intended as a scourge to compel obedience, but rather for the protection of the people of God.   Christ does not drive His people; He calls them. . . .

"Christ never designed that human minds should be molded for heaven by the influence merely of other human minds.   'The head of every man is Christ.'   His part is to lead, and to mold, and to stamp His own image upon the heirs of eternal glory.   However important organization may be for the protection of the church, and to secure harmony of action, it must not come in to take the disciple from the hands of the Master. . . .

"Those who drafted the form of organization adopted by Seventh-day Adventists, labored to incorporate into it, as far as possible, the simplicity of expression and form found in the New Testament.   The more of the spirit of the gospel manifested, and the more simple, the more efficient the system.

"The General Conference takes the general supervision of the work in all its branches, including the State conferences.   The State conference takes the supervision of all branches of the work in the State, including the churches in that State.   And the church is a body of Christians associated together with the simple covenant to keep the commandments of God and the faith of Jesus.

"The officers of a local church are servants of that church, and not lords, to rule over it with church force.   'He that is greatest among you shall be your servant.'   Matt. 23:11.   These officers should set examples of patience, watchfulness, prayer, kindness, and liberality, to the members of the church, and should manifest a good degree of that love to those they serve, exhibited in the life and teachings of our Lord."

BURYING HIS IDOL

THE WESTERN HEALTH REFORM INSTITUTE

CHAPTER XI

Health and Temperance

THE beginnings of health reform among Adventists date back to early times. It was but natural that a people who loved the Bible, and endeavored earnestly to weave its precepts into their daily lives, should ultimately adopt physical practices somewhat at variance with those of the world. The advent belief itself seems to call for a full dedication to God, as in the prayer of the apostle Paul in behalf of the church at Thessalonica: "The very God of peace sanctify you wholly; and I pray God your whole spirit and soul and body be preserved blameless unto the coming of our Lord Jesus Christ."

This is illustrated in the story told by one of the old pioneers of how the movement against the use of tobacco began among the Adventists of New England. One of the believers was plowing in his field, and the day being somewhat warm, he stopped at the end of the furrow to rest his horses. Meanwhile he took out pipe and tobacco for his own refreshment. As he sat there smoking, his mind reverted to the subject which lay nearest his heart,— the return of the blessed Saviour. Stretched out before him lay the quiet landscape, and above a sky of the purest azure, broken only by the presence of one large snowy-white cloud. Quite involuntarily he began to question himself: "What if my Lord and Master were to come to earth this day? What if I should behold Him now on this white cloud? Should I be ready to meet Him?" Then after a pause, "Should I wish Him to find me just as I am this moment — with my pipe in my mouth?"

Such questionings were not uncommon among the believers, and the idea of the Lord's imminent appearing brought no dismay to sincere and earnest souls who were longing for the great event. But in the present instance the thought was a little disquieting, considered from the viewpoint of his immediate occupation. The question, "Should I like to have my Saviour come and find me smoking?" presented some ground for doubt. The more the man thought about it, the less he felt that he could honestly answer in the affirmative. There was a contrast between that filthy clay pipe and the pure white cloud,— his eye told him that; moreover, his heart told him that there was a deeper spiritual contrast between the expected Saviour and any habit intended primarily to satisfy the cravings of a perverted appetite.

The man was not much given to dreamy reverie. His mind was soon made up. He rose from his meditations, laid his pipe and his tobacco pouch in the furrow by his side, put in the plowshare, turned over the sod, and buried his idol. That evening there was a prayer meeting in the neighborhood, and this brother, when his turn came for testifying, told of his morning's meditation in the field, and of its result. He did not argue, he only told his experience,— what he had thought and what he had done. The other brethren saw the matter in the same light that he did, and they, too, buried their pipes.

It was a small thing in itself, but it was a beginning on right lines, and it opened the way for other reforms, which were to come at the proper time. The principle that had actuated these farmers in giving up their well-loved pipes was a fruitful one. There was no better way for them to decide whether or not a given habit should be continued, than to ask, "Is it in harmony with the profession of one who is looking for the return of his Lord? Is it a help toward the higher life? Does it make for purity and holiness? or is it a mere means of gratifying the senses?"

The same principle continued to lead in the further reforms that were identified with the advent movement, although in time, with the more general spread of a knowledge of hygienic principles, scientific reasons came in for their full share of attention. As lovers of truth, the Adventists did not turn a deaf ear to the teachings of science concerning the proper care of the body.

The foregoing experience in the giving up of tobacco occurred among Adventist believers in the spring before the disappointment, in the autumn of 1844. And while abstinence from tobacco early became somewhat general among the Adventists who kept the seventh day, it was not till the early fifties that articles against its use began to appear in the columns of the *Review*. In a selected article in the issue of Dec. 13, 1853, we find the following:

"The person that uses tobacco cannot be as good a Christian as he could be without it. Religion, for its full development, demands all our mental powers. . . . This drug impairs them. It accordingly must follow that, in proportion to their derangement will be the defect of their action; so that in this sense it may be said with truth, that the person that uses tobacco cannot be as good a Christian as he could be without it."

In the same year, Mrs. White, in the supplement to her book, "Experience and Views," referred to tobacco using as a habit that must be given up. She further suggested that if all should "study to be more economical in their articles of dress, depriving themselves of some things which are not actually necessary, and should lay aside such useless and injurious things as tea and coffee, giving to the cause what these cost," they would be blessed in so doing.

About two years later there appeared in the *Review* (Dec. 4, 1855, page 79) the following record of an action taken at a Vermont conference:

"At a general church meeting held at Morristown, Vt., Oct. 15, 1855, at which there were delegates from most of the churches in the State, the subject of the use of tobacco by members of the church was introduced.

"After hearing remarks from several portions of Scripture, such as 2 Corinthians 7:1; James 1:21; 1 Corinthians 10:31, and some of the sayings of Christ on the subject of self-denial, to enforce the above; and some other portions of inspiration; it was, without a dissenting voice,

"*Voted*, That the use of tobacco by any member is a serious and bitter grief, and greatly lamented by the church; and after such members have been labored with, and properly admonished, as long as duty seems to require, if they do not reform, the church will then deem it their duty to withdraw from them the hand of fellowship.

"By order of the church.

(Signed)   "STEPHEN PIERCE."

J. H. Waggoner, who had himself experienced great benefit from giving up tobacco, was an enthusiastic advocate of the reform. For over ten years the columns of the *Review* were used to educate the Adventist people to a view of their calling

17

and work which would exclude tobacco, and the effort was successful.

Tobacco fully out of the way, attention began to be devoted to other physical reforms; but it took time and patience to achieve results. The first Seventh-day Adventist to practise health principles comprehensively and to advocate them in a wise and tactful way, was Joseph Bates. Something has already been said of his faithful labors in behalf of the 1844 movement, and later in advocating the claims of the Bible Sabbath. It remains to study the man somewhat in the character of a health reformer.

Thrown at an early age among sailors, he was disgusted with their intemperate habits, and kept himself from excess; but it was not till he had become master of a vessel that he finally gave up the use of spirituous liquors. In the course of a long voyage to South America, he noticed that he had a greater desire for the one glass of ardent spirits that he was allowing himself daily than for his dinner, and he became alarmed. After reflection he decided that he would take no more of it. A year later he also gave up wine, and still later all other intoxicants, including cider and beer.

It is a little apart from the subject of this chapter, but it may not be out of place to mention that the next reform in the captain's life was to give up the use of profane language; then he threw away his tobacco, and after winning moral victories on all these points, he was brought fully under the gracious influence of the Holy Spirit, and became a converted man. His life thus illustrates what may be said to be a cherished belief of Seventh-day Adventists, as it has come to be of many thoughtful men and women,— that when a man accepts the health principles, he puts himself in an attitude of mind more favorable to the reception of spiritual truths.

Upon returning from the voyage during which he had given his heart to God, Captain Bates remained at home for more than a year, devoting his energies to various religious and philanthropic enterprises. On the day of his baptism, which occurred in the spring of 1827, he solicited the aid of the minister who performed the ceremony in the formation of a temperance society. Failing to interest him, he started out alone. The Congregational minister put down his name, likewise the two deacons, and others to the number of twelve. Then a meeting was called, and the Fairhaven Temperance Society was the result. The members were largely sea captains who had had abundant opportunity to observe the evil results of liquor drinking. At first the pledge obligated the signer to "abstain from the use of ardent spirits as a beverage." Later it was found necessary to exclude the use of all intoxicating drinks except for medicinal purposes. This caused the members to be known as "tee-totalers."

The society thus formed in Fairhaven was one of the earliest organizations of the kind in this country, and rapidly grew in numbers and in favor with the public. Many of the citizens of New Bedford attended the meetings, and from the interest thus aroused, a society was formed in that town, and others in other places. Then came the Bristol County Temperance Society, and this was soon followed by the Massachusetts State Temperance Society, whereupon, temperance papers, tracts, and lecturers began to multiply throughout the land.

Captain Bates made one more voyage, sailing out from New Bedford in the late summer of 1827. Not long after his return, he organized, with the aid of associates, the Fairhaven Seaman's Friend Society, and interested himself in various religious and philanthropic enterprises, at the same time proceeding to improve a small farm which his father had bequeathed to him.

His next step in hygienic reform was to give up tea and coffee, finding that they had a slightly stimulating effect upon his system. It was somewhat later that he discontinued the use of flesh meats and of all richly seasoned viands, and adopted a diet of plain, wholesome food. He was of a modest and retiring nature, and never mentioned his dietetic habits unless questioned. When asked why he did not eat meats, rich pastries, and condiments, he usually replied: "I have eaten my share of them." But though he practised his principles very unobtrusively, he never swerved from them, often when traveling making his principal meal a very meager one in preference to partaking of things he believed to be injurious.

Of the effects of this wholesome régime, maintained oftentimes under difficulties, James White, who met the retired sea captain for the first time in 1846, has the following to say:

"When I first became acquainted with Elder Bates, he was fifty-four years of age. His countenance was fair, his eye was clear and mild, his figure was erect and of fine proportions, and he was the last man to be picked out of the crowd as one who had endured the hardships and exposure of sea life, and who had come in contact with the demoralizing influences of such a life for more than a score of years. It had been eighteen years since he left the seas, and during that time his life of rigid temperance in eating as well as in drinking, and his labors in the pure sphere of moral reform, had regenerated the entire man, body, soul, and spirit, until he seemed almost re-created for the special work to which God had called him."
—"*Christian Temperance and Bible Hygiene,*" pp. 252, 253.

While Captain Bates was the first of the Adventist leaders to throw emphasis upon the health principles as part of the message intrusted to that people, his efforts would have been less fruitful in permanent results had they not been heartily seconded by Elder and Mrs. White, who first brought the whole subject of healthful living as an issue before all the Adventists. With them, as with Captain Bates, it was largely a matter of personal experience. Like other persons devoted to great reforms, they studied the subject of hygiene with a view to adopting those habits of eating and drinking and working which would enable them to accomplish most in the service of the Master. They accordingly sought heavenly guidance, studied the Bible for basic principles, read the best accessible works on hygiene, and finally, in the early autumn of 1864, paid a three weeks' visit to the Dansville health institute in New York, then under the supervision of Dr. J. C. Jackson.

Their attention had been especially directed to the matter by Elder White's breakdown under the heavy strain of anxiety and labor incident to the war. He was stricken with partial paralysis on Aug. 16, 1865, and while in answer to prayer the use of his right arm was restored, he did not rally from the shock, and physicians gave little hope, declaring they had not known a case of recovery from so severe an attack. Under these conditions, after five weeks of careful nursing at home, Mrs. White decided to take her husband to Dansville. Here, though continuing to suffer much from pain and sleeplessness, he gradually improved. After leaving Dansville he continued to practise the principles of hygienic reform, and with his wife's encouragement, began to engage in light outdoor labor.

The visit to Doctor Jackson's institution was of great value to Elder and Mrs. White. The daily lectures in the drawing-room afforded useful information on a wide variety of health topics, and it was also very helpful for them to undergo the hydropathic treatments, and experience their benefits upon their own bodies, as well as to observe the effects upon others.

Another Adventist preacher who came in touch with the Dansville institution about this time was J. N. Andrews, already known to the reader as one of the early leaders in the advent movement. In his youth he did not have a strong constitution, and when he entered the gospel ministry at the age of twenty-one, it was the opinion of his friends that he had not long to live. Severe labor in forwarding the interests of an unpopular truth further depleted his strength, and gave rise to a combination of disorders that made life a burden to him. When a knowledge of healthful living first came to him, he was suffering from dyspepsia, sleeplessness, nervous prostration, and chronic catarrh in an aggravated form. He had been obliged to give up brain work entirely, and to labor in the open air; but by adopting the health principles,— which included the disuse of flesh meats and irritating condiments and of all highly seasoned foods, and the use of a simple, natural diet,— he was very soon able to resume his career as a minister of the gospel, and to perform much additional labor of a literary character.

J. N. Loughborough and R. F. Cottrell likewise passed through personal experiences that made them zealous advocates of health reform. But they did not rest satisfied with simply relating their own experiences. They taught the health principles from the desk and in the homes of the people. Elder and Mrs. White were especially forceful in the presentation of man's obligation to obey physical laws. They argued the matter on the higher ground of duty toward God and toward one's fellow men. Health reform was a great movement that was going forward under heavenly direction, and a reform people like the Seventh-day Adventists could not ignore it. Elder White argued thus:

"Every real reform — every movement that tends to improve man's present condition or to affect his future happiness — is under the direct providence of God. This is true of the great cause of hygienic reform. . . .

"It is with great pleasure that we consider this matter from a Bible point of view. The Bible is to us the voice of Infinite Wisdom, the highest and safest authority; and it contains a vast amount of testimony touching the subject of health. Christian temperance is taught on almost every page of the New Testament. We thank God for science; and we also thank Him that, on the subject of hygiene, science and the Word of God are in harmony."—*"Christian Temperance and Bible Hygiene," by Mrs. E. G. and James White, pp. 211, 212.*

He connected hygienic reform with the doctrine of Christ's soon coming:

"Admitting that we are living in that brief period divinely allotted to the work of preparing for the second advent of the Son of God, and the change to immortality, how timely is the introduction of the subject of hygienic reform among us,— a reform which changes false habits for those of Christian temperance, and purity of soul, body, and spirit!"—*Id., p. 212.*

"Would we be the adopted sons and daughters of the Almighty? Then we must shun the excesses of this degenerate age, and perfect that holiness which consists in physical as well as moral cleanliness. Our God is the embodiment of purity. Into heaven 'there shall in no wise enter . . . anything that defileth.' The throne of God, the tree of life, and the river of life, clear as crystal, will be charming in their purity. We believe it to be but a little while to the ushering in of the day of immortal blessedness; and should we not feel unutterable longings for that purity . . . which is

necessary in order to be meet for the inheritance of the saints in light?"—
Id., p. 213.

With such stirring words he roused the people to a sense of the importance of healthful living. In the light of his luminous treatment of the subject it appeared perfectly clear that Seventh-day Adventists could not but be health reformers. Their whole training fitted them to take the lead in physical as well as spiritual reform. In his own words:

"Seventh-day Adventists took up the subject of hygiene from religious principle, and they adhere to it in the love and fear of the God of the Bible. They have a living, growing interest in the reform as taught among them, because of its harmony with science, with their own invaluable experience, and with the Word of God. Their ministers teach it to the people publicly and at the fireside, and they practise it, so far as possible, wherever duty calls them. This people also carry out the reform in their social relations with kindred and friends, at home and abroad. This straightforward course makes them practical as well as theoretical teachers of hygienic reform. And this is no more than might be expected. A people who have moral courage to leave the deep rut of human custom, and observe the seventh day of the week as the Sabbath of the Lord, purely from principle, should be found firm and true in all reforms. To be out of joint with the rest of the world for two days in each week, is neither convenient nor profitable. The observance of the Bible Sabbath is frequently attended with pecuniary loss. It is also decidedly unpopular; and nature shrinks from taking a step that carries one so far from the world. And the high sense of truth and duty that leads this people to a conscientious observance of the Sabbath of the Bible, also leads them to adopt and carry out the principles of hygienic reform.

"Seventh-day Adventists have taken their position upon unpopular points of theology from hearing sermons and reading works which appeal to their moral and intellectual faculties. The grand themes upon which they dwell with delight and profit are the comparison of prophecy with history; the origin, nature, and perpetuity of the divine law; and that purity . . . which is requisite to heirship to the future inheritance.

"While thousands are induced to take a position in matters of religion simply because their feelings are wrought upon, and while tens of thousands adopt a religion simply because it is popular, Seventh-day Adventists are moved by appeals to the noblest powers of the human mind. Such a people should be ready to follow truth wherever it may lead them, and properly to estimate reforms wherever they may exist. And having, from reason and conscience, taken their position on the subject of hygienic reform, they are prepared to defend it, and to reap the benefits of it."—
Id., pp. 214, 215.

The work of reform was not sudden, nor by fits and starts, but went steadily forward step by step. Writing in the *Health Reformer* in 1870, Elder White says:

"The attention of our people was first called to the harmful effects of tea, coffee, and tobacco about twenty years ago. For thirteen years the voice of truth, pleading in the name of Christian temperance, was heard among us, warning us against these slow poisons, before our attention was called to any further advance in habits of life. This was all that could be borne till victory should turn in favor of purity and health, and against these popular evils. The good work went steadily on, until our tables were cleared of tea and coffee, and our homes and persons were free from the stench of tobacco. . . .

"But the good work of reform did not end here. About seven years ago the attention of our people was especially turned to the importance of thorough ventilation, and to the relation of proper food and clothing to health. The question of flesh eating came up, and was fully and candidly discussed. It was decided that flesh was less nutritious than bread,— an opinion sustained not only by the best medical authorities in our country and Europe, but by the experience of thousands who have tested the matter for themselves. While we admit that flesh is a food, we deny that it is the best food for man. It stimulates the system, but does not nourish and build it up, as do grains, fruits, and vegetables. Besides this, animals are liable to be more or less diseased; and by partaking of their flesh, man receives their diseases into his own system.

"It is stated upon good authority that while wheat, corn, barley, rye, and oats contain seventy-five parts nutrition and twenty-five parts waste, pork, beef, and mutton contain only twenty-five parts nutrition and seventy-five parts waste. On this hypothesis, one pound of meal contains as much nutriment as three pounds of meat. The poor man may figure thus: The rich pay fifty cents for three pounds of meat, which contain no more value in nutrition than one pound of good, unbolted wheat meal, costing only four cents."— *Id., pp. 224-226.*

Not only did the reform proceed gradually and in a certain order with the denomination as a whole, but individuals were advised to use moderation, and make changes in their habits one at a time. James White writes:

"Is a man a tobacco user, a tea and coffee drinker, a meat eater, taking his three meals? Let him begin with tobacco, and put that away. Then let him leave off the use of tea and coffee, eat less meat, and make his third meal very light. He will find this a heavy tax upon his system. He may all the time *feel* worse; but what of that? There is a glorious victory ahead. Soon he can dispense with flesh meats altogether. His appetite will become natural, and he can take simple, healthful food with a keen relish."— *Id., p. 224.*

It will readily appear from the foregoing that the advocacy of health principles on the part of these early pioneers was not only enthusiastic, but was marked by moderation and good sense. They spoke from definite personal experience; but they also based their teaching on broad scientific principles, and they appealed to the noblest human feelings. Still, if one remembers how exceedingly difficult it is to bring about reforms of a somewhat sweeping character when they have reference to daily physical habits so ingrained as to seem to be part of the very life, one cannot but feel that something more is requisite besides the teaching and example of these men. And there was something more, without which it is hardly likely that the move-

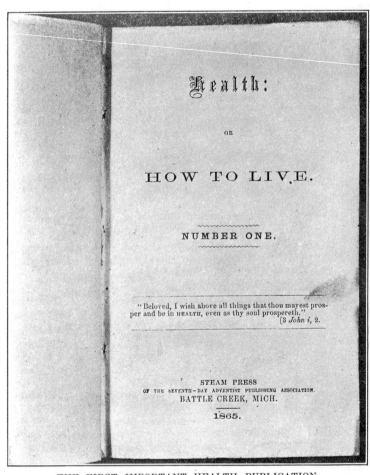

Health:

OR

HOW TO LIVE.

NUMBER ONE.

"Beloved, I wish above all things that thou mayest prosper and be in HEALTH, even as thy soul prospereth."
[3 John i, 2.

STEAM PRESS
OF THE SEVENTH-DAY ADVENTIST PUBLISHING ASSOCIATION.
BATTLE CREEK, MICH.

1865.

THE FIRST IMPORTANT HEALTH PUBLICATION

ment would have been successful; without which, indeed, the worthy pioneers from whom we have quoted, would have lacked in large part the clear, strong conviction from which they spoke.

In the year 1863, while attending a tent-meeting in Otsego, Mich., Mrs. E. G. White received special light relating to health reform. Again at Rochester, N. Y., in 1865, the subject was opened up before her in vision, and more fully as to its essential nature and its relation to other truths of the Bible. In her own words:

" The health reform, I was shown, is a part of the third angel's message, and is just as closely connected with it as are the arm and hand with the human body. I saw that we as a people must make an advance move in this great work. Ministers and people must act in concert."—" *Testimonies for the Church*," *Vol. I, p. 486.*

" There are but few as yet who are aroused sufficiently to understand how much their habits of diet have to do with their health, their characters, their usefulness in this world, and their eternal destiny. I saw that it is the duty of those who have received the light from heaven, and have realized the benefit of walking in it, to manifest a greater interest for those who are still suffering for want of knowledge. Sabbath keepers who are looking for the soon appearing of their Saviour should be the last to manifest a lack of interest in this great work of reform. Men and women must be instructed, and ministers and people should feel that the burden of the work rests upon them to agitate the subject, and urge it home upon others."— *Id., pp. 488, 489.*

About this time there came out a book entitled, " How to Live." It was published at first on the instalment plan, appearing in the form of small pamphlets which contained, with other matter, a series of articles by Mrs. White on the subject, " Disease and Its Causes." In these articles the responsibility properly to care for the body was clearly stated, and much valuable information was given in reference to diet, food, dress, ventilation, and the care of children. This series of articles may be said to contain the seed principles from which the whole health teaching of the denomination, including much of what we have quoted in the previous pages, was an outgrowth.

The writer took different ground from contemporary hygienists in laying stress upon the moral influence of health reform, always enforcing obedience to physical laws as one of the Christian duties.

" Many have expected [runs one of the paragraphs] that God would keep them from sickness merely because they have asked Him to do so. But God did not regard their prayers, because their faith was not made perfect by works. God will not work a miracle to keep those from sickness who have no care for themselves, but are continually violating the laws of health, and make no efforts to prevent disease. When we do all we can on our part to have health, then may we expect that the blessed results will follow, and we can ask God in faith to bless our efforts for the preservation of health. He will then answer our prayer, if His name can be glorified thereby. But let all understand that they have a work to do. God will not work in a miraculous manner to preserve the health of persons who are taking a sure course to make themselves sick by their careless inattention to the laws of health."—" *How to Live*," *No. 4, p. 64.*

The second article in the series was devoted chiefly to the care of children, and touches on the principles of Christian education. Parents are advised not to allow their little ones to have their brains crammed with book knowledge at the expense of normal physical development:

" During the first six or seven years of a child's life special attention should be given to its physical training, rather than the intellect. After this period, if the physical constitution is good, the education of both should receive attention. Infancy extends to the age of six or seven years. Up to this period, children should be left like little lambs, to roam around the house and in the yard, in the buoyancy of their spirits, skipping and jumping, free from care and trouble.

" Parents, especially mothers, should be the only teachers of such infant minds. They should not educate from books. The children generally will be inquisitive to learn the things of nature. They will ask questions in regard to the things they see and hear, and parents should improve the opportunity to instruct, and patiently answer these little inquiries. They can in this manner get the advantage of the enemy, and fortify the minds of their children, by sowing good seed in their hearts, leaving no room for the bad to take root. The mother's loving instruction at a tender age is what is needed by children in the formation of character."— *Id., No. 2, p. 44.*

Dress reform is another subject that received timely attention in the series. Women were urged to discard constricting, injurious corsets, in order that the lungs and other organs of the body might have full play, to clothe the limbs warmly, and to wear dresses that would clear the filth of the street.

The progress of health principles was not to depend wholly upon teaching the principles from the desk and by means of publications. An institution was to be founded for the treatment of the sick on rational principles. Mrs. White wrote:

" I was shown that we should provide a home for the afflicted, and those who wish to learn how to take care of their bodies that they may prevent sickness. We should not remain indifferent, and compel those who are sick and desirous of living out the truth, to go to popular water-cure institutions for the recovery of health, where there is no sympathy for our faith."—" *Testimonies for the Church*," *Vol. I, p. 489.*

Such an institution, it was pointed out, would, if rightly conducted, be a means of helping the patients who might resort to it, spiritually as well as physically. While their bodies were being benefited by the treatments given, their minds might be opened to spiritual truths, and their lives brought into a closer relation with the will of the heavenly Father. Such an institution, moreover, was to be placed in a position to assist the worthy poor, and for this a plan was proposed:

" Those to whom God has intrusted means should provide a fund to be used for the benefit of the worthy poor who are sick and not able to defray the expenses of receiving treatment at the institution. . . . Unless those who have an abundance give for this object, without calling for returns, the poor will be unable to avail themselves of the benefits derived from the treatment of disease at such an institution, where so much means is required for labor bestowed. Such an institution should not in its infancy, while struggling to live, become embarrassed by a constant expenditure of means without realizing any returns."— *Id.*, *pp. 494, 495.*

The instruction calling for a health institution was first given at the General Conference which convened in May, 1866. And although it looked like a large undertaking to a people few in numbers and of small resources, yet there was no delay in carrying it out. The residence of Judge Graves, with eight acres of land, on the outskirts of Battle Creek, Mich., was purchased, and a two-story addition was built and fitted up as treatment-rooms. A call was made through the *Review* of June 19, 1866, for persons to take stock. The members of the church in Battle Creek had already subscribed liberally. The institution was held in trust for a time until the Michigan State Legislature could pass legislation authorizing such a corporation. It was legally incorporated April 9, 1867, under the name of the Western Health Reform Institute. Meanwhile it was opened for patients at the appointed time, Sept. 5, 1866, about $11,000 of stock having then been subscribed.

A note in the *Review* of September 11 called attention to the rapidity with which the enterprise was conceived and carried out:

" We have only to look back to our Conference in May last, less than four short months ago, for the time when this matter first began to take practical shape among our people. Now we behold an elegant site secured, buildings ready for operation, a competent corps of assistants on the ground, . . . a sum bordering on $11,000 already subscribed for stock in the enterprise, and the institute opened and operations actually commenced. In no enterprise ever undertaken by this people, has the hand of the Lord been more evidently manifested than in this thing."— *Review and Herald, Sept. 11, 1866; Vol. XVIII, No. 15, p. 116.*

The institution thus brought into being was pleasantly situated on high ground in what was known as the " West End " of Battle Creek, then a flourishing manufacturing town, with a population of about 5,000. A grove of trees separated the

THE GREAT PHYSICIAN

main building from the street in front, and in the rear was a diversified landscape of hill and valley and stream. It was a suitable location for an institution which was to exemplify the principles of right living as a means of recovering and preserving the health, and though the equipment was rather meager, it was adequate to the immediate needs.

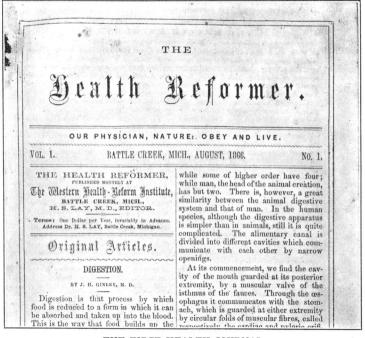

THE FIRST HEALTH JOURNAL

The opening of the Health Institute marked an era in the history of the development of our work. It not only gave tangible outward expression to the health principles as a definite phase of denominational belief, but it supplied an effective instrumentality for the propagation of those principles. It represented, on the side of the Adventists, a new and enlarged vision of the world's need, and of the duty resting upon the Christian church to supply that need. The healing ministry of Christ was seen to be a manifestation of divine love which should be continued in the world through the instrumentality of the church. The practice of health principles and the use of simple hydropathic means of treating disease were regarded as a means of co-operating with the divine power, which alone can truly heal. Disease was seen to be the result of transgression of natural law; and the duty and privilege of Christians to obey all these laws, and teach others to obey them, appeared to be a part of the everlasting gospel.

It was with a view of giving publicity to the health principles that a monthly magazine was started in the month of August, 1866, a short time before the opening of the institute. It bore the name of *Health Reformer,* which was later changed

H. S. Lay, M. D. Phebe Lamson, M. D. Kate Lindsay, M. D.

to *Good Health.* A modest success from the start, it soon attained a very representative circulation, and was widely recognized as an effective advocate of hygienic reforms. Elder and Mrs. James White put into the development of this magazine and of the Health Institute the same enthusiastic labor that they had given to the publishing and evangelistic work, and Mrs. White especially carried a heavy burden for the maintenance among the helpers of the institute of a high degree of spirituality and consecration.

Meanwhile no effort was spared to increase the efficiency of the institute as an agency for the scientific treatment of disease. Dr. H. S. Lay, the first head physician, had not only enjoyed a wide medical practice covering seventeen years, but had been connected with the medical faculty of a hydropathic institution, and thus had a first-hand knowledge of the water treatments.

Dr. Phebe Lamson, the first lady physician employed by the institution, was a woman of talent and ability, and thoroughly devoted to the work. Among other physicians who bore responsibilities in the early years of the institution were Doctors J. H. Ginley, John F. Byington, William Russell, and M. G. Kellogg, the last named being the first Seventh-day Adventist physician to write a popular work on hygiene. Doctors J. H. Kellogg and Kate Lindsay became connected with the institution somewhat later, and did much to make it a success.

In the hands of these faithful men and women, and supported by the prayers and active co-operation of the whole denomination, the institute, although by no means free from embarrassments, both financial and otherwise, and often failing fully to realize the high ideals for which it stood, nevertheless made steady advancement, and enjoyed such a growth of patronage that it was obliged to enlarge its facilities from time to time, first renting cottages, and finally, in the spring of 1877, putting up a brick-veneered building four stories in height and 136 feet in length, which, with equipment, cost $100,000. The rooms of this building were taken as rapidly as they could be completed. Seven years later, in 1884, it became necessary to add a five-story extension on the south, including a dining-room with accommodations for 400. There followed next a five-story hospital to provide accommodations for the rapidly growing surgical work; and then a large extension on the north of the main building, and a nurses' dormitory, a separate building east of the main building.

Meanwhile the work of popularizing the health principles had been powerfully aided by the organization, early in 1879, of a society known as The American Health and Temperance Association, which in a few years obtained a following of 15,000 pledged members. It was largely by means of this organization that considerable quantities of health and temperance literature, including a Health Almanac, were circulated, and lectures given in many different parts of the country, resulting in the raising up of a considerable body of constituents.

The further development of this work will be considered in later chapters.

ELDER AND MRS. JAMES WHITE

THE FIRST CAMP-MEETING, WRIGHT, MICH.

CHAPTER XII

The Camp-Meeting Era

THE year 1868, which marked the sending out of the first missionaries to the Pacific Coast, also witnessed the holding of the first Seventh-day Adventist camp-meeting. It was convened in Wright, Mich., in the month of September, and was a gathering of great significance in the growth and development of the denomination. Elder and Mrs. White, and others closely associated with them, felt the need of a deepening of the spiritual life, and it was their conviction that the need would be most effectively met by a gathering out in the open air in some quiet place, where the people could give themselves uninterruptedly to seeking God.

There were some fears, however, that good order and discipline might be difficult to maintain in such a gathering. Therefore James White regarded this first meeting in the open as something of an experiment; and he was governed by this feeling in the instructions he gave for making the necessary preparations. It was not thought best to invest money in family tents, as they might not be needed for future meetings. The families that came were advised to procure each eighteen yards of heavy factory cotton, and it was suggested that after the cloth had been used for temporary tents, it could be employed for other purposes.

The camp was pitched in a grove of sugar maples on the farm of E. H. Root, near the town of Wright, Ottawa Co., west Michigan. In an editorial Elder Uriah Smith wrote:

"There were nineteen tents from churches in Michigan, one from Olcott, N. Y., and one each from Oakland and Johnstown, Wis., making in all twenty-two tents on the ground, besides the Ohio and Michigan large meeting tents, each sixty feet in diameter. These, arranged in a circle around the preachers' stand and the seats for the people, in the edge of the beautiful grove, made it a most pleasant and inviting spot."— *Review and Herald*, *Sept. 15, 1868; Vol. XXXII, No. 12, p. 172.*

The tents, which were of various sizes according to the number of persons to be accommodated, were mostly constructed with side walls of rough boards, the roof and ends being of factory cotton. The two large tents near the center were used for services only in case of rain, the speaker's stand and the great majority of the seats being under the trees outside. The seats were of rough boards laid on logs arranged longitudinally end to end. Logs alone were also used for seats. The rostrum, which stood out in the open, measured about ten by twelve feet, and was provided with a canopy. The camp was lighted at night by means of a number of wood fires which were kept burning on elevated boxes filled with earth. For the comfort of the campers in wet or chilly weather, a log fire was kept burning in the outskirts. There was no grocery stand. Food was prepared in the farm houses near by, and brought warm to the camp. Bread wagons drove in from Berlin, the nearest village.

The bookstand consisted of three planks supported on posts so as to form a triangular inclosure, within which the attendant stood. Six hundred dollars' worth of books were sold at the meeting. Tracts and periodicals also received attention. One of the survivors remembers Elder White's saying, as he scattered a handful of tracts over the congregation, "The time is coming when these tracts will be scattered like the leaves of autumn."

The meeting was opened on Tuesday, September 1, with a season of prayer at the speaker's stand. No further service was held till five o'clock, the campers being busily engaged erecting tents and making other preparations. At that hour Mrs. White gave an address, taking up the spiritual needs of the churches, and setting forth fully the special objects for which the meeting had been called.

The ministers present included Elder and Mrs. James White, J. N. Andrews, Joseph Bates, J. H. Waggoner, I. D. Van Horn, R. J. Lawrence, R. F. Andrews, C. O. Taylor, N. Fuller, and John Matteson. Among the prominent truths presented were the facts concerning the investigative judgment, and the need of a special preparation in order to stand before the throne of God. Elder White enjoyed great freedom as he in his discourses enlarged on the special work intrusted to Seventh-day Adventists, and urged higher ideals of personal holiness and greater activity in the promulgation of the truth. Mrs. White and J. N. Andrews also enjoyed great freedom of spirit, their messages being pointed, but tender and sympathetic.

I. D. VAN HORN

The preaching met with a prompt response on the part of the congregation, as was seen in the social meetings, of which two or three were held each day. There was a willingness to repent of backsliding, and an earnest longing to come up on higher ground spiritually. Some had encroached upon the Sabbath, others had neglected family worship, and all had to some extent partaken of the spirit of the world. Parents made confession to their children, children to parents, and the spirit of grace and of supplication was poured out upon all. When the invitation was given on Friday for those who had no hope to make a start, more than sixty responded; and when the call was made for backsliders who wished to start anew, about three hundred pressed forward. There were other similar occasions. Fathers brought their children, friend labored with friend, brothers who had been alienated for years came forward hand in hand, mingling their tears of forgiveness and brotherly love.

Not only were the general meetings seasons of great solemnity and power, but a spirit of consecration and of praise pervaded the grounds. Little meetings were held between times in the various dwelling tents. At all hours the sound of praise and song and testimony could be heard over the camp, while out in the woods were groups of two and three engaged in prayer and intercession.

A severe rainstorm on Sunday lessened the attendance from the surrounding neighborhood; but as it was, there were fully 2,000 people present. Meetings were held in both large tents. J. N. Andrews spoke on prophecy in the Michigan tent in the morning; in the afternoon Mrs. White preached on the elevating tendency of Christianity. Tracts were freely distributed to the crowd. The weather becoming more favorable in the evening, James White spoke from the outdoor stand, his subject being the law and the gospel.

Monday, the closing day, was given to social meetings and labor for inquirers. The members eagerly pressed forward with their testimonies, every heart seeming to overflow with praise and thanksgiving. Early Tuesday morning the campers left the spot made sacred by the evident presence of God, and returned to their homes with a new sense of the responsibilities resting upon them as a people intrusted with a great spiritual message. The meeting thus brought to a close, was, up to that time, in the words of the *Review* editor, " the largest, the most important, and by far the best meeting ever held by Seventh-day Adventists."

The camp-meeting in Wright was followed by one in Clyde, Ill., September 23-28, and by a meeting in Pilot Grove, Iowa, October 2-7. These gatherings were also seasons of great spiritual uplift. The next year, 1869, Elder White announced in the *Review* camp-meetings for Ohio, Michigan, New Hampshire, New York, Wisconsin, Minnesota, and Iowa, the first one beginning August 10 and the last closing October 19. Giving advice as to the location of these meetings, he mentions the following essentials:

" 1. A central and accessible point, near a railroad.

" 2. Dry grounds, large trees, as far apart as possible, and yet furnishing a complete shade.

" 3. Good water, and ample grounds for retirement.

" 4. There should be a good chance to pitch one or more large tents in which to hold meetings in case of storm."

The arrangements in these early meetings were much the same as those at Wright. The tents were mostly rather large ones, and were used for sleeping purposes. They were divided lengthwise into two compartments, with a passageway between the curtains, one side being assigned to the men from a certain church, and the other to the women. There were no bedsteads, but plenty of clean, fresh straw was provided.

The cooking at the earliest meetings was done Indian fashion in the open air. A little later it became customary to hire a number of cookstoves, which would be placed at convenient places under the trees for the free use of the campers. A large iron kettle for cooking warm gruel was hung over an open fire. Every morning the gruel was furnished free to all persons in the camp. Sabbath was sometimes set apart as a fast day; but if it turned out cold and damp, there was sure to be a supply of hot gruel for the campers.

The arrangement of the tents was always with a view to orderly effect. The plan, to begin with, was circular. Later the circle gave way to the street arrangement, which proved more suitable for a large number of tents. The crude, home-made tents were gradually replaced with the best products of the various factories, and the camp came to take on a pleasing appearance. The meetings were presently held in large assembly tents, and it was only on occasions of overflow that the seats outside the walls would be used. The seats, too, were duly supported on boards set on edge, and provided with backs for the comfort of those who used them. A well-stocked grocery stand and a large dining pavilion were other features of the later camps.

In spite of the large crowds that attended these meetings, excellent order prevailed on the grounds. Lights in the tents were required to be put out at a certain hour, and all talking had to cease at the appointed time. The camp lights were kept burning throughout the night, and watchmen were appointed to patrol the grounds.

The camp-meetings were a marked feature of the denominational work in the late sixties and early seventies, and they undoubtedly accomplished great things in the direction of deepening the spirituality of the believers, and bringing into the body a larger sense of unity of aim and effort. While they have continued to the present day to wield a strong influence for good, there can be no doubt that in those early formative years their influence was proportionately far greater. Probably the years 1870-85 would cover the period during which the camp-meeting underwent the most rapid development and achieved the most decided results in the building up of the denomination.

In such Western States as Iowa, Wisconsin, and Minnesota, where the believers were very largely of the farming class, the camp-meetings developed certain characteristics of their own. Adventists in attendance came in their covered wagons, and oftentimes were several days on the road coming and going.

Those living at the greater distances would start early, and the train of wagons would gradually grow in length as it passed through the nearer towns, till it became a very long one.

A typical camp-meeting of this general character was held at Marion, Iowa, in the early summer of 1870. Let us join one of the smaller trains of wagons as it nears the meeting place.

On a bright morning in June we leave the hospitable home of a believer, in company with about thirty persons, including Elder and Mrs. James White, who have come by rail from Michigan. There are five wagons loaded with people and baggage; the roads are good, and the air invigorating. At six o'clock in the evening the party encamp for the night, pitching three large family tents on the grounds of a good-natured farmer, who furnishes plenty of clean straw. Preparations having been made for the night's rest, a brief religious service is held, attended by the farmer host and his neighbors.

At four-thirty the next morning all are up, the tents and baggage have been packed, and the company is on the road, most of its members walking to keep warm. At seven o'clock a halt for breakfast is made on the banks of a clear stream. The horses are watered, fires are made of dry bark, a hot drink is provided, and after " looking to God in thanksgiving and petition for His blessings," breakfast is served. About one o'clock the camp is reached. It is the day before the meeting is to begin; but a large number of people are already on the ground, and new companies are arriving hourly.

The camp occupies a sandy knoll liberally sprinkled with trees. The large meeting tent stands in an open place in the center, and the smaller tents are pitched under the trees around it in an orderly fashion. The large tent is fully seated, but the seats continue beyond and around it, so that during services fully half the large audience is sitting under the trees. The speaker's stand is several rods from the large tent, the walls of the latter being raised so that all can hear.

The next morning, Sabbath, the rising bell is rung at four-thirty, and at five o'clock the campers are seen going to the stand for the morning prayer and social service. Short prayers and testimonies fill the hour. Breakfast comes next, and after that, morning worship in the various tents. In twenty-five different tents the people are singing twenty-five different tunes, and a person standing in the middle of the circle hears only what one of the campers calls a " sort of sacred, sublime confusion." But each tent company is following its own tune, and great benefit is derived from these small district meetings.

At nine-thirty there is a general social meeting. At a quarter before eleven, W. H. Littlejohn enters the stand, and preaches a sermon from Revelation 14: 12. At 2 P. M. Mrs. E. G. White addresses the congregation with great freedom. By a rising vote some hundreds covenant to live a more devoted life. Then sinners are called forward for prayers, and about thirty respond. At six o'clock services are held in about half the tents, all the campers gathering into them as far as room permits, and hearts are touched and tears flow freely as testimonies are given to the praise and glory of God.

But it is becoming very close in the crowded tents, so after an hour has been spent in this way, James White calls all into the large tent, and addresses them for an hour on the general interests of the cause. Later in the evening a sermon on some phase of the message is attended by a large crowd from the surrounding neighborhood.

Sunday morning the social seasons at the stand and in the family tents are held as on the day previous. At ten-thirty James White preaches from 1 Peter 3: 15, giving some of the leading reasons for our faith to a large and attentive audience. At two o'clock the congregation is still larger, and Mrs. White speaks with freedom and power. Strong men who entered the grounds an hour ago entirely indifferent to religion, are weeping like children, and the whole audience is deeply moved. When the service is closed, the people seem loath to leave. As the crowd slowly move out on the road, more than 700 teams are counted, and the number of people is estimated at fully 3,000. In the evening the audience is comparatively small because of a storm. The next day the good meetings continue, a number coming forward for special prayer in the forenoon service. The baptismal candidates number twenty-eight, one of them being a Methodist class leader.

The time has come to break camp, and a farewell meeting is held immediately after dinner, closing with an earnest prayer, after which tents are quickly taken down and packed up, and the teams begin to move off, after the last hearty hand-shaking.

Elder and Mrs. White left this meeting to go to similar gatherings in Illinois and Minnesota, after which they went to New England, attending, during that summer and autumn, fifteen camp-meetings in as many different States.

Meanwhile the message was making headway also in the East. In this part of the field, where the work had its beginning, there had been a steady though not so rapid growth as in the Middle and Far West.

Vermont, the first of the Eastern States to put a tent in the field, was also the first to be formed into a conference, the organization taking place at a meeting held on June 15, 1862. A. S. Hutchins, a former Freewill Baptist preacher, who had accepted the truth in 1852, labored long and faithfully in Vermont, and came to be regarded as a father by all the Sabbath keepers in the State.

Oct. 25, 1862, witnessed the organization of the New York Conference, which included in its membership the Adventist churches in Pennsylvania. The organization was effected at a representative meeting held at Roosevelt, N. Y., October 25, David Arnold being elected the first president. Hiram Edson, S. W. Rhodes, C. O. Taylor, and R. F. Cottrell were among the active laborers in this portion of the field.

A. S. HUTCHINS

John Byington, founder of the company of believers in Buck's Bridge, N. Y., helped to build the first Seventh-day Adventist meeting house in the East. He was born at Hinesberg, Vt., in 1798. At the age of thirty he moved with his family to Potsdam, St. Lawrence Co., N. Y., where he settled on a farm. He was a member of the Methodist Episcopal church; but when a number of his associates in that church decided in favor of slavery, he lent his influence to organize a Wesleyan Methodist church, consisting only of persons who were opposed to traffic in human beings. In those days his home was always open to the Indian and the African, and many of the latter did he help in their efforts to get over the line to freedom.

When the claims of the Bible Sabbath were brought to his attention, Brother Byington made a careful study of the subject, and became convinced that it was the truth; but he had a family of six children, most of whom were just merging into manhood and womanhood, and he dreaded the result if he should make a change in his church affiliations. He prayed that, if it was the Lord's will that he should keep the seventh-day Sabbath, he might receive some unmistakable evidence. In one short week his youngest daughter sickened and died. As he sat by her bedside and watched the young life ebbing away, he felt that God was speaking to him in that terrible affliction, and resolved that no matter what it cost, he would step out and obey the commandments. His wife joined him.

The following year Elder and Mrs. White visited his home. In time there grew up in the neighborhood a company of Seventh-day Adventists. For three years the Sabbath meetings were held at Brother Byington's house at Buck's Bridge. Then a church building was erected.

In 1857, at the request of James White, Brother Byington moved with his family to Michigan, settling in the southern part of the State. For the next fifteen or more years, he spent his time largely in driving about in his carriage, visiting the little companies of Seventh-day Adventists, giving them further instruction, and establishing them in the truth. He was closely associated with Elders White and Andrews and other leaders in aggressive plans for the work of the denomination; and when it was decided, at the General Conference of 1863, to elect General Conference officers, he became the first man to hold the office of president. He was re-elected the following year, and was succeeded in 1865 by James White.

Among the most active workers in New England in the late sixties and early seventies was S. N. Haskell, of South Lancaster, Mass. He was born the 22d of April, 1833, in the little town of Oakham, Mass., his parents being members of the Congregational Church. He was married when just under eighteen, and a year later, in 1852, heard his first advent sermon, which deeply interested him. He talked of that sermon to every one he met, and was presently asked by a neighbor why he himself did not preach, and replied that he would if his friends would get an audience together. The man did so, and young Haskell, not willing to " back down," as he said, repeated the sermon he had heard, although under great embarrassment.

In the following year Mr. Haskell resolved to give himself to preaching if he received evidence of his call in some one's being converted under his labors and wishing to be baptized. In the course of that summer he was sent on an evangelistic tour to Canada, and held meetings for ten days at a point known as Carrying Place, five miles from Trent. The school-house was crowded, and many stood at the open windows. He says of his experience at this time, that he was so busy each day planning his sermon for the evening that he had no time to talk with the people personally and inquire into their religious experience. But while he was walking to meet his next appointment, which had been given out for an adjoining neighborhood, he was overtaken by a man driving a farm wagon, who invited him to ride. The man told him that he and his wife had attended the meetings, felt that they had experienced conversion, and wished to be baptized. Some days later he returned to the neighborhood where he had held the ten days' meetings. and found about twenty-five persons who gave evidence of conversion. He took this experience as an evidence that he should give his life to preaching.

In the course of a second trip to Canada, in the same year. he met William Saxby, of Springfield, Mass., who gave him a copy of " Elihu on the Sabbath." He took the little tract into the woods with him at Trent, on his way to his destination at Carrying Place, and after studying the subject for the entire day, decided to keep the seventh-day Sabbath until he received further light. About the same time he learned that there were people who, on Biblical grounds, refrained from eating swine's flesh, and he decided to give up the use of that kind of food.

The Sabbath seemed so clear to him that he attended the First-day Adventist Conference in Worcester, Mass., in the summer of 1854, fully persuaded that he could convince every member that it was his duty to keep the seventh day. It was a great disappointment to him when his friends would not even listen to him. However, Thomas Hale, of Huberston, Mass., invited the young Sabbath keeper home with him, and in a short time he and his family, another family of four members, and certain others began the observance of the Sabbath.

In the following winter Joseph Bates visited S. N. Haskell at his home. He preached to him and his wife from breakfast till dinner, and then till evening, and the same night he addressed the members in the little church. Thus it went on for ten days, at the end of which time Mr. Haskell felt that he fully understood the doctrines of Seventh-day Adventists.

S. N. Haskell visited Battle Creek, Mich., for the first time in the year 1868, and was deeply impressed with the zeal of the brethren who were carrying responsibilities at the center of the work. As he listened to the earnest appeals of Elder and Mrs. White, calling for every believer to take an active part in the work, he resolved to do all in his power to forward the cause of present truth. Shortly after his return to New England he organized the first tract and missionary society in his own house in South Lancaster, Mass.

At this time among the Adventists in six New England States there was but one tent. Brother Haskell felt the need of a tent in his work, and as the brethren did not see their way clear to purchase one, he and P. C. Rodman, of Rhode Island, a First-day Adventist preacher who had begun the observance of the Sabbath, purchased a fifty-foot tent, and had it pitched on the ground of the first New England camp-meeting, held between South Lancaster and Clinton, in the summer of 1870. At the camp-meeting the four States, New Hampshire, Massachusetts,

A MODERN ASSEMBLY TENT

Rhode Island, and Connecticut, were organized into one conference. S. N. Haskell was ordained and elected president.

Tent-meetings were soon being held in different parts of New England and New York. The Eastern camp-meetings also grew in influence and power, and while the Adventists in attendance were not so numerous as in a few of the Western gatherings, the attendance on the part of the general public was in some cases even greater than in the West. Especially cheering was the large outside attendance, also the interest manifested, at the camp-meeting at Groveland, Mass., held in the summer of 1876. The camp was pleasantly situated in a grove of oaks and pines, along one edge of which ran the Boston and Maine Railroad. A few rods beyond the railway was the Merrimac River, where steam yachts landed passengers every hour on Sunday and twice daily on other days. There were fifty-five family tents on the ground, and the meetings were from the first marked by great spirit and life.

Elder Haskell had taken care to have the meeting widely announced in the leading papers of New England, and the interest on the part of the public was keen from the start. Moreover, Miss M. L. Clough was at hand from the first to report the meetings, and as her full and spirited reports began to ap-

GROUP OF FAMILY TENTS

pear in the prominent papers, the attention of the people was widely attracted.

The following description given by a reporter for the Haverhill *Publisher*, appearing in the issue of that paper for August 29, will give a fair idea of the attendance on Sunday:

" Sunday was the great day at the meeting in the woods at Bradford, by Seventh-day Adventists, bringing together the largest assembly of people ever convened in this region for a similar purpose. . . . The railroads were taxed beyond the utmost capacity of all their preparations for the occasion, and large numbers were prevented from attendance by not finding means of conveyance at the time the trains started, or by not finding the trains moving when their effervescent inclinations were just active enough to stimulate them to visit the scene. We understand there were thousands at the station in Lawrence who could not be accommodated with conveyance, all the cars at command being literally packed to overflowing. It was the same at this station, and in the afternoon we noticed a train of sixteen heavy-laden cars slowly pulling out for the camp. In addition, two steam yachts were very busy, and omnibuses and barges were constantly running, while private carriages without number thronged in the way thereto. Had the cars run every half hour, they would have been full, and a much larger number of people would have passed over the road. As it was, it is thought fully twenty thousand visited the grounds during the day. But this was only an experimental occasion; another year an improvement can be made in the facilities for travel.

"The speaking through the day was almost continuous, it being in part an exposition of the doctrines of the sect, and was, therefore, 'seed sowing;' in addition there were two addresses on temperance by Mrs. White, of California."— *Review and Herald, Sept. 7, 1876, p. 84.*

Mr. and Mrs. White each spoke twice, the former on the leading doctrinal features of the Adventists' belief, the latter on her favorite theme, Christian temperance. Her addresses were received with great favor, and she was urged to speak the following day at the Haverhill City Hall under the auspices of the Reform Club. She did so, and the hall, with a seating capacity of 1,100, was filled. Mrs. White spoke with her usual power. In the words of one who was present:

"She struck intemperance at the very root, showing that on the home table largely exists the foundation from which flow the first tiny rivulets of perverted appetite, which soon deepen into an uncontrollable current of indulgence, and sweep the victim to a drunkard's grave. She arraigned the sin of mothers in giving so much time to the follies of dress, instead of giving it to the moral and mental elevation of their households; and the sin of fathers, in wasting time, health, and means on the gross indulgence in tobacco in its various forms, instead of uniting with their companions in noble efforts to dot our land with model households, where the parents shall occupy their proper positions, and the children come up with well-balanced and well-disciplined powers, to act a self-reliant and manly part in the world, and thus shut off recruits from the great army of tobacco and liquor devotees. Her remarks raised the audience to a high pitch of enthusiasm, which was manifested by several outbursts of applause while she was speaking, and by hearty hand-shakings and words of approval at the close."— *Ibid.*

Not only was an excellent impression made upon the thousands in attendance at this meeting, but a goodly number made the decision to keep the Bible Sabbath. On Monday morning, after an appropriate discourse, Dores A. Robinson, later a pioneer worker in Africa and India, was ordained to the gospel ministry. In the afternoon thirty-three candidates were baptized in the waters of the Merrimac.

J. N. LOUGHBOROUGH

FIRST PACIFIC PRESS BUILDING, OAKLAND, CALIF.

CHAPTER XIII

Expansion West and South

Mission to the Far West

AN important step was taken by the denomination in the spring of 1868, when it decided to open a mission in California. The work had begun in the East, as we have seen, then it had moved west as far as Rochester, N. Y., where for the first time the denominational organ, the *Review and Herald,* was printed on a press of its own. In 1855 the headquarters were moved to Battle Creek, Mich., from which, as a center, evangelistic work, by the use of schoolhouses, tents, and halls, had been carried on chiefly in Michigan, Wisconsin, Illinois, Iowa, Indiana, and Ohio. The time had now come to carry the message to the Far West, and a train of providences opened the way for this to be done.

D. T. Bourdeau attended the General Conference which convened in Battle Creek, May 28, 1868, with all arrangements made to enter a new field of labor, feeling strongly impressed that he would receive such a call at the meeting. When M. G. Kellogg, then resident in California, made a plea for laborers to be sent to that State, Elder Bourdeau immediately volunteered to go, believing that to be the field of labor for which he had been constrained to make himself ready. J. N. Loughborough was impressed in the same way, and he also gave public expression to his convictions of duty. The brethren assembled made the matter a subject of daily prayer until May 31, when it was decided that the proposed mission should be undertaken, and that Elders Loughborough and Bourdeau should have it in charge.

James White thereupon appealed through the *Review and Herald* for $1,000 with which to purchase a tent and send these laborers to the Pacific Coast. The transcontinental railway lacking some hundreds of miles of completion, the party journeyed by way of the Isthmus of Darien, arriving July 18, 1863, in San Francisco, where they were entertained at the home of a believer. It was naturally the desire of the one or two families of Adventists in San Francisco to have the tent pitched first in that city, but the brethren found on inquiry that a suitable lot could be obtained only on payment of a very high rental. As the situation was presented before the Lord in a season of prayer, the minds of the brethren were led out in the direction of the country to the northwest of San Francisco.

On the following day a man who was a stranger to the Adventists called at the house where they were staying, and invited them to pitch their tent in Petaluma. He belonged to a little church in that town, whose members called themselves "Independents." They had seen a notice in an Eastern paper to the effect that two evangelists had sailed for California with a tent, intending to conduct a series of religious services, and they had prayed that if these men were servants of God, they might have a prosperous voyage. Elder Loughborough wrote:

"The night following that prayer meeting, one of their prominent members dreamed that he saw two men kindling a fire to light up the surrounding country, which seemed to be enveloped in darkness. As the two men had a fire kindled and shining brightly, he saw the ministers of Petaluma trying to extinguish the fire by throwing on brush, turf, etc.; but all such efforts only increased the flame. As he was watching this, he saw that the men lighted a second fire in another quarter, and that some of the same ministers ran to quench that fire, but with no better success than in the first instance. In his dream he saw that this work was continued until the two men had five fires brightly burning, and the light was shining most beautifully. Then he saw these ministers, together with others, in council, and heard them say, 'It is no use. Let them alone. The more we try to put out the fires, the better they burn.'"—"*Rise and Progress of Seventh-day Adventists*," by J. N. Loughborough, p. 277.

The man was further given to understand in the dream that the two men he had seen kindling the fires were the evangelists coming to California with a tent. He told the dream to his brethren, saying that he should recognize the two men on seeing them. This further roused the interest and curiosity of the little company of " Independents " in the expected tent evangelists, and it was one of their number who called at the house where Elders Loughborough and Bourdeau were staying, and invited them to Petaluma. The man had learned, on inquiry at the dock, that a tent had arrived from the East, and had been delivered to such a street and number. Calling at the place thus indicated, he found the men he was looking for.

The result was that the tent was pitched in Petaluma on Aug. 13, 1868, and the meetings then begun were continued until October 16. The man who had had the dream recognized Elders Loughborough and Bourdeau as soon as he saw them, and both he and all the members of the " Independent " church co-operated heartily in giving the meetings a good start. Six of them ultimately accepted the Adventist views; the others joined in the opposition, which was vigorous. The five ministers of Petaluma all united in opposing the Adventist evangelists. One of them, in introducing the subject of the tent-meetings in the pulpit, said if the men had confined themselves to preaching, he would have said nothing, but their books were in every house. He was not far wrong, for already by that time the evangelists had sold about $300 worth of books in the place, and the instruction in Bible truth thus imparted was undoubtedly influencing the minds of the people.

In the course of the winter, meetings were held in Windsor, and in the Piner District, lying to the west of Santa Rosa. Early in April, 1869, the tent was pitched at Piner for a general assembly of the Adventists in California, to last over two days, at which time there came together seventy believers. At this meeting a temporary organization was effected, known as a " State Meeting," which took upon itself the responsibility of sustaining by tithes and offerings the evangelistic work west of the Rocky Mountains.

From the middle of April to the sixth of June a tent-meeting was held in Santa Rosa, followed by one in Healdsburg. While the latter meeting was in progress, one of the preachers would go over to Santa Rosa to meet with the believers there on the Sabbath. A trustee of the schoolhouse three miles west of Santa Rosa, had invited Elder Loughborough to make use of the building on June 12 for such a gathering, but when the hour for the meeting came, the building was closed against the Adventists. They accordingly held their meeting under the boughs

19

of a wide-spreading oak. Scores of teams passing along the adjoining highway soon carried the word throughout that section of the country, and awakened everywhere sympathy and support for the work. The people determined that the Adventists should have a meeting place of their own in Santa Rosa. One man gave two building lots and $500 to start the enterprise. Others pledged from $50 to $100, and soon a sufficient sum of money was in hand to erect a neat house of worship 60 x 40 feet, which was ready for use Nov. 1, 1869.

By the spring of 1871 there had been raised up in Sonoma County five churches of Seventh-day Adventists, the ministers of other denominations in each place strongly opposing the work. At a Methodist camp-meeting held that summer, the ministers met in council are said to have decided to " let the Adventists alone," because the more they opposed the doctrine, the more it spread.

The city of San Francisco was next to hear the advent message, the tent being erected on the south side of Market Street, between Fifth and Sixth Streets, June 16, 1871. Elder Bourdeau having been recalled East, D. M. Canright had been sent to take his place. The interest to hear was good, and the meetings were continued in halls, with the result that by the first of December there was a company of believers numbering more than fifty, the whole number of Sabbath keepers in the State then being 208. The tithe for the year was more than $2,000.

In the course of the summer of 1872 a tent-meeting was held in Woodland, Yolo County, which resulted in a church being raised up also in that place. In the following October the first Adventist camp-meeting in the State was held at Windsor, lasting one week. The camp consisted of thirty-three tents in addition to the sixty-foot circular tent in which the meetings were held. Elder and Mrs. White attended, and their message was heartily received by the believers. They remained in the State till the end of February, 1873, holding meetings with the various churches and companies, and giving much appreciated instruction in various phases of the truth. On February 15 and 16 the California Conference was organized at a meeting held in Bloomfield, Sonoma County, the Sabbath keepers then numbering 238.

The message next entered what was then the quiet little city of Oakland. In the middle of the year 1873 there was a solitary sister here who kept the Sabbath, and she had been alone in her faith for a long time. First a brother from San Francisco joined her in prayer meetings held in a little back parlor. The neighbors were invited, and occasionally one would drop in, on which occasions the brother would explain the prophetic charts the best he could. In October J. N. Loughborough held a few meetings in Oakland, after which six signed the covenant, and a Sabbath school and tract society were organized. Among those who embraced the Adventist views at this time was John I. Tay, who was afterward used to bring the advent message to the inhabitants of Pitcairn Island.

At the end of the following April the tent was pitched on the grounds of the city hall in Oakland, and in the latter part of May another sixty-foot tent was erected in East Oakland, services being held in both for some weeks. The question of local option being just then to the fore, a good deal of attention was given to the denominational views on temperance. Elder and Mrs. White, who had returned to California toward the end of 1873, took a prominent part in these meetings, Mrs. White's temperance addresses drawing large crowds and making a deep impression. When the tent efforts were brought to a close, there was a church of fifty members meeting regularly in a hall on the corner of Broadway and Twelfth Streets.

On June 4, 1874, Elder White began to issue an eight-page semimonthly paper, *The Signs of the Times,* as a further means of spreading the Adventist principles on the Pacific Coast. After issuing six numbers, he arranged with the California Conference to take charge of the paper, and returned East to obtain means to put the enterprise on a strong footing. At the General Conference held in August of that year it was proposed to raise $6,000 east of the Rocky Mountains for this purpose, provided the brethren on the Coast would raise $4,000, secure a suitable site, and erect a building. Elder George I. Butler brought this proposition to the California brethren assembled at the Yountville camp-meeting in October, and they responded by raising $19,414 in coin. The Sabbath keepers in California then numbered 550, and the yearly tithe amounted to more than $4,000.

At the close of this very successful camp-meeting, a 60 x 120-foot tent was erected at a central point in San Francisco, and a series of meetings was held, which further strengthened the work in that city. Elder Butler took a prominent part in these meetings, besides laboring among the churches.

In February, 1875, Elder and Mrs. White returned to Oakland, accompanied by J. H. Waggoner and other workers, and on February 12 a special session of the California Conference was called to consider the location of the printing office.

The decision was finally reached to purchase two lots on the west side of Castro Street, between Eleventh and Twelfth. Streets. James White and John Morrison took the deeds of the lots in their own names, the understanding being that when a publishing association should be formed, they would deed over

to it as much land as should be considered necessary for the use of the corporation.

The Pacific Press Publishing Company was formed in Oakland April 1, 1875, with a capital stock of $28,000. The central portion of the lots on Castro Street was duly turned over to the corporation, and a building was soon in course of erection, of the same shape and size as the three buildings of the Review and Herald in Battle Creek, the material, however, being wood instead of brick. The *Signs* was moved into its new quarters on Friday, Aug. 27, 1875.

Meanwhile the message was advancing in the rapidly growing city of San Francisco, where the company of believers found it difficult to carry on their work satisfactorily in rented halls.

There was urgent need of a church building; but lots were expensive, and the company of believers, with their very limited resources, did not feel able to undertake the responsibility of securing a suitable house of worship of their own.

It had been revealed to Mrs. White, however, that San Francisco would be an important evangelizing center, and if a suitable place of worship could be provided, it would greatly facilitate the work. The brethren were accordingly called together about the middle of April, 1875, and the facts placed before them.

The response was immediate. Search was made for a lot, and one on Laguna Street, which ordinarily would sell at $6,000, was obtained for two thirds of that sum. The necessary means came in answer to prayer, and as a result of self-sacrificing liberality on the part of the members. There were many special providences. A sister promised to give $1,000 if she could sell her place. The property was placed in the hands of a real estate agent, who said she had valued it too low, and sold it for her within a fortnight for a thousand dollars more than she had expected to get. Another member who had taken hold heartily to do his best, though he had very little, shortly received, to his astonishment, a legacy amounting to $20,000. Elder White sold his house in Battle Creek in order to put the money into this enterprise.

In due time a commodious church building was put up, measuring 35 x 80 feet, the total cost being $14,000. The building was dedicated April 2, 1876. By the end of that year there had also been provided a suitable house of worship for the believers in Oakland.

From California the message began to spread into adjoining States in the Far West. In the spring of 1878 some California Adventists who had moved to Nevada, sent in a request for a minister to open work in that State. Elder Loughborough, responding to the call, found at St. Clair, Churchill County, ten Sabbath keepers. After meetings had been held for one month, the number was doubled. This little company paid the expenses of Elder Loughborough's visit, and pledged $200 for a fifty-foot tent to be used in the State. The tent was erected at Reno, and meetings were held till August 18, at which time twenty-one signed the covenant. The number of Sabbath keepers in the State was then forty-five, with tithe amounting to $500 a year.

In Oregon, likewise, the pioneer work was done by a few faithful families who visited their neighbors and handed out tracts and papers. An interest having been created in this way, I. D. Van Horn entered the State, and was instrumental in raising up four churches and building three meeting houses, one at Milton, and one each at Walla Walla and Dayton in Washington State.

In the same way the truth entered the other States bordering on California, and went beyond. In the early eighties believers were reported in Arizona and New Mexico.

The message was also being carried over the line into British Columbia, where the nucleus was formed of what some years later became a very strong union conference. Eastern Canada had already been entered at an earlier period, and there also the interest gradually grew.

Beginnings in the South

It was about the year 1860 that Isaac Zirkle left the valley of Virginia and settled in Indiana, where he soon afterward was made acquainted with the Adventist doctrines through the labors of the Brothers E. B. and S. H. Lane. Letters sent by him to his relatives in Virginia roused their interest and curiosity, and Henry á Rife, of Timberville, began to correspond with S. H. Lane, with the result that E. B. Lane and J. O. Corliss accepted an invitation to go to Virginia. They arrived in New Market on Friday, Jan. 28, 1876, and were entertained at the home of John and Elizabeth Zirkle.

An appointment was given out for a meeting at the Oakshade schoolhouse on Sunday, January 30, at which time Elder Lane delivered a sermon on John 5: 39 to an attentive audience. The next meeting was held on the evening of January 31 in Polytechnic Hall in the village of New Market, Elder Corliss speaking from 1 Timothy 4: 1. The further use of the hall was refused by the owners, but Mr. Brock, a grocer of the town, secured the Methodist Episcopal church for the Adventist services.

Meanwhile Elders Corliss and Lane, not knowing that the way was open for further services in New Market, began services the next night in a small chapel in a neighborhood known as Soliloquy, three miles northwest of New Market. Meetings were conducted in both places until February 26, when some of the members of the Methodist church showing a deep interest in the doctrines taught, the further use of that church was denied. The services were continued for some months at Soliloquy, where a number of people manifested a deep interest in the truths taught.

With the opening of spring a fifty-foot tent was purchased in Philadelphia, being paid for by personal friends and supporters of the two young ministers. It was pitched at New Market, and the opening meeting was held Sunday, May 7, 1876. By this time the country was pretty well stirred over the Adventist doctrines, and the Disciples challenged the ministers to a public debate on the Sabbath question. Elder Lane accepted the challenge, and the ensuing discussion, held in the Disciple church at Eninburg, May 9, greatly extended the interest and brought from many quarters new invitations to preach.

The meetings in New Market closing on the 22d of May, the tent was next erected at Mount Jackson, on land belonging to Mr. Moore, where meetings were opened May 26 and continued till July 9. The tent was then taken to Newport, Page County, where it remained for about six weeks, being removed thence to Leaksville. In the course of the meetings held at this place, considerable opposition was stirred up among the Disciples of Luray, the adjoining county seat, as a result of which a discussion of four days' duration was held in the courthouse between J. O. Corliss and C. S. Lucas, a Disciple minister brought there for the purpose. At the close of the meetings in Leaksville the tent was taken down and stored for the winter.

Meanwhile services had been held from time to time at Soliloquy, and toward the close of the year a church was organized in that place, which worshiped first at Soliloquy, then at Liberty, and finally at New Market, which name it bears today.

The first baptism was administered at Smith's Creek, near New Market, Mrs. Elizabeth Zirkle and Miss Sallie A. Keyser being the candidates. Others followed shortly, and before the close of the first year's labor, more than fifty had been baptized.

The General Conference took note of these efforts in Virginia and other similar work in the Southern States, and passed the following resolution at its session held in September, 1876:

"*Resolved,* That we feel a deep interest in the spread of present truth of late in the Southern States, and that we will aid this work as fast and as far as our means and men will allow."

In the summer of 1877 the Virginia tent was erected at Middletown, Frederick County, and at Front Royal, Warren County. Some persons received the message in both places, but no church was organized. Soon after these efforts Elders Corliss and Lane returned to Michigan, and for some time there was no Adventist minister in Virginia. More or less labor was put forth in the course of the next few years, especially in the Middle Road schoolhouse in Frederick County, and to the west of that place, in the hills around Mount Williams; but no sustained effort was made.

The Virginia Conference was organized by J. O. Corliss at Liberty, near Quicksburg, March 4, 1883, A. C. Neff being elected the first president, followed later by R. D. Hottel. At the same time a State tract society and a Sabbath School Association were organized, the conference membership numbering at the time less than one hundred. In June, 1883, J. O. Corliss

R. D. HOTTEL   A. C. NEFF

opened tent-meetings at Fairfax Court House, Fairfax County, not far from the home of Reuben Wright, and continued them till the end of July. He was assisted by M. G. Huffman and B. F. Purdham. Several accepted the Adventist teaching, and were baptized.

The first camp-meeting was held at Valley View Springs, near New Market, beginning Aug. 8, 1883, the tent erected at Fairfax Court House being taken down to be used in connection with the gathering. The General Conference laborers present were George I. Butler, president of the General Conference, and I. D. Van Horn. After this the work gradually advanced in Virginia, Sabbath-keeping companies being raised up and churches organized in various parts of the State, for both white and colored members.

Texas

The work was pioneered in Texas by laymen who had gone from other parts of the country and settled in that State. One of these, John Ethan Rust, was a native of Vermont who had accepted the Adventist views in 1865, while convalescing from a wound received in the Civil War. He lived for some years in Battle Creek, Mich., where he was well known to Joseph Bates, James White, and other pioneers in the work. He moved to Texas in the spring of 1875. A letter from him appeared in the *Review* of April 29, 1875, in which he told of his arrival in Rice, Navarro County, March 19. He wrote that he knew of but two other families in the State who were keeping the Sabbath, and urged the sending of workers.

Sometime during 1875 M. E. Cornell went to Texas from Oakland, Calif., and delivered a course of lectures in the First Baptist church of Dallas; by arrangement with the members of the Young Men's Christian Association of that city. Five persons accepted the message. Elder Cornell then left to labor in other places.

Soon the new converts were pleading for help, and D. M. Canright was sent to answer the call. He arrived in Dallas May 5, 1876, and found eleven ready for baptism. The brethren had been holding their services in a rented hall not far from the Union Station; but they had erected a large temporary tabernacle of boards decorated with evergreens for Elder Canright's use.

Instruction having been given on baptism and organization, Elder Canright, on the first Sabbath after his arrival, organized a church of eighteen members. The following day eleven persons were baptized in a lake about two miles distant. Services continued to be held nightly, and on the next Sabbath, after the sermon and a social meeting, six additional persons were baptized, and ten new members added to the church, making a total of twenty-eight. E. G. Rust was ordained deacon, and the ordinances of the Lord's house were celebrated. On Sunday a tract and missionary society was organized, with thirty-two members.

A few months later Elder R. M. Kilgore went to Texas, and remained for some time, holding meetings and raising up companies of Sabbath keepers in various parts of the State. In the summer of 1877 he drove fifty miles from Dallas to Cleburne in Brother Crawford's carriage, accompanied by wagons containing the tents and lumber for the seats. On arriving in Cleburne they put up their assembly tent and a small dwelling tent.

Handbills were circulated, and the people came out readily. Twelve or fourteen took their stand for the Sabbath at this place. The tent was next pitched in Peoria.

In the summer of 1878 a series of meetings was held at Rockwall, beginning August 8. On November 12-19 the first Texas camp-meeting was held at Dallas, Elder and Mrs. James White, George I. Butler, and S. N. Haskell being present. It was at this camp-meeting that the Texas Conference was organized.

R. M. KILGORE

Tennessee

One of the earliest Adventists in Tennessee was W. D. Dortch, of Springville. In the year 1876 he received from his brother, who was living in Texas, some tracts setting forth the belief of Seventh-day Adventists. He was then twenty years old, and had never before heard of such a people; but when he saw that the seventh day was the Sabbath, he immediately decided to observe it, supposing that he was the only Sabbath keeper in the State. His mother, a zealous Methodist, was greatly grieved at the time, but within a year both his parents and all his brothers and sisters were keeping the Sabbath.

When the Adventists first began to do aggressive work in Tennessee, there was a good deal of opposition. In one of the earliest tent efforts, the tent was burned to the ground. But the work advanced in spite of the opposition, and in the place where the tent was burned, the first Seventh-day Adventist meeting house in Tennessee was erected. A number of the brethren, chiefly in Henry County, were imprisoned for working on Sunday. But the prejudice died down in time, and some of those who had been leaders in the opposition became extremely friendly.

Arkansas

In the late seventies an Adventist minister entered Arkansas from Missouri, held a few meetings, and baptized several persons, but the work was not at that time followed up. A new beginning was made in March, 1883, when E. W. Crawford, of Dallas, Texas, went to Fayetteville and began to canvass for the first subscription edition of " Thoughts on Daniel and the Revelation." In three months he took about $100 worth of orders. He found the people interested in the prophecies, and he urged that the General Conference send a minister to that field.

In response to this request, Elder and Mrs. D. A. Wellman, of Michigan, were sent to Arkansas. Elder Wellman began his labors in the central part of the State, holding meetings at Argenta and Little Rock, and then went to Springdale, in the neighborhood where Brother Crawford had been canvassing. Here the attendance was so large that the tent could not hold the audience.

Elder and Mrs. J. W. Scoles arrived in time to assist in this effort. After they had labored together for several months, Elder Wellman died of pneumonia, the funeral service being held in the tent. The meetings were continued by Elder Scoles, and a church was organized with the aid of E. Van Deusen, who arrived there at the time of Elder Wellman's illness. The twenty-one members in this church gave sufficient money to erect a neat little church building, the first one to be owned by the Adventists in Arkansas.

J. G. Wood was sent to Arkansas in the winter of 1884-85, and continued to labor in the State till the spring of 1888, when George I. Butler, then president of the General Conference, called a meeting at Springdale to organize a conference. At that time there were 226 members in the different churches, and seventy or more isolated members. J. P. Henderson was elected the first president of the conference.

J. N. ANDREWS

President of the General Conference, from May, 1867, to May, 1868; and first missionary to a foreign land, in 1874.

CENTRAL EUROPEAN PUBLISHING HOUSE, BASEL, SWITZERLAND

CHAPTER XIV

The Central European Mission

In the previous chapter we have seen the Adventists gradually awakening to a sense of the extent and greatness of the work committed to them, and sending out laborers to different parts of the United States, even as far as to the Pacific Coast. They were now, in the providence of God, to enter Europe.

In the year 1864 there returned to the old country a Polish convert to Protestantism from the Roman Catholic Church, by the name of M. B. Czechowski. He had heard the Seventh-day Adventist views at a tent-meeting held at Findlay, Ohio, and had at least nominally accepted the doctrines, though not connecting definitely with the movement. Desiring to go to Europe as a missionary, he sought and obtained the support of the First-day Adventists. Entering Europe under their direction, he began to labor in the Piedmont Valleys, where, in spite of hardships and opposition, he remained about fourteen months. He thereupon entered Switzerland, established a paper called *The Everlasting Gospel,* which was published regularly for two years, and continued to preach not only on the second advent, but also on the Sabbath and the other truths peculiar to Seventh-day Adventists.

On New Year's Eve, at the beginning of 1867, a little company of believers at Tramelan pledged themselves to keep the Seventh-day Sabbath, and in the following July eight candidates were immersed at nightfall. About two months later there was another baptism, at which four candidates, also from Tramelan, observed the rite. A series of meetings held at Chaux-de-Fonds resulted in raising up converts also in that place, and the number of believers steadily grew.

Mr. Czechowski left Switzerland in the winter of 1868-69, to enter upon active propaganda of the same truths in Rumania, where his unfamiliarity with the language made progress slow, though here also some converts were made to the truths taught. The later life of this first messenger of Adventism to enter European territory was unfortunate. He died at a hospital in Vienna early in 1876. Though working in an independent and rather irresponsible way, this man had planted good seed; some of it had fallen into good ground, and was to spring up and yield an abundant harvest.

JAMES ERZENBERGER

Later, after Mr. Czechowski had left them, some of his followers in Switzerland learned providentially, through a stray copy of the *Review and Herald*, of the Adventist publishing house in Battle Creek, Mich., and opened up correspondence with the brethren there. They appealed for help, and were invited to send a representative to the General Conference to be held in Battle Creek in May, 1869. The invitation was accepted, and James Erzenberger, a young German Swiss, was sent on this mission, but arrived in June, too late for the conference. Nevertheless, he remained for a time, to become more familiar with the truth and to acquire some knowledge of the English language. He was soon able to speak in English at various camp-meetings. He returned to Switzerland in September, 1870, feeling well repaid for his visit. In June, 1870, Ademar Vuilleumier came to America to spend some years in preparing himself for the work of preaching the message in his native land.

These visits from abroad, combined with the earnest calls for help that continued to come from time to time, led to the establishment of the Central European Mission. It was at the General Conference in August, 1874, than J. N. Andrews was selected to open up work in Europe. He sailed from Boston September 15, accompanied by his son Charles M. and his daughter Mary F. and by Ademar Vuilleumier. The party arrived at the city of Neuchâtel, Switzerland, about a month later.

On November 1 there was held at Neuchâtel the first general meeting of European Seventh-day Adventists, representatives being present from the companies in Tramelan, Locle, Chaux-de-Fonds, Fleurier, Bienne, and Buckten. No very definite conclusions having been arrived at, a second meeting was appointed to be held at Locle two weeks later. At this meeting it was decided to raise the sum of 2,000 francs for the purpose of spreading the truth by means of publications, and the brethren present showed their earnestness and willingness to help, by giving 1,800 francs on the spot. A committee of three, consisting of J. N. Andrews,

ALBERT VUILLEUMIER

Albert Vuilleumier, and Louis Schild, was appointed to take the oversight of the work during the ensuing year.

A still more general meeting of believers was convened in January, 1875, at Chaux-de-Fonds, " for the transaction of business, for the celebration of the ordinances, and for the worship of God." It was decided at this gathering that Elders Andrews and Erzenberger should visit certain German Sabbath keepers in Elberfeld, Prussia, from whom communications had been received, the sum of 300 francs being raised to defray the expenses of the trip. The day after the meeting the brethren accordingly started for Elberfeld, lying 300 miles to the north.

On their arrival they found a company of forty-six Sabbath keepers scattered over a considerable territory. These persons formed the congregation of J. H. Linderman, a former preacher of the Reformed Church. In 1850 Mr. Linderman had been led by his own study of the Scriptures to embrace the Bible doctrine of baptism by immersion, in which he was followed by part of his congregation. On further study of the Bible, he found that it afforded no basis for Sunday observance. He accordingly stepped out once more, and began to observe the seventh day as the Sabbath. This further change of views was naturally a cause of separation between himself and the congregation which had followed him on the doctrine of baptism. For three years he kept the Sabbath alone; but in course of time his example and teaching began to produce an effect, and others joined him.

The Seventh-day Adventist brethren learned of these Sabbath-keeping Germans through a wanderer who was given a night's lodging at the house of one of the sisters living near Basel. When told of the Adventist belief, he in turn informed his hostess that there were people of the same faith near Elberfeld, and gave her the address of Pastor Linderman. This opened the way for correspondence with J. N. Andrews, and led to the ensuing visit. When these brethren, who, for aught they knew, were alone in keeping the seventh day, learned of the Sabbath reform message that was being preached in America, and had now begun to be given also in Europe, their hearts were greatly cheered, and they wept tears of joy.

Upon closer acquaintance it was discovered that this little company of Sabbath keepers had also been led, by their unaided study of the Scriptures, to look for the soon coming of the Saviour, and like their brethren in America, they had given up tobacco, almost universally used in that part of the country, and observed great simplicity in dress. They were employed, for the most part, in weaving, the looms being set up in their own homes, an arrangement especially favorable to Sabbath keeping. After spending about a month holding meetings with this company and others who could attend, Elder Andrews returned to Switzerland, leaving Brother Erzenberger to follow up the interest.

Letters were now coming from various parts of Switzerland, Germany, and Holland, from persons who had seen the advertisements the brethren had inserted in the leading newspapers, and who wished to know more about the Adventist doctrines. It was necessary, therefore, to provide tracts and other literature in the leading European languages, in order that honest inquirers might receive the light they sought. Elder Andrews again applied himself diligently to the study of the French language, and began to print a series of tracts, the first of which were issued at Neuchâtel. Later a Basel publisher was employed.

At the second annual meeting, held at Bienne, Dec. 12, 1875, and attended by a good representation from the various small companies, it was reported that there had been published in French during the year 10,000 copies of the tract, " Which Day Do You Keep, and Why? " and 3,000 copies each of " The Millennium," " The Second Advent," " The Two Thrones," " The Judgment," and " The Sanctuary." The chief business of this conference was the organization of a tract and missionary society, modeled on the lines of those already in operation in America, in order that the literature now available might receive the widest possible circulation by the united efforts of all the believers. Instruction was also given on the subject of systematic benevolence, and pledges were taken to the amount of $460.

Meanwhile the message was being preached in various places. In the previous June, Albert Vuilleumier had baptized a company of twelve at La Coudre, and in August the rite was administered to eight persons at a charming spot near the north end of Lake Neuchâtel. The truth was also making some headway in Germany, under the labors of James Erzenberger, who found an especially good interest in the city of Solingen, near Elberfeld, where he held a course of meetings, resulting in the raising up of a company of sixteen, eight of whom were baptized on Jan. 8, 1876.

About this time a new impetus was given to the work by the arrival of D. T. Bourdeau and his family, who were sent from America to labor among the French people in Switzerland and France. They settled at Locle, Switzerland, whither Elder Andrews also removed, and Elder Bourdeau, who knew the French language, having been educated in Canada, began a course of lectures in March. The meetings were well attended, and among those who accepted the truth was Louis Aufranc, the leading teacher in a school of that city.

The time had now come when the brethren felt able to begin the publication of a monthly journal to give further publicity to the message. The new journal was called *Les Signes des Temps* (The Signs of the Times), and Basel, lying on the boundary line between Switzerland and Germany and not far from France, was wisely chosen as a publishing center, and as the headquarters of the European Mission. To this place Elder Andrews accordingly moved with his family in the spring of 1876. The first number of the new journal appeared in July, and monthly issues, of eight pages each, followed with a good degree of regularity.

In the autumn of 1876, Elder Bourdeau entered upon a year's campaign in Southern France, which resulted in the baptism of seventeen persons in Valence, as well as the raising up of isolated believers in other localities. Following this he spent a year in southern Switzerland.

The publishing work being now well under way in Basel, with the *Signes* entering upon its second volume, Elder Andrews resolved upon making a tour into southern Italy, where a few were keeping the Sabbath. These persons had accepted the Adventist views under the labors of Dr. H. P. Ribton, a graduate of Dublin University, residing in Naples, whose attention had first been drawn to the Sabbath truth by means of publications sent to a friend of his by Seventh Day Baptists in England, and who had later read Adventist literature from Basel. The conditions being very unfavorable to public effort, it seemed wise for Elder Andrews to devote his time mostly to visiting the people in their homes. Before leaving, he had the pleasure of baptizing Dr. Ribton, together with his wife and daughter, at a beautiful retired spot in the harbor of Puteoli, probably near the point where the apostle Paul landed on his journey to Rome. Later Dr. Ribton removed to Alexandria, Egypt, where he and three Italian brethren were slain in the massacre of Europeans that took place June 11, 1882.

On returning from Naples, Elder Andrews visited the historic Piedmont Valleys, and gave further instruction to the believers there who had first embraced the Adventist views under the labors of Mr. Czechowski. These descendants of the Bible-loving Waldenses manifested the same love of truth that characterized their brave forefathers. Accustomed to privation and hardships such as one seldom meets with elsewhere, they had developed something of the strength of their own mountain fastnesses. They had also escaped in large measure the corrupting influences which had been at work elsewhere in Italy.

The annual meeting of the Swiss brethren for the year 1877 was held at Bienne, September 30 and October 1, at which time it was reported that the paper *Les Signes* had nearly four hundred subscribers, and that seventeen French tracts had been printed in editions of 5,000 each, and two in editions of 10,000.

In December, 1877, the force of workers was strengthened by the arrival of Mr. and Mrs. William Ings and Miss Maud Sisley. These workers came to assist in the publishing work, and were met in England by J. N. Andrews, who used the opportunity to look for type and other printing materials, so that in future our own brethren could do the whole work of composing. Early in 1878 the publication of tracts in German and Italian was accordingly begun. A portion of a building at 68 Müllerweg was occupied as a typeroom, and the office facilities were further increased.

The work in Europe had now reached such a state of development that further counsel with the leaders in America was deemed advisable. J. N. Andrews accordingly attended, by request, the General Conference held in Battle Creek, Mich., Oct. 4, 1878. He was accompanied by Elder and Mrs. D. T. Bourdeau, and by his daughter Mary, a girl of seventeen, who had been in failing health for some months. The journey and the treatment at the Battle Creek Sanitarium failed to restore her, and she passed away on November 27. Elder Andrews himself was in feeble health at this time, and remained in America till spring, taking part in the special session of the General Conference held in April, 1879. He sailed in May, accompanied by his niece, Miss Edith Andrews, and by Miss Anna Oyer; but owing to extreme feebleness, he made a short stay in England, not arriving at Basel till near the end of August.

Meanwhile the publishing and evangelistic work had been going steadily forward, James Erzenberger, who had returned from Germany, having labored with success in various parts of Switzerland, and conducted baptisms at Morges and Tramelan.

About this time public opinion was greatly agitated over the subject of temperance, and the strong stand taken by *Les Signes* against alcoholic stimulants made for it friends in influential quarters. Elder Andrews was elected an honorary member of the leading temperance society in France, and his periodical was given honorable mention in the reports of the society, as a journal exerting a widespread influence on the side of total abstinence. As a result of the temperance agitation and of sending sample copies of the paper through the post, the circulation materially increased, so that at the Tramelan conference, held in 1881, the monthly edition was reported at 3,500 copies.

In the spring of 1882, S. N. Haskell, at the request of the General Conference, visited the mission. His visit was of importance in giving a new impetus to the tract and missionary work carried on by the churches. At the close of the conference at Tramelan, a general gathering of laborers working in different parts of Europe, was convened at Basel, the object being to give them an opportunity to compare notes, and together lay some general plans for the further prosecution of the work. The meeting, which proved to be the first session of what came to be known as the European Council, lasted three days, delegates being present from Norway and England, in addition to those from different parts of Switzerland. J. N. Andrews was chosen chairman, and A. A. John, then laboring in England, secretary, and C. M. Andrews, treasurer. About the same time the printing office was moved to a new building on the corner of Weiherweg and Belchenstrasse, which also served as a home for the mission family.

The increasing feebleness of Elder Andrews making it necessary to provide further help, it was voted at the General Conference in America, held in Rome, N. Y., Dec. 7, 1882, that B. L. Whitney and his family join the mission. They arrived in Basel the following July, and a little later D. T. Bourdeau returned with his family from America, and resumed his labors, after an absence of five years.

The meeting which convened at Basel October 19 was more widely representative than any hitherto held, there being present, in addition to the Swiss brethren, representatives from Germany, Italy, and Rumania. The financial report indicated that the contributions during the year had been double those of any preceding year, a result owing largely to the zeal and interest in church missionary work which S. N. Haskell's visit had encouraged.

At this meeting, requests were made on behalf of the brethren in Italy and Rumania, that papers be published in the languages of those countries, as a means of spreading the truth. The conference not having the means to enter upon these new enterprises, resolutions were passed requesting the General Conference in America to take the matter under advisement, and pledging the help of the European members in carrying out whatever action might be taken.

While this conference was in session, J. N. Andrews, the revered leader in the work, who had been rapidly failing for some weeks, passed away peacefully October 21, one of the last acts of his life being, with trembling hand, to assign to the mission $500, which was pretty much all that remained of his earthly possessions.

He had laid the foundation of a work whose greatness and extent he and his associates little realized, and he had toiled faithfully at writing and translating until within a few days of his death. His going was an irreparable loss,— one which brought great sadness to the hearts of the brethren gathered out of various parts of Switzerland and other countries, who looked to him as to a father. Yet it was no time to repine. They must close up the ranks and continue the battle, taking to themselves new courage from the loyalty and earnestness of their fallen leader, and resolving to conse-crate themselves unreservedly to the unfin-ished work.

J. N. Andrews was born at Poland, Maine, in 1829, and had labored in the mes-sage for about thirty-five years, the last nine of which had been spent in laying the foundations of the work in Europe. His character was marked by rare personal hu-mility combined with fervent zeal and ag-gressiveness in forwarding the interests of the cause. He was fond of books and hard study, and without enjoying the advantage of a college education, had, by his own ef-forts, gained a good working knowledge of Latin, Greek, and Hebrew, as well as a thor-ough acquaintance with church history.

Entering upon his labors in Europe, Elder Andrews applied himself vigorously to the study of the French language, and was soon using it with a good degree of fluency both in writing and in speaking. In Amer-ica he had been editorially connected with the *Review and Herald* almost from the be-ginning, and he had been the sole editor of the French paper, *Les Signes des Temps,* which had proved such an effective means of spreading the Adventist views in Europe. He had also written a number of tracts and pamphlets, throwing light upon such sub-jects as the sanctuary, the United States in prophecy, and the messages of Revelation 14; but he left as his best literary legacy to the denomination, " The History of the Sabbath and the First Day of the Week," a book which came out first in the early sixties, and now, after sixty years, still holds its place in the front rank of the standard denominational works.

Monument at Grave of J. N. Andrews, Basel, Switzerland.

Elder Andrews was married in the autumn of 1856 to **Miss** Angeline S. Stevens, who died in 1872. There were four **chil-**

dren, of whom one, the eldest and only son, still survives, and has occupied for years a trusted position in the leading denominational publishing house.

J. N. Andrews was not an old man, but his constitution was weak to begin with, and the anxiety and hardships incident to the undertaking of work in a new field, under trying conditions, put it to a severe strain. Had it not been for the health principles, which gave him, as he fully believed, a new lease of life, he could not have accomplished a tithe of what he did. Had he been more careful to avoid intemperance in labor, and to provide himself with needed comforts, he would undoubtedly have lived longer; but this was too much to expect of one who took thought ever for others rather than for himself. It was much that such a man was permitted to begin the work in Europe, and there, as in his native country, his name will ever be fragrant with memories of noble, self-denying labor in behalf of the cause he loved better than his life. He had a worthy successor in B. L. Whitney, who already for some months had shared the responsibilities of the mission.

The conference being in session in Basel at the time of Elder Andrews' death, appropriate action was taken, expressing on the part of the brethren their deep sense of the loss sustained, and their determination to give themselves to the work which remained. The tract society was reorganized for aggressive work on the model of those recently put in operation in America, and plans were laid for a general missionary meeting to be held at Chaux-de-Fonds shortly after the close of the conference, for giving instruction in home missionary work with papers and books. At this meeting, liberal orders were given by the brethren for clubs of *Les Signes,* the monthly edition of which had risen to 6,000 copies.

About this time there was likewise formed a Sabbath School Association, followed by the organization of Sabbath schools in the various churches and companies.

The General Conference in America having taken favorable action respecting the matter, the year 1884 witnessed the first issue of three new periodicals, the *Herold der Wahrheit,* an eight-page German monthly of the same size and form as *Les Signes des Temps; L'Ultimo Messagio* (The Last Message), a sixteen-page quarterly in Italian; and *Adevarulu Present* (The Present Truth), a Rumanian quarterly. The German paper began with an edition of 5,000, and enjoyed the loyal support not only of the German-speaking Swiss and the few Sabbath keepers in Germany, but also of brethren who spoke only French themselves, but were glad to have a share in making the truth known to the Germans. The other two papers came out in editions of 2,000 each.

The visit of George I. Butler early in the year 1884, was a source of great encouragement to the laborers in Central Europe. After holding a workers' meeting in Basel and visiting various parts of Switzerland, Elder Butler made a tour into the Wal-

B. L. WHITNEY   J. H. WAGGONER

densian Valleys, and traveled southward as far as Naples, also visiting the Sabbath keepers in Rumania.

Churches having now been regularly organized, it was decided to effect conference organization according to the plan followed in America. A meeting was therefore appointed to be held at Bienne, May 24-27, 1884, to which all the churches sent delegates. At this, the largest general meeting held thus far, there were present about 123 persons. Under the direction of Elder Butler, a conference was organized, including the five churches in Switzerland. To this conference were then added by request the German churches at Vohwinkel and Solingen, raised up by James Erzenberger; the church at Naples represented by A. Biglia; and the company at Pitesti, Rumania, represented by Thomas Aslon. The usual conference officers were elected, B. L. Whitney being made president.

Immediately following the Bienne conference, the second session of the European Council was called at Basel, and was attended by representatives from nine different nations. At this meeting a thorough organization was effected, which provided for each mission field represented an executive board of three, the board for the Central European Mission consisting of B. L. Whitney, D. T. Bourdeau, and A. C. Bourdeau.

A. C. BOURDEAU   D. T. BOURDEAU

Considerable attention was given at this council to the publishing interests of the Central European Mission, and it was decided to purchase a lot, looking toward the erection later of a suitable building to be used as a printing office and as a home for the family of workers. Definite plans for the building were held in abeyance till Elder Butler could return to the States and counsel with the other members of the General Conference Committee.

The brethren in Europe had not long to wait. In the latter part of July word came to proceed immediately with the erection of the proposed publishing house, which, after some vexatious delays, owing to building regulations, was duly completed. Built of brick and stone, it was a substantial structure, with a ground plan 64 x 76 feet, and a height of four stories, including the mansard roof. It contained, in addition to spacious accommodations for the publishing work, a neat chapel seating 200, and apartments for the family of workers. It was favorably located, overlooking on the south a large government park used as a parade ground. The combined cost of the building and lot, including machinery for the printing establishment, was about $60,000.

With the publishing interests thus well provided for, additional attention began to be given to the field evangelistic work. D. T. Bourdeau, who had gone to Branges, France, at the call of a brother who had embraced the Sabbath from reading *Les Signes,* found a community, largely Catholic, which gave intelligent heed to the word preached. It being a farming community, and the busy time of the year, meetings could not be held till nine o'clock in the evening. Nevertheless, the attendance was good, and a sufficient number accepted the truth to allow of the organization of a church.

Elder Bourdeau next labored at Bastia, on the island of Corsica, where a young Baptist evangelist had begun to observe the Sabbath as a result of reading *Les Signes.* In this place a company of twelve believers was raised up. Elder Bourdeau went thence to Naples and other parts of southern Italy, where he established the believers and awakened an interest on the part of others. During the winter of 1884-85 he delivered a course of lectures in Torre Pellice, Italy, at the close of which additions were made to the company of believers and a church was organized.

Meanwhile A. C. Bourdeau was meeting such decided opposition in Pitesti, Rumania, that he found it necessary to conduct his meetings in private houses. He baptized several new members, and organized a church of fourteen. He afterward labored in western France, where a number accepted the truth.

James Erzenberger resumed labor in Gladbach, Prussia, and also gave a course of lectures in a near-lying city. Albert Vuilleumier had good success laboring as a colporteur in various parts of Switzerland.

At the European Council held in the summer of 1884, a resolution was passed, extending to Mrs. E. G. White " a hearty and urgent invitation to visit the different fields in Europe as soon as possible," and also requesting that W. C. White accompany her and give the brethren at Basel the benefit of his experience in the publishing work. The General Conference in America, at its next session, having seconded this call, the visit was made, Mrs. E. G. White and W. C. White with his family arriving at Basel Sept. 3, 1885. One week later the Swiss Conference convened, and continued till September 14. There were present in all nearly 200 brethren and sisters, including delegates from Germany, France, Italy, and Rumania.

The conference had at this time one ordained minister, seven licentiates, and ten churches, with a membership of 224. The tithe for the year amounted to something over 8,000 francs. The report of the tract and missionary society showed that since its organization, late in 1883, it had distributed 137,039 pages of tracts and books and 39,920 journals; 9,066 missionary visits had been made; and offerings taken up in addition to the tithe amounted to about 10,000 francs. The Sabbath School Association reported eleven schools, with a total membership of 251.

An essential feature of this conference was the practical discourses on Christian living given by Sister White, which exerted a strong influence upon those in attendance. Fourteen candidates were baptized, and Albert Vuilleumier was set apart to the gospel ministry.

Immediately at the close of the conference, the European Council met for its third session, which lasted ten days. The attendance was large, the various European fields being well represented. Reports were rendered by the ministers, showing widespread interest to hear the truth.

The report of the publishing work showed encouraging progress. The office at Basel had sent out during the year 131,000 copies of the periodicals in the French, German, Italian, and Rumanian languages. It was also publishing thirty-one different tracts and pamphlets in French, fourteen in German, and seven in Italian.

Plans of labor were fully talked over. The question was raised whether it would be well to make use of tents in working the cities. The counsel given by Mrs. White was in favor of this method of work, and the scarcity of halls in many cities pointed in the same direction. It was accordingly decided that the Swiss Conference purchase two tents, one each for the French and German work. The General Conference was requested to furnish a tent for use in Italy. Tents were also voted for England and Sweden.

At this meeting, too, the foundations were laid for the colporteur work in Europe. The idea had largely prevailed that it was impossible to sell our books on the commission basis, and that canvassers could not maintain themselves in the field without the aid of a salary. Mrs. White took the position that the commission plan was workable in Europe as well as in America, and cheered by her encouraging words, the brethren determined to give the system a thorough trial. The outcome was a complete success.

Officers were elected for the coming year, B. L. Whitney continuing as chairman of the executive committee.

The morning talks by Mrs. White, covering a wide range of practical subjects, were a marked feature of the meeting, and did much to unite the hearts of all the laborers on the work that lay before them.

The winter following the council witnessed aggressive work in various centers. D. T. and A. C. Bourdeau gave a course of lectures in the city of Geneva, while James Erzenberger and Albert Vuilleumier labored in Chaux-de-Fonds. Presently L. R. Conradi, who had come over from America, joined Elders D. T. Bourdeau and J. Erzenberger in a public effort at Lausanne, conducted simultaneously in the French and German languages, at the close of which twenty-one persons were baptized and organized into a church. In the summer of 1886 A. C. Bourdeau and his assistants conducted a tent effort at St. Germain, Italy; while D. T. Bourdeau, J. Erzenberger, and A. Vuilleumier pitched their tent in Nîmes, France, and L. R. Conradi started on a tour through Russia.

THE FIRST SABBATH SCHOOL LESSONS

Written by Elder James White by the roadside at the dinner hour, using his lunch basket as a writing table. These four lessons appeared in the first number of the *Youth's Instructor*, in 1852.

THE PENNY COLLECTION

A Sabbath school of pioneer days, held in a farm house. On the stroke of the bell, the members filed past the collection box with their penny offerings.

CHAPTER XV

The Organization and Work of the Sabbath School

In the early days of the advent movement little was done in a denominational way for the spiritual instruction and upbuilding of the children and youth. They attended meetings of various kinds with their parents, and the preaching, while not directed especially to them, was marked by directness and simplicity, and not ill adapted to the needs of the young. The temptations from without were many. It was not an easy thing to endure the scoffs and jeers or the silent contempt of schoolmates and acquaintances; for to be an Adventist in those days meant, if not persecution in some form, then at least a reputation for singularity and aloofness, from which the young people often suffered more than their parents.

But if the children had little done for them in an organized way, many of them had the inestimable privilege of being under the care of prayerful fathers and mothers. They knew that their parents loved the truth more than life, and were making

daily sacrifices in order to forward its interests.   They knew,
too, that they themselves had been dedicated to God from the
cradle, and that fact had a saving influence upon them.

These children were early taught habits of devotion.   Bible
religion had a large place in the homes of the pioneers; it was
not crowded out by pressure of worldly cares.   In most families
worship was held regularly two or three times a day, and it was
not a brief, formal service.   The portion of Scripture was generous, the prayers offered by father and mother were instinct
with the hope of a soon-coming Saviour, and the children themselves took part both in prayer and in the reading of the Scriptures.   If the home was provided with a musical instrument,
evening worship was usually accompanied by the singing of
advent melodies.

Meetings conducted by adults especially for the children and
youth do not seem to have been held in early times, but we find
occasional references to gatherings for prayer and Bible study
under the direction of groups of earnest young people.   Ellen G.
White as a girl was active in organizing and carrying on such
meetings at the time of the advent movement of 1843-44.   James
White, himself a young man in those days, had a keen interest
in the children, and wherever he went, his preaching appealed
to young as well as old.   In the course of his tour among the
Freewill Baptist churches of Maine in the winter and early
spring of 1842-43, he had seen many children and young people
awakened by the advent message.   A little group of awakened
youth at West Gardiner kept together after he left, and held
meetings by themselves.   About a year later, when he was in
the neighborhood, a messenger came twenty miles to get him
to go to Gardiner and baptize these youth.   Their parents had
opposed the idea, telling the children that the pastor of the
church would baptize them; but they had insisted that the young
minister whose preaching had touched their hearts, should perform the ceremony, and they had their way.

There were people in the church who had serious doubts
about the propriety of baptizing children, and some had even
tried to intimidate these lambs of the flock.   " What kind of
experience does Mr. White suppose these babies can tell? " asked
a rigid Baptist minister.   The large schoolhouse was crowded at
the appointed time, and these unfriendly ministers were there
to watch the proceedings.   Elder White had a few seats vacated
in front, and in response to his call twelve boys and girls of
ages running from seven to fifteen years came forward.   He
took for his text the words, " Fear not, little flock; for it is your

Father's good pleasure to give you the kingdom." The children were cheered and comforted by the discourse, and at its close they rose one by one, and by the aid of judicious questions each of them gave evidence of a clear, intelligent experience. When the call was made for any who were opposed to the baptism to rise, no one rose. The children were accordingly led down into the watery grave, and duly presented to their parents with smiles of joy on their young faces.

In the early days of the Seventh-day Adventist denomination, the children at various times had some special labor put forth in their behalf, but the work was more or less irregular and spasmodic. While Elder and Mrs. White were residing at Oswego, N. Y., soon after their marriage, they enjoyed marked success in laboring for the children and youth in the company of believers in that city, and a considerable number dedicated themselves to the service of the Master.

Some years later, when the work was yet in its infancy in Ohio, J. H. Waggoner went to the church at Lovett's Grove, and seeing a good many children, told the leader, Oliver Mears, that something ought to be done for them. Brother Mears thought the matter over, and the next Sabbath told the members what the minister had said. He proposed that every Sabbath, after the regular meeting, prayer should be offered to God, that He would save the children. "Bear the children in your arms to the Saviour," said the good elder, "and may the Lord come in and convert them." After four such meetings for prayer had been held, a little girl stood up and said, "I want to be a child of God." There was not one of those little ones that did not follow. The floodgates were open, and parents and children rejoiced together that the Lord had graciously answered prayer in imparting also to the younger members of the flock a desire to serve Him.

The early camp-meetings afforded excellent opportunities, which some were not slow to improve, of laboring in the interests of the young people. At the beginning the facilities were of the most meager kind. At the camp-meeting held in Lansing, Mich., in 1876, one of the sisters gathered some children together and held a meeting with them while they sat on a large log in the woods. Similar efforts were put forth by others, and valuable personal work was done between the meetings, resulting in the conversion and baptism of a goodly number of young people at all the important camp-meetings. I. D. Van Horn, in his camp-meeting tours in the early eighties, was often asked to conduct meetings for the children, and his tender, heart-to-heart talks on such practical subjects as conversion, repentance, and obedience to God's law are gratefully remembered by not a few men and women of today, whose young feet he directed into the paths of peace.

Perhaps the earliest systematic and thoroughgoing effort in behalf of the children and youth was made at the camp-meeting held in Mankato, Minn., in the summer of 1883. O. A. Olsen, then president of the Minnesota Conference, had especially requested Elder George I. Butler, the president of the General Conference, to bring with him a man who would give special attention to the young people. The man thus brought was R. A. Underwood. Associated with him in the effort was Lewis Johnson, one of the Minnesota laborers. A fifty-foot tent was set apart for the work, and in it these men held meetings daily at 8 A. M. and 5 P. M., devoting the intervening hours largely to personal work for the young people, either individually or in groups of two and three, in retired places in the grove. For a time they also held meetings with the children, but they found so much to do for the youth and young people, that the children were later turned over to some of the sisters, who held suitable services with them.

At the close of the camp-meeting 125 persons were baptized in the Minnesota River, the large majority of the candidates being young people who were making their first start to live the Christian life. From this time onward, meetings for young people and also for the children became a regular feature at all Seventh-day Adventist camp-meetings, and ministers in visiting the various churches took an increasing interest in the welfare of the younger members of the flock.

It was a great boon to the children of the early days when in the summer of 1852 the *Youth's Instructor* began to make its monthly visits to the homes of Seventh-day Adventists. James White had always felt a deep interest in the children; but that summer, while traveling with Mrs. White from Rochester, N. Y., to Bangor, Maine, his mind was especially burdened on the subject, and he determined to provide some form of systematic religious instruction for the children and youth. One day when he and Mrs. White had eaten their luncheon under the trees, he sat down by the roadside and began to write out some Scripture lessons for the children, which duly appeared in the first number of the *Instructor*. " We give four Sabbath school lessons in this number," wrote the author, " one for each week, and hope the parents will establish Sabbath schools even where there are but two or three children in a place. And we expect the children will read the lesson over many times, so as to be able to answer all the questions."

Thus was the Sabbath school work begun in the denomination, and little did any one then realize what dimensions it would take on in later years. In those days each school developed along the lines of its own special needs, and there was not much uniformity. During the long periods when no printed lessons were furnished, the various schools selected certain books of the Bible, and went through them slowly, taking a few verses a week.

Among the schools that earliest developed efficiency during this period when each school had to look out for itself, special mention is due those at Rochester and Buck's Bridge in New York State. John Byington was the leader in the latter school, and he did much to put it on vantage ground. In the year 1855 the Battle Creek Sabbath school began its career. Dr. M. G. Kellogg was the leader who did most for it in those beginning days. It was often an uphill struggle. He says:

"For months the life of this poor weakling of a Sabbath school hung by such a brittle thread that it was a question whether the succeeding Sabbath would find it alive; but by patient perseverance and much strong crying unto God for help, it not only lived, but gradually became a stronger factor for good than I had expected."—"*Early History of the Seventh-day Adventist Sabbath School Work*," by L. Flora Plummer, p. 7.

When Dr. Kellogg left Battle Creek, G. W. Amadon succeeded him as superintendent.

The adult portion of the Sabbath school membership was often called the " Bible Class." Unprovided with lessons or helps of any kind beyond reference Bibles, the members often displayed a zeal and earnestness commensurate with the real importance of the study. William Covert, one of the pioneers in this work, has the following to say of the spirit and methods of the early Sabbath schools:

"It is my mind now that I spent five years in Sabbath school work before regular periodical lessons were provided. In my class we went twice through the books of Daniel and the Revelation, verse by verse, and thought by thought. We had Brother Smith's books on Daniel and the Revelation for reference. We would go as far as we could in one lesson, and next Sabbath begin where we closed the Sabbath before, and thus proceed through an entire book. The average lesson comprised five or six verses. We also studied the book of Romans and the book of Hebrews, and others of the epistles, in the same way.

"I enjoyed our Sabbath school study then as much as ever in my life. We had reference Bibles, and brought in kindred matter that we found in other parts of the Scriptures to help us understand that particular part that we were using for the lesson. In fact, it was a regular Bible study week by week, month by month, and year by year, with us then. I became so engaged in my Sabbath school study that I often remained up nights till

21

ten or eleven, and possibly sometimes till midnight, to be sure that I should have a good lesson. Much of the time I was a teacher, and I felt that I must make the lessons a real blessing to the class. The five years that I spent in this way laid the basis for my Bible education, and then I was asked to enter upon the work of the ministry. The request was largely due to the study that I had given to the Bible in our Sabbath school.

" In those times we made no Sabbath offerings. Parents and friends provided themselves and their children with such helps as we used, without mentioning the matter of expense to the school. We did but little reviewing, but spent more time in our lesson recitation and study than we do now. Our opening exercises were one song and a prayer, and the report of what the lesson had been the previous Sabbath; this probably occupied fifteen minutes, and then we would spend about forty-five minutes with the lesson. If we visited churches, we had to find out what that church was studying and where the Sabbath school lesson was to be found for that church. We had no uniformity in the matter, each school did what it thought was for its best interest."— *Id., pp. 8, 9.*

It was hardest for the children in those days, for the teaching was so often beyond them. In many Sabbath schools the children's tasks consisted chiefly of learning and reciting portions of Scripture, and into this exercise they entered heartily. Often the brighter ones would recite in a clear voice and without making a single mistake from twenty-five to fifty verses. They seemed to enjoy the exercise, and there was some good-natured rivalry in attempting to learn the largest number of texts. The early efforts to provide instruction for the children were not very successful. In one school, lessons were arranged to begin with Genesis, taking several chapters each Sabbath; in another school the book of Revelation was selected for old and young, and it was reported that the children " were pleasantly entertained with this wonderful book."

But better days were coming for the children. Lesson books were to be supplied in time, that would be not only highly instructive, but also attractive, because adapted to the needs of the child mind. The history of lesson making may be given briefly. Thirty-six lessons appeared in the first volume of the *Instructor*, nineteen being original and seventeen selected. Then there was a series of eight lessons on the sanctuary, after which none were supplied for a period of eight months. Then there appeared a series of fifty-two lessons prepared by R. F. Cottrell, covering the most essential features of the denominational belief. These lessons, appearing first in the *Instructor*, were afterward issued in book form, under the name, " The Bible Class." Two thousand copies were published in 1855. Then for several years no fresh lessons were issued.

In 1863 a series of thirty-two lessons adapted for use in advanced classes was published in the *Review and Herald*. The questions in these lessons were based upon the books, " Thoughts on Daniel," by Uriah Smith, and " History of the Sabbath," by J. N. Andrews.

In 1869 Prof. G. H. Bell prepared two series of lessons, which appeared in the *Instructor*, lessons from the Old Testament beginning with creation week, for the children, and studies on the book of Daniel, for the youth. Out of these Professor Bell developed the series of " Progressive Bible Lessons." These were the first steps toward classification.

These lessons were the beginning of the extended series in the form of books of fifty-two lessons each, which briefly covered the whole Bible history from Genesis to Revelation. The series of eight books, all by Professor Bell, were in general use throughout the denomination for many years. They did much to interest the children in the Bible, and made them familiar with the foundation truths of revelation.

In 1868 and 1869 there also came into most of the Sabbath schools of the denomination a more effective organization. Superintendents, secretaries, and other officers began to be appointed for definite terms, teachers were made to feel a larger sense of responsibility, and pupils were more carefully classified. A regular program was provided. Beginning with the year 1870, the *Instructor* was issued semimonthly, and its more frequent visits helped to build up the Sabbath schools.

Under Professor Bell's inspiring leadership the Sabbath school in Battle Creek, Mich., attained a rare degree of efficiency as an agency for training the mental as well as the moral and spiritual faculties. The method of recitation had all the system and formality of a day school. Not only was a strict record kept of the attendance, but the scholarship also was noted. The test of perfection, in the words of one of the students, was the giving of a clear, connected synopsis of the entire lesson from beginning to end. This synopsis must be given without any prompting from the instructor, and in good English. Another exercise consisted in letting one pupil begin the synopsis, another carry it a little farther, and a third or fourth carry it to the end, the instructor indicating just how far each should go, and then calling on another member to continue. Unless the pupil could take part without hesitation in such a recitation, his scholarship was not perfect.

But while the Sabbath school flourished in places like Battle Creek, where gifted and consecrated leaders had charge of the work, in most places it was not on a firm foundation, and its importance was but dimly recognized. When a minister came

around, it was considered quite proper to omit the Sabbath
school exercises entirely, and the work done was sometimes so
weak that not a great deal was lost. It must be said to the
honor of James White that he strongly opposed the practice of
allowing the Sabbath school to give way to the preacher. He
said:

"We here enter a solemn protest against the course of some of our
preachers and some of our churches in suffering the Sabbath school to be
set aside on those Sabbaths when the church is favored with the labors of
a minister. This should never be. This is the very time to strike a blow in
favor of the school. And not only should the Sabbath school be held at the
usual time in the morning, but the minister should be there on time to a
minute, to set an example for the entire school. . . . He should lift just
where superintendent and teachers should be lifting. And if they are not
lifting at the right points, he should be prepared to instruct them properly."
— Id., pp. 11, 12.

Plans were adopted in the summer of 1877 that very materially advanced the interests of the Sabbath school work. It all
came about very quietly. One evening Professor Bell, then superintendent of the Battle Creek school, asked the teachers who
were assembled at the home of W. C. White, whether they
thought it feasible to develop an organization which would bring
all the Sabbath schools of a State together for mutual helpfulness
and support. The outcome of the suggestion was the appointment of a committee which drafted plans for a State Sabbath
School Association. These plans having been communicated to
them, the members on the Pacific Coast gave their approval,
and forthwith organized, in the month of August, 1877, the California State Sabbath School Association. A few weeks later
a similar organization was formed in Michigan, and immediately
entered upon its work.

When the General Conference convened in Battle Creek in
March, 1878, there was held in connection with it a meeting of
Sabbath school representatives, at which a constitution was
adopted for a General Sabbath School Association. At the next
session of the association, held the following October, it was reported that twelve State associations had been formed.

The question of taking offerings at the weekly meetings of
the schools received some consideration at the association meeting in October, 1878. A few doubted the propriety of receiving
money on the Sabbath day, but the majority decided in favor
of the offerings, and a resolution was passed, asking teachers
and pupils to contribute a penny or more weekly.

At the close of the year 1878 the first combined statistical
report of the Sabbath schools was issued. It reads as follows:

	No. of Schools	Membership	Attendance
Michigan	43	1,753	1,227
Missouri	14	412	230
Minnesota	12	673	344
Illinois	16	482	314
New England	16	396	281
New York	7	231	145
Iowa	16	679	410
Totals	124	4,626	2,951

—"*Early History of the Seventh-day Adventist Sabbath School Work*," by L. Flora Plummer, p. 15.

At the second annual meeting of the General Association, held in the latter part of 1879, it was reported as a further evidence of progress that a Sabbath school had been conducted at every camp-meeting held that summer and autumn. The announcements of these camp-meeting schools are quite prominent in the *Review*. Here is a typical one:

"There will be a grand Sabbath school exercise in the big tent on the Ohio camp-ground at 9 A. M. Sabbath morning. Every person on the camp-ground will be invited to take part in these exercises; hence let all come prepared to do so. The lessons for the day will be the regular lessons in the *Instructor*. The infants' division will recite Lesson VI, ' Beasts, Creeping Things, and Man,' in ' Bible Lessons for Little Ones.' Let the children give this lesson in story form, commencing at the first, and telling all about it without being questioned.

"We shall expect the members of each division to give a synopsis of their lessons for a general exercise. For a concert exercise, the school will repeat the books of the Bible in their order."— *Ibid.*

The year 1885 is a memorable one in the annals of the Sabbath school as witnessing two important advanced steps: First, the *Sabbath School Worker* was established as a quarterly. Second, the Upper Columbia Conference took action at a session held at Milton, Oreg., in favor of using all the Sabbath school offerings for missions. The small sum of money for missions supplied in this way was increased by a gift of $700 from the California schools, the money being devoted to the Australian field, where work had just been started. In 1886 the name of the general organization was changed to the International Sabbath School Association, and in the following year the association adopted the plan of giving to missions the surplus donations. During that year, the needs of Africa were presented to the schools, and a gift of more than $10,615 was raised to begin operations at the first African mission station.

The *Instructor* began to be issued as a weekly in 1878, and at a meeting of the executive committee of the International

Sabbath School Association held in November, 1889, it was voted to request the Pacific Press Publishing Company to issue a child's paper which should contain Sabbath school lessons for the little children, and also helpful reading matter of a general kind suited to their needs. The first number of the paper thus called for, named *Our Little Friend,* appeared on the 4th of

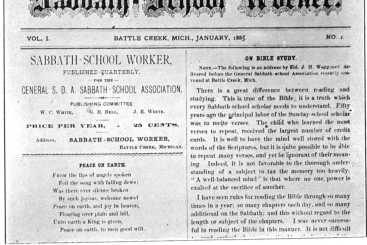

FIRST NUMBER OF THE *WORKER*

July, 1890, the editorial committee being W. N. Glenn, Jessie F. Waggoner, and Fannie Bolton. It had only four pages to begin with; but it met with instant favor, and has ever since continued to furnish lessons for the primary pupils.

The smaller children thus being provided with weekly lessons, there began to be expressed on the part of some a desire to have lessons for the older children in periodical form instead of in book form, as had been the custom. After due deliberation the executive committee made the recommendation that senior and intermediate divisions study the same subject, but that the lessons for the intermediate division be prepared by a different writer and adapted to the special needs of the youth. Beginning with January, 1891, the schools very generally recognized three divisions,— senior, intermediate, and primary,— and studied lessons respectively in the *Lesson Quarterly, Youth's Instructor,* and *Our Little Friend.* In course of time there came to be two grades of lessons in *Our Little Friend,* known as the first and second primary.

At the same time it was suggested that where it was possible to provide for it, another division be formed for children five years of age and under, to be known as the kindergarten. The beginning of this division really dates back considerably farther.

FIRST NUMBER OF *OUR LITTLE FRIEND*

Already in the late seventies some provision began to be made for this class of members. The problem was most successfully solved in the school at Battle Creek. About 1878 the attendance in that church of very small children became so large that it was necessary to make special arrangements for their instruction. They were, accordingly, brought together first in the northeast entrance of the gallery of the Tabernacle, and later in the south vestry on the first floor.

No printed lessons being provided for these children, teachers were selected who could prepare oral lessons from the simplest stories of the Bible, the lessons being illustrated with bright crayon drawings on large sheets of paper. After a time Lillian Affolter, a trained kindergarten teacher, was elected superintendent of the division, and began to develop lessons for the children, which she would go over with the teachers each week, thus bringing uniformity into the work. Under her care the division was organized in 1886 into a regular department of the school. The lessons that she prepared, together with the songs used, were published as a kindergarten book entitled, " Bible Object Lessons and Songs for Little Ones," coming out in the year 1892.

The program followed by the earliest Sabbath schools provided for no reviews. Little by little the custom came in of conducting a general review of the day's lesson before the whole school, after the individual classes had gone through it. This custom was followed for a long time. About 1890 some leading Sabbath school workers tried the plan of conducting first a review of the previous Sabbath's lesson, so as to get an advantageous approach to the lesson of the day. This latter plan in time prevailed.

Sabbath school officers were at first elected once in three months. At the meeting of the International Society held in 1893, it was definitely recommended that the term of office be extended to six months. The schools were not slow in adopting the plan, and it prevailed generally till the year 1915. Since that time Sabbath school officers, by recommendation of the General Department, hold office in most of the schools for one year.

The first envelopes prepared especially for Sabbath school contributions were used in 1893. They were of heavy manila paper, and contained an announcement that the contributions for that year would be given to India. For several years, envelopes of this kind were issued from time to time, each for the benefit of a certain mission field.

Quite a succession of song books represent the growing needs of the schools. The first specially prepared book, the " Song Anchor," was published in 1878. It contained 150 pages of songs, new and selected, and was a great boon to the Sabbath schools, which, previous to its appearance, had been obliged to use the denominational hymn book or introduce some Sunday school book. For some eight years it was universally used in the Sabbath schools of the denomination. " Joyful Greetings," compiled by J. E. White, appeared in 1886. The " Gospel Song Sheaf," by F. E. Belden, was published in 1895. " Christ in Song " first appeared in 1900. It was a larger and more varied collection than any of the others, and has continued in general use ever since.

The *Sabbath School Worker,* probably the largest single factor in the building up of the work, has had to fight for its existence. Sometimes it has for the time being fought a losing battle, but in the long run it has come off victorious. Beginning as a quarterly in 1885, at 25 cents a year, it had a list of 1,800 subscribers at the end of the first volume. Nevertheless the association decided at its meeting in the autumn of 1886, "that the matter now contained in the *Worker* be published in the *Instructor*, in the form of a monthly or quarterly supplement, as the editors may find necessary." The new plan was not satisfactory, however; so the *Worker* was resuscitated. It came out in January, 1889, as a sixteen-page quarterly, being published at Oakland, Calif. In the following year the increasing interest in the Sabbath school work called for a monthly, and the *Worker* was raised to that status, its price being changed to 50 cents. It has continued in this form, with a steadily increasing influence, up to the present time, barring a period of two years following shortly after the General Conference of 1901, during which time it was merged with the educational magazine.

An account of the Sabbath schools of the early days would not be complete without some reference to the home schools, of which there were a goodly number, and some of which especially had very fruitful careers. In the late sixties a fairly well-to-do brother failed in business, and lost all. He went west with his wife and four children, and began over again. There was one other believer in the neighborhood, an elderly sister. These seven persons organized and carried on for years a home Sabbath school. A minister calling on them thought to propose studying the lesson with them on Sabbath morning; but their studying had all been done during the week. When nine o'clock came, every one was in his place, and the school proceeded with the same order and deliberation as if there had been a membership of five hundred. Needless to say, all four children grew up in the love of the Bible, and one of them became a successful minister.

In another neighborhood where there was no church, two or three families met together in the capacity of a Sabbath school. As the neighbors became interested, they joined, and the school increased in interest and enthusiasm. Out of this Sabbath school have come three ordained ministers, several efficient canvassers, and five foreign missionaries.

Following the reorganizing of various denominational activities at the General Conference of 1901, the Sabbath school entered upon a new and very fruitful phase of its history, in the course of which it came to exert a still more powerful influence on the denomination, especially as regards the successful financeering of extensive mission enterprises. Some account of these developments will be given in a later chapter.

GEORGE I. BUTLER

President of the General Conference, 1871 to 1874, and 1880 to 1888.

G. H. BELL   SIDNEY BROWNSBERGER

CHAPTER XVI

Christian Education

THE subject of Christian education early engaged the attention of the believers in the advent message. At the time of the disappointment in 1844 and after, the children of Adventists were subjected to not a little petty persecution on the part of their schoolmates, who would call them " Millerites," ask them when they were " going up," and otherwise taunt them. Later the keeping of the Sabbath made a wall of separation between the children of Adventists and those of their neighbors, and caused the former to be regarded with unfriendly eyes.

But apart from these annoyances, the parents felt in their hearts that the spirit of the education given in the public schools did not harmonize with the spirit of the movement with which they were connected. That education was to prepare for the world; they wished their children prepared for heaven. Nevertheless, education of some kind was essential. Most Adventists sent their children to the public schools, but tried in various ways to counteract the evil influences to which they were subjected.

Some feeble attempts were made to provide denominational schools. In Battle Creek, which in those early days had one of the strongest churches, a private school was started by Louise M. Morton, a woman of some education, who also wrote for the magazines. She conducted the school in the second church building, which had been erected in 1857, and charged a tuition fee of 25 cents a week for each pupil. The school was a fair success as long as it was carried on; but the teacher went away, and the school was closed. Somewhat later elementary instruction was given in a kitchen in the same neighborhood, with about a dozen pupils. Still later J. F. Byington conducted a school of some size in the church. But nothing enduring in the way of a denominational educational institution was provided until the matter was taken in hand by Prof. G. H. Bell. The arrival of this remarkable man in Battle Creek may be said to have marked the beginning of our educational work.

Professor Bell, like other leaders in the denominational work, was of New England ancestry, both his father and his mother being descended from Revolutionary stock. His people moved west, and settled near Watertown in northern New York, and there he was born in April, 1832, the eldest of a family of twelve children. Later the family moved to Oberlin, Ohio, where the son took some studies at the well-known college of that name. His work was reluctantly broken off when other removals took the family to Hillsdale and finally to Grand Rapids, Mich. In spite of poor school advantages, the young man by earnest, persistent application made good progress in his studies, and continued to cherish the hope of one day going to college; but the death of his father, leaving him to shoulder the chief burden in caring for the large family of brothers and sisters, made such a thing impossible. He continued to improve his time, however, and at the age of nineteen took charge of his first country school. The young man's ability as a teacher won early recognition, and it was not long before he was filling good positions in some of the best schools of the State.

He first went to Battle Creek in 1866, in the company of a friend who sought relief for some physical ailment at the recently founded Western Health Institute. The next year he went on a similar errand himself, his health having suffered from prolonged overwork and a lack of knowledge of physical laws. While staying in Battle Creek, he not unnaturally became interested in the doctrinal beliefs of Seventh-day Adventists. His earliest denominational affiliations had been with the Baptists. Later he had joined the Disciples, believing them to be possessed of advanced truth. For similar reasons, after thoroughly investigating every point of doctrine and comparing it with the plain teaching of the Bible, he finally entered the Seventh-day Adventist communion, of which he continued a consistent member to the time of his death.

His school had a modest beginning. While engaged for the sake of his health in light outdoor labor on the sanitarium grounds, he was very companionable with the boys of the neighborhood, who occasionally consulted him about their lessons, and invariably found his suggestions extremely helpful. Presently the sons of Elder James White, Edson and Willie, told their

ANOTHER LANDMARK

The old building where Professor Bell conducted his first school in Battle Creek, Mich.

parents that Mr. Bell's explanations of difficult problems in arithmetic or puzzling constructions in grammar were a great deal more convincing than those given by their teachers, and asked why they could not take lessons of him instead of going to the public school. Other people heard of Professor Bell's genius as a teacher, and he was encouraged to start a school, and did so, conducting it at first in a cottage on Washington Avenue near the sanitarium. As the attendance increased, the school was moved to a frame building that had served as the first printing office, the teacher using the lower story as a home for himself and his family, while he conducted his classes on the upper floor. The school was a pronounced success from the start. The instruction was at once sympathetic and thoroughgoing; the children made rapid progress, and enjoyed their work,

Meanwhile the denomination, urged on by the representations of Elder and Mrs. White and other leaders, was gradually coming to realize the need of an educational institution of larger scope for the preparation of workers. An editorial note appeared on the last page of the *Review,* dated April 16, 1872, which plainly set forth the reasons why such an institution was necessary, and called for an expression of opinion on the part of the constituency. It also invited prospective students to write in, giving information concerning the extent of their acquirements, and indicating what subjects they wished to pursue. In the *Review* of May 7 a further article appeared, explaining more fully the nature of the proposed institution, and in the issue of June 4 G. I. Butler, then president of the General Conference, strongly commended the new enterprise to the consideration of all the members. He fully believed it to be in the order of God that a school should be started in Battle Creek in connection with the other institutions growing up there, and he expected to see " this comparatively small beginning [the school carried on by G. H. Bell, which had opened under General Conference auspices June 3] amount to something very important before the message shall close." He continued:

" We want a school to be controlled by our people, where influences of a moral character may be thrown around the pupils which will tend to preserve them from those influences which are so common and injurious in the majority of the schools of the present day; and in this school we want a department in which those who would labor in the ministry, or in other public positions of usefulness, may receive that instruction which will qualify them for the duties of those positions."— *Review and Herald, June 4, 1872, pp. 196, 197.*

The subject was discussed at the camp-meetings that summer, as well as in the current numbers of the *Review,* and at the General Conference convening at Battle Creek, March 11, 1873, the following resolution was passed:

" *Resolved,* That while it becomes our duty to pray to the Lord of the harvest to send forth laborers, we also regard it as our duty to establish a school, guarded by sound moral and religious influence, where those who give themselves to the work of the Lord may discipline their minds to study, and at least qualify themselves to read, speak, and write the English language correctly; where our people can send their sons and daughters with comparative safety; and where men and women may study those languages especially now spoken by the people of those nations from whom we hope to gather a harvest of souls to the Lord."— *Review and Herald, March 11, 1873, p. 108.*

It was further —

" *Resolved,* That the establishment of the school be placed in the hands of the General Conference Committee."— *Ibid.*

During the summer and autumn the work of raising means for the necessary buildings went forward vigorously, able articles appearing in the *Review* from time to time, in order to keep the subject continually before the constituency.

At the next session of the General Conference, held Nov. 16, 1873, the committee that had the matter in charge was able to report pledges already in hand to the amount of $54,000. The conference thereupon appointed a committee of seven to organize an educational society and secure a site for the main building. The committee consisted of the following persons: George I. Butler, James White, S. N. Haskell, Harmon Lindsay, Ira Abbey, J. N. Andrews, and Uriah Smith.

A plot of twelve acres of land, the home of a wealthy Quaker, on Washington Avenue in the " West End " of Battle Creek, was purchased Dec. 31, 1873, as a site for the proposed institution. Seven acres were retained for the college campus, the remaining five being cut off in two strips on the south and west sides, to be used largely for the homes of members of the faculty. Legal organization was effected in March, 1874, the committee of seven incorporating as " The Educational Society of the Seventh-day Adventists," and in the course of the summer and fall a three-story brick building, in the form of a Greek cross, was erected on the spot from which the former residence had been removed.

In the meantime, while these preparations were under way to provide suitable accommodations for the new institution, the school itself was conducted in temporary quarters, with a steadily increasing interest and attendance.

On June 3, 1872, G. H. Bell, who had been engaged in private teaching for several years, opened a school under the auspices of the General Conference Committee. It met in the frame building already mentioned, which had been the first home of the publishing association. There were twelve pupils present on the opening day, and the number soon increased to twenty-five. Somewhat later an evening grammar class of fifty pupils was organized. When the fall term began, September 12, the attendance was so large that the school had to be moved to the church building, which it occupied for more than a year. With the opening of the fall term of 1873, the management of the school passed into the hands of Sidney Brownsberger, a graduate of the University of Michigan, and a successful teacher of ten years' experience.

At the opening of the winter term, Dec. 15, 1873, the school, having an enrolment of 110, was removed to the new third building of the Review and Herald office, which had just been completed. Steam-heated and provided with desks, it was a decided improvement over the church, which was very inadequately warmed by two stoves. With the opening of the third term G. H. Bell resumed his connection with the school as head of the English department.

BATTLE CREEK COLLEGE
First building, erected in 1874.

In December, 1874, the school was transferred to the new building, with rooms for the science department in the basement, study and recitation rooms on the first and second floors, and a large chapel and assembly room on the third floor. The new building was dedicated Jan. 3, 1875.

School had been in session only two or three weeks when a severe frost burst the boiler, making it necessary for teachers and students to return to their previous quarters in the Review office till the advent of warm weather, when repairs to the boiler could be safely made.

Various suggestions were made as to a name for the new institution. Some urged that it be named James White College, in honor of the man who had done so much to bring it into existence. The name finally adopted was Battle Creek College.

In the early years of the institution there were no dormitories, and students made their own arrangements for board and room. Quite a number found homes with members of the Battle Creek church, the usual charge being $2.50 a week for board, room, and plain washing. Students whose means were very limited usually boarded themselves, their food costing them from fifty cents to a dollar a week. In the course of time some of these students began to club together so as to enjoy some social privileges. The club rate for room and board was usually $1.50 a week when there were two in a room. The membership of some of the clubs grew very large, employees of the Review office often joining them in order to cut expenses.

Meanwhile the members of the board and the faculty, while grateful for what had been accomplished, regretted that the students were so largely subject to outside influences except while attending lectures and recitations. They desired also to carry out more fully the instruction given through Mrs. White, to the effect that useful labor with the hands should be combined with book study in such a way as to give a symmetrical, all-round training.

Influenced partly by these considerations and partly on account of poor health, Professor Brownsberger resigned his position in the spring of 1881, having given eight years of efficient service. He was succeeded by Prof. Alexander McLearn. The new president had but a limited knowledge of the Adventist belief, including education, and was therefore unable to develop the school on the essential principles to which the denomination had dedicated it. Prof. G. H. Bell, the real founder of the school, did all he could to uphold the high ideals of earlier years. By the spring of 1882 the lack of harmony between these two strong-minded men brought about a situation in the faculty and student body that was working disaster to the interests of the college.

George I. Butler, president of the General Conference, with S. N. Haskell and J. H. Kellogg, who were also on the board, stanchly upheld the views of Professor Bell, who was contending for the foundation principles for which the college had been brought into being, and gave him their hearty support; but in

22

view of the very unfortunate situation that had been created, Professor Bell thought it best to resign. When the institution opened its doors again, in the autumn of 1883, although it was once more established on a right basis, with W. H. Littlejohn as president, the former head of the English department, to the great loss of the school and the regret of all its well-wishers, did not rejoin the faculty, his talents being brought into requisition for laying the foundations of another educational institution.

HEALDSBURG COLLEGE

It is an interesting fact that the school year of 1882-83, during which the doors of Battle Creek College remained closed, witnessed the founding by the denomination of two new schools, — South Lancaster Academy in the East, and Healdsburg College in the Far West. The latter, situated in Healdsburg, Calif., was the earlier by a few days. It opened its doors, April 11, 1882, and had an enrolment during its first year of 152 students. Work was begun in a ten-room house. In the course of the first school year the institution was started as a college. An additional five-acre lot was bought, and a commodious dormitory erected. About $27,000 was raised for the purpose, mostly in California. Sidney Brownsberger, who had been recuperating his health in northern Michigan, was called to the presidency of this school, and served in that capacity for five years.

In taking charge of this second educational institution of the denomination, Professor Brownsberger was able to draw on his previous experience at Battle Creek. Especially did he desire to carry out more fully the instruction that had been given concerning the combining of physical with mental labor.

In the early period of Healdsburg College, gardening, horticulture, carpentry, printing, and tent-making were among the industries carried on, and while this part of the school work at times lacked the supervision of highly skilled instructors, it was taken up with enthusiasm by the pupils, and entered into their building of a symmetrical character.

The general interest taken by the leaders of the denomination in the industrial phase of education, may be gathered from the action taken at the session of the Educational Association held in connection with the General Conference which was convened at Oakland, Calif., in the autumn of 1887.

The committee on resolutions at that time brought in recommendations, which were unanimously adopted, approving the increased facilities that had been provided during the previous year for work in industrial lines, and urging that further efforts be made in the same direction, and such advanced steps taken as experience might indicate necessary. It was further recommended that a pamphlet be prepared for general circulation, setting forth the advantages of manual training in the education of our youth, and removing misconceptions in regard to it.

At this same meeting Mrs. E. G. White gave a short address, in which she bore positive testimony to the value of the manual training department, saying that, in comparing the profit and loss of the work, it should be estimated, not upon a mere money basis, but in the light of the judgment. She enlarged upon the importance of a symmetrical education. The physical powers should be taxed as well as the mental. Parents should not be permitted to have their children excused from physical labor; for to neglect education in the practical duties of life is wholly to unfit the individual for the responsibilities of home making.

South Lancaster Academy was opened to students on the 19th of April, 1882, under the principalship of G. H. Bell. There were only eight pupils present on the opening day, but by the end of the first week there were eighteen, and this number increased to twenty-four before the close of the term. At this school, also, industrial training was undertaken, and the principles of Christian education were carried out with conscientious care. Manual labor at the beginning had to be carried on by means of ax and saw. A huge supply of cordwood was piled up in an adjoining lot, and morning after morning, by lantern light in winter, the boys were busy cutting it into stove lengths. The woodpile helped not a few of those early students to pay their way through school. Later on, harness-making, printing, cobbling, and broom-making were all taught, and every young

SOUTH LANCASTER ACADEMY

man was required to make himself reasonably proficient in one or another of these handicrafts.

The general character of the work carried on at South Lancaster is briefly sketched in a report of a meeting held in the interests of the school in the autumn following its opening, at which Professor Bell explained the principles followed:

" The speaker proceeded to show that the popular method of filling the student's mind with that which is not practical, and hurrying him through a certain course in order that he may obtain a diploma, is not true education. True education begins on the inside, at the core, with that which is practical. It builds up and strengthens a symmetry of character that, by and by, in after-life, will show itself in some grand, good, and noble work for the world. The school at South Lancaster seeks to attain to this ideal. The teachers at this school have experienced that study and physical labor must be intermingled in order to make a good school. Hence the time of the students there is divided into labor, study, and recitation hours; and the best of results are seen, both as to physical health, mental discipline, and progress in study."

The school at South Lancaster was first held in what had once been a carriage house, but was later used, first as a church, then as a tract society office. It measured only 20 x 25 feet, so it became necessary to furnish additional room even during the first term. The school was also conducted for a time in the

STUDENTS' HOME, SOUTH LANCASTER, MASS.

South Lancaster church building. Meanwhile S. N. Haskell had been raising money in the field, and by the autumn of 1884 a new academy building, 60 x 65 feet, and a students' dormitory, 36 x 88 feet, were ready for dedication.

Professor Bell continued in charge of the academy for about two years, being succeeded as principal by D. A. Robinson, who in turn was succeeded by C. C. Ramsay. In 1888 G. W. Caviness came from Iowa to take the principalship. During his term of service, covering six years, the school made a substantial growth in efficiency, while a very general interest in the principles of Christian education was awakened throughout the constituency. J. H. Haughey, Frederick Griggs, B. F. Machlan, and C. S. Longacre occupied the position of principal in succession following Professor Caviness, and under their guidance the institution continued to prosper. Sarah J. Hall, who succeeded

Professor Bell as head of the English department, occupied that position with distinction until her death, twenty-six years later.

Meanwhile the central college at Battle Creek had been training a goodly number of promising students. It, too, had developed industrial departments of the same general character as those at Healdsburg and South Lancaster, but it had given more attention to the college studies.

SOUTH LANCASTER FACULTY, 1884

In the autumn of 1885 W. H. Littlejohn was succeeded as president by W. W. Prescott, of North Berwick, Maine, a graduate of Dartmouth College. After completing his college course, Professor Prescott had taught for some years in the public schools, and at the time of his call to Battle Creek he was conducting a publishing business in Montpelier, Vt. He brought to his work not only a liberal education and good administrative ability, but high ideals of Christian service. During his ten years' term of office, Battle Creek College made rapid advancement both in numbers and in efficiency. Before that time there had been good individual teaching, but under his fostering care the work of the institution was unified and strengthened, and the whole brought up to a high level of efficiency.

As a result of the steadily increasing attendance it had been necessary to provide additional buildings. The first dormitory, known as South Hall, was erected in 1884. Two years later, in the summer of 1886, a large addition was made to the main building on the south, and in 1887 a handsome brick dormitory, known as West Hall, was put up for the use of lady students, South Hall thereafter being used exclusively to provide accom-

BATTLE CREEK COLLEGE
At the time of its greatest growth and prosperity

modations for the young men. In the early winter a further large addition was made to the main building on the north.

In the year 1887 Professor Prescott was made secretary of the Educational Department of the General Conference, and began to devote his energies to building up the denomination's educational interests throughout the country. In this work he was very successful. The reports that he made from time to time to the General Conference, and the addresses delivered at camp-meetings and other large gatherings, created a widespread interest in Christian education, and really marked the beginning of a denominational program for the young people. The new schools which arose in course of time, and the further working out of the educational ideals of the denomination, will be taken up in a later chapter.

JOHN G. MATTESON

FIRST HEADQUARTERS BUILDING IN SCANDINAVIA
Purchased by Elder Matteson at Christiania, Norway, in 1878.

CHAPTER XVII

The Scandinavian Mission

IT fell to the lot of a little company of Norwegians in southern Wisconsin to form the first church of foreigners organized by Seventh-day Adventists. The story takes us back to the middle of the nineteenth century. In the spring of 1850 Andrew Olsen and Ole Hegland Serns, small farmers living near Christiansand, in southern Norway, emigrated with their families to America. They came, not as many others, to better their financial condition, but in the vague hope that in this new land of promise would be found the spiritual light that their souls longed for. For years they had felt oppressed by what they deemed an increasing coldness and formality in the Lutheran Church, and had longed for something better. More recently they had also come to feel, partly through some words accidentally dropped by evangelists of the Society of Friends who had held meetings in their neighborhood, that the doctrines taught by the state church were not in harmony with the Scriptures. Especially did they question the validity of Sunday observance in view of the plain statement of the Bible that the seventh day is the Sabbath.

345

Troubled by these and other doubts, and eagerly hoping for light and truth, they set their faces westward, and after a long voyage in one of the sailing vessels of those days, supplemented by travel by river steamer, canal boat, and lake steamer, and finally by ox team, they found themselves in a wooded section of country in the township of Oakland, Jefferson County, Wisconsin, some seventy miles west of Milwaukee, then the nearest railway town.

Here they found partial relief from their spiritual troubles by joining the Methodist Church. The Methodism of those early times was an advance on Lutheranism as they had known it in the Old Country; it was more charged with vital godliness, more devout, more brotherly. Nevertheless, the new immigrants were not entirely satisfied with Methodism. They felt that there was wanting that perfect loyalty to the teachings of Holy Writ which they had hoped to find in the church that would be after the apostolic order. Especially were they troubled over the Sabbath question. When the minister, praying in church on Sunday morning, would call that day the holy Sabbath, it seemed to them that he was striking a false note. The solemn words of Scripture rang in their ears, " The seventh day is the Sabbath of the Lord thy God; in it thou shalt not do any work."

Feelings and convictions of a similar character were cherished also by the heads of two other families, Tarel Johnson and Sören Loe, who had come from the same district in Norway in the year 1849, settling first in Illinois, but later joining their friends in Oakland, Wis. They had also become members of the Methodist Church, and were troubled with the same doubts. These last-named families, moreover, had made the acquaintance of Gustav Melberg, a Swede, who was observing the Sabbath.

All four families finally decided to settle the matter in question by a prayerful study of the Word, determined, if they found that the Bible taught the sacredness of the seventh day, to step out and obey the commandment even though it should involve the severing of their church connections. This decision was arrived at toward the end of the year 1854, and the proposed period of prayer and searching of the Scriptures was continued during the whole of the winter. With the arrival of spring they reached their decision, and held their first Sabbath meeting about Easter time in the house of Andrew Olsen, there being present, besides his own family, Sören Loe and his wife, thus making four adults. Tarel Johnson and Andrew Serns had already begun to observe the day, but were not at this meeting.

These four families stepped out to keep the Bible Sabbath, and thus formed the first group of Sabbath-keeping Scandinavians in America. The Methodist Church disfellowshiped them on the ground of heresy, and they experienced much opposition from their former brethren; which, however, only confirmed them in the position they had taken. Within two and one-half years, the original number had doubled, and eight families in that quiet rural community were joyfully keeping the day set apart by Jehovah.

But now more truth was to come to the little band of believers. On a Sunday early in 1858 some of the younger members, who could understand English, heard a sermon on immersion, given in the neighborhood, and reported it to the others. There followed another period of earnest Bible study, after which the company, with ranks somewhat depleted, took its stand definitely in favor of adult baptism by immersion. This new step, while it occasioned the loss of some of the original members, brought in a few new ones, and all pressed forward a united band, determined to follow the Bible in all matters of doctrine.

About this time the little company of Norwegian Sabbath keepers came to the notice of the Adventist believers in Koshkonong, a settlement near by, as a result of which Waterman Phelps, one of their preachers then living near Hebron, came over in April, 1858, and began meetings in the neighborhood. Progress was a little slow at the first; for the preacher knew not a word of Norwegian, while most of the adults understood little or no English, and there was no interpreter. But those who did know a little whispered what they could understand to those who sat near them. The result was apparent confusion; but the minister was patient and the people eager to learn. Thus the main points of his discourses were eventually understood, with the result that almost the entire company accepted the message. The month of May witnessed the first baptism, Andrew Olsen and his wife going forward with others in the ordinance. Further baptisms followed at fairly frequent intervals, and in the last week of that year a number of the young people, among them Ole Andres, the eldest son of Andrew Olsen, followed the example of their parents, and were formally numbered with the company of believers.

Much patient labor was put forth by Waterman Phelps, and the company was fully established on the foundation of Bible truth. It was organized as a Seventh-day Adventist church in December, 1861, by Isaac Sanborn and W. S. Ingraham, and came to be known as the Oakland church. Elder Phelps was present, but would not himself become a member, being opposed to organization. Not long after that he ceased to labor in the ministry.

In 1864 it was decided to build a church on a plot of ground centrally located, donated by Andrew Olsen. The building is still in use, though by far the greater portion of the charter members rest under the sod of the churchyard. Three of the families, namely, the Olsens, Johnsons, and Sernses, have contributed eight sons to the Adventist ministry, while the youngest of the Olsen daughters sleeps in a missionary's grave in South Africa.

As soon as they had themselves embraced the truth, the company of believers at Oakland began to pray most earnestly for a minister who could carry the message to their countrymen. God answered their prayers. In the early autumn of 1863, the message reached a young Baptist preacher, John G. Matteson, of Poysippi, Wis., who had come to this country from Denmark. He was first interested in the subject of Christ's second coming by reading First-day Adventist literature. Then he read some numbers of the *Review and Herald* lent him by P. H. Cady, of the Poysippi Seventh-day Adventist church. The thoughtful perusal of these papers made him a Seventh-day Adventist. Late in the autumn he walked forty miles to attend the quarterly meeting of the Mackford church. On returning to Poysippi, he devoted some months to preaching the truth to the members of his congregation in that town, where from thirty to forty began to observe the Sabbath, this being the next oldest Sabbath-keeping Scandinavian church in America. Somewhat later, in the summer of 1864, he visited the believers at Oakland, and great was the joy of the Scandinavians there to hear for the first time the third angel's message preached in their own tongue.

The next four years Elder Matteson spent in traveling and preaching, mostly among the Scandinavians of Wisconsin and Minnesota, where as a result of his labors a goodly number of churches were raised up, as well as many scattered Sabbath keepers. Later he labored also in Iowa and Illinois. In 1870 he received a letter from a Scandinavian in Chicago, inviting him to come to that city and preach on the second coming of Christ. He accepted the invitation, and found a company of interested persons, who hired a hall for him in the neighborhood of Milwaukee and Alston Avenues, and had the meetings advertised in the Scandinavian papers. The attendance was small, but those who came seemed deeply impressed with the truths taught, and in due time a small company of believers was raised up. In the fall of 1871, about the time of the great Chicago fire, these persons bought a lot at 1244 West Erie St., and put up a house of worship, which was the first Seventh-day Adventist church to be erected in a large city. This soon became the center of a growing interest among the Scandinavians of Chicago.

For the most part, however, the labors of Elder Matteson and his associates were put forth in the country districts and under conditions that may be called primitive. In those days the preacher's physical endurance was quite as often put to the test as was his knowledge of the Bible, and he learned the valuable art of sleeping soundly on a hard bed. It was not because there was any lack of hospitality on the part of the people for whom he worked. They gave the best they had. But they themselves often lived in humble log cabins, many miles from the nearest railway station, and they were so busy clearing land for their crops that they had little time to think of household conveniences.

On a certain occasion Elder Matteson went to visit a Norwegian brother who had not seen a Sabbath keeper for several years. His cabin was sixteen miles from the nearest railway station, and this walk the preacher took through mud and snow often knee-deep. He reached his destination about an hour after sunset. The one-room log cabin would have been small enough had it been used exclusively for living purposes; but in it were gathered the farm implements and the winter's supply of potatoes, pumpkins, corn, and other crops, so that it was difficult to move about. However, if house room was small, not so the hearts of the host and hostess. The preacher received a hearty welcome, and spent many pleasant hours with that family, unfolding the promises of God; and when, some days later, he left to visit others, the honest farmer brought him on his way rejoicing.

Later in the winter Elder Matteson came to a little log cabin about nine o'clock one cold night, seeking shelter. The man and his wife and three children were already occupying the only bed the place afforded, but the preacher was made welcome, and was asked to help himself to the straw in the adjoining stack to make up a bed. He took an armful of the straw, and spreading it out on a small open space in the center of the crowded cabin, covered it with his rubber coat, and then wrapping himself in his shawl, lay down to enjoy a night's rest.

Advent Tidende.

"Her er de Helliges Taalmodighed; her ere de, som bevare Guds Befalinger og Jesu Tro." Jab. 14:12.

| 2det Bind. | Battle Creek, Mich., Januar, 1873. | Nummer 1. |

Advent Tidende
trykkes maanedlig af det
Syvende-Dags Advent Trykkeri Selskab,
Battle Creek, Michigan.

John Matteson, : : : Redacteur.

Bestemmelsen af dette Blad er, at opmuntre til practisk christelig Religion, at forklare Prophetierne, samt forsvare Guds Befalinger og Jesu Tro.

Betingelser: En Dollar om Aaret, altid forskudsviis. Frit til de Fattige.
Adresseer: Advent Tidende, Battle Creek, Mich.

Babel.

Paa Pilegrims Vandring al Verden omkring,
Mit Øie beskuer mangfoldige Ting,
Snart onde, snart gode, snart gamle snart ny,
Paa Havet, paa Landet, i Stad og i By.

En Dag paa min Vandring jeg satte min Fod
Just lige ved Bredten af Euphrates Flod,
Paa Sinears Slette, hvor Babylen laae.
Mit Hjerte betænkte, mit Øie bejaae.
1 Mos. 10:10.

Saa rædsomt et Skue jeg aldrig har seet,
Retfærdige Dommer! hvad er der dog skeet!
Den frugtbare Slette, den yndige Plads
Er bleven en Grushob, et stinkend' Morads.

Jeg ofte har studset ved Sodomas Grav.
Der er, som vi vide, det styggeste Hav.
Men Babel! det Mudder, hvori du nedsank,
Nu flyder og ryger, som Værme og Trank.
1 Mos. 19:21; Jer. 51:42.

Jeg saae en Flok Røvdyr, der gave et Skryd,
Som var i mit Øre den føleste Lyd.
Her Strudsunger, Drager og Skovtrolde sprang.
O Lodningebandse, o djævelske Sang!
Es. 13:21, 22.

O Babel! hvorledes har Bladet sig vendt!
Det deiligste Rige, som Nogen har kjendt,
Er blevet fuldkastet, fortærvet og fort.—
O Nimrod, o Nimrod! hvad haver du gjort?
Es. 13:19; 1 Mos. 10:8.

J Oprør, i Hovmod, i Trods mod din Gud
Med Folket du drager til Sinear ud,
En fattet Beslutning i Hjertet dig sad:
Velan! lad os bygge et Taarn og en Stad.
1 Mos. 11:2, 4.

Og Planen, du lagde, den udført du har;
Thi Babel dit Riges Begyndelse var.
Og Staden opvor'de, og Taarnet blev stort.—
Men Nimrod, men Nimrod! hvad haver du gjort?
1 Mos. 10:10.

Du vældige Jæger og Herster, er stærk;
Dog Herren formaaer at forstyrre dit Værk;
Han Sproget forvirrer, og blander det saa
Den Ene kan ikke den Anden forstaae.
1 Mos. 10:9; 11:7.

Og Folket adspredtes—og Tiden svandt hen,
Og saa saae man Babel paa Bene igjen;
Opbygget, saa man maae forkerdes derved;
Thi Sædet blev her for Ugudelighed.
Dan. 4:30.

Dit baaliske Tempel, den Gudernes Bo,
Te hængende Haver og Euphrates Bro—
Alt viser din Vellyst, din Lurus og Pragt,
Og Guden, med hvem du har sluttet en Pagt.

Du Folkene uden Afladelse slog,
Med Vold og med Grumhed du Stræk dem indslog.
For Plager, for Kjøv og for Riis man dig strøv,
Thi over al Jorden du Slaahammer blev.
Es. 14:4-6; Jer. 50:23, 51, 20.

O Babel! du blev til Forfængelighed.
Din Høihed er kastet i Helvede ned.
Hvor var du, hør var du . . . men nu er det gaaet
Dig, som den Prophet Esaias har spaaet.
Es. 14:11; 13:19, 22.

Men hvad der især har din Undergang voldt,
Er ikke, at du var vellystig og stolt;
Men, at du udrakte din vældige Haand,
Og plaged' Guds Folk i dit Fangenskabs Baand.

Du har dem bespottet, og voldt dem Fortræd,
Da ved dine Floder se sadde og græd.
Du haardhjertet var imod al deres Nød,
Du Aarsag har været til mangen Eens Død.
Ps. 137. Jer. 51:49.

Tyrannisk, hovmodig og frek i dit Sind,
Du vilde dig trodse i Himmelen ind.
J Hjertet du sagde: der sætter jeg mig,
Min Throne skal være den Høiestes liig.
Es. 14:13, 14.

Saa haard i dit Hjerte, som Marmor og Staal,
Du fyldte omsider dit Syndelals Maal.
Og saa foer du lige til Helvedes Port.—
Al Nebuchadnezar! hvad haver du gjort!
Es. 14:5; Jer. 51:34.

THE FIRST SCANDINAVIAN PERIODICAL
This is No. 1 of the second volume of the *Advent Tidende* (Advent Herald).

350

The work of Seventh-day Adventists in the Middle West was in those days in its early stages. Funds were scarce, and ministers' salaries were very precarious. Moreover, work among the foreigners was not quite so likely to attract notice as that among Americans. So while Elder Matteson traveled and labored incessantly, and was instrumental in raising up a considerable number of strong churches and companies of believers, he received from the conference for his first four years' work only $20, while the small donations that came in from time to time from the brethren among whom he labored hardly sufficed to meet necessary expenses. His wife and family, from whom he was separated often for months at a time, had to work hard and exercise the closest economy in order that he might remain in the field.

The first minister to join Brother Matteson in preaching the message was J. F. Hanson, a Baptist preacher living in Freeborn County, Minnesota. The two sat down together, Bible in hand, to study the points upon which Baptists and Adventists disagreed, the subjects chiefly considered being the Sabbath and the nature of man. When the study was at an end, Elder Hanson was convinced, and with his family embraced the truth. In the autumn of 1869 O. A. Olsen, a son of Andrew Olsen, one of the pioneer Sabbath keepers, began to preach among the Scandinavians of Wisconsin, and a little later Lewis Johnson, O. A. Johnson, and others entered the ministerial field.

Reading matter in the mother tongue being eagerly called for, Elder Matteson wrote a tract on the Sabbath question, and went to Battle Creek to get it printed, but met with a somewhat discouraging reception. The few publications issued in German and Dutch had had a poor sale, and the association did not see its way clear to issue more foreign publications just then, not having the necessary compositors. Brother Matteson thereupon obtained permission to learn the art of typesetting, after which he set up his own tracts, which were in due time printed, and followed by others.

Later the growth of interest among the Scandinavians, comparatively few of whom could read English, brought about a demand for a periodical in their mother tongue. To supply this demand the *Advent Tidende* (Advent Herald), a 24-page monthly, edited by Elder Matteson, began to be published at the office of the Review and Herald in 1872. This journal, which was enlarged at the beginning of the second volume to thirty-two pages, was the first foreign periodical issued by the Adventists. In addition to its American circulation, it came to have a considerable number of readers in Denmark and Norway, as a result of which calls kept coming from these countries for the living preacher, and Elder Matteson began to lay plans to carry the message to his home country.

Before following him thither, however, let us briefly trace the beginning of the work among the Swedes in America. Some of them attended services held by Brother Matteson, and became members of the companies and churches of Danish-Norwegians that he raised up. Others joined American churches. The first Swede to give special attention to the work among his own countrymen was Dr. Charles Lee. He was a practising physician who had embraced the Adventist views at Wasioja, Minn. He labored in Iowa and Minnesota, trying to the best of his ability to carry the message to his countrymen. Being without funds, he traveled on foot, and often suffered for lack of the necessaries of life. Nevertheless he was able to come up to the Minnesota Conference of 1873 with a report of more than fifty Swedish converts to the Adventist belief. In later years Dr. Lee became discouraged, and left the denomination, but the work that he had done remained.

Another Swede, who had a somewhat remarkable experience in accepting the Adventist faith, was C. Carlstedt. A short time before he heard of the Adventists, his mind was turned to the book of Revelation, and to the blessing promised those who should hear the words of that prophecy, and keep the things written therein. He accordingly applied himself earnestly to the study of the book, meanwhile praying for light on the prophecies therein contained. He had continued thus for a few weeks, when his attention was providentially called to the Seventh-day Adventists, and in the book published by them entitled, " Thoughts on the Revelation," he found the light he had been seeking. Mr. Carlstedt went to Battle Creek about the beginning of the year 1874 to take charge of the Swedish paper published by the Adventists.

A number of the Swedes who first became identified with the Adventist denomination were interested by means of reading matter. It was in this way that the message first came to the Swedes in Iowa. About the year 1870 a Norwegian sister who had embraced the Adventist views under the labors of Elder Matteson, was impressed to send some Danish tracts to a Swedish friend in Wisconsin. These tracts were the means of converting the friend, who thereupon sent some of the tracts to her brother, a man by the name of A. G. Swedberg, living a few miles northwest of Waukon, Iowa. She followed up the tracts by a personal visit, as the result of which the brother began to keep the Sabbath. Being a local preacher, his conversion to the Adventist faith gave rise to some uneasiness in the neighborhood; and Pastor Hamren, a Swedish Baptist preacher, was requested to deal with the heresy. Mr. Hamren had been educated and brought up as a Lutheran in Sweden, but had joined the Baptists. He had thus learned the lesson that truth is not always on the popular side, and he investigated the Adventist views, with the result that he also became a Sabbath keeper. Another Swedish Baptist minister was sent for, but he, too, became so far convinced of the truth of the Adventist teaching that he did little to oppose it. At length a minister was found who had the heart to exclude the Sabbath keepers from the Swedish Baptist church. Not long afterward, J. N. Andrews visited Waukon, and made the acquaintance of Hamren, Swedberg, and others of the same nationality who had accepted the faith.

Among the American brethren who took a special interest in the development of the Swedish work in these early days, was James Sawyer. He had but an imperfect knowledge of the Swedish language, but was very diligent in the circulation of the Swedish paper, *Sanningens Härold,* and of Swedish tracts. He was able to arrange with an agent to distribute Swedish reading matter in Portland, Maine, and many persons of that nationality passing through this important shipping center were thus brought to a knowledge of the Adventist views.

A. G. Swedberg embraced the truth about the year 1871. For a number of years his son, August Swedberg, edited the Swedish paper, *Sanningens Härold,* which was started in 1874; he also translated a number of the leading tracts and books into the Swedish tongue. The Swedish paper, like its sister journal in the Danish-Norwegian language, began to be sent to the old country, and the calls kept coming from all three Scandinavian countries for an Adventist preacher.

In the spring of 1877 Elder Matteson decided that the time had come to respond to these calls, and after advising with the leaders in Battle Creek, he sailed with his wife for Denmark. They arrived at Vejle, a beautiful town in southern Jutland, June 6, and began to visit among the interested ones. About fourteen miles from Vejle were three families who were keeping the Sabbath, and on Sunday Elder Matteson held a meeting attended by thirty. On another Sunday he spoke in the Methodist chapel at Vejle on the second coming of Christ; but this door was soon closed to the Adventist doctrine.

Elder Matteson next went to Alstrup, a small country town in northern Jutland, where he spent the autumn and winter, at first living by turns at the homes of interested persons, and later occupying a rented house, which he also used as a hall for meetings. At Alstrup there was an excellent interest to hear. The houses were too small to accommodate the crowds, so recourse was had to the barns. Meetings were also held at a point six miles from Alstrup, on the farther side of a large swamp. Here the preacher's life was threatened. At both places some began to observe the Sabbath. Results also followed in Fanö, a small island off the west coast, and at Ringsted, on the island of Sjælland, a small church being organized in the latter town.

In the autumn of 1878 Elder Matteson went to Christiania, Norway, being invited thither by a man of influence who had become interested through reading Adventist literature. Trondhjem, Bergen, and Stavanger were also visited, and in October, 1878, the brothers Andrew and Knud Brorsen having in the meantime come over from America to assist in the work, Elder Matteson left the Danish interest in their hands, and took up his headquarters at Christiania. He began meetings in two large rooms in his house. He announced his subject — the second coming of Christ — in the papers, and the people began to come an hour before the time. They filled all the rooms and the stairs, and many had to go away. Thus the crowd continued night after night.

On Jan. 1, 1879, a gymnasium was hired for use every Sunday evening for three months. It was intended to accommodate six hundred; but the people crowded in, filling every available nook and corner, till there were often more than a thousand present. The donations fully met expenses, and soon several persons began the observance of the Sabbath. When the doctrine of the soul's immortality was attacked, the opposition became intense; but those whose hearts God had touched came out and obeyed the truth, and on June 7, 1879, a church of thirty-eight members was organized. Elder Matteson, who had first to appear before the authorities and present under oath a declaration of his faith, was elected elder. In the course of the winter Andrew Brorsen had come from Denmark to assist in the work, and in the spring J. P. Jasperson and his wife came over from America, bringing with them Elder Matteson's children.

Before the organization of the church the opposition had taken the form of bringing pressure to bear upon the owners of public halls so that none could be had for meetings. The believers accordingly stepped out in faith, and purchased on easy terms a property containing an old building of considerable size, which could be used in part for a meeting hall, in part for a printing office, and in part as a home for workers. The cost was $14,580, the payments to be made in semiannual instalments, extending over a period of years. The meeting hall, which with adjoining rooms could accommodate 400 persons, was dedicated in June, 1879, there being then eighty members in the church.

Meanwhile the publishing work was receiving its full share of attention. In January, 1879, *Tidernes Tegn* (Signs of the Times) began to come out as a weekly sheet in editions of 1,500 copies, some of which were sold, the others given away. In April of the same year it was made a regular subscription paper of eight pages, issued semimonthly, at 54 cents a year. In June a hand press was purchased, after which both the paper and tracts were printed at Elder Matteson's home, his children largely doing the work. To circulate this reading matter, the church members were organized into a tract society, which in the first six weeks of its existence put out more than 67,000 pages of tracts and 600 papers.

In the meantime the work had been going forward in Denmark under the fostering care of Knud Brorsen, so that Elder Matteson was able to organize in that field a small conference in the summer of 1880. A little later he returned to America to obtain help for the further enlargement of the work in Scandinavia. After attending the General Conference, he spent the following winter among the Scandinavian brethren in the West. Returning to Norway in the spring, he bought a cylinder press, and began issuing a monthly health journal, *Sunhedsbladet,* which soon had a list of several thousand subscribers. Two years later, in 1883, a Swedish health journal was started, and then a Swedish religious journal, *Sanningens Härold* (Herald of Truth). The publishing work after a few years became self-sustaining, and proved an effective means of spreading a knowledge of the message, 115,000 papers being printed in the year 1884, besides thousands of tracts and small books.

From Norway the work naturally extended into the neighboring country of Sweden, which, as we have already seen, was supplied with literature from the Christiania publishing house. Tracts and papers had also been sent thither by believers in America, and an interest had sprung up to hear the Adventist views fully presented. In response to calls, J. P. Rosqvist, who had been assisting in the work in Christiania, was sent to

Sweden, and began labor in April, 1880, at Amot. Thence he went to Grythyttehed, where he remained four months, after which a church of forty-seven was organized, there being an excellent interest and practically no opposition.

When Elder Rosqvist returned, a year later, however, he met with decided opposition, being called before a church council and formally forbidden to preach any more in Grythyttehed. He continued, was fined, and refused to pay the fine, saying that if he had sinned against God, money could not atone for it, and he could not have sinned against man by preaching God's word. In the following January he was arrested and sent to prison at Örebro, his arrest and imprisonment being made possible by an old law, seldom enforced, which provided for the punishment of any who teach doctrines leading to division in the state church.

On leaving prison, after nine days, he was invited to the house of a merchant of Örebro, where he breakfasted and spent some pleasant hours with the family. He then left Örebro and resumed his labors at Grythyttehed, where his audiences were larger than before. In March another warrant was sworn out for his arrest, but it was technically incorrect, and the case was deferred till the fall session of the court, when he was again fined. After this he was liable to sudden arrest in any part of Sweden; nevertheless, through the good providence of God, he was able to keep on with his work.

In the year 1882 Elder Matteson visited Sweden, and a conference was organized. Brother Rosqvist continued his labors till 1883, when he went to America to labor among the Swedes in that country, O. Johnson taking his place in Sweden.

The workers in Scandinavia were greatly encouraged by the visits of S. N. Haskell in 1882 and George I. Butler and B. L. Whitney in 1884. In the latter year the working force was increased by the arrival of A. B. Oyen and E. G. Olsen, the former taking the management of the publishing house in Christiania, and thus setting Elder Matteson free to devote himself largely to evangelistic work.

Stockholm, the capital of Sweden, already had a few Sabbath keepers who had accepted the faith under the labors of Elders Rosqvist and Johnson. In the fall of 1884 Elder Matteson began preaching in a large hall, assisted by O. Johnson. Two courses of lectures were given, and fifty converts were added to the church, making a membership of sixty-six.

In the following spring a similar effort was begun in Copenhagen, the capital of Denmark. Work had already been started there in a quiet way by Knud Brorsen, who had hired a small hall and advertised his meetings in the papers. A young woman came, and was overjoyed to find that the prophecies of Daniel and the Revelation were to be the subject of study. She opened her home for Bible studies, and was the first person to take her stand for the truth. A little later a young student at the university began to keep the Sabbath, and others became interested. When Elder Matteson began meetings in a large hall, the little handful of believers worked earnestly to secure a good attendance, but the people were so given to pleasure seeking that it was difficult to direct their attention to the truths of the Bible. A few additions were made to the company of believers; and when the church was organized, there were seven ready to join it, in addition to the laborers, Elders Matteson and Brorsen.

It was a small number indeed that came together and signed the covenant in that great city; yet out of these seven, one became an ordained minister whom God has used in raising up a number of Adventist churches in different parts of Denmark; another became the founder and superintendent of what is now one of the largest and most influential Adventist sanitariums in the world; and a third, the young woman who first took her stand for the truth, has been engaged for many years in self-supporting medical missionary work, during which time she has been able to educate several promising young people for work in the denomination. Moreover, while the number at the beginning was small, the Copenhagen church had an encouraging growth, so that within about a year of its organization it was able to report a membership of upwards of forty.

While the evangelistic work was thus progressing in the three Scandinavian countries, the publishing house in Christiania was keeping pace with it. It accordingly became necessary to consider the erection of a larger building. The matter received favorable consideration at the General Conference of 1885, and the Scandinavian brethren proceeded without further delay to carry out their plans for a combined mission hall and printing office. The building, which was dedicated March 14, 1886, contains a hall seating 700 persons. It measures 46 x 69 feet, has two stories and a basement, and is favorably situated on one of Christiania's leading thoroughfares.

In the spring of 1886 the staff of laborers in Scandinavia was further re-enforced by the arrival of O. A. Olsen with his family, N. Clausen and his wife, and John Lorntz. A tent purchased in England was pitched at Moss, a little town on the

Christiania Fiord, for the holding of the first tent-meeting in Scandinavia. The brothers O. A. and E. G. Olsen conducted the nightly services, and at the close of the season organized a church.

On the arrival of the workers from America, Elder Matteson removed with his family to Stockholm, where he spent the summer in evangelistic work. In the autumn of the same year,

CHRISTIANIA PUBLISHING HOUSE

a book depository was opened in that city, and efforts were put forth to enlarge and strengthen the corps of colporteurs.

Early in the year 1887 a three months' school for colporteurs and Bible workers was conducted by Brother Matteson. It was attended by twenty promising young people, who supported themselves while going to school by canvassing for books and papers in the city of Stockholm. The hours for instruction were in the early morning and in the evening, leaving students free to work in the city from nine to five o'clock each day. The city was divided into districts, and each student visited his district twice during the three months. The first time he introduced the health magazine, and the second time he took orders for the only subscription book then published in Swedish, " The Life of Christ," by Mrs. E. G. White. At the same time O. A. Olsen conducted a similar school in Christiania, Norway.

In the summer of 1887 there was held on an island near Moss, in a grove of fragrant pines and firs, the first European camp-meeting of Seventh-day Adventists. Among those who attended this meeting were D. A. Robinson and C. L. Boyd, with their families, who were on their way to South Africa; Mrs. E. G. White and W. C. White, then visiting the leading centers of our work in Europe; also J. H. Waggoner, from the States; B. L. Whitney, from Basel, Switzerland; J. H. Durland, then laboring in England; and some other workers.

In connection with this camp-meeting, the European Council was held, and plans were laid for aggressive work in various parts of Europe. At this meeting, also, the Norway Conference was organized, with four churches and a membership of about two hundred, O. A. Olsen being elected president.

There were a number of family tents on the ground, but the majority of the people in attendance found lodging in houses in the neighborhood. The attendance from the outside was reasonably good, and the interest encouraging. Mrs. White's testimony was a source of great help and encouragement to the believers present, representing the various Scandinavian churches and companies, as well as to the body of workers assembled from various parts of Europe.

Following the camp-meeting in Norway there was held in Stockholm the annual meeting of the Swedish Conference, which was attended by a goodly number of believers from different parts of Sweden. Also at this meeting the instruction by Mrs. White was greatly appreciated, and did much to give the members larger views of the message, as well as to foster the sense of unity.

At the beginning of 1888 mission schools were again conducted in Christiania and in Stockholm, on the same plan as those held the previous year, and with an increased interest and attendance. After the close of the school in Stockholm, J. G. Matteson went to Copenhagen, and conducted a similar school there for the benefit of the workers in Denmark. Shortly after the close of this school, he returned with his family to the United States, in order to perform important literary work and help to foster the Scandinavian interests in this country. He attended several camp-meetings during the summer; and although his health was feeble, in the fall and winter he conducted large mission schools in Minneapolis and Chicago on the

CAMP-MEETING HELD NEAR MOSS, NORWAY, IN 1887

same general plan as those carried on in Scandinavia. After a short stay in Galveston, Texas, and in other places, he presently settled at Boulder, Colo., where the disease that had attacked his lungs was stayed for a time, and he carried on a fruitful work, in editing, translating, and instructing a small group of younger men who were associated with him, chiefly O. A. Johnson, Zechariah Sherring, and A. Christiansen. He also for a time taught Bible in the Danish-Norwegian Department of Union College. He died of tuberculosis at Santa Monica, Calif., busy at work until the last.

Elder Matteson ably pioneered the work among Scandinavians, both in America and in Europe, for which his name will ever be held in grateful remembrance. He was a man of deep Christian experience, who entered fully into the spirit of the advent message. His work as both editor and preacher was strongly spiritual, and his influence was ever in the direction of self-denying effort in behalf of the cause he loved.

As a pioneer preacher and gospel messenger, going into new places, arousing an interest to hear, and winning adherents among a people naturally slow to change their religious affiliations, he was unsurpassed. His activity as a preacher, moreover, was strongly backed up by his literary toil. From the time when he went to Battle Creek and set up with his own hands his first tract on the Sabbath question, till the end of his faithful life, his pen was never idle. Books, tracts, and articles for the papers poured forth from him in a never-ending stream, and his work during the closing years of his career in developing the literary talents of younger men, was not the least of the services he rendered the cause of Adventism. His one large book, " Prophecies of Jesus," of 566 pages, illustrated, was published in 1895.

O. A. OLSEN

President of the General Conference, 1888 to 1897

A WORKERS' COUNCIL

Taken in front of the British Mission House, Ravenswood, Shirley Road, Southampton, in 1882.

CHAPTER XVIII

The Work Established in Great Britain

IN Great Britain two of the outstanding truths of Seventh-day Adventism, the Sabbath of creation and the imminence of Christ's second coming, had, as noted in earlier chapters of this volume, been nobly witnessed to, the former through several centuries, the latter by Edward Irving and other devoted ministers in the early decades of the nineteenth century. England, moreover, had led the nations of the world in the great missionary movement inaugurated at the close of the eighteenth century. It was, therefore, with feelings of special interest that Seventh-day Adventists prepared to open work on British soil.

The country was first visited from this continent by William Ings, born in Hampshire, England, but brought up in America, who reached Southampton, May 23, 1878. He remained at this time only two weeks in England, but soon returned to resume his labors, and after sixteen weeks was able to report ten Sabbath keepers. He continued to labor in England till the beginning of 1882, devoting his energies largely to ship missionary work in the port of Southampton. He not only brought the advent message to the attention of a large number of captains and sailors, but through them he was able to send thousands of pages of reading matter to many remote parts of the world, the seed thus sown being destined in time to give returns in an abundant harvest.

While pushing the work forward to the best of his ability, Elder Ings was calling for more help from America. In re-

WILLIAM INGS

sponse to his appeals, J. N. Loughborough went over at the end of December, 1878, and preached his first sermon at Shirley Hall, Jan. 5, 1879. Meetings were also held in Coxford, a suburb of Southampton, and both there and in the city proper some additions were made to the ranks of believers. In the course of the spring a sixty-foot tent was purchased, which was pitched in Southampton about the middle of May, the first meeting being held on Sunday, the 18th, with an audience of 600. Seventy-four discourses were given; and though the weather was unfavorable, the attendance continued good, and when the series closed on August 17, the company of believers in Southampton numbered about thirty.

Early in January, 1880, a national tract and missionary society was organized, with a membership of thirty-six. A club of *Signs of the Times* was ordered from America, and systematic missionary labor was begun by the sending out of these periodicals through the mails to persons whose names were obtained in various ways. Letters were sent out with the papers, and many interesting responses were received, sometimes as many as a hundred in a month. Papers were also to a limited extent sold from house to house.

Adventists administered baptism for the first time in Great Britain on Feb. 8, 1880, when six candidates were immersed by J. N. Loughborough. Others followed in the course of the next few months. June 18 the tent was pitched a second time at

Romsey, a village eight miles from Southampton. J. N. Andrews, though in feeble health, came from Basel to assist in this effort. The series of meetings had to be closed early, owing to severe damages inflicted by a gale; but not until some additions had been made to the company of believers. During the same summer several signed the covenant as the result of a three weeks' effort at Taunton, Somerset, among them being Henry Veysey, an experienced teacher, who afterward rendered useful service on the faculty of Battle Creek College.

On Nov. 15, 1881, Elder Loughborough sailed for America to attend the General Conference, which convened that year on the first of December, at Battle Creek, Mich. In response to his call for help, there accompanied him back to Great Britain A. A. John and his family, of Illinois; George R. and Mrs. Drew, of California; Miss Jennie Thayer, of Massachusetts; and his own son and daughter, the party reaching Southampton Jan. 25, 1882.

Elder John began labor in Grimsby, Lincolnshire, by lending packages of tracts from house to house, following up the effort by preaching in halls and on the street, and by writing for the local press. A church and a tract and missionary society were organized at Grimsby in 1884, and at Ulceby, a near-by village, in 1885. Somewhat later a church building, the first owned by Adventists in Great Britain, was erected at Ulceby.

George Drew spent a few weeks in London, going from there to Grimsby and Hull, where his sales of books and papers sometimes were as high as $45 a week. In April, 1883, he settled in Liverpool, where he continued with zeal and energy to carry forward the ship missionary work. One of his early converts, a ship captain from Finland, himself engaged in the work in his native land, and was the means of bringing the message to the attention of many.

Brother Drew not only sold books and papers, but sent large parcels of literature for free distribution to many different ports, the captains of the various vessels distributing them for him. He had been a sailor himself from early youth, and had risen to be captain of a vessel when the message found him in San Francisco. He continued the distribution of literature until a short time before his death in 1905.

Meanwhile the tract and missionary work was steadily growing. The churches continued to use the American *Signs of the Times*, to which they began in 1882 to attach a supplement giving interesting local particulars in reference to the work in England. Tracts were also published in increasing quantities, and early in May, 1884, during the visit of George I. Butler, then president of the General Conference, it was decided to issue a sixteen-page monthly about the same size as the *Signs of the Times*.

The printing office was moved from Southampton to Grimsby, and M. C. Wilcox, who with J. H. Durland had come over from America, was appointed editor. The first number of this paper, called *The Present Truth*, bore the date of May, 1884, the

FIRST PERIODICAL ISSUED IN ENGLAND

subscription price being two shillings and sixpence (60 cents) a year. The first year about a thousand copies were subscribed for by friends of the cause. The paper continued to be issued monthly until the European Council of 1885, when it was decided to issue it as an eight-page semimonthly, and to illustrate it. Later it was enlarged to sixteen pages and issued weekly. It has continued to the present day to exert a strong influence in behalf of the truth in Great Britain.

In the spring of 1885 the staff of workers in Great Britain was further strengthened by the arrival of Elder and Mrs. S. H. Lane and Elder R. F. Andrews. The latter labored chiefly in Ireland, amid many difficulties, but not without some fruit. Elder Lane joined Elder Durland in a series of meetings in Exeter, where a few accepted the truth. Later they conducted meetings in a tent in Risley, a village in Bedfordshire, where a considerable stir was made and six accepted the Sabbath.

The visit of Mrs. E. G. White and W. C. White in the same year (1885) proved a great encouragement to the believers in Great Britain, and helped to establish them in the faith. Mrs. White addressed large audiences in the town hall at Grimsby and elsewhere, her labors being well received by the public.

In the year 1887, S. N. Haskell visited England to counsel with the laborers and assist them in making any change that might seem necessary to facilitate the progress of the work.

" THE CHALONERS "

The mission home where work was started in London by S. N. Haskell.

The periodical *Present Truth* had then been coming out regularly for three years, and its circulation was increasing. It was decided to issue the paper from London. Suitable premises were secured at number 451 Holloway Road, in the north of London, and the printing plant and workmen were transferred from Grimsby to their new home, which was to be the headquarters of our work in England for about twenty years. A city office where Adventist books and other publications would be on sale was rented in the well-known Paternoster Row.

At the time this move was made there was only one Seventh-day Adventist in London, the city in those days having a population of about five million. Evangelistic work was begun at once. S. N. Haskell had been accompanied by three trained

Bible workers, Jennie Owen, Helen McKinnon, and Hettie Hurd. These young women began to seek out homes where Bible readings were desired, and they soon found themselves fully occupied. A large house — " The Chaloners," in Anson Road, Tufnel Park, not far from the publishing house — was secured as a home for the workers. A large room on the first floor was used for meetings on Sunday nights, and it was not long before a Sabbath school began to be held regularly. The first baptism took place June 9, 1888, and in the same year a church was organized. About a year later the membership in London had grown to sixty-five.

In the late autumn of 1891, J. S. Washburn came over from America, and began to labor in Bath. He held his first public service Jan. 10, 1892, in a centrally located hall, with an audience of thirty. The interest and attendance steadily increased, so that early in April he was speaking on Sunday night to an audience of 500. Later he moved into a hall seating 1,500 people. Opposition sermons were preached, and tracts were put out to warn the people against the doctrines taught. About eighty persons began to keep the Sabbath as a result of these meetings.

The remarkable success attending the meetings in Bath was doubtless owing in no small part to the fact that George Stagg, a colporteur, had been faithfully circulating the *Present Truth* for five years previous to the coming of Elder Washburn, and of the number who finally joined the church fully half attributed their interest in the teachings of Adventists to the reading of the paper.

In October, 1893, Evangelist Washburn began a series of meetings in Southampton in a hall that would seat 700. Later he secured the Philharmonic Hall, with seats for 1,100, for a month's services, two meetings being held each day and four on Sundays. Still later both halls, occupied by attentive audiences, were used for a time. Francis Hope and H. R. Hanson assisted in these meetings. When the series of lectures was brought to a close, the number of Sabbath keepers in Southampton had been increased to 120. Elder Washburn's next field of labor was Kettering; later he spent several years in Wales.

When D. A. Robinson left England to open a mission in India, he was succeeded by H. E. Robinson, who remained about a year in the country, residing most of the time in Plymouth, where he raised up a strong church. He was succeeded by W. W. Prescott, who had general charge of the British field from 1897 to 1901. During his tenure of office, beginnings were made in the direction of a sanitarium, a health magazine, a health food factory, and a training school. The sanitarium had to be closed, owing to the failing health of Dr. D. H. Kress, the superintendent, but the work was later taken up and carried on with success. The health food factory, situated in Surrey, burned to the ground; but through the efforts of H. G. Butler the business was put on its feet again, the factory moved to Birmingham, and a good patronage built up. The training school held in the winter of 1899-1900, by W. W. Prescott and E. J. Waggoner, brought definite results in deepening the experience of the workers, and giving them a broader knowledge of the message.

The first general meeting for Great Britain was held in a suburb of Bath in 1898, and was an occasion of great blessing to the believers throughout the field.

About this time there came over from America three experienced laborers, E. E. Andross, M. A. Altman, and S. G. Haughey. Elders Andross and Haughey held a tent-meeting in the city of Birmingham in the summer of 1900, which resulted in bringing out a large company of Sabbath keepers. In the same year a company was raised up in Leytonstone, in the northeast of London.

On W. W. Prescott's being recalled to America in 1901, the British field was placed in charge of O. A. Olsen, under whose administration the United Kingdom was divided into five parts; namely, North England, South England, Scotland, Ireland, and Wales, each having its own administration, and all uniting together to form the British Union Conference. During Elder Olsen's term of office the English Training School began its fruitful career under the leadership of H. R. Salisbury. The publishing work was greatly strengthened by the arrival of W. C. Sisley, who took the oversight of the printing office. The sanitarium work also was placed on a firm basis.

O. A. Olsen being called to the presidency of the Australasian Union, he was succeeded in Great Britain by E. E. Andross, during whose administration an estate of fifty-five acres, lying in the vicinity of Watford, in Hertfordshire, about seventeen miles north of London, was purchased as a permanent home for the publishing, educational, and health institutions of the denomination in Great Britain. The estate, which is known as Stanborough Park, contained a manor house, which was used for a school building the first year, and later for a sanitarium. Substantial brick buildings were erected under the direction of W. C. Sisley for the publishing work and the health food business, and somewhat later a building was put up for the training college. Elder Andross continued to have charge of the British field till the failing health of his wife made it necessary for him to return to America. His place was taken by W. J. Fitzgerald.

Before giving some further particulars in reference to the growth of the publishing, educational, and health work in Great

W. C. SISLEY

Britain, it may be well to give a brief account of the beginnings of the evangelistic work in Ireland, Scotland, and Wales.

About the year 1888, R. F. Andrews spent some months in evangelistic work in Ireland. He found the field a difficult one; nevertheless his labors were not without fruit. Among his converts were a mother and several daughters by the name of McKinstry. This family was related to Mrs. Bell, the mother of Isaac Bell and Dr. J. J. Bell, both of whom later embraced the Adventist faith. For a time S. H. Lane was associated with Elder Andrews in the work in Ireland. In 1889 William Hutchinson began to work in Banbridge, where about a score of substantial people, including six members of the Bell family, took their stand for the truth. A number of these became excellent canvassers, and carried our leading subscription books to many parts of Ireland.

In the summer of 1890, William Hutchinson, assisted by Francis Hope, held the first tent-meetings in Ireland, first at a small town called Tanderagee, in the county of Armagh, and later in Coleraine, a city of about 7,000. The results were meager, and from that time on the work was carried on chiefly by the use of halls.

When Elder Hutchinson returned to the States, he was succeeded by O. O. Farnsworth, who labored with Francis Hope at Belfast, and was successful in raising up a small company of Sabbath keepers. On returning to Ireland in 1895, Elder Hutchinson built a portable tabernacle, which he used for evangelistic efforts in a number of places, being assisted at different times by S. Hollingsworth and D. McClelland. In the effort at Portadown, Samuel Joyce accepted the truth. He was ordained elder of the church at Banbridge, and later became general field secretary for the British Union Conference.

M. A. Altman and R. Musson entered Dublin in 1906, and were able in time to raise up a small company of believers. Elders Musson and Whiteside brought out a company also at Carnglass in County Antrim. In 1908 J. J. Gillatt took charge of the Irish mission, and was successful the following year in bringing to completion the plans begun by Elder Altman to provide a church building for Belfast.

There were faithful Sabbath keepers in Glasgow as early as 1874, when J. N. Andrews spent a short time there on his way to the Continent.

At the General Conference of 1891 it was voted that N. Z. and Mrs. Town go to Glasgow, Scotland, with a company of colporteurs, to pioneer the work in that field. He began the work there the same summer, being joined by two brethren from England. In March, 1892, Mr. Town moved to Birmingham, England, and took charge of the book work in Great Britain, the first field missionary secretary to give his whole time to the direction of the book work. At this time Ellery Robinson was devoting himself to the supervision of the paper work in the British Isles.

C. M. Dyer, of London, and R. M. and Mrs. Lamie, who went over from America, were actively engaged in the book and paper work in Scotland in the late nineties. In 1901 H. E. Armstrong was sent to open up public work in Glasgow, the number of believers in that city being about twenty. W. A. Westworth took charge of the work in 1903, and a successful tent effort was carried on by Alexander Ritchie at Kirkcauldy, resulting in the building up of a strong church. Elder Westworth was obliged to return to America on account of poor health, and the work was placed in the hands, first of J. J. Gillatt, and later of A. E. Bacon.

A. A. John and C. H. Keslake did some evangelistic work in Wales, and a band of faithful colporteurs circulated a large number of books, tracts, and periodicals, which brought individuals [1] here and there to decide for the truth. The first sustained evangelistic effort was put forth when J. S. Washburn entered Cardiff in September, 1896. At the outset his meetings were held in small halls, and were not largely attended; but when he secured Lesser Park Hall, with seats for 400, and

---

[1] One of these, W. H. Meredith, was later ordained to the ministry, and became president of the Wales Conference.

began to advertise the lectures, the attendance grew so rapidly that it was necessary shortly to move to Larger Park Hall. It had seats for 2,500, and was provided with an excellent pipe organ. The hall was occupied on Sunday nights for several months, the prophecies, the Sabbath, and other features of the denominational faith being fully presented and creating a widespread interest. The collections were large, for the most part equaling or exceeding the hall rent, and a strong church was organized at the close of the effort.

In the autumn of 1898 Elder Washburn began to hold meetings in Swansea. There were some results, but nothing to compare with those at Cardiff. After this effort, little was done for Wales for several years. Then W. H. Meredith, formerly a Welsh coal miner, who had been associated with Elder Washburn in the meetings at Cardiff and Swansea, conducted a series of meetings in the little mining town of Pontypridd, and was successful in raising up a small company of believers. C. E. Penrose, a Baptist pastor, joined the Adventists, bringing several members of his flock with him. Later W. H. Meredith took charge of the work in Wales, and continued to hold this position till he was called to the presidency of the South England Conference, being succeeded by H. E. Armstrong, who in turn was followed by A. E. Bacon.

The publishing work from its inception was a powerful means of spreading a knowledge of the message in England. *Present Truth* came in time to have a goodly number of permanent subscribers, who had the paper delivered to them weekly by regularly appointed agents. The editorship of the paper passed into the hands of W. A. Spicer when M. C. Wilcox was called back to the States. Elder Spicer in turn was succeeded by E. J. Waggoner, who arrived in England with his family in the spring of 1892, and continued to edit the paper until the summer of 1902. He then returned to America, W. T. Bartlett taking his place.

Aggressive work in canvassing for the large books was conducted under the auspices of the Pacific Press, of Oakland, Calif. In October, 1889, six colporteurs went over from America, and began work in the British field. They enjoyed fair success from the beginning. The publishing work continued under the fostering care of the Pacific Press until the spring of 1892, when the General Conference Association took over the business, and from that time the work was carried on under the name of the International Tract Society, which was legally organized as a limited company in August, 1894.

In 1895 the workers at the International Tract Society, by carrying on Sunday labor, came into conflict with the factory laws. The managers of the office were warned by the authorities to desist from employing women and minors on Sundays. Since these persons had their Sabbaths free, and thus were already enjoying the full benefits of the rest the law was intended to provide, the management did not feel free to turn them away on Sunday. John I. Gibson, secretary of the board of directors, was thereupon called into court to answer to the charge of violating the law, and a fine of £3 was imposed. In default of payment, the authorities seized and sold certain articles of office furniture in order to cover the fine. Meanwhile, the London papers had taken up the matter, and spread the news far and wide that there was a denomination in the country who taught that the seventh day is the Sabbath of the Bible, and that Sunday is, and should be, regarded as a working day. A deep interest was awakened throughout the kingdom, which resulted in the material increase of the circulation of *Present Truth* and of other reading matter containing the advent message.

While very helpful institutes had been held at different times, educational work in England began in the autumn of the year 1901, when Professor and Mrs. H. R. Salisbury went over from America to take charge of Duncombe Hall Missionary College. The first year school opened in January, 1902, and continued twenty-one weeks in Duncombe Hall, in North London, the students occupying private lodgings in the neighborhood.

The next year the school began September 2, and continued thirty-six weeks in Holloway Hall, facing Holloway Road, one of the main business streets of North London. Among the young men who attended this year were a number from America, two of whom, the brothers Frank and Walter Bond, went to Spain to open up work there at the close of the school year. In the fourth year, the school was held at Manor Gardens, two large villas in the neighborhood of Holloway Hall being fitted for school home and classrooms. This year there were seventy-six students, of whom twelve were in the intermediate grades. H. C. Lacey was called over from America to assist in the teaching, and took charge of the Bible instruction.

The fifth and sixth years the school continued in the same place. At the close of the latter year Professor and Mrs. Salisbury left the school and returned to America to take charge of the Foreign Mission Seminary in Washington, D. C.

The seventh year opened with H. C. Lacey in charge. A new school property had been purchased, consisting of an old-fashioned manor house and fifty-five acres of beautiful grounds near Watford, seventeen miles north of London. In 1910 the school was moved into a new brick building erected for its accommodation, which it has continued to occupy. On Professor Lacey's returning to America in 1913, the school was placed under the charge of W. T. Bartlett, who was succeeded in 1915 by Glenn

STANBOROUGH MISSIONARY COLLEGE

Wakeham. The institution, known since its removal into the country as Stanborough Missionary College, has ever kept in close touch with the needs of the field, and from its classes have gone out many successful workers.

By 1925 the faculty of the institution, headed by Prof. G. Baird, principal, numbered twenty teachers, giving instruction in twenty-eight subjects, including normal work, ministerial training, domestic science, carpentry, market gardening, and farming, each of which is so comprehensive as to include more than is sometimes understood by the simple term " subject."

Medical missionary work in the United Kingdom began in the year 1898, when Drs. D. H. and Lauretta Kress went to England at the request of the British Conference committee.

During the greater part of the first year they devoted their time to giving lectures and holding health schools, in which work they were eminently successful. They also began to issue a magazine called *Life and Health,* which continued to be published for nearly a year, and did much to spread a knowledge of the principles of healthful living.

In 1899 a property was rented near Redhill, Surrey, and in September of that year it was opened as a sanitarium. A small class of enthusiastic young people was organized for instruction in nursing, and the prospects were excellent for a growing work,

STANBOROUGH PRESS

when failure of health on the part of Dr. D. H. Kress made it necessary for him to leave the country. The health magazine was accordingly discontinued in the summer of 1900, and the work was in abeyance until the following year, when Dr. A. B. Olsen, having secured his British qualification, began health educational work, conducting health schools, giving lectures, etc. The first number of the new health magazine, bearing the name of *Good Health,* was issued in November, 1901.

In 1902 a small institution containing ten bedrooms and well-arranged bathrooms was opened in rented premises in the city of Belfast, Ireland, Dr. J. J. Bell being placed in charge. Work was carried on here until the autumn of 1906, when the institution was moved to Rosstrevor, County Down, about two and one-half miles from Warrenpoint. This institution was conducted until the first of October, 1911.

As a result of a good health school conducted by Dr. and Mrs. A. B. Olsen at Leicester, England, in 1902, a sanitarium was opened in that city in a building owned by Mr. J. W. Goddard, at a nominal rental of £1 a year. Mr. Goddard also built a suite of bathrooms according to specifications furnished by Dr. Olsen. This institution was for a time under the direction of Drs. F. C. and Eulalia Richards. Eventually it passed into the hands of W. M. Scott, a graduate nurse. The institution had a good patronage, and continued to be under the direction of the British Union Conference until April, 1912, since which time it has been conducted as a private institution.

The buildings occupied by the Caterham Sanitarium in Caterham, Surrey, were purchased March 5, 1903, at the expense of £3,030, of which £2,050 were supplied by the General

STANBOROUGH PARK SANITARIUM

Conference, the remainder being raised by friends of the health work in the United Kingdom. The institution was dedicated and opened its doors for patients on the 30th of the following May, being in charge of Dr. A. B. Olsen as superintendent. From the beginning it enjoyed a good patronage. It soon outgrew its former quarters, acquiring two adjoining villas by purchase and renting others. It was also fitted out with steam heat, and in other ways its facilities were greatly improved. Dr. Olsen continued in charge of the Caterham Sanitarium till the year 1919, when he returned to America. Not long after this it became necessary to close the institution and sell the buildings, because of increasing heavy motor traffic on the road that passed within a few feet of the patients' rooms, the government having established a large military camp in the vicinity.

The Stanborough Park Sanitarium, located on grounds adjacent to the college of that name, was dedicated July 3, 1912, being then in charge of Dr. Charles H. Hayton. In 1922 Dr. W. A. Ruble became the superintendent. The institution has had a good patronage from the opening day, and is exerting a wide influence for good throughout the United Kingdom.

In connection with the sanitarium work, a flourishing nurses' training school is being conducted; also active health propaganda in the form of health lectures given in different parts of the United Kingdom. A Good Health League was organized in 1902, with a central office in London and the *Good Health* mag-

THE HEALTH FOOD FACTORY

azine as its organ. Members joining the league sign the following declaration:

"I am a total abstainer from alcohol and tobacco, and I desire to learn and to follow the perfect way of life in all that pertains to health and purity."

The *Good Health* magazine received a cordial welcome on the part of the reading public. Starting out with an edition of 20,000, it soon had an average circulation of 50,000 a month. Besides meeting its own expenses almost from the start, it has been able to turn over a considerable sum of money to assist in other lines of health work.

The Health Food Factory, also located at Stanborough Park, has likewise prospered, and has contributed liberally to the needs of various lines of health educational work.

J. O. CORLISS

M. C. ISRAEL

HENRY SCOTT

WILLIAM ARNOLD

THE AVONDALE SCHOOL

CHAPTER XIX

Australia and New Zealand

THE Adventist doctrines were first taught in Australia in the late sixties by Alexander Dickson, of Melbourne, a returned missionary. He learned of the views held by this people through Miss Hannah More, of the Mendi Mission, in Africa, who had become an Adventist during a furlough spent in New England. Mr. Dickson for a time labored earnestly in behalf of the Bible Sabbath, but ultimately became discouraged and gave up the truths in whose advocacy he had spent a small fortune.

As early as 1874, Mrs. E. G. White had mentioned Australia as a country where many would accept the message; but not until ten years later was the work finally entered upon. The General Conference, at its session held in November, 1884, adopted a resolution recommending that " S. N. Haskell go to Australia as soon as possible, and superintend the establishment of a mission there," and that J. O. Corliss and other laborers be associated with him in the work. The party set sail from San Francisco May 10, 1885, including, besides the ministers already mentioned, M. C. Israel, Henry Scott, of California, and William Arnold, of Michigan; also the families of the Brethren Corliss and Israel.

Work was begun at Richmond, a suburb of Melbourne, and hall rent being high, the Americans confined their efforts at first to visiting the people in their homes, and making the acquaintance of some of the leading business men. The latter were open-minded and friendly from the start. The members of the working class, on the other hand, were difficult of access, and inclined to be suspicious of new doctrines. As soon as a few began to show an interest, the leading clergymen of the town entered upon a course of bitter opposition; but this helped rather than hindered the progress of the message. Tract distributors were placed in various shops, and papers were also stuck between the pickets of the iron fences inclosing the public grounds, whence the people passing to their daily work would take them.

J. H. STOCKTON
The first to accept the message in Australia.

Gradually results began to appear. One Sabbath, while the workers were assembled for worship, a man called with a copy of the *Signs* which he had taken from a fence picket. He said he had learned the address of the mission from the paper, and wished one of the workers to take part in a gathering to be held in South Melbourne the following Thursday night for the consideration of the Sabbath question. J. O. Corliss attended the meeting, and showed in his handling of the subject so much tact and such a broad knowledge of the Scriptures that he was invited to conduct regular Bible studies at the homes of some of the members. A goodly number assembled for these studies, and eventually fifteen of the young men who attended the first meeting on Thursday night accepted the Adventist views. Two of these men were printers, and their knowledge of the printing business was of great help a little later in the publishing of a paper.

Meanwhile aggressive public work being desirable, and halls and private homes being largely closed on account of prejudice, it seemed best to try to hold meetings under canvas. A 40 x 60-foot tent was accordingly ordered, and pitched in North Fitzroy, one of the suburbs of Melbourne, in September, 1885. The meetings were advertised by means of notices in the various papers and by posters, and the people came out in great numbers, curious to hear the men against whom their pastors had so earnestly warned them. Among others a Presbyterian deacon attended, purchased some tracts, and announced his intention to keep the Sabbath. His brother, greatly disturbed over the matter, asked his son, a well-educated young man, to reason his uncle out of the delusion; and the son attempted the task, with the result that he, too, became a Sabbath keeper, and in turn

W. H. B. MILLER

J. H. WOODS

began to labor for his father and mother, the final outcome being that thirteen out of a family of fourteen took their stand for the truth.

The tent was pitched five times during the season from September to May, 1885-86, in four of the suburbs of Melbourne, and in each place there were some who decided to obey the Word of God. Among the converts was a contractor who labored so earnestly for his father, mother, brothers, and sisters that in a short time nine of them had taken their stand for the truth. The contractor was in business in a large way, and employed many hands. These he called together, and informed them that henceforth there would be no work on Saturday. Some objected. These were paid off, and the others were told that if they chose to do so, they might put six days' work into five by working overtime.

The contractor was just then engaged on a government contract, and was a little behind with it. The work must be finished by a certain date, or payment would be forfeited. The men said they would be obliged to work on Saturday in order to complete the work within contract time. They were told to work on Sunday instead. Some threatened to prosecute the contractor; but a lawyer whom they consulted said to them, " The English laws are founded upon the law of God, and if it should turn out that these men are right in their explanation of that law, it might go hard with you." His advice was that they should not carry the matter further, and it was dropped.

A great interest sprang up in the community, many persons being eager to see the contractor and learn why he worked on Sunday. He accordingly appointed a meeting place, and a crowded house listened attentively while he gave his reasons for observing the Bible Sabbath.

Few families were divided by these early accessions to the Adventist ranks. In most cases all the members of a family heartily embraced the doctrines. The converts were chiefly from the middle class, including school-teachers, printers, foremen of business houses, contractors, and the like. Not one of the early believers was using alcoholic liquors or tobacco at the time he embraced the Adventist doctrines. Thus they were persons who had already taken sides in behalf of certain reform movements, and they wielded a strong influence for good in the community. This fact gave to Adventism at the outset a good standing.

Naturally the loss of a number of members of this type caused not a little uneasiness on the part of the clergy. An effort was made to find a man who would take part in a public debate with Elder Corliss. With a view to preparing for this, several persons provided themselves with a full set of the Adventist books, but after looking them over carefully, they came to the conclusion that it was best not to offer to debate. Nevertheless the opposition continued. Some went so far as to put up flaming posters with the heading, " Christians, beware! " in different parts of the town, and even on the billboards in front of the tent. But the people continued to come, and as the saving truths of the Word were clearly set forth from night to night, those whose hearts God had touched received them gladly.

On Sunday, April 10, 1886, a meeting was held to organize the first Seventh-day Adventist church in Australia. Eighteen persons were present who signed the covenant, seven others applying for admission by baptism. These were baptized on the following Sabbath, and on each following Sabbath for some weeks there were additional candidates until the membership of the church was fifty-five. By the end of May the enrolment of church members had reached nearly the hundred mark, besides more than thirty who had signed the covenant. A missionary society was organized, and a club of 200 papers taken for use in active soul-saving work. A church building was rented for Sabbath meetings.

When the tent meetings in the suburbs of Melbourne were closed at the end of April, Elder Corliss called the believers together on a Sunday afternoon, and told them about the tithing system as a means of support for the ministry, and then read a detailed statement of the expenses incurred in the holding of the tent services. The total amount was about £83. A considerable portion of this had already been paid in contributions; but there remained a deficit of £32, which was made up in a few minutes. It was not even necessary to ask the people to give. Immediately after the reading of the statement, some one said: "I will give £5 toward making up the amount." Then one after another responded so rapidly that it was difficult to set down the names.

The same whole-hearted interest was manifested by the members in the building up of the publishing work. It seemed evident from the first that it would be necessary to publish a paper in order to give character to the work, and reach the largest possible number of people whose hearts were open to new truth. As time passed on, the need came to be so urgent that it was decided to move out by faith, without waiting for word from America. The brethren accordingly approached a large dealer, and made known to him their desire to purchase a complete printing outfit. He asked how much money they had, and was told £10. He then inquired when they could pay the remainder of the bill. They replied: "In about four months."

"Will you give me your note to be paid in that time?"

"We will."

"Are you willing to insure this plant in my favor?"

"We are."

"Then, I am inclined to let you have the outfit; it is not a business way of doing, but I feel impressed to let you have it."

So the office was fitted out with a small gas engine, a large press and a small one, a stitching machine, a paper cutter, type, paper, etc. Two of the young men who had embraced the truth as a result of the Bible studies held by Elder Corliss, sold out their own printing business which they had just started, and united their interests with the new denominational printing office, which was located in a suburb of Melbourne, about four miles from the post office.

In January, 1886, appeared the first number of the monthly periodical, *The Bible Echo and Signs of the Times,* with J. O. Corliss as editor. It was sold by regularly appointed agents, and with its well-written articles on vital scriptural truths, its good make-up, and its freedom from advertising matter, it created a favorable impression wherever it was circulated.

In the course of three months, money had come in to pay all that was still owing on the printing outfit. So the dealer who had advanced the engine, presses, and other things which went to make up the equipment, received his money a month before the note was due. He continued to be a stanch friend of the work.

About this time, too, a beginning was made in canvassing for subscription books. William Arnold, who had come to Australia with the first company of workers, was an experienced colporteur, and he had excellent success in introducing the denominational literature. The first Australian to enter the colporteur field was an elderly man by the name of William Wainman. A plasterer and a bricklayer by trade, he was one of the first to accept the truth in the Melbourne tent-meeting. When he had lost his job and could not get another, owing to his observance of the Sabbath, he gave himself to the book work, and in time came to do very well in it.

Meanwhile the evangelistic work had been going on with undiminished vigor. Immediately following the close of the tent campaign in Melbourne, Elder Corliss went to Ballarat, then a city of 15,000 inhabitants, lying forty-five miles northwest of Melbourne. Elder Israel had been there for some time, engaged in house-to-house work, and a good interest had been built up. A meeting place known as Alfred Hall was engaged, and services were held there regularly till the following spring, with the result that forty-five persons signed the covenant.

From Ballarat Elder Corliss moved with his family to Adelaide, and opened a series of meetings in the town hall of one of the suburbs. Somewhat later the tent was brought from Melbourne and pitched in another suburb of Adelaide, where meetings were also held for some weeks. Following these efforts a church was organized, numbering thirty-five members.

In the spring of 1887, Elder Corliss was obliged to return to the States, owing to failing health. In the same year, W. L. H. Baker, W. D. Curtis, and G. C. Tenney entered upon work in

Australia, the two former enjoying success in evangelistic work by means of tent and hall meetings in various towns and cities, while the latter gave himself chiefly to editorial work. In 1888 meetings were held in Hobart, Tasmania, as a result of which a church was established in that place.

In August, 1888, A. G. Daniells, who had left the United States for New Zealand two years before, attended a general meeting in Melbourne which began August 29 and lasted four days. At this meeting the Australian Conference was organ-

ECHO PUBLISHING HOUSE EMPLOYEES

ized, G. C. Tenney being elected president and Stephen McCullagh secretary. A Sabbath school association and a tract and missionary society were organized at the same time.

At this general meeting it was decided to erect a suitable building to house the publishing interests, the leased premises not being large enough for the growing work. Pledges were taken for this purpose to the amount of £750. Toward the end of the year the new quarters were occupied, though not entirely finished. About the same time the *Bible Echo* was changed to a semimonthly. The Echo Publishing Company was organized under the Companies' Act, its capital being placed at £10,000.

In the spring of 1889, Elder and Mrs. Daniells moved from New Zealand to Australia, where they were occupied with evangelistic work in new places and in further instructing the churches and companies already established.

25

In December, 1891, Mrs. E. G. White and W. C. White landed in Australia, accompanied by G. B. Starr, Marian Davis, and others.

On the 24th of the month a conference was opened in Melbourne, attended by nearly a hundred representatives from churches in Sydney, Adelaide, Tasmania, and Victoria. It was decided at this meeting to take immediate steps to establish a school for the training of workers. This need was provided for

AUSTRALASIAN BIBLE SCHOOL
The beginning of the educational work in Australia was at this place,
George's Terrace, Melbourne.

in rented quarters in the city of Melbourne, where a Bible Training School was temporarily conducted.

Mrs. White's coming to Australia was an event of far-reaching importance in the development of the work in that field. Her labors were in the direction of deepening the spirituality of the believers, and instructing them fully in the principles that underlie the denominational work. When she first arrived in the country, she seemed blessed with even more than her usual degree of strength and energy, and was able to carry heavy responsibilities at the various gatherings of believers.

Her addresses and her wise counsel were much appreciated on the occasion of holding the first Australian camp-meeting, which convened at Middle Brighton, a suburb of Melbourne,

Dec. 29, 1893, and lasted till Jan. 15, 1894. Nearly 500 people were encamped on the ground, and the attendance from the outside was excellent. Thirty-five persons were baptized as a result of the meeting. O. A. Olsen, then visiting Australia, was among the speakers. The success of the gathering far exceeded the anticipations of the brethren, and established camp-meetings as an effective means of spreading a knowledge of the message in Australia, as well as of deepening the spiritual life of the members.

Mrs. White's influence was strongly felt also in the founding of the training school for workers. The selection of a site was a difficult question to settle. A tract of land of about 1,500 acres seventy-five miles north of Sydney, in Cooranbong, N. S. W., was finally selected. The purchase was made at the express desire of Mrs. White, who had seen this piece of land in a dream and had been told that the soil was good. On the other hand, men supposed to have an expert knowledge of soils reported that the land was not suitable for raising fruit. When the location had been finally settled, Mrs. White bought a piece of land and had it planted to fruit. As early as the second year there was such an abundant yield of peaches that the branches had to be propped.

The estate having been purchased, a building formerly used as a hotel, lying something over a mile from the school site, was rented for the accommodation of the students. Four tents pitched in an adjoining field were occupied by some for whom room could not be found in the building. Each morning at six o'clock the faculty and students met together for morning worship and Bible study, and Mrs. White occupied the hour daily for a time at the beginning of the school year, the meetings thus held being fraught with rich spiritual blessings to the school.

In March the young men began to clear the land on the school property, many of them learning for the first time the use of the ax and the saw. It was a season of drouth, and the ground was very hard. Nevertheless ten or twelve acres were cleared for the plow during the first term of school, and over a thousand fruit trees were planted.

Oct. 1, 1896, Mrs. White laid the corner-stone of the first school building. By the end of December that building was nearing completion, and plans were under way for the second, which was to be a one-story structure for use as a kitchen and dining-room. Mrs. White visited the ground when the foundation of this building was being laid, and asked where sleeping-

W. C. WHITE

rooms had been provided for the young men. The reply was that they would occupy the chamber above the sawmill, a very cold, uncomfortable place, wholly unfit for such use. It was finally decided to make the second building two stories instead of one, giving space for sleeping-rooms for the young men at one end of the second story, and a much-needed chapel at the other end.

For some time after the frame of the latter building was up, the work dragged. Available funds had all been used. It lacked only a few weeks of the time fixed for the opening, and there was much yet to be done and no money in the treasury. Mrs. White laid the matter before the church, and called for volunteers. Thirty responded, men and women and children, and they took hold with a will. Every one was put to work, including women and children. Mrs. White's assistants led out. Some helped the men lay the floors, and brought brick for the building of the cistern. Others used the paintbrush. In due time the buildings were ready, and the Avondale school entered upon its career of wide usefulness.

The first faculty consisted of Mr. and Mrs. C. B. Hughes, Elder and Mrs. S. N. Haskell, and Mr. and Mrs. H. C. Lacey. Mr. Hughes was principal, and S. N. Haskell was Bible teacher. The latter held his class daily at an early hour in the morning, and it was attended by a number of persons from the neighborhood, besides the regular students. A school for children was also started at this time.

Not long after the school was well under way, a movement was set on foot for building a church at Cooranbong. For a time the members had worshiped in the loft over the old sawmill in which the school furniture was stored. In winter it was very cold; in summer the sun beating down on the iron roof made the heat almost unbearable. There was nothing about the place to suggest worship. When the second school building was completed, the meetings were held for a time in a room in the second story, but as the school attendance increased, this room was needed for the students.

At a meeting held in August, 1897, when A. G. Daniells and W. L. H. Baker were present to counsel with the brethren in reference to the matter, it was decided to put up a church building, and a suitable location was fixed upon, but for lack of funds it was felt necessary to let the enterprise wait for a time. However, the night following the council, Mrs. White was aroused at an early hour, the situation was brought before her, and she was bidden to give the message of the prophet Haggai: " Is it time for you, O ye, to dwell in your ceiled houses, and this house lie waste? Now therefore, thus saith the Lord of hosts: Consider your ways." "Go up to the mountain, and bring wood, and build the house; and I will take pleasure in it, and I will be glorified, saith the Lord." Haggai 1: 4, 5, 8.

The message was delivered, and met with a hearty response. The very next night a draft for £200 came from friends in

| EDITH M. GRAHAM | ANNA INGELS HINDSON |

South Africa to help pay for a church. Other gifts came in from various sources. The carpenters worked with a will, and just before the close of the school term a neat, commodious house of worship was ready for dedication.

The staff of workers was further increased in the early nineties by the coming of L. J. Rousseau, who devoted himself to educational interests; W. D. Salisbury, who took the management of the publishing house; W. A. Colcord and A. S. Hickox, who gave themselves to evangelistic work; and Anna L. Ingels, who with Edith M. Graham, of Australia, took a leading part in the work of the tract and missionary society.

Mrs. White remained in Australia for ten years, during which time the evangelistic work was put on a very strong basis, and a union conference organization was developed which has served as a model for all the other conferences of the denomination throughout the world. This period of time also saw the college, sanitarium, and publishing house put upon a strong footing.

The Avondale school, known now as the Australasian Missionary College, has been conducted from the beginning on the industrial plan, and has had for the most part a very prosperous career. Like many of our institutions, especially our schools, it had its share of embarrassment and trial. At a time of special embarrassment, E. R. Palmer was called from the Echo Publishing House to help out in the school work, and for two years there was an encouraging growth. Later Prof. C. W. Irwin, from the United States, was with the institution for eight years, during which time further substantial advancement was made.

The industries of the school, such as gardening and fruit-raising, the manufacture of health foods, the printing of island literature, etc., after becoming well established, enabled it to open its doors to large numbers of deserving young people who could not otherwise have obtained an education, and the combination of useful hand labor with book studies has made for all-round development. From the school have gone out devoted men and women, not only to various parts of Australia and New Zealand, but also to many of the islands of the Pacific, to Asiatic countries, and to other parts of the great harvest field.

The Echo Publishing Company, organized some eighteen years previously, was in 1906 removed to Warburton, a rural community forty-eight miles east of Melbourne. At the same time all commercial work was given up, yet the office has kept more than busy supplying the workers with the denominational publications. The Avondale Press, connected with the college, issues two English periodicals and several in native tongues of the South Pacific Islands, as well as tracts and books in various languages. Prominent among the managers of the publishing house have been W. D. Salisbury, W. H. B. Miller, one of the young men who closed out their own publishing business in 1885 in order to work on the *Bible Echo,* and J. M. Johanson.

Australia has from the beginning offered a favorable field for the colporteur. William Arnold, a member of the first company of workers, was successful in introducing the denominational books into thousands of homes, and he was followed in early days by other men who enjoyed similar success. In course of time, however, a backward trend began to manifest itself in this work. Some of the agents became involved in debt, the tract societies slackened their efforts, and the publishing house began to deal directly with the canvassers, the sales meanwhile undergoing a steady decline. Under these circumstances a call was made for an experienced man to be sent from the States to revive the work by putting it once more on a sound basis.

E. R. Palmer, of New England, who had recently been associated with F. L. Mead in conducting canvassers' institutes in various parts of the country, and was then secretary-treasurer of the Oklahoma Tract Society, was sent in response to this

THE SYDNEY SANITARIUM

call. He landed at Melbourne about the first of May, and joining with other experienced leaders already in that field, immediately applied himself to the task in hand. He was first connected as general agent with the Australian tract society, and after about one year, connected with the publishing house as manager of the book and periodical department and with the Australasian Union Conference as general agent. The Australian tract society was later divided into six different societies, each representing a local conference. Secretaries were trained for these societies, who took hold of the work with vim and enthusiasm, and general agents were appointed to train colporteurs and direct their activities in the field. In a short time the book work began to show tangible results, and the sales ultimately increased fourfold. When E. R. Palmer was called back to America in 1901, the work was continued under the leadership of other men, prominent among whom were J. M. Johanson and L. D. A. Lemke.

Health work was begun by A. W. Semmens, a nurse, who started treatment-rooms in Sydney. The interest thus developed took form finally in the Wahroonga Sanitarium, conducted in a suburb of Sydney by Drs. D. H. and Lauretta Kress, who landed in Australia in the autumn of 1900. Later a small sanitarium was opened in Adelaide, and in 1910 another institution of the kind was established at Warburton.

When A. G. Daniells returned to America in 1901, G. A. Irwin took his place as president of the Australasian Union. He was followed four years later by O. A. Olsen, who was succeeded by J. E. Fulton. After the latter was called elsewhere, the direction of the work for a number of years rested with C. H. Watson.

New Zealand

While Elder J. O. Corliss was conducting the various tent efforts that resulted so successfully in Melbourne, Elder Haskell went to the neighboring island of New Zealand, chiefly for the purpose of securing agencies for the monthly paper, *The Bible Echo and Signs of the Times*, which was to come out in January. He found in Auckland a denomination whose members, calling themselves Christians, appeared to have much in common with Seventh-day Adventists. Some of them were accustomed to meet for a sort of class meeting on Thursday nights, in order to discuss different points of doctrine. Elder Haskell was invited to meet with them, and present those doctrines wherein Adventists differ from other denominations. This resulted in a discussion of the Sabbath question with the pastor of the church. Another class of the same character was held at Mount Eden, one of the suburbs of Auckland, and at this one Elder Haskell introduced the subject of the personal and visible coming of Christ.

As a result of these discussions a number began to observe the Sabbath. One of the first in Auckland was Edward Hare, who with his wife soon embraced the Adventist views, and began at once to interest himself in the circulation of the books and papers containing the truth. At his request Elder Haskell visited his father and mother, who resided in Kaeo, 160 miles north of Auckland. The elder Hare, who had been a schoolmaster in Ireland for twenty years, was at the time a local preacher for the Methodists. Elder Haskell occupied his pulpit for three Sundays; he also held meetings in a hall, and visited freely from house to house. Father Hare and his son Robert, also a local preacher, embraced the truth, and Robert sailed shortly for America, where he entered Healdsburg College.

As a result of this first visit of Elder Haskell, two families took their stand for the Sabbath; but their numbers being few, they did not hold public meetings. Returning to the place a few months later, Brother Haskell found that the believers had continued faithful, and the interest had deepened, the opposition also having greatly increased. The people, never having witnessed Scriptural baptism, had strange ideas of it, and were reluctant to move forward; but after the first baptism their objections were fully removed. Three were converted the night after the first baptism, and two days later eight others were baptized. After the second baptism a church of seventeen members was organized, and the ordinances were celebrated at the home of Father Hare. Arrangements were made for a Sabbath school, and the number of believers steadily increased. By September of the same year there were keeping the Sabbath in Father Hare's family alone, some forty persons, including children and grandchildren.

FATHER HARE

In the autumn of 1886, Elder and Mrs. A. G. Daniells, who had been conducting a mission in Des Moines, Iowa, went to New Zealand to labor. A fifty-foot tent, brought from America, was pitched in Auckland, and a series of services covering seventeen weeks was begun on December 29. About sixty persons accepted the Adventist views as a result of these meetings. Elder and Mrs. W. D. Curtis were associated with the effort during the closing month. From the company of believers thus brought out there was shortly organized a church of seventy members, a Sabbath school numbering a hundred, a tract society, a health and temperance society, and a small company of canvassers. Moreover, a house of worship had been erected, and was almost entirely paid for when it was ready for use in the summer of 1887.

Elder Daniells' second tent effort in New Zealand was conducted at Napier in 1888, Robert Hare, who had returned from America, assisting in the work. Here also the meetings were well attended, a church of more than fifty members was organized, and a commodious church building erected.

At the close of the Napier tent-meetings, Mr. Hare removed to Gisborne, where he was able, in the course of a few months, to raise up a company of believers. A house of worship for this church was provided by purchasing a suitable building from another denomination.

In the spring of 1889, Elder M. C. Israel came from Tasmania, and spent some weeks in visiting the New Zealand

THE FIRST CHURCH BUILT IN NEW ZEALAND, AT AUCKLAND

churches. About the same time Elder and Mrs. E. M. Morrison, from America, devoted several months to the building up of the canvassing and Sabbath school work. During the stay of these workers a general meeting was held in Auckland, at which were organized the New Zealand Conference and the tract society.

When Robert Hare was transferred to Australia, early in 1890, M. C. Israel moved with his family to New Zealand. Immediately after the holding of the first annual conference, A. G. Daniells opened tent meetings in Wellington, the capital of the colony, at the same time locating a book depository in the city, and arranging for the introduction of denominational literature by canvassers. He was presently called away, however, to take part in a Biblical institute in Melbourne, and to visit the churches with S. N. Haskell in connection with the latter's third visit to Australia. The results of the effort at Wellington were therefore comparatively meager. Nevertheless, several embraced the truth, and the work was continued under the direction of S. McCullagh, who came from Australia when Elder A. G. Daniells was transferred to that field of labor. A church of twenty-five members was organized in June, 1891.

At a conference held in Napier, April 1-15, 1892, there were present representatives from Kaeo, Auckland, Gisborne, Palmerston, Wellington, Petone, Blenheim, Nelson, Kaikoura, and Dunedin. In the following November Elder and Mrs. G. T. Wilson, of America, took up work in New Zealand, Brother Wilson serving for a number of years as conference president.

The first Seventh-day Adventist camp-meeting in New Zealand, and probably the first south of the equator, was held at Napier March 24 to April 7, 1893. Mrs. E. G. White was present, and spoke on several occasions. Her address on Sabbath, March 25, had a powerful effect upon the audience. She had come to the colony some weeks before the camp-meeting, and had visited some of the churches and spoken in the Theater Royal at Auckland. She remained over till the next camp-meeting, which was held in Wellington in the latter part of the same year, and was an occasion of great blessing to the believers, as well as a means of reaching many new ones. O. A. Olsen was also present at this meeting.

Mission work for the Maoris was established in 1905, with headquarters at Gisborne. Various small books and tracts and a monthly paper have been issued in the Maori tongue. Among the persons connected with this work, mention should be made of Mr. and Mrs. Redward, Mr. and Mrs. Read Smith, who were nurses, and R. K. Piper. Read Smith laid down his life among the Maoris.

A training school originally established in Cambridge, one hundred miles south of Auckland, was in 1912 moved to a more suitable location in Longhorn, about seventy miles north of Wellington.

Australia as a Base for Missions

The work has gone forward on even lines in Australia. The well-thought-out plans for systematic organization of all the various lines of activity, under the leadership of A. G. Daniells, the first president of the union, had much to do with the rapid and harmonious growth that has ensued.

It was a great experience for the members when at the union conference of 1906 the oversight of all the work in the islands of the Pacific was turned over to Australia. There was present at that Sabbath service C. H. Parker, of Fiji, and with him Pauliasi, a native convert, who was ordained at the time. " The Spirit was literally poured out upon us," writes an eyewitness. " God bound off the work of our conference with a manifestation of His power such as none of us had ever before witnessed."

The responsibility thus assumed has been faithfully discharged. Under the leadership of Australasia, the work of giving the advent message to widely scattered groups of islands in the South Seas has been going forward systematically. The Australian believers have given of their best blood that the isles might hear His law. Even so small a conference as Tasmania has given many of its sons and daughters to the island work.

The more remote portions of the mainland are also being worked. West Australia was entered in the middle nineties, and likewise Queensland, Sabbath keepers being found in both.

More recently a mission and a school for aborigines is being carried on at Monamona, near Cairns, in northern Queensland. In New South Wales a similar work is going forward. Both these missions are bearing fruit.

L. R. CONRADI

THE FIRST PLACE OF WORSHIP IN GERMANY

CHAPTER XX

Beginnings Among the Germans

ONE morning in the early spring of 1878 a young man stood at the door of a humble cabin a few miles from the little town of Afton, Iowa, and begged to be taken in as a boarder. He had been engaged to clear an adjoining piece of land, and desired board and lodging at this particular cabin because it was the only one lying conveniently near. The owner, on his part, urged the small size of the cabin, its two rooms scarcely affording accommodations for himself and his growing family. But finally the good-natured persistence of the young stranger won the day, and he was accepted as a boarder on condition that he be content to sleep in the loft, and to forego a warm dinner on the seventh day of the week.

The home thus opened to the stranger, as the reader will have surmised, was a Seventh-day Adventist home. The young man who entered it as a boarder was Louis R. Conradi, a native of Karlsruhe, in the Grand Duchy of Baden, Germany. He had been brought up a Roman Catholic, and was pursuing studies leading to the priesthood when his father's death made it necessary for him to discontinue school work. He accord-

399

ingly applied himself to learn the trade of a cooper, and not long afterward sought his fortune in America, the new land of promise. Here he wandered about a good deal, working at his trade in New York, Chicago, St. Louis, and other large cities, and at length drifted out to Iowa, where he took a job of clearing land, which brought him under the humble roof of James Burton for room and board. It was a different home than any he had known before, and he was not slow to notice the fact. The family life was marked by quiet earnestness and serenity. Religion manifested itself in actions rather than in words. No effort was put forth to ascertain the denominational affiliations of the new boarder, or to induce him to change them for others; but family worship was held morning and evening, and even the children took part, and they prayed for the stranger within their gates. This touched a tender place in the young man's heart. It threw a new light on the whole subject of religion, this kindly interest in a perfect stranger on the part of little children.

When Sabbath came, the farmer hitched up his team and drove to the nearest town, where he and his family attended the Sabbath school and the prayer and social meeting following, in the little Seventh-day Adventist meeting house, while the new boarder looked over the town. The next Sabbath the boarder of his own choice attended the Sabbath school, but went out when the social meeting began. The third Sabbath he attended both. The fourth Sabbath he kept according to the commandment. The prayers of those little children had been answered; God had remembered the stranger within their gates.

These had been weeks, however, of severe struggle. The young man was addicted to tobacco; the power of this evil habit had to be broken. Then there was another and most insidious enemy to whose attacks so many young men succumb,— the enemy of unbelief. Was the Bible true? Did men really know what it taught? And was there any hereafter? A copy of " Thoughts on Daniel and the Revelation " helped to solve these doubts, and threw welcome light on the Bible as a whole, showing its relation to human history, and to the working out of the plan of the ages. But reading, alone, would not have convinced the young German. He had before him a daily demonstration of the meaning of Christianity in the home life of the family who had taken him as a boarder. He heard their daily prayers for help, and saw them answered in the serene peacefulness and quiet beauty of that humble Christian home. It had a wondrous attraction for him; it appealed to all that was best in him, especially the prayers of those little children. And in his great need he himself resorted to prayer. Many an earnest petition for light and guidance and strength did he offer in the lonely woods. And the answer came in abiding peace and the forming of a new life purpose.

Some weeks after he had taken his stand, the young man, having finished the work assigned him on the adjoining farm, found work at a place about fifteen miles from Afton; but regularly every Sabbath he attended the Adventist services in that town, covering the thirty miles sometimes on foot and sometimes on horseback. In July he attended the State camp-meeting, and was baptized. He now gave himself to close study in order that he might be able intelligently to present to others the truth which had become precious to him. Engaged in hard labor for the entire day, he would rise at two o'clock in the morning, in order to have time for Bible study and prayer before the work of the day had to be taken up. He also began holding Bible readings with interested persons in the neighborhood, and for a time taught a class in Sunday school.

In the autumn S. N. Haskell and Maria L. Huntley were holding an institute in Oskaloosa. They learned of the young German through his applying for some German tracts, and telegraphed him to come to the institute. The outcome of the acquaintance thus made was that he attended Battle Creek College the following winter, the Afton church contributing $25 toward his expenses.

Once in college, he applied himself so earnestly to his studies as seriously to undermine his health, meanwhile boarding himself to save money. When his slender resources did not hold out even for the meager fare he allowed himself, and he was confronted with the necessity of leaving school, the way opened for him to enter the employment of the publishing house. Thus he was able to complete the literary course in the spring of 1880, after which he remained in the printing office about a year.

In the spring of 1881 he began to labor for his countrymen in Iowa, first devoting himself to securing subscriptions to the German paper, and later assisting James Sawyer in a tent effort at Sac City. Autumn found him laboring among the Russian-German Mennonites of Brotherfield and Childstown, S. Dak. He spent about three months in faithful labor on behalf of these people, holding meetings in schoolhouses and private homes, and visiting from house to house. The seed was taking root in good ground, but the harvest was yet a little way off. Meanwhile he was called to Milltown in a neighboring county, where there was a company of Sabbath-keeping Germans who were split into factions. After faithful labor extending over some months, things were put right, and it was possible on April 9 to organize the first German Seventh-day Adventist church, with a membership of nineteen.

By this time the situation at Brotherfield had become very favorable. The young licentiate accordingly returned to resume his labors, with the result that a church of thirty members was organized in that place in September, 1881. Then he went on to Immanuel Creek, and there too it was possible, before the close of the year, to raise up a company of German Seventh-day Adventists.

At the Dakota camp-meeting, held in the summer of 1882, L. R. Conradi, the licentiate who had been instrumental in thus making a substantial beginning among the Germans of this country, was ordained to the ministry. In the following summer he joined H. Shultz, who had left the presidency of the Nebraska Conference in order to devote himself to work among his countrymen, in the carrying on of the first tent effort among the Germans of the United States, at Sutton, Nebr.

A year later he conducted a tent effort in Fleetwood, Pa.; and in 1885, assisted by J. S. Shrock, he held meetings in Allentown, Pa., where the attendance at times rose to 1,000 persons. A church of thirty members was organized in the latter place.

The German work in America had its most rapid growth, however, in western Kansas. As early as the spring of 1884 a beginning had been made by L. R. Conradi and J. S. Shrock, and in the course of the following winter a church was established in Hillsboro, which by May, 1885, had attained a membership of 123. Further additions continued to be made to this church, and other companies were gradually raised up in other parts of Kansas, as well as in Wisconsin, Minnesota, and Oregon.

In January, 1886, Elder Conradi, by action of the General Conference, sailed for Europe to answer the call for a German preacher. Shortly after his arrival, he and J. Erzenberger began a series of meetings for the German-Swiss in Lausanne, as a result of which twenty-two persons were baptized in Lake Geneva, and organized into an Adventist church the ensuing spring. In the latter part of June Elder Conradi visited German Sabbath keepers in the Crimea, as recorded in another chapter. The following year he accompanied Mrs. E. G. White and her son, W. C. White, on a visit to the Sabbath keepers in

Rhenish Prussia. In April, 1888, E. E. Frauchiger, one of the converts of the Lausanne tent-meeting, and G. Perk, of Russia, began to do colporteur work in Rhenish Prussia, and Brother Frauchiger began to sell our publications in Würtemberg.

At the General Conference held in the autumn of 1888, it was decided to begin aggressive evangelistic work in Germany.

E. E. FRAUCHIGER

L. R. Conradi, who attended the Conference, was accordingly accompanied on his return to the old country by J. T. Boettcher, J. Klein, and others. Hamburg, the third largest seaport in the world, was chosen as a center. A mission was opened here the following April, at 41 Sophienstrasse, in connection with which regular preaching services were held, supplemented by the holding of Bible readings and canvassing from house to house. The effort thus put forth resulted in the organizing of a church of twenty-five members the following autumn.

In connection with the mission there was held in the course of the summer the first training school for workers in Germany, the pupils numbering eight. At the close of the school in September, 1889, J. Klein, one of the student workers, was ordained to the gospel ministry and sent to Russia to labor.

The first general meeting of Germans in Europe was held at Altona, a suburb of Hamburg, Jan. 28 to Feb. 1, 1891. The meeting was attended by H. P. Holser, then superintendent of the Central European Mission, with headquarters at Basel; and by L. R. Conradi, J. Erzenberger, and other laborers, as well as by representatives from various parts of Germany. At this meeting it was decided to separate Germany and Russia from the Central European Conference, of which they had been a part, and organize them as separate mission fields under the superintendency of L. R. Conradi. At the same time a German tract and missionary society and a Sabbath School Association were organized.

In the course of the winter and spring of 1891 the second session of the training school for workers was conducted at the mission in Hamburg, with an attendance of twelve students. At the camp-meeting held near Basel that summer, J. T. Boettcher was ordained to the ministry, and soon afterward began a series of meetings in Barmen, Rhenish Prussia, which resulted in the raising up of a church of nineteen members.

At the next general meeting, held in Hamburg in January, 1892, the chief question under consideration was the acquire-

HEADQUARTERS IN HAMBURG

ment of a suitable property in Hamburg for the permanent establishment of the work. Offerings were received for this purpose from the members in Germany, to which was added the sum of $15,000, voted by the General Conference in 1893. At the third general meeting for the Germans held at 15a Grindelberg, Hamburg, it was decided to purchase that property for the permanent headquarters of the German work. The mission training school in that year enrolled thirty-two students, six of whom came from Russia, two from Holland, one from Hungary, one from Denmark, one from Switzerland, and the rest from Germany.

When the brethren held their fourth general gathering, in the summer of 1894, it was in a tent pitched in the rear of the mission property on Grindelberg. They then voted to erect a two-story chapel, 35 x 67 feet, alongside the mission building. The ground floor of the chapel was in due time equipped as a printing office, and about the middle of the year 1895 the German paper, *Harold der Wahrheit,* began to be issued biweekly from this office instead of from Basel. Books and tracts in many different languages were also put out in large numbers, the office undergoing enlargement from time to time to accommodate the rapidly increasing business till it had taken on large proportions.

To meet the growing educational needs, H. F. Schuberth came over from America in the autumn of 1894, and took charge of the training school. A further advanced step was taken in the development of the educational work when it was voted, at a meeting held in Magdeburg in July, 1896, to secure permanent quarters for the school. After looking about in various places, the brethren finally fixed upon the " Klappermuehle " estate, lying in the heart of Germany, near the village of Burg, not far from the city of Magdeburg. The property includes some ninety acres of tilled field, meadow land, and forest, through which runs the Ihle, a small stream furnishing water power for running the gristmill from which the estate takes its name.

In November of the same year the school opened its doors, with one teacher, Otto Luepke, and seven pupils. Later more pupils came in, and there was an addition to the staff of instructors in Dr. A. J. Hoenes, who taught in the nurses' department. The small schoolroom had only twenty-four seats, and it served also as meeting hall and business office. Dormitory accommodations were very meager to begin with, the young men sleeping in the large loft over the mill. This arrangement was, however, only temporary.

In 1900 two provisional buildings were put up and occupied for school purposes, to be used afterward as workshops; and after July of that year there was a two-room schoolhouse, which would accommodate about forty pupils, the attendance by that time running from thirty to forty.

The permanent plan for the school, which came to be known as the Friedensau Missionary Seminary, began to be revealed in the erection in 1902 of the south wing of the present school building. On the first floor of this there was a large assembly room that would accommodate fifty pupils. On the second floor were living rooms for the young women, and on the third floor the young men were accommodated.

In 1904 the school building at Friedensau was completed, including four spacious classrooms, forty-nine living-rooms for

Herold der Wahrheit

„Prüfet aber Alles, und das Gute behaltet." 1. Theff. 5, 21.

| 1. Jahrgang | Basel, Schweiz, Januar 1884. | No. 1. |

Herold der Wahrheit

— eine —

Religiöse Monatsschrift

Herausgegeben von der Gesellschaft der

Adventisten vom siebenten Tage.

— Gewidmet: —

Der Erklärung biblischer Wahrheiten, insbesondere der Prophezeiungen, die sich auf die Wiederkunft Christi beziehen und der vorbereitenden Vorbereitung auf jenes Ereigniß.

Abonnements-Preis portofrei

1 Exemplar jährlich . . . Frc. 3.— Mt. 2.40
5 — 10 „ . . . . . 2.50 „ 2.—

Bureau: Weiherhalde 20, Basel.

Der Jahrgang dieser Zeitschrift fängt mit Januar an. Man kann aber auch im April, Juli mit October darauf abonniren. Zeigt uns vor den Abonnementsbetrag in Briefmarken oder deutschen Reichsmark einzusenden, so kann man solches thun. Es werden jedoch alle schriftlichen Mittheilungen sowie Geldsendungen portofrei erbeten.

Adresse: L. R. Conradi,
Bureau des „Herold der Wahrheit"
Basel, Schweiz

Das Kommen des Herrn.

Unser Gott kommt und schweiget nicht. Fressendes Feuer gehet vor ihm her, und es ist ihn her ein großes Wetter. Er ruft Himmel und Erde, daß er sein Volk richte. Versammelt mir meine Heiligen, die den Bund mehr achten, denn Opfer. Und die Himmel werden seine Gerechtigkeit verkündigen; denn Gott ist Richter." Pf. 50, 2-6.

Wir befinden uns am Vorabend des größten Ereignisses, das die Welt je gesehen hat und von dem die größte Veränderung für Gläubige und Ungläubige abhängt. Es ist dieses das Kommen unseres Herrn Jesu Christi zum andern Mal, wenn er mit großer Kraft und Herrlichkeit und als König aller Könige, und Herr aller Herren erscheint, um alles sich zu unterwerfen. Wir wollen nun sehen was der Psalmist in unserem Texte über dieses Ereigniß sagt.

Schon das erste Wort ist sehr auffallend— „Unser Gott." Es ist ein Wort, das der Jude Gottes nachspürt. Nur ein Kind Gottes kann es in Wahrheit aussprechen. Ein solches Kind ist Glied der Familie und mit seinem himmlischen Vater verwandt. Es wurde durch das Blut Christi erlöst und nahe gebracht. Es ist ein Erbe der Verheißungen des ewigen Bundes und Mürbe Christi. Es kann aufwärts blicken und sagen: „Mein Freund ist mein und ich bin sein." Und wenn der Herr aus Feuerflammen vom Himmel kommen wird, wird es von denjenigen gesagt werden können: „Siehe, das ist unser Gott, auf den wir harren, und er wird uns helfen; das ist der Herr, auf den wir harten, daß wir uns freuen und fröhlich seien in seinem Heil." Es ist nicht zu zweifeln,

dieses Wort gehört der Familie an. Und derjenige, welcher uns die köstlichen Worte „Unser Vater" auf die Zunge legt, wacht auch tröstig auf jene ereignißvolle Stunde vorwärts blicken und sagen zu können: „Unser Gott."

Wir sind nun daran das Kommen Gottes zu betrachten, wenn er in menschlicher Form, als ein verzehrendes Feuer, mit Windwirbel und Ungestüm auf sich her, auf diese Erde kommen wird. Wie nothwendig ist es aber in Wahrheit sagen zu können „Unser Gott," ehe dieses Ereigniß stattfindet. Was wird es doch sein, wenn wir nicht ausrufen können: „Unser Gott." Welche Angst und welches Entsetzen muß sich doch bei jenem Anblick solcher bemächtigen, die nicht zum Vorauss sagen können: „Unser Gott!"

Lieber Leser! Laß es deine Hauptaufgabe sein solches zu erlangen, ehe du einen Schritt weiter gehst. Wenn du in Wahrheit sagen kannst „Unser Gott," wird es dir dann herzlich sein, in die Zukunft zu blicken, und wenn dich dieses Ereigniß zuvöni antreffen zu können: „Unser Gott." Eben deswegen läßt der heilige Geist dieses kleine Wort zuerst an, damit wir uns ernstlich und aufrichtig prüfen möchten, ehe wir zu demjenigen übergehen, das nachfolgt.

„Unser Gott kommt und schweiget nicht." Um diesen Ausdruck „schweiget nicht" recht zu verstehen, müssen wir auf den letzten Theil dieses Kapitels verweisen, wo vom sechzehnten bis zum zwanzigsten Vers gesagt ist: „Aber zu dem Gottlosen spricht Gott: Was verkündigst du meine Rechte und nimmst meinen Bund in deinem Mund, so du doch Zucht hassest, und wirfst meine Worte hinter dich? Wenn du einen Dieb siehest, so läufst du mit ihm, und hast Gemeinschaft mit den Ehebrechern. Dein Maul lässest du Böses reden, und deine Zunge treibet Falschheit. Du sitzest und redest wider deinen Bruder, deiner Mutter Sohn verleumdest du. Das thust du, und ich schweige, da meinst du, ich werde sein gleich wie du." Hier führt Gott die bösen Handlungen der Gottlosen an. Es ist gerade dasjenige, was während sechs tausend Jahren auf unserer Erde vorgegangen ist. Die Menschen nahmen Gottes Bund in ihren Mund; sie gaben vor der Gottseligkeit zu huldigen, verleugneten aber ihre Kraft. Unter dem Deckmantel der Frömmigkeit wurden die größten Sünden begangen. Gott wurde „gehabt" und sein Wort hinter sich geworfen. „Ehebruch," „Falschheit" und „Verleumdung"—solches sind von den Übeln, die heute im Schwange gehen. Und während dieser ganzen Zeit schweigt Gott. Er ließ den Menschen in seinem gottlosen Wesen nachgehen, ohne mit dem Herrn seiner Gerechtigkeit einzugreifen. Eben deswegen trug der Unglaube: Wo ist Gott? Sollte Gott sehen können? Wenn es einen Gott gibt, warum läßt er sich nicht merken? Entweder ist kein Gott, oder er ist gleichwie wir." Auf solche Weise ist es ja bisher Welt vor sich gegangen— der Gottlose „grünete wie ein Lorbeerbaum" der Gerechte vergoß Thränen darüber und Gott schweig da-

zu. Es wird jedoch nicht immer so gehen. „Unser Gott wird kommen und nicht schweigen." Er wird kommen die Menschen zu stellen, um den Unbußfertigen vor Augen zu stellen, was sie gethan haben. Und die sündlichen Handlungen der Bösen, welche in diesem Psalm verzeichnet sind, werden von der Geschichte als die herrschenden Grundzüge der Welt bezeichnet, und im zweiten Timotheus, Kapitel drei durch Gottes Geist aufs Neue angeführt. Es sollen in den letzten Tagen besonders blühen.

Welches werden jedoch die Herolde seines Kommens sein? Fressendes Feuer geht vor ihm her, und um ihn her ein großes Wetter. Solches wird auch durch den heiligen Gott bestätiget, wenn er durch Paulus spricht: „Euch aber, die ihr Trübsal leidet, Ruhe mit uns, wenn nun der Herr Jesus wird geoffenbaret werden vom Himmel, sammt den Engeln seiner Kraft, und mit Feuerflammen, Rache zu geben über die, so Gott nicht erkennen, und die, so nicht gehorsam sind dem Evangelio unsers Herrn Jesu Christi, welche werden Pein leiden, das ewige Verderben von dem Angesicht des Herrn, und von seiner herrlichen Macht."

Von einem Ende der Christenheit bis zum andern wird dann ein verzweiflungsvolles Geschrei zum Himmel emporsteigen. Die Gottlosen werden die Berge und Felsen anrufen, daß sie über sie fallen und sie vor der Gegenwart des Lammes verbergen möchten. Dann wird von vielen Lippen, die nun über die Predigt von Jesu spotten, das laute und dringende Rufen vernommen werden: „Herr, Herr, thue uns auf!" aber zu spät. „Und die Menschen werden verschmachten vor Furcht und vor Warten der Dinge, die kommen sollen auf Erden." Einige jedoch werden in jener allgemeinen Verwirrung ihr Freuden ihre Häupter erheben, denn sie wissen, daß ihre Erlösung nahet. Welch Glück wird es doch sein, in jener feierlichen Stunde der kleinen Heerde anzugehören und auszutreten in Frieden: „Unser Gott."

Was wird der Herr dann thun? Er wird Himmel und Erde rufen, „daß er sein Volk richte." Solches wird durch Paulus, der durch den Geist Gottes spricht, folgender Weise bezeugt: „Denn das sagen wir euch, als ein Wort des Herrn, daß wir, die wir leben, und überbleiben in der Zukunft des Herrn, werden denen nicht vorkommen, die da schlafen. Denn er selbst, der Herr, wird mit einem Feldgeschrei und Stimme des Erzengels, und mit der Posaune Gottes hernieder kommen vom Himmel, und die Todten in Christo werden auferstehen zuerst. Darnach wir, die wir leben und überbleiben, werden zugleich mit denselben hingerückt werden in den Wolken, dem Herrn entgegen in der Luft, und werden also bei dem Herrn sein allezeit."

Das Wort „darnach" zeigt, daß nachdem die Auferstehenden mit den noch lebenden Heiligen zusammen genommen sind, und bevor die Kinder Gottes den Herrn entgegen gerückt werden, noch eine kleine Zwischenzeit stattfinden wird. Diese wird durch herzliche Begrüßung, innige Umarmung und Ausdrücke der Freude ausgefüllt werden. Und nach diesem werden sich students, and workrooms, and a neat chapel, the whole costing about $35,000.

Every extension of room has been accompanied by an increase in the number of students, young men and women coming from many different parts of continental Europe to receive a training for effective service. In one year as many as seventeen different nationalities were represented. In the early days the

GERMAN TRAINING SCHOOL, FRIEDENSAU

largest group of students, aside from Germans, came from Russia.

In the period before the World War more than 300 evangelistic workers went out from the school, and 200 nurses. In the training of the latter the school had the efficient co-operation of the Friedensau Sanitarium. This institution, which was opened in 1901, not only was able to care for a large number of patients yearly, but had under its direction nurses working in a number of the leading cities of Central Europe.

Meanwhile evangelistic work was being carried on in various parts of the German Empire, and in spite of unfavorable circumstances, chiefly in the nature of restrictions of various kinds, honest hearts were gladly accepting the advent message. A few representative instances may be cited.

Rhenish Prussia may be said to be the cradle of German Adventism. As early as 1884 two small churches were organized at Elberfeld and Solingen, respectively, the members being in part persons who had begun the observance of the Sabbath as a result of the teachings of Elder Linderman in the seventies. From this small nucleus the work gradually reached out into other parts of the historic country drained by the Rhine. In time there were flourishing churches at Essen, the center of its iron works, at Cologne, Barmen, and Bonn. In other parts of Prussia the work has grown with equal rapidity, the number of churches and companies in or near Berlin numbering more than twenty in 1925.

In southern Germany the truth has made progress under trying conditions. Sabbath keepers were reported in Bavaria in the early years of the work; but up to May, 1907, there was no official recognition of the denomination in that country, and believers were fined at different times from 25 to 50 marks each for attending Adventist meetings. Baptisms had to be held in secret, and public worship was conducted in a way to attract the least attention. At first the believers organized local societies under the name, " Society of Christian Men and Women." The first of these was conducted in Augsburg, the second in Bayreuth. These societies, however, were greatly limited in their rights. After repeated appeals had been made to the government, a special decree was secured by which Adventists were given the privilege of holding church property and preaching freely throughout Bavaria without even asking permission of the authorities.

In the summer of 1908 a series of lectures was held in the city of Augsburg, famous as the place where the Augsburg Confession of Faith was framed and adopted. The lectures were given in a tent, a new thing for the people, and a good interest was awakened. The daily papers without solicitation began to print encouraging reports of the services, and the interest constantly increased. Presently the clergymen of the city became aware of the situation, and began to write articles against the Adventist teaching. These our brethren took pains to answer, the result being a greatly increased interest. In due time there came to be a flourishing church in Augsburg.

In Munich, the residence city of the prince regent of Bavaria, and a great educational center, sometimes called the Athens of modern Europe, the message received a great impetus about the same time. A man who posed as an Adventist minister began to preach in certain sections of the city. The city authorities were alarmed over the errors he preached, and began to inquire whether he really represented the Adventists. When they were informed to the contrary, they had him arrested for making false representations. Thereupon the articles which had been printed in the public press against us were by order of the magistrate recalled. Moreover, in order to have a trustworthy statement, the publishers of the Bavarian Year Book for 1909 forthwith solicited a short but comprehensive sketch of the origin, development, organization, and present financial standing of Seventh-day Adventists, as well as the principal points of their faith. This was furnished, and proved very helpful to our workers.

Evangelistic work in Saxony was begun under G. Perk, who, being a foreigner, was sent out of the country in 1902. K. Sinz, a native of the country, continued the work, but for a time under great difficulties. At every meeting there were two or three detectives present to make note of all that was said or done. In course of time the surveillance became less strict, the authorities finding that Adventists have no ulterior aims beyond helping their fellow men. They were merely tolerated, however, the denomination having no official standing.

In spite of these difficulties the truth spread rapidly, and in 1908 the believers were organized into a conference.

The further growth of the institutional and evangelistic work in Germany will be dealt with in a later chapter.

STEPHEN N. HASKELL

This photograph was taken on his eighty-fifth birthday.

HOME OF THE FIRST TRACT SOCIETY

CHAPTER XXI

Home Missionary Activities -- Death of James White

THE present chapter will cover two main topics: first, the early beginnings and full development of the organization known as the International Tract Society; and, second, the closing years and the final passing away of the man whom God had especially used in laying the foundations of the advent movement. The junction of these two topics in the one chapter is the more appropriate inasmuch as James White was from the beginning exceedingly active in the circulation of Adventist literature, and it was under his fostering care that the new organization grew in strength and exerted its widespread influence for good.

The early Adventists may be said to have been, all of them, purveyors of tracts and papers. Firmly convinced of the truth of the doctrines they held, they coveted the opportunity to place the evidence before their fellow men.

Tract societies of various kinds suited to the local needs followed close after the general organization of churches in 1862. They were first brought to a high degree of efficiency in

411

the New England Conference, under the leadership of S. N. Haskell. He visited Battle Creek in the late sixties, and was deeply impressed with the views of Elder and Mrs. White concerning the systematic distribution of literature. Shortly after his return to New England, in the early part of 1868, he organized in South Lancaster, Mass., what became known as the Vigilant Missionary Society.

The membership consisted originally of nine women who met every Wednesday afternoon at three o'clock to pray and

MARIA L. HUNTLEY   MARY L. PRIEST

talk over plans for Christian work. During the week they visited their neighbors as they had opportunity, and passed out tracts and papers. They also sent papers through the post to names obtained in various ways, and this phase of the work came in time to occupy a large share of the attention of the members.

The activities of the original Vigilant Missionary Society of South Lancaster took on quite a range. One of the members, Maria L. Huntley, began the study of French in order that she might conduct missionary correspondence with interested persons who spoke only that language. Another, Mary Martin, undertook to learn German in order to work for persons of that nationality.

The society did more than distribute literature. It sought in other ways to advance the interests of the kingdom. There were a number of cases of healing by prayer. Correspondence was carried on regularly with lonely Sabbath keepers, who were supplied with literature and encouraged to distribute it among their neighbors. As a result of this correspondence, some back-slidden members were led to make a new start, while many faithful ones had their hearts cheered and encouraged, and their purpose to press forward greatly strengthened.

To carry out the work successfully, agents were appointed who were to report semimonthly on all cases that came under their observation, and the society would then appoint some person to correspond with the persons thus named. These agents in time extended throughout the Eastern, Middle, and Western States. At the close of the second year the society had twenty-eight members, with fourteen corresponding agents working in nearly as many different States. In that year the members sent out 554 letters and received 325 communications in reply. In 1874 it had a membership of forty-six, thirty-two corresponding agents in three different languages, and was carrying on correspondence with 450 persons in eighteen different States and in such foreign countries as England, Switzerland, New Zealand, and China.

About the year 1871 S. N. Haskell organized the New England Tract Society in connection with the conference of that name. The original Vigilant Missionary Society then became an auxiliary of the larger organization, which served to bring all local societies together. Directors were also appointed, each of whom had charge of a certain section of territory known as a district. It was the duty of these directors to see to the appointment of a librarian in each church, to whom he would intrust a supply of literature for church use, the librarian to collect the money for the same and hand it to the director. The latter was to hold a district quarterly meeting in the interests of the tract society work at least two weeks before each general quarterly meeting. He was to collect funds of all kinds in his district, and send in the money once a quarter to the conference treasurer.

James White, always keenly alive to any new efficiency developed in the field, learned of the work of the New England Tract Society, and with Mrs. White paid a week's visit to South Lancaster to study the organization. He then on the spot wrote an account of it, issued in pamphlet form, urging other conferences to follow the example of New England.

The work of these societies was also referred to at the General Conferences of 1871 and 1872, and at the session held in the spring of 1873 resolutions were passed expressing satisfaction with the progress made, and suggesting the advisability of consolidating the various societies into a general organization which could be properly represented at the regular meetings of the General Conference. At this meeting, moreover, action was taken recommending " that S. N. Haskell visit the various conferences in the interests of the tract and missionary work." This he did, with the result that during the summer and autumn of 1873 local and State tract societies were organized very generally throughout the country, and a systematic literature campaign was inaugurated.

The strength of the organization was shown early in the year 1874. A call had been made in the *Review* of Dec. 18, 1873, for 10,000 new trial subscriptions to the *Review and Herald* and the *Health Reformer*. The tract societies took it up, and within a very few weeks they had sent in more than 13,000 names with the accompanying cash. Moreover, they also raised $5,000 to meet delinquencies in the way of unpaid back subscriptions to the *Review, Instructor,* and *Reformer.*

In the same summer the General Conference in session at Battle Creek organized a general tract society, to hold the State and local societies together and promote the work of circulating books, tracts, and papers throughout the country. The officers of this larger organization, known as the General Conference Tract and Missionary Society of Seventh-day Adventists, were as follows: *President,* James White; *Vice-President,* George I. Butler; *Treasurer,* Benn Auten; *Business Agent,* S. N. Haskell. The appointment of a secretary was left to the General Conference Committee. Miss Maria L. Huntley, one of the leading spirits in the original society in South Lancaster, was appointed to this office, and for many years devoted her whole energies to the task.

One great factor in the promotion of this work during the year 1874 was the publication of a monthly paper, *The True Missionary,* which contained, besides much helpful instruction, full statistical reports from the various societies, as well as interesting letters from individual workers describing various methods tried and the results achieved. It was thought well to publish such matter in a separate paper in order that the *Review* might devote its space largely to doctrinal articles dealing with the message, and thus be used as a pioneer missionary paper. At the close of the year it seemed best, however, to discontinue the *Missionary,* and use the columns of the *Review* for instruction in all branches of denominational work. Following this for a time a new periodical was issued for general distribution, *The Voice of Truth,* which was largely made up of doctrinal

The True Missionary.

VOLUME 1.   BATTLE CREEK, MICH., JANUARY, 1874.   NUMBER 1.

"Go ye into all the World, and Preach the Gospel to every Creature." MARK 16:15.

GIVING.

THE sun gives ever; so the earth—
What it can give, so much, 'tis worth;
The ocean gives in many ways—
Gives paths, gives fishes, rivers, bays;
So, too, the air, it gives us breath—
When it stops giving, comes in death.
Give, give, be always giving;
Who gives not is not living.
The more you give
The more you live.

God's love hath in us wealth upheaped;
Only by giving it is reaped.
The body withers, and the mind,
If pent in by a selfish rind.
Give strength, give thought, give deeds, give pelf,
Give love, give tears, and give thyself.
Give, give, be always giving;
Who gives not is not living.
The more we give
The more we live.

— *British Workmen.*

THE SPIRIT OF SACRIFICE:

An Appeal for Men and Means to Send the Truth to Other Nations.

BY ELLEN G. WHITE.

DEAR BRETHREN AND SISTERS: I deeply feel the necessity of our making more thorough and earnest efforts to bring the truth before the world. In the last vision given me, I was shown that we were not doing one-twentieth part of the work we should for the salvation of souls. We labor for them indifferently, as though it was not a question of very great importance whether they received or rejected the truth. General efforts are made, but we fail to work to the point by personal effort. We do not approach men and women in a manner that impresses them that we have a personal interest for them, and that we feel deeply in earnest for their salvation, and do not mean to give them up. We hold too much at a distance those who do not believe the truth. We call them and wait for them to come to us to inquire for the truth. Many will not be inclined to do this, for they are in darkness and

them to him, but there are so very few who have the spirit of sacrifice. Some will hand out readily of their means, and feel that when they have done this, there is no more required of them. They make no special sacrifice in thus doing. Money is good so far as it goes, but, unless accompanied by personal effort, will go but a little way toward converting souls to the truth. Not only does God call for your money, brethren, but he calls for you. While you have given of your means, you have selfishly withheld yourselves. One earnest worker in the vineyard is worth more than a million of money without men to do the work. This giving of yourselves will be a sacrifice if you have a correct estimate of the work, and realize its claims. Christ our pattern was an earnest worker. He not only left the royal courts of Heaven, and for our sakes became poor, that we might have infinite riches, but took human nature, and by personal labors he came close to man, that he might reach him where he was, in his error and blindness. He withheld not himself. He gave all. He suffered deprivation, and reproach, and hatred of those whom he came to bless and save, and finally sacrificed his life in the work. And now, says Christ, I have done all this for you, what are you willing to do for me? I have given you an example.

Who, we ask, will follow the example of his Lord in self-sacrifice and disinterested benevolence, to save his fellow-men? There are young men and women and those of middle age who have had experience in the truth, but do not advance in the divine life and increase in the knowledge of our Lord and Saviour Jesus Christ, and they do not know the cause. One cause of their lack of spiritual strength, and of their not being full-grown men and women in Christ is, they are not workers with Christ. If they would work for Jesus, their sympathies would be brought in close union with Christ, and they would grow in

the work for the time. The night soon cometh, in which no man can work. Satan is earnest, zealous, and persevering in his work. If he fails to accomplish his purpose the first time, he tries again. He will try other plans, and work with great perseverance to bring in various temptations to ensnare souls. He never becomes so discouraged as to let souls entirely alone. If the zeal and perseverance of Christ's followers in their efforts to save souls were equal to Satan's efforts to deceive them to their eternal loss, we should see hundreds embracing the truth where we now see one.

God calls for men and women to qualify themselves, by consecration to his will and earnest study of the Scriptures, to do his special work for these last days. He calls for men now who can work. As they engage in the work in sincerity and humility to do all they can, they will be obtaining a more thorough experience. They will have a better knowledge of the truth and better know how to reach souls and help them just where they need to be helped. Workmen are needed now, just now, to labor for God. The fields are already white for the harvest, and yet laborers are few. There are those among us who could work if they were awake to the wants of the cause, and were willing to bear burdens. God calls for men and women, who are followers of Christ, to volunteer to work under his dictation to rescue souls from ruin. All who engage in the work of presenting the truth to others must have true courtesy, and Christian politeness, and sincere love for souls, so as to make, not general efforts merely, but personal efforts.

I have been shown that, as a people, we have been asleep as to our duty in regard to getting the light before those of other nations. Is it because God has excused us, as a people, from having any burden or special work to do for those of other tongues that there are no mis-

articles taken from the *Review.* It was intended as a pioneer missionary paper for use east of the Rocky Mountains, but it soon gave way to *The Signs of the Times,* published on the Pacific Coast.

The sense of personal responsibility rested heavily on the hearts of the members of the society, and urged them on to ever-increasing labors. " Many times," writes one of the isolated Sabbath keepers, " my companion and myself would sit down by the fire at home and study; but feeling that to be a wrong to others, get up, put on our wraps, take some tracts or periodicals, and visit our neighbors one or two miles distant perhaps, and try 'once more' to say a few words, oftentimes ill-chosen and untimely perhaps, but the best we could do with our limited gifts."

The methods used were various. Personal work was usually confined to the neighborhood, but it might go much farther. Here and there a brother would undertake a somewhat extended trip with horse and buggy. James Harvey wrote from North Liberty, Ind.:

"I have now spent twenty days in going from house to house, offering our publications to the people, and explaining these things, and praying with some of the families. I have visited 220 families, and sold 52,986 pages, for which I have realized $40.59. I furnished the Young Men's Christian Association of Logansport, Ind., with four of our bound books, and gave away some tracts."

He went on to say that he was kindly received everywhere, he and his horse being entertained mostly free of charge, and the people thankfully receiving the tracts and papers he was distributing. He reported one family of four who had decided to keep the Sabbath, while others were carefully investigating the subject.

A good measure of personal sacrifice went to the upbuilding of the work in the early days. One member, a sister in very limited circumstances who greatly needed new spectacles, had earned a little money by nursing, and hoped, when she had collected what was due her, to have enough to buy the spectacles. But on her way to make the purchase, she stopped to put some papers in the rack at the post office. While doing so, she noticed how old and rough-looking the rack was, and then and there decided to provide a new one with the spectacle money. She went immediately to the cabinetmaker, and ordered the new rack; then returned home to endure the pain in her weak eyes for an indefinite period, till more money could be laboriously earned for the purpose. It is pleasant to be able to add that the good woman's sacrifice was rewarded, so that within a short time she had both the rack for the public and the glasses for herself.

The work often produced results far exceeding what might have been expected from the feeble efforts put forth. A believing sister, accompanied by her son, visited one of the Southern States, to remain for the winter. Of her experience Miss Huntley wrote:

" Conscious of her weakness and unworthiness, she made it a subject of prayer that God would give her *one soul* as an evidence of His love and care. She took with her the *Review* and some tracts, and with earnest, broken pleadings that God would encourage her with this token, she endeavored to let her light shine, and waited for an answer to her prayers. Impressed with the simple, confiding devotion of a Swede who was living in the family where she boarded, she lent him some *Reviews.* Soon he confessed himself convinced that the Adventists had the truth, and that he ought to keep the Sabbath. The next to become interested was a son of the gentleman in whose home she boarded, fifteen years of age. Then the mother began to read and ask questions. An older son coming home about this time, his attention was called to the subject."— *Review and Herald, Dec. 16, 1880, p. 394.*

When this sister returned to her home in the North, none of these persons had definitely taken their stand; but she followed up the interest with papers and tracts, and in a short time all four had embraced the Adventist faith. One of the young men went to Battle Creek College to prepare for a place in the Lord's work.

In the early days in California, there was a believer who formed the habit of placing a tract in the hands of a friend whenever opportunity offered. When J. N. Loughborough visited that section of the country, five persons thus supplied with tracts had begun to keep the Sabbath and were ready for baptism. Moreover, one of the five himself began to circulate tracts, with the result that he also brought out a small company of believers, and wrote in to seek advice about organizing them into a Bible class.

Papers and tracts were also sent to foreign lands, and correspondence was opened up that led in not a few cases to the raising up of Sabbath keepers. This work outside of America gradually came to be left largely in the hands of the General Conference Tract Society. It was in line with this larger mission that came to be mapped out for the general society, that its name was changed at the General Conference held in Rome, N. Y., the early winter of 1882, to the International Tract Society. Under its new name the organization continued to flourish greatly, and probably did more than any other one agency to spread the advent principles during the next ten years in all parts of the world.

The business of the International Tract Society was to send out literature, which consisted chiefly of papers and tracts, mostly in the English language. This literature was supplied by the society free of charge, and was always carried free. The carrying was done mostly by ship captains, themselves oftentimes indifferent to the contents of the papers, but willing to

JAMES WHITE
President of the General Conference, 1865 to 1867 ; 1868 to 1871 ; 1874 to 1880.

418

be accommodating to a society devoted to the business of distributing religious literature.

The society came to have corresponding agents in a great many parts of the world, who acted as distributors of literature. These agents were persons who had become interested in the denominational belief, and nearly always they ultimately became Sabbath keepers, and formed the nuclei of churches afterward organized in those places.

Closing Days of James White

It was in the palmy days of this new and very efficient organization that James White began to lay off the burdens he had been carrying so long and so faithfully. He had lived the strenuous life during those eventful years which had seen the rapid development of the denomination's publishing business east and west, the founding of the Health Institute and of the Rural Health Retreat, the establishment of the Central European Mission, the building up of a flourishing college at Battle Creek, and finally the inception and full development of the International Tract Society, which was doing so much to bring the advent truths to the attention of the larger public, both in America and in foreign lands.

Although other faithful men had been taking up some of the burdens that Elder White had carried almost alone for many years, yet he remained to the last the supreme embodiment of that zeal and enthusiasm for righteousness which was making the Adventist people a power for good in the world. He could not in the nature of things be less than the foremost man of the denomination; whether occupying a leading office or not, his brethren looked to him for leadership, and they never looked in vain.

The closing years of James White's life were largely devoted to the building up of the work on the Pacific Coast. He saw large possibilities in that part of the country, and put forth his best energies in realizing them. His services to the new publishing work in California included, not only wise management of a growing institution, but enthusiastic advocacy of the needs of the work at the various camp-meetings in the East and Middle West, with the result that thousands of dollars were raised, by means of which the new enterprise was put on a sound financial footing.

He took an equally leading part in the evangelical work in the Golden State. The ship missionary work in the harbor of

San Francisco was the object of his special care. The tent-meetings held at Woodland and Oakland, and the hall meetings in San Francisco, profited much by his earnest labors. Both Elder and Mrs. White saw the need of houses of worship for the cities of Oakland and San Francisco, and they labored un-

THE "DIME TABERNACLE," BATTLE CREEK, MICH.

tiringly till a substantial church had been erected in each of these important cities, at an aggregate cost of $35,000.

When, in 1879, Elder White accepted for the last time the presidency of the General Conference, he had labored continuously in the cause he loved for upwards of thirty-five years, and was entering upon his eleventh year as president. It was the year in which the Battle Creek Tabernacle, the fourth in order of the Adventist church buildings in that city, was dedicated. The building was erected at a cost of $25,475.17, and it accommodated on that occasion fully 3,500 persons. The erection of the Tabernacle was a fitting climax to the career of Elder White, representing as it did the freewill offerings of Adventists in many different parts of the country, and also of the people of Battle Creek themselves, including many not of that faith.

In the following year Elder White was succeeded in the presidency by George I. Butler, a member of the committee who had been for years ·carrying heavy responsibilities. Brother White entered his sixtieth year enjoying a fair degree of health, and as busily engaged as in any previous year in fruitful work for the Master. In company with Mrs. White he attended a camp-meeting in Charlotte, Mich., making the journey thither by carriage. On the way, owing to a sudden change in temperature, he contracted a severe cold, and though he rallied sufficiently to take an active part in the meeting, he did not recover his strength. Shortly after their return to Battle Creek, both he and Mrs. White were prostrated with malarial fever, to which Elder White succumbed on the morning of August 6, 1881, aged sixty years and two days.

The funeral was deferred to the following Sabbath, at which time almost the whole city came out to pay their respects to the man who, whatever his religious views, was regarded as one of its foremost citizens. Uriah Smith preached the funeral sermon. Mrs. White, who had not risen from her sick-bed since the death of her husband, was borne to the Tabernacle to be present at the funeral. At the close of the discourse she rose and spoke for about ten minutes, her simple, heartfelt words deeply moving the vast audience.

It was the largest funeral that Battle Creek had ever seen. But more impressive than the size of the gathering was the feeling of deep personal loss that prevailed among the employees of the Review office and the other institutions which Elder White had been so largely instrumental in building up, and in fact throughout the denomination it was as if a beloved father had been taken away, one who sustained an intimate personal relation to every believer and was deeply concerned for his welfare.

James White was essentially an organizer. He was a good example of his own saying: " Leaders and generals are not made by appointment, or by the vote of the church; but they are born." From the time when in a threadbare coat and patched trousers he attended those earliest conferences of the advent believers in the East, he made himself felt not only as a preacher of force and spirituality, but even more as a far-seeing leader. He was always looking ahead. When others were harping on little things, he was massing the large fundamental principles for which the denomination was to stand, and showing how all could unite in giving them to the world. He was of an eager, impetuous nature, and not seldom gave offense; but no man was more ready to confess his faults, and he numbered among his warmest friends men who at some time or other had felt that he had wronged them, but had also experienced the hearty, sincere way in which he could make matters right.

Aggressiveness was an outstanding quality of the man. He was constitutionally opposed to anything like standing still. When it was a time for action, nothing disgusted him more than to have his brethren advise delay, urge the careful weighing of consequences, and seemingly make a virtue of doing nothing. " Some people," he said one day, " think that all a train needs to make it go is to put on the brakes."

He was a good judge of human nature, and showed rare discernment in selecting the men who were to share the responsibility for a rapidly growing work. If he was at times impatient over blunders, he was also generous in his praise of good work. Earnestness and activity pleased him. He could forgive many mistakes if they sprang from zeal and a desire to accomplish things. He would have said with Moody, " Blundering do-somethingism is better than faultless do-nothingism." As a preacher his success lay in his earnestness and zeal for the Master, and his large grasp on the realities of the eternal world.

James White was remarkably successful in originating and fostering institutions. His activities covered a wide range, and were everywhere attended with good results. The oldest of these institutions was the Review and Herald publishing house, which was the creature of his fostering care even from its infancy. Single-handed he managed it for years, and after he had turned it over to the denomination, its continued success was largely owing to the fact that the policy he had inaugurated was carried out at practically every point. Not to mention the other large publishing house on the Pacific Coast, which he likewise started and watched over for some years, the substantial success of the Health Institute, and of the *Health Reformer* which advertised it throughout the country, was also to be attributed, under God, to the business sense and sagacity of James White. Battle Creek College, the first of the educational institutions of the denomination, was likewise started under his leadership.

These various institutions not only accomplished great good under his management, but they were successful financially. Elder White had the genius for making things pay for themselves. His policy was the farseeing one that commands confidence. Things seemed to grow in value as he took charge of them, and gave them opportunity to develop.

If we compare James White with John Wesley, the founder, under God, of the Methodist denomination, we shall see that the two men had much in common. There was in both the same broad vision, the same irrepressible energy, the instinct for making things go. The two men were of course far apart educationally. John Wesley was a finished scholar; James White had little beyond a common school education. But both were excellent organizers, and each at his death left behind him a denomination destined to grow rapidly and along very much the lines marked out for it during the lifetime of the founder.

Needless to say, James White's marked ability as a great religious leader has not been generally recognized outside of the denomination. Like other men of his type, he did not seek worldly recognition; he was too busy doing the Master's work. Many a personage looms large in the encyclopedias of biography, whose real accomplishments did not equal those of this comparatively unknown man of faith, prayer, and achievement.

URIAH SMITH

REVIEW AND HERALD BUILDINGS IN 1873

CHAPTER XXII

Growth of the Publishing Work

IN the preceding chapter we have seen the development of a system of organization by means of which the printed page bearing the message of present truth was having year by year a steadily growing circulation. In the present chapter we shall consider the growth of the facilities for the manufacture of books, periodicals, and tracts, and also the inception and subsequent development of the work of circulating our subscription books, which has come to occupy so large a share of the energies of our publishing houses.

The little two-story frame building that received the printing outfit when it was moved to Battle Creek from Rochester, N. Y., in 1855, did not long suffice for the growing needs of the work. When the Review and Herald Publishing Association was organized in 1861, it proceeded at once to remove the frame building to an adjoining lot on Kalamazoo Street, and to erect in its place a two-story brick building in the form of a Greek cross, the main portion being 26 x 66 feet. Ten years later it was necessary to erect a second building of the same plan and dimensions as the first; and in 1873 a third. In 1876 the first and third buildings, standing side by side on Main Street, were united by a central structure of three stories, having a mansard roof, which gave it another story. Subsequently the roofs of the two original buildings, which now formed wings

425

of the main building, were changed to mansards, making them three stories in height. In 1881 a large pressroom was built in the rear on Washington Avenue. Subsequent additions and enlargements provided upwards of 50,000 square feet of floor space, devoted to all the various activities of an up-to-date publishing house, the largest institution of the kind in the State of Michigan.

GEORGE A. KING   "Thoughts on Daniel and   D. W. REAVIS
the Revelation "
The First Colporteur   The First Subscription Book   The First Purchaser

Meanwhile the idea of reaching the public by means of the printing press was growing in the minds of the leaders of the denomination. Said James White,

"The press is the right arm of our strength. Our field is the world, and as the number of our efficient preachers is small, a large part of the work of giving the last message must of necessity be accomplished by our publications."—" *Life Sketches,*" *p. 371.*

The rise and development of the tract societies in the early seventies helped to create a growing demand for Adventist literature. Much was done also by the preachers of that day, who carried with them a generous supply of books and tracts, and relied as much upon literature as upon sermons to convince the people of the truth of their message. But the most important step in the history of the denominational publishing work was the adoption of the plan of selling books by subscription. This plan was first proposed by Mrs. E. G. White in a testimony dated 1879.

George A. King, of Canadian birth, was the first among Adventists to make practical use of this method of putting out literature. He had enjoyed a good measure of success in taking subscriptions for the *Health Reformer,* and he felt confident that if he could have a fair-sized book, he could take orders for it in the same way. So he set himself to convince the brethren. At the General Conference held in camp in Battle Creek, Mich., in 1880, he could have been seen with two small black books under his arm, going around among the leading delegates and

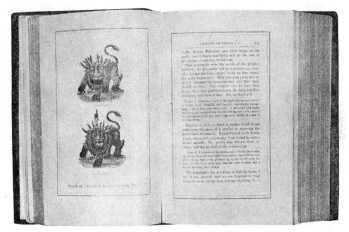

TYPE PAGE OF THE FIRST SUBSCRIPTION BOOK

urging the printing of a large book to be sold by subscription. The two small books were "Thoughts on Daniel" and "Thoughts on the Revelation," which, he said, taken together, would make one good subscription book. He had his way. The brethren put out the book, and it had a good sale. "The Great Controversy" followed, and by the year 1889, 75,000 copies of that excellent book had been sold. Later, "Bible Readings" appeared, and a number of others.

The colporteur work thus begun was gradually built up all over the country, men known as State agents taking the oversight of it in conferences. For a time the president of the Review and Herald Publishing Association had general supervision of the colporteur work in the East, and the head of the Pacific Press looked after the work in the West. Later a man was appointed who gave his whole time to this work.

In these early years the International Tract Society rendered valuable help toward getting the work on a practical business basis. At its annual session in 1886 the society passed resolutions which were generally adopted, and have been instrumental in keeping the work on a right basis up to the present time. It was provided that the State tract societies should act as sole agents of the publishing houses for all religious subscription books, with the understanding that a competent man was to be kept in the field to superintend the work. No agent was to be allowed to solicit orders for more than one book at a time except by consent of the State agent. The State

THE FIRST POWER PRESS

societies were to furnish their local agents with books at one half the retail price. The latter were required to confine their activities strictly to the territory assigned them, and were to furnish prompt reports of all work done.

With system and order thus guaranteed, a high degree of efficiency soon began to be displayed, and many of the most promising men in the denomination devoted themselves to the sale of its literature. The Kansas Conference was the first to enter heartily into the plans outlined by the International Tract Society, but the work there succeeded so well that the other conferences soon swung into line.

The same plans, with slight alterations to meet local needs, were gradually adopted in Europe and Australasia, and there also they proved successful. About 1889 companies of colporteurs were sent into the South, then under the direction of the General Conference; also north into Manitoba. William Arnold made a trip to the West Indies, and during an absence of nine months sold 1,260 copies of " Daniel and the Revelation."

Thus the work went on with steadily increasing interest. The sales advanced rapidly, and the two large publishing houses were at times put to the strain to supply the growing demand for books and other literature. At length, in 1892, there came a decline. The work had gradually been taking on too much the complexion of mere salesmanship. The books sold so readily that the colporteur did not always realize his need of divine

C. H. JONES   F. L. MEAD

grace in order to render acceptable service. The immediate cause of the decreasing sales was the influx of hard times. Money was scarce, and people could not afford to buy books at standard prices. The colporteurs urged that prices be reduced, and when the publishing houses did not see their way clear to comply with this demand, the general agents encouraged their men to sell smaller books. Moreover, on the plea of economy the conferences began to try to get along without a State agent, and some of the districts did likewise. The publishing houses, no longer requiring their large facilities to put out a message-filled literature, began to occupy themselves largely with commercial work.

This situation continued till 1901, when a general strengthening of the denominational organization brought help and

SOUTHERN PUBLISHING HOUSE, NASHVILLE, TENN., IN 1925

succor also to the colporteur work. Progress was slow at first, but with the re-establishment of right principles, confidence was restored, and in a few years the sales of denominational literature were not only on an ascending scale, but were showing remarkable records.

It was in the year 1901 that the Southern Publishing Association was incorporated at Nashville, Tenn. At the General Conference held in the spring of that year Mrs. E. G. White made earnest appeals in behalf of the Southern work, and a very considerable interest was aroused. The association was at first a non-dividend-paying stock company, receiving funds toward its support from Seventh-day Adventists in the North. It occupied in those early years a property on Jefferson Street, purchased a few months before by J. E. White, and by him transferred to the newly organized Publishing Association, which added to the original two-story brick building quite a large three-story frame structure. This building, illy adapted at best for a publishing house, was sold a few years later. The equipment was moved to 24th Avenue, North, in 1906.

In 1907 the association was reincorporated as a non-stock constituency association, under the name it now bears,— The Southern Publishing Association of Seventh-day Adventists, thus coming under the direct management of the denomination. It occupies a modern brick building having a floor space of approximately 50,000 square feet. This enlargement has been brought about chiefly in the last few years, during which time there has also been a replacing of the old equipment with the best modern machines.

The special field of the association is the Southern States, which it supplies with trade and subscription books, as well as tracts and pamphlets. It also publishes the *Watchman,* a monthly magazine used all over the United States in aggressive evangelistic work. There are two branch houses, located respectively in Fort Worth, Tex., and Atlanta, Ga. The present manager is M. F. Knox, formerly secretary and treasurer of the institution.

Brief Survey

The progressive growth and development of the denomination's publishing interests may best be understood by a brief survey of its history by decades. The first period of ten years began with the publication, early in 1845, of an article by T. M. Preble on the Sabbath, and ended with the close of the year 1854. It saw the publication of a number of tracts, the *Pres-*

PACIFIC PRESS, MOUNTAIN VIEW, CALIF., IN 1925

ent Truth, and a small hymn book, also the establishing of the denominational organ, the *Review and Herald.* For the first nine years of this period, the Adventist literature was given away, the cost of publication being met by donations. In the closing year, 1854, J. N. Loughborough at a tent effort he was conducting in Michigan, offered the literature for sale. He made up packets containing one copy each of the denominational tracts and pamphlets, which he sold at 35 cents a packet.

The next decade, 1855-64, saw the publishing work removed to Battle Creek, Mich., and there installed for the first time in a home of its own. Later a substantial brick structure took the place of the first building, and the work was definitely organized as the Seventh-day Adventist Publishing Association.

In this period a beginning was made in foreign work, with the translation by D. T. Bourdeau of one of the Adventist tracts into the French. The value of a complete set of Adventist publications at the end of this second decade was $3. The total sales of the period amounted to $17,500.

The third decade, 1865-74, marked definite progress in the foreign work. J. G. Matteson translated and set up with his own hands a series of tracts in the Danish-Norwegian language. He also edited a Scandinavian hymn book, which came out in 1870. Two years later the *Advent Tidende,* a 24-page Danish-Norwegian monthly edited by J. G. Matteson, began to appear. In June, 1874, another enterprise of vast importance was launched, the first number of a new weekly, the *Signs of the Times,* issued in Oakland, Calif. The sales of this period amounted to $73,000.

The fourth decade, 1875-84, began with the organization of the Pacific Press Publishing Company. This step was followed the next year by the issue of the first number of a French 16-page monthly, *Les Signes des Temps,* in Basel, Switzerland. Three years later, publishing was begun in Christiania, Norway. In the closing year of the decade a German paper began to be issued at Basel, a Swedish paper in Christiania, and the first number of the *Present Truth* came out in England. It was in this period, too, that a beginning was made in publishing subscription books in America. The sales amounted to $371,000.

The fifth decade, 1885-94, marked in its early years a rapid advance in sales, owing chiefly to the success which attended the sale of subscription books. It saw the establishment of large, well-equipped publishing houses in Basel, Christiania, London, and Melbourne, and the inauguration in all these foreign fields, as well as in America, of a flourishing subscription book busi-

WORLD SALES, 1845-1924 (80 YEARS)

1845-1854 ....$ 2,500.00
1855-1864 ....   17,500.00
1865-1874 ....   73,000.00
1875-1884 ....   371,000.00
1885-1894 .... 3,969,000.00
1895-1904 .... 3,144,000.00
1905-1914 ....14,095,000.00

Total for 70 years $21,672,000.00

Eighth Decade

1915 ....$2,174,591.94
1916 .... 2,181,340.27
1917 .... 2,937,422.88
1918 .... 3,566,500.00
1919 .... 5,215,000.00
1920 .... 5,682,972.35
1921 .... 4,764,521.06
1922 .... 3,656,481.31
1923 .... 4,067,460.00
1924 (estimated) 4,500,000.00

Total for 10 years 38,746,289.81

Total for 80 years $60,418,289.81

ness. It saw also a tentative effort to put the whole of the publishing interests into the hands of a central organization, whose trustees were to be elected by the General Conference. This movement, which seemed at the time to make for unity and denominational control, went so far as to put the foreign publications of the denomination largely in the hands of the General Conference Book Department. A number of new books and tracts were likewise published under the same auspices. At the General Conference of 1897, held at College View, the plan was definitely abandoned. The slight decline in sales in America in the closing years of this decade was due to the general tendency, already referred to, toward taking up the sale of smaller books. The total sales amounted to $3,969,000.

The sixth decade, 1895-1904, witnessed to the full the disastrous results of doing without general and State agents in the interests of economy, and employing the energies of the publishing houses on commercial work while the canvassers sold 25-cent books. The record for the year 1898 dropped as low as $200,000, which was less than one fourth of the sales in 1891, under the earlier policy of large books and strong leadership. In the closing years of the decade, however, the situation began to improve, as a result of the change of policy which came in with the general reorganization following the General Conference of 1901. The sales for this period amounted to $3,144,000.

The seventh decade, 1905-14, witnessed steady and rapid advancement. Lost ground was retaken, and much more in addition. The publishing houses giving their undivided energies to the production of truth-filled literature, had to work overtime to supply the growing demands of the colporteurs. The work was thoroughly organized and manned with efficient leaders, and it was vitalized throughout by a strong missionary spirit. The rapid advancement in the sales of this period is indicated in the accompanying diagram.

The eighth decade, 1915-24, showed a further encouraging increase in the total sales of our denominational literature, the sales in 1915 amounting to $2,174,591.94; for 1924 the total reached the sum of $4,500,000. There was some fluctuation from year to year. The highest figure reached was in 1920, when the total sales amounted to $5,682,972.35. The period ended with a total of $38,746,289.81 for the ten years, making a grand total of $60,418,289.81 for the eight decades covered by our publishing work.

Among the men who have been prominent in developing the subscription book business of the denomination, a few names

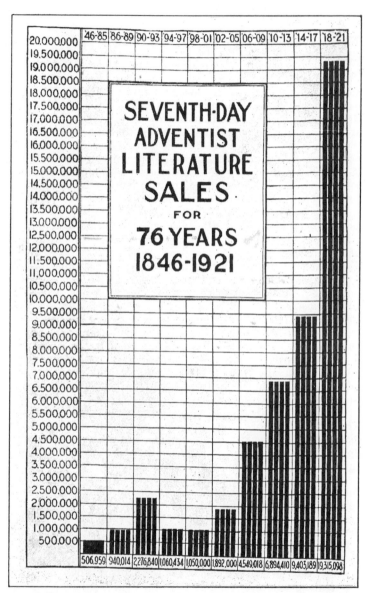

SEVENTH-DAY
ADVENTIST
LITERATURE
SALES
FOR
76 YEARS
1846-1921

46-85	86-89	90-93	94-97	98-01	02-05	06-09	10-13	14-17	18-21
506,959	940,014	2,276,840	1,060,434	1,050,000	1,892,000	4,549,018	6,894,410	9,403,189	19,315,098

may be mentioned. Capt. C. Eldridge was manager of the Review and Herald publishing house when this work was getting on its feet. A. R. Henry, W. C. Sisley, S. H. Lane, and I. H. Evans followed in succession in Battle Creek, Elder Evans being manager when the institution was removed from Battle Creek, Mich., to Washington, D. C., in 1903. He was succeeded by S. N. Curtiss, who was manager until 1912.

C. H. Jones has directed the activities of the Pacific Press Publishing Company almost from the beginning, and his strong leadership has been widely felt out in the field. F. L. Mead had general oversight of the canvassing work of the denomination while the subscription book business was making some of its best early records, and also in its years of decline. E. R. Palmer was sent to Australia in 1895. After putting the canvassing work in that field on a strong footing, he returned to America to take the position of secretary of the Publishing Department of the General Conference, which he filled until 1912, being then called to the management of the Review and Herald Publishing Association. He was succeeded as secretary of the General Conference Publishing Department by N. Z. Town. At the General Conference of 1913 Brother Town was re-elected to the position of secretary of the Publishing Department of the General Conference, and W. W. Eastman was made secretary for the North American Division. In 1920 H. H. Hall, a man of large experience in that line of work, became associate secretary of the Publishing Department. His first duty was to visit some of the foreign fields to render assistance to them in solving their publishing problems. In this he was eminently successful.

An interesting feature of the work from the beginning has been the question of how most effectively to train the new men. In the early nineties the canvassers' school came into vogue, and was successfully employed in various conferences. The first such school was held in Vilas, S. Dak., in the winter of 1891-92. The canvassers had done hard and faithful work during the spring and summer, and the prospects were good for delivery, when hot, dry winds from the south ruined the crops. It was impossible to make deliveries, and the canvassers were destitute.

Under these circumstances the conference, at the suggestion of G. A. Wheeler, the State agent, decided to conduct a four months' school for the benefit of these workers. Bible instruction was given by Elder S. B. Whitney, studies in the subscription books were given by the State agent. There were also classes in the common branches. In the spring the conference provided each of the young men with a new suit of clothes and a $5 bill, and sent them out to take orders. Every one had a successful summer, and the next winter there was another session of the school. Other conferences adopted the plan. But the school sessions gradually became shorter and shorter, and the gatherings came to be known as institutes, the time being given chiefly to the study of the various subscription books.

It may be well, in bringing this chapter to a close, to call attention once more to the very large place which the publishing work fills in the activities of the denomination. Before there were half a dozen ministers preaching the message, the paper, *Present Truth,* began to appear. Before a single conference had been organized, even before the denomination had taken a name, the Central Publishing Association was organized at Battle Creek, and the first step in Europe and later in Australia was to get the message out in the form of papers and tracts.

The success of the subscription book business, moreover, has grown out of the essentially evangelistic character of the work. The Adventist colporteur is much more than a mere salesman. He goes forth as a gospel worker, introducing into the homes of the people literature whose life-giving power he knows himself from personal experience, and he is always ready as the way opens to speak a word in season to him that is weary. Especially in the more remote country districts the agents enjoy many opportunities of bringing light and help to longing souls.

A colporteur at work in a sparsely settled district of Montana came to a little cabin one evening. At first thought he was inclined to go farther; but a voice seemed to urge him to stop, and he did so. There lived in the cabin a man and his wife and three children, one of whom was away from home. He canvassed the man for " The Great Controversy," and took his order. He also remained for the night, and before retiring held family worship with the family. The next morning he was urged to stay longer, and he remained over the Sabbath. When he returned that way a little later, the family were observing the Sabbath. They had also discarded pork and unwholesome foods, and were carrying out the principles of healthful living as far as they knew them. They were baptized at the next camp-meeting. (See *General Conference Bulletin,* 1901, page 363.)

The determining factor in a great many cases, however, has been the mere reading of the books apart from the personal ministrations of the colporteur. "I have never yet seen a Seventh-day Adventist preacher," runs a typical letter written to the *Review* from Indiana. "I was converted by reading your works and comparing them with the Scriptures. The *Review* and the books are the only preachers I have seen of this faith. I highly prize the weekly visits of the paper. I am trying to lecture on the Sabbath, as best I can."— *Review and Herald, July 6, 1876, p. 32.*

Another representative case is reported by W. W. Eastman, associate secretary of the Publishing Department for the North American Division. A young man from northern Quebec came to the United States about 1880. In some way he came in contact with a Seventh-day Adventist, from whom he learned the views of that people and accepted them. Soon after this he returned to Quebec, where he persuaded the young lady of his choice also to accept the Adventist views. The young people were presently married, and brought up a family of children, all of whom became active members of the denomination, one of the daughters taking the nurses' course at a sanitarium. During the thirty-odd years in which this was going on, the family continued to pay tithe regularly into the denomination; yet in all this time they never once saw a Seventh-day Adventist minister. But they had in their home a well-filled bookcase of our denominational books, and had been regularly taking the leading denominational publications.

One marked feature of the publishing work in recent years has been the rapid growth of the publishing houses in foreign lands. This has not been an unaided growth. The parent institutions in America have rendered material assistance. They have taken of their earnings to purchase buildings and equip them, and then have sent trained men to act as managers and superintendents. By means of the plan known as the Big Week, which has been in operation for a comparatively short time, they have raised large sums of money in addition to what they have given from their own earnings. The Big Week, so called, is a week once a year in which all colporteurs and other employees of conferences and publishing houses, as well as the full membership in the various conferences, unite to give their net earnings, preferably from the sale of books and papers, toward the support of the new publishing houses in foreign lands. The plan has been successful in putting a number of these institutions scattered over the world on a good financial footing.

MISSIONARIES TO THE PACIFIC ISLANDS

Mrs. E. H. Gates   Mrs. J. I. Tay   E. H. Gates   J. I. Tay   A. J. Cudney

HATTIE ANDRE'S SCHOOL ON PITCAIRN ISLAND

CHAPTER XXIII

Island Missions

THE launching of the missionary ship "Pitcairn" marks an era in the missionary history of Seventh-day Adventists. With the dedication and subsequent voyages of this little ship the hearts of Adventists for the first time were drawn out in behalf of the natives of the many groups of islands in the great Pacific. The enterprise thus set on foot was in the fullest sense a missionary enterprise, and it evoked among young and old an enthusiasm commensurate with its importance.

The whole thing had its beginning in the little island of Pitcairn, whose romantic story is too well known to need repetition in this connection. At an early period in the history of the denomination, James White had heard of the devout character of the inhabitants, and had been able by some means to send them a large box of Adventist publications. No word had come from the islanders in acknowledgment of the unordered consignment of reading matter, and apparently no further thought was given to it, literature in those days being sent out freely to many parts of the world.

There was one Adventist, however, who felt a deep personal interest in the island. When John I. Tay first went to sea, in

441

his sixteenth year, he was presented with a Bible and a book entitled, " The Mutiny on Board the ' Bounty.' " While serving on board the United States sloop-of-war " Housatonic," he again had his attention drawn to the island by a conversation with a member of the ship's company who had visited it. A number of years later, while doing ship missionary work in Oakland harbor, he met the captain of the " Ocean King," who had recently called at Pitcairn and spoke in high terms of its inhabitants.

His interest in the subject was thus newly aroused, and Brother Tay determined to make an attempt to visit the island. He succeeded in obtaining passage on the " Tropic Bird " to Tahiti, whence he hoped to be able by another vessel to reach Pitcairn. He sailed as ship carpenter, and was to have his Sabbaths free on condition that he receive no wages. The " Tropic Bird " left San Francisco July 1, 1886, and arrived in Tahiti July 29. On making inquiries at this place, Brother Tay was informed that only one vessel went to Pitcairn, and he might have to wait two years.

The event was more favorable. In the first week in September the British man-of-war " Pitcairn " sailed into the harbor of Tahiti, and it was soon noised about that the captain intended to make a call at Pitcairn. Brother Tay was accepted as a passenger, and at daybreak Monday morning, October 18, had the privilege of seeing with his own eyes the romantic little island which for so many years had been an object of unique interest to him.

He went ashore with the members of the crew, and when it was learned that he wished to stay on the island for a while, the bell was rung on Tuesday morning at six o'clock, and all the inhabitants came together to consider the question. When the vote was finally taken, it was unanimous and favorable. In the afternoon of the same day the ship sailed away. That evening the islanders held their regular weekly prayer meeting. The newcomer was invited to speak, and gave a short talk on the love of God, which seemed to interest the audience. On the following day he visited the people from house to house, and was everywhere kindly received. Thus runs a contemporary record:

" The third day of his [Brother Tay's] stay, he asked some of them if they would not like to have a Bible reading. At this time he was stopping at Simon Young's house, and all together there were eight at his first Bible reading. The first subject taken up was the ' Sanctuary.' A short time was spent on this occasion, and the next day the reading was finished with two or three more present. A reading was appointed for the following day. At this time Simon Young, the pastor, was present, and about a dozen were in the congregation.

"It was soon found that the house was too small, and it was suggested that they go to the schoolroom. This was in one end of the church. He had with him a set of charts, and hung them up as he began the reading of Daniel 2 and 7. With their knowledge of the Bible, when it was told them what these symbols were designed to represent, the interest was wonderful, and so continued every day.

"The people generally had their breakfast about eight o'clock and dinner at five in the afternoon, sometimes earlier and sometimes later. It was arranged that he was to dine at one house one day, and at another the following day, and so on.

"The first Sunday he was there he went to their meeting, and was asked to speak. Standing near his seat, he talked for half an hour on the Sabbath question. Then Tuesday evening at the prayer meeting he spoke again by request, and as he talked of the Sabbath, one said, 'I will keep it,' and then another, and so said a goodly number all around him. It is ever thus that the Scriptures affect the unprejudiced child of faith.

"Brother Tay then thought that they ought to have a Sabbath meeting; and the magistrate, being present, said they could, and there should be no disturbance. So a meeting was appointed for the next Sabbath morning. Friday evening he called on the magistrate's sister, and asked her if she thought her brother would be at the meeting. She said she did not think he would. As Brother Tay did not want any division, he went to the magistrate himself, and talked the Sabbath question to him for an hour, until he was thoroughly aroused over the subject. The next morning the bell was rung, and everybody on the island turned out to the meeting. Simon Young took his text and preached a sermon on the Sabbath question. Others talked about it, and another service was held that day, and the principal talk was of the Sabbath. The next day, Sunday, the whole island went to work, and they have never kept Sunday since.

"About five weeks after reaching Pitcairn, a yacht came down from San Francisco, by the name of the 'General Evans.' Here, it seemed, was the opportunity for him to leave the island; but the work was not yet finished off. He wished to give them the third angel's message. Providentially, a strong wind storm came up for a few days, and it was impossible for the boat to leave. Brother Tay improved this opportunity by holding Bible readings on this topic. He left many books with them, a law and a prophetic chart, also, and instructed Sister McCoy, in whose care they were, to see that they were used.

"They then wished to be baptized, but he told them that the regulations of the church to which he belonged did not allow a deacon to perform this ceremony, but he believed the Lord would accept them under the circumstances if they expressed the desire, and then when the proper time came, they could be baptized. Brother Young thought this was right. . . .

"The last thing to be done was to go from house to house talking with them, and encouraging them to hold firm. Finally, just five weeks from the time he landed, the boat was ready, and he took his departure. Before the yacht sailed, Simon Young thanked him for his coming to the island, and for the work that had been done there."—"*The Story of the 'Pitcairn,'*" *pp. 20-22.*

Thus was the advent message given to the Pitcairn islanders. Perhaps the rapidity with which they accepted the new doc-

"THE PITCAIRN"

trine was due in part to the fact that the Adventist tracts and papers sent to the island years before had not been wholly unread. The seed had been sown, and only needed watering to spring up and yield an abundant harvest.

When Brother Tay returned to California and told the brethren of his experiences on the island, there immediately sprang up a deep interest, not only in Pitcairn, but also in the other islands of the Pacific. When the General Conference was convened in November, 1887, the following recommendation was duly brought before that body:

" 1. That a vessel of suitable size and construction for missionary purposes be purchased or built, and equipped for missionary work among the islands of the Pacific Ocean.

" 2. That the cost of building and equipping said vessel for two years' cruise shall not exceed the sum of twenty thousand dollars ($20,000).

" 3. That such a vessel be made ready for service early in the year 1888.

" 4. That the duly elected officers of this body for the coming year constitute a committee who shall be empowered to put in execution the provisions of this bill, and also to appoint other persons, as their judgment may dictate, to act with them in carrying out the project."— *General Conference Bulletin, Nov. 14, 1887, p. 2.*

The matter was referred to a committee of five, which finally reported, in view of the urgent needs of enterprises already on foot, that the building of a missionary ship be postponed till the next annual session of the General Conference. This report was adopted.

At the meeting of the General Conference Committee held in April, 1888, it was decided to send A. J. Cudney, of Nebraska, to Pitcairn Island. He was to be accompanied by John I. Tay, and after baptizing the believers on the island, the two missionaries were to visit other islands in the interests of the message.

Elder Cudney, finding no means of reaching Pitcairn directly, took ship for Honolulu. After waiting there for a time, he at length accepted the offer of one of the members to fit out a schooner then offered at a forced sale. In this vessel he started for Pitcairn, intending to call at Tahiti to take on board John I. Tay, who had sailed from San Francisco July 5. The vessel on which Elder Cudney sailed, was never heard from after leaving Honolulu. Brother Tay waited for a time at Tahiti, and then returned to America.

The attempt to send an ordained minister to Pitcairn Island having thus failed, the General Conference assembled in the autumn of 1889 took action authorizing the purchase or building and equipping for service of " a vessel of suitable size and construction for missionary operation among the islands of the Pacific Ocean." The vessel was to be ready for service early in 1890, and a board of three persons was to be appointed to superintend the carrying out of the Conference decision.

At the same meeting the International Sabbath School Association took upon itself the task of raising the funds for building and equipping the proposed missionary ship, thus making the first effort of the denomination in behalf of the heathen, a distinctly Sabbath school enterprise. Indeed, there is little doubt that it was this assumption on the part of the Sabbath School Association of the financial responsibility that made the General Conference Committee willing to go forward with the enterprise.

The building committee appointed by the General Conference consisted of C. H. Jones, C. Eldridge, and J. I. Tay. These men contracted with Captain Turner, whose shipyards lay in the Straits of Carquinez, about thirty miles north of Oakland, to build a two-masted brigantine of upwards of a hundred tons' burden, the cost of the vessel alone, rigged for the sea, to be within $12,000.

The Sabbath schools, which were enthusiastically raising the building money, were invited to suggest an appropriate name for the ship. More than a hundred names were sent in. " Glad Tidings " seemed to meet with somewhat general approval; but there was a widespread interest in the little island whose inhabitants, having unanimously accepted the Adventist views, were awaiting baptism, and the name finally decided upon was " Pitcairn."

The vessel was launched on a beautiful moonlight night late in July, in the presence of a number of members of the Oakland church, as well as people from the region around. The dedicatory services were held in Oakland on the afternoon of Sept. 25, 1890. The trim new vessel, decorated with her flags, ensigns, and streamers, was moved to the wharf at the foot of Washington Street, Oakland, thus giving opportunity to a large number of people to come within hearing distance. It was the time of the California camp-meeting, and the day was mild and balmy. A large crowd assembled, and many eyes gazed eagerly on the stanch little craft which was so soon to begin its voyage across the broad Pacific. The leading address was given by O. A. Olsen. C. H. Jones presented the report of the building committee, J. N. Loughborough gave the invocation, M. C. Wilcox read an original poem, and R. A. Underwood offered the dedicatory prayer.

The missionaries carried by the ship on its maiden voyage were E. H. Gates, A. J. Read, and J. I. Tay, with their wives. Capt. J. M. Marsh stood at the head of the crew, every member of which was a Seventh-day Adventist. The missionaries and crew totaled fourteen persons.

On Oct. 20, 1890, the ship weighed anchor, and passed out through the Golden Gate, accompanied by the prayers of a denomination which was enthusiastically entering upon a new field of activity. On November 25 the island of Pitcairn was sighted, and in a short time the missionaries had landed and were being joyfully welcomed by the inhabitants.

THE LANDING, PITCAIRN ISLAND

Meetings were held, instruction was given in various lines, and one fine day eighty-two persons were baptized in a quiet little cove formed by coral rocks. When the missionary ship sailed on to other island groups, Elder and Mrs. Gates remained on Pitcairn to give instruction to the church, and to labor for the spiritual upbuilding of its members.

Elder and Mrs. Read were left at the Society Islands. Brother Tay, who had been the pioneer in the island work, died at Suva, Fiji, Jan. 8, 1892, and Captain Marsh died June 3, 1892, in New Zealand.

The ship returned to San Francisco in November, 1892. It started on its second cruise on Jan. 17, 1893. The company of missionaries included B. J. Cady, J. M. Cole, and E. C. Chapman, with their wives, also Dr. M. G. Kellogg, Miss Hattie Andre, and J. R. McCoy. Miss Andre took up work on Pitcairn Island, where she organized and conducted a church school. The other workers filled urgent calls from various islands in the South Pacific.

In the Society Islands the interest was great, and the ruling classes joined in the request for a teacher. One of the old chiefs, in presenting the plea, said: " The people of Raiatea have for a long time refused to allow any missionary to come among them. Now God has softened their hearts, and they ask you to give them a missionary. Don't refuse, lest they go back to serving the devil, and you be to blame for it." Professor and Mrs. Cady were left in response to this request, with E. C. Chapman and his wife to assist them. Dr. M. G. Kellogg took up work on the Tongan Islands.

The " Pitcairn " sailed out of the Golden Gate for her third cruise June 17, 1894, Capt. J. E. Graham being in charge. The following missionaries were on board: D. A. Owen and family, Dr. and Mrs. J. E. Caldwell, Mr. and Mrs. G. O. Wellman, Lillian White, Mr. and Mrs. R. G. Stringer, Mr. and Mrs. Buckner, J. R. McCoy and his daughter, and Miss Maud Young.

The first stop was made at Pitcairn, where J. R. McCoy and his daughter and Mr. and Mrs. Buckner were left to labor. Mr. and Mrs. Wellman and Lillian White were first left at Tahiti; but on the return voyage they were taken to Raiatea to assist Professor Cady. Mr. and Mrs. Stringer, and Sarah Young, who had been taken on board at Pitcairn, were landed at Rurutu. Dr. and Mrs. Caldwell and D. A. Owen and family stayed for a time on Rarotonga.

The " Pitcairn " returned in safety to San Francisco, and in course of time made a fourth and a fifth cruise among the Pacific islands. As time went on, steamship lines were started, which afforded fairly good facilities for reaching the islands. The " Pitcairn " was accordingly sold in 1900.

The island field has been grouped into two grand divisions, known as Eastern and Central Polynesia. Eastern Polynesia includes those islands in the eastern part of the Pacific Ocean which lie south of the equator, namely, the Society, Cook, Austral, Marquesas, and Tuamotu groups, as well as Gambier, Pitcairn, and a few other single islands. The greater number of these islands are under the French government. The Cook group and Pitcairn, with a few adjacent islands, are the only British possessions in this part of the Pacific.

There is no regular means of transportation between these islands. When one wishes to visit any of the smaller ones, the voyage must be made on a small sailing vessel, and it is uncertain when an opportunity will offer to leave the island. Each group has a dialect of its own, but there is more or less resemblance between the dialects.

Two written languages are used in the fields entered by Seventh-day Adventists, namely, Tahitian and Rarotongan. The latter prevails in the different islands of the Cook group. In all the other islands in Eastern Polynesia the Tahitian language is largely used, Tahiti being the political and commercial center of the French possessions in this part of the world.

John I. Tay was the first Seventh-day Adventist missionary to visit Tahiti. He spent some time in Papeete on his way to Pitcairn.

Work in the Society Islands was begun in 1891 by Mr. and Mrs. A. J. Read, who sailed with the first company of missionaries on the " Pitcairn." They returned to the States, and were succeeded at Tahiti in 1893 by Mr. and Mrs. G. O. Wellman, who remained there but a short time, and later went to Raiatea. In 1893 Mr. and Mrs. B. J. Cady took up work in this group. They made their headquarters at Raiatea, lying 120 miles west of Tahiti. Soon after this the pioneer workers in Tahiti returned to the States, and it was left with B. J. Cady to foster the growing work in both Raiatea and Tahiti, with the assistance of other workers, who came and went. For a time a printing press was maintained at Tahiti. Later the printing press was given to another island field which had greater need of it, and since that time our Tahitian printing has been done by the Avondale Press in Australia.

When Mr. and Mrs. Cady first began work in the islands, there was a general desire on the part of the young people to learn English. They accordingly took a number into their home, and imparted to them a knowledge of the English language and of the Bible. As the school grew in interest and numbers, they were able to secure possession of a farm, which furnished work to the students for a number of years, Miss Anna Nelson, Mr. and Mrs. George Beckner, H. L. Fowler, and Mr. and Mrs. G. L. Sterling being connected with the institution at different times as teachers and assistants. Other schools were carried on with some success.

There are three organized churches on the island of Tahiti, each provided with a church building. Believers are also found in Raiatea, Huaheine, Morea, and some smaller islands.

Cook Islands

Six islands compose the group known as the Cook Islands, the chief of which is Rarotonga. The story of how the gospel was given to the natives of the latter is a deeply interesting one. John Williams had landed two native workers with their wives; but the Rarotongans treated them so badly that they were compelled to go on board the ship again.

J. R. McCOY
Magistrate on Pitcairn Island

When Williams learned of their cruel treatment, he deemed it advisable to postpone working in Rarotonga till a more favorable time. But as they were about to sail away, Papeiha, one of the workers who had been ashore overnight, said to Williams: " Take my wife to her people, but let me return to the shores of this heathen land, and preach the gospel to its needy inhabitants." They tried to persuade him to remain on the ship, but binding his Tahitian Scriptures on his head, he jumped into the sea and swam ashore. His heroic action was not without prompt effect upon the Rarotongans. They marveled at the man who was willing to risk his life to give them the gospel, and before many months they were helping him to build a meeting house.

Our work in Rarotonga began about 1896, J. D. Rice and Dr. J. E. Caldwell and his family, with a Pitcairn Island sister to assist them, being the first workers. The doctor soon became known by a term indicative of his reform methods of treatment; for the natives called him " Dr. Vai Vera," the English equivalent of which is " Dr. Hot Water." His nurse they called " Hot Water Bag." Doctor and nurse had their hands more than full from the beginning, and as time went on, they were able to see some fruit of their efforts in the conversion of souls.

When the island field was taken over by the Australasian Union Conference, Elder Piper was sent to labor in the Cook group. He sailed from Australia in 1901, and remained in the islands for six years. He was relieved by W. H. Pascoe, who was obliged to leave on account of sickness, and was succeeded in turn by Frank E. Lyndon, of New Zealand. When Brother Lyndon succeeded to the superintendency of the Eastern Polynesian Mission Field and settled in Tahiti, he was succeeded at Rarotonga by G. L. Sterling, who had previously labored in the Society group.

There was on Rarotonga a neat little church building made of coral lime, and a mission property of about thirteen acres provided with buildings. The church membership was small. In former years there was a school of some size, but later the school work was discontinued. It was resumed in 1922, and we now have a flourishing institution. After some years, G. L. Sterling left the work in Rarotonga in charge of Mr. and Mrs. R. K. Piper, and himself entered Aitutaki, another island of the group. He raised up a church on this island, and the work became firmly established.

Our Cook Island paper, the *Tuatua-Mou* (Truth), which began to be issued in 1906, has been exerting a wide influence. We have in the Rarotongan language these books: " Steps to Christ," " Daniel and the Revelation," " Christ Our Saviour," and " Bible Readings."

Pitcairn Island is associated with the Society Island Mission organization. It was visited by B. J. Cady in 1904 and again in 1907. The school work carried on for a number of years by Hattie Andre was later conducted by M. W. Carey, who labored in the island from 1907 to 1912. He was succeeded by R. Adams. There were about sixty pupils in attendance. In January, 1914, a camp-meeting was held on the island, which was a season of rich spiritual refreshing. J. R. McCoy, for a number of years chief magistrate of Pitcairn Island, has labored successfully in other islands.

Central Polynesia

The Central Polynesian Mission, now known as a conference, includes the Fiji, Samoa, and Friendly (or Tonga) groups. Pioneer work in the last-named group was done in the nineties by Mr. and Mrs. E. S. Butz under whose labors a company of Sabbath keepers was raised up and a school established, taught by a sister from Australia. A church building was erected in 1904. In 1909 a second school was opened, in purchased quarters, and some new members were added to the company of believers. W. W. Palmer, then director of the mission, was succeeded in 1911 by A. G. Stewart. There are believers on the islands of Tonga, Vavau, and Haapai. E. E. Thorpe began the work in Vavau. The first laborer in Haapai was a native Christian from Fiji.

Early in the history of our work in Samoa a sanitarium was opened by Dr. F. E. Braucht, to be carried on by others after his departure. Delos Lake and W. E. Floding were for a time engaged in evangelistic labor, both leaving on account of impaired health. J. E. Stead labored in the island for a number of years. A. H. White and H. T. Howse both had a part in the work, which has progressed but slowly. The book, "Christ Our Saviour," and a number of tracts have been translated and published. L. E. P. Dexter has engaged in missionary nursing among the people.

Fiji

Fiji was visited a number of times by the missionary brigantine "Pitcairn," and it has the honor of being the last resting place of John I. Tay, who died in Suva. J. M. Cole began to labor in Fiji in 1895, but was obliged to return to America on account of ill health. In 1896 J. E. Fulton and family left New Zealand for Fiji, which became their home for a number of years. Elder Fulton applied himself earnestly to the mastery of the language, and in 1897 began to preach to the natives and to hold Bible readings among them. A small missionary cutter was provided by the General Conference, with which to tour among the different islands. The first full course of sermons on the Seventh-day Adventist doctrines was given in 1899, and was successful in bringing out a company of Sabbath keepers, including some natives of influence.

The mission building was erected at Suva Vou, a suburb of Suva, the chief port on the largest island, Viti Levu, and the *Rarama* (light), our native paper, began to be issued in 1900, and has continued to the present day. An abridged edition of "The Great Controversy" was put out in 1903, and a hymn book with one hundred hymns set to music was published two years later. A physiology of 125 pages came out in 1908, a revised edition of "Bible Readings" in 1912, and "Early Writings" about the same time. Besides these, numerous tracts have been issued and widely circulated.

C. H. Parker and his wife labored for a number of years in Fiji, and were prominent in the work in that field. Elder

Parker succeeded as superintendent when J. E. Fulton was called to take the presidency of the Australasian Union.

The school work, begun in the early days in connection with the mission at Suva Vou and later carried on at Buresala on the island of Ovalau, was for a time in charge of S. W. Carr, a graduate of the Avondale school. He was succeeded in 1907 by A. G. Stewart. In 1908 Mr. and Mrs. G. E. Merriott joined

J. E. FULTON

C. H. PARKER

the mission, and somewhat later Miss A. N. Williams took charge of the girls' school. A fine corps of native laborers have been developed in Fiji, who are carrying on active missionary work in various parts of the island group.

The mission school at Buresala has grounds comprising 270 acres of well-wooded and fertile land, and is undergoing improvement at the hands of the students, who are under the care of G. Branster, principal. The improvements include the cultivation of land, making new roads, building houses, etc. Excellent success has attended the raising of crops, for which good prices are obtained at Levuka, the nearest European settlement and former capital of this group. One of the students trained in this school was sent to New Guinea. Other students are at work in the various islands of their own group. In a smaller school on another island, the youth are prepared to enter the training school at Buresala.

Pauliasi Bunoa was one of the first natives to accept the Adventist views in the Fiji Islands. It was while working as a translator that he was brought to a conviction of the truth. He was at first very much perplexed over the doctrines, and he talked with other missionaries to get their advice. They said to him: "You do not want to be unsettling yourself over these

PAULIASI BUNOA AND HIS WIFE

things. You have been a worker among us for thirty years, and see what has been done. These people do not understand the language. Do not allow them to unsettle you."

"Yes," he replied, "these people may not understand the language, but they understand the Bible, and they prove these things from the Bible. I want to know the truth."

After Pauliasi had begun to keep the Sabbath, other teachers came to Suva Vou, and began to oppose the Adventists. One of these missionaries asked Pauliasi why he had given up his former belief. He replied that it was because the Bible confirmed what the Adventists taught. The missionary began to talk about the blessedness and triumphs of the church which was keeping Sunday. "Tell me from the Book," said Pauliasi; "then I will keep it." He was ordained to the gospel ministry at the Australasian Union Conference held in 1906.

Another interesting case is that of Ambrose, a chief of high birth, who would have been king under the old government. He invited the Adventists to the town and gave them land; but he was a drunkard, a wife beater, and one of the most inveterate gamblers on the island. Twice he had been banished by the government. When J. E. Fulton first settled on the island, the people told him: "Look out for old Ambrose. He will do anything for money. If he thinks there is anything in it, he will profess to be a Christian." When Ambrose began to attend the meetings night after night, Mr. Fulton remembered these words. A number came out and professed conversion, but Ambrose was not among them.

Finally one Sabbath, at an early morning meeting, when the believers had bowed in prayer after reading the Scriptures, and a few had prayed, the old chief began to pray, and weep, and confess his sins, and to plead for mercy. Then he arose, and after humiliating himself in the sight of his townspeople by telling them what a wicked man he had been, he asked them to pray for him; and then and there he gave himself to Christ. From that day he was a different man. He did not change in everything at once; but as he saw the light, he walked in it. His conversion was a wonder to many, who could not deny that a marvelous transformation of character had taken place in the old chief.

Other faithful members might be mentioned who have given equally clear evidence of a thorough change of heart. Shortly after J. E. Fulton left the little church he had raised up, there was a great feast in the village, in the course of which the natives donned their old war dress and danced and sang and feasted. The leader of the company of Adventists, knowing the peculiar fascination of such a feast, appointed a meeting for the same hour, and all the members assembled. Tavita preached to them for an hour, but as the service was about to close, he heard the sound of the music and dancing still going on, and he said: " Brethren, the music is still on over there; we cannot leave yet. I will begin and preach the sermon over again." So he spoke for another hour.

At five o'clock the music was still heard; so the leader turned to the old chief and said, " Ambrose, will you talk to the brethren a little while? " So Ambrose exhorted them to be faithful. After he had finished, Tavita called on the Sabbath school superintendent to talk. As he finished, the sun was setting, and he said: " We will have our evening prayer now." A number took part in prayer, and then the service closed. And though it had lasted the whole afternoon, and in full hearing of the festive dance and music, not even one of the children left the church until it was all over.

In Fiji, as in other parts of the field, the message is carried effectively by the printed page. One little incident may be given as an illustration:

Early in the history of our work four young men from the interior of the largest island of the group were passing our mission station toward evening, and sought shelter there. Mr. Fulton permitted them to remain overnight with the native young men of the mission. In the evening, worship was held as usual, a portion of Scripture being read, followed by prayer, in which the young men were not forgotten. Again in the morning there was worship, and they were prayed for. Before they left, Mrs. Fulton took the prophetic chart, pointed to the image of Daniel 2, and gave them a short Bible study. They asked questions about the pictures of the various beasts, and she gave some explanations also of these symbols. Then they took their departure.

Nine years later Mr. Fulton was at the training school at Buresala, and one of the native men came up and shook hands with him, saying, " Don't you know me? " He had to acknowledge that he did not. The man identified himself as one of the four boys who had stayed overnight at the mission. He went on to say that before leaving the seacoast, he had secured a copy of our Fijian paper, *Rarama,* and also a copy of " Bible Readings." Afterward, when he opened the book and saw the image of Daniel 2, he remembered the Bible study.

Still he was a careless young man, and did not then go more deeply into the matter. But he gave the book and paper to his brother, who was a sort of preacher in one of the mountain settlements. This brother seriously read the book and the paper, and studied his Bible, as a result of which after four years he decided to obey the truth. He told his townspeople of his decision, and they were displeased, and said that he must leave, as they did not wish him any longer to teach their children. But one old man asked him to explain his views.

The young man with much fear and trembling took his Bible and read the proof texts. When he had finished, the old man said, " Matthew, you may stay with me." Thereupon others invited him to stay with them, till it was quite evident that he was once more in favor with the people. But he said he would not stay unless he might bring to them a missionary who could teach them more of the truth he had learned to love. To this they assented.

The work in Fiji received a very special impetus in the closing year of the World War, when the Spirit of God worked mightily in the inland portions of Viti Levu, causing the people of various villages to unite in earnest appeal for the living preacher. As our workers went inland in response to this call, they were welcomed with great demonstrations of joy, and they found whole villages keeping the Sabbath and seeking further instruction. The chief of one of these villages said:

" It may be asked why we accept this faith now and not before. This is God's time. His word has come to us, and we have been awakened. . . . In coming into this faith, we came for all there is in it. We came for cleansing. We cast away the old life. We cast away our tafia, our grog, and our unclean food; and we intend to stand steadfast to the truth of God."

In seven weeks over 400 new converts were baptized, more than in the preceding twenty-five years. This marvelous outpouring of the Spirit in the interior gave new hope and courage to the workers throughout Fiji.

Because the Adventists in Fiji were taught to give up smoking and leave off all unclean foods and drinks, the native people gave the denomination a name of their own. They call us " Lotu Savasava " (The clean church). J. E. Fulton, and after him Mr. Parker, received letters addressed to " Ai Talatala in Lotu Savasava " (The preacher of the clean church).

Detached Missions

Work was begun on Norfolk Island by Mr. and Mrs. S. T. Belden, who raised up a company of Sabbath keepers. Mr. Belden dying, the work was carried forward by his wife. A. H. Ferris was sent to the island in 1909, and others later. The mission property consists of a house and twenty-eight acres of good land. There is also a church building.

In 1912 the message was carried from Norfolk to Lord Howe Island, where there is also now a company of believers.

Late in the year 1908, Mr. and Mrs. S. W. Carr, formerly of the Fiji Mission, and B. B. Tavode, a Fijian, began work at Port Moresby, New Guinea, also known as Papua. They were joined the following year by Mr. and Mrs. Gordon Smith, and by Solomana, a Rarotongan educated at the Avondale school. Lectures were given on the message, and a European planter was among the converts. A plot of 150 acres of land was secured at Bisiatabu, twenty-seven miles inland from Port Moresby. Mission buildings were erected and school work entered upon for people who had never before heard the gospel. Results were slow, but patient, persistent labor had its reward. The first Papuan convert was baptized in 1920.

The New Hebrides

The first Adventists to open work in the New Hebrides were C. H. Parker and H. E. Carr, with their wives. They began their effort in Atchin in 1912, being at that time the only European missionaries on the island. Mr. and Mrs. Carr were shortly obliged to return to Australia because of malaria. The others remained and put up a mission house. In the winter of 1913-14 the feeling against foreigners was at its height. European traders were driven into banishment, and the native inmates of a Presbyterian mission station were killed within sight of the Adventist headquarters. Three times our missionaries had to barricade their doors to save their lives. Parker was urged to flee, but he felt it his duty to remain, and he gained greatly in influence over the natives by so doing. Little by little the natives assumed a more favorable attitude. A. G. Stewart succeeded Brother Parker.

NORMAN WILES AND HIS WIFE

From Atchin the message was carried to the adjoining coast of Malekula, the home of the Big Nambus, many of them at that time still cannibals. Elder Parker had begun work among these people, and Elder Stinnes made occasional visits to them. On one occasion he came upon the villagers when they had their preparations under way for a cannibal feast. Nevertheless they welcomed the missionary, and asked for a permanent worker. Owing to the uncertain character of the islanders, the commissioner refused his permission, but advised instead that we open work in Espiritu Santo, the largest island of the group. This was accordingly done, J. R. James being placed in charge of the new mission. Shortly afterward the chief of the Big Nambus sent some of his men over to Santo to plead once more for a teacher, and this time the commissioner gave his consent.

Norman Wiles and his wife, from Atchin, responded to this call, and built a mission home on Malekula. He was making good headway in reducing the language to writing when the fever attacked him, and he had to lay down his work. Mrs. Wiles, after burying her husband, returned to Atchin, first by a sea voyage in a small boat, then inland through villages of hostile tribes. This true woman had only one request to make,— that a worker be sent back to Malekula to raise the standard once more among the Nambus. Thus another mission field is marked for the message.

Solomon Islands

In May, 1914, Mr. and Mrs. G. F. Jones, who had been laboring in Sumatra, opened a mission in the Solomon Islands. They took with them a portable house and a mission launch. The chief magistrate gave them a cordial welcome, and they were able to secure a satisfactory location at Viru, in the Marovo Lagoon, on the island of New Georgia. The natives took hold enthusiastically to clear the land. No less than a hundred different dialects are spoken in the Solomon group.

G. F. JONES

While the natives of this island were, until very recently, sunk in the depths of savagery, they listened eagerly to the gospel as expounded by our missionaries, and began at once to erect churches and school buildings. Within three years of the early beginnings it seemed that the work had grown sufficiently to hold a general camp-meeting. G. F. Jones accordingly sent a message out to the various missions, asking them to come together for such a meeting, and 350 responded to the call, coming in their little canoes from many different directions. The meeting was a decided success.

The rapidly growing work called for additions to the staff. D. Nicholson was one of the first to join G. F. Jones, and others followed. A number of native young men were placed under training, and developed into efficient workers. Aside from the island of New Georgia, where the work began, evangelistic efforts are under way in Vella Lavella, Rendova, and Ronongo. Something like 1,500 islanders are regular members of our Sabbath schools, and the number is steadily growing under the superintendency of H. P. B. Wicks.

SEVENTH-DAY ADVENTISTS IN THE CHAIN GANG

BEHIND PRISON BARS

CHAPTER XXIV

The Organization and Work of the Religious Liberty Association

THE National Religious Liberty Association was organized at Battle Creek, Mich., on the evening of July 21, 1889. Its purpose was well summed up by the president at the first annual session, held in the autumn of the same year. " A few men," he said, " believing in civil and religious liberty, organized for the purpose of combating anything and everything that has a tendency toward uniting church and state."

The animating principle of the organization was no new one to Seventh-day Adventists. They had been teaching it from the beginning. Like the Baptists, from whom in a sense the denomination may be said to have sprung, Adventists regard the church as a distinctly spiritual organization, owing spiritual allegiance to Christ alone, and seeking from the state nothing more than the protection which that power is intended to give alike to all its citizens.

Adventists were not occupying new ground in opposing religious legislation. It was a development which their views of prophecy led them to expect. Already in the middle of the nineteenth century, years before the Blair Sunday bill, or any similar piece of legislation, had been brought before Congress, Adventists had in their literature taken the position, based upon the prophecy of Revelation 13: 11-17, that there would arise here in the United States an intolerant hierarchy similar to the papacy of the Middle Ages, which, taking advantage of certain circumstances, customs, and prejudices, would seize upon the civil power of the government, and use it for the accomplishment of its own ends.

Hence the organization of the National Reform Association, followed by other developments looking in the same direction, and especially persistent efforts to induce Congress to subvert the principles of the national Constitution, together with manifestations of intolerance and persecution in a number of States, all seemed to demand that some steps be taken to meet the issue, and to make the most of the opportunity for warning all the people of the impending danger.

The immediate cause of the organization of the Religious Liberty Association was the rapidly increasing activities, not only of the National Reformers, but of certain other religious organizations having for their aim and purpose to commit the United States to religious legislation. Efforts in this direction were made early in the history of the Republic. In 1811 the synod of Pittsburgh was petitioning Congress to prohibit mail stages from traveling on Sunday, and to close the post offices on that day. In the following year the General Assembly of the Presbyterian Church sent in a petition to the same effect. Similar requests and petitions came from various sources in the course of the next few years, and early in 1830 the time seemed opportune for some kind of answer. Col. Richard Johnson, of Kentucky, then serving as chairman of the House Committee on Post Offices and Post Roads, made a statement of the principles involved. He pointed out that conscientious people cherished widely different opinions. He said:

" The memorialists regard the first day of the week as a day set apart by the Creator for religious exercises, and consider the transportation of the mail and the opening of the post offices on that day the violation of a religious duty, and call for a suppression of the practice.

" Others, by counter-memorials, are known to entertain a different sentiment, believing that no one day of the week is holier than another. Others, holding the universality and immutability of the Jewish decalogue, believe in the sanctity of the seventh day of the week as a day of religious devotion, and, by their memorial now before the committee, they also request that it may be set apart for religious purposes. *Each has hitherto been left to the exercise of his own opinion, and it has been regarded as the proper business of government to protect all and determine for none.* But the attempt is now made to bring about a greater uniformity, at least in practice; and *as argument has failed,* the Government has been called upon to interpose its authority to settle the controversy."—" *American State Papers,*" *by W. A. Blakely, pp. 245-248. Also "American State Papers," class vii, p. 229 et al. (Library of Congress).*

The report went on to point out the limitations of Congress in dealing with such matters:

" Congress acts under a Constitution of delegated and limited powers. The committee look in vain to that instrument for a delegation of power authorizing this body to inquire and determine what part of time, or whether any, has been set apart by the Almighty for religious exercises. *On the contrary, among the few prohibitions which it contains, is one that prohibits a religious test, and another which declares that Congress shall pass no law respecting the establishment of religion, or prohibiting the free exercise thereof. . . .*

" *If Congress shall, by the authority of law, sanction the measure recommended, it would constitute a legislative decision of a religious controversy, in which even Christians themselves are at issue. However suited such a decision may be to an ecclesiastical council, it is incompatible with a Republican legislature, which is purely for political, and not for religious purposes.*"— *Id., pp. 248-250.*

This comprehensive statement of the fundamental principles gave a temporary quietus to the attempts to commit Congress to religious legislation. Some years were to elapse before the question would be generally agitated again.

In 1863 there was launched an organization known as the National Reform Association, whose avowed purpose, as stated in Article II of its constitution, was:

" To secure such an amendment to the Constitution of the United States as will declare the nation's allegiance to Jesus Christ and its acceptance of the moral laws of the Christian religion, and so indicate that this is a Christian nation, and place all the Christian laws, institutions, and usages of our government on an undeniably legal basis in the fundamental law of the land."— *Id., p. 343.*

Moreover on May 21, 1888, there was introduced into the Fiftieth Congress a bill prepared by Senator H. W. Blair, of New Hampshire, designed to secure nation-wide Sunday observance. The original title read:

" Bill to secure to the people the enjoyment of the first day of the week, commonly known as the Lord's day, as a day of rest, and to promote its observance as a day of religious worship."— *Id., p. 360.*

A hearing was given in the interests of this bill on Dec. 13, 1888, the advocates of Sunday laws occupying the entire time, with one exception. A. H. Lewis, D. D., a leading minister and

AMERICAN SENTINEL.

" Corrupted Freemen are the worst of slaves."

VOLUME 1.   OAKLAND, CALIFORNIA, JANUARY, 1886.   NUMBER 1.

The American Sentinel.

PUBLISHED MONTHLY, AT THE

PACIFIC PRESS PUBLISHING COMPANY,
OAKLAND, CAL.

Entered at the Post-office in Oakland.

"A Christian Nation."

THE idea which is advocated by some, that this may be made a Christian nation by simply making a change in the Constitution, was thus pertinently commented upon by the Janesville, Wis., *Gazette*:—

" But independent of the question as to what extent we are a Christian nation, it may well be doubted whether, if the gentlemen who are agitating this question should succeed, they would not do society a very great injury. Such measures are but the initiatory steps which ultimately lead to *restrictions of religious freedom*, and to committing the Government to measures which are as foreign to its powers and purposes as would be its action if it should undertake to determine a disputed question of theology."

An Unprofitable Alliance.

IN regard to the supposed benefit of the church by State patronage, or an alliance between the Church and the State, Lord Macaulay speaks as follows. These words are worthy of careful consideration:—

"The ark of God was never taken till it was surrounded by the arms of earthly defenders. In captivity, its sanctity was sufficient to vindicate it from insult, and to lay the hostile fiends prostrate on the threshold of his own temple. The real security of Christianity is to be found in its benevolent morality, in its exquisite adaptation to the human heart, in the facility with which its scheme accommodates itself to the capacity of every human intellect, in the consolation which it bears to the house of mourning, in the light with which it brightens the great mystery of the grave. To such a system it can bring no addition of dignity or of strength, that it is part and parcel of the common law.

"The whole history of Christianity shows, that she is in far greater danger of being corrupted by the alliance of power, than of being crushed by its opposition. Those who thrust temporal sovereignty upon her treat her as their prototypes treated her author. They bow the knee, and spit upon her; they cry, 'Hail!' and smite her on the cheek; they put a sceptre in her hand, but it is a fragile reed; they crown her, but it is with thorns; they cover with purple the wounds which their own hands have inflicted on her; and inscribe magnificent titles over the cross on which they have fixed her to perish in ignominy and pain."—*Essay on Southey's Colloquies.*

The American Sentinel.

IT is well known that there is a large and influential association in the United States, bearing the name of the "National Reform Association." It is popularly known as the "Religious Amendment Party," because it is endeavoring to secure a religious amendment to the Constitution of the United States. As stated by the world, its object is "to put God in the Constitution." According to its own avowal its aim is to procure—

"Such an amendment to the Constitution of the United States (or its preamble) as will suitably acknowledge Almighty God as the ultimate source of its authority, Jesus Christ as its Ruler, and the Bible as the supreme rule of its conduct, and thus indicate that this is a Christian nation, and place all Christian laws, institutions, and usages, on an undeniable legal basis in the fundamental law of the land."

The president of this association is Hon. Felix R. Brunot, who has held that position almost from its origin. Its present list of vice-presidents, to the number of two hundred, embraces bishops of churches, judges in the highest courts in the land, governors, and representative men in various secular positions, presidents of colleges, doctors of divinity, and professors of theology in large numbers. In fact there is no other association in the land which can boast such an array of names of eminent and influential men. It employs its agents and lecturers, who are presenting their cause to the churches and to the people, and who almost everywhere report unbounded success in their efforts. It has also a paper, the *Christian Statesman*, as its organ to advocate its cause.

While there are many people in the land who are opposed to, or look with suspicion upon, the movements of this party, there is no paper published in the United States, which has for its distinct object the vindication of the rights of American citizens, which, we solemnly believe, are threatened by the actions and aims of this association. That light may be disseminated on this subject, we have commenced the publication of THE AMERICAN SENTINEL. That such a paper as this is needed, we think we can make apparent to every individual who will read our paper, who will hold prejudice in abeyance, and examine our reasons with candor.

While so many really think they are doing God service in their efforts to change the form of our Government, and we are willing to give them credit for thinking so, we are aware that they will look with disfavor upon our work, and some, who do not understand our motives

or our reasons, will be ready to class us, and all who indorse our positions, with the base of the earth, assuming that we are striking at the foundations of morality and religion. But they are much mistaken in their estimate. We promise to do or say nothing against the plainest principles of morality and religion. So far from that, we shall try to set before our readers the true relation of morality and religion, and show that this relation is not correctly presented by this "amendment party."

But the objector will say: "There can be no harm in recognizing Jesus Christ as the Ruler of the nation, and his laws as the rule of our lives." We know that this plea is plausible—we may say it is *taking* with nearly all-religious people. Yet it is specious, plausible in the eyes of those only who have not examined the end to which it necessarily leads. Let us notice some of the things which must attend the success of their efforts, and some principles bearing on the subject:—

1. The Constitution of the United States must be so amended as to permit laws to be made which shall legalize the laws and institutions of Christianity, or of that which they may claim is Christianity. They ask that these laws, institutions, and usages shall be " put on a legal basis." Of course to be put on a legal basis they must be made matters of legal enforcement. That this is the object of that association, real and avowed, we promise to clearly show.

2. To carry this amendment into effect, any person who refuses to obey the laws and usages of Christianity must be subjected to penalties for his neglect or disobedience. As no law can exist without a penalty, no institutions or usages can be placed on a legal basis without authorizing penalties for their enforcement. This is undeniable.

3. A person can be convicted of a misdemeanor only before a court of justice, on the text of the law and the hearing of evidence.

4. The court is necessarily constituted the judge and exponent of the law; and, therefore, if disagreement arises as to the meaning of the law, or as to what constitutes a misdemeanor in the premises, the court is the authority, and the sole authority, to which appeal must be made.

5. And, therefore, if a question arises as to what is or what is not Christian law, usage, or institution, it must be determined by a court of justice! Or, if it be said that it need not be left to the decision of a civil court, but such questions may be referred to an ecclesiastical court,

editor among the Seventh Day Baptists, was permitted to speak for a few minutes. He weakened his cause, however, by admitting the right of Congress to legislate on the subject, and only asked an exemption in favor of his people.

At this point Seventh-day Adventists, who had been entirely ignored, asked the privilege of a hearing, and were allowed about an hour and a half. A. T. Jones, the chief spokesman, made it very clear that Adventists were not seeking an exemption clause, that they would oppose the bill just as much with as without such a clause, because they regarded the principle of legislation in behalf of a religious institution as in itself fundamentally wrong. Senator Blair, who presided at the hearing, interrupted the speaker again and again, but finally admitted that the argument presented was logical and sound throughout.

A report of this hearing, which brought Adventists for the first time somewhat prominently before the national legislative body, was printed in pamphlet form, with additional material on the subject of religious legislation, and widely circulated throughout the country.

Meanwhile there were various cases, especially in the Southern States, of Adventists' being fined for garden and field labor on Sunday, and everything pointed to the need of enlightening the general public as to the principles of religious liberty. It was in view of these circumstances that Adventists thought it wise to organize an association which should give its particular attention to this one thing. The movement first took shape in the appointment in December, 1888, of a press committee of three " for the purpose of devising and carrying out plans for the dissemination of general information to the public, on the question of civil and religious liberty." C. Eldridge, M. B. Duffie, and W. H. McKee, the members of the committee, had much other work to do; but they were instrumental in securing the publication of a number of articles and reviews in various papers.

In January, 1889, W. H. McKee, who was acting as secretary, was furnished an assistant in A. F. Ballenger. The work thus re-enforced rapidly grew in extent and efficiency. Early in February a new press committee was appointed by the General Conference Committee, consisting of the following seven members: C. Eldridge, A. T. Jones, D. T. Jones, W. A. Colcord, J. O. Corliss, J. E. White, W. H. McKee. The committee organized on the 10th of February, and immediately sought the co-operation of the various conferences, who were asked to appoint State press committees and select local agents as far as possible in all places where a newspaper was published.

The members of the committee also engaged in field work, J. O. Corliss appearing at the second hearing on the Sunday rest bill before the Senate Committee on Education and Labor, and A. T. Jones addressing committees of the legislatures of Ohio and Indiana, which had under consideration resolutions favoring the bill. Copies of the pamphlet entitled, " Civil Government and Religion," were placed in the hands of all members of Congress.

When it was learned that the Arkansas Legislature was considering a bill to repeal the exemption clause, J. O. Corliss was sent to appear before the committee that had the bill in charge. His representations and the liberal distribution of literature brought about the defeat of the bill. In the early summer, lectures on religious liberty were given in a number of large cities, and reported in the leading papers.

Meanwhile the need of a larger and more representative organization was making itself felt. Accordingly the committee drafted a declaration of principles and a constitution for a new body, to be known as The National Religious Liberty Association, and then adjourned *sine die.* The new organization was brought into being at a mass meeting held in the Tabernacle at Battle Creek on the evening of July 21, 1889. A constitution and by-laws were adopted, and 110 persons signed the following declaration of principles, thus becoming charter members:

" We believe in the religion taught by Jesus Christ.

" We believe in temperance, and regard the liquor traffic as a curse to society.

" We believe in supporting the civil government, and submitting to its authority.

" We deny the right of any civil government to legislate on religious questions.

" We believe it is the right, and should be the privilege, of every man to worship according to the dictates of his own conscience.

" We also believe it to be our duty to use every lawful and honorable means to prevent religious legislation by the civil government, that we and our fellow citizens may enjoy the inestimable blessings of both religious and civil liberty."—" *National Religious Liberty Association* " (*tract*), *p. 1.*

The officers elected were largely persons who had been active members of the press committee, the president being C. Eldridge; the secretary, W. H. McKee; assistant secretary, A. F. Ballenger. There was no delay in getting to work. The secretary wrote:

" Immediately after the organization of the association, all but one member of the executive committee left the city to fill appointments to which they had been detailed: President Eldridge to work in the Southeastern and Southern States; J. O. Corliss to accompany him to Georgia, and take charge of the defense of Day Conklin, who was there under arrest for Sunday labor; A. T. Jones to make a lecture tour through the Northwest and California with the especial purpose in view of exerting an influence in the constitutional conventions of the States about to be admitted; D. T. Jones to work in the Southwestern States, and the secretary and assistant secretary in the Central States.

" In all of these sections the members of the committee presented the subject of the organization of the association, and took memberships. Wherever possible, the question of religious legislation, in its different phases, was given prominence and discourses were delivered. As a result of this labor, a complete or partial organization was effected in Ohio, Indiana, Illinois, Michigan, Minnesota, Wisconsin, New York, Maine, New England, Vermont, North Carolina, Virginia, West Virginia, Georgia, Florida, Arkansas, Texas, Kansas, Missouri, Tennessee, Nebraska, Colorado, Wyoming, New Mexico, Louisiana, the Atlantic States, and Canada.

" The appointments made for the secretary and assistant secretary were filled by them, and in the course of the trip over 3,000 newspapers were corresponded with, to more than half of which articles were sent explaining and emphasizing the position of the association on the question of religious legislation."— *General Conference Bulletin, Oct. 25, 1889; Vol. III, p. 77.*

The association held its first annual meeting in Battle Creek, Oct. 24, 1889, in connection with the twenty-eighth session of the General Conference, there being present 109 delegates from twenty-nine States. A more perfect organization was effected at this meeting, and plans were laid for aggressive work. In the year following, the membership steadily increased, the month of July alone adding 439 new names to the list. When the organization had been in existence about a year, the vice-presidents, secretaries, and press agents in the various States numbered seventy-five; the local press agents, one hundred. Lectures had been given in many parts of the country, and large mass meetings held at important centers; over 1,500,000 pages of reading matter had been circulated, and 300,000 signatures had been secured to the petition against religious legislation. A thousand dollars had been spent in defending members prosecuted under State Sunday laws.

The association took care to be well represented at Washington, where the fight was on. The Blair Sunday rest bill, whose first appearance in the Fiftieth Congress has been related, was presented again before the Fifty-first Congress, its title being slightly changed so as to seem less religious in nature. There was also brought in the Breckenridge bill compelling Sunday observance in the District of Columbia. Both measures were successfully opposed by the association, and incidentally much was done in the way of enlightening the general public as to the essential character of Sunday laws.

The activities of the association as an organization for the defense of Sabbath keepers who exercised their Constitutional right to labor on Sunday, were various and exerted a widely felt influence. The case of R. M. King, a farmer living in Troy, Obion Co., Tenn., may be given as typical. At the first annual meeting of the association in the autumn of 1889, word was received of his arrest and impending trial. Col. T. E. Richardson, a well-known local lawyer, was engaged, and argued the case; but it was decided adversely, subjecting King to a fine of $75 and costs. The case was appealed to the State Supreme Court, which reaffirmed the decision of the lower court. The association then took the case to the United States Circuit Court for the western district of Tennessee, on a writ of habeas corpus, Judge Hammond presiding. Here also the decision, rendered Aug. 1, 1891, was adverse.

It was the intention to carry the case to the United States Supreme Court, but Brother King died in the meantime. In his case, and practically all others, it was amply proved that the work complained of was done very quietly, and could not in any sense be regarded as a disturbance. The chief reason for prosecution seemed to be that Mr. King had become a member of a recently organized church of Seventh-day Adventists, and local prejudice took the form of enforcing an obsolete Sunday law in order to retard the growth of the denomination in that part of the State. The result, as usual, was precisely the opposite. Leading newspapers, North and South, took up the matter, and gave the case the widest possible publicity, and the editorial articles were mostly in favor of Mr. King.

The Atlanta *Constitution* of June 20, 1890, says, among other things:

"The case is a most interesting one. It seems that Mr. King, who is a farmer, was indicted for quietly working on his own premises, 'not in sight of any place of public worship,' he disturbed no one by his work, but it was held that 'the moral sense' of the people had sustained a shock by seeing work done on the Sabbath, and this statement was made against him at his trial. . . .

"Whatever the merits of the case may be, Mr. King can count on public sympathy; for from the statement of it in the Tennessee papers, he appears to be a sadly persecuted man, and the history of the case thus far smacks of injustice and a religious intolerance which is novel in its Puritan severity. The man appears to have been dragged from court to court, and jury to jury, subjected to great pecuniary expense, fined twice for the same offense — if an act like his, committed in accordance with the rules of his sect, can indeed be called an offense.

"The case is a peculiar one, and the final decision of the United States Supreme Court will be awaited with great interest."— *The Home Missionary, July, 1890; Vol. II, p. 153.*

The New York *World*, in an editorial June 23, 1890, went even more fully into the principles involved:

"Whatever the judicial ruling may be, as to the constitutional power of a State to enforce such laws, there can be no doubt that their enforcement in such cases as that of Mr. King, is a gross violation of natural rights, and rights of conscience. It is not contended that Mr. King disturbed any neighbor in the enjoyment of a quiet Sunday, but merely that his working on Sunday and his observance of Saturday as his Sabbath instead, was an offense to the moral sense of the community, and a violation of the laws of the State.

"If it was so, it is high time for the community in which Mr. King lives, to discipline its moral sense, and for his State to re-arrange its laws in conformity with that principle of individual liberty which lies at the foundation of American institutions.

"The principle involved is simple, and its application plain. The State has nothing to do with religion, except to protect every citizen in his religious liberty. It has no more right to prescribe the religious observance of Sabbaths and holy days, than to order sacraments and to ordain creeds."— *Id., p. 152.*

The Chicago *Tribune* of June 18, 1890, related the facts at some length, and said the whole country would watch the progress of the case with great interest, as it involved a question which had not before engaged the attention of the national Supreme Court.

"So long [it continued] as the labor of Adventists on Sunday does not interfere with the rights of the Mosaic and Puritanic people on the same day, the prosecution of them seems neither more nor less than persecution."

There were a number of similar cases. On the 27th of May, 1892, the grand jury of Henry County, Tennessee, indicted five farmers living near Springville. These men, whose neighbors testified that they had not disturbed them in the least, were nevertheless found guilty, and some of them, as well as others later, were put in the chain gang along with hardened criminals, and made to work with them on the public roads.

One of the most powerful agents in arousing public attention during these early years of the association, was the *American Sentinel*, issued weekly, and wholly devoted to the promulgation of the principles of religious liberty.

The further activities of the denomination in the field of religious liberty will be dealt with in a later chapter.

A GROUP OF RUSSIAN WORKERS

GERHARDT PERK READING THE TRACT IN SECRET

CHAPTER XXV

Beginnings in Russia

WE have seen, in an earlier chapter, how the Adventist truths were accepted by a company of Germans in Milltown, S. Dak., who were organized into the first German Seventh-day Adventist church. The members of this church had come to America from the Crimea, where they still had relatives and friends. To these, accordingly, they began to send Adventist tracts and papers, and in 1883 one of them, Jacob Reiswig by name, resolved to return to the homeland and follow up with personal labor the interest aroused by the printed page. He had come to America with his family in 1878, and had begun to observe the Sabbath as a result of reading a tract left at his house by a colporteur. He was uneducated and stuttered badly, yet from the time when he first became an Adventist, he was a successful personal worker, distributing a large amount of literature from door to door, and talking with the people as he had opportunity.

When he decided to return to Russia that he might communicate to his friends and acquaintances the message so dear to his own heart, he was acting solely on his own responsibility.

471

He neither asked nor received the aid of church or conference. His method of labor was much the same as it had been in America. He knew the power of the printed word. His trunk was well stocked with tracts, and though he was so poor that he had to sell his boots in order to procure money to complete the journey, his supply of literature was intact when he reached his destination.

He began work without delay. It was not lawful to teach the Adventist doctrines in public, but the old man went from village to village, seeking out the people in the market places, and in various ways calling their attention to the advent truths. He would hand a tract to any likely-looking person, and ask him, in his stuttering way, if he would kindly read a few paragraphs aloud for him. Then he would ask the reader what he thought of it. The outcome would usually be a quiet talk on Scriptural truths. He also called on people in their homes, and on the pastors themselves as well as on the members of the flock. And although the contents of the tracts came to be pretty well known in certain quarters, and considerable opposition was aroused, not even the pastors could find it in their hearts to molest the kindly old man who merely asked people to read for him, and then invited them to give their opinion of what they had read.

After a stay of two years, Jacob Reiswig returned to the States to acquire a fuller knowledge of the faith, and in other ways prepare himself for more effective service. In 1887 he packed his trunk with tracts and books the second time, resolved to devote his remaining years to spreading a knowledge of Adventism in the Crimea. During his second stay in America he had learned from his grandchildren to sing a number of advent songs, and he found his new acquirement a great help in gathering little companies of interested listeners at the market places, where he could distribute his tracts among them, and discuss Bible subjects.

After several additional years of patient, persistent labor for the Master, he was finally laid to rest. When he died, his son, with whom he was staying, carefully packed in the old man's coffin what remained of the precious tracts and pamphlets, to be buried with him. At the funeral service the pastor said: "If every one lived as this old man did, they surely would all go to heaven." This testimonial from the pastor set the people to thinking still more deeply over the ideas contained in the tracts. Some had already begun to observe the Sabbath, and others soon joined them.

The persons thus brought to a knowledge of the Adventist views were all German-speaking descendants of German colonists, settled in southern Russia. The first Russian-born German to embrace the Adventist views was Gerhardt Perk. At conversion he became a member of the church of the Brethren, but in 1882 there came into his hands a tract entitled, " The Third Angel's Message," which made him acquainted with the belief of Seventh-day Adventists. The tract had been sent from America three years before to a neighbor, who kept it very secretly. Finally he came to Mr. Perk and said: " For three years I have had some very dangerous publications in my house. I have never given them to any one to read. Indeed, these publications are so dangerous that even an earnest member of the Brethren Church might be led astray by them."

Naturally Mr. Perk began to be curious. " Possibly," he thought, " these publications have some connection with the great falling away at the revealing of Antichrist." He asked his neighbor to let him have the publications, that he also might read them in secret. For a long time the man was unwilling; but finally he consented to lend a tract, on condition that its contents be not divulged. Mr. Perk took it out into the haymow, and read it through three times, after which he copied the address of the publishers. He was convinced then and there that what he had read was the truth; but he dared not say anything to his neighbors.

In the same year he became a colporteur for the British and Foreign Bible Society, who sent him first to Moscow and afterward to Siberia. He had written meanwhile to the publishers of the tract in America, and had received a further supply of Adventist publications, which had confirmed the impression made by the first tract; but he lacked courage to obey what he believed to be the truth.

While trying to sell Bibles in Siberia, he passed through an experience that taught him to trust God implicitly. He started for a Siberian city by the name of Irbit, where there is held annually a fair that brings large numbers of people from the region round about. On the way to this place, he lost his entire stock of Bibles, worth about a thousand dollars. For four weeks he sought the lost property in vain. Meanwhile the fair had been held, and with it had passed the opportunity to sell the books. He had been working for the society only a short time, and was fearful of losing his position. Finally he resorted to fasting and prayer, which he continued for three days. On the third day his prayer was answered, and he found his books.

A further providence enabled him to dispose of the entire lot in a single day. Near the place where he had been staying was a large railway shop employing thousands of hands. He asked the director if he might sell his books in the factory, urging that the Bible had in it power to make men better. Not only did the director give him permission to sell the Bibles, but he sent a man along with him, who practically told the men that they were to buy the book. Thus the books were disposed of, and at the close of the day there were only a few damaged copies left.

RUSSIAN COLPORTEURS

This experience gave Brother Perk courage to come out boldly and become the first Seventh-day Adventist in Russia. When later he received a letter from L. R. Conradi, suggesting that he take up the sale of Adventist publications, he was glad to resign his position with the Bible Society. Not long afterward he accompanied Elder Conradi on the latter's first trip through Russia, which was to mark the beginning of our organized work in that empire.

The tour was made in the summer of 1886. On July 12 the two men left Odessa by steamer for the Crimea. In Eupatoria, they found some German Baptists, who invited them to their village, some thirty-five miles north. The invitation was accepted, and the brethren remained with these Baptists two days, holding several meetings, and convincing some of the truth of the advent message. The Baptists then took them to Demir-bulat, where a Mennonite brother had been keeping the Sabbath for four years.

Resuming their journey, they arrived on Friday evening, July 16, at Japontschi, where a small company of believers had been holding Sabbath meetings. There were twelve in the company, and as many more within a circuit of fifty miles. It being harvest time and the mails slow, several weeks were required to allow of all the believers' being notified. But as the people were anxious to hear, meetings were begun at once, the attendance steadily increasing. On Friday evening the subject of the Sabbath was taken up, and then opposition began. The windows were smashed the following night.

The next week Elders Conradi and Perk traveled thirty miles south to Avell, where several Sabbath keepers were living, and after holding two meetings there, drove forty miles to Berdebulat, where an appointment had been made for the believers to assemble from various quarters because there was water for baptism. Here nineteen signed the covenant to keep the commandments of God and the faith of Jesus, thus laying the foundation for the first Seventh-day Adventist church in Russia. An elder and a deacon were chosen and ordained, and baptism was administered to two sisters in a backwater of the Black Sea, many of the inhabitants in the near-by Russian village looking on from the housetops.

Returning from the baptism, the members celebrated the ordinance of humility, and were preparing to partake of the Lord's Supper when Elder Conradi was called out to appear before a sheriff, Brother Perk accompanying him to act as interpreter. On their appearance before the sheriff, their passports were forthwith demanded, and they were confronted with an accusation of teaching Jewish heresy, and of baptizing two women into this faith. A Russian brother was also called, and likewise the two women who had been baptized, and many questions were asked them. Finally two of the brethren became responsible for the appearance of Elders Conradi and Perk at Perekop the following day. This done, the meeting which had been so rudely interrupted, proceeded, and the following morning, after a short parting meeting, the men were on their way to Perekop, where they arrived at two in the afternoon of the same day, and reported to the authorities.

On presenting themselves before the *isprafnik*, the highest officer of the district, and delivering to him the sealed letter from the sheriff, they were promptly placed in confinement, and in the evening were conveyed to the district prison, which was to be their home for forty days. Mr. Conradi was allowed to write letters to the American consuls at Odessa and St. Petersburg, and send a dispatch to B. L. Whitney at Basel; but these must first be sent to Simferopol, and not till more than a week later were they returned to be sent to their proper destinations. Even then a blunder was made in conveying the telegram, so that not till nearly two weeks after the arrest did the word get to B. L. Whitney, who promptly laid the case before the American minister at St. Petersburg.

On the second Sabbath the judge called L. R. Conradi down to the office, and examined him at great length, after which he asked him if he would be satisfied if he was released on bail for 1,000 rubles. If so, he was to sign such a statement. This he did, and thereupon his companion was examined. The brethren, understanding that the sum of 1,000 rubles would be accepted as bail, made earnest efforts to sell their crops and raise the sum, which they offered to the authorities; but they were informed that the money would be accepted for Perk, but not for Conradi.

The prisoners, who had been allowed to buy their own food, now decided to try the prison fare, in order to save their money. They were accordingly served two and one-half pounds of heavy black rye bread a day, and at noon a dish of soup, usually *borscht,* a sour vegetable broth with some meat in it, served in liberal quantities in a small wooden tub.

On August 19 a letter came from the American consul at Odessa, and some days later a communication from the American minister at St. Petersburg, both officials promising to do what they could for the early release of the prisoners.

Sabbath, August 28, was spent in fasting and prayer. That evening cheering letters came to the prisoners from home, and from the brethren in Basel, which the jailer was good enough to hand them direct, instead of sending them first to Simferopol, as he had been doing with others.

On September 8 the *isprafnik* for the first time gave L. R. Conradi some encouragement that he might be released on bail. On the morning of the 9th the prisoners were called down into the office, and had handed them a whole bundle of letters that they had written, and had supposed were long ago in the hands of their friends, one of them being to Mrs. Conradi, who had thus not had a line from her husband during the thirty days' imprisonment. About seven o'clock they were marched over to the office of the judge, who told Mr. Conradi that the trial might come off in three, six, or twelve months, or not at all; but he was to have liberty to leave Russia whenever he chose.

Returning from the judge's office, the prisoners had their money and clothing returned to them, paid for the scanty favors they had received, and then started in a lumber wagon for Berdebulat, where they arrived in the evening. It was a joyful meeting. The brethren at Berdebulat had been in as much uncertainty as the prisoners. Somewhat later Oscar Roth arrived, having come from Switzerland to see what could be done for the relief of the prisoners. The day was Friday, and fortunately the meeting for the next day had been appointed for Berdebulat. Thither came accordingly the brethren from Japontschi. A long meeting was held that evening, and another on the Sabbath, in which the organization of the church and the tract society was perfected.

On the evening after the Sabbath Elders Conradi and Perk were driven to Japontschi, where they met friends who had come thirty miles from the south, bringing with them some

FIRST RUSSIAN CHURCH AT ST. PETERSBURG (Petrograd)

persons who had embraced the Adventist views since the imprisonment. The meeting began at nine o'clock in the evening, and lasted until almost daybreak. After a few hours' rest, the people came together again. Several joined the church, and others expressed their desire to be baptized at the earliest opportunity. All fell in heartily with the principle of tithing.

On Sunday afternoon L. R. Conradi was invited to lead the meeting of the Mennonite Baptists, and general regret was expressed that he could not remain longer. Several who had joined in the accusation expressed regret that they had done so, and the fact of the imprisonment increased the demand for Adventist literature.

After holding meetings in several other places, and spending a day at Biten, the old home of the brethren belonging to the Milltown church in Dakota, Elders Conradi and Perk returned to Eupatoria September 15, leaving behind them in the Crimea, where their experiences had been a good deal like those of the early Christians, both as to eager interest on the part of some and opposition on the part of others, about fifty Sabbath keepers, with prospects for a rapidly growing work.

From Eupatoria they returned to Odessa, where they made the acquaintance of the American consul, who had shown a genuine interest in their welfare. Here it was decided that before returning to Switzerland, L. R. Conradi and Oscar Roth should visit some of the German colonies in eastern Russia. Accompanied by Brother Perk, they accordingly embarked on the Black Sea, sailing east to the mouth of the Dnieper, then up that river to Alexandrovsk, where they took the train to Wisenfeld, the home of Brother Perk. In this place they spent two days, and visited most of the Sabbath keepers. Their next stopping place was Saratov on the Volga, a city having then upwards of 100,000 inhabitants, many of them Germans.

Immediately on their arrival they were told that the Lutheran ministers, learning from the papers of L. R. Conradi's proposed visit, were prepared to secure his arrest at the first opportunity. The brethren were accordingly careful to avoid offense. On the morning of the arrival, it being Sunday, Elder Conradi spoke by request to a select company of interested persons. In the afternoon he visited a family of Sabbath keepers living in the outskirts of the city.

On the following day the brethren left Saratov in order to visit Conrad Laubhan, of Kansas, who had returned to his native country in the spring and was residing in the little Russian village of Tscherbakovka. They found that he had been hindered from holding meetings by the elders of the Lutheran church, but by personal effort some had begun to observe the truth, and others were investigating. After a few days spent in counseling concerning the work, the brethren returned to Saratov, where a meeting was held on the Sabbath. Here Brethren Conradi and Roth took leave of Brother Perk, who was to remain in Russia and continue to labor in behalf of the truth, while they returned to Germany and Switzerland.

In the same year in which L. R. Conradi first visited the believers in the Crimea, a beginning was made in the Caucasus. Many years ago some German Mennonites, at the invitation of the emperor, had settled in this part of Russia. When the original promise of complete religious liberty was not kept, many of them emigrated to America. One of these, Neufeld by name, who had embraced the Adventist views in Kansas, returned to the Caucasus in the summer of 1888, and labored with such diligence that a number of believers were won for the truth.

The following was especially good in the colonies of Alexanderfeld and Wohldemfürst in Kuban, whose inhabitants by adopting immersion had cut themselves off from the body of Mennonites, and were ready to receive further light from the Word. In these colonies and in the near-lying town of Eigenheim, inhabited chiefly by Esths from the Baltic provinces, L. R. Conradi found, on his second visit to Russia in 1890, some

GROUP AT THE RUSSIAN BALTIC CONFERENCE

200 believers. About half this number were able to assemble together for a general meeting in Eigenheim, at which careful instruction was given in various phases of the message and in plans for their future growth.

The work thus begun was destined to grow rapidly, though under adverse conditions. Severe persecution was visited upon the believers; a number were imprisoned for their faith, and others were banished. In one flourishing church the authorities seized all the men, and sent them in chains in the midst of winter to the other side of the Caucasus Mountains, near the Persian border. "Now," the priests said, "this thing will stop. There are only a few women and children left. They cannot do anything." But the women said: "God lives. If we ever worked, we will work now. The worst they can do is to send us where our husbands and fathers have gone." They went to work with a will, and in a little while the church had doubled its membership.

Meanwhile the husbands and fathers had carried the message with them to their place of exile, and there, too, a flourishing body of believers was growing up. Thus the efforts to stop the work really gave it a new impetus, and the decree of banishment became a means of carrying the advent message into regions where it would not otherwise have penetrated at that early date. In the same manner the work was begun in Siberia. While the believers were meditating sending workers to that large field, but were hindered for lack of money to meet traveling expenses, the government came to their rescue by sending several faithful workers into banishment. They went accordingly, at government expense, and were successful in leading many an honest soul into the full light of the gospel.

Progress was also being made in other parts of the great empire. The ordained ministers most active in these early years were Jacob Klein and Conrad Laubhan. The former had his passports taken from him, and suffered imprisonment for a time; but even during his confinement the truth continued to make advancement, and earnest men and women risked their all in order to walk in the way of God's commandments.

In the early years the work in Russia was carried on in connection with that in Germany, the earliest Sabbath keepers being, as has been seen, descendants of German colonists. Along in the nineties Russia was set apart as a separate mission field, and in 1901 it was divided into the southern and northern mission fields. D. P. Gaede, a descendant of the Mennonite colonists already referred to, who had gone over from America in 1900, took charge of the work in the northern division, and it developed rapidly under his fostering care.

In 1903 South Russia was organized as a mission field, and Daniel Isaak was sent there to labor. Two years later the field was organized into a conference with Elder Isaak as president. The people were eager to hear the message, but the opposition was great. When meetings were held in Sevastopol, the attendance was greater than the hall could accommodate, and thirteen were baptized in the Black Sea. Among those who accepted the truth were members of the navy, who were imprisoned, one for two years, and the other for two years and a half. The leading officer accused them severely; hence the rigorous sentence. They were sent to a northern province called Archangel, where it is very cold. There they were commanded to work on the Sabbath, and on Sundays to go to the Greek church, and join in the exercises and pray to the images. On declining to do this, they were flogged; but they remained true. Some months after this, the Russian laborer baptized three other sailors belonging to the navy, who, with tears in their eyes, said, " If the Lord permits, we will follow these faithful brethren."

A meeting was held in the autumn of 1908 in Alexandrovsk, a city of 30,000. After securing the permission of the governor, services were opened in the largest hall in the city. Four hundred attended the first meeting, and 800 the last. Among those in attendance were four Russian priests and a Greek Catholic missionary. When the third night came, the priests could no longer keep their seats. They arose and wished to speak; but permission was not granted them, because our brethren were not allowed by the official regulations to depart from their program. The priests then jumped upon the seats and shouted, and so did those in the audience who sided with them. Our own people left the hall, followed by the priests, who promised to tell the people what they had to say in the church the following Sunday morning.

When the conference closed, the whole congregation rose and expressed heartfelt gratitude for the privilege of listening to such soul-stirring truths. Then they added, " Will you now leave us as sheep without a shepherd? "

At this meeting our first Russian native minister was ordained. He received his preparation for the work in the school at Friedensau. He there learned the German language, and became thoroughly acquainted with the principles of present truth. Then he returned to Russia, and labored in various parts as a Bible worker and licentiate, having the previous year raised up a good church at Sevastopol.

More recent developments in Russia are dealt with in a later chapter.

C. L. BOYD

I. J. HANKINS

A. T. ROBINSON

W. S. HYATT

A NATIVE TEACHER'S BIBLE CLASS

CHAPTER XXVI

African Missions -- Part I

SOMETIME in the seventies J. N. Loughborough was conducting a series of tent-meetings in northern California. Among the persons who attended was a man by the name of William Hunt, who came in from a near-by mining camp. He manifested some interest in the doctrines taught, and on going away was liberally supplied with tracts and pamphlets. Years afterward a request came from this man, then in the diamond fields of South Africa, for a further supply of Adventist literature. He reported himself as keeping the Sabbath, and he received from the denominational publishing house papers and tracts in considerable quantities, which he passed on to persons who were willing to read them. Among those who received this literature was a Mr. Van Druten, who became deeply interested.

Meanwhile, the Spirit of God was also working upon other minds. Peter W. B. Wessels, a member of a large Boer family, had had an experience in trusting divine power for physical healing; and when he saw the binding claims of the Bible Sabbath, he promptly obeyed the Word. His attention was called to the matter by a friend who, referring to some remarks of Mr. Wessels to the effect that healing by faith is a Bible doctrine

483

and should be observed in the church, replied, " If you want to follow the Bible strictly, why do you not keep the Bible Sabbath? " Mr. Wessels at once applied himself to a careful study of what the Bible teaches in regard to the Sabbath; and as the result of his investigations, he began to observe the seventh day. A short time after he had thus taken his stand for

SOUTH AFRICAN SENTINEL

" WATCHMAN, WHAT OF THE NIGHT?"

No. 1.   CAPE TOWN, JANUARY 1, 1902.   VOLUME VIII.

"WHOSO offereth praise glorifieth Me, and prepareth a way that I may show him the salvation of God."   of the glory of His grace." Ephesians 1 : 5, 6

LOOK in the margin of the Revised Version, and you will find this as the exact rendering of the words of the Lord, recorded in Ps. 1 : 33. That praise does reveal the salvation of God, is shown by the fact that God is our salvation, and that He dwells in the praises of His people. Ps. 22 : 3.

PRAISE is the way of salvation. "Out of the mouth of babes and sucklings Thou hast perfected praise, because of Thine enemies, that Thou mightest still the enemy and the avenger." Matt. 21 : 16.

BUT it is true of simple thanksgiving, that it is all that is necessary for salvation. Men who once knew God became heathen solely because "they glorified Him not as God, neither were thankful." Rom. 1 : 21. Let us see how it is that praise and thanksgiving open the way for God's salvation.

IT is very simple. Thanksgiving is an acknowledgement of favours received. It is the recognition that something has been done by another. It is plain, therefore, that if we "in everything give thanks," we shall be continually recognising

A HYMN OF PRAISE.

Up to the throne of God is borne
The voice of praise at early morn,
And He accepts the punctual hymn
Sung as the light of day grows dim.

Nor will He turn His ear aside

Bible truth, he made the acquaintance of Mr. Van Druten, and was surprised to hear from him of the existence in the United States of a denomination that observed the Bible Sabbath.

The parents of Peter Wessels were then living at Wellington, not far from Cape Town. He wrote to them of his convictions, and cited the texts of Scripture that had convinced him. They applied themselves in turn to the study of their Bibles, and in due time were convinced and accepted the Bible Sabbath. Other members of the family and some not of the family followed their example. There was now a little company of believers in South Africa, and they began to plead earnestly for a minister, Mr. Van Druten sending £50 to the headquarters at Battle Creek, Mich., to pay traveling expenses.

In response to this call, Elders D. A. Robinson and C. L. Boyd, with their wives, and George Burleigh and R. S. Anthony, colporteurs, were sent to Africa, arriving in Cape Town in July, 1887. Somewhat later the staff of workers was further increased by the arrival of I. J. Hankins, A. Druillard, and A. T. Robinson, with their wives. Elder Robinson had general charge of the work for some years.

THE SANITARIUM, PLUMSTEAD, SOUTH AFRICA

In 1892 the Cape Conference was organized, with headquarters at Cape Town. Two periodicals, *The South African Sentinel* and *The South African Missionary,* began to be published. A suitable building was erected at Claremont, a suburb of Cape Town; and a training school was put in operation, with Prof. E. B. Miller, of Battle Creek College, as principal. A privately owned sanitarium was also erected at Claremont. At Plumstead, another suburb of Cape Town, an orphanage was founded, the buildings being subsequently enlarged and transformed into a sanitarium. At Kimberley, a great industrial center, a workingmen's home was opened as a philanthropic enterprise, and conducted during the Boer War, and later was made into the Kimberley Treatment-Rooms.

Natal, the Orange Free State, and the Transvaal were for a time mission fields connected with Cape Colony. In 1902 they were organized as an independent mission field, and at the next annual meeting were made into a conference, with G. W. Reaser as president. The headquarters and book depository, together with a school and treatment-rooms, were at Pietermaritzburg, in Natal.

THE OLD DUTCH COTTAGE
Home of the Sentinel Publishing Company before the Big Day gift was made.

The work advanced somewhat slowly among the white population of South Africa. The country was visited by S. N. Haskell in his trip around the world in 1889 and 1890, and later by O. A. Olsen and W. W. Prescott. Elder Olsen went there again in 1897, and spent about a year in building up the various branches of the work. W. S. Hyatt, J. M. Freeman, E. R. Williams, and H. J. Edmed labored successfully in that field.

When the South African Union Conference was organized, in 1902, W. S. Hyatt was elected president. Later R. C. Porter had the general oversight of the work for some years. In 1913 W. B. White, former president of the Atlantic Union, went to Africa to take the presidency of the union. He was followed in 1920 by B. E. Beddoe. Africa was organized as a division in 1919, and W. H. Branson was appointed vice-president of the General Conference for the division.

Following the return of E. B. Miller to America, J. L. Shaw went to Africa in 1897, and took charge of the school at Claremont. When he was sent on to India in 1901, the school work was left chiefly in the hands of Charles H. Hayton and W. A. Ruble. In 1909 C. P. Crager, of Ohio, took charge of the school. He was succeeded by J. I. Robison.

THE NEW PUBLISHING HOUSE
Purchased and equipped by one Big Day's effort in the Review and Herald territory.

The colporteur work received a new impetus when G. H. Clark, an experienced worker in the Columbia Union, went to Africa to lead out in that branch of activity. The equipment of a new publishing house in 1921, under the management of J. G. Slate, put the publishing work on a strong footing.

The foregoing paragraphs have dealt very briefly with the progress of the work among the white population of South Africa. We shall now consider the various mission stations, at which work is carried on in behalf of the native races. A few words may be said first of some efforts put forth in behalf of the natives in connection with the regular evangelistic work of the conference.

In 1895, while S. N. Haskell was at Beaconsfield, a Kafir teacher, named Richard Moko, listened to the presentation of truth and received the message, continuing firm in spite of much opposition. He was granted a missionary license in January, 1897, and was sent to Kimberley to engage in work among the natives there.

The following March a night school was opened for the natives of Kimberley, in charge of Joel C. Rogers. During the day, Richard Moko would go among the people, selling books, tracts, and papers, and talking with them about the truth. When Elder Rogers left Kimberley to labor elsewhere, Moko went on with the school. O. A. Olsen, calling there some months later, was able to baptize four natives. One of these, David Kalaka, belonged to the Basutos, and also owed his first knowledge of the truth to his association with S. N. Haskell. When the latter had visited Basutoland, Kalaka had been with him for a few days as guide. They had read the Bible together and prayed, each in his own tongue, and though each could understand but very little of what the other said in conversation, a deep impression had been made. Later Kalaka had gone to Kimberley to attend a Bible class conducted by Elder Olsen for him and a few other natives, to prepare them for work among their people.

In dealing with the further development of work in behalf of the natives of Africa, we shall consider the various missions one at a time, taking them up for the most part in chronological order.

The Solusi Mission

Earlier attempts had been made to carry the gospel to the Matabeles: but owing to the hostility of the native rulers, little progress was made until in 1893 Lobengula was overthrown, and the British government took possession of the country. The time seemed opportune to our brethren in South Africa, and a fund of £500 was raised to begin mission work for the natives. A. T. Robinson, who had general oversight of the work, interviewed the Hon. Cecil J. Rhodes, then prime minister of Cape Colony and managing director of the British South African Company, which controlled the territory of Southern Rhodesia, and secured from him a grant of 12,000 acres lying thirty-five miles west of Bulawayo, for the establishment of a self-supporting mission.

In May, 1894, the committee, consisting of Peter Wessels, A. Druillard, and five other brethren, started for Matabeleland to select a site for the mission buildings. They arrived in Bulawayo on the 4th of July, having had to trek 700 miles with ox teams from the terminus of the railroad at Vryburg. They located the mission farm, built a few huts, purchased 200 head of cattle, and returned to the Cape, leaving one of their number in charge.

In the following year, G. Byron Tripp and W. H. Anderson and their wives, and Dr. A. S. Carmichael, coming from America by appointment of the General Conference, left Cape Town to take the long, toilsome journey to what was then known as the Zambesi Mission. Fred Sparrow met them with ox teams at Mafeking, whence they trekked 600 miles to this new frontier mission site.

The plot selected was then a barren waste of sandy bush land, interspersed with large kopjes, or mounds, of stone. It was unimproved, and without buildings, excepting the three native huts put up by Peter Wessels and those who accompanied him. The country was just being opened, and facilities were of the rudest kind.

The missionaries had been only eight months on the farm when the Matabele rebellion broke out, obliging them to repair to Bulawayo under an armed government escort. Rooms being held at prohibitive prices, they lived in their wagon. It required some ingenuity to plan for the accommodation of three families and Dr. Carmichael, who was single, in the one wagon, but the missionaries were equal to the emergency. It was arranged that Fred Sparrow, wife, and baby, should occupy the front end of the covered wagon, and Byron Tripp, wife, and boy the back end, while W. H. Anderson and wife and Dr. Carmichael found suitable quarters underneath.

At the end of ten weeks the supply of food was exhausted, and from that time on they had to buy their food at war prices. When five months had passed, and prices in Bulawayo were extremely high, flour costing $37 a hundredweight, eggs $6 a dozen, cabbage $5 a head, and other things proportionately, Brethren Tripp and Anderson decided to risk making trips to the farm. The country being infested by hostile natives, who kept the city in a state of siege, these trips had to be made at night and on foot. Mr. Tripp would spend one week at the farm, then he would return, and his place would be taken the following week by Mr. Anderson, each bringing back with him such supplies as he could carry. In the course of these night trips the brethren had several narrow escapes, but the good hand of God was over them, and they were not captured.

When the war was over, a severe famine visited the district, and large numbers of the natives perished. The Solusi Mission took into the home thirty native children, twenty boys and ten girls, these children forming the nucleus of the first mission school. One of them, a baby boy of two and a half years, was found playing on the veldt by the side of the dead body of his mother. Another was found in the hole of an ant bear, with an ugly gash in his forehead and one in the back of

SOLUSI MISSION CHURCH MEMBERS

his head, where he had been struck with some blunt instrument and left for dead. In a near-by hole were the dead bodies of two other children, killed and left in the same manner. The living child was taken to the mission, and grew up to be a very bright and capable youth.

The famine over, the missionary workers began to show some effects of the trials and privations through which they had passed. Dr. Carmichael was first to fall. He took the dreaded malarial fever; and his system being weakened by hardships and exposure, he soon succumbed, dying on Feb. 26, 1898. He was in the prime of life, full of energy, and devoted to his work, and the only physician within reach of the mission, any member of whom was liable to come down with the fever. A week later, Byron Tripp, the superintendent, fell a victim to the same disease. On April 2 his little son died, and was laid by the side of the father in the mission cemetery. Just one month later

Mrs. F. B. Armitage passed away in Kimberley, whither she had been sent in a vain attempt to save her life.

In October of the same year, W. S. Hyatt, then president of the South African Union Conference, visited the mission, and counseled with the workers concerning the extension of the work. In the spring of 1899 the mission was re-enforced by the arrival of a considerable company of workers, including F. L. Mead, with his family, who took up the work laid down

SUPERINTENDENT'S COTTAGE, SOLUSI MISSION

by Byron Tripp. Shortly after his arrival, two outstations were opened, one at Umkupuvula, twenty-three miles distant, in charge of J. A. Chaney; and another at Somabula, 140 miles northeast of Bulawayo, under the charge of F. B. Armitage. After three years of strenuous labor, F. L. Mead was stricken with apoplexy while en route to Cape Town in the interests of the mission work, and was laid to rest in Kimberley cemetery. For about nine months Mrs. Mead and her son and daughter worked on at the mission; then they returned to Cape Colony, Mrs. Mead being called to serve as matron at the Claremont Union College, where she died in February, 1904.

In April, 1902, Mr. and Mrs. M. C. Sturdevant went to Solusi to join W. H. Anderson in the mission work. About this time the industrial training feature of the mission was further developed, with the result that it became more nearly self-supporting. Later Mr. and Mrs. Claude Tarr, J. R. and Mrs. Campbell, and others shared in the work at Solusi. When W. H. Anderson pushed farther up into the wilds of north-western Rhodesia, M. C. Sturdevant succeeded to the superintendency of the Solusi Mission; and when he in turn left to start a new mission in Mashonaland, the work was taken in hand by Mr. and Mrs. W. C. Walston.

The mission premises at Solusi have undergone very considerable changes in the years that have elapsed since the first settlement. There is an air of thrift and prosperity about the place. Extensive fields of beans, peanuts, sweet potatoes, and mealies (Indian corn) stretch out on every side, and there is a large herd of cattle. The buildings, which are well arranged, include a church, a school building, a girls' dormitory, dairy, barns, and several cottages, all built of brick, with iron roofs. There are also fruit trees and ornamental trees, with flower gardens and well-laid-out walks. The school inspector for the Solusi district, who visited the mission and extended his stay over two days, gave a favorable report of every department.

The number of pupils ranges from sixty-five to one hundred twenty. A church was organized at Solusi June 25, 1902, with a membership of twenty-four. There has been a steady growth since that time. There are about thirty other schools, with an average attendance of from thirty to one hundred pupils each.

The Somabula Mission

In 1901, Mr. and Mrs. F. B. Armitage (Mrs. Armitage was formerly Mrs. Tripp) settled on the Lower Gwelo Native Reserve, and began mission work with eight pupils brought from Solusi. Their outfit consisted of a wagon and ten oxen. Mission work was begun upon a site six miles west of the present location, where the school soon had upwards of thirty pupils. There the workers remained about three years, during which time eight natives were baptized. Soon after the removal to the present site, six miles nearer Gwelo, the school had an attendance of over forty.

The Somabula Mission church, consisting of nineteen members, was organized by W. S. Hyatt in 1905. In that year Mr. and Mrs. F. B. Armitage found it necessary to leave Rhodesia on account of repeated attacks of fever. W. C. Walston took charge of the work. In 1910 the enrolment in the mission school reached sixty-eight. In the autumn of that year Brother Walston was called away to take the superintendency of the Solusi Mission, and T. J. Gibson became superintendent at Somabula.

The farm area at Somabula includes 100 acres of cultivated land, several acres of garden, and a small orchard. The mission has had a steady growth. In 1920 the superintendent, J. N. de Beer, reported eighteen outschools within a radius of a hundred miles.

Nyasaland

The first Seventh-day Adventist to enter Nyasaland was a student of Battle Creek College, George James, who had a great desire to reach the natives of the interior. He went to Nyasaland in 1892, and after convincing one missionary of the Sabbath truth, proceeded on his way. He died of fever on his return journey down the coast.

Malamulo [1]

The Malamulo Mission occupies ground close by the spot where David Livingstone pitched his tent for a few days' rest. Thither he called the chiefs to arrange with them for additional carriers for his caravan. So tells Kwitamule, one of the underchiefs still surviving, aged and decrepit, but proud of having seen and talked with the famous missionary. " When the great and good white man was ready to move on," continues the chief, in the soft, expressive tongue of his race, " I went with him across the little stream at the foot of your garden, and there we said ' *Tsalanibwino* ' [good-by]. I never saw him again. I was distressed that I could not go with him, but a great fever was on me, and I could not walk well."

After Livingstone, other white men came, one of whom bought this tract of land for a few bundles of cheap red cloth. He sold it in turn to a German planter, who cleared the land, and planted part of it to coffee, and part to guavas, bananas, lemons, and other fruits. He also erected a good dwelling house with wide verandas, and a long building for the storage of coffee, both with good iron roofs. The estate was next sold to the Seventh Day Baptists, who paid $12,500 for it, intending to run the coffee plantation as a means of support for their missionary operations. Finding it not a financial success, the Baptists sold the estate to the Seventh-day Adventists about the beginning of 1902, and their minister, Joseph Booth, worked with us for a short time. His services being discontinued, T. H. Branch and his family entered the field. About a year after the departure of Mr. Booth, J. H. Watson came to lead out

---

[1] In this report of the Malamulo Mission the writer has followed very closely a narrative kindly furnished by Mrs. J. C. Rogers.

in the work; but six months had not passed till he lay under the trees at the foot of the garden, and his young widow and little son were on their way to the Cape. For four long years T. H. Branch faithfully carried on the work, without change or rest, until the coming in May, 1907, of Mr. and Mrs. J. C. Rogers, when he and his wife returned to the States to put their children in school.

Up to that time the place had been known as " The Plainfield Mission Station," a name given to it by the Seventh Day Baptists, in honor of Plainfield, N. J., the headquarters of that

NATAL-TRANSVAAL CAMP-MEETING, JOHANNESBURG, 1909

denomination. But the name was unfortunate in that it meant nothing to the natives. Within a week of his arrival, Mr. Rogers called the four native teachers together, and after prayerful consideration, it was decided to call the place the Malamulo Mission (the mission of the commandments).

The school had in 1907 an enrolment of about sixty names; but the greater number were middle-aged married people, the women coming to school with their babies on their backs, and being sadly hampered in their efforts to learn by their home cares. Few of them could be looked on in the light of prospective teachers. Mr. and Mrs. Rogers accordingly gave themselves to prayer to the intent that more young men of impressionable years might be led to come to the mission for training.

The prayers were signally answered, for at the beginning of the new school year in August, 1907, a company of more than two hundred young people flocked to the school. The little grass-and-wattle shed that served as church and schoolhouse literally overflowed with the crowd that poured into it, and classes were obliged to find recitation-rooms under the shade trees in the vicinity of the church. Most of these young people came as boarding pupils, paying their expenses by working on the estate. This gave the missionaries a better opportunity to form their characters, and the result is seen today, when no small number of these young persons are faithful members of the mission staff.

This sudden growth at headquarters created a demand for outschools in the near-lying villages. The first of these was opened by Mr. and Mrs. S. M. Konigmacher. The same year

WORKERS ATTENDING A SOUTH AFRICAN CONVENTION

the most faithful of our native teachers, with his wife and family, opened a school in another village.

Vacation months are seasons of recruiting, every student returning to his home with the firm intention of bringing back with him from one to ten of his boy friends. Sometimes a boy brings more than ten. It is very inspiring, on opening day, to see a happy-faced boy come up leading his group of boys whom he has influenced to come to the school. The vacation months of 1908 were given to the erecting of a good burnt-brick church, which was greatly needed. The divine help was manifest from the first. The bricks were made from the clay of ant hills apparently a thousand years old, trodden into mud by willing native feet, and shaped into brick by native hands, then burned in fires made from native wood on the farm. The furniture was also made by the natives, from mahogany wood grown, cut, and polished on the mission property. When the building was finished, there were just three items which were not furnished by the work of native hands,— the glass of the windows, the linoleum of which the blackboards were made, and three wall maps.

In 1909 the same dairy which had been producing a dozen or so pounds of butter a week, had its business decidedly increased by the purchase of some excellent stock, and was able to furnish, with only slight expenses for upkeep, a cash income of from $100 to $125 a month. In that year rubber trees were planted in some of the old coffee fields, and some cotton was raised.

The aim of the school work has been to develop and draw out the best traits of the young people who attend, with a view to fitting them for future usefulness. Naturally, special attention is given to the preparation of evangelistic school-teachers, there being the greatest demand for such, and the majority of those who show a fitness for this work are eager to take it up. At the close of 1912 nearly a hundred young men were already serving as teachers or assistant teachers. Others were developing in mechanical lines, and such were used in the carpenter shop, and in building and field operations. Others take to tailoring, domestic or overseer's work, and nearly all have shown great faithfulness in what they have undertaken.

The mission was for a time undermanned with white workers; and this caused heavy burdens to fall on those who stood at its head. Two sisters, the Misses Ina and Etta Austen, joined the mission force in 1910; but the elder was obliged to return before the end of the first year. The other, Miss Etta Austen, remained nearly two years, having charge of the girls' home. In November, 1910, G. A. Ellingworth arrived and took the position of business manager and overseer of the rubber and cotton fields. A year later, C. Robinson, previously connected with the mission in Rhodesia, came to Malamulo to act as superintendent during the absence of J. C. Rogers on furlough.

The Musofu Mission

S. M. Konigmacher, of the Barotseland Mission, did some prospecting for a new mission site in the year 1916. He fixed on a spot near the Congo border, twenty-two miles from the railway station of Bwana Mkubwa. A school was started, and the native young people flocked in. By 1919 there was an attendance of about 200, and the school had an actual enrolment of 150.

The Songa Mission

W. E. Straw and F. R. Stockil prospected for this location, which is on the Lulwelwe River, ten miles east of the larger Lomami River, and a hundred miles north of Bukama, the terminus of the Congo railway. C. Robinson, who had labored formerly in connection with the Nyasaland missions, secured from the government a grant of 1,000 acres, and with the assistance of G. Willmore superintended the erection of the necessary buildings.

The Kolo Mission

Basutoland, which includes the most elevated and mountainous portion of South Africa, has been called " The African Switzerland." On the grassy hills and mountains thousands of cattle, sheep, goats, and horses find pasture, while the fertile valleys yield abundant crops of mealies, kafir corn, wheat, and pumpkins, which furnish the food supply for a population of nearly 250,000 natives.

The conversion and baptism of David Kalaka, a Basuto, has been related in the early pages of this chapter. He returned in 1898 to Kolo, near Mafeking, on the southwestern border of Basutoland, where he gave an account of his new faith to his friends. The chief invited him to start a mission, and J. M. Freeman joined him in opening Kolo station. J. A. Chaney was also one of the early workers.

The Emmanuel Mission

Toward the close of 1909, M. E. Emmerson and H. C. Olmstead, with Murray Kalaka as interpreter, made a trip into the northern part of Basutoland to locate a new mission station. The old chief Jonathan, who controlled the district, gave his consent to the undertaking. The mission site, which was changed three times, but always for the better, has about twenty-five acres of good land, and is situated on a main road eleven miles from a railway siding. A native day school and an evening school for herd boys have been in operation almost from the beginning. There is also a flourishing Sabbath school. Several meetings are held weekly. A. P. Tarr, a former student of Battle Creek College, was for a time in charge of the training school. F. MacDonald, medical missionary and superintendent, reported a church membership of fifty-five in 1919.

HOME OF W. H. ANDERSON, BAROTSE MISSION
Taken July, 1908

TREKKING TO A NEW MISSION SITE

BRITISH EAST AFRICA
A group of missionaries sent from England.

CHAPTER XXVII

African Missions -- Part II

Northern Rhodesia

LITTLE is known of the history of Northwest Rhodesia previous to the coming of the white man. The inhabitants were continually warring among themselves, and were often raided by their powerful neighbors, the Matabeles. Although the country was filled with game, the prevalence of the tsetse fly made it in large part uninhabitable for the white man; but when in the providence of God the time had come for the land to be opened, He allowed the rinderpest to pass through the country, and destroy the game by thousands. With the destruction of the game, the tsetse fly disappeared from large areas, thus opening the way for civilization. Moreover, the British government put an end to the wars.

The Rusangu Mission

Lewanika, the native chief, visited England at the coronation of the late King Edward VII, and on his return he invited more missionaries to enter the country and teach his people. W. H. Anderson was one of the missionaries who accepted this invitation. He left Bulawayo, Southern Rhodesia, in July, 1903, accompanied by five native boys as carriers from the Solusi Mission. Reaching the end of the railway, he began an 800-mile trip through the country. The first day out a hired native stole his load, and ran away. With him went the supply of fruit, salt, and sugar that Mr. Anderson had laid in for the journey; so these things had to be omitted from the bill of fare during the next three months.

It is a difficult thing to start on foot to locate a mission farm in a territory covering some thousands of square miles. Elder Anderson had scarcely begun his work when he was taken with a severe attack of dysentery, and thought his end had come. He left a last message for his wife and child, and lay down on the veldt to die; but the carriers took him to the camp of a hunter, where he remained for two weeks. Then, though still weak and emaciated, he resumed his journey. In three months the work was completed. He had located a farm on the Makoe River, where there was a spring of fresh water and good soil. Later the railway was built so as to pass directly by the farm.

In 1904 W. H. Anderson returned to America, where he received sufficient money to make a start in the new territory. In May, 1905, he again crossed the Zambesi at Victoria Falls, and began the journey of hundreds of miles with a span of eighteen untrained oxen. With his wife and child, he arrived at the Rusangu Mission July 3, and at once began to build a house. There was famine in the land, food was very scarce, and many of the natives were perishing from hunger. His own teachers, who had come from the station at Solusi, could be supplied only half rations. Nevertheless, there was no complaining, and not one of them turned back. The ground was soon plowed, and sixty-five acres of mealies (maize) planted. The crop was a good one, and never since then has the mission lacked food. Although the accommodations were very poor to begin with, the natives came to the school, and there were soon forty or more pupils in training. When the wet season came on, it brought fever, and often Mr. and Mrs. Anderson and the little girl were all three in bed at once. Still their lives were spared, and the work prospered. When G. A. Irwin, then vice-president of the General Conference, visited the mission in 1907, the rains had washed out the gable ends of the house, and likewise the chimney. He kindly promised £150 to pay for the materials for a better house. Brother Anderson himself made and burned the bricks, and with the help of A. Gibson, who had joined the mission in the meantime, the house was ready for occupancy by the end of that year. In August of the same year a church was organized, the charter members being those who had come from the church at Solusi. In October, the first convert was baptized.

WORKERS IN THE ZAMBESI UNION

Late in November Mrs. Anderson was stricken with blackwater fever, and her husband took her to the hospital at Livingstone. A little later she was taken down to the Colonies, and died at Cape Town in February, 1908.

Mr. Anderson carried the work alone until June, when Mr. and Mrs. H. C. Olmstead, of California, went to his assistance, but they had not been on the mission farm more than three weeks when Mr. Olmstead came down with the fever, and had to leave. The first outstation was opened in 1907, and another in the following year. These two outstations, and the fifty pupils in the home station, were thus left in the sole charge of Mr. Anderson until in March, 1909, when he was joined by C. Robinson, a graduate nurse from the Cape. In June of the same year, J. R. Campbell arrived with his family, and now further enlargement was possible. Mr. Robinson accordingly opened three outschools north of the Kafue River.

Meanwhile Elder Campbell devoted himself to the study of the native language with such success that he was able presently to act as translator.   There being no books for school work in the vernacular, " The Gospel Primer " was printed first, and then a reader.   The British and Foreign Bible Society supplied copies of the Gospel of Mark, and still later Sabbath school lessons covering a year were prepared.   The expense of these publications was met by a second tithe, paid by the members

J. V. WILSON'S MISSION HOME

of the mission church.   Elder Campbell read the proofs for a translation of the New Testament issued by the British and Foreign Bible Society.

Later the country was explored to the east and south, along the banks of the Zambesi, and sites staked out for nine additional outschools, to be opened as teachers could be supplied. When C. Robinson left the mission to take charge of Malamulo, in Nyasaland, Mr. and Mrs. Boekhout took his place.

This new station in Northern Rhodesia, known at first under the name of Pemba, was later called the Rusangu Mission. Among the laborers were S. M. Konigmacher from Nyasaland, and J. V. Wilson from Solusi.   The natives reached by it were the Batongas, the Barotses, and other tribes.

In 1920 W. H. Anderson made a trip through northeastern Bechuanaland as far as the Zambesi, where the Fasubea tribes live. Their chief received him kindly, and asked for teachers. J. V. Wilson accordingly, a few months later, took some native teachers into the country and started school work.

The Maranatha Mission

Mission work was begun in Kafirland in 1905, under the general direction of G. W. Shone, assisted by R. Moko. Mr. Shone erected a little house in the native district of Deb Nek. He and· Mr. Moko labored in the villages round about, selling books and working among the natives as the way opened.

In 1906 he secured a ninety-year lease of a farm of 400 acres, situated some twenty-five miles east of Grahamstown, on the Great Fish River. On this mission farm work proper began. In 1907, Mr. Shone was called to enter the Dutch work, and F. B. Armitage took his place at the mission. He erected in 1908 a church, which also served as a school building, and a shop, both buildings being of stone. In the same year a small day school was opened. In October, F. B. Armitage and W. S. Hyatt made a wagon trip into Kafirland, holding evening services, illustrated by the stereopticon, among the natives, and giving their days largely to treating the sick. They made another trip later in the year, and early in 1909 went over the same ground and gathered up children for the boarding school, which was begun that year under the charge of G. A. Ellingworth.

In 1910, Mr. Armitage was requested to go to Natal, and open up work among the Zulus, and W. S. Hyatt took his place at Maranatha. Forty-eight pupils were enrolled in the last term of that year, and fourteen were baptized. Early in 1911 the Maranatha church was organized, with a membership of twenty-seven. A little later six new members were baptized, giving the church a total membership of nearly fifty. In January, 1911, W. S. Hyatt, R. C. Porter, and Dr. George Thomason took a ten days' trip among the natives, holding illustrated services in the. evening, and giving medical help to the sick. During these few days, Dr. Thomason treated 197 cases.

W. S. Hyatt being called to take the presidency of the Cape Conference, Claude Tarr took over the superintendency at Maranatha. Miss Victoria Sutherland, a student from Claremont, was active in the school work. The mission had some drawbacks in early years, owing to drouths, but in more recent years the farm has yielded excellent crops.

When in 1919 the school work was moved in order to get nearer to the heart of Kafirland, the Maranatha farm passed into the ownership of Charles Sparrow, who still maintains some of the missionary features. The school was moved into the Transkei district, where it occupied a farm property near Butterworth in the Cape Conference, and is known as the Bethel Mission Training School. There is also an outstation, from which work is done for the Tembus and the Pondos.

The Tsungwesi, or Inyazura, Mission

The occupation of Southern Rhodesia by the pioneer white settlers began in 1891. Until then, the Mashonas, a peaceable class of natives, had been periodically raided by their neighbors, the more warlike Matabeles, and then came a war between the Europeans and the natives. In 1896 occurred a native rebellion, followed by the cattle plague known as the rinderpest. The great Boer War, beginning in 1899, further interfered with the settlement of white men in that part of Southern Rhodesia.

M. C. Sturdevant, superintendent of the Solusi Mission, desiring to push farther into the interior, went to Mashonaland in March, 1910, to look up a mission site. The government directed him to Mr. Folks as a gentleman who might give some information in reference to a suitable site. Mr. Folks told Mr. Sturdevant that he was about to surrender his own farm to the government in order to return to England, and suggested that it might prove suitable for the mission. After carefully investigating the character of the soil and the water supply, Mr. Sturdevant decided to accept the offer, and the government was pleased to set the land aside for mission purposes, with the understanding that a tract of similar size be deducted from the land belonging to the Solusi Mission.

The Folks farm consists of 3,666 acres, and has a fertile soil watered by two rivers, the Tsungwesi and a tributary, both of which flow during the entire year. It lies near Inyazura Siding, a station on the Salisbury-to-Beira Railway. In the early records is found the name Tsungwesi, but it is now known as the Inyazura Mission. The improvements on the farm, when it was taken over, consisted of fifteen acres of plowed land and four native huts. The place is surrounded by hills and mountains, and the scenery on every side is beautiful.

The four huts already mentioned provided shelter for the first year. Early in 1911 bricks were made and burned; and by the end of November, Elder Sturdevant and his family were occupying a comfortable, six-room brick cottage. A new school building, 24 x 40 feet, was built of poles set perpendicularly, and plastered inside and out with mud, roofed with grass, and provided with brick seats plastered with mud. To these buildings were added a store, tool shop, and a large dining-room, all with iron roofs, besides a number of huts, lion-proof cattle kraals, and a mule stable.

MEMBERS OF A MISSION CHURCH

The mission school was opened Jan. 1, 1911, with twelve students, who boarded at the mission. By the end of 1912 the enrolment had grown to seventy-three, of whom forty were boarding students. F. B. Jewell was for a number of years in charge of the school work. W. Hodgson, who had charge in 1919, reported a church membership of ninety-five, with one outschool.

During the first half of the year 1911, Claude Tarr assisted in the mission work, giving M. C. Sturdevant an opportunity to take some needed rest. About this time the lions were becoming very troublesome. One afternoon Mr. Sturdevant took his gun and some native boys, and went in pursuit of a lion which had done considerable damage on the farm. They found the beast in a secluded spot among some rocks. After it had received four rifle shots, it charged upon Mr. Sturdevant. He had not time to insert a rifle cartridge, and so fired a load of buckshot full into the face of the animal, which immediately reared and fell backward on the rocks dead.

The Zulu Mission

F. B. Armitage, formerly of the Solusi Mission, opened up a mission for the Zulus near Ladysmith, Natal, in 1910. During the first two years the work was carried on in temporary quarters, Mr. Armitage meanwhile giving much of his time to searching out and negotiating for a permanent home. In 1912 the Spion Kop farm was purchased, so named from a portion of the hill which included one of the famous battlefields of the Boer War. The work at Spion Kop was begun in a three-room sod house. The students worked hard, and by 1913 suitable buildings had been put up, and one outschool was in operation. The Zulu church then numbered twenty-five. Hubert Sparrow assisted in the work.

On the West Coast of Africa

One of the earliest believers on the West Coast of Africa was F. I. U. Dolphijn. He learned of the Adventist views by receiving from the captain of a vessel which was anchored for a while in the harbor of Apan, a roll of Seventh-day Adventist papers sent out by the International Tract Society. The reading of this literature led him, in the year 1888, to begin the observance of the Sabbath. Five years later E. L. Sanford and K. G. Rudolph, entered the field as the first Adventist workers in that part of Africa. Sickness brought this first effort to naught.

The next company of Seventh-day Adventist missionaries to go to the West Coast of Africa consisted of D. U. Hale, superintendent; Mr. and Mrs. George T. Kerr, medical missionaries; and G. P. Riggs, a colporteur. These persons landed at Cape Coast Castle Oct. 4, 1895. A mission site was duly selected,— 5,760 acres donated by a native named Essien. Once more, however, the work was broken up by serious illness. Mr. Riggs contracted dysentery, and had to hasten home. He died in a hospital in Liverpool, Jan. 8, 1897. Brethren Hale and Kerr moved some of their things to the mission site, and began to build. While thus engaged, Mr. Kerr was stricken with black-water fever. Careful nursing restored him; but when he was attacked the second time, in April, 1897, the doctor ordered him sent to Cape Town, South Africa.

During that spring, Elder Hale baptized five faithful Sabbath keepers, but he had struggled through several severe attacks of the fever before Mr. Kerr left. When in June of that year he had recovered from a severe attack of black-water fever, it was recommended that he return to the States. The mission work was then left in the hands of two of the converts, F. I. U. Dolphijn and G. P. Grant. For six years no further aggressive work was done.

In the early spring of 1903, D. U. Hale and his family returned to the mission, where they found Brother Dolphijn bearing faithful witness to the truth. At this time J. D. Hayford was also taking an active part in trying to get the mission established. But sickness soon showed itself again, and Elder Hale came down with his third severe attack of black-water fever. For two weeks he was not expected to live; but by the most careful nursing, he finally rallied. Before he was able to sit up, three of his children were in the hospital with him. The doctor urged that to remain would be nothing less than suicide, and so Mr. Hale and his family reluctantly left that field.

At the General Conference of 1905 it was voted that D. C. Babcock, who had been laboring in British Guiana, be sent to the West Coast of Africa, to revive the work of that mission. He and his family settled first at Freetown, Sierra Leone, from which place he paid a visit to the Gold Coast. It was decided that Sierra Leone was the proper place in which to establish the headquarters of the work in West Africa. Thus an acquaintance was gained with the people, and a number of books were sold. Early in 1906 a mission house was built on the mountain side in the suburbs of Freetown. When the workers moved into this house, their health greatly improved.

Shortly after this, Mrs. Babcock was requested to open a school for children, and did so. The enrolment ran up to 125.

It was decided next to conduct a tent-meeting. A new 40 x 60-foot tent having been erected in the city of Freetown, the first meeting was held on the evening of January 10, with a crowded congregation. The interest increased each evening, the nightly congregations for six weeks ranging from 600 to 1,500. At the close of this effort, a church was organized, with a membership of thirty-one, and plans were laid for the erection of a meeting house.

L. W. Browne, a West Indian, who had received some training in the United States, arrived at the end of April, 1907, and rendered valuable assistance. One of the results of the tent-meeting was to bring into the truth two young men, R. P. Dauphin and C. E. F. Thompson, who soon became valuable workers.

In August, 1907, Mr. and Mrs. Babcock went to the Gold Coast and held a series of tent-meetings. Several young men accepted the message, one of them, Samuel Morgue, becoming

TRAVELING IN THE WEST AFRICAN "BUSH"
D. C. Babcock and his family on the road.

actively engaged in the work. On their return to Sierra Leone in November, it was decided that L. W. Browne, C. E. F. Thompson, and R. P. Dauphin open work at Waterloo, twenty miles from Freetown. This effort also was successful, and a little company of believers was gathered out and a church organized. In May, 1908, L. W. Browne sailed for America, his health being somewhat impaired.

To accommodate the increased attendance at the school, a small building was erected near the mission home at the beginning of 1908, which was also used as a house of worship. The Mission Board was now asked to make an appropriation of $1,500 with which to secure better facilities for the education of more mature young people who could be trained as laborers. The request was granted, and Mr. and Mrs. T. M.

French, of Union College, Nebraska, were sent to take charge of the work. They arrived in August, 1908, and school was opened in 1909, with a fair number of students.

In November of the same year this work of missionary training was removed to Waterloo, where the students were able to do something on the land to help meet expenses. A year later a repair shop was opened in connection with the school, and this furnished further opportunity for the boys to earn their way.

Early in 1909, urgent requests having come from the Gold Coast, C. E. F. Thompson went to Kickam and Axim, and conducted a series of meetings among the Nsimbia people. A year later, D. C. Babcock visited these points, held further meetings with the people, and baptized about fifty believers, organizing churches at Kickam and Axim.

The first general meeting on the West Coast was held in October, 1910, and was attended by representatives from all parts of the field, there being present about one hundred members, including the pupils from the Waterloo school. In view of the urgent calls for further help on the Gold Coast, where three schools were being conducted at this time, Mr. French volunteered his services. Leaving the school at Waterloo in charge of W. H. Lewis, who had recently come over from America, with I. W. Harding as teacher, he settled with his wife at Axim. Two weeks later Mrs. French succumbed to the fever. She was a faithful and efficient worker, and her death was a great loss. Mr. French's health being in a precarious condition, he was advised to return to the States for a furlough, and he sailed in February, 1911. During his absence, C. E. F. Thompson took charge of the work on the Cold Coast for a time, until he, too, was broken down in health, dying of Bright's disease, March 25, 1912. He had been trained at Kingston College, Jamaica, and was well prepared for the work. When it became necessary for Mr. and Mrs. Lewis to remove to Freetown on account of failing health, the work at the school was taken up by Mr. and Mrs. F. S. Bolston, of the Washington, D. C., Foreign Mission Seminary. After an absence of a little more than a year, Professor French returned, and once more had oversight for a time of the training school.

In the year 1912 a resthome for the West Coast missionaries was opened at the Canaries, under charge of Mr. and Mrs. B. B. Aldrich, trained nurses. In April, 1912, the corps of workers was further re-enforced by the arrival of Dr. E. W. Meyer, of Washington, under whose direction treatment-rooms were fitted up in a building first erected in Freetown for school purposes. Dr. Meyer enjoyed excellent success in his labors as a medical missionary.

Early in 1912, following a general evangelistic tour by the superintendent, work was opened at two new stations, one at Metotoka, among the Timnies; and another at Gbamgbama, among the Mendies. Work was naturally interrupted at the time of the World War, but it has since been resumed.

D. C. Babcock began work in Nigeria in 1914. Accompanied by two West African workers, he traversed a considerable part of the country, founding a school for the Yornbas at Lalupon in southern Nigeria. In the course of a few months two other schools were in operation, and the interest was growing. In 1917 Elder Babcock was compelled by failing health to return to America. E. Ashton, of England, carried on the work for a time. Others took it up later. In 1924 Nigeria reported a baptized membership of 314.

British East Africa

Work was begun in British East Africa in 1906 by A. A. Carscallen, who was sent out by the British Union Conference. A site was selected near Kisumu, Kavirondo Bay, on the northeastern shore of Victoria Nyanza. A piece of land containing about 320 acres was purchased for $244, and a stone mission house erected, also a schoolhouse, and blacksmith and carpenter shops. In 1907 the company of workers was re-enforced by the arrival of Mr. and Mrs. J. D. Baker and Miss Thompson, of England, the latter marrying Mr. Carscallen.

The Kavirondos were not only living in the darkest heathenism, without even having heard the name of Christ, but they had no written language. The missionaries accordingly applied themselves to reducing the language to writing, and in due time Mr. Carscallen had prepared the manuscript for a grammar, a primer, and a Kavirondo-English dictionary.

Meanwhile they were diligently working for the conversion of the natives. Gendia, the first mission station, was on a high point near Kisumu, in the midst of a thickly populated area, and from it could be seen a hundred Kavirondo villages. Late in 1908, during a visit from L. R. Conradi, a new site was secured, and the Wire Hill station was founded, J. D. Baker taking charge. B. L. Morse and H. H. Brooks arrived in the same year, and joined in the growing work. In 1911 the first fruits were gathered in, sixteen students being baptized. In the following year twenty-four were baptized.

In 1913 a station formerly used by the government was sold to the missionaries, and a new work started there. Two other sites were granted in 1914, one being in the Kisi country, among the people of a different tribe. In 1914 three additional stations were opened among the Kavirondos, and the one among the Kisi was reopened.

Communication between the various stations is facilitated by the use of the mission schooner, which plies on the lake. There is a small press, on which a monthly periodical is printed in the Kavirondo tongue.

The work was more or less broken up during the World War; nevertheless 100 believers were baptized in that period. In 1920 and 1921 the British Union sent out some new workers, headed by W. T. Bartlett, in order that those who had been long in the field might have a furlough. The government made a grant of ten acres for a hospital at Kisi, which was placed under the charge of Dr. G. A. Madgwick, a former superintendent of the Stanborough Park Sanitarium.

The British and Foreign Bible Society announced in 1921 that it had accepted a translation of the Epistles prepared by A. A. Carscallen, other parts having been translated by other men. This gave the whole of the New Testament to the Kavirondos.

The Pare Mission

This and the following mission were located in what was formerly German East Africa, but is now the Kenya Colony, under British mandate.

The first workers were J. Ehlers and A. C. Enns, who arrived at Dar-es-Salaam, a port on the East African Coast, some twenty-five miles south of Zanzibar, Nov. 12, 1903. Before the end of the month a mission site had been secured among the native people in the Pare Mountains. The allottment consisted of thirty acres of cultivated land lying in a healthful region 3,600 feet above sea level. Suitable buildings were erected, and the mission received the name Friedenstal (Vale of peace).

In the spring of 1904, L. R. Conradi visited the mission, and brought with him four additional laborers, one of whom was obliged to leave shortly, owing to an attack of fever. Two new stations were opened in the district in 1906, namely, at Kihuiro and Vuasu. Early in 1908 the first fruits were gathered in, six of the young men receiving baptism.

Meanwhile E. Kotz and B. Ohme had been hard at work reducing the native dialect to writing, and translating into it suitable evangelical literature. A Chassu grammar prepared by E. Kotz was published by the German government. In the course of the year 1909 six new schools were opened, bringing 350 pupils under the instruction of missionary workers. Twenty-six pupils were baptized that year. At the urgent invitation of three chiefs, a school was opened also at Kiranga, with sixty-seven pupils.

The work continued to go steadily forward, the year 1913 witnessing 133 baptisms, and the ordination of five native deacons. The mission published in the Chassu language, besides the grammar already mentioned, a song book, primer, reader, and the Gospel of John. It put out in the Swahili dialect, which is derived from the Arabic, a collection of Bible readings and a monthly paper, the latter prepared on the cyclostyle.

When the World War broke out, the membership at the Pare station was 256, with 2,338 natives under instruction in the schools and outschools. There was considerable scattering of the converts during the war. In 1921 the British Union sent three families from Kenya, one to reopen the Pare Mission, the other two to work along the southeastern shore of the Victoria Nyanza. In that year the British and Foreign Bible Society announced that it would issue the New Testament in a new language of the Pare Mountain tribes, the translation being made by E. Kotz.

The Victoria Nyanza Mission

The southwestern shore of the Victoria Nyanza was explored in 1909 by A. C. Enns, of the Pare Mission. In the following year he and E. Dominick settled at a point known as Majita. They were no sooner encamped than a troop of boys marched up to them, and saluting like soldiers said, " We've come, Mr. Missionary." They meant they had come to go to school; but they were willing first to work for money with which to clothe themselves. The school was started in February, about a month after the arrival of the missionaries. The school building, 50 x 16 feet, was intended to accommodate 160 pupils, seated close together; but within four days of the opening no less than 600 boys and 175 girls applied for admission.

In 1912, B. Ohme came from Pare to take the general oversight of the Victoria Nyanza Mission. There were then five stations and fourteen missionaries. Three additional stations were established in that year, work being begun among the

Wasukumu people. At the annual conference held toward the end of the year, the field was organized into three main districts, — Majita, on the east shore of the lake; Busegwe, the interior lying east of the lake; and Usukuma, the interior lying southeast of the lake. At that time there were 1,214 pupils in the several schools. Two years later there were twelve stations and eight outstations, with twenty-two missionaries and twenty-three native assistants.

Dr. F. W. Vasenius entered upon medical work in the Busegwe district. The mission was provided with a schooner to ply on the lake. Manuscripts were prepared for a dictionary, a hymn book, the four Gospels, and for primers in the various districts. Since the World War the mission with its outstations has been largely in the hands of native teachers.

The Abyssinian Mission

In the year 1907 the first Adventist missionaries to Abyssinia, J. Persson and P. N. Lindegren, sailed for Suez and Massawa. They were sent by the Scandinavian Union Conference, and they traveled by rail and cart to Asmara, in the Italian colony of Eritrea, where they were able to secure a language teacher. Having obtained a fair knowledge of the language, they entered the country proper, and in 1909 settled on an Italian homestead of seventy-five acres, lying a mile out of Asmara. The next month came Dr. and Mrs. F. W. Vasenius and V. E. Toppenberg, a nurse; also L. R. Conradi. In the following year a mission home and school were erected. E. J. Lorntz, of Norway, assisted in teaching the natives. Somewhat later Dr. Vasenius and Mr. Toppenberg were transferred to the Victoria Nyanza Mission field; and H. Steiner came from Switzerland to serve as director.

The mission farm had a remarkable deliverance in 1913. Hosts of locusts were devouring every living thing around them, and they fell upon the mission fields. As the workers prayed for deliverance, they were thankful to see great flocks of birds coming from every direction. Storks and other birds settled in the fields, and entirely destroyed the locusts.

The first fruits of the Abyssinian Mission appeared in 1914, when three converts were baptized, an Abyssinian priest and two deacons. During the World War the mission was looked after by natives. In 1921 V. E. Toppenberg returned to resume work, having been sent by the Scandinavian Union.

33

The North African Mission

As far back as 1886 a Spanish Protestant in Oran, Algeria, accepted the Adventist views through reading our French periodicals. He was active in spreading a knowledge of the truth, and was joined by others, so that a worker coming over from Switzerland in 1889 was able to organize a church; but the opposition was strong. The leader, a baker, lost all his business, and moved from the city. Eleven members left for South America, and the company of believers was eventually broken up. In 1909, U. Augsbourger, of France, began evangelistic work among the French-speaking people in the city of Algiers, and some accepted the message. S. Jespersson, who conducted treatment-rooms for a time, was obliged to leave, owing to ill health. In 1912, P. Badaut entered the field, meetings being held in Constantine, east of Algiers. A year later, Mr. and Mrs. W. E. Hancock, formerly of Guatemala, and R. T. E. Colthurst, of the West Indies, were appointed to this field, the former settling in Oran, and the latter in Mustapha. It was intended that Elder Hancock should open work in Morocco, but the outbreak of war made it necessary to postpone such a move. The city of Algiers was reported as having thirty members in 1919, there being churches also in Oran and Relizane.

Egypt

In the late nineties several Armenian Adventists moved to Egypt, where they did what they could to spread a knowledge of the message. About the same time, J. Lenzivgir, an Italian, began to do ship missionary work at Port Said, and in 1889 Mr. and Mrs. L. F. Passebois and Miss Schlegel, trained nurses, settled in Cairo, where they conducted a restaurant and health home, and did some Bible work. A Copt minister, working for the Presbyterians in Upper Egypt, came across the tract, " Is the End Near? " sent for further publications, and ended by accepting the Adventist views and becoming an active worker. At the time of a visit from L. R. Conradi in 1901, a church was organized in Cairo, baptism being administered in the river Nile.

W. H. Wakeham took general charge of the work in 1902. A small book on the prophecies of Daniel was published in the Arabic, and had an extensive sale. Elder Wakeham was obliged to leave Egypt in 1906, owing to the breakdown of his wife's health. Mrs. Wakeham died before the ship reached England.

In the autumn of the same year, Mr. and Mrs. J. J. Nethery were appointed to the field. An apostasy breaking out among the Armenian and Syrian believers reduced the number temporarily. Elder Nethery returning to England, the work was for a time directed from Syria. In 1909 a Coptic believer, A. A. Elshaneed, began to work in Luxor, near ancient Thebes. In the same year, George Keough, of England, went to Egypt, working

GROUP OF BELIEVERS AT CAIRO, EGYPT

at first in Cairo, and afterward in Luxor. Somewhat later he took the superintendency of the field. In 1912 calls came from Beni Addi, near Assiut, on the Nile. On visiting that place, Elder Keough found one man who had kept the Sabbath for six years and another for two years. A series of meetings was held, and a company of sixteen believers was brought out. Some work was also done at this time in Assiut.

In the spring of 1914 the territory was grouped in two main divisions, Elder Keough taking Upper Egypt, with headquarters at Beni Addi, and Elder W. C. Ising taking Lower Egypt, with headquarters at Cairo. Shortly after the outbreak of the World War, Elder Ising was interned on the island of Malta. In the antiforeign uprising after the war, Elder Keough was unharmed, while the other Europeans in that district were slain. The fact that his life was spared could not be regarded otherwise than as providential.

D. A. ROBINSON

H. R. SALISBURY

J. L. SHAW

H. C. MENKEL, M. D.

PIONEER WORKERS IN INDIA

CHAPTER XXVIII

Missions in India and Burma

INDIA, the home of the Hindu, the Mohammedan, the Parsee, the Jain, and the animist, and the birthplace of Buddhism, has been called the most powerful citadel of ancient errors and idolatry in the world. The population of India and Burma is over three hundred million, and Christian missions have been carried on in these countries for upwards of two hundred years.

The work of Seventh-day Adventists in India and Burma, as in most other mission fields, was pioneered by colporteurs. Late in 1893, A. T. Stroup and William A. Lenker were sent to India as canvassers, and were joined by Mr. and Mrs. Masters from Australia. They began their work early in the year 1894, and for about two years gave their best efforts to introducing the denominational literature in the cities of India.

The pioneer in zenana work was Miss Georgia Burrus, now Mrs. L. J. Burgess, who landed at Calcutta in January, 1895. Miss Burrus was sent out by the Mission Board, which paid her traveling expenses with the understanding that she was to work the first year on a self-supporting basis and study

517

one of the native languages. Her funds soon ran low, but help was providentially provided from a source then unknown to her. A man who had recently accepted the Adventist views in Africa sold his billiard table for £100, and sent the money in quarterly instalments to Miss Burrus to enable her to continue her study of the Bengali language.

In the year 1895, Mr. and Mrs. D. A. Robinson and Miss Mae Taylor, now Mrs. Quantock, landed in Calcutta. Miss Taylor took up the study of the Bengali language, and united with Miss Burrus in the Bible work. Some time later D. A. Robinson, who went to India to take general charge of the work, opened up mission headquarters in Calcutta. His first efforts were for the English-speaking people of that large city. He conducted a series of meetings in a hall at 154 Bow Bazaar Street in the autumn of 1895, and continued the effort through the winter with an increasing interest. In the spring and summer of 1897 these meetings were transferred to the Corinthian theater. The Dalhousie Institute was also used for public meetings. A small company of believers was gathered out as a result of this effort, and regular Sabbath meetings began to be held in a rented hall on Free School Street.

Meanwhile the staff of workers had been further increased by the arrival in 1896 of Dr. and Mrs. O. G. Place, Mr. and Mrs. G. P. Edwards, Miss Samantha Whiteis, and Maggie Green (Mrs. I. D. Richardson). Dr. Place opened a sanitarium in Calcutta, and operated it until his return to America, being succeeded by Doctors R. S. and Olive G. Ingersoll.

In May, 1898, the first number of a monthly magazine, *The Oriental Watchman,* appeared. It was edited by W. A. Spicer, who had come over from England in the same year. The first edition of 1,500 copies was distributed free; but the magazine soon had a paid subscription list of 4,000. The denominational books were also being sold at this time in Bengal and Bombay by Ellery Robinson; in South India and Ceylon by R. W. Yeoman; and in the northwest, far into Kashmir, by I. D. Richardson; while H. B. Meyers, who had accepted the truth in Calcutta, carried the literature into the Malay States and Burma.

Something had also been done in a philanthropic way. At the time of the Santal famine in 1895, D. A. Robinson and his coworkers were active in their efforts in behalf of the suffering natives. An orphan school had been opened in Karmatar, 168 miles to the northwest of Calcutta, and here some of the most needy children were gathered in to be cared for and taught the Christian religion. This work was under the immediate direction of Mr. and Mrs. F. W. Brown, who had recently come over from America.

The work thus well begun in the several lines received a severe setback when D. A. Robinson, superintendent of the mission, and F. W. Brown, of the orphanage, died of smallpox in 1900. The leadership devolved on W. A. Spicer, who carried it forward until the General Conference of 1901, when he was called to the secretaryship of the General Conference. He was

OLD HEADQUARTERS AT LUCKNOW
Office of the India Union Mission and Watchman Press

succeeded by J. L. Shaw, formerly principal of the college at Cape Town, South Africa.

For five or six years the work was carried on in much the same way as it had begun, by means of English publications. The denominational literature continued to be widely circulated. In 1904 an English edition of *Good Health* was introduced, and continued to be used for six years, until in 1910 *The Herald of Health,* published in India, began to appear. The Watchman Press office was opened in May, 1903, at 38 Free School St., Calcutta, under the charge of W. W. Quantock. In the year 1905 it was moved to Karmatar, and placed under the charge of J. C. Little. In 1909 it was transferred to Lucknow, and W. E. Perrin became the manager. In 1924 it was again moved, this time to Poona. Its full name is The Oriental Watchman Publishing Association.

During all these years constantly increasing evangelistic work was being done for the natives. Miss Georgia Burrus, after spending two years in learning the Bengali tongue, began to do house-to-house work in the city of Calcutta and its suburbs. Her first two converts, Noniballa and Kiroda Bose, were widows. In a high-caste Hindu zenana, Noniballa first met Miss Burrus and heard from her the story of the cross. Her heart was touched, and she decided to cast in her lot with God's people. Scaling the walls of the compound by night, she made her way

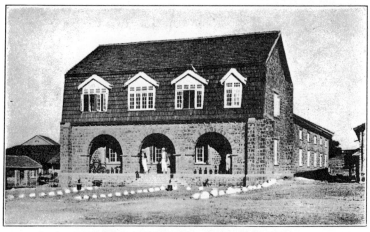

THE NEW PUBLISHING HOUSE AT POONA

to Miss Burrus, who gladly took her in and instructed her in the way of salvation. Noniballa later came to America, but continued her membership with the home church in India. The next native convert was A. C. Mookerjee, a great-grandson of William Carey's first convert. He first came in contact with the mission workers at the sanitarium in Calcutta, and was the means of giving the message to various members of his family, who accepted it and became workers in different capacities.

Educational work was carried on from the beginning. In the spring of 1896, Misses Burrus and Taylor opened a girls' school in Calcutta, which was a help to them in perfecting their knowledge of the language and in getting into the homes of the people. Kiroda Bose was employed as a teacher in this school. A second school for girls was opened in Baliaghatta, a suburb of Calcutta, and about the same time an orphanage for boys was opened in the same city. After two years this school was moved to Karmatar, where it was continued until 1906. A number of the present native workers in the Bengali language were taught in this orphanage. It was in connection with this institution that the first English school was started, under the direction of Thekla Black, with Anna Orr as head teacher. In 1911 the English school was revived and opened in Mussoorie, with Mrs. Edith E. Bruce in charge.

NATIVE WORKERS IN INDIA

These various agencies were showing some results, but it was felt by those who had the general oversight that if the work of giving the message to the natives of India was to be carried forward successfully, it must be put on a somewhat different basis. The new missionary recruits, instead of being called upon almost immediately after their arrival to fill some of the openings, must be assigned to a definite language to begin with and master it. At the conference of workers held toward the close of 1906, it was unanimously decided that persons attempting to learn a native tongue should have their whole time for the undertaking. Moreover, their course was to be marked out for them somewhat definitely, and dates set for the various examinations.

Following the council, Mr. and Mrs. J. S. James were located in Bangalore, South India, to open work among the Tamil-

speaking people; and Mr. and Mrs. R. R. Cook were assigned
to the Santal work in West Bengal. Property for a mountain mission was purchased at the hill station of Mussoorie,
North India, and dedicated in 1907. Mr. and Mrs. L. J. Burgess
(L. J. Burgess and Miss Burrus had recently been married)
moved to Dehra Dun, on the plains below Mussoorie, where
they continued evangelistic work in the Hindi and Urdu tongues.

As a result of following the above-mentioned plan, J. L. Shaw
was able to report at the General Conference in 1909 that work

H. R. SALISBURY WITH HIS STUDENTS AT MUSSOORIE

had been opened up in eight different languages. Some of the
workers, he said, " were far enough along to give themselves
fully to evangelistic work, while others were still spending most
of the time in study of the language." Workers were then engaged among the English, Bengali, Hindustani, Burmese, Tamil,
Marathi, and Santali people.

Aggressive evangelistic work among the English-speaking
people, especially of the large cities, was carried on by J. M.
Comer in Calcutta and South India, and by G. W. Pettit and
G. F. Enoch in Bombay.

As the work grew, the need arose for a more extensive
organization. At the conference in Lucknow held in the autumn
of 1910, India was definitely organized into a union mission
under the superintendency of J. L. Shaw, the whole field being
divided into five missions; namely, Bengal, North India, South
India, Burma, and West India. The further development of
the work in India will be considered under these five heads, as
follows:

Bengal

Adventists began their work in India in the province of Bengal, the largest of the governmental divisions of British India. Lying largely in the delta of the Ganges and Brahmaputra Rivers, Bengal is a highly fertile province, famine being practically unknown. It is also the most highly developed district educationally, Calcutta, the principal city, having several colleges and fine universities, as well as a good system of public schools. The country is very malarious, however, many of its inhabitants dying yearly from this cause. The first superintendent of this part of India was J. C. Little, who while engaged in his itinerating work, was attacked by cholera, and died Aug. 10, 1910. W. R. French was sent to take his place, and he arrived in India in time to be present at a meeting in 1910, when the general organization was effected.

At this meeting Bengal was organized into a mission, with four stations, namely, Karmatar, Babumohal, Gopalgunj, and Calcutta. Karmatar, the first Seventh-day Adventist vernacular mission station, was opened in 1901, being first operated as an orphanage and afterward as the original headquarters of the Watchman Press, established in 1898. Educational work was a feature of this station from the beginning. Within a few years five village schools were in operation, besides one English intermediate school. Sabbath schools were organized in the village schools, with an attendance larger than that on week days. The intermediate school was opened in 1913, and soon had an attendance of sixty boys, including children of some high-caste parents. Medical work is done in the dispensary, where large numbers of suffering natives receive medical care, and have their attention directed to the great Physician.

The Babumohal Mission had its beginning in the year 1900, when W. A. Barlow secured a small plot of land near Simultala, a town in the Santal country, where in due time he opened a school for boys. This was the first Seventh-day Adventist boarding school among the Santal people, and by means of it the first Santal converts were obtained. Two outschools were started, with an attendance of about thirty, one a night school for shepherd lads, and the other a village day school. A beginning was made in getting out literature in the Santali language, tracts and a hymn book being among the first publications.

Work was begun at Gopalgunj by L. G. Mookerjee, who with his wife began as a self-supporting worker, but was afterward engaged in labor under the Mission Board. With their own money Mr. and Mrs. Mookerjee erected a dwelling for themselves, a church, a dispensary, and a house for native workers. Mrs. Mookerjee's health failing, they went to America for a year. On their return it was not thought best for them to continue the work in that region. Mr. Mookerjee was accordingly given charge of the Calcutta Bengali church and the literature work in Bengal, and A. G. Watson was placed in

AMONG THE JUNGLE VILLAGES OF WEST BENGAL

charge of the Gopalgunj station. Colporteur work is being carried on by a number of the natives. The whole of the district lying in the delta of the Brahmaputra River, for a portion of the year, is flooded with water, which necessitates the use of boats as a means of transportation. A twenty-five-foot motor launch, bought by appropriation of the General Conference in 1910, has been a great help in the development of the mission. There is a boys' school in the district, with a large attendance, nearly all the pupils being Hindus.

In Calcutta, public meetings were conducted regularly in a rented hall, and there was a slow but steady growth in the membership. A half dozen colporteurs are employed in the sale of denominational literature. The sanitarium work inau-

gurated by Dr. Place, and continued by the Doctors Ingersoll and H. C. Menkel, was in course of time discontinued, and
treatment-rooms were started, which are operated successfully
at the present time. Dr. V. L. Mann went to India in December, 1911, to supply the place of Dr. Menkel during his furlough, and has since been engaged in medical work. Dr. Menkel
in time opened treatment-rooms in Simla.

ON A SCHOOL INSPECTION TRIP IN INDIA

North India

The removal of the union headquarters of the printing office
to Lucknow in 1908 strengthened the work in North India,
which is the most populous of the five divisions, having 130,-
000,000 inhabitants within its borders. In 1910 Mr. and Mrs.
L. J. Burgess established an industrial school among the Garhwal people in the Himalayas, near Dehra Dun. They opened
this school in response to urgent requests from the native people. Land was donated by the government, and people gave
freely toward the expense of erecting a school building, and
also helped the missionaries to build a dwelling house. The
Garhwal district being located in the Himalaya Mountains,
where the climate is cool, it is a good place in which to carry
on the education of Hindustani workers.

The progress of the work in North India has not been without opposition. John Last, a zealous evangelist who preached

WORKERS AND BELIEVERS OF THE SOUTH INDIA MISSION

Photograph taken at a general meeting held at Coimbatore, May, 1916.

in the streets of Patala, was attacked by Mohammedan fanatics in 1911, and beaten to death. In 1913-14, while Mr. and Mrs. Burgess were absent on furlough, the work was in charge of C. C. Belgrave, a West Indian who acquired the Hindustani language in British Guiana, among the Hindus there engaged on sugar plantations. In 1914 the school at Garhwal had its first baptism.

Temporary school work was opened in Dehra Dun by Mrs. Alice O'Connor, who had obtained a knowledge of the Urdu. Later Mrs. O'Connor joined Misses Kurtz and M. B. Shryock in school and dispensary work at Najibabad. This work had an encouraging growth, and in 1913 a brick mission house was erected. Dr. V. L. Mann, who has had general oversight of other dispensaries and is editor of the health journal at Lucknow, has done much work in connection with this mission.

About 1910 work was begun among the Hindu women of Lucknow by Miss Vera E. Chilton. In 1913 a call came from the Punjab province, which had not been entered by a Seventh-day Adventist worker. A native Christian minister, leader of a body of 1,200 natives, not connected with a religious society, met S. A. Wellman while traveling, and accepted the Sabbath truth. He urged that work be begun in the Punjab. Dr. Mann and F. H. Loasby accordingly made a tour of the region with a wagon and tent outfit, treating the sick and teaching the essential truths of the message. They finally located at Lahore.

South India

The South India Mission includes the southern portion of British India and Ceylon, with a population of 60,000,000. Our work began with the Tamils, a race who have shown themselves unusually susceptible to the Christian religion. Moreover about a thousand of the Tamils had been paying some regard to the Sabbath for a number of years. J. L. Shaw, in company with G. F. Enoch and J. S. James, visited these Sabbath-keeping Tamils for the first time in the autumn of 1908. The people gave our workers an enthusiastic reception, and a number of them showed a deep interest in the gospel.

At the special request of these Tamil Sabbath keepers, Elder James settled among them, and began to apply himself to the study of the language. The people of the Tinnevelli District came forward with an offer of two acres of land adjoining their village on the north, where buildings could be erected for the carrying on of work. In the spring of 1908, Elder James took up his abode in the village, and began to work for the people. In the following summer he put up a mission bungalow at a cost of $1,300. As he became familiar with the language and began to give definite instruction, a controversy arose among the people, some taking a definite stand for the Adventist faith and others opposing it.

Meanwhile a dispensary was opened, where an average of one thousand persons a month were treated, and a school was started. To begin with, the teachers in this school were not of the Seventh-day Adventist faith, but when they had had

A TAMIL BIBLE STUDY CLASS

opportunity to study the truth, they were glad to identify themselves with it. The attendance soon numbered about one hundred. By 1913 fifteen of the boys and girls of the school had been baptized, and sixty-six adults had accepted the message and received baptism, while many others were interested and counted themselves as Adventists.

In 1910 work was begun in Trichinopoli, a city with a population of 150,000, by a Tamil brother who had heard the message in Singapore. The interest was followed up by G. G. Lowry, who, however, was soon compelled by Mrs. Lowry's failing health to leave the field. While J. S. James was absent on furlough in 1913-14, the work in South India was in charge of V. E. Peugh. On Elder James' return, accompanied by Mr. and Mrs. E. Morrow, Mr. Peugh and a Tamil evangelist began work in the town of Pondicherry, on the east coast, where several persons had accepted the Sabbath through reading the Adventist literature.

The work in South India has been carried forward largely by means of literature. Almost the first work attempted after entering the field was the translation into the Tamil language of four tracts: " Herald of His Coming," " The New Testament Sabbath," " Is the End Near? " and " Which Day Do You Keep, and Why? " In 1912 a colporteurs' institute of three weeks' duration was conducted in the city of Trichinopoli, at which nine men were in attendance. This institute marked the beginning of aggressive work with literature in South India. While it was in progress, a Hindu printer was getting out the first issue of our Tamil quarterly, *The Present Truth,* which was finished and delivered to the workers on the last day of the institute. " After the men had been assigned their territory," writes J. S. James, " we knelt around this pile of papers, 3,000 in all, and asked God to bless those who were to carry them to the people and those who should read them." In the course of the next nine months the workers secured 1,250 yearly subscriptions among an excellent class of people, altogether disposing of 9,525 copies.

West India

Work in West India has been carried forward under the leadership of G. F. Enoch. While acquiring the Marathi language, he opened up work at Lanovla, a semi-hill station near Bombay, where a number of English-speaking persons accepted the truth. A permanent station was established at Panwel, a village of 10,000 in a thickly populated district bordering on Bombay. A school and dispensary were opened here, and A. G. Kelsey joined in the work. In 1912 Mr. and Mrs. M. D. Wood, who had formerly labored in India under the direction of the Methodists, returned to take up work for the Seventh-day Adventists. Mrs. Wood, being a medical missionary, began work in a dispensary at Kalyan, a railway junction near Bombay. Nine acres of land were purchased and a mission house erected. A branch dispensary was later opened at Igatpuri. As a result of the work in the two dispensaries and the evangelistic labors of Brethren Enoch, Wood, and their associates, a Marathi church came into being.

Burma

Work in Burma was begun by colporteurs, who sold large quantities of books and papers to the English-speaking people.

In 1902 H. B. Meyers, who had been engaged in canvassing, began to hold public meetings in the city of Rangoon, as a result of which several began to keep the Sabbath. At the conference held in Calcutta, Maung Maung, who had been working at his own charges for the Burmese people for several years, made an earnest appeal for help, in response to which Mr. and Mrs. H. H. Votaw were sent to Burma, arriving in Rangoon early in January, 1905. Elder Votaw entered upon aggressive evangelistic work in Rangoon, and had the pleasure of seeing the number of Sabbath keepers (there being only three when he arrived) increased in the next few years to sixty. He was ably assisted by two native workers, Maung Maung and David Hpo Hla, who made great personal sacrifices in accepting the truth, and gave themselves unreservedly to the work. In 1909 Elder Votaw appealed for a teacher to take charge of the industrial school which was called for by Buddhists in North Burma. R. B. Thurber, who was sent out in response to this call, established an industrial school at Meiktila, with thirty acres of land, buildings and shops.

The school occupies a unique position in that it has practically no Seventh-day Adventist constituents to draw from, and the money for its maintenance is raised among non-Adventists. When Mr. Thurber went to Burma in 1909, he wished first to learn the language, but calls for the opening of the school were so loud and frequent that the work was finally begun in a rented building with practically no facilities. After a number of obstacles had been overcome, the school was provided with twenty-five acres of " freehold land " on high ground overlooking the lake. There were a large school building, 38 x 78 feet, with tile roof, cement floor, and double mat walls; a house for one teacher; house and stable for cartmen and bullocks; a temporary workshed, with living quarters for the teachers of carpentry and cane work; and finally a spacious workshop of the same size as the school building.

In the morning the boys are taught English and Burmese; in the afternoon they work at their trades or at outdoor labor. Three different trades are taught. The members of the carpentry class make chairs, tables, clothespresses, and other furniture. They also work on the buildings. The boys in the cane department make cane chairs of various models, stools, wastepaper baskets, and the like. The shoe department is crowded with orders for new shoes and repair work. In addition to the ordinary Burmese sandals and slippers, the students make regular American shoes, for which there is a great demand.

The accommodations provide for an attendance of 140. There is a waiting list, and thus the school is always full. Most of the pupils are Burmese, but there are some Indians, Chinese, Karens, and Eurasians. The boys are paid something from the start. As they become more skilled, the wage is increased until some receive as much as five cents an hour. A few are able to earn practically all their expenses, but usually the cost of tuition and board is about $15 a year more than the average boy can earn. The Meiktila Industrial School was for years the only

BOYS' SCHOOL IN BURMA

trade school in Burma. Those who helped to start the institution are well pleased with it, and give it their hearty support.

The circulation of literature has occupied from the beginning a large place in the work in Burma. The Burmese people are fond of reading, and gladly welcome the colporteur. The sales of some of our workers have reached as high as $300 a month. Strange to say, while other denominations have been at work in Burma for something like a century, Seventh-day Adventists were the first to sell their books and papers. Our first attempt to sell reading matter in the Burmese language was made in 1911, with a 32-page booklet entitled, " The Signs of the Times and End of the World." At first one of these books and a Gospel sold at one-half cent for the two; then the books sold at one-half cent apiece. Later the booklet and others like it were sold at one cent apiece, which covers the cost of printing. In the first four years more than 14,000 copies of these booklets were placed in the hands of the people of Burma.

An eight-page tract, "The True Mode of Worship," has been widely circulated free of charge. Some 2,000 copies of an eighty-page health booklet have also been sold. In 1912 a twenty-two-page quarterly magazine, at 15 cents a year, appeared. The first three numbers were issued in editions of 5,000. Then the circulation began to increase. The periodical is generally liked, and is exerting a strong influence in favor of the truth.

Later Developments

H. R. Salisbury succeeded J. L. Shaw as superintendent of the Indian field in 1913. It was a severe blow to the work

ORDAINED AND LICENSED MINISTERS OF THE INDIA
UNION MISSION

when, early in the year 1915, the ship "Persia," on which he was crossing the Mediterranean on his return from the General Conference in America, was torpedoed near Egypt, and he was not among the few that were rescued. Somewhat later, India was constituted the South Asiatic Division, with J. E. Fulton in charge, and W. W. Fletcher, of Australia, serving as field secretary. Carrying out this plan, the whole field was divided into four union missions, each under a superintendent: the Northeast, Northwest, and South India, and the Burma.

At the General Conference of 1922 the Northeast Union Mission, under the oversight of H. E. Willoughby, reported a strong English and a Bengali church in Calcutta and seven other native churches in the Bengal Presidency; also several churches among the Santali-speaking people at Karmatar and Saljhari, and a church of Hindus at Ranchi. The territory of this union includes the Bengal Presidency and certain other neighboring states that can be most easily worked from this center. The union has suffered for lack of workers, but the sale of the literature is going forward encouragingly.

The Northwest India Union, under the care of I. F. Blue, forms a triangle of a million square miles. Political uprisings are common, and famine follows any failure of crops. An encouraging work is being carried on by F. H. Loasby and V. L. Mann in the Punjab. The colporteurs are learning to sell our books, and the literature thus circulated is giving rise to many calls for teachers. The mission schools are reported as having an attendance of 500. These are not all conducted in buildings. A tree affording shade is sufficient protection for the village school. Chairs and benches are unnecessary, for the Indians prefer to sit on the ground. The brighter pupils in these village schools are picked out and sent to one of the boarding schools.

The union has two fully equipped treatment-rooms and two dispensaries. The former, located at Simla and Mussoorie, are mainly for Europeans. The dispensaries are at Kalyan and Chuharkana. They minister every year to the physical needs of thousands of natives, who, while they wait their turns, are also given instruction from the Word of God.

Evangelistic work is being carried on at ten stations, in charge of Europeans, from which itinerating tours are taken through the adjacent district. In the region above Hapur, M. M. Mattison is having encouraging success. R. E. Loasby has had charge of the training school at the Bombay Mission, and has also served as superintendent of the mission. There are many openings in the vicinity of Lasalgaon, where the training school is located.

The South India Union Mission, under the leadership of G. G. Lowry, includes the field occupied by the Tamil, Telugu, Malayalam, Kanarese, and Singhalese peoples, numbering all told about 60,000,000. The beginning among the Tamils has been related on an earlier page of this chapter. The number of believers among these people has been more than trebled in the last four years. Two young Tamil men, E. D. Thomas and A. Asirvatham, have been ordained to the ministry. The strongest station in the south is at Prakasapuram, a village near Nazareth, where the work began. Besides day and boarding school,

WORKERS' GROUP AT A CONFERENCE IN LUCKNOW

there is a very live church, which occupies a building of its own, dedicated in 1921. This mission is under the supervision of E. D. Thomas. In the Malayalam country, lying to the west of the Tamil territory, there are one main station and four out-stations, all under the general oversight of H. G. Woodward.

INDIAN LEPER WHO WAS HEALED BY PRAYER

The work among the Telugus has been going on for several years in a small way, but only recently has it been put on a strong basis. There are three well-attended schools. T. R. Flaiz is in charge. Evangelistic work on behalf of the English people was done at Madras by P. C. Poley, and at Colombo by J. M. Comer. The combined attendance at all the schools in the union numbers about 500. From the training school at Bangalore, thirty-five students have gone out into the work. The circulating of de-nominational literature is found to be a very important factor in the progress of the message in South India.

The Burma Union Mission, under the leadership of J. Phillips, reports a growing interest and many new openings. The English church in Rangoon is under the care of I. V. Counsell and Dr. O. Tornblad; the Burmese church is shepherded by D. Hpo Hla, and the Telugu believers are led by T. R. Flaiz. In Upper Burma a new station has been opened at Toung-gyi in the Shan States. The Irrawaddy Delta Mission, having its headquarters in Henzada, has one strong church, with a village school and a school for girls, the buildings for which have been recently completed. R. A. Beckner has been in charge of this mission. The Tenasserim Mission, headquarters for our work among the Karens, reports a very hopeful outlook. In recent years our workers have come in contact with the Klee Bow Karens, who keep the seventh-day Sabbath, and are looking for the second coming of Christ. Mary Gibbs Denoyer, our first worker among the Karens, is still laboring for this people. The industrial school at Meiktila is doing an excellent work.

F. J. HUTCHINS   JOHN ECCLES, M. D.

ANOTHER MEMORIAL OF SACRIFICE

The graves of Elder Hutchins and Dr. Eccles in Bocas del Toro, with their
widows standing by.

THE "HERALD"

The trim missionary schooner is seen at the left, with one of her yawl boats in the foreground.

CHAPTER XXIX

Missions in Central America and the West Indies

IT was a ship captain that first carried a knowledge of the advent message to the islands of the Caribbean Sea. It happened on this wise:

There was established in New York City in 1883 a branch of the International Tract Society, which made large use of the vessels leaving New York Harbor, as instruments for the circulation of denominational literature. One day William J. Boynton, a member of the staff of workers, asked the captain of a ship bound for British Guiana, if he would be willing to distribute a roll of religious periodicals in that country, and he consented with some degree of reluctance.

Not long thereafter a woman living near the wharf in Georgetown, British Guiana, called on an old man with whom she was acquainted, and saw lying on the table in his house a copy of the *Signs of the Times*. When she inquired where it came from, he told her that a few days before a sea captain had stepped ashore, and scattered a bundle of periodicals on the wharf, saying as he did so, " I have fulfilled my promise."

The woman took the paper home with her, and presently began to observe the Sabbath. Others read the paper, and joined her in obeying the truths it taught. After some time the same periodical, considerably the worse for wear, was carefully folded up and sent to a sister living in Barbados. Before it was entirely worn out, several persons in that place had been brought to a knowledge of the advent message.

In the case of some of these persons, it should perhaps be said the conviction that the seventh day is the Bible Sabbath dated still farther back. Years ago, when slavery was still prevalent, a pious black mother of Barbados gathered her children around her, and read to them the fourth commandment out of the Bible, saying in substance: " My children, God made the seventh day holy, and it is the Sabbath. Men have changed it, but some day the true Sabbath will be restored. I may not live to see it, but you will."

The children never forgot the words of their mother, and when the copy of the *Signs* fell into their hands, and they read of a people who kept the seventh day and taught others to keep it, they gladly accepted the truth, saying, " Mother told us so."

It was not long before the new believers entered into correspondence with the International Tract Society in America, with a view to obtaining more literature, and by and by a colporteur proceeded to British Guiana, where during three years he distributed all the literature sent to him. In the *Review and Herald* of Dec. 2, 1886, he reported the holding of the first Sabbath service in that mission field.

Meanwhile further help for the region of the Caribbean had been provided in Mrs. E. Gauterau, of Honduras, who accepted the message in California, and returned in 1885 to her Central American home, taking with her a large supply of reading matter. This she scattered throughout the Bay Islands and in British Honduras, taking pains also to send the names of many interested persons to the International Tract Society. Letters beginning to come in rapid succession from interested persons in those parts, the General Conference, at its meeting in 1886, decided to send G. G. Rupert on a visit to British Guiana, and T. H. Gibbs to Honduras and the Bay Islands. These men started in January, 1887. Elder Rupert was accompanied by

George A. King, of New York, an experienced canvasser, who took with him a supply of our books. The brethren remained in the field about three months, during which time Mr. King sold not far from $1,000 worth of books. Mr. Gibbs found a good interest in the message in the parts of Central America that he visited. He disposed of a number of books, and found reliable persons to act as distributors of literature.

In 1888 Mrs. A. Roskrug, of the island of Antigua, accepted the message while on a visit to London, England. On returning to her home the following year, she began at once to interest her neighbors in the truth, and in the course of time organized a Sabbath school. The church in Antigua was established by D. E. Wellman, who gave a full quarter of a century's service in this tropical field.

William Arnold made his first canvassing trip to the Caribbean also in the late eighties. He made four other trips, working in almost every English-speaking colony in the West Indies, and placing, all told, about 5,000 books.

D. A. Ball was sent to the West Indies in 1890, and visited most of the islands. He found interested persons in many places, and was able to organize companies of believers in Barbados and Antigua. Failing health obliged him to leave at the end of two years, and again the believers had to wait several years for a minister.

Late in 1893 A. Beans and W. Hackett, two faithful colporteurs, settled in the Barbados, and not only greatly encouraged the company of believers, but began to train a corps of West Indian young men for the canvassing work. Soon several of these were in the field, and doing well.

Spanish and British Honduras

The first ministerial help was provided for Central America in 1891, when Mr. and Mrs. F. J. Hutchins began to pioneer the way along the Central American coast, combining ministerial work, dentistry, and book selling. They found eight adult believers in Ruatán, one of the Bay Islands. Soon there were believers also at Utilla and Bonacca. On the latter island, the progress of the message was so rapid that a church building begun as a union church was completed as a Seventh-day Adventist meeting house, nearly all those connected with the enterprise having by that time embraced the message.

It was soon found that the work could be carried forward more rapidly in these islands if the missionaries had a boat of

their own.   Accordingly, the Sabbath schools in the United
States took hold of the enterprise in characteristic fashion, and
the needed funds were provided.   The " Herald," a trim little
schooner of thirty-five tons' burden, was built and put into commission, and for several years, with its " storm king " captain,
as Elder Hutchins was commonly called, was well known along
the coast.   In 1900, the means of communication between the
islands having improved, the " Herald " was sold, a portion of

THE CHURCH BUILDING AT BONACCA

the proceeds being used to purchase mission property in Bocas
del Toro, now in the republic of Panama.   A gasoline launch
was purchased to operate among the islands around Bocas.

In 1895 the work in Central America was strengthened by
the arrival of Elder and Mrs. James A. Morrow, and Frank
Mosebar, a colporteur.   The school started in 1893 in Bonacca
was for a short time in the hands of Mr. and Mrs. H. A. Owen,
who later entered upon work in the interior of Spanish Honduras, being succeeded by Mr. and Mrs. William Evans.   In
1899 F. Holmden and his family settled in Utilla, one of the
Bay Islands, where Winifred Holmden conducted a school which
came to have an enrolment of sixty.   School work was also
undertaken by S. arker Smith and his wife in 1P901 on St.
Andrews Island, belonging to Colombia, where Elder Hutchins
and Dr. John Eccles, a medical missionary, had pioneered the
way.   A few years later the work was taken over by Mr. and
Mrs. J. B. Stuyvesant, of Missouri.

In 1902, after nearly eleven years of faithful labor, F. J. Hutchins was stricken with a tropical disease, and died in Bocas del Toro. His grave and that of Dr. John Eccles, who died four months earlier in the same year, mark this region for the message.

H. C. Goodrich had general charge of the work in Spanish and British Honduras for some years, the mission headquarters and book depository being for a time in Belize. He was succeeded by E. L. Cardey. Spanish Sabbath keepers in Honduras were reported as early as 1905, when A. N. Allen was selling books along the coast. H. Publer and C. A. Nowlan were other colporteurs who worked at this time. Early in 1908 a camp-meeting was held on Ruatán.

In 1907 H. C. Goodrich was made president of the West Caribbean Conference, including Panama, Costa Rica, and Nicaragua, and the islands of St. Andrews and Old Providence. There were then believers in Colon and Costa Rica.

The membership gradually increased as the workers reached out in various directions. In 1920 F. Hardt began to conduct an industrial school for the training of our own youth. The membership, as reported by a later superintendent, W. E. Lanier, amounted to three hundred.

Guatemala and Salvador

The first of these fields has received but little attention. E. L. Cardey in 1908 located the Central American headquarters in Guatemala City. J. B. Stuyvesant settled in the same city in 1913, and W. E. Hancock, E. W. Thurber, and others followed.

Salvador was first entered in 1915, when J. L. Brown returned from Spain and opened work in San Salvador City. C. F. Staben reported sixty-five members in 1919.

West Caribbean Conference

C. E. Peckover began in 1905 to labor for the thousands of Indians working in the Canal Zone. Churches and companies were raised up by him and those who followed. A training school in charge of C. J. Boyd was opened in 1921. It is located on forty acres of land near Imperial on the canal.

Believers in Costa Rica are scattered along the coast, where they work on plantations. There are churches at Port Limon, San Jose, the capital, and in other ports. Along the Mosquito Coast of Nicaragua we have had believers for some years.

Colombia, South America, was early entered by the colporteurs, B. E. Connerly, Gilbert A. Schwerin, and others having a part in the circulation of our literature as far as Bogotá, the capital.

W. E. Baxter, president of the Caribbean Union Mission, reported a membership of 3,603 in 1925.

Venezuela

Venezuela was not entered in a permanent way till F. G. Lane settled in Carácas in 1910. He was welcomed by a small group of people who had met together for years, praying for additional light. Some of them very quickly accepted the advent message. Colporteurs and other workers entered the field, among them D. D. Fitch and W. E. Baxter, the latter becoming superintendent. The work moves forward slowly but steadily.

Jamaica

Work in Jamaica began in 1893. Mrs. M. Harrison, a resident of the island, who had accep'ed the message through reading, visited the General Conference and earnestly pleaded for a minister. Mr. and Mrs. A. J. Haysmer, sent in response to this plea, landed at Kingston in May of the same year, and found there a company of believers waiting to welcome them. In February, 1894, they were able to organize the first Seventh-day Adventist church in Jamaica, thirty-one persons being baptized, and six being received into the church by letter. In March, 1895, F. I. Richardson joined Elder Haysmer in labor on the island, the membership at that time being seventy-four.

The church thus raised up was more than usually active in the circulation of literature, large clubs of the *Signs* being taken, and thousands of pages of tracts and pamphlets given away or lent on the envelope plan. The young men and women who accepted the message were trained to labor as colporteurs, and soon our books were to be found in every parish. Among those who embraced the truth in 1895, were A. H. Humphries, a native preacher, a portion of whose congregation followed him, against no little opposition. The first tent-meeting on the island was held on the race course at Kingston.

F. I. Richardson being called to Africa in 1896, C. A. Hall and his family took up the work in Jamaica. In that year the Spanish Town church was dedicated, and the following year marked the dedication of the Kingston church, the largest church building Adventists then had in the West Indies.

Once it was well under way, the evangelistic work went steadily forward in Jamaica, both in the coast towns and in the villages of the interior. The training school in Mandeville is successfully preparing workers.

In 1925 C. E. Wood, president of the Jamaica Conference, reported sixty-seven churches, with a membership of 2,430.

FIRST JAMAICA CONFERENCE

A group of workers and believers, taken on the occasion of a visit from Elder W. A. Spicer.

British Guiana

After struggling alone for six years, the believers in British Guiana rejoiced in the arrival of Mr. and Mrs. W. G. Kneeland, who settled in Georgetown in 1893, and at once gathered the believers together and reorganized the work. Elder Kneeland also pushed out into the unentered portions of the Guianas, along the coast and up the great rivers, finding in many places faithful ones who were glad to receive the message.

Philip Giddings, a native of British Guiana, who had spent a few years at the college and sanitarium in Battle Creek, Mich., returned to his native land in 1895. With him were Dr. and Mrs. B. J. Ferciot, who intended to open up medical missionary work, but owing to medical restrictions, were not able to do so.

In July, 1895, Elder Kneeland was able to organize the Bootooba church, on the Demarara River, which included among its members three aboriginal Indians. A little later a colored brother who was a school-teacher carried the truth to some of the Indian tribes living near the mouth of the Essequibo River, holding his first meeting under the shade of a tree in a forest.

The message was joyfully received by a number of these Indians, children of nature, to whom the Sabbath especially made a powerful appeal as being the sign of the Maker of all things. A small church building was put up, and dedicated in December, 1896. The membership included representatives of four races — South American Indian, Hindu, Negro, and Caucasian.

Not long after the dedication, smallpox broke out in these Indian settlements, and many died. As a result the Indians moved farther up the Essequibo River, and the believing ones settled on Tapacrooma Creek, where they erected a new church building, and held regular Sabbath services.

In 1911, O. E. Davis, then superintendent of Guiana, made an effort to begin work among the Indians of the Mt. Roraima district, the meeting point of Brazil, Venezuela, and Guiana. Brother Davis reached the field with his guide and interpreter, but fell ill of fever and died. The last entry in his journal reads thus: " Just finished establishing a mission when I was taken sick." He was buried by the Indians, who erected a building over his grave. More recently there has been planted the Kimbia Mission, among the Indians living 200 miles up the Berbica River, six tribes having called for teachers.

Trinidad

Mr. and Mrs. A. E. Flowers took up work in Trinidad in 1894, assisted by Mr. and Mrs. F. Grant, who were colporteurs. They found a few believers, to whom the truth had been carried by publications. A minister in another island had purchased a copy of " Patriarchs and Prophets," but not caring for it, had given it to a catechist. He in turn gave it to a third person, who accepted the message it bore, and became one of the first Sabbath keepers in Trinidad. Mr. Flowers and Mr. Grant had labored for only a few months when they were stricken down with the yellow fever, to which the former succumbed on the 29th of July, 1894, and was buried in the Port of Spain cemetery. Mrs. Flowers returned to the States in the autumn, and one year later Elder and Mrs. E. W. Webster arrived in Trinidad and took up the work. On Jan. 15, 1897, Elder Webster had the privilege of dedicating at Couva the first Seventh-day Adventist church building in Trinidad.

Trinidad became the headquarters for the South Caribbean Conference, reaching from British Guiana to the Leeward Islands, and having a membership of over 1,600.

In 1925 this mission had twenty-four churches, with 450 members.

Barbados

In 1895 the believers in Barbados, after two years' patient waiting, gladly welcomed Mr. and Mrs. E. Van Deusen, who spent six years in labor among them. Elder Van Deusen not only revived the work in the Lesser Antilles, but pioneered the way into St. Vincent. He enjoyed the privilege of erecting church buildings in Barbados and St. Vincent, the former being dedicated Sept. 30, 1900, the latter two years later. It was

A. J. HAYSMER AND E. VAN DEUSEN WITH THEIR FAMILIES

while he was laboring in St. Vincent that the supposedly extinct volcano, Soufrière, suddenly became active, sending forth smoke, mud, and lava, so that the north portion of the island was overwhelmed.

Beginning with 1890, D. A. Ball labored for two years on the island. Dr. Charles Cave, a West Indian, did sanitarium work in Bridgetown.

Porto Rico

While the message was being introduced into the English-speaking portions of the field, the Spanish portions remained largely unentered. In 1901, however, Mr. and Mrs. A. M.

REPRESENTATIVES FROM THE WEST INDIAN FIELD

Fischer began work at Mayaguez, on the island of Porto Rico. They had settled down resolutely to the task of learning the language, and had just reached the place where they could actually take up the work, when Mr. Fischer was stricken with the fever, and soon succumbed. Mrs. Fischer continued at her post till the arrival of Mr. and Mrs. B. E. Connerly.

RAFAEL LOPEZ

First Porto Rican to accept the message, and become a worker. He was murdered by bandits in 1922, while itinerating in Venezuela.

Under the fostering care of the latter the periodical *El Centinela* had a considerable circulation, and the little printing office issued a number of tracts and leaflets in the Spanish language. William Steele labored in the field for a long period.

The little band of workers in Porto Rico began to reach out a helping hand to Santo Domingo, introducing tracts and papers into that field as they were able. Their efforts in this direction were seconded by the brethren in Port Antonio, Jamaica, where there came to be a flourishing church of 100 members, some of whom volunteered to go and settle in Santo Domingo, and labor there at their trades as self-supporting missionaries.

A school building was erected in 1920 at Aibonito, Porto Rico, near the center of the island, and there B. A. Wolcott opened the first training school. Churches have been established in a number of the towns.

The Porto Rican Mission, under the superintendency in 1920 of C. V. Achenbach, formerly of the Inca Mission, includes the islands of Porto Rico, Santo Domingo, and the Virgin Islands. Seven churches were organized and four church buildings erected in this field during 1918-22. The Year Book for 1925 credits this mission with thirteen churches, aggregating 462 members.

The first general meeting for the West Indies was held in Kingston, Jamaica, Nov. 5-15, 1897, representatives coming from Barbados, British Guiana, British Honduras, Trinidad, and Bonacca, as well as from the various Jamaican churches. Elder Allen Moon, then president of the Mission Board, was in attendance, and the hearts of all the believers were greatly encouraged. At this meeting A. J. Haysmer was appointed superintendent of the West Indian Mission, with Jamaica as the center. At the time of the meeting an epidemic of yellow fever broke out in Kingston, and a company of our missionaries who had reached Montego Bay, whence the " Herald," our missionary schooner, was to take them to their respective missionary fields, were placed in quarantine, first at Montego Bay and later at Grand Cayman Island, for a total period of fifty-two days. Before they were released Mrs. Webster and her little daughter Mabel, and Mrs. Gosmer died of the dread disease. In 1898 fur-

THE FIRST CAMP-MEETING
Held at Ruatan, Bay Islands, Honduras.

ther re-enforcements were received. D. U. Hale settled in British Guiana, J. O. Johnston in Trinidad, A. Palmquist in the Lesser Antilles, G. F. Enoch and F. I. Richardson in Jamaica. These men with their wives made a very substantial addition to the number of workers.

Taking a view of the Caribbean work as a whole, the years 1901-03 were especially marked by widespread evangelistic labor. In the open air, in rude cocoanut booths, and in a few cases in tents, the pioneers preached the message. The missionary and his wife, with possibly a native worker, formed the entire corps. Missionary funds were low, so that the missionaries sometimes even lacked for the necessaries of life. A tent was a great boon when it could be obtained, so much so that one worker who had a tent with a fly over it, offered another worker the bare fly. It was gladly accepted, and for more than two years that worker went from place to place with no equipment but that fly and a few canvas chairs.

When companies of believers have been raised up, it has been necessary to erect a suitable place of worship, there being no available halls, and the private houses not being suitable for holding meetings. Small as has been the cost of these meeting houses, they have severely taxed the resources of the little companies. In some places it was possible to raise money to purchase the wooden frame, in other places the brethren were too

poor to do this, and had to take axes and saws to the forest, and themselves cut uprights, joists, rafters, etc. Oftentimes it was necessary for this timber to be carried piece by piece on the head for miles over rough mountain trails.

The year 1903 recorded some definite advance steps in the Caribbean field. In that year general meetings attended by W. A. Spicer were held in Jamaica and Trinidad. At the former the Jamaica Conference was organized, with a membership of 1,200. The meeting held in Port of Spain, Trinidad, witnessed the organization of the East Caribbean Conference, with a membership of 850 and a territory extending from St. Thomas in the north to the Guianas in South America.

At these meetings it was decided to issue a monthly periodical of sixteen pages to disseminate the truths of the message. The paper thus started, *The Caribbean Watchman,* was sold from house to house, and soon attained a monthly circulation of upwards of 7,000.

The *Watchman* was at first printed by an outside publishing house; but when it had been issued about a year, in 1904, at the session of the East Caribbean Conference held in Bridgetown, Barbados, it was decided to begin to raise a fund with which to purchase a printing outfit. In a comparatively short time a complete printing plant had been installed. Some years later the Pacific Press established a branch house at Cristobal, Canal Zone, after which all printing interests centered there.

PACIFIC PRESS BRANCH, CRISTOBAL, CANAL ZONE

In 1925 the Caribbean Union Mission reported ninety-two churches, with 3,603 members.

Haiti

Haiti, with a population of about one million, nine tenths of whom are Negroes, the remaining one tenth mulattoes, received the message in the first place through the printed page. In 1879, J. N. Loughborough, then living in Southampton, England, sent a box of books and tracts to Cape Haitien. The box not being consigned to any one in particular, it fell into the hands of the agent of the steamship company, who passed it on to the Episcopal missionary stationed in the city, and he in turn distributed its contents among the other Protestant missions. On the following Sunday the Baptist missionary circulated some of this literature among the people in attendance at his service.

One of these, a young Jamaican by the name of Henri Williams, read the literature given him, and with his wife began to keep the Sabbath. He soon established communication with the publishers, and obtained further supplies, which he industriously circulated, thus preparing the way for the living preacher. In time he was joined by a few other earnest souls, among them a young teacher. W. J. Tanner entered the field in 1905, and his labors were blessed, so that at the General Conference of 1909 he was able to report 109 Seventh-day Adventists in the island, eighty of whom had come from the Roman Catholic Church. Since then the work has continued to grow.

There is a thriving company at Port au Prince, that had an interesting origin. When W. J. Tanner visited the place in 1907, he found a respectable old man who had been observing the Sabbath for nine years, during the first seven of which he supposed that he was the only Christian in the world observing the seventh day. He had discovered the truth simply by reading the Bible. It was not long before he had a company of eight or nine who met with him on the Sabbath to study the Bible and the Sabbath school lessons.

At the beginning of the work Mr. Tanner was greatly hampered for want of Bibles. The people would say, " What is the use of having your tracts and books if we have no Bibles? Sell us Bibles, and then we shall be able to read your literature with profit." Application was accordingly made to the agent of the British and Foreign Bible Society at Port au Prince, and the response was liberal. Not only were Bibles furnished at less than the original cost, but our workers were permitted to give away Bibles to those who could not afford them, and to do so at the expense of the society.

When Elder Tanner's health failed, the work went forward under other leadership. Andre Roth took general charge in 1918. In the same year a church building in Port de Paix was finished; 1920 saw the completion of a church for Cape Haitien, and a year later an advantageously located church property was purchased in Port au Prince, the capital of Haiti.

In 1925 the Haitien Mission was able to report twenty churches, numbering all told 700 members.

Cuba

Cuba has about the same area as the State of Pennsylvania, and a population of over 2,000,000, more than 60 per cent of the native population being colored. Work was begun on the island by Mr. and Mrs. I. E. Moore, who entered Havana as self-supporting nurses in 1904. In the following year E. W. Snyder, formerly of Argentina, began work in Havana. Shortly after his arrival a native pastor invited him to address his congregation on the subject of prophecy. At the close of this meeting, one of the most intelligent members asked permission to come to the house of Brother Snyder for regular Bible readings. On coming to receive his first reading, he saw the chart of the ten commandments hanging on the wall, and was impressed with the fourth. He kept the next Sabbath. Moreover, he began at once to labor for his friends, and to circulate reading matter.

In the same year a church was organized in Havana, with a membership of thirteen. Other centers were shortly opened at different points in the city, and in other parts of the island, two of these being in eastern Cuba. In one of the latter, Omaja, is our first church of American settlers. Local schools have been operated on St. Lucia and San Claudis. In 1914 the first training school was opened at Santa Clara, Mr. and Mrs. S. H. Carnahan being in charge. S. E. Kellman, superintendent, reported seven churches in 1919, with a membership of 232. The mission headquarters is at Matanzas.

In 1925 there were eight churches, with a combined membership of 400.

Earthquake at Kingston, Jamaica

In June, 1906, there was a fourth session of the East Caribbean Conference, held in Port of Spain, Trinidad, at which the General Conference was represented by I. H. Evans. The West Indian Union Conference was organized at this time, and arrangements were made for a union conference gathering to be held at Kingston the following year. At this meeting, which convened on Jan. 11, 1907, there were delegates from St. Thomas, Antigua, Dominica, St. Lucia, Barbados, St. Vincent, Grenada, Tobago, Trinidad, British Guiana, Panama, Costa Rica, Spanish Honduras, British Honduras, Cuba, Haiti, and Porto Rico, as well as a large representation from Jamaica, the whole number of delegates and members in attendance being over 400.

The conference opened encouragingly, but was just getting well under way when, on the third day of the session, occurred the awful earthquake which destroyed practically all the business portion of Kingston and severely damaged the adjacent section. The loss of life was estimated at 1,500, and thousands were injured. One of the delegates, Norman Johnston, the treasurer of the West Indian Union, was among the dead. Under the circumstances it seemed best to transact only the necessary business, and then let the workers return to their homes.

This they did, however, with unabated courage, feeling that the earthquake was one of the calamities for which we may look in the last days, and earnestly praying that it might in some degree awaken the careless and unconverted to a sense of their lost and helpless condition. In fact, the terrible calamity did have the effect of causing some to decide for the truth.

At the time of the earthquake a service was being held in the Kingston church by J. A. Strickland, who gives the following account of the experience:

" We were singing No. 732 in ' Hymns and Tunes.' We had reached the third stanza of the hymn,

> " ' Whate'er events betide,
> Thy will they all perform;
> Safe on Thy breast my head I hide,
> Nor fear the coming storm.'

" Just as we finished singing the last line of that stanza, the earthquake was upon us. It came with a moaning, rumbling sound. The earth trembled, and the church building quivered from foundation to roof; then there were two or three seconds of stillness — a deadly, oppressive stillness, such as I never felt before; then a rushing, roaring, rumbling noise, and the storm was upon us, as a wild beast might spring upon its prey. The building shook with a violence that made it difficult for one to stand on his feet; the floor of the church rose and fell like the waves of the sea; the building swayed back and forth, the walls twisted, as if a mighty giant were trying to wrench off the roof.

" Outside could be heard crashing walls and shrieks of people. The timbers of the church cracked as if the building were at the point of a collapse. Falling plaster filled the place with dust, so that a twilight prevailed. The arched brick entrance gave way, and fell with a crash. When the entrance fell, there was a stampede for the door, the people not knowing what had happened.

" I sprang from the pulpit, and got between the people and the door, and began to sing, ' Praise God, from whom all blessings flow.' In a moment there was perfect order, and all signs of excitement had disappeared, and our people sang that grand old doxology, sang it gloriously, prayer was forgotten, and only praise was offered to God.

" When we had finished singing, we hurriedly examined the steps to see if they were safe for the people to stand upon, and then assisted the congregation out, without hurt or harm."—" *The Advent Message in the Sunny Caribbean*," by George F. Enoch, p. 37.

Mexico

Adventists began their work in Mexico in 1893, when D. T. Jones, Dr. Lillis Wood, Ida Crawford, Ora Osborne, and Mr. and Mrs. Alfred Cooper entered the field. School and sanitarium work was carried on with some success, and a well-equipped sanitarium was put in operation in Guadalajara.

It was some years later that the work began to take on more of an evangelistic character. In the summer of 1897, Prof.

G. W. Caviness, formerly president of Battle Creek College, entered Mexico. He settled at first in Guadalajara, where he gave himself to the study of the Spanish language, and as he became able to undertake it, engaged in literary work. Toward the close of 1899, he and his family, with Mr. and Mrs. S. Marchisio, went to the city of Mexico to open up evangelistic work. They took up their permanent abode in Tacubaya, one of the principal suburbs of Mexico City, and began visiting the people in their homes and introducing the few denominational books then printed in the Spanish language.

G. W. CAVINESS

As they visited the Mexican families, they were asked why they did not start a school where the children might learn English. The request being a general one, the school was opened, and about forty pupils of the higher class were soon in attendance. Through these children entrance was gained into many homes, and Bible readings were held in some of them, bringing out different phases of the advent message. A Sabbath school was started in connection with the school, and was attended by a goodly number of children. A school was also opened later at San Luis Potosi, and a school for native children in La Visnaga.

The publishing work began in 1896 with the issuing of a monthly periodical called *El Mensajero de la Verdad.* When George Brown went to Mexico in 1904, it was decided to open a publishing house of our own. A piece of land was bought, a small building put up, and a printing press installed. From this small beginning there was developed a fairly well-equipped printing office. This did all the necessary work until the opening of the branch of the Pacific Press at Cristobal, Canal Zone, which took over all the publishing interests.

S. Marchisio was the first canvasser for Seventh-day Adventist books in Mexico. He entered the country in the summer of 1891. As there were no Spanish books, he sold the English edition of " The Great Controversy," his field being the city of

Mexico, with only about 2,500 English-speaking people. Later he spent some time at the Guadalajara Sanitarium, returning in 1899 to Mexico City, where he began canvassing for the Spanish "Christ Our Saviour" and "Steps to Christ." In Mixcoac, a suburb of this city, fifty copies of "Christ Our Saviour" that he had sold to various customers, were burned by the Catholic priests. Later he began to work with the periodicals.

BAPTISM IN SOUTHERN MEXICO

Professor Caviness baptizing a native Mexican in the Pacific Ocean.

The canvassing work in Mexico had a new start in 1908, when four young men from Los Angeles, Calif., under the leadership of J. A. P. Green, began to work with Spanish "Coming King." Later other and larger books were sold, and with excellent success. More recently "Patriarchs and Prophets" is having an encouraging sale in the country. Most of our churches in Mexico had their beginning in the circulation of reading matter.

At Salina Cruz, in southern Mexico, a young Spaniard received a copy of the paper and some tracts, and made such good use of the light thus received that a little later there were twenty keeping the Sabbath in that locality. The work thus begun extended to the neighboring districts until there were four ad-

CHAPEL IN VISNAGA, MEXICO

ditional companies, numbering fifty Sabbath keepers. These persons are descended from the Zapotecan Indians. They are superior in some respects to the Mexicans in other parts of the country, and are religiously inclined.

In San Luis Potosi, where Julius Paulson for some years carried on a health food business, two families of tinsmiths began to keep the Sabbath through reading matter placed in their hands, and wrote to G. W. Caviness, requesting further instruction. In due time a company of believers was raised up. As the work grew, it extended into the surrounding country, so that soon there were three other small companies in the vicinity of San Luis Potosi.

WEST CARIBBEAN TRAINING SCHOOL

Colporteurs scattered papers and books also in Torreon, and soon an interest developed there. When Professor Caviness went to the place, he found one whole family keeping the Sabbath. After he had held a series of meetings, a half dozen more accepted the truth. Here also the work has continued to grow.

Toward the close of 1911, H. L. Hawson went to Monterey, in the province of Nuevo Leon. He found some interested persons, and the interest grew rapidly till it became necessary to rent a hall for the meetings. Fifteen persons signed the covenant, and a number of others awaited baptism. Scattered about in other parts of the country were a number of small companies of believers who were sending in appeals for help.

Other places where believers were raised up in these years are Salina Cruz, Tampico, Ameca, and Tuxpan.

J. E. Bond, who became connected with the work in 1920, reported a baptized membership of nearly 450, with eight organized churches.

Prof. G. W. Caviness, prominent in the Mexican work for twenty-five years, passed away in 1923.

In 1923 the republics of Mexico, Guatemala, Salvador, and Honduras, with British Honduras, were organized into the Aztec Union Mission, having by 1925 a total of twenty-one churches and a membership of 1,014.

General Organization of the Caribbean Field

U. Bender, and after him A. J. Haysmer, occupied the position of president when the field as a whole was organized into a union conference. H. H. Cobban was for years secretary-treasurer and manager of the publishing work that developed in the Canal Zone. During the Great War the union organization was discontinued, the island fields eastward being then made into a group known as the East Caribbean Missions, for a time under the oversight of C. E. Knight. The republics of Mexico and North Central America were grouped together as the Mexican and Central American Missions, under the general oversight of R. W. Parmele. The taking over of the publishing work by the Pacific Press branch publishing house has stimulated the sale of the denominational literature all through the field.

In 1922 the Bahama Islands, Mexico, Guatemala, Honduras, Salvador, Nicaragua, Costa Rica, Trinidad, Tobago, British Honduras, Panama, Colombia, Venezuela, together with British, French, and Dutch Guiana, were organized into the Inter-American Division, under the superintendency of Elder E. E. Andross, vice-president of the General Conference for that division.

According to the Year Book of 1925, the Inter-American field had twenty-five organized churches and 8,889 members.

J. W. WESTPHAL

F. H. WESTPHAL

F. W. SPIES

F. A. STAHL

HEADQUARTERS AT FLORIDA, NEAR BUENOS AIRES

CHAPTER XXX

Missions in South America

In the older countries of South America, civilization extends far back. Before the Pilgrim Fathers landed at Plymouth Rock, the universities of Lima and Cordoba were graduating numerous students annually, and one finds today in most of the republics well-equipped universities, and a growing number of normal and high schools. Common schools are gradually spreading, and are becoming general in Argentina. There is among the upper classes a refinement of manners, an elegance of dress and appearance, and a natural politeness not excelled anywhere.

Seventh-day Adventists began evangelical work in South America in the early nineties. About ten years later, in 1902, the continent was divided for administration purposes into three main groups: the River Plate Conference (comprising Argentina, Uruguay, Paraguay), the Brazil Conference, and the West Coast Mission (comprising Chile, Bolivia, Peru, and Ecuador). New conferences were organized and new divisions arranged at the union meeting attended by W. A. Spicer in 1906, and again in 1914, when L. R. Conradi visited the field; but in the present chapter the first broad grouping will be followed.

The narrative of Adventist missions in South America naturally begins with Argentina, the first South American country to be entered by a Seventh-day Adventist minister. Argentina has an area of 1,200,000 square miles, which is five times the size of France, and a population of more than 8,000,000. The great Paraná River, with the estuary Rio de la Plata, which drains a large portion of this territory, is the second largest river in the world. Steamers make regular trips up this magnificent waterway and its branch, the Paraguay, to Cuyabá in Brazil, a distance of 2,300 miles. Argentina is also supplied with more than 20,000 miles of railway lines. Buenos Aires, the third city in size on the American Continent, and the metropolis of South America, is the largest Spanish-speaking city in the world. During a single year 30,000 vessels enter its harbor, coming from all parts of the world.

The climate of Argentina, resembling that of California, and the fertility of its soil, together with its stable government, are attracting immigrants from many parts of the world, and the population is growing rapidly. There is freedom of worship; but Roman Catholicism enjoys the patronage of the state.

The Adventist doctrines first found their way into Argentina by means of the printed page. Late in the eighties a small company of believers were baptized in Lake Neuchâtel, Switzerland, in connection with one of our European general meetings. This being a somewhat unusual occurrence, it was reported in one of the newspapers, and was copied by a French Baptist journal, which fell into the hands of a French colonist living in the province of Santa Fé, Argentina. It so aroused his curiosity as to the doctrines held by Seventh-day Adventists that he sent for the denominational publications, and after a time began to keep the Sabbath. He was joined by some of his neighbors, and for several years these people continued to plead for a Seventh-day Adventist minister.

The message was brought to the province of Entre Rios by German believers from the United States. Some of these, reading an article from the pen of Mrs. E. G. White in the *Hausfreund,* decided to move to South America in order to engage in self-supporting missionary work, and spread a knowledge of the Adventist belief among the Germans on that continent. Toward the close of 1889, they left their homes in Kansas, and reached Argentina early in 1890, settling in the province of Entre Rios, north of Buenos Aires. One of them, a previous resident of the country, had for years carried on a correspondence with friends in South America, who had manifested varying degrees of interest. One man had gone so far as to say that he would begin to observe the Sabbath if he had some one to keep it with him. Four Adventist families in all went to

Argentina at this time. When they reached the country, they met many discouragements; but the one man who had promised to keep the Sabbath as soon as he had a companion did not disappoint them, and in time he became elder of a Seventh-day Adventist church.

The first Adventist workers to enter Argentina were three colporteurs,— E. W. Snyder, C. A. Nowlin, and A. B. Stauffer. They were sent out from America in 1891, and pioneered the way not only in Argentina but also in Brazil, and in the Falkland Islands, where C. A. Nowlin found many willing buyers among the English and Scotch sheep ranchers.

F. H. Westphal went to Argentina in the summer of 1894 to labor in German communities. Landing in Buenos Aires August 18, he started a week later for Crespo, in the province of Entre Rios, where the brethren from Kansas had settled. Crespo is a German-Russian colony, containing about 7,000 families, who came to Argentina forty or fifty years ago. The majority are Roman Catholics, some are Lutherans, and others are Baptists. Quite an interest had sprung up regarding the principles of Seventh-day Adventists, and Elder Westphal found many who were anxious to hear the message. Indeed, a number were already keeping the Sabbath. Some of these had come from Brazil years before, in the hope of finding Baptist people to whom they could join themselves. They became acquainted with the Adventist brethren, and joined them instead.

Shortly before the arrival of Elder Westphal, the whole company was tested on the question of Sabbath keeping. Threshing machines were scarce in those days, and it was the custom for the grain raised in a certain community to be taken to one place, each man being obliged to have his grain threshed when his turn came, or be entirely left out. Every day in the week, Sunday included, was used for threshing. The time for the threshing of the grain of the Adventist brethren in two communities fell on the same Sabbath. The brethren were told that if they did not allow their grain to be threshed on that day, it would not be threshed at all; but they quietly adhered to their position that the work should not be done on the Lord's Sabbath. Consequently both threshing machines lay idle on the Sabbath day, and a deep impression was made throughout the neighborhood. The grain of these brethren was not left unthreshed either. After three weeks' labor among this people, Elder Westphal was able to organize a church of thirty-six members, this being the first Seventh-day Adventist church in South America.

36

He next visited San Cristobal, in the province of Santa Fé. The interest in this place had sprung up through the circulation of reading matter. Three brothers and a sister, members of a family of ten, passed through a period of great spiritual darkness, from which they were delivered by earnest prayer. About this time they had an opportunity to read " The Great Controversy." It brought them great spiritual comfort, and they embraced the views of Seventh-day Adventists, and gave their lives to the advancement of the message. There being no streams in this neighborhood, the brethren dug a hole in the ground and filled it with water for the baptism.

From San Cristobal Elder Westphal went to Esperanza, where he met for the first time Lionel Brooking, one of the first Sabbath keepers in Argentina, who was then canvassing for our books. A little later in the year, having learned of a company of inquirers at San Javier, he went to visit them, traveling by boat and stage. In the course of this journey he spent his first night in a native hut, which consisted of one room and a kind of straw-covered shed in front. From the ceiling hung a chain supporting a kettle of water over the fire. After the water became sufficiently hot, a gourd-like cup, into which had been put a quantity of Paraguay tea, was filled with water, and passed around from one to another, being drunk through a tube. When Mr. Westphal allowed the cup to pass by him, and called instead for a drink of plain hot water, the people were so surprised that they could not refrain from comment. Even after he had gone to his bed, which consisted of a board beside the fire with a saddle for his pillow, the people laughed aloud and continually repeated the words, *"Agua caliente"* (Hot water).

On Sept. 10, 1895, Elder Westphal began the first series of tent-meetings in Argentina, the services being held at Diamante. The tent was taken down after a week, but the meetings were continued in various neighborhoods, and resulted in the conversion of fourteen.

Early in October, 1896, the tent was pitched in the province of Entre Rios for a general meeting; but after the meeting had been in progress for only one day, the police issued a decree prohibiting worship in the tent. Later, permission was given to continue the services, but the ministers were forbidden to administer baptism. Nevertheless, when Sabbath morning came and six persons presented themselves for baptism, the brethren resolved to go forward with the rite. As they were about to go into the water, they were informed that if they did so they would be taken to the chief of police in Diamante. The baptism was performed, and they were conveyed to the chief, who asked them many questions. The brethren answered these questions, and said that they would obey the magistrate in all civil matters; but in questions of religion and conscience, they must obey God rather than man. The chief of police, after listening attentively to all they had to say, told them that they were right, and if they desired to hold such meetings again, he would see that they were protected.

N. Z. Town, O. Oppegard, and Lucy Post were among the pioneer laborers in this country. J. Vuilleumier, who joined

A GROUP OF PIONEERS

F. H. Westphal   J. Vuilleumier   O. Oppegard   E. W. Snyder   N. Z. Town

the corps of workers in 1895, found his knowledge of several languages very helpful. In sixteen places where he held public meetings, he used French; in nine, German; in six, Spanish; and in two, English.

In August, 1898, a general meeting was held in the province of Entre Rios, the services being conducted in a tent centrally located for all living in that province. The weather was somewhat rainy to begin with, but the first Sabbath dawned clear and bright, and wagon loads of the brethren and sisters began to arrive from all directions. The three organized churches in the province were well represented, some members having driven a long way to reach the place. The public speaking was done by F. H. Westphal and J. A. Leland.

One of the matters that received attention at this meeting was the starting of a school to train laborers. A brother had offered forty acres of good land at Puiggari, near Diamante, for such an institution. At this meeting it was decided to accept his offer, and steps were taken toward erecting proper buildings. The matter was brought to a head at a general meeting held at Diamante in 1899, when a young man who had come all the way from Uruguay presented himself as a student. It was ascertained that he had closed out a prosperous business in order to enter school and prepare for a part in God's work. Such an appeal could not be resisted. The brethren decided that they must have a school, and set about the matter energetically.

RIVER PLATE ACADEMY, ARGENTINA, SOUTH AMERICA
Bird's-eye view from the roof of the sanitarium.

Elder and Mrs. N. Z. Town had already conducted two short terms of school in their own house in Las Tunas, province of Santa Fé. Six young men attended the first term of two months, studying the common branches as well as the Bible, and also receiving some special instruction in canvassing. When the first term closed, they went into the field and did successful work in introducing the denominational books.

The new building having been erected, the school opened in April, 1890, with an attendance of fifteen, N. Z. Town and J. A. Leland, with their wives, being in charge. The institution which had this humble beginning is known as the River Plate Junior College. New buildings have been added from time to time, and the attendance has steadily grown. A large number of efficient laborers have been trained in this school. W. C. John was principal for a time. Later H. U. Stevens filled the position for a number of years before taking the educational secretaryship of the South American Division. He was succeeded by Prof. J. S. Marshall.

While the school has had many earnest, consecrated students, special interest attaches to one young man, Pedro Kalbermatter. For years Pedro desired to enter the training school in Entre Rios, in order to prepare himself for some branch of the work; but his father, one of the wealthiest cattle men in the country, at first offered serious objections. At length the way opened for the young man to begin school, and with great rejoicing he entered upon his studies. But he had hardly begun when word came that he must present himself for military duty. He answered the call, but with the determination to be true to the Sabbath. For a few weeks he was left free on that day, but soon the test came. When he refused to work on the Sabbath, he was whipped till too weak to stand. Later he gained the consent of the army officials to keep the Sabbath on condition that he would work on Sunday.

He had an interesting experience at his last trial previous to being allowed to keep the Sabbath. The captain had given him permission to state his reasons for refusing to work on the Sabbath before the head officials of the army. He supposed he was to meet only two or three; but was surprised to find a room full, and among them a priest. Hard questions were asked him; but with divine help he answered them all, the priest completely failing in his efforts to confuse him. Finally Brother Kalbermatter asked the priest to produce from the Bible one single command for the observance of Sunday as the Sabbath. The reply was that there was no such command, but that the day was changed by the authority of the Roman Catholic Church.[1]

The Publishing Work

As already stated, E. W. Snyder, A. B. Stauffer, and C. A. Nowlin were the pioneers in the canvassing work in South America. In December, 1891, they arrived at Montevideo; but learning that they would be obliged to pay an import duty on books sent to that port, they decided finally to settle in Buenos Aires and begin work in Argentina. They carried forward the work there with diligence and earnestness, selling books principally among the English, German, and French people, and the seed thus sown has borne abundant fruit. Two persons soon began to keep the Sabbath in Buenos Aires, both of whom later became laborers, one of them undertaking ship missionary work in London, the other, Lionel Brooking, laboring as a colporteur

---

[1] As a result of the experience of Brother Kalbermatter, a change was made in the Argentine law, by which Seventh-day Adventist young men may be exempt from military service on the Sabbath.

in Argentina, chiefly among the French Waldensian settlements. He later took up work in England.

E. W. Snyder sold some books in Montevideo to a German lady, who became an Adventist, and was the means of leading others to a knowledge of the message. At San Cristobal, in Santa Fé, a few persons began to keep the Sabbath as the result of reading books delivered by A. B. Stauffer. C. A. Nowlin labored for a time in the Falkland Islands and in Chile, where he also saw results of his efforts.

The bookmen have often pioneered the way most effectively for the minister. One of our colporteurs, coming across a large Roman Catholic settlement in Ripamonte, in the province of Santa Fé, was unable to take any orders; but he found one man who was willing to accept a copy of " The Great Controversy " as a loan. After reading the book, the man, with his family, began to keep the Sabbath. They were persecuted, but remained firm.

Some time afterward F. H. Westphal visited them. A meeting was held in the neighborhood on Friday evening, after which Elder Westphal returned to this man's house. There were five grown-up sons, besides smaller children. The men lighted their pipes and gathered around the table, telling the minister how deeply they were interested in the truths he had come to explain more fully. The room was soon filled with tobacco smoke, almost to suffocation. The next morning the minister spoke on some of the principles of health reform, and endeavored to show the importance of keeping pure the bodies which are the temples of the Holy Ghost. When he came back to the house in the evening, he found that all the pipes and tobacco had been gathered together in a bundle and hung up in the house. The father explained that one of the smaller children had said it was something connected with evil, and therefore it should be hanged. In the same whole-hearted way these sincere truth lovers accepted the principle of tithe paying and other truths connected with the message.

The first Adventist periodical printed in Spanish, under the name *El Faro* (The Lighthouse), began to be issued from Buenos Aires in July, 1897. A paper was started also in Chile, but the two were finally combined to make one strong periodical, *Las Señales de los Tiempos* (The Signs of the Times), published in Buenos Aires. The name was later changed to *El Atalaya* (The Watchman). In 1905 a cylinder press was purchased and installed in new premises erected in Florida, a suburb of Buenos Aires. About the same time a large new cylinder press was installed and a substantial addition made to the building. In the general plan of having each of our North American publishing houses take a special interest in the publishing work of a foreign field, South America was assigned to the Southern Publishing Association, the manager of which accordingly visited Buenos Aires in 1921, and planned with the brethren there for the advancement of the work.

Medical Work

The first Seventh-day Adventist physician to enter South America was Dr. R. H. Habenicht, who arrived at the close of 1901, and settled with his family in the vicinity of the mission

THE SANITARIUM IN ARGENTINA

school in the province of Entre Rios, Argentina. He began work at once, his wife assisting him. Being the only medical missionary workers in a large district, they led a very strenuous life, sometimes scarcely going to bed for a whole week. The doctor might travel sixty miles in a wagon to see a patient out in the country, and on returning home find ten wagons with patients waiting for him. Among them might be a man wanting to take him fifty miles off in another direction to prescribe for a sick wife.

The doctor's home was at first used to receive the people; but during the summer vacation, the school building was turned into a sanitarium, and within ten days every room was filled. Not having nurses to assist them, Dr. Habenicht and his wife had to give the treatments themselves, and the conditions under which the work had to be done added greatly to the labor.

DELEGATES AT THE SOUTH AMERICAN DIVISION SESSION, 1920, BUENOS AIRES, ARGENTINA

Nevertheless the work prospered, a large number of sick people being helped to a good recovery.

In 1908 Dr. Habenicht was using a part of the school building as a hospital. A year later a sanitarium building was erected, and the sick people filled the rooms even before windows and doors had been placed. Dr. G. B. Replogle joined the staff in 1910, and a nurses' training school was started. From small beginnings there has developed a fully equipped medical and surgical sanitarium, with a staff of four physicians and a strong nurses' training school.

Especially in the early days, opportunities were continually offering themselves for combining evangelical with medical work. One day Dr. Habenicht was called upon to prescribe for a man suffering with malaria. When the treatment had been administered, fourteen persons being there to witness it, the doctor suggested holding a little meeting. The owner of the house having given his consent, the thirty-second psalm was read, followed by a short talk on the goodness of God and His willingness to forgive sins. When the meeting was over, the doctor said he should be glad to visit any other sick people or to hold Bible studies with any interested persons. From that moment his hands were more than full in that neighborhood. The people came from all quarters. Meetings were held nightly, and the house and the yard were full to overflowing. Before leaving the place, he was able to organize a church of thirty-two members.

The Work in General

It was providential that our work in South America had its beginning in Argentina. The message made steady progress there from the first, and that field became in some measure a base of supplies for the Spanish-speaking part of South America. Argentina is now divided into three parts, the North Argentine Conference, with 946 members; the Buenos Aires Conference, with 277 members; the Central Argentine Mission, with 118 members; besides the small Mendoza Mission, consisting of thirty-six members, and the Magellan Mission, which is the most southern Seventh-day Adventist church in the world, with nineteen members.

The Alto Parana Mission

Paraguay and the northern part of Argentina (along the Paraguay and Paraná Rivers) form the Upper Paraná Mission. Elder and Mrs. E. W. Snyder went to labor in Asuncion, the capital of Paraguay, in 1898, finding a few persons who had accepted the message through reading. At Hohenau, in southern Paraguay, the believers erected a church building in 1914, and opened a school. In the same year Pedro M. Brouchy and his wife, who had been trained at the Argentine Sanitarium, opened treatment-rooms in Corrientes. Later Mateo Leites engaged in medical missionary work. Julio Ernst led out in evangelistic effort in this mission field. The work has gone forward steadily but slowly. In 1923 there were two ordained ministers, with 460 members in this mission.

CHURCH AT NUEVA HELVECIA, URUGUAY

Uruguay

About 1895 work was begun among the Waldenses and Spanish-speaking people of Uruguay, some of whom began to keep the Sabbath. F. H. Westphal held some meetings in Colonia Suiza, as a result of which a church was established there.

Meda Kerr and Frances Brockman, medical missionaries, entered Montevideo in 1910. They were followed a year later by F. L. Perry, formerly of Peru, who as superintendent of Uruguay opened mission headquarters in Montevideo, where somewhat later a church was established. In 1923 the superintendent, C. E. Krieghoff, reported companies of believers in Colonia, San Pedro, Miguelete, and in the Russian colony of

Porvenir, besides the original church in Colonia Suiza, to the number of 219.

The Magellan Mission

In 1914 A. G. Nelson began evangelistic work at Punta Arenas, on the Strait of Magellan, where there had been one lone Sabbath keeper for some time. Six years later, on account of his wife's health, he had to move northward, and settled in Chubut. The work on the strait was continued by John Wede-

T. H. DAVIS

F. W. BISHOP

kamper. In Tierra del Fuego, across the strait, some effort has been put forth, and there are individuals here and there who are studying the message.

Chile

T. H. Davis and F. W. Bishop, colporteurs, were the pioneer workers in Chile, beginning their efforts in 1894. A year later Elder G. H. Baber was sent to the field to take up evangelistic work. E. W. Thomann accepted the Adventist views in Santiago, and helped in the translating and getting out of literature. A press was secured, and a Spanish paper started in 1900, called *Las Señales de los Tiempos,* which was later united with the Argentine paper and transferred to the headquarters at

Florida in Argentina. Valparaiso was made the publishing headquarters. A. R. Ogden and H. F. Ketring entered Chile in 1902, and in 1904 F. H. Westphal and William Steele.

Chile was organized as a conference in April, 1907, with F. H. Westphal as president. At the time of the Valparaiso earthquake, Aug. 18, 1906, the building rented for the printing office was wrecked and the stock of books burned. In the following year publishing headquarters of our own were secured in Espejo, near Santiago. Churches have been raised up in Valparaiso, Santiago, Concepcion, and other places. There are a number of isolated believers. Land was secured for a school

TRAINING SCHOOL IN CHILI

in Pua, southern Chile, in 1902, a three-story frame building being erected. Later another building was added. This school was moved from Pua to Chillan, a city of 50,000 inhabitants, in 1921. In its new location the institution occupies a farm containing 160 acres of irrigated land. In 1923 the president of the Chile Conference, W. E. Hancock, reported a total membership of 797.

Brazil

Brazil, the largest of the South American republics, contains within its borders about half of the continent, and has a population of more than 22,000,000, not including a million or more aboriginal Indians.

At the beginning of its history, there was a fair prospect that Protestantism would become the dominant religion. A colony of French Huguenots settled along the bay, opposite the city now known as Rio de Janeiro; and in Pernambuco, in the north, the Dutch had for many years a firm foothold. Had these people succeeded in establishing themselves, the history of Brazil might have been different. But the Portuguese finally conquered the whole country, and with them came the Jesuits, and a whole train of evils, from which the country has suffered during these four centuries.

The people of Brazil spring from three main stocks,— white, Negro, and Indian. Race distinctions are practically nonexistent. The Portuguese language is spoken.

Periodicals first brought the advent message to Brazil. One of our German papers, probably handed to a sea captain in Southampton by a ship missionary, found its way to San Francisco, Calif., and thence to Brusque, in Brazil. There it fell into the hands of a school-teacher who was given to drink. He saw on one of its pages a notice to the effect that further copies would be sent free of charge to persons desiring to read them, and wrote a letter to the editor, requesting such copies. Papers then began to be sent regularly, and the man sold them in order to get money for more drink. But the people read them, and some were convinced of the truth. These corresponded with the brethren at headquarters, and years afterward F. H. Westphal visited Brusque. He remained there only a week; but before leaving he was able to organize a church of twenty-three members. This was the first Seventh-day Adventist church organized in the great republic of Brazil.

São Paulo, the first state in Brazil to receive personal labor from our missionaries, was visited by colporteurs in 1893. Two years later F. H. Westphal, of Argentina, spent some time in labor there, preaching in several towns, and baptizing those who had embraced the message. In the spring of 1896, H. F. Graf met with and encouraged those already in the faith, and baptized several new converts. A year later F. W. Spies, who had been called from Germany, visited the various companies, when still others united with them.

In 1894 W. H. Thurston had begun work in Rio de Janeiro, where he opened a book depository. Espirito Santo was entered by colporteurs in 1894, and in 1896 H. F. Graf organized there a church of twenty-three. The brethren were then without a visit from a minister for fifteen months. Meanwhile, the church elder had died, and the brethren had been subjected to severe persecution. Nevertheless, the cause prospered, and at the time of the second visit twenty-three additional persons were awaiting baptism.

In 1897 F. W. Spies entered the colony of Santa Isabel, in the same state, where the second church in the province was organized. Some time later, the brethren of the Santa Maria church purchased sixty-five acres of land and suitable buildings for the establishment of a church school, which prospered from the beginning.

The province of Minas Geraes was entered by Elder Spies in 1896. During his first day at Theophilo Ottoni, nineteen were baptized, and additions were made later. Here also a church school was started.

At meetings held in Brazil following the organization in 1906 of the South American Union, the Rio Grande Conference was formed, with H. F. Graf as president; and the Santa Catharina and Paraná Conference, with W. Ehlers as president. The province of São Paulo was made into a mission field, with E. Hoelzle for superintendent. The remainder of Brazil northward constituted the North Brazil Mission.

In 1907 F. W. Spies entered Bahia, lying north of Rio de Janeiro, where he baptized a number of believers. These persons had had the knowledge of the true Sabbath brought to them by a man who had discovered the truth by his own study of the Bible, not knowing there were any other Sabbath keepers in the world.

Opposition of a very determined kind has been encountered in parts of Brazil. In the state of Santa Catharina, a man came into a meeting conducted by José Linderman, cut down the hanging lamps with one sweep of his sword, and laid open the evangelist's cheek with another. The final result was the raising up of a good company of believers, one large landholder sending all his tenants to the meetings.

In 1913 and 1914 churches were built in Curityba, the capital of the state of Paraná, and in Teixeria Soares. From 1912 onward mission work has been carried forward in the city of São Paulo. In 1914 tent-meetings were held in the town of Santo Amaro, a suburb of São Paulo. The priests warned the people to stay away, but the effort closed with a company of twenty-six believers and the erection of a church building. In the German-Brazilian colony of Novo-Europa, lying in the interior of São Paulo, meetings were held by J. H. Boehm in 1913-14, a company of Sabbath keepers being raised up and a church built.

In 1925 Brazil had two union conferences,— East Brazil and South Brazil,— with a total of sixty-two churches and 4,156 members.

The Educational Work

For a time a private school was conducted at Curityba in the state of Santa Catharina. Later the interests of this institution were transferred to the Brusque school in the same state, where a building was erected. A school for the southern portion of the field was established at Taquara in the state of Rio Grande do Sul. John Lipke pioneered the work of founding the Brazilian Seminary at Santo Amaro, near São Paulo, where he was later succeeded by T. W. Steen. This is the training center for our work in Brazil.

THE BRAZIL PUBLISHING HOUSE

The Publishing Work

The pioneers of the message in Brazil were the canvassers. A. B. Stauffer went from Buenos Aires to Brazil in 1892, and later was joined by E. W. Snyder, who had been laboring in Argentina. Mr. Stauffer put in many years of faithful work. Midway in the nineties the brothers Albert and Fred Berger entered the field. They usually had two mules each, one to ride and one for carrying books and Bibles. At some seasons of the year they would travel day after day through rain and mud, meeting not a little opposition. They often slept in the woods, for the people whom they were trying to help would turn them away with cursing. More than once they were severely whipped, but they went on their way rejoicing. Many received them with gladness, and they had blessed times in reading the Bible with such and imparting to them a knowledge of its vital truths.

At the beginning there were no Adventist publications in Portuguese; so the work had to be done largely among the German-speaking people. Efforts were made to procure Portuguese literature, and it was found to be necessary to have our own printing office. In 1904 John Lipke, while in the United States, obtained the gift of a printing press and other equipment. But the first location of the press at Taquara, in Rio Grande do Sul, the extreme southern part of Brazil, was not well adapted for a publishing center. Hence in August, 1907, the office was moved to São Bernardo, in São Paulo, where suitable property was bought and has since been enlarged. A new and larger press was purchased, also a gasoline motor and machinery for the bindery. This equipment, together with a press donated by the Hamburg Publishing House, and a small one given by Emmanuel Missionary College, afforded the necessary facilities for printing a number of valuable publications, among them " Steps to Christ," " His Glorious Appearing," and " Christ Our Saviour." Later the large subscription books were published, and the colporteur work was put on a strong footing.

Bolivia

Bolivia, the country of third largest area in South America, has a population of about 2,500,000, three fourths of whom are Indians. There is still much unexplored territory, occupied only by aborigines. Although the masses are ignorant and fanatical, congress has granted religious liberty.

But little has been done to proclaim the third angel's message. A colporteur by the name of Pereiro, from Chile, made several visits, but severe persecution prevented his doing much for the people. Once he was sentenced to death, but escaped.

When traveling from Cochabamba to Oruro, a worker spent the night at a small place called Tapacari. He tried to distribute some papers, but found it dangerous to do so. On the following morning, accordingly, rising before daylight, he slipped papers under the doors of the houses in the principal streets, where he thought the people would probably be able to read. Having done this, he returned to his lodgings, mounted his mule, and rode away; but before he could get out of the town, a hundred or more people carrying copies of the papers, which they were tearing to pieces with many threatening demonstrations, set upon him and his driver, throwing stones and dirt.

When Bolivia was set apart as a separate mission field in 1907, E. W. Thomann, who had made a tour of the leading cities in the interest of *Las Señales de los Tiempos* some years before, and who consequently felt a special interest in the people of that republic, volunteered to make it his field of labor, and was for some years the superintendent and only laborer, meanwhile acting also as editor of the west coast missionary paper, and doing considerable work as translator. He settled at Cochabamba, where he labored not only for the Spanish people, but also, by means of teachers and a duplicating machine, for the Quichua and Aymara Indians.

Work in La Paz, the capital, was begun by Mr. and Mrs. F. A. Stahl in 1909. They did nursing in European families, and began dispensary work for the Indians. Ignacio Kalbermatter and Claire Wightman, a nurse, also labored in La Paz. O. H. Schulz traveled over a wide area, selling books and papers. The first Sabbath keeper was reported in 1912. W. R. Pohle took the superintendency in 1914, and began to hold regular meetings in La Paz. By 1920 it was possible to report a church of twenty-five members in that city.

Reid S. Shepard, who was connected for a time with the mission at Lake Titicaca, began work in 1920 for the Indians at Rosario in Bolivia, south of the lake. An assistant opened an outstation in Iquiaca, twenty miles from La Paz.

Ecuador

Ecuador takes its name from being located on the equator. During the winter, or rainy season, the weather is hot and sultry, and yellow fever and the plague are more or less common, thousands of people dying of these diseases. The climate of the great plateaus of the interior is generally healthful; but the people live under very insanitary conditions, causing disease to be widely prevalent. One rarely meets a person, young or old, who does not smoke cigarettes and use intoxicating drinks.

Our work in Ecuador began in November, 1904, when T. H. Davis, of California, who had started the canvassing work in Chile, settled at Guayaquil, and began the sale of our literature. He visited all but two of the provinces along the coast, and sold Adventist literature in all the towns along the Guayaquil and Quito Railway. In 1905 he was joined by G. W. Casebeer, who, however, was not able to do aggressive work until he had learned the language. In 1907 two persons were baptized, one of them being a young man of good education belonging to one of the principal families of Quito. He entered our training school in Argentina.

37

The conditions under which the work must be carried on in Ecuador were vividly set forth in the following account (slightly adapted), given by G. W. Casebeer of his first visit, in company with his wife and T. H. Davis, to a small town in southern Ecuador which had never before been entered by a Protestant missionary. They took with them a large supply of Bibles and other books. As they began to dispose of these early in the morning, the priests prohibited the sale. He says:

" Nevertheless the work was continued. People bought readily, and in one forenoon the entire stock was exhausted. About eleven o'clock there was an earthquake; people rushed out into the streets praying to their saints for help; and soon the church bells began to ring, calling the people to meeting. The priests told the people that God was beginning to pour out His judgments upon them for having received Protestant missionaries and bought their literature, and that if they did not get rid of us immediately, the Lord would continue His judgments upon them, perhaps destroy them entirely. The fanatical mob soon demanded that we be sent out of the hotel where we were staying, and the owner of the hotel came to us and told us that we must leave immediately. We had made the acquaintance of the mayor of the place, who promised to help us in case of need, so we applied to him, and he persuaded the owner of the hotel to let us stay till the next day. As the next day was Sabbath, we did not wish to leave, so remained in the town three days longer.

" That night, as we studied our Sabbath school lesson by candlelight, with doors and windows open, suddenly there came a shower of stones, brick, and tiles into the room where we were sitting. We shut the windows and doors. Then we suddenly heard a rush on the stairway, and a number of young men came rushing up the steps. We supposed that they were part of the mob come to do us violence, but they promised to protect us with their lives, and offered their homes as a place of refuge if we were not allowed to remain in the hotel. A number of the principal citizens of the place soon appeared, lamenting the actions of their fellow citizens, and offering us protection. The priests commanded the people to burn all the literature that they had received within three days, or else they would be excommunicated from the church. That night the town was lighted up with burning Bibles.

" Soon after leaving this place, the citizens sent word to us by the mayor, whom we met in another town, that they wanted us to return, for they desired to hear more of the message which we preached and to buy more Bibles, as some of them had destroyed theirs. They also said that the two priests who had worked against us had suddenly been stricken with a dreadful disease, and that there was no one there to molest us."

At the union conference in March, 1908, G. W. Casebeer was requested to take charge of the training school at Pua, and William Steele was sent to take up work in Ecuador, accompanied by a young Chilean colporteur. After considerable difficulty a theater was obtained in Ambato, and a short series of meetings held. The attendance ranged from fifty to one hundred fifty. Violence was attempted several times. The theater was stoned, and the workers were attacked on their way home and severely beaten by the mob.

When William Steele was obliged to leave, owing to his wife's failing health, he was succeeded by W. W. Wheeler, who was later joined by Mr. and Mrs. John Osborne, nurses. In 1912 Mr. Wheeler was called to the school in Argentina, and S. Mangold, of that field, took his place. Within a few months Mrs. Mangold died of yellow fever, which made it necessary for the

FIRST HOME OF ORLEY FORD, COTTA MISSION

husband to leave the field with his children. He was succeeded by Mr. and Mrs. C. E. Knight, of Argentina.

Progress has been very slow from the beginning. J. D. Lorenz, superintendent, reported twenty-four members in 1919.

Peru

Peru has 1,400 miles of coast line, and 6,000 miles of navigable rivers. The population is somewhat under 5,000,000.

Our work began in 1905, when the South Dakota Conference volunteered to support a laborer in Peru. F. L. Perry was sent to the field, and found a few scattered Sabbath keepers. After four years' work he was able to report one organized church, four companies, and some isolated believers.

The missionary paper, *El Atalaya,* has been circulated in all parts of the country, and frequently letters are received, asking for further instruction in the truth. The people respond liberally to the efforts put forth, but the opposition is often bitter.

When F. L. Perry visited Puno, on the shore of Lake Titicaca, he found the way open before him as a result of the papers which had preceded him, and in a very few days fifteen adults had decided to keep the Sabbath. From Puno the light spread out through a valley with a population of 40,000 Indians.

One native colporteur had been at work from the beginning. Early in 1909 a canvassers' institute was held, attended by eight prospective workers. At the beginning of the institute two young men who had studied for the priesthood began to observe the Sabbath. They also entered the work. There is a tract

RECEPTION TO MISSIONARY VISITORS

society depository at Lima. Here also H. B. Lundquist opened in 1919 a training school for Peruvian workers.

There are believers in the coast towns. Arequipa, with a moderate altitude, is situated on the railroad running up to Lake Titicaca. In this halfway-up city we have a resthome where workers on Lake Titicaca spend a few weeks from time to time recovering from the effects of the excessively high altitudes of the lake region.

In 1919 Peru reported a membership of 330; in 1923, there were 411 members.

The Lake Titicaca Indian Missions

The interest steadily increased among the Indians of Lake Titicaca, and Mr. and Mrs. F. A. Stahl, who had recently begun work in La Paz, Bolivia, were asked in 1910 to give half their time to the Indians of Peru. From 1911 onward they gave practically all their time to that work. The opposition was intense at times. Ecclesiastical authorities cursed the Adventist work, and ordered it destroyed, but the interest steadily grew. In 1913 six of the Indian brethren were put in jail; but investigation by the government resulted in greater favor and less bitter local prejudice.

In the same year mission headquarters and school and dispensary buildings were completed at Plateria, the natives taking hold with a will. The school had to be closed temporarily, however, because the teacher, Bartoleme Rojas, who had come from Argentina, had no Peruvian certificate. He passed his examinations, however, and in 1914 the school was reopened with

PLATERIA MISSION

eighty-three students, the first school ever conducted for these Indians. The schoolroom had to be doubled in size to accommodate the growing number of pupils, and the Indian brethren cheerfully did the work gratis, transporting lumber and other materials on their donkeys from Puno, the railway station, over twenty miles distant.

The educational work thus well begun at Plateria grew by leaps and bounds. In 1918 there were nineteen mission schools; by the end of 1919 there were forty-six primary schools in operation, forty-five of which were taught by Indian teachers trained at Plateria.

This work in behalf of the Inca Indians, founded by F. A. Stahl, has attracted wide attention. Bishop Oldham, of the Methodist Church, referred to it in the *Missionary Review of the World* as the most remarkable thing that he had seen in South America. A mining man said he couldn't understand what had got hold of these Indians, but added, " I do know that they are better Indians than before. They do not quarrel and fight, and are more industrious, and look cleaner and happier." Members of the Peruvian Senate have strongly commended the work, and expressed their desire for its extension into all parts of Peru as soon as possible.

Elder Stahl remained in the Indian work around Lake Titicaca until his health became so impaired by the high altitude that he was compelled to leave that field. But instead of accepting honorable retirement, he urged before the Mission Board that he be permitted to open a new work, that for the Chuncho Indians, a savage tribe on the Perene River, one of the tributaries of the Amazon. Here at a lower altitude he has made a

PLATERIA INDIAN CHURCH

beginning that bids fair to develop into a no less successful work than that done among the Aymara and Quichua Indians in the Titicaca region.

The Inca Union Mission

In recent years the republics of Peru, Ecuador, and Bolivia have been grouped together to form the Inca Union Mission. The chief interest in this union naturally centers in the work in behalf of the Indians, which has been dealt with briefly in the preceding pages. The reported membership of the entire union in 1917 was 1,128. At the close of 1921 it had risen to 3,716, as reported by the superintendent, E. F. Peterson. In the Lake Titicaca region alone 2,693 have received baptism in these four years, nearly a thousand of them in 1921. There is one church with a membership of 700, and another with over 500. The union has eleven church buildings. It is not an uncommon thing on special occasions to have an audience of a thousand or more. In 1923, Superintendent H. U. Stevens reported a membership of 4,427. Of this number 3,736 were in the Lake Titicaca Mission.

From the beginning, the medical missionary work has been a prominent feature. There is one physician and surgeon, and practically all the workers have had training as nurses.

BAPTISM OF INDIANS

W. W. PRESCOTT

UNION COLLEGE, NEAR LINCOLN, NEBRASKA

CHAPTER XXXI

Growth of the Health and Educational Work

Medical Missions

THE growth of our work abroad, which has occupied the attention in the foregoing chapters, was accompanied by a corresponding growth in the home conferences, and in the various institutions of the denomination. The organization of the American Health and Temperance Association, briefly referred to in the closing paragraphs of the chapter on Health and Temperance, met with general approval, and many responded enthusiastically to the calls it made upon their time and energies.

The society circulated three pledges, one calling for abstention from alcoholic drinks, the second excluding tobacco in all forms, and the third, tea, coffee, and other narcotics. Most of the members signed the third, known as the teetotal pledge.

The work of propaganda was carried on by means of lectures and institutes and the circulation of health literature, including the monthly magazine *Good Health,* books, pamphlets, and tracts, and a Health Almanac, which appeared annually for a number of years.

The association was maintained until 1893, when it was merged into a similar organization known as the Seventh-day Adventist Medical Missionary and Benevolent Association, which was intended to cover the activities of the original society, and in addition to provide for carrying on a line of benevolent work on behalf of the poor and unfortunate. The constituency of the association consisted of the members of the General Conference Committee, the presidents of conferences, all persons contributing $1,000 or more to the funds of the association, and ten persons to be elected biennially by the General Conference assembled. The management of the work was vested in a board of nine trustees.

Among the institutions which the new organization was soon called to administer was the James White Memorial Home for the aged and the Haskell Memorial Home for orphans. The first-named institution was founded by the denomination; the orphans' home, costing $30,000, was built with money donated by Mrs. C. E. Haskell, of Chicago, as a memorial to her deceased husband. Both were maintained at denominational expense, to which the Battle Creek Sanitarium contributed.

The year 1893, which witnessed the building of the Haskell Home, also marked the opening of the medical mission and dispensary at Chicago. A young woman who had been a patient at the Battle Creek Sanitarium expressed on her deathbed appreciation of what had been done for her, and exacted from her father the promise that he would employ a sanitarium nurse to work among the poor of Chicago. The nurse thus appointed began her work in 1892, and was presently joined by other sanitarium nurses, who volunteered to devote several weeks of their time to practical house-to-house effort.

It was to follow up the work thus begun that a medical mission was established at 40 Custom House Place, which furnished wholesome food at the cost of one cent a dish, and a clean bed and warm bath, with laundry privileges, for ten cents. The patronage increased till hundreds of persons were fed daily, and the sleeping accommodations were inadequate to meet the demand. In the summer of 1896 the mission was moved to an adjoining church which had been fitted up as a lodging house. It was thoroughly cleaned and renovated throughout, and after the necessary alterations had been effected, it proved a commodious home for the many activities of the mission. Religious services were held nightly at this mission, and many men hopelessly stranded in the great city were brought to a saving knowledge of the gospel. In course of time missions of a similar character were opened in other large cities of the country.

Meanwhile there was growing up in many of the churches a deep interest in the work of these city missions, which was manifesting itself in various ways. Christian help bands were organized, the members of which took a special interest in the sick poor in their own neighborhood, and in many cases opened their homes to the rescued men who had made a new start in connection with some of the city missions, or for a neglected child, or a young woman who had strayed from the path of virtue, and wished to begin life over again. The city missions also received financial support from the members of the bands, some of whom would give the proceeds of a garden or a portion of the farm crops, or would raise money in other ways to support the work.

Along with this increased devotion to philanthropic work there was gradually developing in the denomination a new interest in the health principles as practised in the sanitariums and taught in the denominational literature. At the large campmeetings instruction in the principles of right living and of Christian help work often formed a prominent feature of the program, and was highly appreciated by those in attendance.

The movement was furthered by a change which had taken place in the early nineties in the personnel of the denomination's sanitariums. Instead of continuing to have in the nurses' training schools pupils who were there chiefly for a professional training, these institutions adopted the plan of accepting only such persons as were desirous of devoting their lives to the missionary phase of the medical work. The classes, instead of becoming smaller under the new régime, rapidly increased in size, the number of applicants often being in excess of the accommodations.

Beginning with the year 1897, there was held for several years, in connection with the Battle Creek Sanitarium, a summer school which was largely attended by men and women desirous of attaining in a comparatively short time the knowledge most needful in order to engage intelligently in various lines of Christian help work. The Medical Missionary Conference held in Chicago in the autumn of 1897, and attended by G. A. Irwin, then president of the General Conference, and a number of other representative men and women, was another means of encouraging this work. Among the workers in attendance at this meeting was Mrs. S. M. I. Henry, formerly an evangelist of the W. C. T. U., who had embraced the Adventist views while a patient at the Battle Creek Sanitarium. Mrs. Henry not only entered heartily into the work of promulgating medical missionary principles, but took up special work for the women of the denomination, which had a far-reaching influence for good.

The Department of Education

While the health work was thus rapidly advancing, there was a corresponding growth and development in the department of education. The denomination had two colleges and one academy, it will be remembered, at the close of the earlier chapter on education. The fourth institution was to be a college for the Mississippi Valley. A beginning was made as far back as the fall of 1888, with the opening in Minneapolis of the Minnesota Conference school, which was held for three years in the basement of the Seventh-day Adventist church in that city, and was successful in preparing a number of young people for work in the field. The accommodations being inadequate, a council was held at Owatonna, Minn., in the spring of 1889, attended by Prof. W. W. Prescott, the educational secretary, and the presidents of a number of the near-by conferences, at which it was recommended that the several conferences of the Northwest should unite in establishing and maintaining a well-equipped educational institution adapted to their growing needs. The General Conference, which was assembled at Battle Creek in the following autumn, voted to establish a denominational college at some point between the Mississippi and the Rocky Mountains, and appointed a committee to select a location.

A number of offers were received from various centrally located cities; but the choice finally fell on Lincoln, Nebr. The citizens donated 300 acres of land lying about four miles southeast of the capital, and the denomination agreed to erect, by July 1, 1891, buildings to cost not less than $70,000. Ground was broken for the main college building on April 10, 1890, and the work went forward rapidly. A. R. Henry had the general oversight of raising the money and handling the property. Some of the land was sold for building lots. W. C. Sisley was architect and superintendent, and J. H. Morrison lent valuable help. On Sept. 24, 1891, the main building and two large dormitories were dedicated in the presence of an audience of Lincoln people who filled the large chapel to overflowing.

The college thus happily opened included, in addition to its English department, complete German and Scandinavian departments, each with its own chapel and regular school program. Prof. W. W. Prescott was the first president, and James W. Loughhead served as principal. The attendance was good from the beginning, and in its second year the institution enrolled 600 pupils.

Meanwhile the attendance at Battle Creek College was not in the least diminished, and the growing needs of the Far West resulted in the opening of a school in temporary quarters in the city of Milton, Oreg. This school was later transferred to Walla Walla, Wash., where suitable buildings were erected

WALLA WALLA COLLEGE

on a plot of land lying about two and one-half miles from the city. The college opened its doors to students Dec. 7, 1893, with W. W. Prescott as president and E. A. Sutherland as principal. Since then the institution has had a steady growth.

Other institutions arose in different parts of the country to supply the denomination's growing educational needs. Keene Academy, situated on a tract of about eighty-five acres in Johnson County, Texas, was opened as a conference school in January, 1894, with an attendance of fifty-six, C. B. Hughes being the principal. In the following year the school was made a training center for the Southwest. The institution has had a steady growth, suitable buildings being added from time to time and the land holdings increased as need arose. When the old college building was destroyed by fire in 1921, a large brick structure took its place. The institution now bears the name Southwestern Junior College.

In that part of the South lying east of the Mississippi River, the educational work of the denomination had its beginnings in Graysville, Tenn., where Elder G. W. Colcord opened a school in 1893. In the course of a few years, this school had grown to considerable size, had passed into the hands of the denomination, and had come to be known as the Southern Training School. When the young ladies' dormitory was destroyed by

C. B. HUGHES   G. W. COLCORD

fire in 1915, it was decided to seek a location removed from town life, where the institution could have a larger development in agricultural lines.

The Thatcher farm, near Ooltewah, Tenn., fifteen miles east of Chattanooga, was purchased in 1916, and the new school opened its doors in October of the same year. Some of the farm buildings were used to begin with; but not for long. A commodious girls' dormitory was the first permanent building to be erected. Then followed the young men's dormitory, and in the fall of 1924, the administration building was ready for occupancy. Industrial buildings, barns, and cottages have been provided as needed. The school estate, which is in the foothills of the Smoky Mountains, comprises 600 acres, nearly half of which consists of fertile valley and upland soil.

The institution supplies the higher educational needs of the Southeastern and Southern Union Conferences, and is known as the Southern Junior College. Its annual enrolment is upwards of 250.

Academic and intermediate schools have been started and are being conducted in practically all the conferences.

Simultaneously with the growth in educational institutions and the number of students attending them, there sprang up in the denomination generally a new interest in the fundamental principles of Christian education. The movement received a definite impetus from an educational convention held in Harbor Springs, Mich., in the summer of 1891. This convention was the first gathering of its kind held by the denomination. It was

GRAYSVILLE ACADEMY

conducted under the general leadership of Prof. W. W. Prescott, much important instruction being given by Mrs. E. G. White. The spiritual character of the work of the denominational teacher was clearly brought out, and likewise the importance of making our educational institutions contribute very definitely to giving the message to the world. A large number of our leading educators were in attendance at this gathering, and they went back to their work with a new inspiration and a broader vision of its great possibilities.

Another step in the development of our educational system was taken when President Prescott, on his return from a trip around the world, gave a series of chapel talks before the students of Battle Creek College, on the schools of the prophets. The talks were based on the Bible and the writings of Mrs. E. G. White, and following their delivery an attempt was made to bring the work of the college more directly into line with the denominational needs. Renewed emphasis was placed upon the Bible classes, and greater efforts were made to make the Bible in spirit and purpose the basis of all the teaching.

Some of these ideas, owing to favoring circumstances, were carried out more fully in the new college at Walla Walla than in the older institution at Battle Creek. E. A. Sutherland, in giving a report of the Walla Walla school at the General Conference of 1897, mentioned certain concrete features of the class work which seemed to the delegates to be a successful carrying out of certain principles which the denomination had been seeking to embody in its educational work. Professor Sutherland was accordingly invited to take the presidency of Battle Creek

SOUTHWESTERN JUNIOR COLLEGE

College, in order that the experience he had gained in directing the work of the smaller institution in certain channels might become more widely available in connection with the leading denominational college. Prof. G. W. Caviness, who had served as head of the institution for nearly three years, accepted a call to missionary work in Mexico.

The school continued in Battle Creek for about four years, efforts being made to strengthen the industrial branches, and in other ways to make it a more effectual instrument for the preparation of workers. It was then decided, in order to develop more fully the industrial features of the institution, that the college should be removed to a rural district. A suitable tract of land containing 272 acres was finally bought near Berrien Springs, Mich., in the summer of 1901. The summer term of school was conducted in tents, and for the remainder of that first school year the instruction was given in the old courthouse of Berrien County. Meanwhile the most necessary buildings were being erected by student help, under the direction of an experienced architect, and in the course of a few years the institution, which had received the name Emmanuel Missionary College, was fairly well equipped for its work, and was carrying on a full course of training, in which industrial features, chiefly various lines of agriculture, were strongly emphasized.

Another feature of the work that received special attention was the training of church school teachers. The educational plan of the denomination did not, to begin with, include church schools. Colleges and academies had been carried on for about

EMMANUEL MISSIONARY COLLEGE

twenty years before a comprehensive plan was adopted for giving the little children of the denomination the privilege of Christian schools. It was in 1894 that Mrs. White first called attention to this need. Three years later, when E. A. Sutherland was placed in charge of Battle Creek College, a definite plan was inaugurated for the building up of a system of church and intermediate schools. Earnest efforts were made to stir up the churches to a realization of their need of denominational teaching for their children, in order that they might be willing to furnish the needed moral and financial support. At the same time a movement was set on foot to gather in Seventh-day Adventist teachers employed in the public schools, and imbue them with a true missionary spirit, so that they would be willing to take charge of church schools and work hard to make them a success at a salary considerably less than they had been receiving. Normal work was carried on at Emmanuel Missionary College, to train teachers for this important line.

All these efforts were in a measure successful. The churches responded heartily to the call; they put up buildings, and raised money to pay the teachers' salaries, and then gladly sent their children to these schools. The teachers on their part, if not so fully versed in the principles of Christian education, had the spirit of the work, and made a willing sacrifice of time and money in order to put the schools on vantage ground. As a result of all-round co-operation the church school propaganda went rapidly forward, and in a few years hundreds and then thousands of Adventist children were enjoying the benefits of a Christian education.

In the year 1904 the college at Berrien Springs having been placed in a position where its future seemed assured, E. A. Sutherland and P. T. Magan, who had been closely associated in the work of building up that institution, resigned in order to undertake educational work for rural districts in the South. After considerable looking around, they finally purchased a 400-acre farm near Madison, Tenn., about two miles from the Gallatin Pike and ten miles from the city of Nashville. The farm had an old dwelling house and barns, and a few cattle. The soil, originally good, was much the same as that of a great many other farms in the South, where neglect to vary the crops has caused needless deterioration.

In taking up their new work, Professors Sutherland and Magan were joined by two other members of the faculty of Emmanuel Missionary College, and by a few students. With this nucleus they opened their school in the autumn of 1904, naming it The Nashville Agricultural and Normal Institute. The institution had for its chief aim the training of teachers who were to go into the most needy portions of the South, and establish rural schools of a certain kind. They were to be schools which would not confine their attention to the ordinary book studies, but would teach the boys and girls, and as far as might be possible, their fathers and mothers, how to make the land productive, and also to solve other practical problems having to do with the daily life. It was decided that needed buildings at the Madison School should be put up as the way opened, and by student labor. Meanwhile teachers and students made the best of existing conditions.

Practical farm problems received prompt attention. In the school dairy herd unprofitable animals were gradually replaced with blooded stock, and in the course of a year or so the dairy products had obtained recognition for their quality in the leading stores of Nashville. Other problems have been dealt with in a similar way, the students thus having daily object lessons in scientific farm and dairy management.

The rural schools started and carried on by young men and women trained at this institute have already run up into the thirties, and their work is telling strongly for good in many different communities.

The sanitarium connected with the Madison school had a small beginning. "When the school was first started," writes Professor Sutherland, "there came to its doors from the city of Nashville a sick man who begged to be taken in for the sake

COLUMBIA HALL, WASHINGTON MISSIONARY COLLEGE

of the fresh air, quiet life, and wholesome diet he could get there. From this simple beginning there has developed the medical department of the institution, which consists of plain, one-story cottages accommodating fifteen or twenty patients, and affording them rational treatment at a moderate expense. The buildings were erected by the students of the school."

Very soon after the removal of the denominational headquarters to Washington, D. C., in 1903, there arose a demand for an educational institution that could supply the needs of near-lying fields. Washington Missionary College was accordingly incorporated in July, 1904, and opened its doors for the reception of students the following November. It was then known as Washington Training College, and later, when giving its attention especially to the training of workers for the foreign field, it bore for some years the name of Foreign Mission Seminary. At the General Conference of 1913 it was decided that the institution should resume its status as a senior college.

The college is situated in Takoma Park, a suburb of Washington, lying about eight miles northwest of the Capitol building. The buildings which have been added from time to time, largely by the use of student labor, include Columbia Hall, two dormitories recently enlarged, and a science building, which also accommodates the printing plant. There is a building also for woodwork. The enrolment for 1924-25 was upwards of 300.

Healdsburg College, whose rise and early development were recorded in a previous chapter, was found unequal to the growing needs of the Pacific Coast, and it was decided to move to

BOYS' DORMITORY, PACIFIC UNION COLLEGE

a location where the industrial features could have room for development. A suitable location was found on Howell Mountain in Napa County, seven miles from St. Helena. The holdings of the institution, known as Pacific Union College, comprise 1,800 acres of land, most of which is heavily wooded. There are 100 acres of rich valley land, twenty of which are in fruit.

In these quiet surroundings, there has grown up an educational institution which is well fitted to give its students an all-round training for the duties of life. Almost entirely as a result of student labor, commodious buildings have been erected, including College Hall, dormitories for men and women students respectively, a normal building, gymnasium, printing plant, and others. C. W. Irwin was president of this college from its founding till 1921, when he was succeeded by W. E. Nelson. The annual enrolment is about 400.

In Canada an interest in Christian education was manifested early in the development of our work. One of the first church schools was conducted in Quebec. Somewhat later, academies were carried on at Williamsdale, Nova Scotia, and at Lorne Park, Ontario. The latter institution was moved to Oshawa, on the northern shore of Lake Ontario, in 1912, and became the training school for the Eastern Canadian Union. In 1915 it also became the training center for French workers. The name of the school was changed in 1916 to Eastern Canadian Missionary Seminary; and later to Oshawa Missionary College.

In like manner, what was originally Alberta Industrial Academy, at Lacombe, Alberta, became in 1919 Canadian Junior College. The institution is located on a farm of 198 acres, lying two miles northwest of the town of Lacombe. The build-

LOMA LINDA HOSPITAL

ings are commodious, and the number of students is steadily increasing.

In order to make it possible to provide a thoroughgoing medical education and at the same time develop qualities that make for success in the mission field, the denomination founded its medical school, the College of Medical Evangelists, which was organized and chartered as a medical college in 1909. The institution is located at Loma Linda, San Bernardino Co., and in Los Angeles, Calif. The estate in San Bernardino County contains 300 acres, including extensive orchards and farm lands, as well as the grounds of the Loma Linda Sanitarium.

The equipment and work of the institution have been of such a character that it has been placed in the " A " class by the American Medical Association. Dr. W. A. Ruble, the first president of the college, was succeeded in 1914 by Dr. Newton G. Evans. Dr. P. T. Magan became dean in 1916.

G. A. IRWIN

President of the General Conference, 1897 to 1901

SKODSBORG SANITARIUM

CHAPTER XXXII

Advancement in Europe and the Near East

BEFORE recounting further developments in Europe, it will be in the interests of clearness to speak very briefly of the work as a whole. The reader will remember that after the death of Elder J. N. Andrews in 1883, Elder B. L. Whitney succeeded to the leadership of the Central European Mission. He continued in charge till his death in 1889, after which the chairmanship of the European Council was held for six years by D. A. Robinson, who, however, resided in London, England, where he devoted himself chiefly to the building up of the work in Great Britain. In 1895 H. P. Holser became chairman of the council and director of the Central European Mission, with headquarters at Basel, Switzerland. He continued to be associated with this work till a short time before his death at Cañon City, Colo., in 1901.

With the rapid growth of the work among the German-speaking people the center of the denominational activities on the Continent gradually shifted to Germany. About the beginning of the twentieth century, Hamburg became the headquarters of the Adventist work in Europe, and the chairmanship of what came to be known as the European Division fell to

L. R. Conradi, under whose leadership very substantial growth was made both in Germany and in Russia, and in various other parts of Europe and the Near East.

The plan of the present chapter will be to take up first the developments in such countries as Scandinavia, Great Britain, Switzerland, Germany, and Russia, which have already been dealt with in earlier chapters, and then to pass on to the work in countries not yet mentioned.

H. P. HOLSER

Scandinavia

Norway passed through a severe crisis in 1899, when at a time of financial panic the Christiania Publishing House found itself unable to meet its obligations, and passed temporarily into the hands of receivers. The brethren in America, however, came to the rescue, and raised more than $90,000 in order that this institution, which had long been an important witness to the truth in Scandinavia, might pay every one of its creditors in full. Thus the fair name of the denomination was kept untarnished in Scandinavia, and business men in Christiania were deeply impressed with a sense of the Christian integrity of the leaders in the advent movement.

The strongest church is still in Christiania, the capital and metropolis of Norway. But there are churches also in Stavanger, Bergen, Trondhjem, and still farther north. Norway was first organized as a conference in 1887. It was later subdivided into three conferences, but still later a single organization was found to be more advantageous. In 1924 the Norway Conference had forty-nine churches, with a membership of 2,054.

Visiting nurses developed an interest in Christiania, which grew until it was thought best to establish treatment-rooms, and finally a small sanitarium.

Lapland, in the extreme north, has had a few believers for a number of years. In 1914 J. J. Hokland opened work among these interesting people, with Karlsjok and Finmark as headquarters.

In Sweden a school was founded on a farm of 500 acres, near Nyhyttan, in the late nineties, which has been a means of training a number of workers. Karl Mattson had a large share in building up this institution. Until recently, nearly all the evangelistic work has been done in the central and southern parts of the country. There are excellent treatment-rooms in Stockholm; and also in the summer the school buildings at Nyhyttan are used for the accommodation of patients. Colporteurs are carrying our denominational works to every part of the country. The 1925 Year Book reported forty-four churches in Sweden, with an aggregate membership of 1,483.

Denmark has as its leading institution a large and well-equipped sanitarium at Skodsborg, north of Copenhagen, with a patronage of the best people of the country, including members of the royal family. The institution has a history in which are recorded many divine providences. It was in the year 1897 that steps were taken to start a medical institution in Denmark. The committee looking for a proper location found on the sea road leading out from Copenhagen a large villa formerly occupied by King Frederick VII. It, with an adjoining house and the land surrounding them, was for sale for 70,000 kroner (about $17,500). The owner was a widow, and when she learned what the place was wanted for, she ultimately reduced the price to 50,000.

Friends of the enterprise came forward with gifts large and small, with which the necessary alterations were quickly put under way; but reliance was placed upon a promise of very substantial assistance from a friend in America with which to pay the contractors and meet the first payment on the property. When the word came that the promise could not be fulfilled, it looked as if the enterprise was ruined; but the workers took the matter to God in prayer; the contractors made better terms for payment, and the work went on. Meanwhile the first payment, deferred six months, was almost due. Once more money was promised; but two weeks before it was to be paid, the word came again that it could not be sent. There followed days of earnest prayer for deliverance. Then four days before the money had to be paid, the whole sum came as a gift. Thus it was possible to open our first sanitarium in Scandinavia May 1, 1898.

Almost from the beginning the institution was filled to its utmost capacity, though little or no advertising was done. Workers gave up their rooms to patients, and crowded together where they might. Among the guests were persons of great influence. Parish and city councils sent patients at public expense, though other hospitals were available, and physicians in the large hospitals sent their patients, declaring that the results of the treatments given were surprising.

The institution has been enlarged from time to time by the erection of a number of substantial buildings with all modern improvements. It also owns and rents cottages. It has trained a large number of excellent nurses. The number of patients in the summer months runs up to 350. At that time of the year there has to be a waiting list. The institution has been from the beginning under the supervision of Dr. J. C. Ottosen, supported by Drs. N. P. Nelson, A. Andersen, and Miss Jensine Iversen, and other members of the staff.

The union school for Norway and Denmark, also located at Skodsborg, has an annual enrolment of about 100, and is doing excellent work in training laborers for the two countries. It occupied at the first a substantial building at Frederikshavn, on the northern coast of Jutland, M. M. Olsen being the principal. Later it was moved to Skodsborg, the Frederikshavn building being used for sanitarium purposes. At Skodsborg, E. Arnesen was in charge for many years. The school now occupies buildings of its own at Naerum, a village near Skodsborg.

In 1912 the Danish Conference, originally organized in 1880, was divided into two, but later was again united into a single conference, with forty-four churches, and 2,375 members. J. C. Raft, who returned to Denmark from America in the nineties, was for many years closely connected with the work in Denmark, conducting from time to time series of meetings in Copenhagen and elsewhere.

Finland

Work in Finland was begun in 1892, when O. Johnson and two Bible workers from Sweden went to Helsingfors to labor among the Swedish-speaking people in that city. Meetings were first held in Elder Johnson's private house. Later an interest was awakened in certain country districts, so that by 1898 three churches had been raised up. In that year John Hoffman took general charge of the work. Already some of the denominational books had begun to be printed in the Finnish language. Colporteurs enjoyed good success. Institutes for their encouragement and training were held in Helsingfors and Abo.

A missionary boat, which cruised among the islands off the Baltic Coast, was maintained for some time, and proved useful in circulating literature. In 1901 Fred Anderson joined the group of workers, and A. Boettcher, of Hamburg, was placed in charge of the publishing work in Helsingfors, where books and tracts and a periodical were issued. Finland was organized as a conference in 1909, and from that time on the work has taken a wider range, being no longer confined mainly to the Swedish-speaking portion of the population. At the end of 1912, L. Muderspach, then conference president, reported three new churches organized that year, and twice as many colporteurs in the field as in the previous year. About this time Prof. V. Sucksdorff. of the National University, accepted the Adventist Views, and for a time served as president of the conference. A. Rintala, a Finnish laborer, has been directing the work in recent years. In 1924 Finland had twenty-one churches, with an aggregate membership of 1,051.

Iceland

Iceland has an area nearly equal to that of Ireland, and though it lies just below the arctic circle. it is surrounded by the Gulf Stream, so that the climate on the coast is not very severe. The winters are mild, but the summer temperature is so low that grain will not grow to any extent. and potatoes are about the only vegetable that can thrive. The population is small, Reykjavik. the metropolis, having a little over 6,000 inhabitants, the other cities being mere fishing villages.

The inhabitants are chiefly descended from the Norwegians who went to the island in the ninth century because they resented the rule of Norway's first real king, Harald Haarfagre. They have kept their customs and their language almost unchanged for a thousand years, their isolation making this possible.

Seventh-day Adventists began their work in Iceland in November, 1897, when David Ostlund with his family reached Reykjavik. His first task was to learn the language, which is an extremely difficult one. He then began to preach and to translate and to issue a paper. In 1901 he was able to report sixteen Sabbath keepers, and a flourishing monthly periodical, besides two books translated and published. In the autumn of 1905 a meeting house seating about 250 people was finished in Reykjavik.

In 1911, Olaf F. Olsen took the superintendency, and his labors have been blessed to the building up of the work on a strong basis. Nils Anderson, of Denmark, has been prominent in the colporteur work, traveling on horseback and afoot into the most remote parts of the country, and circulating a large number of denominational books. As many as 10,000 copies of the Icelandic edition of " Christ Our Saviour " have been sold in a single year.

The Faroe Islands are in a sense an outlying mission field for Iceland. O. J. Olsen visited the Faroes from Iceland during the World War, and organized a church there.

The Scandinavian Union as a Whole

The Scandinavian Union Conference was organized in 1901, P. A. Hansen being elected president. He was succeeded by J. C. Raft. During the World War the work progressed in all three of the Scandinavian countries, the membership increasing by 2,712, and the tithe rising from $31,700 to $118,000. During the war period the union committee voted $20,000 as a gift to the General Conference for its missionary operations.

In the plans laid following the war the Scandinavian Union had the Abyssinian Mission assigned to it, and was also asked to exercise a fostering care over the Russian Baltic States.

Germany

There were in Germany in the year 1908 a little over 7,000 members. By 1914 the number had doubled. Evangelistic work in the large cities has been very successful, there being twenty organized churches in and around Berlin. In 1908 the first tent-meeting was held, with such good results that a year later eleven tents were in use, some of which had been donated by American conferences. The field is grouped in two main divisions,— the East German and West German Unions, with an aggregate of 606 churches and 24,524 members.

The Hamburg Publishing House issues some fourteen periodicals in various languages, and books and tracts in a still greater number of tongues. In 1912 a large four-story building was erected to provide additional accommodations for the growing business of the Hamburg house. Nearly a thousand colporteurs in various parts of Europe are engaged in selling the denominational publications. F. W. Spies led out in the colporteur work in 1905 before he was called to South America. H. Böx has been longest in the field. Even during the World War he was at times released from his noncombatant duties in the army, and allowed to hold institutes in various places. On these occasions he carried a paper from the military authorities to the effect that " all persons should give aid and assistance to Herr Böx, leader of the Seventh-day Adventist colporteur work."

The Friedensau school reports seventeen different languages represented among its pupils. Until the Great War, it had a regular department for the training of Russian workers. In recent years the school at Friedensau has been serving particularly the needs of the East German Union. A new training school was opened in 1921 at Kirchheim-Teck, near Stuttgart, with O. Schuberth as principal. The school property thus acquired was furnished, having been used before the war to house a commercial school. In 1921 there was also bought a hotel property at Neandertal, near Düsseldorf, where a school for West Germany is carried on, with W. Müller as principal in 1925.

Holland and Belgium

Work was begun in Holland when Elder R. G. Klingbeil began canvassing among the German river boatmen of Rotterdam, at the same time studying the Dutch language. Believers sprang up in Rotterdam, Amsterdam, Leyden, and The Hague. Jacob Wibbens began to labor in 1901. In the following year, when the general outlook was encouraging, heretical teaching concerning the sanctuary crept in, resulting in the loss of a number of believers. The movement shortly came to naught, however, and some returned to the fold. In 1909, Holland and Flemish Belgium were separated from the West German Conference, and a year later were made a separate mission field. The largest church in Holland is at The Hague. Churches are also to be found at Rotterdam, Amsterdam, Leyden, Leeuwarden, and Utrecht. Captain Christiansen engaged in ship missionary work for years at Rotterdam.

The work in Belgium has progressed but slowly.

Russia

In Russia the work has continued to make progress in spite of great opposition. Permission was obtained in 1908 to establish a publishing house in Riga, which proved of great advantage to the colporteurs who had previously been obliged to obtain their books from Hamburg. In 1909 the Greek Church held a Congress in Kief, attended by a thousand priests, at which resolutions were adopted, condemning the work of Adventists. J. T. Boettcher, who was then in Kief, obtained permission to address the Congress, and occupied an hour and a half in explaining to an attentive audience the fundamental principles of our faith.

In the year 1910 a representative of the government attended the whole series of Adventist conferences and general meetings, and wrote a full account of our work, which was issued as a government document, making a book of 100 pages, and sent to officials throughout the empire. The work states, among other things, that " Seventh-day Adventists in Russia have a determined zeal to win souls, but their whole organization is primarily a missionary one, and every member is expected to help forward the work of the third angel's message." Subsequently the publishing house at Riga was closed by government order, but it was found possible to turn the business over to a private corporation, which does all the required printing at a low rate.

In 1913, Russia was divided, for administrative purposes, into two parts, the Eastern and Western Union Conferences, O. E. Reinke becoming president of the former, with headquarters at Petrograd, where were then four churches, and J. T. Boettcher taking the oversight of the Western Union Conference, with headquarters at Riga.

Following the Great War the whole Russian field was reorganized to such an extent that the denominational Year Book for 1925 lists the following:

	Organized	Reorganized
Soviet Russia Federation of Unions	1920	
North Russian Union Conference	1920	
Central Russian Conference	1910	
Neva Conference	1912	
Northwest Russian Mission	1922	
White Sea Mission	1912	
West Russian Union Conference	1913	1924
Wolhynian Conference	1923	
Podolian Conference	1920	
Black Sea Conference	1919	
Central Dnieper Conference	1919	
Lower Dnieper Conference	1924	
Kiev District Mission	1917	
Upper Dnieper Mission	1924	
Crimean Mission	1920	
South Russian Union Conference	1920	1924
Don Conference	1920	
North Caucasian Conference	1901	
Transcaucasian Mission	1912	
Central Caucasian Conference	1920	
Voronezh Mission	1920	
East Russian Union Conference	1913	1924
German-Volga Conference	1911	1924
Saratov-Tambov Mission	1911	
Samara-Ural Mission	1911	1924
Turkestan Mission	1911	

Siberian Union Conference

Early in the history of our work in Russia, exiles for the Word of God carried the advent message to Siberia. In 1908 this large territory was made a mission field of the Russian Union. K. A. Reifschneider, who pioneered the work, settled in Omsk. In the winter of 1908-09 he traveled some 2,000 miles, mostly by sleigh, in order to visit believers and give further instruction to inquirers. The message was carried over into

GROUP OF RUSSIAN WORKERS

Manchuria by soldiers who took part in the Russo-Japanese War. In 1909 five Sabbath keepers in Harbin appealed for a Seventh-day Adventist minister. A man in Tobolsk, hearing of the Adventists, traveled south to Turkestan and thence on to Omsk, nearly 2,000 miles, to meet a minister and learn the truth more fully. In 1910, E. Gnädjin, our first native Russian minister, was sent to Manchuria, and after two months' labor, he reported twenty-six baptized believers.

A few German-Russian believers moved to Turkestan about 1908, and twelve months later a company was reported at Auli Ata, and also at Askhabad, near the Persian border. J. Ebel was sent to this field in 1909. Five years later there were four churches in and about Tashkent.

The advent message was carried to the Transcaucasus by two Seventh-day Adventist families who had been banished to that region shortly after the truth first entered Russia. The first church was organized in 1908 by H. J. Loebsack, our oldest minister in the Russian work. About the same time a church was organized in Tiflis. Dr. V. Pampaian worked for a long time among the Armenians, and won some of them to the faith. He was bitterly opposed, however, and had to flee for his life. In 1909, Elder Loebsack reported a visit to a colony of Molokanes, from whom eighty-six believers had been gathered out. Nearly 200 members were reported in and about Etschmiasin, near the Persian border.

The denominational Year Book for 1925 gives the Siberian organization as follows: The Siberian Union Conference, reorganized 1924, embracing the conferences of Central Siberia, organized 1920, and West Siberia, organized 1911; together with the Irtysch, the East Siberian, and the Dalne Wostotschnaja Missions. The Siberian Union reported at that time eighty churches, with a total membership of 2,210.

Austria

Work was begun in Austria by J. P. Lorenz, who began in 1902 to conduct meetings quietly in Prague, where several had begun to keep the Sabbath through reading. The preaching was in German, one of the brethren translating into the Bohemian when necessary. Some time later L. Mathe entered Vienna. The laws generally forbidding public Protestant propaganda, Adventists in Lower Austria organized, at the close of 1907, a reading and lecture association called a " Society of Christian Men and Women." Under the law such societies had the right to hold open assemblies. Similar societies were organized in other provinces. One was called the " More Light Society." All these public meetings had to be opened by a native Austrian. Singing of hymns and public prayer were forbidden.

In 1911 work was opened in Triest, on the Adriatic, and a company there accepted the truth. A year later the message began to be preached at Spalato, in the province of Dalmatia, and baptisms were presently reported. About the same time a society was organized in western Galicia. A colporteur began work in Czernowitz, capital of Bukowina, in eastern Galicia. He was put in prison the first day, but was later released, and immediately began to sell more books. Six persons were baptized in that city as a result of his labor.

Opposition was general throughout Austria. Some of the societies were broken up by the authorities. Colporteurs and other workers cheerfully went to prison, but the work continued to advance. When the war broke out, the work in many places almost came to a standstill. " Our church hall and bookcases in Vienna," wrote G. W. Schubert, " were put under seal." Since the war there has practically been greater freedom in religious worship. For a time only occasionally did intolerance manifest itself. But everywhere there is seen a tendency toward a reestablishment of the old order.

Hungary

As far back as the middle of the sixteenth century there were Sabbath keepers in Hungary. A nobleman named Ossi Andaras, of the Szekely Hungarians, during a long illness made a careful study of the Bible, as a result of which he was convinced that the seventh-day Sabbath was the only one enjoined by the Scriptures. On regaining his health, he began to teach this truth publicly, and was joined by a goodly number of his countrymen. In course of time, there came to be some seventy towns and villages whose inhabitants observed the seventh day instead of Sunday.

Then persecution arose, many were deprived of their homes and property, and others were exiled. Some held fast, and as late as the latter part of the nineteenth century, when the government gave permission to the Jews to observe their Sabbath, there were to be found in Hungary quite a number of Christian Sabbath keepers also.

L. R. Conradi, who made a special trip to Hungary in 1891 to seek out these earlier Sabbath keepers, met in Kolozsvár Mr. and Mrs. Rottmeyer, German Baptists, who became convinced of the truth and were the first German people to accept the advent message in Hungary. Mr. Rottmeyer was an employee of the British Bible Society for Transylvania, and he rendered excellent help in establishing the work in Hungary.

J. F. Huenergardt, also coming from Germany, in 1898, found twelve believers. He soon learned the language and began to labor for the Hungarians and Slovaks. He baptized fifty converts during the first year of his labors. In 1904 work was begun in Budapest, where ultimately believers to the number of 250 were raised up, with three separate churches. Suitable literature was prepared, and colporteurs were trained to carry it to the homes of the people.

Late in 1911 the Hamburg Publishing House started a branch in the city of Budapest. It was a decided success. Among the publications of this house were the Hungarian monthly, *Az Arato* (The Reaper) in editions of from 10,000 to

15,000; the Rumanian monthly, 2,000 to 3,000; a Serbian quarterly, with a circulation running from 10,000 to 12,000; and a Bohemian quarterly, with a circulation of about 2,000. In 1924 the Hungarian Conference had forty-three churches, with a membership of 1,006.

Bulgaria

There were believers in Rustchuk, Bulgaria, in the early nineties; but not till 1898 was regular work in that country begun. Meetings were held in Sofia, and a church established there. The two Balkan wars and the Great War scattered the believers. Following the war, Stefan Konstantinoff held meetings in Sofia, and thirty accepted the message. In 1925 there were in the Bulgarian Mission eight churches, with a total membership of 200 adult believers.

Jugo-Slavia

In 1907 J. F. Huenergardt baptized a Serbian from Belgrade, who had studied the truth and gone over the boundary line into Hungary to receive baptism. Serbians receiving the message in Hungary sent books and tracts into their own country, and in this way the seed was sown in Serbia. In 1909-10 a Serbian brother did some Bible work in Belgrade. He was imprisoned again and again, till his health failed; but he continued to work, and by 1911 there had grown up a little company of believers. After the Balkan War of 1912-13 practical freedom of worship was enjoyed. The Serbian work was reorganized in 1920 as the Jugo-Slavian Mission, with nineteen churches. The headquarters are at Novi-Sad, where we have a small printing establishment that issues a Serbian paper, *The Messenger of Peace.* R. Schillinger is the superintendent. In 1925 this mission reported fifty-three churches, with a total of 729 members.

Rumania

The early beginnings of the work in Rumania have already been recorded in the chapter on the Central European Mission. Elder A. C. Bourdeau preached the message there in the early eighties; but the effort was not followed up, and the believers scattered. Some years later a number of German-Russian Sabbath keepers moved into Rumania, near the Black Sea, and as a result of their efforts the work took a new start. L. R. Conradi visited these colonists in 1892, his visit resulting in the organization of a church.

Systematic work for Rumania began when Pastor Ginter settled in Bukharest in 1904, and began to study the language. He found sixteen believers, and started meetings before he had fully mastered the language. Armed policemen sat in the congregation to arrest the speaker in case he should say anything against the state religion. At the end of 1908 the church at Bukharest had grown to 108, the members representing twelve nationalities.

The interest kept growing. Late one night in 1909, three peasants appeared at the door of Mr. Ginter, the superintendent. When asked what they wanted, they replied: " We seek the way of salvation, and have heard that from this man it may be learned." They had walked fifty miles. In that same year Mr. Ginter, being expelled by the authorities for his religious work, took up his residence on the Bulgarian border, directing the work of the native Rumanians who could not be expelled. In time, P. P. Paulini, a Rumanian who had been attending our school at Friedensau, succeeded to the leadership, and since then the work has gone steadily forward.

The first general meeting, held in the city of Ployeschi in 1911, was seriously disturbed by the priests, who raised a tumult. In the following year a meeting was held in the same place, a good hall being secured, and by the mayor's permission public services were held for the first time in connection with a conference session. Priests gathered their sympathizers together, and made an attack on some of the believers; but public sentiment turned against them. From that time on, public meetings have been held by permission of the authorities. In 1913 a second Rumanian church and a German church were organized in Bukharest.

During the World War there were many special deliverances, and after it was over, our people enjoyed greater freedom. In 1920, Rumania was organized as a union conference with 2,000 members. By 1924 there were in the Rumanian Union Conference 169 churches, with 4,947 members.

Poland

When the advent message first began to be preached in Germany, there came to be believers among the Poles in eastern Prussia. Churches were organized in Warsaw and in Lodz. After the war, territories containing a number of believers were added to the Polish republic. The Polish Union Mission formed in 1920, with L. Mathe as president. There are alto-altogether about 500 members, the headquarters being at

Teschen, east Silesia. The 1925 Year Book reports fifty-nine churches in the Polish Union Conference, with a total of 1,356 members.

The Latin Union Conference

The Latin Union is the name given to a large group of countries speaking the Latin tongues. It includes France, Italy, Spain, Portugal, Belgium, and all Switzerland, except the German-speaking portion in the north.

On the organization of this union in 1902, Prof. B. G. Wilkinson became its superintendent. He was recalled to America in 1905. In the same year the headquarters were moved from Paris to Geneva, and a union school was opened at Gland, Switzerland, in 1904, with J. Vuilleumier in charge. This school began with fifteen students, and with a tent fly as a roof; but at the close of the school year every one of the students went into conference work. The school was later well housed at Gland, where it was successfully operated until 1921, when it was removed to Salève, France, where it has had very encouraging success, with A. G. Roth as principal.

In 1905 the Latin Union Mission became the Latin Union Conference, with L. P. Tièche as president. Later A. V. Olson was called to the presidency of this union, which was and is enjoying a good degree of prosperity. According to the Year Book for 1925, this union had seventy-seven churches and 3,033 members.

France

France was entered in 1876 when D. T. Bourdeau, working under great difficulties, brought out and baptized a company of believers in Valence, and also labored in other places. In 1888 an attempt was made to put the colporteur work in France on a self-supporting basis, E. P. Auger from America and a brother from Switzerland leading out in the effort; but the influence of the priests was too strong to allow success at that time. During the winter of 1901-02, Elder B. G. Wilkinson held an institute for the French workers in Geneva, and a year later conducted a similar school in Paris. Among the young men who received training in these institutes were U. Augsbourger, A. Vaucher, and Paul Steiner. The French paper, under the editorship of J. Vuilleumier, was transferred from Basel to Paris. A church was organized in Paris, and that city was made the headquarters of the French work. Professor Wilkinson returned to the States in 1905 to teach Bible in the college at Washington D. C. H. H. Dexter continued the work.

In 1907 the northern part of France was constituted the North France Mission, with Paris as headquarters, the rest of the country constituting the French Conference, with H. H. Dexter serving as president. The work in France has gone forward but slowly. In 1908 an Adventist church was raised up in Montpellier, and about the same time a series of meetings held in Lyon brought out a small company of believers. The membership in Paris gradually increased. Churches were also raised up in Marseille, Grenoble, and Rouen. During the war a strong evangelistic effort was conducted by A. Vaucher in the city of Paris. More recently Dr. J. Nussbaum, by doing evangelistic work in connection with his medical practice, was able to raise up a church at Le Havre, the well-known seaport.

Italy

Torre Pellice, the headquarters of the historic Waldensian church, heard the advent message in 1865 from the lips of the ex-priest, M. B. Czechowski. At that time Mme. Catherine Revel accepted the Adventist teachings, and continued faithful to them for nearly twenty years, until D. T. Bourdeau's visit to Torre Pellice in 1884, when he held a series of meetings, as a result of which a small church was raised up. Later A. C. Bourdeau, and for a time Mrs. E. G. White, held meetings in the neighborhood, but the work was not followed up, and the little company of believers in time grew so small that it did not meet regularly. J. D. Geymet and Joseph Curdy in turn labored in the valleys. Dr. H. P. Ribton did some faithful work in Naples, as recorded in an earlier chapter, but his untimely death brought that effort to a standstill.

In 1902, Elder and Mrs. Charles T. Everson and Mrs. Josephine R. Schell were sent from California to take up work in Italy, and settled in Rome. There were then in Italy about thirty believers, most of them in Torre Pellice. In the course of his labors, Elder Everson organized a church in Rome, and also one in Gravina, in southern Italy. At the General Conference of 1909, Elder Everson was recalled to America, and the work in Italy was placed in charge of L. Zecchetto, who had been working among the Italians of New York. He labored chiefly in the regions about Florence. After the World War there was renewed activity in soul-winning. Believers have been gathered in from Florence, Genoa, and other cities. In 1921, R. Werner, then superintendent, reported 118 members, with churches in Balsorano, Govitza, Torre Pellice, Montalto, Pisa, Bara, Gravina, and in central Sicily, besides scattered believers.

In the summer of 1924 an advance move was made in Italy by securing, in Florence, the scene of Savonarola's labors and of his martyrdom in 1498, ground excellently located for a headquarters building, a depository, mission offices, and living apartments. This is the first real estate acquired by Seventh-day Adventists in Italy, and it means much for our work there.

Spain

Work was begun in Barcelona in 1903 by the Brothers Walter G. and Frank Bond from California. In the following year they were joined by W. Robinson, of Wales, who continued for a time to assist in the work. In the same year the first three converts were baptized in Barcelona. Some of the earlier believers developed into faithful colporteurs and Bible workers. These often suffered persecution, but went on their way rejoicing. In a number of instances workers were in a remarkable way saved out of the hands of violent mobs. John L. Brown, of Mexico, entered Spain in 1911, and met with excellent success in the further development of the colporteur work, especially in the sale of the larger books. In 1912, E. Forga, formerly of Peru, moved to Barcelona to edit the Spanish paper and do some book translating. It was a great blow to the work in Spain when the superintendent, Walter Bond, was taken away by death in 1914. Only a year before, Sister Lola Casals, a native Bible worker of beautiful character and fine ability, was laid to rest. Not long afterward E. Forga died. Frank Bond served as superintendent through the war, and until 1920, when he was succeeded by C. E. Knight, of the East Caribbean field. At that time there were eight churches, with 230 members. *Las Señales de los Tiempos* (The Signs of the Times), a sixteen-page monthly magazine, is printed in Barcelona.

Portugal

Mr. and Mrs. C. E. Rentfro were the first Seventh-day Adventist workers to set foot in Portugal. They landed in Lisbon in October, 1904, and began the study of the language. For use in their missionary endeavors, they had a few Portuguese tracts, and made use of the Brazilian paper. In course of time they were joined by a Portuguese colporteur, and were enabled to raise up a company of believers. In 1911, Paul Meyer went to Portugal and became superintendent of the field. His labors have been attended with some encouraging results. There are companies of believers in Lisbon and Oporto.

Belgium

An aged Baptist, of Liège, began to keep the Sabbath in 1895 as the result of reading Adventist literature, and in the same year C. Osberger, a Swiss colporteur, was sent to labor in that city. A year later he was joined by C. Grin, of Basel. In the following year J. Erzenberger organized a church of ten in Jemeppe, near Liège. In 1902 Brother Grin, at that time the only worker, began to labor near Charleroi, but died soon after. J. Curdy, of Switzerland, entered the field in 1903. R. G. Klingbeil, from Holland, labored for a time. Work went on in Ant-

GLAND SANITARIUM

werp, Brussels, and other places during the war. In 1920 Belgium was organized as a conference, with Jacob Wibbens as president. After a time he was succeeded by A. J. Girou.

Leman Conference (French Switzerland)

The beginnings of our work in French Switzerland have been recorded with some fulness in an earlier chapter. When B. L. Whitney's failing health made it necessary for him to return with his family to America, the superintendency of the work fell to H. P. Holser. Owing to Sunday law restrictions, it seemed best to reduce the printing work, and to transform the large building into a sanitarium, over which Dr. P. A. de Forrest was placed in 1895. A food factory was opened in connection with the sanitarium. In 1904 this property was exchanged for an estate of ninety acres, with buildings, at a little place called Gland, on Lake Geneva, between the cities of Geneva and Lausanne. Here, in ideal surroundings, the sanitarium work has since been carried forward. The food factory was moved at the same time. The patronage increasing, it was necessary to make substantial additions to the sanitarium building which came to have accommodations for more than a hundred patients. The training school work which had been carried on successfully for several years at Gland, was later transferred to the Latin Union Training School at Haute-Savoie, France. The church in Geneva developed special strength. During the World War it received considerable additions, H. H. Dexter conducting a series of services in a theater. After the war U. Augsbourger reported a membership approaching a thousand.

The Mauritius Mission

The Latin Union has a general oversight of the work in Algiers, which has been dealt with briefly under Africa. It has also a mission on the island of Mauritius, which had its beginning in this way: Mlle. R.. Le Meme went from Mauritius to Switzerland to recover her health. For years she had felt a special interest in the prophecies of Daniel and the Revelation, and seeing an announcement to the effect that these prophecies were being explained at a certain place, she attended our meetings and accepted the truth. On her return to the island, she interested her friends, and a call was sent for a preacher. Paul Badaut responded, and by the end of 1914 there was a church there of twenty-eight members. When Brother Badaut returned to France in 1920, the work on the island went forward under the supervision of M. Raspal. There were 150 members at the close of 1921.

The Latin Union After the War

In the reorganization following the World War, A. V. Olson, of Eastern Canada, succeeded L. P. Tièche as head of the Latin Union, and J. Vuilleumier was called back from Canada to assist in editorial work. L. L. Caviness was sent over from America to serve as union secretary for the educational and young people's work. A permanent location for the union training school was secured at Collonges sous Salève, in France, five miles south of Geneva. At this point two hotel buildings were purchased, together with a small piece of land and a good spring of water. In the summer of 1921 a number of young people went out into the colporteur field under the leadership of J. A. P. Green, who had lately come over from the Spanish-American field. A number were successful in earning scholarships, and the school had an enrolment the first year of seventy-five, who represented all the different fields of the Latin

Union. The membership of the union, as reported at this time, amounted to exactly 1,999, with sixty-seven churches. By 1925 the number had increased to 3,033 members, with seventy-seven churches.

Turkey

It was a humble instrument that was chosen to be the first bearer of the third angel's message to Turkey. About 1838 there was born in Asia Minor, on the shores of the Black Sea,

LATIN UNION TRAINING SCHOOL IN FRANCE

a Greek by the name of Anthony. He became a shoemaker by trade, and emigrated to the United States, where he attended a Seventh-day Adventist camp-meeting in California. Although his knowledge of English was limited, he obtained an understanding of the truth, and promised the Lord on that campground that if He would send him a purchaser for his shoe shop, he would immediately return to his own country and give the message to his people.

On returning home the first person who came to him was a man who wished to buy his business. He sold, and was soon off for Turkey. He went at his own expense, and on his way to the home of his childhood he stopped for a short time in Constantinople. Supposing that everybody would be as glad to hear the message as he had been, he went directly to the Protestant churches, and there proclaimed it, but he was not favorably received. However, he remained in the city, and continued to talk his views as he had opportunity, till finally the Protestants reported him to the authorities as a disturber of the peace. He was arrested and kept in prison as long as his money lasted. On being released, he found work with a manufacturer of shoes, who, however, paid him only half wages because he kept the Sabbath. Nevertheless, he found time on Sundays and on the evenings of other days to spread a knowledge of the faith.

At this time he was rooming with a man by the name of Baharian, with whom he had been acquainted before he went to America. Baharian had a son who was attending college at Aïntab, and to this son he would send from time to time the tracts that Mr. Anthony gave him. The son spent the summer season of 1890 in Constantinople, where he met Mr. Anthony at the home of his father, and received from him the loan of two books, " Daniel and the Revelation " and " The History of the Sabbath." He read these books, and was convinced of the truth of the Adventist views. At the invitation of H. P. Holser, then superintendent of the Central European Mission, he went to Basel, and remained there till the spring of 1892, when he returned to Turkey to preach the message.

Meanwhile Mr. Anthony went on with his work. He was often in prison for preaching. When the chief of police forbade him to preach any more, he replied that he could not comply with such orders, saying: " I am not my own. I gave myself to the Lord, and He commands me to preach, and I must preach. If you put me in prison, I will preach. I can do nothing else than what the Lord commands me."

On one occasion he was cast into prison because he distributed tracts, and the authorities promised to release him if he would agree not to do so any more. At first he thought he could do this conscientiously and work in some other way; but while the officer was accompanying him to his home to receive a written guaranty to this effect, it occurred to him that the Lord might be pleased to have him work with tracts. He accordingly told the officer that he could not give the required guaranty, and was taken back to prison. When in course of time he was released, he returned to his work. He was a man of great simplicity of character. He had come back to his home country to carry the good tidings, and he devoted his energies unreservedly to this one thing, leaving the rest with God.

When Z. G. Baharian returned to Constantinople, he and Mr. Anthony began holding meetings in a sort of hotel. The first person to be interested was a Greek colporteur of the American Bible Society by the name of Abraham. He brought with him to the meetings a tailor whose name was John Isaac.

John Isaac brought his brother-in-law with him. The study that day was on Daniel 8. On the fourth Sunday the sanctuary question was taken up. In the course of a few weeks Mr. Isaac began to keep the Sabbath. About the same time an Armenian brother embraced the Adventist views, also his sister, who was later married to Brother Baharian. Thus in the course of a few months there had come to be six Sabbath keepers in Constantinople.

By this time the believers had got out some tracts in Armeno-Turkish, and some in the Greek-Turkish language, which they distributed as they were able. They also rented a house, and made public announcement that meetings would be held on Sabbaths and Sundays. This provoked opposition, and Brethren Anthony and Baharian were both arrested. After investigation the authorities let them go, but advised them not to make any public announcements of their meetings.

The six believers in Constantinople having been baptized in the sea in 1892, the brethren began early in 1893 to work in the villages outside of Constantinople. At Bardizag four persons began to keep the Sabbath. The message was also carried to Ovajik, where a well-known Protestant by the name of Minas Beurekian accepted the Adventist views. Elder Baharian coming thither to labor in 1894, three more persons accepted the truth; but great opposition arose, and a mob surrounded the house of Beurekian, and broke the windows. Baharian's life was in imminent danger, but the village police took him in charge, and saw him safely to Bardizag. The interest in Ovajik developed still more rapidly after this tumult, and soon there was a Seventh-day Adventist church there of thirty members.

In 1894 H. P. Holser visited Turkey, and Z. G. Baharian was ordained to the ministry. The two men then visited various parts of Cilicia. Elder Holser on this occasion spent some time with the company in Constantinople. He instructed the brethren more fully in the message, and finally organized a church of twenty members.

In 1904 Dr. A. W. George was sent to take charge of the work in Turkey, and opened a medical mission in Constantinople. At that time Elder Baharian, with other workers, was in prison for a year. Treatment-rooms were established in 1906 by Dr. and Mrs. George on a site overlooking the Sea of Marmora; but it was soon necessary for them to leave Turkey, owing to broken health, Dr. George dying at Friedensau the following year. C. D. AcMoody began his labors in 1907, holding meetings and conducting baptisms in the vicinity of Constantinople and

Brusa, as well as in other places. In the summer of 1907 the Constantinople church was prohibited from assembling in a hall, and therefore came together in an open common on the Asiatic shore of the Bosporus. In July of the same year seven were baptized in the Sea of Marmora, two of them being Jews, two Greeks, and two Armenians. At the opening of the year 1908, Mr. and Mrs. Robert S. Greaves, of Canada, landed in Smyrna to begin work.

It marked a new era for our work in Turkey when in July, 1908, a constitution was granted, guaranteeing freedom of speech and of the press. A general meeting was called at Beirut, Syria, in September of that year, at which for the first time the workers could preach and sing and pray without restriction. In the following winter a Bible institute was successfully conducted. C. D. AcMoody was obliged to leave the field in January, 1909, on account of illness, dying in America two years later. The directorship was taken over by E. E. Frauchiger, of Germany. In the spring of 1909, in the course of the massacres of Christians by Moslems in the regions of Adana and Tarsus, six of the Adventist brethren were slain.

The work has been attended with danger all the way along; but there have been many remarkable providences and many deliverances. At the 1911 European Council, held in Friedensau, Germany, A. Buzugherian, of Smyrna, told of one time when the workers were anxious to come together to hold a Bible institute, but the government repeatedly refused to grant the necessary permission. Just about that time the government shut them all up in prison, together with Z. G. Baharian, their leader. So they had their Bible institute behind the bars.

Elder Baharian made a trip through eastern Asia Minor in 1910, finding open doors everywhere. The workers often met with violence, however, from the Armenian Christians as well as from the Turks. A school was conducted in the winter of 1910-11 in Constantinople, the Greek, Turkish, and Armenian being the principal tongues used in the classroom. A book depository has been established in Constantinople, and Turkish tracts are sold from house to house.

Just before the World War, the number of believers in Turkey was about 350. During the war the believers were badly scattered. Z. G. Baharian, the faithful leader, came to his end in 1915, evidently being killed and robbed by a Kurdish driver who had agreed to take him part way on one of his long journeys. It was not an unexpected end. This apostle of our day was like one of old, " in perils oft; " he knew what it was to face death in many forms; but he went on with his work till the last.

Henry Erzberger, of Switzerland, had charge of our work in Constantinople during the war. Even in those troublous times the Constantinople church grew in members. Miss D. Keanides, the secretary-treasurer of the mission, was summoned before one of the local courts to answer for her correspondence. After being kept some time in prison, where she labored on behalf of the depraved women who were her associates, she was brought before the tribunal, who allowed her to explain at length our denominational teachings. She was listened to with respect, and then politely dismissed, so impressed were these hardened men with the sincerity and truthfulness of the prisoner.

About the same time A. Buzugherian was marvelously delivered from massacre, he and his wife journeying by camel over deserts for thirteen days to Egypt and safety. As soon as the war was over, this brother was back in his field of labor.

Syria and Palestine

H. P. Holser visited Palestine early in 1898, and on his return made a call at a general meeting in Hamburg for volunteers to open work in that country. Mr. and Mrs. J. S. Krum responded. They began by doing colporteur work among the German colonists at Jaffa (the Joppa of the Bible). In 1900, F. Hoerner, from the Basel Sanitarium, opened a medical mission in Jaffa. Later Mr. Krum established such a mission in Jerusalem, which he operated himself for a while, being in course of time relieved by Mr. and Mrs. J. Jespersson, trained nurses from Basel. J. G. Teschner, a German nurse, sent to Jerusalem to assist Mr. Jespersson, died of fever a few months later.

In 1905 W. H. Wakeham, who served as superintendent of the Levant, visited Syria and Palestine, and held the first institute for Armenian workers at Aintab, six young men being in attendance. A brother from Iconium, who was baptized at this institute, reported five others in that city who were observing the Sabbath. Sabbath keepers were also reported from Beirut, Cyprus, Alexandretta, Tarsus, and Adana. In 1908 Elder and Mrs. W. C. Ising settled at Beirut. Two years later Elder Ising baptized two converts in the brook Cherith. In the following year a tent-meeting was held on Mt. Carmel, in the midst of a German colony. In 1913 Elder Ising visited believers in Bagdad and Mosul, near the site of ancient Nineveh, who had been for some time sending tithes to the mission. Elder H. Erzberger was appointed director of Syria in 1913, and the following year visited the regions east of the Jordan, where an interest had been awakened among the Arabs as a result of colporteur work. He was interned during the war and for some time thereafter on the island of Malta.

Greece and Albania

Prof. W. E. Howell with his family entered Greece in May, 1907, following the council at Gland. They settled in a suburb of Athens, and began the study of modern Greek. Professor Howell was recalled to America in 1909 to resume educational work. Before leaving Greece he visited Albania, where an interest had developed. He also translated some tracts into modern Greek. In the same year R. S. Greaves baptized the first believers in Albania, who had learned of the truth through one of Professor Howell's tracts. F. Scior began work in Salonica in 1909. During the Balkan War, Loxandra Keanides, a nurse, worked in the hospitals of that city. Workers were withdrawn during the World War. Not till 1921 did R. S. Greaves return to resume his work, which is progressing slowly, but steadily.

The Persian Mission

F. F. Oster, of Walla Walla College, Wash., entered Persia in 1911, working among the German-speaking residents about Urumiah, and at the same time studying the Persian language. He was joined later by O. Staubert and his wife. Mr. Oster settled at Maragha, twenty-five miles south of Tabriz, where he began to work among the Turks and Persian-speaking Syrians. Shortly before the outbreak of the Great War he journeyed through Turkestan on horseback, and did evangelistic work, going over some of the ground covered by Joseph Wolff when he was preaching the advent message in connection with the movement of 1844. Maragha was exposed to the Kurdish raiders, who began to ravage Persia as soon as Turkey entered the war. The inhabitants, accordingly, had to flee. Elder Oster and his wife and four-months-old baby were in the stream of refugees. The first day Mrs. Oster was in the saddle fourteen hours. They reached Tabriz, the city of refuge, in safety. The headquarters of the mission is at Tabriz, Persia, F. F. Oster being director.

A Great General Meeting

In the foregoing pages an attempt has been made to give a very brief summary of the advancement of the work in various parts of Europe and the Near East. A few closing words may be said concerning the work as a whole. The General Conference Council held at Friedensau in the summer of 1911, was a practical demonstration of the remarkable growth and development of the work in Europe during the previous twenty years. There were gathered together on this occasion people from practically all the important countries of Europe and from many parts of Asia and Africa, to the number of over 3,000. This

FRENCH PUBLISHING HOUSE

large company was accommodated partly in a great encampment of tents and partly in public buildings on the estate. The huge canvas tabernacle was crowded to its fullest capacity. While reports were being made and sermons preached, there were two interpreters, one standing on either side of the rostrum, other interpreters doing the same thing for little groups of listeners gathered in various parts of the tent. However, while representing all these different nations, the meeting was marked by perfect oneness of feeling, and seemed to form a remarkable fulfilment, in part, of the beautiful scripture which says that they shall come from the east and the west, and the north and the south, and sit down in the kingdom of God.

A. G. DANIELLS
President of the General Conference, 1901 to 1922.

GENERAL CONFERENCE HEADQUARTERS
Takoma Park, Washington, D. C.

CHAPTER XXXIII

The General Conference of 1901

IN order to appreciate the full significance of such a meeting as the General Conference of 1901, it will be necessary to go back somewhat in the narrative, and consider certain developments in the history of the organized work of the denomination, which naturally led up to the situation that confronted the delegates to this historic conference, and led them to take the action they did. When James White passed away, in 1881, at the age of sixty, after guiding the destinies of the denomination for more than thirty years, the denominational organization may be said to have existed in germ, but there was to be growth and expansion in many directions to keep pace with a rapidly growing work.

The General Conference at Minneapolis in the autumn of 1888 marked a crisis in the spiritual development of the denomination. The issues seemed on the surface to center about certain men and their theological views, but it was really a conflict of fundamental principles. The work of the previous years had been aggressive and thoroughly successful, viewed from every standpoint. George I. Butler, succeeding James White, had proved a strong, resourceful leader, who worked hard himself and inspired others to work hard. The evangelistic work of the denomination was successful, the camp-meetings were large and enthusiastic gatherings, the publishing houses were prosperous, the colporteurs were selling books at a marvelous rate. Elder Butler's visit to Europe had given an impetus to the work there, and his talks at large gatherings in this country stirred up new interest in the regions beyond, and moved the brethren to contribute toward their support.

Nevertheless, with all these manifest tokens of prosperity, something was lacking. The tent-meetings were conducted with spirit and efficiency. The discourses given were well-thought-out expositions of the denominational doctrines, and were effective in bringing men to a recognition of the fact that Adventist teachings harmonized with the Bible. But there was gradually growing up a feeling of satisfaction with doctrines which could be so easily defended, an emphasis on certain argumentative features of the denominational belief, to the exclusion of the deeper, more spiritual elements. There was lack of that brooding over the deeper things of experience in the gospel, that eager yearning after spiritual power, that sense of man's utter helplessness in the presence of God, of his sole dependence for salvation on the merits of a risen Saviour.

This outstanding need of the denomination — a greater emphasis on that fundamental doctrine, righteousness by faith — made itself felt at the Minneapolis meeting. The studies and counsels at that conference resulted in the end in bringing an accession of new spiritual strength to the Adventist people, though for some time no little controversy continued over the method of setting forth the great fundamental doctrine of righteousness by faith.

The choice for the presidency at that conference fell on O. A. Olsen, who had been sent to Scandinavia in 1886 to labor. His engagements there made it necessary for him to remain in Europe till the following spring. When he came to this country, the situation that had been precipitated at Minneapolis was still a perplexity. Some evidently did not apprehend the spiritual bearings of the question at issue, nor realize how fundamental were the truths involved.

Nevertheless these men, with all their weaknesses, were standing for advanced truth in the way of a more spiritual conception of the whole system of doctrine professed by Seventh-day Adventists. It was the perception by Mrs. E. G. White of this great fundamental fact that led her, in the beginning, to take the course she did in commending the work of these men, and to emphasize in the messages that are preserved in the bound volumes of " Testimonies for the Church," the vital necessity of laying hold of the truths presented.

It was under these circumstances that Mrs. White began a series of meetings in Battle Creek, intended to bring the brethren there to realize their need of a new and more spiritual view of the great reform truths they were preaching, and to show tenderness and love toward their fellow workers.

These meetings were held partly in the Review and Herald chapel, partly in the east vestry of the Tabernacle. O. A. Olsen often led out in the consideration of the situation and its demands upon God's people. Mrs. White bore a very plain testimony, holding up day after day the great spiritual truths connected with the advent message, and insisting on the need of every one's entering into a fuller Christian experience than many had yet known, and of all uniting heartily together in giving the message to the world.

The result of the giving of this instruction was a marked accession of spiritual power in camp-meetings and other representative gatherings. The ministerial institutes which were held in different parts of the country in the early nineties, were also an effective means of following up the interest aroused in the deeper truths of the message, and they afforded to many workers a new experience in their own souls, and added power in soul-winning.

Simultaneously with this emphasis on the spiritual import of the denominational teaching, there came a revival of interest in the health and philanthropic work, which resulted in bringing that branch of activity into sympathetic touch with the body as a whole, and caused a great army of young people to enter the nurses' courses in the sanitariums and not a few to enter medical schools.

The outbreak of persecution for Sunday labor in several of the Southern States, and the efforts of certain organizations to secure the passage of various Sunday bills through Congress, likewise roused the denomination to a sense of its responsibilities to push forward the work of giving the advent message while it should have the opportunity. The Religious Liberty Association was accordingly organized, and its nation-wide activities resulted in carrying light and truth to many who might not have received it through other channels.

The foreign missions of the denomination came in for increased consideration during these years. Doors were opening on every hand. In Germany and Russia and other parts of Europe people were eagerly receiving the message. Urgent calls for laborers came from Central and South America, and the work was opening encouragingly in South Africa. The missionary ship " Pitcairn " was cruising among the islands of the Pacific, and finding openings everywhere. These open doors were so many signs that God's providence was preparing the way for the world-wide work to which Adventists believed themselves called.

But there was one important thing that was lacking, namely, an adequate system of finance for supporting mission enterprises. The local conferences used their tithe for the home work. The annual offerings and a portion of the Sabbath school offerings were all that the Foreign Mission Board could regularly depend on for its rapidly growing work. Meanwhile drouths were seriously affecting crops in the West, and the country as a whole was suffering from financial depression. The sales of the colporteurs materially decreased, and other branches of the work were affected.

Under these circumstances some of the believers who had property and wished their money in safe keeping, offered it to the General Conference at a low rate of interest. The money was accepted, and a considerable indebtedness was thus incurred. It was one means of meeting a trying situation, but it was not going to the root of the difficulty. What needed to be done was to provide regular and adequate financial support for the growing foreign work. This was not accomplished till some years later.

At the General Conference held in College View, Nebr., in the spring of 1897, there was a general overhauling of the policies and work of the denomination in view of the rapid growth of recent years, and an effort was made to provide for a more general distribution of responsibilities. In harmony with this generally prevailing conviction, it was decided to have the work as a whole administered in three grand divisions; namely, the United States of America, Europe, and Australia, it being understood that the interests of the cause in countries situated in other parts of the world would be looked after by the Foreign Mission Board.

There were other changes effected at the Conference, but they were of minor consequence. A good deal of concern was felt over the debts which the General Conference had incurred, but nothing effective was done in the way of providing a remedy. G. A. Irwin was elected president of the General Conference;

O. A. Olsen, president of the European Division; and A. G. Daniells, president of the Australasian Division.

The Conference of 1899 was on the whole uneventful. When, therefore, the delegates assembled in Battle Creek for the Conference of 1901, it was with the generally prevailing conviction that the situation was practically the same as it was four years earlier, only the work outside of the United States had grown far more rapidly than at home; hence the need for a broader policy was so much the more urgent. There was also a generally felt desire that the medical missionary interests of the denomination, which had likewise been passing through a period of growth and expansion, should somehow be brought more directly into union with other branches of the denominational work, in order that ministers and physicians might the more successfully labor together for one common end.

These two main needs were clearly voiced by Mrs. E. G. White at a meeting of representative men, held a day or two previous to the opening of the Conference, and met with general approval on the part of the delegates. In harmony with the prevailing desire for a change of policy,— a reorganization of the strength of the denomination on a scale commensurate with the larger needs,— it was agreed at the outset to talk over freely, in a large gathering composed of representative persons, both ministers and laymen, the most urgent needs of the hour, and the best way to meet those needs. The body of men thus brought together was far more numerous and more widely representative than any ordinary committee on plans and recommendations would have been. By its very size it commanded respect, and it included so many different minds, all able to give counsel, that its recommendations, when finally reported to the Conference, were almost invariably found to be in line with the wishes of all the delegates.

The general results of this Conference of 1901 were of a far-reaching character. They may be summed up under three main heads:

First, it effected an enlargement of the General Conference Committee from thirteen to twenty-five members, thus bringing in representative laymen, such as physicians, managers of publishing houses, and prominent educational men, also the heads of important mission fields. The advantage gained by this substantial increase in the number of the men who were to mold the policy of the denomination between the sessions of the General Conference, are obvious. It put the work on a world-wide basis, and gave tangible expression to the desire to have all the interests of the cause well represented when plans were laid for its furtherance.

With a committee thus widely representative in character, the brethren in foreign fields could not longer feel that important decisions adversely affecting them and their work were often made by a small group of men. Moreover, the inclusion of several prominent medical men tended to cement the union between the medical missionary work and other branches of denominational activity. The bringing in of men identified with the publishing work, helped to bring about that denominational

REVIEW AND HERALD IN 1925

control of the book business which was in the minds of the brethren six or eight years before, when they contemplated a General Conference book concern; at the same time it avoided the serious danger that threatened the other plan of centering so much responsibility in Battle Creek.

The second important change brought about at this Conference was the beginning, at least, of an attempt to distribute the available funds of the denomination where they were most needed. The important fact was pointed out that the field is not North America, but the world; hence the tithe paid by the people of America was not necessarily to be used in America, but anywhere in the great harvest field where it might be most needed. Hence Michigan or Ohio, with thousands of Adventists in a comparatively small population which had already enjoyed an opportunity to hear the message, could not consistently retain its large tithe for exclusive use within its own borders, while England, France, and Russia, to say nothing of such mission fields as China and India, with their teeming millions who had had little opportunity to hear the message, struggled on with a very few workers and a tithe entirely inadequate to the requirements of the field.

By this it is not meant, of course, that the General Conference took action calling upon the local conferences to hand over their tithe to be used in these needy fields; but the principle involved in this wider distribution of the denominational funds was plainly set forth and its reasonableness acknowledged.

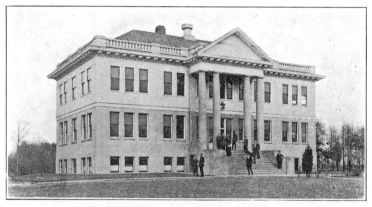

WASHINGTON MISSIONARY COLLEGE
The first administration building, but later used for science and arts departments.

A third achievement of the Conference of 1901 was the adoption of the plan of organizing groups of conferences, as union conferences, each under a union president, who should have supervision of all the conferences in his union, and preside over representative gatherings of delegates at proper times, when the immediate affairs of the union would be considered. This plan relieved the General Conference at its biennial sessions, and the General Conference Committee between sessions, of a large amount of work of a more or less local character, at the same time providing by means of the union gatherings for prompt and careful consideration of all the needs of the section.

The full importance of this move was not realized at the time. It not only relieved the members of the General Conference Committee of a large amount of administrative detail, but it placed responsibility upon a larger number of men throughout the country, who were thus brought into close relations with the general work.

A. G. Daniells, president of the Australasian Division, was elected to succeed G. A. Irwin as head of the General Conference, and it fell to him to carry out the reforms inaugurated at this Conference, Elder Irwin accepting a call to take charge of the work in Australasia. W. A. Spicer, who had succeeded D. A. Robinson as superintendent of the Indian Mission, was called to the secretaryship of the General Conference, his place in India being taken by J. L. Shaw.

The Conference of 1903, held in Oakland, Calif., was a remarkable meeting in its way, but perhaps its most important

THE WASHINGTON SANITARIUM

achievement was in supplementing the work done in 1901. Action was taken outlining a plan for reorganizing institutions so as to bring them fully under the control of the denomination. The forward movement in behalf of foreign fields inaugurated at the Conference of 1901 was greatly strengthened, and the General Conference departments, which had been foreshadowed in the general plans adopted at the earlier Conference, were carried through to organization.

It was in the years immediately following this Conference that the first health institution founded by this people, the Battle Creek Sanitarium, passed out of the control of the denomination, to the sorrow and regret of its best friends and well-wishers. It was painful to see this institution cut off from the advent movement with which it had been connected from its humble beginnings nearly forty years before; but as matters stood, it seemed to those immediately concerned that either the movement or the institution would have to change if the two were to work together harmoniously. In fact, as the situation developed, it became apparent to the General Conference Committee that some of the medical workers were not in full sympathy with the fundamental teachings of the denomination. Under these circumstances those who occupied positions of responsibility could not consistently encourage the young people of the denomination to go to Battle Creek to receive their training.

While this unfortunate situation was developing in Battle Creek, our other health institutions and the medical workers connected with them throughout the world were more or less in perplexity. It was a time when men considered their relation to the reform work represented by the Adventist people as a whole, and made their decisions on principle. With few exceptions the physicians and nurses took their stand with the denomination, and loyally supported the Medical Department, which was in due time organized on the same basis as the other departments. They co-operated also in such an adjustment of the question of ownership of the various medical institutions as would bring them strictly under denominational control, and make it impossible for a sanitarium founded by the denomination to take itself out of the hands of the organization.

One of the far-reaching decisions made at the Conference of 1903, was " that the General Conference offices be removed from Battle Creek, Mich., to some favorable place for its work in the Atlantic States." The removal of the headquarters of the Review and Herald Publishing Association, which had lost its main building by fire, Dec. 30, 1902, was likewise suggested. Both these important moves were rapidly effected.

The committee appointed to secure a location for the General Conference offices spent some time in looking at sites in the neighborhood of New York City and in other parts of the East, but found nothing favorable till they began prospecting in the vicinity of Washington, D. C. A beautiful plot of land of some fifty acres, lying in the town of Takoma Park, about eight miles north of the Capitol, was at length secured, at the merely nominal price of $6,000. On this ideal site were erected in due time buildings for a sanitarium and a college. Smaller building sites were also secured in that portion of the town lying within the District, about a mile nearer the Capitol, on which the General Conference administrative building and the office of the Review and Herald Publishing Association were erected.

REVIEW AND HERALD TEMPORARY HEADQUARTERS

On moving to Washington, D. C., in 1903, this building, 222 North Capitol St., was occupied until the permanent office in Takoma Park was erected.

The removal to Washington was in harmony with the instruction given through the spirit of prophecy,— that the headquarters of the work should be in the more populous East. Many years before, the cause had moved West and grown into strength. The eastward move of the General Conference and the Review and Herald office seemed to the people a signal of advance, and brought courage and hope. In the new location a freer field was found for the full development of the new policies which the delegates of the 1903 Conference had marked out for it.

When the search for the new location began, the spirit of prophecy had given no definite counsel as to the exact place. But while the committee on location were still at their task, messages began to come, urging attention to the advantages of the national capital as headquarters for our work. As the brethren considered these counsels, all felt assurance in selecting the various sites for the General Conference and publishing, educational, and sanitarium interests in Takoma Park, Washington, D. C. On the removal, much was said by the national press in approval of the foresight shown by our denomination in choosing the national capital as its headquarters. The results have fully justified the counsels given.

GROUP OF SANITARIUMS IN NORTH AMERICA

STUDENT BODY, WALLA WALLA COLLEGE

CHAPTER XXXIV

Educational and Health Activities [1]

THE beginnings of our educational work were set forth somewhat fully in a previous chapter. It is gratifying to be able to say here that the fundamental principles that were clearly enunciated when our first college was brought into being in 1874, are still recognized. While the work has grown rapidly, and has taken on proportions little dreamed of by the founders, the reform ideas that gave rise to our first humble efforts to educate our own children, are still precious in the eyes of parents and fruitful among our young people. Adventist schools are founded and carried on for the purpose of giving Adventist young people such a fitting up for life as will enable them to act worthily their part in this world, and be ready for higher service in that better world beyond.

How far our schools are successful in carrying out these ideals must be judged from the records. Out of sixty-five college graduates that came from one of our colleges in 1921,

---

[1] In writing this chapter, the author has drawn freely from the reports of the educational secretaries given at the General Conferences of 1918 and 1922. In some cases the language of the reports has been used with but slight modification.

fifty-two were in our own work a year later, or still in school, or making Christian homes. In another college, all except six of the graduates in three years went into our work, or were taking special courses intended to fit them for better serv-

FOREIGN MISSIONS CLASS, UNION COLLEGE, NEBRASKA

ice. These examples are typical. They are taken from our American colleges; but the schools in Europe and Asia and Africa and South America are not one whit behind our American institutions in this matter of giving their young people such a training as will fit them to take an active part in the great work of giving the gospel to the world.

In Africa, in India, and in the Far East, and also in South America, the Christian school is our principal evangelizing factor. In Africa, out of seventeen organized conferences and missions, fourteen are operated essentially on a school basis. At Malamulo, in our Nyasaland Mission territory, the outschools number more than fifty, and there are literally thousands of young men and women in training. In South America, the Indian mission schools enroll some 2,500 students yearly, and there have been as many as 1,000 baptisms in one year.

While the evangelizing character of our schools here in the homeland may not be quite so outstanding, yet it is, nevertheless, a large factor. Statistics show that of the young people who are educated in our own educational institutions, a very large proportion continue true to the principles that are dear to us, while of those whose training is received in institutions not of our planting, the large majority go the other way. The educational work is a definite part of the work of this denomination. Adventist schools were born of a spiritual necessity, to serve the needs of a spiritual movement.

There are certain fundamental characteristics that have come to be associated with Seventh-day Adventist schools. They may be briefly summed up as follows:

The Bible is faithfully taught in all the years of school life. The teaching in all classrooms is related to the fundamental principles taught in the Bible, which is the source of spiritual truth. Those studies are emphasized which contribute most directly to the spiritual objectives that led to the founding of our schools. Manual labor is honored as having a definite place in an all-round preparation for life. The cultivation of correct physical habits is emphasized. Well-planned missionary activities form a large factor in the school program.

It has been the policy of the Educational Department to emphasize those phases of school work which best lend themselves to the needs of the denomination, at the same time endeavoring to maintain balance and all-round efficiency. When the church school work was new and the support of the teachers was precarious, it was, at times, difficult, if not impossible, to maintain those high intellectual standards that are necessary to the fullest success; but as time has gone on and the supply of well-trained teachers has become more nearly adequate to the demand, the efficiency of the church schools has been greatly increased.

The intermediate schools, academies, and colleges have been passing through a similar experience. While holding strongly to their denominational features, they have gradually strengthened their courses from the intellectual standpoint, at the same time improving their facilities and equipment. The various educational conventions held under the auspices of the Educational Department have been a strong factor in raising the efficiency of these schools.

At the convention held in College View in the summer of 1906, certain general plans were adopted which have since been followed. A course of sixteen years, extending from the beginning year of the primary grades to the end of the fourth year of the college course, was then decided upon, and the work in the grammar grades and also in the four years of the preparatory or academic course, was made to correspond in a general way with the work given in the same years in the public high schools.

The convention held in Berrien Springs in the summer of 1910 marked the organization of sections representing the various departments with a view to the working out of syllabi covering the first twelve years. Important decisions were also made at this meeting with reference to approved textbooks. The educational council held at our college near St. Helena, Calif., in the summer of 1915, which was followed by conventions conducted in connection with other important colleges in the country, was successful in establishing more definite standards of education, and increased the efficiency of the schools and colleges by bringing about oneness of aim and methods.

The convention held at Colorado Springs, Colo., in the summer of 1922, was the largest and most representative gathering of the kind ever held by Seventh-day Adventists. It was the first real world convention in which the educational institutions of countries outside the United States were fairly well represented.

At this convention much earnest work was done in the direction of maintaining the distinctive ideals that called forth the establishment of Seventh-day Adventist schools, and of resisting worldly influences and policies that would neutralize our efforts to educate our young people for effective service in the work of the denomination. Emphasis was placed on the industrial features of our educational work, not only as a means of enabling students to work their way through school, but also as a valuable part of development in character and in physical skill.

The spiritual principles underlying the training of our young people received much attention. It was encouraging to note the perfect unanimity in such matters of the large delegation made up of educators from all parts of the world field.

When the Educational Department was first organized, Frederick Griggs, then serving as principal of South Lancaster Academy, was called to the chairmanship. He continued as head of the department until the spring of 1910, when he resigned to accept the presidency of Union College, and was succeeded by H. R. Salisbury. At the General Conference of 1913, Professor Salisbury was asked to take the superintendency of the India Mission field, his work as general secretary being taken

MISSIONARY VOLUNTEERS, SOUTH LANCASTER, MASS.

by J. L. Shaw, the former superintendent of India. Somewhat later, Professor Griggs was released from Union College to take the educational secretaryship of the North American Division, and in the winter of 1915, on the resignation of Professor Shaw, he was made educational secretary also of the General Conference.

At the General Conference of 1918, W. E. Howell was elected educational secretary, Frederick Griggs accepting a call to the presidency of Emmanuel Missionary College at Berrien Springs, Mich. At the Conference of 1922, W. E. Howell was re-elected secretary of the Educational Department, and C. W. Irwin, who had entered the department the previous year as associate secretary, was re-elected to that office. Otto John served as assistant secretary from 1918-22, when he was called to the presidency of Union College in Nebraska. In 1921 Flora H. Williams was called to serve as assistant in elementary and home education, and one year later C. A. Russell was appointed assistant secretary in secondary and elementary education. Sarah Peck did valuable service in the department from 1918 to 1923 as assistant in elementary and normal education, especially in the development of textbooks for the elementary grades.

The growth in the number and efficiency of our educational institutions the world over, has been of a most encouraging nature. In North America, there has been growth in the num-

COLPORTEURS AT EMMANUEL MISSIONARY COLLEGE, MICHIGAN

ber of academies and intermediate schools, and in many cases considerable enlargement of the various college plants. Washington Foreign Mission Seminary, after doing excellent work of a special kind in training missionaries for the foreign fields, entered the class of senior colleges in the autumn of 1914. South Lancaster Academy began to give junior college work about the year 1915; and in 1923, as Atlantic Union College, it entered the class of senior institutions in the training of ministers.

Canada has developed two strong training centers,— Oshawa Missionary College at Oshawa, Ontario; and Canadian Junior College at Lacombe, Alberta. South America has five educational centers. Work for the Spanish is conducted at Camarero, Argentina, at Chillan, Chile, and at Lima, Peru; for the Portuguese at Santo Amaro, near São Paulo, Brazil; and for the Indians at Juliaca, near Lake Titicaca, Peru. The training school at Juliaca has government recognition, so that the principal is able legally to appoint teachers for the outschools.

In Europe, some important steps forward have been taken. Stanborough Missionary College, our regular training school for Great Britain, has raised its standards. Its courses of instruction have been so arranged that their unique content may serve as a means of training workers for the cause. The training school at Friedensau, which had to be closed during the war, has resumed its work in a stronger way than ever before, and is turning out a large number of efficient workers for the large German-speaking field.

Germany also has two new academies, one in the west and one in the south. Norway has recently established an academy at Onsrud, while similar schools in Sweden, Finland, and Denmark have been strengthened. The Latin Union school has been moved from Switzerland to France, where it is housed in substantial and well-furnished buildings at Collonges sous Salève, in Upper Savoy, and has an enrolment three times as great as it had before.

There was also for a time a school in Prague for the training of workers, but it has been temporarily closed to secure better conditions for work. Short-term schools are being conducted in Poland and Jugo-Slavia, and in 1922 a school was opened in Constantinople. Following the organization of the new Baltic Union Conference in 1923, a new training school was established in a beautiful country location a few miles outside of Riga. Substantial work has begun also in the establishment of elementary schools in several leading countries of Europe.

In the Far East a complete system of schools is in process of development, with a central college at Shanghai, intermediate schools at various centers in China, and training schools in Korea, Japan, the Philippines, and Singapore, all increasing year by year in size and in strength. In India four training schools for Indians are doing good work, with a fifth in process of establishment. One school for Europeans, of the junior college type, is conducted near Mussoorie, India, in the foothills of the Himalayas. These, together with their outschools, enroll nearly 1,400 students. The average increase in enrolment during the four years 1918-22 amounts to 220 per cent, one union showing 400 per cent.

In Africa the old Kenilworth Union College plant for Europeans has been moved up country, and established on a large farm at Spion Kop in Natal. Not only have our native schools advanced in their march from the Cape into the Rhodesias and Nyasaland, but the Congo Tanganyika Territory and Kenya Colony have been entered, and the drive has begun from the north into Abyssinia. There is renewed activity also in Upper West Africa, while our first schools have just been established in Portuguese West Africa and Southwest Africa. All through the African field, much improvement is being made in the educational facilities and in the standards of teaching.

The Australasian Missionary College, at Cooranbong, New South Wales, received new inspiration and much practical help from the labors of Prof. W. W. Prescott in 1922 and 1923, and is continuing to make excellent progress under the principalship of Lynn H. Wood. A small but substantial school is

COLPORTEURS AT BROADVIEW THEOLOGICAL SEMINARY, ILLINOIS

being conducted in West Australia, while New Zealand is caring for her promising youth in a growing institution on her own soil.

There is a renewed interest in education in the West Indies, Mexico, Fiji, the Hawaiian Islands, and other centers in the South Pacific, and word comes that new schools have recently been started in Sumatra and North Borneo. Our latest word is of a school in Alaska, and another to be started there for the native Indians.

The growth of our educational work as a whole may be understood by setting forth a few figures:

At the close of 1912, the denomination had 573 elementary schools, employing 674 teachers, with an enrolment of 15,602. In the same year there were ninety colleges, academies, and intermediate schools, employing 631 teachers, and having an enrolment of 8,205, and property valuation of something over $2,000,000.

At the close of 1922 there were 1,259 elementary schools, employing 1,718 teachers, and having an enrolment of 34,034, and an annual maintenance cost of $601,752.59. In the same year there were 123 colleges, academies, and intermediate schools, employing 1,159 teachers, with an enrolment of 15,505, and the value of the school property amounted to more than $5,000,000.

The total number of students in colleges, academies, and intermediate schools the world over in the school year 1921-22, was 15,505; the number the same year in the elementary schools was 34,034. This gives a grand total of 49,539. This number of students, compared with the church membership of the same year, gives a percentage of 23.73, while the percentage ten years earlier stood at 20.38. Thus a larger proportion of our children and young people are enjoying the privilege of attending a denominational school than was the case ten years ago.

Extended visits made by the Educational Secretary of the General Conference from 1920 to 1924 to Europe, South America, Africa, and India, have brought rich returns in clarifying the aims and methods of Christian education, in broadening the conception of world education in the home field, and in giving unity and coherence to the work as a whole.

The Health Work

Following the separation of the medical work from the parent institution at Battle Creek, a number of smaller sanitariums sprang into existence, until they became quite numerous in the United States. Treatment-rooms were also established in many cities. Today our medical work is represented by a system of sanitariums, hospitals, treatment-rooms, dispensaries, health food factories, cafés, and cafeterias reaching into many lands.

Conference sanitariums, treatment-rooms, hospitals, and dispensaries now number fifty-five, representing an investment of nearly $5,000,000. Institutional work is carried on in eighteen countries. More than 2,500 workers are employed, including 172 physicians, 1,080 nurses, besides other employees. More than 100,000 patients are cared for annually in these institutions, which have an income of about $3,000,000. The charity work, based on moderate rates, is about $100,000 per annum. There are also fifty or more sanitariums and treatment-rooms under private ownership or control, which represent the denominational health principles, and in many ways help forward the work.

Outside of the United States there are the sanitariums at Calgary, Alberta, and Victoria, British Columbia, Canada; Entre Rios, Argentina, South America; Watford, England; Skodsborg,

Denmark; Gland, Switzerland; Zehlendorf, near Berlin, and Bad Aibling, Germany; Plumstead, South Africa; Sydney and Warburton, Australia.

Several health homes, hospitals, and dispensaries are to be added to the list of health institutions in foreign lands. At Shanghai, China, much has been done toward establishing a sanitarium and nurses' training school. Other places in China have their dispensaries and hospitals. At Soonan, Chosen, a dispensary hospital has long been established. Dr. Riley Russell and his assistants at this one center in one year treated

SANITARIUM NURSES, SKODSBORG, DENMARK

17,000 patients. He also was able in a few years to baptize more than 500 converts. India has a number of dispensaries.

A feature of interest is the way our stronger denominational sanitariums are assisting to start the work in new centers. The Washington Sanitarium, at Washington, D. C., which has grown to large dimensions under the superintendence of Dr. H. W. Miller, made a cash donation of $10,000 toward the establishment of the Shanghai Sanitarium, and is undertaking to equip that institution by a liberal per cent of later earnings. It is also rendering relief to the medical work in Europe. The St. Helena Sanitarium has been helping in a similar way. The sanitarium at Skodsborg, Denmark, which has grown, under the fostering care of Dr. J. C. Ottosen, its superintendent, to be our largest denominational sanitarium, is rendering needed help in connection with the medical work in various parts of Europe.

It is particularly in the dispensaries in mission lands that medical work finds its largest field. It may not be favored with beautiful buildings, well situated and well equipped. It is in the number of persons who receive material relief from their ailments, that these medical missionary enterprises make their best records. We are fortunate in possessing today a number of these health centers which, while ministering to the body, find thus more ready access to the soul. Those in charge report to us that many favorable opportunities for evangelism are offered through the physical help rendered.

Our medical work among the Inca Indians of Peru shows the large possibilities of medical work as an evangelizing agency. In the pioneer stages of this work, as reported by Elder F. A. Stahl, probably 90 per cent of the conversions are an outgrowth of medical work. It is the same among the savages of central Peru. There are twenty-three medical workers in the Inca Union, mostly couples of whom both man and wife are nurses. The sick often come as early as four o'clock in the morning, and keep coming all through the day.

We are probably safe in saying that fully 200,000 persons each year are numbered as patients in our sanitariums, hospitals, and dispensaries throughout the world. Figures, however, cannot represent the real good accomplished. In India, China, Africa, among the Inca Indians of Peru, in various island fields, and in other places where our missionary doctors and nurses are at work, there is gross ignorance of the simplest principles of health, hygiene, and sanitation. Disease conditions of all kinds are very prevalent. Medical help of any kind is scarce. The good that is accomplished in these places is measured by the amount of suffering that is relieved. The multitudes who suffer on, without help, tell the need of what is yet to be done.

It is the hope of our Medical Department to see the medical extension plan successfully developed to the point where many small enterprises may be established in fields that keep calling so piteously for help. Almost endless possibilities of doing good are held out by those in charge of these fields.

A large health educational work is done by our medical institutions. Each one is supposed to stand as a center of light, radiating truth concerning the better way of living, teaching the laws of health, and following rational principles in the treatment of disease. The influence of Christian physicians, nurses, and other helpers, does its part in bringing spiritual help to those who come for physical relief. Taken as a whole, our sisterhood of sanitariums and allied institutions represent a large sphere of educational influences. How strong a factor for evangelism this work may be, only the judgment of the great day can tell.

For many years we have operated training schools for nurses. Probably 3,000 or more young men and women have been sent out from our institutions to fill various positions of responsibility and usefulness. The twenty-three training schools now conducted have a constant full attendance of young people selected from among the best the denomination offers. From the yearly output of graduate nurses it is our hope to meet the demands of the home and foreign fields for true missionary nurses.

In more recent years, since the appointment in 1921 of Miss Kathryn L. Jensen as assistant secretary, the oversight of our nursing work has been more definite, and special attention is being given to fitting workers for denominational needs. Out of 208 nurses graduated in 1921, 109 are engaged in some branch of our organized work. Eight of these are in foreign lands, ninety in sanitariums, seven in academies, and four in conference work. Institutes and summer schools for graduate nurses are being held, with a view to keeping in close touch with the large number of trained medical workers.

In co-operation with the General Conference Educational Department a most important field of usefulness is opened to our nurses. School nurses are being placed in our academies and colleges, who take oversight of the health of the school family, and give instruction in certain phases of health training. Extending to our church school work, nurses are rendering further help through the health inspection of the children. Already excellent results are seen from this recent step.

Health training is carried still farther through the course in home nursing which is offered to our churches. Several thousand of our sisters and a number of brethren have taken this course, and have qualified for the certificate that is offered by our General Conference Medical Department. The value of this instruction may not fully appear until we come to the time of another epidemic. In the meantime our people are being instructed in disease prevention, simple treatments, and home care of the sick, all of which is helpful in our homes and among our neighbors.

An important feature of our medical education is in the operation of our College of Medical Evangelists at Loma Linda and Los Angeles, Calif. This unique institution, the only one of its kind in the world, was established for the purpose of training medical missionary physicians and other medical evangelists. A number of thoroughly qualified doctors have been graduated from the school, of whom several have responded to calls from the mission field. We are hopeful that the future will see many well-trained men and women go from this institution to the ends of the earth, carrying the gospel of good health and the ministry of helpful spiritual service. The standing of our medical school, as far as medical and legal requirements are concerned, has been assured. Its rating is the highest, and its students do highly creditable work at every examination and test.

Through several health journals our health principles are being given to the public month by month in thousands of copies. *Life and Health,* which title succeeded that of the old *Pacific Health Journal,* first published in 1885, has a monthly circulation of 50,000 copies. The British journal, *Good Health,* also has a good circulation. Other health publications, some in various languages, are doing their part to carry the health message. Tracts, pamphlets, and bound books add to the volume of printed pages doing the same.

Our health food activities are flourishing. With ten food factories, many food stores, cafés, and cafeterias, this feature of our health work occupies a wide field of usefulness. The health food business of the Australasian Union deserves notice. With several factories, a large wholesale depot, many retail stores, and a system of affiliated cafés, it represents an enterprise of widespread usefulness and influence. The food sales of a single year amount to $750,000. The profits are largely used for the support of church schools.

Our health work stands distinctly as one of reform. Through parlor lectures in our sanitariums, by schools of health, in nurses' classes, in the schoolroom, through our publications, by means of our health food products, and by every means by which we can work, we are endeavoring to sound the call of reform. This means to point out the better way of living, make plain the laws of health, and urge obedience to them. It enables us to present these laws as the laws of God, and to point men and women to Him as the Healer alike of body and soul.

I. H. EVANS

THE OLD MISSION IN HONAN
It was here that our publishing work was first started in China.

CHAPTER XXXV

Missions in China

THE awakening of China, accomplished in large part since the opening of the twentieth century, may well be regarded as the most remarkable event of modern times. That a people numbering more than one fourth the population of the globe, boasting a civilization reaching back into prehistoric times, and which had for centuries kept itself rigidly aloof from the rest of the world, should now suddenly throw open all its doors, and show an eager interest, not only in the culture and civilization of the once hated foreigner, but also in his religion, is indeed more than remarkable. It defies explanation except as the operation of a divine providence which is everywhere going out before the people of God and opening the once closed doors in order that the gospel of the kingdom may be preached throughout the world for a witness to all nations.

In reviewing as we do in this chapter the missionary operations of Seventh-day Adventists in China, it has seemed best, in the interests of clearness, to consider the country by sections, taking up one after another the various groups of provinces into which for missionary administrative purposes the country has been divided, and relating the facts concerning the founding of the leading mission stations.

It is only within recent times that Adventists have opened work in the Middle Kingdom. Mention was made of China's needy millions at the General Conference in 1899, but no definite action was taken in the direction of beginning missionary operations there until 1901, a year memorable among Seventh-day Adventists as marking for them the beginning of a really world-wide missionary activity. At the General Conference held in the spring of that year, it was voted, at their own request, to send Mr. and Mrs. J. N. Anderson to China, and a little later it was decided that Miss Ida Thompson, Mrs. Anderson's sister, should accompany them.

South China Union Mission

The work thus begun was in a part of the celestial kingdom now designated as the South China Union Mission, including the provinces of Kwangtung, Fukien, French Indo-China, the British colony of Hongkong, and the islands of Taiwan (Formosa) and Hainan. The party of three took up residence at first in Hongkong to learn the language, and to follow up the work of Abram La Rue, a colporteur and Bible worker who had there engaged in self-supporting missionary effort since 1888. Brother La Rue had entered upon this work of his own accord, and maintained himself by selling health foods and religious books and papers. He labored chiefly in Hongkong, which is not a part of China proper, but his efforts were extended also to Shanghai and other parts, where he sold a large number of the standard denominational books and distributed many thousands of papers and tracts. His work was chiefly with English-speaking people, such as merchants, sailors, soldiers, and dock laborers; but he carried no little burden for the large Chinese population in Hongkong, and managed, with the assistance of Mok Man Cheung, a colonial court translator, to have two Seventh-day Adventist tracts translated into the Chinese. These tracts he diligently circulated; but not knowing the language, he was unable properly to follow up the work.

When J. N. Anderson and his associates arrived in January, 1902, Brother La Rue was nearly fourscore years of age, and was rapidly becoming too feeble to help in the cause he loved. The new workers accordingly devoted a part of their time, while studying the language, to following up the interest already developed, and Elder Anderson was able after some months to baptize nine persons on profession of their faith, including six members of the crew of H. M. S. " Terrible."

At the end of October, 1902, the band of workers in South China was re-enforced by the arrival of Elder and Mrs. E. H. Wilbur, who first settled at Canton, in the province of Kwangtung, but later took up work at Hongkong, thus releasing Elder and Mrs. Anderson and Miss Thompson, who thereupon began to labor at Canton. They opened a school for boys, and one for girls under the charge of Miss Thompson, and applied themselves diligently to the study of the Cantonese dialect.

In 1906 J. P. Anderson joined the workers in South China. He began studying the Hakka dialect, preparatory to taking up work among the Hakka-speaking people who lived in the central and north-central parts of the province of Kwangtung. He settled pres-

ABRAM LA RUE

ently in Waichow, a city which served well as a center for the work among the Hakka-speaking people. In addition to the main station at Waichow, there came to be several widely scattered outstations, that were looked after by the workers residing at Waichow. The membership was more than 500 in 1920. At Waichow Mrs. J. P. Anderson died, after doing very valuable work in the schools and in translation, having attained an unusually thorough knowledge of several languages.

During the year 1907 two new stations were opened in Kwangtung Province for the Cantonese-speaking people, one at Fatshan, about ten miles from Canton, under the charge of Dr. Law Keem and his wife; the other at Kongmoon, about fifty miles from Canton, under the charge of Elder and Mrs. Wilbur. The mission at Fatshan, which has a population of half a million, later passed into the hands of one of our native workers, who is carrying on a dispensary and treatment-rooms.

Work was begun in the southwestern part of Kwangtung by August Bach, a German missionary who had worked for many years in South China. He was brought to a knowledge of the doctrines held by Seventh-day Adventists by reading the book, "Thoughts on Daniel and the Revelation," and by falling in with some missionaries of this denomination who were on their way to Korea. After spending some weeks at the headquarters

DR. LAW KEEM

of the mission in Shanghai, he went in the fall of 1909 to the southwestern part of Kwangtung Province, and opened work in the city of Pakhoi. A considerable interest developed, resulting in the organization of a church in Pakhoi and the opening of outstations.

The Cantonese Intermediate School for young men and the Bethel Girls' School were both near the city of Canton. These schools were in operation for a number of years, and did much to forward the work. The school for young men is still in operation. In 1920 the Cantonese Mission was reported as having twelve stations. The Year Book for 1925 reported thirty-two churches and 2,154 members in the South China Union Mission.

Central China Mission

In September, 1905, work was begun in Hunan, the last province to be entered by Protestant missionaries. P. J. Laird and his wife (Dr. Emma Perrine Laird) were the first to carry the advent message into this province. They settled at the provincial capital, Changsha, opening a dispensary and a school for the Chinese. Mr. Laird, a former missionary of the Church of England, knew the language, and thus could enter at once upon evangelistic work.

Elder and Mrs. Laird were compelled to return to America on sick leave in 1910, and some months later Elder and Mrs. R. F. Cottrell moved to Changsha to take oversight of the work in that field. In the fall of 1911, C. P. Lillie and his wife were sent out by the Mission Board, and after spending a few months in Shanghai, they joined the workers in Changsha.

O. B. Kuhn, who later became director, operated tent-meetings with good success in various Hunan towns. He reported 340 believers in 1920, with about a thousand persons receiving regular instruction. As a result of the faithful labors of a colporteur, the people in the province of Kwangsu began to call for a laborer. Early in 1914, Dr. Law Keem, responding to these calls, settled in Wuchow. Very soon a number were keeping the Sabbath. Later Dr. Law opened a dispensary at Nanning, far up the river, and there died. Dr. and Mrs. Roy Falconer and Paul Williams were sent to labor in this field, and there Mrs. Falconer was stricken down. One hundred members were reported in 1920, with two schools in operation.

Work at Amoy, in the southern part of the province of Fukien, was first opened as an outstation by the company in Canton. Later it was placed in charge of Elder and Mrs. W. C. Hankins, who arrived from the States in 1905. They were joined by B. L. Anderson and his wife.

The way had been prepared for these workers at Amoy by Pastor Keh, a former ordained minister of the English Presbyterian Church, whose conversion to the Seventh-day Adventist faith well illustrates the value of personal work. Timothy, a young Chinese who had embraced the truth at Singapore under the labors of R. W. Munson, was sent up to Amoy to learn the language of that province. He was to attend the school of the London Missionary Society, and went with the determination to make at least one convert to the advent message among the students. He failed to make any deep impression upon any of the young men in the school; but he early made the acquaintance of Pastor Keh, a prominent native worker among the Presbyterians.

The preacher's attitude was at first decidedly antagonistic; but Timothy perceived that he was a man of deep earnestness and consecration, and applied himself patiently to the task of convincing him of the truth. He sought occasion to converse with the pastor, and the two frequently went together to the hills, where they both talked and prayed over the question at issue. At length Timothy had the great joy of seeing his friend begin the observance of the Sabbath. Not long thereafter Keh presented his resignation to the Presbyterian Board, and began to preach for the Adventists. The interest spread throughout the Amoy district, which is in southern Fukien. A high school, started in connection with the mission, became a regular intermediate school for the training of workers. By 1920 thirty-nine Chinese workers had come out from this school. The mission buildings and school are situated on the island of Kulangsu, which is a part of Amoy.

Foochow, in the northern part of Fukien Province, was entered by Pastor Keh in 1913. The following year a church was organized, and a school for boys and one for girls were put in operation, the former growing into the Foochow Intermediate School for workers. The membership of this mission was reported as 255 in 1920.

An interest sprang up almost spontaneously at Swatow. Some began to keep the Sabbath as the result of a brief visit made by Pastor Keh while en route for Canton; while at Chaochowfu, some twenty-five miles inland from Swatow, there was found on a second visit quite a company of adults keeping the Sabbath according to their best light, some having already discarded wine and tobacco. These people pleaded long and earnestly for a foreign worker to come and give them further instruction. In response to this call, W. F. Hills and family were sent out by the Mission Board in the fall of 1911. T. K. Ang, a Chinese worker, has had a very active part in the work. Believers numbered nearly 300 in some thirty centers in 1920.

Chinese believers from Hunan carried the message over to Hupeh. F. A. Allum and Esta Miller rented a hall in Hankow, called the Chicago of China. A church was raised up, and Hankow became the headquarters of the Central China Mission. The membership was 220 in 1920. Kiangsi, a province worked hitherto only by colporteurs, reported sixty believers in 1920. In that year a mission station was opened at Kiukiang on the Yangtze, E. H. James being in charge.

The province of Shensi was just entered by Dr. A. C. Selmon and Frederick Lee in 1915. They visited and gave further instruction to certain persons who had become interested through reading matter. Not long afterward, S. G. White opened a mission station in Sianfu. When it became necessary for him to leave because of failing health, the mission was carried on by native workers. Revolutionary activities and banditry have made the province a difficult one to work.

In the fall of 1903, Drs. H. W. Miller and A. C. Selmon, with their wives, who were also physicians, and two nurses, Misses Simpson and Erickson, were sent to China by the Mission Board. This company at first located at Sintsai, in the province of Honan, the work in this province having been opened two years previously by E. Pilquist. After remaining in Sintsai for about a year, Dr. and Mrs. Miller moved to Shangtsai, Dr. Selmon and his wife to Siangcheng, and E. Pilquist to Loshan.

Elder and Mrs. F. A. Allum, of Australia, went to China in the spring of 1906, and joined Dr. Miller in the work at Shangtsai. In the following year the company in Shangtsai moved to Sinyang, a city in the south-central part of Honan, on the Hankow-Peking Railroad, where they were joined by Esta Miller and Orvie Gibson. J. J. Westrup, who had come to China in 1905 and settled at Loshan, moved to Shangtsai, and followed up the interest there.

The work in Honan having spread over a considerable territory, it was deemed advisable to secure a central location where

FRUIT OF THE GOSPEL IN CHINA

the foreign workers could reside, and from which they could conveniently visit the outlying stations. The city of Chowkiakow, with a population of 200,000, was chosen, and in time became the center from which numerous outstations could be carried on under the charge of evangelists or colporteurs. As an outgrowth of an institute, the first training school in Mandarin was started at Chowkiakow, O. A. Hall being principal and Pauline Schilberg one of the teachers. C. P. Lillie, director, reported a membership for the Honan Mission of 427 in 1920.

The intermediate school work was transferred to a rural district near Yencheng. Here first R. F. Cottrell and after him M. G. Conger built up a strong institution. The Yencheng Hospital Dispensary began its work under Dr. D. E. Davenport in 1916. Later as the work grew Dr. H. C. James joined the staff. The Central China Mission had, in 1925, twenty-four churches, with 1,346 members.

East China Mission

The East China Union Mission includes within its territory the provinces of Anhwei, Kiangsu, and Chekiang. The first active evangelistic work in this field was begun at Yingshan, in the province of Anhwei. D. B. Liu, of Honan, was acquainted with an evangelist of the Independent Chinese Church living in Yingshan, to whom he sent Adventist literature. The result was that this evangelist, D. D. Han, and several others in Yingshan, accepted the message. Mr. Han went to Shanghai, and spent some time with the workers there, after which he was baptized and returned to Yingshan, where he entered upon a very fruitful evangelistic campaign. Frederick Lee and his wife, on coming out to China in 1909, were asked to locate in Yingshan, and they, together with Dr. and Mrs. M. M. Kay, had charge of the work there until the spring of 1912.

During the summer of 1910, China held her first National Exposition in the city of Nanking. A company of evangelists and colporteurs was sent there under the direction of F. A. Allum and E. Pilquist, to improve the opportunity of reaching the large crowds that would come from all parts of the empire.

In 1919 the director, H. J. Doolittle, reported a membership of 225 in Anhwei Mission, including northern Kiangsu and the city of Nanking. In the latter city are the mission headquarters; also the interdenominational language school for missionaries, where a number of our workers have studied the Mandarin tongue.

Although our printing establishment for China was moved to Shanghai in the province of Kiangsu, in 1908, yet no continuous evangelistic work was started for some time, due to the fact that no one was able to speak the Shanghai dialect. In the spring of 1911, F. E. Stafford and Mrs. Bothilde Miller, with the aid of F. K. Li, of Honan, began a series of meetings, which soon brought out a company of inquirers. Since then the interest has been steadily growing, Director K. H. Wood, with the assistance of other workers, having held evangelistic meetings from time to time. Shanghai is the headquarters not only for the East China Union, but also for the Far Eastern Division, the organization and officers of which, as well as the institutions connected with it, are dealt with in a later chapter.

Southern Chekiang, which has a language of its own, was entered by G. L. Wilkinson in 1918. He settled in the chief city, Wenchow, and began study of the language. He was joined a year later by F. P. Greiner. The way had been pioneered by a native evangelist. A membership of 300 has been reported from this mission. By 1925 the East China Union Mission had twenty-five churches and 1,053 members.

North China Mission

The North China Union, which was organized in 1919, includes the provinces of Chihli, Shantung, and Shansi. Peking, the capital of China, is the headquarters of this union. H. M. Blunden was in charge at first, followed by Frederick Lee, whose series of evangelistic meetings had to be discontinued when war broke out between the political factions, placing the capital under military rule. After that a severe famine further wasted the territory. One church is reported.

In the Shantung province work was begun by F. E. Stafford, who made a short itinerating trip in the Chefoo district, selling and also giving away our literature.

The headquarters for the Shantung Mission is at Tsinanfu, where a small industrial school has been started. Evangelistic services were begun in the same city by W. J. Harris. H. L. Graham, the director, reported sixty members in 1921, with inquirers numbering 200. In 1925 the North China Union Mission reported three church organizations, with a total membership of 179.

Shantung is the birthplace of Confucius, a lineal descendant of whom is numbered among the believers in the advent message.

West China Mission

The West China Union includes the provinces of Szechwan, Yunnan, and Kweichow, with an area of 432,433 square miles and a population of 85,900,000. Nearly all traveling must be done by foot or pony, in a sedan chair, or by boat. It takes forty days to travel through this field from east to west, and fifty to cover the ground from north to south. The inns that must be patronized on the road are in comfort far inferior to the average barn. The country is infested with robbers.

In 1914, F. A. Allum and M. C. Warren made a trip through the gorges of the upper Yangtze as far as Chungking, and there opened a mission station. They traveled by house-boat, and were thirty-nine days going up the river. In the season of high water, steamers cover the distance in about five days. Chungking is a city of 700,000, and the leading commercial center of west China. F. A. Allum followed up the interest in this place. A substantial building was erected near the center of the city, which provides a large chapel, a street chapel, reading-room,

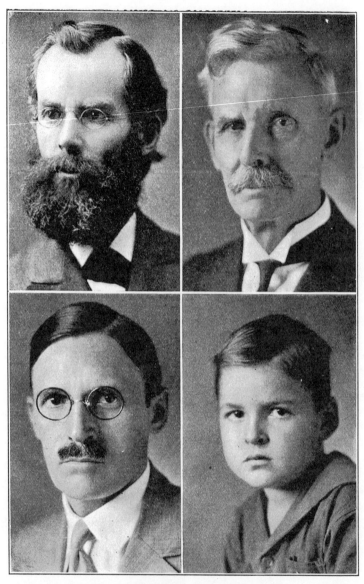

FOUR GENERATIONS OF MISSIONARIES

J. N. Andrews, our first foreign missionary ; C. M. Andrews, who went to Europe with his father ; Dr. J. N. Andrews, missionary to western China ; and " Bobbie," who is with his parents in China.

a schoolroom for boys and one for girls, as well as homes for some of the Chinese workers. Colporteurs are working the city and surrounding territory, and a chain of outstations is being opened.

The West Szechwan Mission has its headquarters at Chengtu, the capital of Szechwan, with a population of over half a million. Pioneer work in this field was done by Mr. and Mrs. C. L. Blandford, who entered the field in 1917, and labored on alone for four years, in sickness and war and plague, hoping monthly that help would come. Not till the fall of 1921 was it possible to send Mr. and Mrs. S. H. Lindt to assist them. Outstations were then opened. As the work was being thus established on a strong footing, Mrs. Blandford was removed by death.

The Tibetan Mission, located near the border of that inaccessible country, was founded by Dr. and Mrs. J. N. Andrews, who had been engaged in evangelistic and dispensary work in Chungking. In June, 1919, they packed their goods and supplies on a native boat, and started with their little son for Tatsienlu. The trip up the Yangtze and Meir Rivers occupied nearly two months, including one shipwreck, in the course of which their books and other belongings were thoroughly soaked. At Tatsienlu, where a fire broke out and burned to within a few doors of them, they have opened a dispensary, and thither both Tibetans and Chinese come for help. They were alone for two years, and then were joined by Mr. and Mrs. Leroy I. Shinn. The medical work is appreciated, as is shown by the record of over 1,000 calls in one month. The Tibetans apparently do not fear operations. Dr. Andrews reports one of his patients as saying: " I have a little pain in my stomach. Won't you cut me open, and see what is the trouble? "

Tatsienlu has been called " The gateway to Tibet," and is virtually a Tibetan city, so Dr. Andrews is enjoying the privilege of ministering to the people who have been most completely cut off from a knowledge of the gospel. A dispensary building has been erected, also a home for the missionaries, and literature in the Tibetan tongue is being printed on a press furnished by the Review and Herald, and carried into Tibet.

Dr. Andrews and his family returned to the United States on furlough October, 1923, and started on the return trip to their field of labor July, 1924. Their journey through a wartorn and bandit-infested country, though marked by hardships and dangers, was made without serious mishap, except the loss of much-needed supplies. They found their mission station, closed during their absence, unharmed, and conditions for the renewal of their work rather more favorable than when they left the year before.

Yunnan and Kweichow have been occupied more or less by colporteurs, and the former has had some visits from itinerating evangelists; but no stations have been opened at the present writing. In 1925 this mission reported two churches and eighty-four members.

MISSION HOME OF DR. J. N. ANDREWS

Manchurian Union Mission

Korean believers who moved over the Chosen border were the first Adventists in Manchuria. Adventists entered the field in October, 1914, when Bernhard Petersen and O. J. Grundset with their wives settled in the city of Mukden. They had spent a year in Shanghai studying the language, and were the first American missionaries to enter upon permanent work in Manchuria. They first began meetings in their compound, setting apart one of the rooms as a chapel. When the room became too small, the landlord allowed them to remove a partition, thus doubling the seating capacity. The meetings were begun in the fall; in the following summer nine persons were baptized, and shortly afterward the first church of eleven members was organized. When the crowds became too great to be accommodated in the compound, quarters were secured on one of the busy thoroughfares.

The second summer there were fourteen baptisms, and the interest to hear was steadily increasing. In 1916 the mission secured property of its own on one of the busy streets, meanwhile retaining the other assembly place for a chapel. Later, in 1921, the latter was replaced with a good church building.

The mission has secured for residential purposes a piece of land outside the city, where three houses have been erected, furnishing homes for the missionaries.

A station was opened in the Kirin Province in 1916, O. J. Grundset taking charge of the work and settling at Changchun. There also land has been secured outside the city, and houses have been erected for the missionaries. The Manchurian Union Mission, organized in 1919, reported in 1925 nine churches, with 205 members.

General Meetings in China

Late in 1906, Elder W. W. Prescott paid a visit to China, spending nearly three months in counseling with the workers at the different stations and studying the situation with them. At the close of his visit a general meeting of all the foreign workers in China was held at Shanghai.

I. H. Evans visited China in the latter part of 1908 and the early part of 1909, and gave some time to a careful study of the field. In the spring of 1909 a general meeting of all the members of the China Mission was held in Shanghai. At this time the field was reorganized, and made to constitute a union mission. Elder Evans returned to China in the autumn of 1910 as vice-president of the General Conference and superintendent for the Asiatic Division, and took over the supervision of the work in China, as well as in Japan and Chosen. His wide experience enabled him to give wise counsel in organizing and pushing the work in the field. He was also successful in arousing a deep interest in its needs in America, thus increasing the flow of means and of qualified workers.

During the years 1913-18, when I. H. Evans was serving as president of the North American Division, A. G. Daniells found time to interest himself effectively in the development of our work in China and other parts of the Far East.

Pioneer Conditions

Our work in China for a number of years was largely of a pioneer character. The missionaries went into new places and rented Chinese quarters, which they fitted up the best they could in order to make them habitable; but no amount of repairing can convert an old Chinese dwelling into a sanitary place in which to live. The floors are always low and damp, the walls are water-soaked from one year to the next, and the neighboring houses press in so closely on all sides that there is no chance for proper ventilation. Compelled to live under such conditions, our workers were subject to considerable illness, and a number had to return to the homeland on sick leave. The death toll, however, has not been large.

Abram La Rue passed away in 1903, at the ripe age of eighty-four. His declining years were gladdened with the

DR. H. W. MILLER AND HIS FAMILY

thought that younger and stronger hands than his were taking up the work he loved, and broad plans were being laid to give the message to China's teeming millions.

Mrs. Miller, wife of Dr. H. W. Miller, who died in the spring of 1905, was called away in the morning of a beautiful life; but she died happy in the thought of being laid to rest in a great needy mission field, and anxious only that her death should not discourage others from responding to the calls.

Seven years later, in the spring of 1912, Esta Miller died at his post of duty, young and burning with enthusiasm for the work of the Master, yet submissive to the divine will. Gertrude Thompson died in the summer of 1912 of malignant malaria. Miss Thompson had been in the field for only a little over two years, and was just getting a good command of the language, and coming to the place where she could do effective work for the Chinese people.

As these pages are being put into type for printing, Doctor H. W. Miller, with his present wife and their family, is preparing to return to China, his heart having long been in that field.

General Missionary Activities

In the foregoing pages an attempt has been made to give the reader some general account of the different parts of the field entered and the placing of the workers. It remains to treat in somewhat greater detail the various branches of missionary activity in China, and the conditions under which the work is carried on. The account naturally groups itself under four main heads: First, educational, consisting of the conducting of day schools and boarding schools; second, medical, consisting of the carrying on of dispensaries or hospitals; third, publishing, involving the printing and circulation of the denominational literature; fourth, and most important of all, the direct evangelistic and pastoral work, consisting of preaching the gospel on the streets and in halls, the holding of Bible studies in the homes of the people, and further instructing and baptizing the believers and organizing them into churches.

The Educational Work

Perhaps the most striking change that China has undergone in the last few years is that involved in the reorganization of the national educational system. Previous to August, 1901, education in China consisted of memorizing the old Confucian classics; but at this date an imperial decree abolished the ancient curriculum, and directed that in future candidates be examined in the Western arts and sciences. It was also decreed that schools and colleges be established throughout the empire.

Not only was this action taken officially, but China's leading men came out boldly in favor of popular education. Said Chang Chi Tong, an old and trusted statesman:

"Convert the temples and monasteries of the Buddhists and Taoists into schools. Today these exist in myriads. Every important city has more than a hundred. Temple lands and incomes are in most cases attached to them. If all these are appropriated to educational purposes, we guarantee plenty of money and means to carry out the plan. Buddhism and Taoism are decaying, and cannot exist; while the Western religion [Christianity] is flourishing and making progress every day. We suggest that seven temples with their lands, out of every ten, be appropriated to educational purposes."

And best of all, the people are doing this. It is not such an uncommon thing to see workmen tumbling the idols out of a temple, and replacing them with tables, chairs, and other furniture for a modern school. Even the girls and young women are being provided for, whereas formerly they could get an education only in mission schools. In 1906 the viceroy of Nanking sent four Chinese women to Wellesley College to be educated, this being the first instance of the government of China sending women abroad to be educated.

Of course, official action in itself could operate but slowly if the people held back; but this is not the case in modern China. The people there are hungry for knowledge; and as soon as they learn something themselves, they are eager to pass it on to others. One of our workers, visiting some villages in the interior, was surprised to find the children in one village fairly well versed in the Scriptures. They knew the leading Bible characters, and could answer many questions correctly. This was the more strange because all the women and most of the men were illiterate. Where, then, had these children learned to read? They were asked if they had a school or chapel. The answer was in the negative. "Where, then, did you learn these things?" There was a man in the village, reported one of the boys, who taught the children for a little while every evening.

The missionary sought out this self-appointed teacher, and found that he was a farmer living in a little mud-brick house with a straw roof and no floor. He was a poor man, too, and had to pay a high rent for the field he tilled; but every day, when the evening meal was finished, he gathered about him his own children and others who were free to come, and gave them a short lesson. The big rice sieve, turned bottom up over a grain basket, formed the table around which the children clustered, while the humble farmer taught them the intricacies of the Chinese alphabet. First they would recite in concert, naming the new characters after their teacher. Afterward each child would take a turn in reading by himself, the teacher giving him necessary help. After a few words in explanation of what had been read, the school was closed, and the table became a rice sieve again. Then the farmer would say: "Come, children, we must work the harder now to make up for the time spent in reading." And the children would go to their work with the same eagerness as to the reading.

Our school work in China has been carried on largely with the most primitive facilities, in low, dark houses with mud walls and thatched roofs. The students sit on narrow benches without backs, but they get their lessons. The quarters for the boarding students are small and cramped. The Bible is the chief textbook. The elements of arithmetic, geography, and physiology are also taught. The girls learn to sew, and some schools are provided with a knitting machine and appliances for other lines of industrial work.

In our schools we have the children of Sabbath keepers, both boys and girls, and brighter children it would be hard to find. We have the parents, too, for hardly a quarter of the male population of China can read, and among the women not one in a thousand recognizes the written characters. But they are all eager to learn. Then we have children and adults who have not yet embraced the Adventist views, but are anxious to learn to read, that they may study the Bible for themselves.

In addition to these elementary schools, mostly of a local character, there was opened in Honan, in the fall of 1909, the China Union Mission Training School. The faculty consisted of Dr. H. W. Miller, principal, Miss Pauline Schilberg, assistant, and two Chinese teachers. The attendance at the beginning was twenty-eight. Dr. Miller's health having failed, he was compelled to return to the States in the spring of 1911, and F. A. Allum took charge of the school.

The revolution which started in the fall of 1911 put a stop to the school work for the time being, and when conditions in the interior quieted down in the spring of 1912, it was felt that the quarters provided were so cramped and unsuitable for carrying on school work that it would be better to wait until the fall of 1912, and then open the school in the place where we planned to secure a permanent site for the institution. It was decided that Nanking would best serve the interests of the field. Quarters were accordingly rented there, and the school opened October 8 with an attendance of about fifty young men. Later this training work was carried on by the Shanghai Missionary College. In 1925 it was moved to Nanking, where suitable buildings have been provided for permanent educational work.

The Medical Work

Our medical work, as indicated in a preceding chapter, began in Honan, one of the central provinces of China. Honan is a vast, fertile plain, supporting a population of 35,000,000, with an average of 500 persons to the square mile. The inhabitants are for the most part farmers and small merchants. For a long time bitterly hostile to the foreigner, these people are today fully in accord with the new spirit which is actuating

China generally, and welcome the teachings of the missionary. Previous to the Boxer Rebellion of 1900, Honan did not have a single mile of railway, and only a few of the larger cities were provided with post offices. Now there are in the province hundreds of miles of railroad, including a trunk line from north to south, and another from east to west; while every city and town of importance has regular mail service. Moreover, manufacturing enterprises, such as modern cloth weaving, glass making, and the like, are springing up on every side; rich coal deposits are being opened, and new economic conditions are arising in consequence.

Nevertheless in all matters concerned with hygiene and sanitation the densest ignorance prevails. Surgery as practised by the native physician is barbarous. The suffering of the Chinese women in cases of difficult childbirth is beyond description. Bound by their crude superstitions, the people believe that angry gods and evil spirits are the chief cause of disease; hence the treatment applied is some form of sorcery, and includes puncturing with needles, blistering, cauterizing, and all manner of cruel, useless, and dangerous methods.

Owing to lack of proper hospital facilities, our physicians have been obliged to confine their efforts largely to those diseases which yield quickly to treatment. In the dispensaries in Honan alone, they have saved the lives of hundreds of persons who had taken poisonous doses of opium with intent to commit suicide. As a general rule, these poor people do not come back to thank their rescuers, not because they are naturally unthankful, but because their lot in life is so hard that they really wish to die. The majority of these victims of hard circumstances are women.

It is difficult for a foreigner to appreciate the situation of the Chinese woman. She never has a home as we understand it. As a child she is considered to belong, not to her parents, but to the home of the boy to whom she is engaged. And on her wedding day she is sent weeping away from all she has known and loved, to that which is unknown and dreaded. She is more than fortunate if her mother-in-law treats her with consideration. Her husband is not supposed to speak to her for the first few days, and except among Christians, he rarely learns to love her. The home is dark and gloomy, often including cattle among its inmates. The walls of the best room present nothing more cheerful than hideous images. There is no outlet for the smoke of the cookstove, and the bare earth floor is cold and damp. Even in the coldest winter weather there is no cheerful fireside, but only a pan of coals buried in ashes over which the feet may be warmed.

In such home surroundings the Chinese woman enters upon her life of monotonous toil. There will be few moments of leisure for her. She must pick the cotton, spin the thread, weave the cloth, and make the garments for the household. She must cook the food, grinding the flour herself, and often she must go to the field to help gather in the crops.

Where the missionaries come closest to these women, and perhaps help them the most, is at the dispensary; but even here their gross ignorance and superstition stand in the way. If a woman musters up courage enough to come to the mission for relief, her neighbors get together and discuss the case. They say, if she takes the foreigner's medicine, she will have to eat their doctrine also. Or they declare that receiving the treatments will make her childless, or that she will die within a hundred days, etc. Nevertheless, some of the women do come, and in so doing find relief from much unnecessary suffering.

The Publishing Work

In 1905 a small printing office was opened by Dr. H. W. Miller in Shangtsai, Honan, and a monthly paper, the *Fuh Yin Hsuen Pao* (Gospel Herald), began to appear. A few tracts, a hymn book, and some small schoolbooks for primary work were also issued. In March, 1907, the printing office was moved to Sinyang, also in the province of Honan, a suitable building being erected to receive it. The printing work was suspended during the major portion of 1907 and 1908, while Dr. Miller was taking a furlough in the States.

At a meeting of the China Mission committee held early in 1908, the publishing interests received further consideration, and it was decided to sell the printing office in Honan, and establish the publishing work and mission headquarters at Shanghai, where Dr. Miller took up his residence on his return from America.

Literature has from the first proved an effective means of reaching the Chinese, who are eminently a reading people, and have the highest respect for the printed page. To be sure, the problem is somewhat complicated when one remembers not only that the Chinese language is extremely difficult to master, but that there are many dialects to reckon with. China has a written language (the so-called " classical ") which is understood by all the educated classes throughout the country. The Mandarin, or official language, is understood by approximately three hundred million people. In addition to the Mandarin, there is the Amoy dialect, which is spoken by more than twelve million persons; the Cantonese, spoken by twenty million; the Shanghai-Soochow, spoken by twenty million, and understood by forty-four million. The Shanghai dialect is spoken within a radius inland of about 120 miles of Shanghai. The Hakkas, living in the province of Kwangtung, are believed to number from eight

PUBLISHING HOUSE IN SHANGHAI, CHINA

to ten million, and near them are the five million who speak the Swatow dialect, somewhat resembling the Amoyese. There are also five million Mongols, about that number of Ningpos, three million Hainanese, and three to five million Tibetans, included in this complex language problem.

In order to reach all the people, we need some literature in all these various languages. Nevertheless, we are already reaching, through our monthly paper in the Mandarin and classical, representative people in all parts of China. At present we have a goodly number of pamphlets and tracts and a few illustrated books in the classical tongue. Books and pamphlets have also been issued in the Mandarin tongue. Besides these there are pamphlets in the Cantonese, and a song book in the Shanghai dialect. Our paper, the *Shi Djao Yueh Bao* (Signs of the Times) comes out monthly in both the Mandarin and the classical language, the combined monthly edition exceeding fifty thousand copies.

The Evangelistic Work

Evangelistic work is being carried on, as indicated in the preceding pages, over a wide area. Progress must in the nature of things be slow. The converts require much help and instruction before they are ready to be baptized. In Honan our church is called "The true doctrine church," and it is generally recognized as holding up a high standard of conduct for its members.

The interest to hear is especially great in the villages inland, and there much of the best work is done. For example, Mr. and

NATIVE COLPORTEURS, HUNAN, CHINA

Mrs. Westrup took up their abode in a country village of about 200 inhabitants, and within a short time were able to baptize twenty-three converts. For a time they conducted a boys' school with twenty students and a girls' school with about thirty in attendance.

People come in from all sides to inquire. The women show fully as great an interest as the men; but they are heavily burdened with work. Often missionaries hear it said by these patient toilers as they gather in village groups: "I should like to go to meeting, but we women are always busy; there is no time to go. How can the gospel be for us?"

Itinerating in China is often attended with danger from robbers. Missionary Nagel tells of one such experience. He was returning to his home in Waichow from a trip to Canton, in a flat-bottomed river boat with three decks, pulled by a launch. He writes:

" We were almost half way home, and had come to a place in the river where a small island made the channel very narrow. Two other missionaries and myself were on the top deck, visiting and watching the country, when suddenly we heard the crack of rifles, and the balls whizzed all about us. One of the German missionaries fell, hit in the head. I dropped flat on the deck and crawled into a small cabin. The robbers, armed with knives, revolvers, and rifles, soon waded out and boarded the vessel. They carried off everything they could lay their hands on, including the coat off my back and the shoes from my feet. I did what I could for the wounded missionary, and the captain at my request sailed back for Canton, where we took him to the hospital."

As soon as one of the Chinese receives the truth, he begins to work for others. Converts are largely made in this way. The chief work for the missionaries to do is to train workers, organize the field, and direct in the work, giving further instruction for the building up of the believers. The active propaganda is largely done by the Chinese workers, sometimes before they are themselves fully instructed.

The eagerness of the Chinese to learn is very touching. One of our colporteurs met a man of thirty-five whom he succeeded in interesting in the gospel. The man was a vender of hot sweet potatoes, and a day's earnings would rarely exceed five cents, on which small amount he had to support a blind brother and an aged mother. Nevertheless he bought a copy of the " Gospel Primer," to the mastery of which he diligently applied himself at night. With some help he was able to read the book through. Then he began to read the easier parts of the Bible. He is now a converted man, and can read almost anywhere in the Bible. Two years ago a little company of believers was raised up in his village, and he was elected deacon. When this brother prays or tells the gospel story to a crowd of people, it is hard to believe that only a few years ago he was a poor, ignorant idolater, living in the grossest darkness of heathenism.

Perhaps this somewhat informal sketch of missionary operations in China may best be brought to a close by a few reports of some typical general assemblies held in different parts of the country. The first general meeting was held in Siangcheng, Honan, at the close of the year 1907. It was attended by fifty Chinese Sabbath keepers, mostly from Siangcheng and Shangtsai, and was a season of great spiritual refreshing, as well as of advancement in a fuller knowledge of the truth. Men brought their pipes and burned them, women unbound their feet, and all together sought that complete purification of heart and life which is to make ready a people prepared for the coming of their Lord. A change has indeed come to China.

From this time on, general gatherings of a similar character have been held from time to time. I. H. Evans writes:

" At a meeting held in May, 1911, in Changsha, Hunan, there was an attendance of more than seventy Sabbath keepers, and a congregation more eager to hear the Word of God could not be imagined. They had come from thirty to sixty miles, not a few of them on foot, leaving their work, their crops, their stores, in order to study God's Word. We held five meetings, a day, and finally had to leave Elder Cottrell with this large company of people still thirsting for more instruction, and with no help to give it to them except a sick wife."

About the same time a general meeting was held in Chowkiakow, Honan, beginning the first of May. It was attended by all the workers in Honan and by some from Anhwei, as well as by the students in the school, and when the weather was reasonably favorable, by large crowds from the city.

At this meeting for the first time a call was made for sinners, especially the heathen, to come forward for prayers. In the words of a worker:

" Brother Allum spoke the first evening, and the audience was a large one. At the close of his sermon, he asked if there was one sinner, one heathen, who would show to the world that he wanted to be a Christian by rising to his feet and coming forward. When no one moved, he knelt down and besought the Lord to give conviction to some poor soul. Then another call was made, and one sinner came forward, then another, and another, till nine precious souls had separated themselves from the congregation, and were seeking the Lord. On the following night three more came forward.

" On Friday night Dr. Selmon spoke for about twenty minutes, after which an excellent social meeting was held. Then followed a call to sinners, to which forty responded, coming forward to seek God. The next night fifty-four sought the Lord, and the last night there were seventy. During the week there were over 200 heathen who thus testified to their desire to seek the God of the Bible."

At the General Conference session of 1922, in San Francisco, I. H. Evans, vice-president of the Far Eastern Division, said:

" Thirteen provinces of China proper have been entered by our foreign mission workers, and already we have in China and Manchuria a church membership of 4,277."

According to the 1925 Year Book, by 1924 the number of members in China alone had increased to 4,816. Thus encouraging progress is being made.

43

W. T. KNOX

Treasurer of the General Conference, 1909 to 1922, a period of great foreign mission expansion.

FIRST SESSION OF THE JAPAN CONFERENCE, 1917

CHAPTER XXXVI

Missions in Japan, Chosen, and the Philippines

ADVENTISTS began their work for the Japanese people in the city of San Francisco, where a mission school was conducted in their behalf for several years in the early nineties. As a result of this work, a number of young Japanese accepted the truth, and several of them afterward attended Healdsburg College.

In 1896 this school was closed, and Prof. W. C. Grainger, formerly president of Healdsburg College, who had been in charge of it, sailed for Japan. He was accompanied by T. H. Okohira, a young Japanese who had accepted the truth at a tent-meeting in Southern California and had been a student at Healdsburg. The two settled at Tokio, and a year later were joined by Professor Grainger's wife and younger daughter.

As a result of careful study of the situation, it was thought best to work in educational lines. The Shiba Bible School was accordingly organized, classes in English Bible being conducted at such hours of the day as would best accommodate those who desired to attend. The pupils who came to these Bible classes were mostly attending regular schools in the city, but availed themselves of the Bible instruction for the purpose of gaining a better knowledge of the English language.

The first church was organized in Tokio in June, 1897, with a membership of thirteen. The Sabbath school connected with this church had an attendance of sixty. About the same time

T. H. Okohira opened up work in Kobe. Among the first converts in that city was a young lady who afterward became his wife. Another convert, H. Kuniya, shortly entered the work, and a few years later was ordained to the ministry.

W. C. GRAINGER

In 1898, the force of workers having been increased by the arrival of B. O. Wade and W. D. Burden and their wives, it was decided to start educational work in another part of the city. Both schools prospered, the classes being crowded with eager students, and the workers having many opportunities for personal work. While most of the pupils were interested merely in the study of English, and not in Christianity, nevertheless there were a number of converts, some of whom have proved stanch believers and earnest workers in the cause.

In the summer of 1899 an advanced step was taken when Professor Grainger began to publish a small monthly paper, *Owari no Fukuin* (The Gospel for the Last Days). The periodical thus started has continued to the present time, but with two changes of name, the present name meaning " Tidings of the Message." The list of paying subscribers has never been large, but the paper has been circulated widely through the mails, copies being sent to representative persons in all parts of the country. In this way many have become interested in the truth, and some have accepted it.

It was a severe blow to the work thus well started when Professor Grainger fell sick and died in October, 1899. His wife and daughter remained in the field for a year after his death, and then returned to California. One year later, in the autumn of 1901, Elder F. W. Field and his family, from Ohio, arrived in Japan. A few months later it was necessary for Mr. and Mrs. Wade to retire on account of broken health.

In the fall of 1906, Elder and Mrs. H. F. Benson, of Ohio, arrived in Japan, and at once gave themselves to the study of the language. Elder Benson served as secretary and treasurer of the mission, and later engaged in educational work. Miss

Etta Cornish came in 1909 to take up work for the young ladies. In June, 1910, Elder F. H. DeVinney and his wife from New York State were sent to take general charge of the field, F. W. Field returning to the States the following year. Still later we find V. T. Armstrong superintendent of this union.

While Japan presents openings for medical missionary effort, the conditions are peculiar. Many of the people are densely ignorant concerning the causes of disease and its proper treatment, and yet Japan has an excellent system of medical schools, from which trained physicians are being graduated year by year and are settling in all parts of the country. Hence there is not so great need of dispensary work as in other mission fields. Medical work consequently must be carried on chiefly by other means.

Our first medical missionary workers in Japan were Drs. S. A. and Myrtle S. Lockwood, who arrived in the country in October, 1902. After some months' study of the language, it seemed advisable to open a small sanitarium, and Kobe, lying 375 miles to the southwest of Tokio, at the entrance of the famous inland sea, presented a favorable opening. A suitable building was rented, and the institution opened June 1, 1903. The patronage was encouraging from the start, and every patient became a stanch friend of the institution. Among the patients were many broken-down missionaries who were glad to receive needed medical help in Japan rather than retire from the field permanently or on furlough. When the Doctors Lockwood were obliged to return to the States on account of Mrs. Lockwood's failing health, Dr. and Mrs. W. C. Dunscombe succeeded to the work, arriving in Kobe in May, 1907. Later a private sanitarium, especially for the Japanese, was carried on for a time by Dr. Kiku Noma, a Japanese lady physician.

The question of training workers early occupied the attention of the Mission Board. During the winter of 1908-09, a three months' school term was held, nearly all the regular workers employed in the mission being called in at that time to receive a course of training. Bible, history, physiology, and English were the principal subjects taught, and a rented house furnished the necessary accommodations for the most of the students in attendance. Prof. H. F. Benson had general charge of the school.

The following winter a school was held on similar lines, lasting four months, and a year later the term was extended to five months. Young men and women receiving the message during the summer were taken into the school the following winter, where they were grounded in the truth and trained for some line of work. The attendance during the first three years averaged about twenty-five. This school in time grew into the Japan Mission Training School, located at the headquarters compound, just outside the city of Tokio. P. A. Webber succeeded H. F. Benson as principal. In 1924 the school had a faculty of nine, with A. N. Nelson as principal and H. F. Benson science instructor.

TRAINING SCHOOL, TOKIO, JAPAN

Mention has already been made of the monthly periodical *Owari no Fukuin*, which was started in the days of Professor Grainger. In 1908 and 1909 special efforts were put forth to increase the circulation of the paper. Companies of two or three workers were assigned territory, and canvassed the people from house to house for subscriptions, also selling single copies. In towns of considerable size a campaign of this sort would be conducted previous to holding a series of meetings. Illustrated numbers were prepared several times a year, and were sold in large quantities by the students and other workers. This periodical work has continued to grow with the development of the work as a whole.

The next publications to be put out after the starting of the periodical were a series of Bible readings printed on single sheets. These were followed by a translation of "Steps to Christ" in pamphlet form. Later "His Glorious Appearing" was issued, also translations of a number of standard tracts.

Some small original tracts, dealing in a very simple way with gospel principles, were also put out, with special reference to the needs of the field.

For a time all the printing was done by outside publishing houses. Later the printing of the paper was done in our own rented rooms, and some tracts were also issued; but a considerable part of the printing was still done in Yokohama.

C. N. Lake went to Japan in 1911, and rendered excellent help in the printing office. He returned to America on account of Mrs. Lake's failing health. In 1914 a suitable building was erected in Tokio for the mission and publishing quarters, and A. B. Cole became manager. This building was damaged in the earthquake of Sept. 1, 1923, but has been restored.

Evangelistic effort put forth in Japan has shown results which are meager when compared with those in other lands, but there has been a fairly steady growth. In 1905 a tent was given by friends in America, and the first series of meetings was held in Tokio. The police feared that there would be disorder, but finally gave their consent for the meetings to be held, a representative of the department being present at each service. Perfect order prevailed, and a good impression was made. From this time on a series of meetings was held each summer in a city of some size which had in the previous winter been worked by canvassers. Later two additional tents were purchased.

THE TOKIO CHURCH

The immediate results of these tent efforts have never been large, the Japanese people in general not being much given to attending Christian meetings. The tendency is to take one's stand at the door, and after listening awhile, to go away. Such an attitude is not favorable to a thorough study of the Scriptures, which is essential in order to arrive at a full knowledge of the truth. Nevertheless, lectures on the life of Christ and on hygiene are well attended, and by following up the public effort with Bible readings and personal work in the homes of the people, it is found possible to make a deep impression.

The present laws of Japan allow full liberty to the Christian evangelist; but there is much prejudice to be met, especially on the part of the Buddhists. The younger generation are the freest to accept the gospel, yet there are exceptions, and some old people have taken hold with great earnestness. The principles of the old feudal system, by which the rights of the individual were subordinated to the interests of the family, the village, and the nation, still prevail generally in Japan, especially in the rural districts. Western education has made remarkable progress in the country, but it is making agnostics of many of the most promising young men, and thus greatly hindering the efforts of the missionary.

The work has grown somewhat more rapidly of late. There were reported in 1924, nine churches, with a combined membership of 390.

Chosen (Korea)

The message was first carried into Korea from Japan. In May, 1904, a Korean passed by a Seventh-day Adventist meeting hall in Kobe. A sign hanging by the door, written partly in Japanese and partly in Chinese characters, aroused his curiosity, and he stopped a moment to study it. He was able to determine from the Chinese characters that it was a Christian meeting place, but he could not make out the Japanese characters giving the name of the denomination. A Japanese brother sitting inside saw him standing at the door, and beckoned him to come in.

Although neither could understand the language of the other, they soon conceived the idea of carrying on a mutual interchange of thought by writing, using the Chinese characters, which were familiar to both. After some conversation carried on in this way, the Korean left, but he came again, and again. After he had in this way enjoyed a series of Bible studies, he brought with him a fellow countryman, who was also a Christian, and the two men continued their studies till they were convinced of the truth. The time having come for them to leave Kobe, they were baptized at midnight before sailing.

The first of these men went to Honolulu, whence he kept up a regular correspondence with Brother H. Kuniya in Kobe. The second returned to Korea. On the return voyage he met another Korean, Lim Ki Pao, to whom he passed on the new-found truths. Mr. Lim readily accepted all, and upon his arrival at Chinnampo, began to teach the Adventist views to his relatives and friends. In a few weeks thirty persons had accepted the truth, as far as it could be presented by this brother, and they united in sending an earnest request to H. Kuniya to visit them and give them further instruction. He responded to the call, and labored for several weeks among the country villages between Chinnampo and Pingyang. The interest being a very encouraging one, he was later joined by

DEDICATION OF A KOREAN CHURCH

Elder F. W. Field, who arrived at Chinnampo early in September. Two of the Korean brethren accompanied Elders Field and Kuniya as they visited the various small companies of believers and scattered ones who had become interested. Four little churches were organized as the result of this effort, having an aggregate membership of fifty, besides which there were a number of isolated believers, who later united with other churches.

Before returning to Japan, the brethren held a general meeting for the new believers at Chinnampo, which was attended by between thirty and forty of the new converts. The ordinances of the Lord's house were celebrated, the emblems being spread upon a little Korean table the size of a common tray and about a foot high. The meeting was blessed with the signal presence of God, a sweet spirit of fellowship being manifested by all the believers.

The beginning thus made in Korea was in due time followed up. At the General Conference of 1905, W. R. Smith was requested to make Korea his field of labor. He settled finally at Soonan, on the railway, near Pingyang, where a company of believers had been raised up by Korean workers. Miss Mimi Scharffenberg, of Wisconsin, went to Korea in 1906 to engage in school work. During the year 1908, the force of workers was further enlarged by the arrival of C. L. Butterfield and his family, Dr. and Mrs. Riley Russell, and Miss May Scott.

In the fall of the same year, during the visit of I. H. Evans, it was decided to separate Korea from the Japan Mission, and organize it as a separate mission field, with C. L. Butterfield as superintendent. Since that time, other workers have entered the field, including Howard M. Lee, Harold A. Oberg, and R. C. Wangerin, with their wives. The mission headquarters were finally established at Seoul. Following the General Conference of 1909, W. R. Smith settled at Wonsan, and the work has become well established in that part of the field as the result of his efforts. In 1910, R. C. Wangerin established a new station at Kyongsan in southern Korea. A church of forty-five members was presently raised up and a church building erected.

Medical missionary work has been a prominent feature of the Korean Mission. On their arrival in the country in 1909, Dr. and Mrs. Riley Russell opened a little dispensary in Soonan. Its walls were of mud, and it had a grass roof; but in the first four years the doctors treated more than 20,000 patients, at the same time making frequent evangelistic tours into the surrounding country, preaching and baptizing. The original building has been replaced by a well-built modern structure, properly equipped for the work, and the people are still coming long distances to be cured of their diseases.

School work was begun in 1907 by W. R. Smith and Mimi Scharffenberg. The training school at Soonan is located on a farm of forty-five acres. The original school building was small, with mud walls, and the students lived in dormitories of the same character. These buildings have been replaced with good brick buildings. Beginning with 1910, H. M. Lee had charge of the school, and was assisted by Miss May Scott. Besides the training school, there are also a number of primary schools.

The publishing work was first carried on in connection with the school at Soonan. The outfit in 1909 consisted of an old George Washington proof press set up at one end of the school building and a small font of type. After six months it was moved to Seoul, and then was moved about a number of times, till it finally found a home in 1912 in a substantial building erected at the headquarters in Seoul. The hand press was succeeded by a cylinder press of Japanese make. In the fall of 1910 a twelve-page monthly began to appear, which was later

GRADUATING CLASS, SOONAN, KOREA, 1916

increased to twenty-eight pages. The average circulation of this paper was upwards of 5,000 copies a month. The people were eager to read our publications. Our colporteurs, under the leadership of J. C. Klose, sold books as religious books never were sold before in Chosen.

Considering the unsettled condition of the country, politically, during the last few years, the growth in number of believers has been encouraging. Superintendent Butterfield reported a church membership in 1921 of 1,147 and a Sabbath school membership of 2,565. By 1925 there were twenty-one churches, with a total membership of 1,399. The mission was then in charge of H. A. Oberg.

The Philippine Islands

R. A. Caldwell entered Manila, on the island of Luzon, in 1905, and devoted himself to the circulation of books in English and Spanish. J. L. McElhany labored for two years among the

English-speaking people of the islands. Work for the Filipinos was begun by L. V. Finster in 1908. He devoted the first year to the study of the Tagalog language and to getting out some tracts. Then followed meetings and Bible studies, with the result that in 1911 it was possible to organize a church of eighteen members. Shortly after this, Elder Finster held his first tent-meeting. The tent was pitched in three different places,

PHILIPPINE COLPORTEURS

and the audiences were large. Within a year the church membership had grown to 100, with many more keeping the Sabbath.

A monthly journal in the Tagalog tongue was started, and small books and tracts were issued. E. M. Adams joined the staff of workers, and F. G. Ashbaugh sold Spanish books on the island of Panay. A church building and a mission home were erected in Manila, and a small printing house was established.

In 1913, Leon Roda, a Filipino, was sent to northern Luzon, where he labored among the Ilocano people. Four years later the work thus begun was organized as the North Luzon Mission, under the oversight of R. E. Hay, the headquarters being at Vigan on the northwestern coast. The press at Manila is issuing a paper in the Ilocano tongue; also books for sale by colporteurs. The Sabbath school enrolment in this mission field was already 325 in 1920. Only five years later the field had eighty-nine churches, with a total membership of 4,690.

Spanish books were early circulated on the island of Cebu, but they did not reach the masses of the people. In 1914, Dr.

U. Carlos Fattebert opened a medical mission in Argao, and in that year our press at Manila published 51,000 pages of tracts in the Cebuan tongue. The work advanced more slowly than in Luzon. Director S. W. Munro reported seventy-three members in 1920.

In 1920 Dr. Fattebert planted a station in Misamis on the island of Mindanao. He himself opened a medical office, while Mrs. Fattebert began to do Bible work in the homes of the people.

E. M. Adams started a mission in Iloilo on the island of Panay in 1914. At that time there were about thirty observing the Sabbath as a result of the work of colporteurs, some of these being in the western province of Antique, where they had come out under the labors of F. A. Ashbaugh. In time the message was carried also to the island of Negros, lying to the eastward. A church school was started at Jaro, near Iloilo. A paper and books in the Panay language are printed in Manila.

The Central Southern Luzon Conference, which includes the region about Manila and beyond, where the message won its first converts, baptized 500 converts during 1920. The Manila church building has a seating capacity of 700. The headquarters of the Philippine Union Mission is at Pasay, a suburb of Manila. Here likewise is located the Philippine Academy, established in 1917, with thirty-six students, under the principalship of I. A. Steinel. It had 230 pupils in 1920. In 1925, O. F. Sevrens was principal, with a faculty of twelve teachers.

The publishing house, which stands near the school, finds its one great difficulty in supplying the rapidly growing demands for literature. C. N. Woodward, who saw the plant grow from small beginnings to its present dimensions, reported $50,000 worth of sales in 1918, and it has since gone beyond that mark. In 1924 it was issuing publications in eight of the native languages. In 1920 the union field secretary, J. J. Strahle, had at times eighty colporteurs in the field.

BROADVIEW COLLEGE AND THEOLOGICAL SEMINARY

PACIFIC PRESS, INTERNATIONAL BRANCH, BROOKFIELD, ILL.

CHAPTER XXXVII

Work Among the Foreigners in the United States [1]

The Scandinavians

THE story of the beginnings of the work among the Scandinavians in this country, under the labors of Elder J. G. Matteson, has been told in some detail in an earlier chapter. When Elder Matteson went to Denmark in 1877 to begin work in that country, the general oversight of the work among the Scandinavian Sabbath keepers in America was left in the hands of Elder O. A. Olsen, who, however, continued to devote the larger share of his time to work among the Americans. When he was called to Europe in the spring of 1886, the oversight of the work was left largely in the hands of Lewis Johnson, who was then laboring in Minnesota.

Elder Johnson had heard his first Seventh-day Adventist sermon in a schoolhouse in Iowa in 1875, he being then a licensed preacher among the Methodists. He observed the next Sab-

---

[1] This chapter has been allowed to remain as it was when O. A. Olsen, then secretary of the department, looked it over shortly before his death in 1915. Recent developments in this department will be given in a later chapter.

bath, and began at once to labor for his friends and associates, with the result that a Seventh-day Adventist church was organized at West Dayton, Iowa, of which he was chosen elder. A little later he gave himself to the ministry, and labored for some years among the Scandinavians of Iowa, Illinois, and Dakota. In 1880 he went to Minnesota, which continued to be his chief field of labor for the next eight or nine years. In 1889 he was called to succeed O. A. Olsen as superintendent of the work in Scandinavia.

During these years there continued to be an encouraging growth among the Scandinavians in America, but there was a lack of qualified laborers. On Elder Olsen's return to America, in the spring of 1889, he saw the need of educational facilities for the training of foreign workers. Arrangements were accordingly made for the holding, in Battle Creek the following winter, of schools for the Scandinavians, the Germans, and the French. J. C. Ottosen, then a medical student in Denmark, was secured as principal and head teacher of the Scandinavian school, and Elder and Mrs. M. M. Olsen were placed in charge of the school home. There were others who assisted in the teaching. Thirty pupils presented themselves on the opening day, and the attendance later increased to fifty.

At the session of the General Conference in the winter of 1889-90, plans were laid for the erection of a college in the Middle West, with departments in German, Swedish, and Danish-Norwegian. The plans thus laid resulted in the building of Union College, at College View, Nebr.

At the close of the school year a number of the most promising Scandinavian pupils were sent to Copenhagen, Denmark, where they could pursue advanced studies under favorable conditions, Elder and Mrs. M. M. Olsen going with them to take charge of the school home. Among the students sent to Denmark for preparation, mention should be made of P. E. Berthelsen, who first taught in the Scandinavian Union School in Frederikshavn, Denmark, and later for a number of years was at the head of the Danish-Norwegian Department of Union College, near Lincoln, Nebr.

Work Among the Germans

The advent message first found its way to some German families in Dakota about 1875. These families learned of the Adventist views by reading a few tracts put in their hands by Danish and American believers in Dakota, and a few of them began to keep the Sabbath. No ministerial labor was put forth on their behalf until the year 1881, when L. R. Conradi was sent to Dakota to labor especially for the Germans, and in course of time organized three German churches, as already recorded in a previous chapter. He followed up this work with labor on behalf of the Germans in various parts of the Middle West, and also raised up some churches in the East. When he was called to Europe at the beginning of 1886, the German Sabbath keepers in the United States numbered about 500. A good beginning had been made, and especially in the Middle West a substantial class of people had accepted the Adventist views.

On Elder Conradi's departure for Europe, the German interests in the United States were put in the care of Henry Shultz, who remained at the head of the work for sixteen years, until the organization of the field into union conferences put the oversight alike of the German and American work into the hands of the regular conference officers.

Elder Shultz first came in contact with Seventh-day Adventists in the summer of 1872, when Charles L. Boyd and J. S. Hart were holding a tent-meeting at Stromsburg, Nebr. Elder Shultz was then a class leader in the church of the United Brethren, and did not attend the meetings at the tent. But when the neighborhood became greatly stirred over the Adventist preaching, he was asked to make a public defense of Sunday keeping, and promised to do so.

He immediately set himself to what he considered would be an easy task of assembling an array of scriptures in favor of observing the first day of the week. For three weeks he searched his Bible, as he said, " night and day," and then he knew why the minister had said he could do nothing.

At first he was angry with the Bible because it did not back up his position; then, as the truth gradually came home to his heart, that not only were there no texts in favor of Sunday observance, but the Bible most clearly taught the sacredness of the seventh day, he found himself in the throes of a great mental struggle. When it seemed too hard for him, he cried unto God, and received the answer in a feeling of great calm in his soul and a flood of light which invested the Sabbath of creation with a beauty and sacredness that had never attached to the first day of the week.

On the following Sunday he stood up in his church to give the report of his investigations on Sunday keeping as taught in the New Testament. He told his fellow church members of his prolonged studies and of the struggle, and ended with the words: " You will do as you please, but I and my house have

44

decided to obey God by keeping His commandments." That evening twelve heads of families signed the covenant, and the following spring Elders R. M. Kilgore and C. L. Boyd organized a Seventh-day Adventist church at Stromsburg, and ordained Henry Shultz as elder. The little company met with much opposition, but seemed to thrive on it, so that at the end of two years there was a membership of nearly 200.

In 1874, Henry Shultz received a license to preach from the Iowa-Nebraska Conference, and two years later he was ordained to the ministry. For a time his labors were almost entirely among the Americans; but his heart was in the German work, and when the way opened for him to give his entire time to labor among his countrymen, he was glad to do so. During the sixteen years in which the work was under his leadership, there was a steady and rapid growth of German Sabbath keepers in the United States, chiefly in the West.

At the General Conference of 1905, G. F. Haffner was appointed to take the general oversight of the German Department in the United States, Henry Shultz taking up labor among the Germans in California, where he has been instrumental in raising up strong German churches. Under Elder Haffner's administration, the work continued to grow. There are at the present time about 4,000 German Sabbath keepers in the western portion of the United States and Canada. Of these, about 800 are in North Dakota, 700 in Oklahoma, and nearly 400 in Kansas. The believers are grouped in more than 100 churches, of which sixty have church buildings of their own. They have thirty-six ordained and licensed ministers and four Bible workers.

German Work in the East

German work in the East was begun by L. R. Conradi in the autumn of 1888, when he conducted a series of meetings in Fleetwood, Pa., resulting in the organization of a German church. Later he held meetings at Allentown, where a deep interest was manifested in the message preached, and a church of about forty members organized. When Elder Conradi departed for Europe, the German work in the East was left without a leader, and remained at a standstill for some years. In fact it hardly held its own, the Fleetwood church becoming in time incorporated with the English church at Reading, and the Allentown church also becoming largely English in membership.

The next distinctly German church to be organized was brought out in Brooklyn, N. Y., in February, 1899, with a membership of sixteen. In 1902 a small German church was organized in Jersey City, and in 1907 a church of seventy-two members was organized in Milwaukee. Later, German churches were organized in Philadelphia, Manhattan, Cleveland, and Chicago. These churches, usually small to begin with, have enjoyed a steady growth. They number, all told, seventeen, and have a combined membership of over 800, besides about 100 scattered believers, making the total number of German Sabbath keepers east of the Mississippi River about 900.

Besides these, a considerable number of the English churches are largely composed of Germans. In the summer of 1911, J. H. Schilling was released from the presidency of the East German Union in order to take charge of the German work east of the Mississippi. After that time G. F. Haffner confined his labors to the western portion of the United States and Canada, and the German work both east and west prospered under the adequate supervision thus afforded.

Educational work among the Germans began in the autumn of 1888, when L. R. Conradi came back from Europe to conduct the first German training school in Milwaukee, Wis. The school had an enrolment of over thirty, and it was successful in developing some faithful workers. In the winter of 1889-90 a German training school was conducted in Battle Creek under the auspices of the General Conference, H. F. Schuberth being the principal instructor. The next attempt at educational work among the Germans was a mission school conducted in New York City by O. E. Reinke. From this school came a number of workers to assist in the German work in the East.

The French

So far as is known, Elders D. T. and A. C. Bourdeau, French Canadians, were the first persons of French blood to embrace the Adventist views. Their labors, referred to at some length in a previous chapter, were largely among the English-speaking people. Nevertheless, from time to time they bestowed some labor on their countrymen, both in Vermont and in Canada, as the result of which a few French families embraced the Adventist views and began to keep the Sabbath.

In 1872, D. T. Bourdeau went to Robinsonville, Brown Co., Wis., where a French family had begun to keep the Sabbath as the result of reading a tract on the subject prepared by himself and James White. After some labor in this place, Elder Bourdeau was able to organize a Seventh-day Adventist church. In the following year he held meetings at Serena, St. Anne, and Kankakee, in Illinois, churches being raised up in the two last-named places.

At this point, D. T. Bourdeau was called to labor among the French-speaking people in Europe. When he returned, in the summer of 1888, he and Paul E. Gros conducted four tent efforts in the vicinity of Robinsonville, Saint-Saveur, and L'Erable, Ill., as the result of which the number of believers in Robinsonville was materially increased and a meeting house erected. Later Elder Bourdeau returned largely to the work among the English. Elder Gros spent some time in working among the French in Wisconsin, but he also soon entered upon other work.

In the winter of 1889-90, and also in the following year, an effort was made to conduct a small school in Battle Creek for the training of French workers.

The canvassing work among the French Catholics of Illinois was begun in 1889 by Brother E. P. Auger. Later Brethren Muller, Roy, Berton, Curdy, and Vuilleumier gave some of their time to the circulation of Adventist literature among the French.

The work among the French in America has gone forward somewhat slowly, owing chiefly to the lack of qualified laborers who could give undivided attention to the work.

The Hollanders

The first Hollanders in America to become interested in the Adventist teachings were a few persons of that nationality in Grand Rapids, Mich., who had received some Adventist tracts in their own language. In 1886 B. F. Stureman held a few Bible readings with these families, as a result of which twelve persons began to observe the Sabbath. In the autumn of the same year it was decided to publish a paper in the Holland language in order to forward the work among the people of that nationality. The first number of this periodical came out Feb. 16, 1887, John Kolvoord being editor. A year or two later, as the result of correspondence, M. J. Van der Schuur came over from the Netherlands to receive further instruction in the doctrines, and to labor in behalf of the Hollanders in America. He began his ministerial labor in Kalamazoo, Mich., in the spring of 1889. About the same time Brother Stureman was laboring at Fremont. In the autumn, Brother Van der Schuur went to Baldwin, Wis., and spent some time giving further instruction to a little company of believing Hollanders in that town. During the summer of 1890 he and Brother Stureman labored together in the city of Holland, Mich.

Organization of the General Conference Foreign Department

It was not until the General Conference of 1905 that a separate department was organized for carrying on the foreign work in the United States. In that year for the first time the number of incoming foreigners exceeded one million. Elder G. A. Irwin was elected head of this department, which had for its object the promotion and extension of the knowledge of present truth among the people of foreign nationality in the United States and Canada. Plans were laid for definite leadership in the various nationalities, G. F. Haffner being appointed superintendent of the German division, S. Mortenson of the Swedish, and L. H. Christian of the Danish-Norwegian division. This arrangement proved satisfactory to the foreign nationalities represented, and new interest began to be manifested in the different lines of work. Something was done also to spread the message among the Italians, Bohemians, Slovaks, and Hungarians of New York and Brooklyn.

At the General Conference session of 1909, the various departments of the General Conference received careful study, and the organization was further perfected by placing each under the general direction of a secretary, subject to the supervision of the General Conference Committee. At that time Elder O. A. Olsen was appointed secretary of the North American Foreign Department, Elders Haffner, Mortenson, and Christian being reappointed to their former positions as superintendents.

The next move of importance in connection with the Foreign Department was made at the General Conference Council held in College View, Nebr., in the autumn of 1909, when it was decided to discontinue the foreign departments at Union College, which had been conducted there from the beginning of the school, and to establish in their place three separate schools in different parts of the country. This decision was made in order to increase the facilities for training laborers who could do efficient work for the various nationalities represented in this country. Soon after the close of the Council, the various committees set to work to find suitable locations for these schools.

The Danish-Norwegians were the first to secure a location. They found at Hutchinson, Minn., about sixty miles west of Minneapolis, a college property built by the Lutherans, but then in the hands of real estate agents, who offered it for educational purposes at less than one third its original cost. The building is a four-story structure of pressed brick, containing forty-six rooms for students, together with recitation-rooms, a dining-hall, a chapel seating 400, and a good gymnasium. The grounds consist of a ten-acre campus surrounded by 150 acres of woodland. The property was purchased for $22,250.

The Swedish brethren found, twelve miles west of Chicago, a good farm property of seventy-eight acres on which there were several substantial buildings, which they bought for

HUTCHINSON THEOLOGICAL SEMINARY, MINNESOTA

$20,000. Chicago being the most important Swedish center in the United States, it was very desirable to locate the school in that quarter.

The Germans ultimately located at Clinton, Mo., securing a large college building of solid brick with 110 rooms, standing on a farm of 112 acres. The original cost of the college building alone was $75,000. The whole estate was purchased for $27,600.

Necessary changes and repairs were made with energy and despatch, and the three schools opened their doors to students Sept. 28, 1910, less than a year after the action of the Conference Committee authorizing their establishment. Their combined enrolment during the first year was more than 200.

In addition to the establishment of these schools, a French Department was opened at South Lancaster Academy in 1911, and a Russian Department has been added to Harvey Academy, at Harvey, N. Dak., which had an attendance the first year of twenty-seven Russians. In the autumn of the same year the

International Bible Training School was started in Brooklyn, N. Y., the school term continuing for thirty weeks. Altogether, eighteen were enrolled as students, including Italians, Bohemians, Slovaks, Hungarians, Rumanians, Germans, Russians, and Scandinavians. The instruction was given in English, but colporteur and Bible work was done in the city in all the languages represented. The students carried on house-to-house

CLINTON THEOLOGICAL SEMINARY, MISSOURI

visitation, distributed invitations to meetings, and held Bible readings as the way opened.

Concurrent with the operation of these schools there has been an increased activity in evangelistic work among the various nationalities.

When the Foreign Department was reorganized, in 1909, there was not a single active laborer among the millions of French in the United States and Canada. The Latin Union Conference in Europe was accordingly requested to supply a French laborer, and responded by sending Gustav Roth, who, with his family, landed in Boston July 28, 1910. He took hold of the work vigorously in the New England States and in Canada, and there was a decided revival of interest in this branch of the work. In the autumn of 1911, Jean Vuilleumier was released from his work in Switzerland, and came to Canada to work among the French of that country. He conducted tent work in Montreal and at other important centers, experiencing considerable opposition, but also finding many honest inquiring souls.

Work among other foreign nationalities is being carried on to a limited extent. In 1910, A. Boettcher was called to take supervision of the work in the Eastern division, among all the foreign nationalities except the Germans and Scandinavians. In the following year he conducted a tent-meeting at Newark, N. J., with an excellent interest and encouraging results. The Hungarian church in New York City grew steadily in membership, and developed some workers. A tent-meeting was held among the Finns in Brooklyn, in the summer of 1913, which resulted in raising up a little company of believers. The church at Newark, N. J., composed of Slavs, Bohemians, and Poles, erected a chapel in 1913. They also held a series of meetings in Passaic. A Rumanian Bible worker labored for a time among her countrymen in Cleveland, Ohio. R. Calderone developed a growing work among the Italians of Chicago. A church numbering over forty members was organized, worshiping in a church building of its own on Erie Street, formerly occupied by the Scandinavian Sabbath keepers in that part of the city. Elder Calderone was assisted by Miss Vesta Cash, a Bible worker who had learned the language, and was giving her whole energies to the work among the Italians. There was also in Chicago a Hungarian who visited among the interested persons of his nationality, and saw some results of his efforts.

Also among the Hollanders the work had been for some years practically at a standstill. While not so numerous as the French, the Hollanders are represented in this country by hundreds of thousands, and are among the most intelligent and thrifty of our foreigners. The Adventists of this nationality are chiefly located in Michigan. At a representative meeting held at Grand Rapids in the spring of 1911, request was made that a laborer be provided as soon as possible to work among the Hollanders of this country.

The outlook for the future of the Foreign Department is a bright one. The work is fraught with great possibilities. America is still the land of opportunity. In its early history it was for many years a refuge for the oppressed of Europe. People came here in order that they might freely worship God according to the dictates of conscience. Some are still coming here for that purpose. Many others are coming to us because living conditions are better than in the congested portions of Europe. Some find employment in the factories and coal mines of our Eastern States; others seek homes on the great prairies of the Mississippi Valley, or continue their journey farther west. They come to us from every country of Europe, the men for the most part honest, industrious, accustomed to toil; the women worn with labor and hardships, but with hope in their hearts. And they come to stay, having bidden final farewell to their native lands, in order to make a new start in this land of promise.

Until recent years they came at the rate of about a million a year, with the result that today the population of this country is one third foreign. Indeed, in thirty-three of our largest cities the foreign population is greater than the native, and in Milwaukee and Fall River the percentage of foreigners is actually more than four fifths. New York not only has more inhabitants of German than of native descent, but it has more Germans than any city of Germany except Berlin. It has double the number of Irish people that are to be found in Dublin, and more Italians than Naples or Venice.

The foreigners in our great cities for the most part live in settlements of their own. They retain their native language, their peculiar customs and traditions. Thus they present to the gospel worker a home mission problem of the greatest magnitude; but also a great opportunity. In the words of the Rev. A. R. Bailey:

"The coming of this great foreign army to us spells opportunity and responsibility for the church of the living God. For years we have been sending men and money to foreign fields with the gospel. It seems as if God has looked down upon us and says, 'You are too slow. You will never evangelize the world at the rate you are now working.' So he has stirred up these people to come to us, and with the coming of these millions from foreign lands the church and every individual Christian ought to see the greatest opportunity for evangelism that has ever been given to any people."

MRS. L. FLORA PLUMMER

THE
EVER-WIDENING CIRCLE

SABBATH SCHOOL
Record for Thirty-seven Years
$10,315,183.90 TO MISSIONS

CHAPTER XXXVIII

The Sabbath School and the Young People [1]

AT the General Conference of 1901 plans were laid for taking over the Sabbath school along with other branches of the work and making of it also a separate department. The eighteenth meeting of the International Sabbath School Association, held in the Tabernacle at Battle Creek, Mich., April 18, 1901, was accordingly the last meeting of the kind. At the close of the General Conference, Sabbath school workers were appointed

---

[1] For much of the material in this brief sketch of the recent growth and development of the Sabbath school the writer has drawn freely from the pamphlet by Mrs. L. Flora Plummer, entitled, "From Acorn to Oak," in some cases only slightly adapting the language.

by the General Conference Committee. L. Flora Plummer was selected to serve as corresponding secretary, and a committee of ten was chosen to form a department committee. The office of the corresponding secretary was for a time at Minneapolis, Minn. In October, 1903, it was moved to Washington, D. C., occupying quarters temporarily at 222 North Capitol St. At the same time the department committee was reorganized so that its members could be called together for counsel at any time.

Further help being required in order to care for the growing interests of the work, G. B. Thompson was called to Washington in 1904, and for some years devoted a portion of his time to the Sabbath School Department. Mrs. Plummer being unable to remain in Washington, her place was filled for a few months by Mrs. Flora L. Bland. In July, 1905, the former secretary resumed her work in the office. In December of the same year the department moved into the quarters it has since occupied in the office building of the General Conference at Takoma Park, D. C.

The period from 1906 to 1912 was a memorable one in the annals of the Sabbath school because of the strenuous and successful effort put forth in behalf of missions. The missionary spirit had been steadily growing, Sabbath school offerings were increasing, but a considerable portion of the funds was still used for local expenses. In 1906 the Vermont Conference sent in a Sabbath school report showing that all the schools in that conference had given all their regular Sabbath contributions to missions. The effect was instantaneous. Mrs. Plummer writes:

"Like a mighty rushing tide that could not be stayed or turned aside, the missionary idea enveloped the Sabbath schools, and in six short years of time every school, from the large one at headquarters to the remotest one in the uttermost parts of the world, was giving its all to missions."

The quarterly report for September, 1912, showed that the goal had been reached. The Sabbath schools in all the conferences, and in the mission fields as well, had given all their offerings to missions. Once the principle had been established that all the offerings should go to missions, the fund rapidly grew, and it was not many years before the Sabbath School Department was giving fully one half, and then three fourths of the total amount of funds used for carrying on the work of missions. Said W. A. Spicer,

"There is no agency but the Sabbath school that can hold an envelope before each believer in the denomination every Sabbath, and solicit an offering for missions."

Since the year 1912 the department has followed the plan of having all the offerings that come in on the thirteenth Sabbath of the month go to a designated field. A leaflet known as the *Missions Quarterly,* giving interesting particulars concerning the field, is sent out to all the schools. Thus the pupils are gradually made conversant with the needs of various missions, and the knowledge thus gained makes for larger offerings. The thirteenth Sabbath was first known as Dollar Day, the goal for which the various Sabbath schools have been striving being to make the amount received equal in dollars to the membership of the church.

The birthday offerings, for many years given by the children at the rate of a cent for each year of their age, have recently, in some Sabbath schools, become general among the adults, who usually give a dollar as a thank offering in commemoration of the many blessings received since the last birthday.

At the General Conference of 1913, G. B. Thompson retired from the Sabbath school work in order to accept the secretaryship of the North American Division Conference, which was formed at that time. Mrs. L. Flora Plummer, who had served as corresponding secretary since 1901, with a few months' interruption, was elected secretary of the department. Rosamond Ginther joined the department as assistant secretary about a year later. In January, 1920, J. S. James responded to the call to serve as associate secretary.

The organization of the work in the field is simple and effective. Each conference has a Sabbath school secretary, who reports the work of the schools in the conference direct to the Sabbath School Department. In the case of foreign fields, there are union secretaries and secretaries of divisions, who are usually persons who read and write English. It is from these division secretaries that the formal reports come in to the department.

The evidences of interest and growth in fields outside the United States have been very encouraging. In Europe the work suffered during the World War, but it was not at a standstill; for when the great struggle was over, the reports that came in showed that there had been a gain in membership of 20,000.

In the Far Eastern Division the Sabbath schools are very generally adopting the latest methods, and are growing in interest and in membership. Sabbath school conventions, rally day programs, and interesting thirteenth Sabbath exercises are common in that great field.

In Africa, well-organized and ably manned schools are a marked feature of the various mission stations. The division secretary writes:

" We are trying to keep pace with the Sabbath School Department in all the world, taking one advance step at a time and making no provision for backward steps."

The Australasian Union shows growth in its home field and in the island mission fields under its supervision. From the Solomon Islands, where the members are converts from raw heathenism, a missionary writes:

" All who come to church attend the Sabbath school, chiefs and all, old and young, coming in by canoes and perhaps going without food in order to attend. I have never yet known a native to come late. Once when there was no canoe available, the natives swam the entire distance across the lagoon, rather than break their perfect attendance record, and reached the school on time."

In the South American Division there are Sabbath schools in the large cities, and there are schools hidden away in the forest, many days' journey on horseback from the railway. The secretary writes:

" The most southern school in the world is located at Punta Arenas on the Straits of Magellan, and is the fruit of Brother A. G. Nelson's work, who has labored in isolation for nine years to plant the truth in the southern end of the continent."

The growth of the work as a whole may be gathered from a few figures. At the close of 1923 there were 2,736 Sabbath schools in the United States and Canada, having a combined membership of 109,663. Outside these countries there were 4,336 schools, with a membership of 140,310. Adding these together, we have in all the world 7,072 schools and a membership of 249,973.

The growth of mission funds in the world may be indicated by the varying lengths of time it has taken to raise a million dollars for missions. The general secretary gives the following figures:

First million dollars	25 years
Second million dollars	3 years, 3 months
Third million dollars	2 years, 3 months
Fourth million dollars	1 year, 9 months
Fifth million dollars	1 year
Sixth million dollars	9 months, 3 weeks
Seventh million dollars	8 months, 3 weeks
Eighth million dollars	9 months, 1 week
Ninth million dollars	9 months, 2 weeks
Tenth million dollars	9 months, 2 weeks
Eleventh million dollars	8 months, 2 weeks
Twelfth million dollars	7 months, 2 weeks

It would be a mistake, however, to think of the Sabbath school chiefly as an institution for raising funds. It is a school in the full sense of the word, and as such it is exerting a very definite influence. Sabbath after Sabbath our people all over the world meet together and study the same lessons, though in many different languages and dialects. Thus all are drawn together in the unity of the faith, and advancement is made along even lines in the knowledge of the Scriptures.

In the work of the individual Sabbath school the needs of various ages are carefully looked after. The classification calls for five regular divisions,— senior, youth, junior, primary, and kindergarten. Two lesson themes are provided, one for the senior and youth's divisions, and one for the three divisions of children. These lessons are prepared some time in advance, for they are in use all over the world, and in many cases must be translated.

The aim is to give instruction of a practical nature, adapted to the needs of the hour, and calculated in the long run to insure on the part of the faithful student a saving knowledge of the Scriptures. The appreciation of the instruction thus sent out is indicated by messages that come from the fields from time to time. " Keep the Sabbath school lesson manuscript coming to us as long as you can," was the word that came from Russia just before the darkest days of the war.

One of the definite things which the department is endeavoring to realize is a complete membership: " Every believer in the Sabbath school." By organizing a home department for those who from sickness or other reasons are unable to join any other division of the Sabbath school, this goal is possible of attainment. In fact, it has been reached in some conferences. The daily study of the lesson, perfect attendance, and personal work for pupils, are features that have received much attention.

The quality of the teaching has been very considerably improved by the adoption, beginning with the year 1910, of a Teachers' Reading Course. The outline for the studies to be pursued is published in the *Sabbath School Worker*, the course beginning each year in February and ending with November.

As a spiritual force in the denomination the Sabbath school is making itself felt more strongly from year to year. Mrs. Plummer writes:

" The office of the Sabbath school is to make religion and the Bible lovable from a young person's point of view. . . . Therefore the Sabbath school must reflect what attracts children — brightness, color, sweet sounds, rhythm, free expression, justice, confidence, love."

But the school ministers equally well to the needs of the adult.

"The Word of God is the active agent in the conversion of sinners and the development of Christians, and the study of that Word is the center, the very heart, of all Sabbath school effort."

Organization and Work of the Young People's Department

The development of the organized strength of the young people of the denomination was not attained at a bound; it was a process of slow growth. A previous chapter has recorded the work of the Sabbath school, that first organization directed primarily toward supplying the need on the part of the children and young people of systematic instruction in the Bible. The next step in advance was the holding of services especially for young people in connection with the camp-meetings. This effort also bore rich fruit for the kingdom.

Simultaneously with the development of these camp-meeting efforts to help the young people, there began to be additional stress laid upon active missionary work of various kinds, and in many churches societies were organized that held weekly meetings for the study of mission fields, and to wrap and send out papers to interested persons. In these meetings the younger members of the church often took a leading part, both in getting up the programs and in doing the work.

The success of these initial efforts led many to feel that still more might be accomplished if the work were to be planned in such a way that the responsibility for it would fall more directly upon the young people, thus developing their powers of leadership and their staying qualities.

In response to this demand, local societies began to make their appearance in various churches. One of the earliest of these was organized by Luther Warren, then a boy in his teens, in connection with the church at Hazelton, Shiawassee Co., Mich., in 1879. The members of this society met at stated times for united prayer and to lay plans for Christian work. They bought and circulated tracts and papers, conducted correspondence with interested persons, and also engaged in local effort in behalf of the sick poor.

Similar local organizations appeared from time to time in the early nineties. In Australia, A. G. Daniells, encouraged by a communication from Mrs. E. G. White dated Dec. 19, 1892, organized a young people's society of twenty members in connection with the church at Adelaide, South Australia, which had a successful career of some years, amply demonstrating the possibilities for good that lay in such societies.

In Battle Creek, Mich., there was organized in the autumn of 1895 the Loyal Workers' Society, with a membership of about fifty. The members of this organization had a constitution and by-laws closely resembling the Christian Endeavor Societies. Meetings were held fortnightly, the members also attending the weekly missionary meetings of the church and devoting their best energies to making them a success. The activities of the society otherwise were much the same as in those already mentioned. This society also continued for several years, and was finally merged into a similar body, the " Young People's Self-Improvement Society," which rented a hall in which to hold its meetings, and was intended to minister to the social and educational as well as the religious needs of its members.

All these societies were, however, of a local character and immediately adapted to meet local needs. The Sunshine Bands, formed by Luther Warren in various churches, were the first attempt in the direction of a general organization for the young people. Elder Warren had labored much among young people, and understood their needs. He was encouraged, moreover, in his efforts by repeated references to the need of this work in the writings of Mrs. E. G. White. The first of these to come to his attention appeared in an article in the *Signs of the Times* dated May 29, 1893. The writer asks:

" Young men and young women, cannot you form companies, and as soldiers of Christ, enlist in the work, putting all your tact and skill and talent into the Master's service, that you may save souls from ruin? Let there be companies organized in every church to do this work. . . .

" Will the young men and young women who really love Jesus organize themselves as workers, not only for those who profess to be Sabbath keepers, but for those who are not of our faith? "— *Signs of the Times, May 29, 1893, p. 455.*

In the following October there were published extracts from Mrs. White's writings containing the following suggestion:

" Let there be a company formed somewhat after the order of the Christian Endeavor Society, and see what can be done by each accountable human agent in watching for and improving opportunities to do work for the Master. He has a vineyard in which every one can perform good work. Suffering humanity needs help everywhere."—" *Extracts from Letters from Mrs. E. G. White, Relative to Medical Missionary Work," dated Oct. 2, 1893.*

An article by the same writer appeared in the *Youth's Instructor* of Aug. 9, 1894, in which the idea of young people's work was further dealt with:

45

"Let young men, and women, and children go to work in the name of Jesus. Let them unite together upon some plan and order of action. Cannot you form a band of workers, and have set times to pray together and ask the Lord to give you His grace, and put forth united action? You should consult with men who love and fear God, and who have experience in the work, that under the movings of the Spirit of God, you may form plans and develop methods by which you may work in earnest and for certain results."

On June 11, 1894, Luther Warren organized the first of the so-called Sunshine Bands, at Alexandria, S. Dak. It proved a success, and was soon followed by others in that conference. Aug. 30, 1896, a convention of Sunshine Bands was held at Bridgewater, S. Dak., attended by delegates from Alexandria, Parker, Sioux Falls, and Montrose. Bands were organized in Battle Creek the following year, and in May, 1899, a monthly journal bearing the title *Sunshine* was started, and continued for nearly a year.

The good work done by these bands began to attract general attention in the denomination, and the Ohio Conference, at a State meeting held at Mount Vernon in April, 1899, passed a resolution favoring the further development of the idea. At the camp-meeting held the following August, State officers were chosen for a young people's organization, the members of which were known as Christian Volunteers. They signed the following declaration:

"Recognizing the preciousness of God's gift to me, I volunteer for service for Him anywhere in the wide world that His Spirit may lead, and in any form of service that He may direct."—"*Missionary Volunteers and Their Work*," by Matilda Erickson, p. 15.

In Iowa, Della Wallace, the tract society secretary, encouraged the movement, and societies were formed at Sigourney, Des Moines, and a number of other places.

The first action of the General Conference was taken at its session of 1901. The resolution ran:

"We approve the movement to organize young people's societies for more effectual missionary service; and we recommend that a committee of nine or more representative persons be appointed to form a plan of organization, and report it to this Conference for consideration."—*Id., p. 17.*

This committee was duly appointed. It brought in a report encouraging the formation of societies for the young people, asking the conferences to connect the work with the Sabbath school or missionary department, and requesting from the General Conference the appointment of a committee to give further study to the matter, and push forward the work. The committee also advised the opening of a department in the *Instructor* to be devoted to the advancement of these societies.

The general oversight of the work was provided for at a meeting of the General Conference Committee held in May, 1901, when it was decided to connect it with the Sabbath School Department of the General Conference, then located at Minneapolis, Minn., Mrs. L. Flora Plummer being the secretary.

The department committee, after due deliberation, decided upon a very simple form of organization. It adopted as a motto the words of Paul, " For the Love of Christ Constraineth Us," and took for the aim of the movement, " The Advent Message to All the World in This Generation." The pledge read:

" Loving the Lord Jesus, and desiring to be of service in His cause, I associate myself with the Young People's Society, to take an active part in its work, and by•the grace of Christ, to do what I can to help others, and to send the gospel of the kingdom to all peoples, at home and abroad."— " *Early History of the Seventh-day Adventist Young People's Work*," by *Mrs. L. Flora Plummer, p. 11.*

The following suggestions concerning the details of the organization were sent out for the guidance of the local societies:

" NAME: Young People's Society of Seventh-day Adventists.

" OBJECT: Association for Bible study and mutual encouragement in every good work.

" MEMBERS: Young people who love Jesus and desire to engage in active service in His cause, may be members. Membership implies the duty of faithfulness in all that tends to promote the object of the society.

" MANAGEMENT: The church and Sabbath school officers shall form an advisory Committee to act with the officers elected by the Young People's Society, in arranging for the meetings and work of the society."

The officers were to be a leader, an assistant leader, a secretary, and a treasurer.

When the Sabbath school secretary began to develop the work, only three out of fifty conferences had a young people's secretary. The other conferences being slow to appoint officers, the department decided to consider the Sabbath school secretaries as serving in both capacities until separate secretaries should be appointed. Progress began to be made, though slowly at first. The camp-meetings of 1902 showed that the Young People's Society was becoming a growing factor in the denominational work, and was already wielding an influence for good.

Printed helps in the way of programs for meetings and for other purposes were supplied. The *Youth's Instructor* bearing date of June 27, 1901, contained the first department devoted to the young people's work, the lessons being based on " Steps to

Christ." Beginning with 1903, topical studies of the leading doctrines of the denomination were taken up, " The Great Controversy," " Early Writings," and " Rise and Progress " being used as helps. Later, studies were given on the life of Paul, on mission fields, and on " The Ministry of Healing."

At the General Conference held in Oakland, Calif., in the spring of 1903, the secretary gave a general report of the work. Various lines of missionary effort were being carried on. Books and papers were being sold, branch Sabbath schools conducted, cottage meetings and Bible readings held, jails visited, and contributions made to missions. The conference passed a resolution approving the efforts put forth, and requesting ministers and other workers to give the organization their hearty support.

In the autumn of the same year the Sabbath School and Young People's Department was moved to Washington, D. C., the work thus coming into direct touch with the General Conference management. Early in the following year suitable reporting blanks were provided, and a thirty-two-page manual containing extracts from Mrs. White's writings and other helpful material was published. From October, 1904, till June, 1905, the work was in the charge of Mrs. Flora L. Bland. At the end of this time Mrs. Plummer returned to her post. At the General Conference of 1905 the department was able to report that the work had practically doubled in the last two years.

An important advance step was taken at the General Conference Council held in Gland, Switzerland, in May, 1907, when the following recommendation was passed:

" WHEREAS, There are in our ranks many thousands of young people for whom the most earnest and vigorous efforts should be put forth to fully instruct them in the gospel of our Lord, and lead them to give themselves to the work of the third angel's message; and,

" WHEREAS, The special blessing of God has attended the efforts among our young people put forth under the fostering care of the Sabbath School Department, until it has grown to such an extent that it is difficult for this department to give this work the attention and help which it needs; therefore,

" *Resolved*, That in order that this work may be properly developed, and thus an army of workers properly trained for service, a special department, with the necessary officers, be created, the same to be known as the Young People's Department of the General Conference."—" *Early History of the Seventh-day Adventist Young People's Work*," *pp. 21, 22.*

In carrying out this action of the Council, Prof. M. E. Kern, head of the department of history in Union College, was called to the position of chairman of the new department, and Miss Matilda Erickson (Mrs. E. E. Andross) was made secretary,

G. B. Thompson, Frederick Griggs, H. R. Salisbury, Mrs. L. Flora Plummer, Meade MacGuire, C. L. Benson, Mrs. Fannie D. Chase, and others being members of the advisory committee.

The department thus organized benefited greatly by the holding, in the summer of 1907, at Mount Vernon, Ohio, of the first General Conference Sabbath school and young people's convention. The meeting lasted from July 10 to 21. The program had been planned with painstaking care, in order that all the most vital features of the work might receive attention. Very careful study was given to choosing a distinctive name for the organization, and although it seemed rather long, the name decided on was Young People's Society of Missionary Volunteers. This has been gradually shortened to simply Missionary Volunteer Society.

This convention gave the young people's work a great impetus throughout the country. It opened the eyes of the secretaries in attendance to the great possibilities that lay before them; it gave them light on such subjects as the getting up of programs, the organizing of working bands, the duties of the various officers, and the need of regular reporting.

From this time the work made steady progress. The yearly Morning Watch Calendar, first issued in 1908, has become an institution, being used by old as well as young. The course of study in Bible doctrines, and denominational history, leading up to the Standard of Attainment, is year by year being taken by a larger number of young people, who are thus obtaining a practical knowledge of the denominational teaching. The reading courses, senior, junior, and primary, are likewise being followed by an ever-increasing number. In the Bible Year the young people and others are encouraged to read their Bibles through again and again.

In giving his report at the General Conference of 1922, the general secretary, M. E. Kern, made interesting comparisons showing the growth of the work in the seventeen years that had elapsed since the organization handed in its first report at the end of the year 1904. The membership had increased from 2,182 in 1904 to 43,968 at the end of 1921. During this period the denomination increased 162 per cent, and the Missionary Volunteer membership, 1,900 per cent. Furthermore, the increase in missionary activities and in offerings to missions was even greater than in membership. The offerings reported in 1904 amounted to $332.33; for the year 1921 they were $223,000, an annual average gain of $1,309.09 for seventeen years.

During the World War a number of the young men in the army organized Missionary Volunteer Societies, and the results were often very gratifying. One young man in a government tuberculosis hospital gathered a group of five men for Bible study, and won every one of them to the truth. This society of six constituted a 100 per cent Missionary Volunteer Society: they all belonged to the prayer band, all observed the Morning Watch, and every member reported weekly.

Very fruitful work has been done in various churches in encouraging the young people to reach the Standard of Attainment, which indicates a measure of proficiency in the knowledge of Bible doctrines and denominational history. In one of the Eastern conferences a Missionary Volunteer leader, who was a Bible worker, organized a small Standard of Attainment class, which was increased in size by inviting non-Adventist acquaintances to join. Out of those members of this band who had previously known nothing whatever of our work, five accepted the message, two developed into Bible workers, two young men and two young ladies went away to one of our schools, and one young man who had been working in a milk house became a church school teacher.

Aside from its regular work, the Missionary Volunteer Department has carried on two special campaigns. In the year 1918-19 the Volunteers raised more than $30,000 toward the relief of Armenian orphans. A little later they busied themselves with gathering clothing for needy Adventists in Europe. Something over four hundred boxes of this clothing were shipped from New York, the ocean freight alone amounting to more than $4,000.

Another accomplishment of recent years has been the getting out of complete manuals for both the Junior and the Senior divisions of the society. Help from the home office is being supplied to the outlying fields. M. E. Kern, the general secretary, made an extended visit to Europe in the summer of 1920, to Australia and the South Seas in 1922-23, to South America in 1923-24, and to the Far East in 1925. Meade MacGuire, associate secretary, recently spent a year or more in the Far East and a summer in Europe. H. T. Elliott, elected associate secretary in 1922, visited the European societies in the summer of 1925.

The growth of the organization in Europe since the Great War has been very encouraging. At the Zurich General Conference Council, held in 1920, there were daily consultations with the union secretaries. Following that meeting, J. F. Simon, of Kansas, was sent to Europe to serve as assistant Missionary Volunteer secretary for the division, and L. L. Caviness went over to serve as secretary for the Latin Union. Professor Simon has thus far devoted his time largely to Germany, where we have within the Adventist ranks more than 8,000 young people. In the Latin Union the work has made encouraging progress, the societies increasing from four to twenty-seven, and the membership from 73 to 507. In the Scandinavian Union, where Steen Rasmussen took charge of the young people's work in 1920, reading courses have been started in five languages, institutes have been held, a Missionary Volunteer Day observed, goals set and reached, and aggressive work done all along the line.

In the Far East the work is progressing steadily under the leadership of S. L. Frost. In South America, under the guidance of C. P. Crager, the Missionary Volunteers are also making advancement. The young Indians of Peru, who cannot report in writing, hold up their fingers as the various items are read off to indicate what they have done. In Africa, too, there have been many encouraging developments, and the natives show real enthusiasm for the various volunteer activities.

The work of the organization as a whole may well be summed up in the following combined report of its various branches and societies for the year 1924:

Young people converted	4,465
Persons taking the Reading Courses	11,254
Standard of Attainment certificates issued	1,584
Members who have read the Bible through during the year	4,572
Reporting members	22,107
Mission offerings	$164,033.50

MRS. E. G. WHITE SPEAKING IN THE BATTLE CREEK TABERNACLE, AT THE GENERAL CONFERENCE SESSION, 1901

Seated on rostrum, left to right: H. E. Rogers, L. A. Hoopes, B. F. Stureman, P. T. Magan, G. A. Irwin, S. H. Lane, W. C. White, S. N. Haskell, Dr. David Paulson, J. N. Loughborough. The old men on the stairs are from the James White Memorial Home.

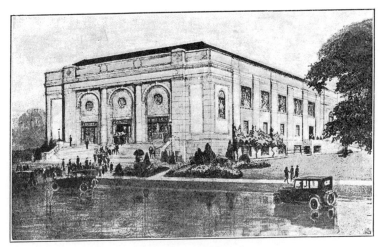

THE NEW TABERNACLE

Architect's drawing of the new building replacing the one destroyed by fire, Jan. 7, 1922.

CHAPTER XXXIX

Recent Departmental Activities

A NUMBER of the more important developments of the work in America in the last few years have been in connection with the various departments and bureaus which have their center at the denominational headquarters in Washington, D. C. Some of these agencies have been treated in earlier chapters as fully as space will permit; others only in their beginning stages. The present chapter will be devoted to later developments of those which have already had some mention, and to a brief statement concerning the general character of others of more recent origin.

The Home Missionary Department

In a previous chapter we considered the home missionary activities of the denomination carried on in connection with the International Tract Society. Closely connected as that organization was from the first with the publishing houses, and with the local tract depositories, the society for a time, in the middle nineties, did some publishing of its own, chiefly of tracts and pamphlets. At the General Conference of 1897 the headquarters of the society were moved to New York City, where it ceased to print, and returned to its original work — the distribution of soul-winning literature.

After the General Conference of 1901, at which the work of the denomination as a whole was carefully considered, and important changes in organization effected, the International Tract Society ceased to function. With the new impulse given to foreign missions at that Conference, the denomination soon came to have representatives of its own in all the leading countries of the world, and the work of distributing our publications in such lands could be done to best advantage by these missionaries.

Meanwhile the home missionary work, especially the circulation of tracts and papers, was fostered by the General Conference Publishing Department, operating through the several publishing houses, and conference tract societies. D. W. Reavis and A. J. S. Bourdeau at different times were connected with the General Conference Publishing Department, in the interests of this line of work.

But as the work of the denomination grew in magnitude and in complexity, the need was felt of a more definite organization of the lay members of the denomination for missionary endeavor. Action was accordingly taken at the General Conference of 1913, placing the promotion of home missionary work on a departmental footing. Miss Edith M. Graham, who had been a successful worker in Australia, was appointed general secretary of the Home Missionary Department for the world field, and F. W. Paap was associated with her, and asked to give special attention to the work in America.

The plan adopted involved not only the selection of a home missionary secretary for each union and local conference, but the thorough organization of the work in each church.

In carrying out this plan there were developed a comprehensive reporting system, a Home Missionary Manual, a series of "Lessons for Church Missionary Institutes," and materials for monthly programs in the several churches.

The development of these plans speedily resulted in a large increase in the volume of home missionary work, not only in America, but throughout the world. There were encouraging gains in almost every line of missionary activity, especially in periodical sales and Harvest Ingathering receipts. And the growth has been healthy and continuous.

In July, 1918, the department suffered a great loss in the death of Miss Graham. She had a special gift for securing widespread co-operation. " God's people are willing workers," she used to say; " all they need is training in service, and encouragement."

Following the death of Miss Graham and the resignation of F. W. Paap, which occurred a few months later, the direction of the Home Missionary Department passed into the hands of C. V. Leach as secretary and H. K. Christman, assistant. Under their leadership progress in missionary conventions and institutes was especially marked.

In 1921 J. Adams Stevens was called from his work as home missionary secretary of the Pacific Union Conference to the secretaryship of the General Department, and he, with his associate secretaries, has continued the good work begun, leading the men and women comprising the church membership of the denomination into ever-widening fields of service.

Two of the newer important lines of missionary endeavor under the immediate charge of this organization are (1) The Harvest Ingathering for Missions, and (2) the Big Week literature effort. While every Seventh-day Adventist has a distinctive duty in connection with each of these campaigns, the responsibility rests with the Home Missionary Department to organize and rally the lay members in the local churches, and lead out in this plan for raising additional funds for the support of foreign missions.

Largely as a result of the loyal co-operation the lay members have given to the annual Harvest Ingathering campaign, it has been possible to place in the mission treasury during the last eleven years since the establishment of the Home Missionary Department, about four million dollars, solicited in the main from non-Adventists, and representing an important addition to the regular funds raised within the denomination. Moreover, during the last five years, since the birth of the Big Week effort, large sums for immediate investment in establishing and equipping printing plants in mission fields, have been gathered in, and great good has resulted.

The Religious Liberty Department

The Religious Liberty Department is an outgrowth of the general plans adopted at the General Conference of 1901. In earlier years the efforts of the denomination to educate the people upon the true principles of separation of church and state, had taken the form of an organization known as the Religious

Liberty Association, which has been dealt with in a previous chapter of this book.

Adventists oppose Sunday laws, not because they are inconvenient, but because they contravene the great principle of separation of church and state, which was so clearly laid down by our Saviour in Matthew 22: 21, and recognized in a broad way for the first time in human history at the founding of the American Republic.

It was an advantage to the Religious Liberty Department to have the denomination, in the year 1903, set up its headquarters in the District of Columbia. K. C. Russell was called to head the department when it was created. The work had hardly begun when two Sunday bills were before Congress. Largely as a result of the endeavors of the department, these bills failed to pass, and a number of others introduced in the immediately succeeding years met a like fate. When, shortly before the General Conference of 1913, K. C. Russell was asked to enter upon city evangelistic work, his place was filled by W. W. Prescott. S. B. Horton was also connected with the General Department for a number of years, and later served as religious liberty secretary for the Lake Union. At the General Conference in 1913, C. S. Longacre, former principal of South Lancaster Academy, was elected head of the department. He was reelected to the position in 1918, and again in 1922. In recent years W. F. Martin has been associated with him in the work, his especial field being the Pacific Coast.

The newspaper and magazine press in America is generally on the side of religious liberty, and many members of the legal profession have boldly championed its cause. Some of the most prominent jurists and statesmen in America are stanch supporters of the principles of religious freedom.

In recent years the Religious Liberty Department has not only had to oppose the enactment of drastic Sunday laws before Congress and the State legislatures, but it has come to the defense of private and church schools, when menaced by hostile legislation.

The religious liberty work was organized on a departmental basis in the European Division Conference during the summer of 1924, when the secretary of the department visited that field. The time seemed opportune for an aggressive campaign in the Old World. Judges, lawyers, editors, and leading statesmen were coming to the front, championing the rights of the minority sects. The ministers of state were given opportunity to read our literature and examine the principles we advocate, and, seemingly at least, were convinced that Seventh-day Adventists have a message of hope and freedom that the world needs. On the whole the religious liberty outlook in Europe is encouraging.

The Bureau of Home Missions

A previous chapter, devoted entirely to the work of the Bureau of Home Missions, brought the narrative down to the sudden death of its secretary, Elder O. A. Olsen. He had recently returned from an extensive trip in the West, and was making strenuous efforts to have things in readiness for the opening of the first session of the new school for foreign workers which was to be conducted in Chicago. In fact, it was over-exertion while hunting up suitable accommodations for the incoming students, that brought on the attack which resulted fatally on Jan. 22, 1915.

Coming to this country from Norway at the age of five, Elder Olsen began his ministry among the Scandinavians of Wisconsin. For a period of years, both before and after his term as president of the General Conference, he labored in Scandinavia and other parts of Europe. It was therefore singularly fitting that the last five years of his busy life should be given to labor among the foreign nationalities in North America. He greatly enjoyed this work, and was happy in the associations it brought to him. Following the General Conference of 1913 he served as vice-president for North America. In this capacity he traveled widely over the country, attending camp-meetings and other representative gatherings, where he labored for the spiritual uplift of believers, a work which always lay nearest his heart.

After the death of Elder Olsen the work of the Bureau of Home Missions was for a time looked after by Steen Rasmussen, who had been for some years closely associated with it. At the General Conference of 1918, L. H. Christian, who had formerly had charge of the work among the Danish-Norwegians, was elected secretary of the bureau. When he was called, somewhat later, to administrative duties in the European Division, P. E. Brodersen succeeded him, and continued in charge of the work till the spring of 1924, when he was called to South America. The bureau was then taken over by M. N. Campbell, former assistant secretary of the General Conference.

During all this time the work of the bureau has gone steadily forward. What were feeble companies of foreign believers a few years ago, have since developed into strong churches. For example, in the report of 1913, mention was made of work

SECRETARIES OF GENERAL CONFERENCE DEPARTMENTS, 1925

N. Z. Town
J. A. Stevens
M. N. Campbell

M. E. Kern
Mrs. L. Flora Plummer
C. S. Longacre

W. E. Howell
A. W. Truman, M. D.
W. H. Green

718

among the Russians of North Dakota. There were at that time seven organized churches, with a membership of 200. At the General Conference of 1922, the report showed thirteen churches and twelve companies of Russians in North Dakota, with a total membership of 700. In the school year 1921-22 there were 125 Russian young people enrolled in the Russian department in three of our schools.

In the report of 1913 reference was made to " a small beginning " among the Italians of Chicago. The Chicago Italian church in 1924 had a membership of considerably over a hundred. Moreover, there is an Italian church in New York, with a rapidly growing membership, whose weekly mission offerings averaged 93 1-3 cents a member in a recent year. There is also a Polish church in Chicago. More recently the Ukrainians are showing a deep interest in the message, and a number are embracing the Adventist views.

The work among the Jews, especially fostered from the beginning by F. C. Gilbert, has been definitely connected with the Bureau since 1911. The interest in our publications on the part of the Jews seems to be growing. In 1920, 55,000 magazines were circulated among them; in the following year the number was 100,000, in addition to about 75,000 copies of a tract entitled, "Seventh-day Adventists — Who They Are and What They Believe." In 1921 there were also circulated 50,000 copies of a Yiddish paper on the subject of religious liberty. The Jewish periodicals are beginning to make friendly references to our work. We are receiving calls for our literature from Jews in South America, Switzerland, Holland, and other parts of the world, where our work is attracting the interested attention of these widely scattered people.

The work of the Bureau of Home Missions, as a whole, is operating at present in thirty languages, and other tongues are being added as rapidly as possible. In the four years preceding the General Conference of 1922, there were won to the truth from among the foreign-language-speaking people in America, 4,457 new believers, and seventy-five new churches were organized. Since that Conference, 2,696 converts have been won and forty-seven new churches organized. The first two quarters of 1924 saw 428 new converts, and the organization of seven new churches. These foreign Sabbath keepers contribute to the cause an annual tithe of more than $500,000 and mission offerings amounting to $345,000.

The three seminaries, founded to train workers and educate the youth of foreign parentage, opened under favorable circumstances, and all have done good work in training an increasing number of recruits for this large field of labor.

The Brookfield publishing house is issuing publications in twenty-eight foreign languages. Its sales for 1924 showed a gain over those of the previous year. Its 386,000 copies of foreign Harvest Ingathering papers were printed in eighteen languages. Harvest Ingathering work among the foreigners opens up a profitable avenue for the inflow of mission funds. The sale of foreign subscription books has rapidly increased. Samuel Lombard delivered $4,700 worth of Italian books in a single year. Workers among other nationalities were also meeting with good success.

The Press Bureau

At the denominational headquarters in Washington, D. C., a Press Bureau has been maintained since 1912, to assist the evangelistic workers in getting publicity for the message through the newspaper press, especially in telling of the progress that is being made at home and abroad, and in proclaiming the principles of civil and religious liberty.

W. L. Burgan, a former member of the reportorial staff of the Baltimore *Sun,* is secretary of the bureau, the work of which has steadily grown in influence and importance. There are today hundreds of newspapers in the United States and Canada, and a number in Europe, Asia, Africa, South America, and Australia, that are devoting space to the fundamental truths of our message.

The Home Commission

At the Fall Council of the General Conference Committee held at Boulder, Colo., in October, 1919, action was taken creating a committee to be known as the Home Commission, consisting of the secretaries of the General Conference departments of Education, Young People's Missionary Volunteers, Sabbath School, Medical, and Home Missionary, with certain other persons, M. E. Kern being appointed chairman. With the beginning of the year 1922 the organization was completed by the selection of A. W. Spalding as secretary and Mrs. Flora H. Williams as assistant secretary.

In the fall of 1921 active work was begun by members of the commission, who held Home Institutes in churches, dealing with basic questions and problems of the home life. This plan of teaching has been extended as far as possible, including a line of study at the camp-meetings.

Upon the appeal of Mrs. W. L. Bates, a Bible worker with experience in mothers' societies, the Home Commission at the beginning of 1923 began the monthly issue of Mothers' Lessons, and the organization of Young Mothers' Societies in the local churches. These Mothers' Lessons include story-telling, nature study, health, and home culture, the last covering the principles of house management, child training, and the establishment of ethical and spiritual conditions in all home relations.

The Ministerial Association

The Ministerial Commission dates from the General Conference of 1922. Further attention was given to the subject at the Spring Council of 1923, at which time action was taken, changing the name of the organization to the Ministerial Association. A. G. Daniells, the general secretary, is largely devoting his time to the work, which consists in the awakening and fostering of a higher and deeper Christian experience of its members, and in general of the whole membership of the denomination; also in conducting a Ministerial Reading Course; and in gathering data that may be of use to those engaged in evangelistic effort. The association further seeks the aid of conference officers and ministers in searching out young men and encouraging them to study for the ministry.

The majority of the members of the advisory council were in attendance at the Spring Council of 1925, and due consideration was given to the interests of the association. The secretary made an encouraging report of the progress attending the Ministerial Reading Course work for the last three years. A standing committee of five was appointed to give careful study to the selection of books for future Reading Courses.

Definite plans were adopted for the production of literature along devotional and inspirational lines, and it was urged that special instruction be given at the camp-meetings covering the entire range of Ministerial Association work. Mrs. J. W. Mace was appointed office secretary.

E. W. FARNSWORTH

Son of the first Seventh-day Adventist, William Farnsworth, Washington, N. H.,
and an ordained minister of the gospel since 1876.

"ELMSHAVEN," HOME OF MRS. E. G. WHITE, NEAR ST. HELENA, CALIFORNIA

Mrs. White may be seen in her wheel chair in the balcony.

CHAPTER XL

Growth at Home and Abroad

PLANS of a comprehensive, far-reaching character require time for their working out. It was not until the General Conference of 1905 that the full significance of the reorganization effected four years earlier began to appear.

The presence of Mrs. E. G. White at the General Conference of 1909, and the instruction she was able to give, added much to the success of the meeting. It was at this conference the decision was made to have one man give his entire time to the organization and development of the work among the foreigners of North America. O. A. Olsen, who had just served for four years as president of the Australasian Union, was called to this office.

At this conference, also, the Western Canadian Union, including the provinces of Manitoba, Saskatchewan, Alberta, and British Columbia, was formally received into membership as a separate union.

In this connection a further word may be said of the eastern portion of Canada, known at this time as the Canadian Union, but later to be designated as the Eastern Canadian Union. Its

territory included the provinces of Ontario, Quebec, New Brunswick, Nova Scotia, Prince Edward Island, and Newfoundland,
and it reported at this conference forty-four organized churches,
with a total membership of 1,200. Various other actions were
taken; but these were all matters of minor importance compared
with the time and attention given to the foreign fields.

The General Conference of 1909 was emphatically a missionary conference. The great problems it dealt with were
chiefly missionary problems. The reports that received most
attention were those from the mission fields, telling not only of
work already accomplished, but of much more that remained to
be done. It was not a note of discouragement that was struck,
but one of large hope and confidence. "We are well able to
go up and possess the land," was the sentiment of every heart,
the only question being as to ways and means.

The Conference grouped together India, China, Japan, Chosen (Korea), and the Philippine Islands as the Asiatic Division,
and elected I. H. Evans, who had been serving as treasurer of
the General Conference, to the superintendency of this great
territory, in order that his large experience in administration
and finance might be used in putting the work in these far-off
mission fields, on a thoroughly sound basis.

W. T. Knox was called to the treasurership of the General
Conference, and to him fell the chief responsibility of working
out the details of mission finance, and providing a steady flow
of means for the support of the rapidly extending work. The
growth in the regular offerings in the years following this
Conference was very encouraging.

The General Conference of 1918 was held in San Francisco,
Calif. It was decided at this meeting to discontinue the full
division organization for North America, which had been inaugurated at the Conference of 1913. A. G. Daniells was re-elected
president of the General Conference, and I. H. Evans, who had
been president of the North American Division for the four-
year period, 1913-18, was elected vice-president for the Asiatic
Division. Moreover, in view of the growth in the great mission
fields of the Far East, India and Burma, which had been added
to the Asiatic Division, were separated, and placed in charge of
H. R. Salisbury, the Far Eastern Division henceforth consisting of Japan with her dependencies, China, the Malay States,
Indo-China, the Dutch East Indies, Borneo, and the Philippines.
E. E. Andross was made vice-president for North America.

Europe was represented at this conference by L. R. Conradi
and a few leading brethren. Measures were taken to render

necessary assistance to our brethren in the countries devastated by the Great War.

The Conference of 1918 was remarkable for one thing: Mrs. E. G. White was not present, and there was no message from her pen addressed to that particular Conference. The trusted spiritual leader, whose messages of encouragement and reproof had been exerting a powerful influence over all branches of the work for more than sixty years, had passed away.

Since returning from Australia in 1900, Mrs. White had made her home near St. Helena, Calif. She had attended the General Conferences of 1901, 1905, and 1909, and had sent a stirring message to the Conference of 1913. She had also visited many different parts of the field, carrying with her everywhere a strong influence to build up the work along even lines, and especially emphasizing the need of a higher spirituality on the part not only of workers, but of laymen. In this country, as in Australia, her pen had been fully employed, not alone with a very extensive correspondence, but also with the preparation of a number of literary works dealing with various phases of Bible truth. Though she was active until the last few weeks, her general health had been failing for some years. The end was probably hastened by a fall about the middle of February, 1915, which caused fracture of the left femur.

The devoted servant who had labored so untiringly in the interests of the cause, died at her home, July 16, 1915. The sunny upper chamber in which her last weeks were spent, breathed an atmosphere of peace and tranquillity. The last words she uttered were characteristic of the faith and courage that went with her through her life: " I know in whom I have believed."

Services were held at " Elmshaven," her home near St. Helena, and in Oakland, and also at Battle Creek, where interment was made in the presence of a large number of sorrowing friends. S. N. Haskell preached the sermon in the Tabernacle, which many years ago Mrs. White and her husband had been largely instrumental in erecting. A. G. Daniells, the president of the General Conference, and for years closely associated with Mrs. White, presented a sketch of her life. The servant of God rests from her labors, but her influence continues. It is doubtful if that influence was ever stronger among us as a people than it is today.

The delegation at the General Conference of 1922 was the largest in the history of the denomination, numbering 582, of whom 461 were from North America, and 121 from other parts

RESTING PLACE OF ELDER AND MRS. JAMES WHITE, BATTLE CREEK, MICHIGAN

Photograph taken at the burial service of Mrs. E. G. White, July 24, 1915.

of the world. In this assembly, as in every Conference since 1901, the demands of the world field were paramount. No new principles were enunciated, no really new plans were made; but the work was considered in its world-wide aspects, and action was taken for pushing it forward to completion.

At this meeting, A. G. Daniells was relieved of the heavy administrative burdens he had carried for twenty-one years, and W. A. Spicer, who had been intimately associated with him in the work, having served continuously as missions and general secretary since 1901, was called to the presidency. W. T. Knox retired from his work as treasurer, and J. L. Shaw was elected to that office. C. H. Watson, of Australia, was elected vice-president. There were some other changes in personnel which are noted in the chapters dealing with the various lines of work. A. G. Daniells was chosen secretary of the General Conference, and C. K. Meyers associate secretary.

There was one familiar figure absent from the General Conference of 1922. George I. Butler, president of the General Conference for eleven years, had passed away. In the last few years of his life he held no administrative position, but was active in writing for the denominational papers, and also did some preaching. Elder Butler had a large place in the affections of the rank and file of our people. His death occurred at Healdsburg, Calif., July 25, 1918.

A very few days later, R. C. Porter, another of our honored leaders who was born and brought up in Iowa, and was baptized by Elder Butler at the age of thirteen, passed away at his old home in Hamilton, Mo. Elder Porter began his ministry in Nebraska, and later became president of the Minnesota Conference, of the Atlantic Union Conference, and after that of the South African Union Conference. At the General Conference of 1913 he was called to the presidency of the Asiatic Division, where the hardships incident to long journeys under tropical conditions brought on a physical breakdown. Elder Porter was a keen Bible student as well as an able administrator. He was greatly loved by his associates, and the work prospered under his care. He died July 29, 1918, a little more than sixty years of age.

Though they remained a little longer with us, it seems appropriate in this connection to mention two other standard-bearers who were associated for many years with the work of the message. S. N. Haskell was in fair health at the General Conference of 1922, and sat on the platform with others of the honored pioneers in the movement. Soon after the meeting was over he began to grow weaker, and was obliged to give up his work. The end came at National City, Calif., the revered leader being then in his ninetieth year.

Elder Haskell was of New England. stock, and born at Oakham, Mass., April 22, 1833. He came to a knowledge of the advent message through reading our publications, and early in his work began to show a special interest in organized efforts

THREE VETERANS
S. N. Haskell   J. N. Loughborough   G. I. Butler

to circulate our tracts and papers. His eminent services in connection with the International Tract Society and as a pioneer worker in Australasia, South Africa, and Europe, have been recorded in earlier chapters. During the last few years of his life he devoted his time to literary work, and to the conducting of Bible studies at camp-meetings and other large assemblies. His favorite hour for these studies was at half-past five or six in the morning. The presentation was marked by quiet earnestness, the attendance kept up well, and the people felt that they were fed spiritually.

J. N. Loughborough was not able to attend the General Conference of 1922, his advanced age making any such strain inadvisable. The active career of our revered brother is dealt with at some length in early chapters of this book. He was prominently connected with the beginnings of the advent movement, being ordained to the gospel ministry at the early age of twenty-two, and continuing his work faithfully till the infirmities of age made it necessary to lay off the heavier burdens. Elder Loughborough pioneered our work in California and in Great Britain, and was for a number of years very closely associated with Elder and Mrs. White in the building up of the general interests of the cause.

In 1908, being then seventy-six years of age, Elder Loughborough began a tour of the world, in the course of which he visited all our leading centers in Europe, Africa, and Australia. His presence everywhere imparted new life and interest to believers, for he could speak authoritatively concerning many features of the work in its beginning. After returning from this trip, he settled at Lodi, Calif., occasionally making short trips to camp-meetings and other gatherings, where his accounts of early experiences were listened to with great interest.

Elder Loughborough was the author of many tracts and pamphlets as well as of that well-known work, " The Great Second Advent Movement." He wrote much for our leading papers. To the very end of his long life he took a lively interest in all things pertaining to the early history of our work, and was indefatigable in his efforts to assist any who were endeavoring to get data on the subject. The last few years were spent quietly at the St. Helena Sanitarium, where he passed away April 7, 1924, being then ninety-two years of age.

There is one laborer fortunately still with us, and yet so fully identified with the aggressive evangelistic work carried on in the Middle West and other parts of this country in the eighties, that it does not seem out of place to mention his name with those of men with whom he was so long intimately associated. When E. W. Farnsworth addressed the delegates on the second Sabbath morning of the General Conference of 1922, there were many gray-haired men present who in their early youth knew him as the most eloquent and untiring of camp-meeting preachers in the days when camp-meetings were great events. Elder Farnsworth served for years on the General Conference Committee, and has done very acceptable work as a Bible teacher; but it is as a preacher of the word that his name will always be held in loving remembrance. No man in the denomination ever gave himself more unreservedly to this great calling, and no one reached a larger number of people with the definite gospel message. May he long be spared to us!

VICE-PRESIDENTS OF THE GENERAL CONFERENCE, 1925

L. H. Christian   I. H. Evans   O. Montgomery
J. E. Fulton   C. H. Watson   E. E. Andross
P. E. Brodersen   W. H. Branson   A. W. Cormack

OFF TO THE MISSION FIELDS

A group of missionaries on the deck of the S. S. "Empress of China," about to sail for the Orient.

CHAPTER XLI

Recent Developments Outside of North America

IN giving the reader some idea of the recent progress in countries outside of North America, we shall not attempt a complete recital of what has been done. To write the annals of the last ten years would require a book all by itself; for the work has grown rapidly, and the number of those who have acted a leading part is very considerable. We shall simply record a few representative facts and incidents, and shall give these largely in the words of those who are on the ground doing the work. The following pages are accordingly based largely on reports made by delegates at the Council held in Des Moines, Iowa, in the autumn of 1924. We have also drawn freely from the recent jubilee number of the *Review and Herald,* which came out about the same time. The reader will kindly note that these pages are intended to be illuminating and suggestive rather than complete.

Europe Since the War

The territory included in the European Division is Europe and those portions of Asia and Africa not included in other divi-

731

sions. Since the World War, conditions in some countries have been almost as hard as while the great conflict was going on. The financial situation has perhaps been the most difficult to deal with. But the message is going with power. When a preacher hires a large hall in any of the great centers, it is sure to be filled.

Our books are being widely circulated, though many of the colporteurs spend a portion of their time in prison. Yet they go right on with their work, just as the apostles used to do. The gospel is everything to these people.

The year 1924 marked the fiftieth anniversary of our work in Europe. Ten union conferences had their annual meetings during the year. At one of these there were present more than 5,000 Adventists on the Sabbath; at another, 2,000. Hearts and doors are open everywhere. In the summer of 1924 our brethren in Russia held a conference at Moscow, attended by eighty-five delegates from all parts of Russia and Siberia. The government turned over to them one of the largest halls in Moscow, and advertised the meetings. We now hold open-air meetings in Russia, and baptize our converts in a stream on Sunday, with a crowd to witness the ceremony.

From very small beginnings in Europe in educational, sanitarium, and publishing institutions, we now (1925) have eighteen schools, with an aggregate attendance of 1,050 students; and four sanitariums, with a capacity for 700 patients. We are printing the truth in twenty different places, and in seventy-five languages. More than 1,200 colporteurs are busy the year round selling our publications, among which are included thirty-one periodicals.

Our mission funds everywhere show similar growth. For example, in 1888 our brethren in England contributed $700 to the work. In 1923 they contributed more than $140,000. The early efforts of Elder Matteson in Scandinavia cost less than $500 a year; last year (1924) the Scandinavian Union raised in tithes and offerings more than $185,000 for work in their own borders and in foreign fields. In Germany the work began later, hardly before 1886; but there it won its greatest triumphs, so that while their currency remained stable, our German conferences did their full share in supporting the general cause. In 1914 we had 14,234 believers in the three German unions; ten years later the membership was 32,011. In Russia the membership doubled from 1914 to 1924. In the Catholic countries of the large Latin Union, with its population of 140,000,000, the work is making a good growth, and is largely self-supporting.

The European Division also has large mission interests. In 1901, shortly after our first missionaries from America started for the Orient, Europe sent missionaries into Africa, and later into Asia. Today we have missionaries, schools, and churches in Sierra Leone, Nigeria, and the Gold Coast, Algeria, Tunis, Morocco, Egypt, Abyssinia, the British possessions of East Africa, in Mesopotamia, Persia, the Holy Land, and Asia Minor. Our people in Europe feel that they should carry the message not merely to the countries of Europe, but also to the large sections of the mission field which have been assigned to the European Division. Since the World War the European conferences have sent out more than sixty missionaries to foreign fields.

The Far Eastern Division

The territory of the Far Eastern Division of the General Conference includes the countries of Japan, China with her dependencies, eastern Siberia (extending to Lake Baikal), Siam, the Federated Malay States, Indo-China, the Dutch East Indies, Borneo, and the Philippine Islands. The combined population is 640,000,000.

The field is divided into eleven union missions, which are subdivided into forty-four missions and two organized local conferences. Each union mission is administered by an executive committee, the chairman of which is called the superintendent; while each local mission is presided over by a local committee with its chairman, who is called the director.

There are in the employ of the Far Eastern Division, 282 foreign workers and 486 native workers. Should we include the native teachers in our schools, the employees in the printing houses and sanitariums, and the colporteurs, the working force would number 982 natives. This would make, including natives and foreign workers, a total working force of 1,278.

We have, in the countries named, five advanced training schools, which are prepared to give fourteen grades of work. In addition to these, there are twelve intermediate schools that carry work to the ninth or tenth grade, and 131 church schools.

There are five printing plants,— one each in Japan, Korea, China, the Philippines, and Malaysia. In 1923 we sold more than $170,000 worth of literature, printed in twenty-eight languages. We are publishing twelve periodicals, five of which are missionary magazines, with an aggregate monthly circulation of 100,000.

The condition of the masses almost everywhere is pitiful, and yet it has been difficult to secure help to promote medical

MEMBERS OF THE EUROPEAN COUNCIL, SKODSBORG. DENMARK

missionary work. We have a little dispensary in Korea, where our workers can minister to the people and give treatments to the sick. The number who can be helped is limited, however, by meager facilities and few workers. In' Honan, China, there is a hospital dispensary that was built up by the faithful work of Dr. D. E. Davenport and his co-laborers. In Shanghai we have tried to conduct a little sanitarium, but are greatly hampered in carrying on our work by lack of funds. We have a little dispensary hospital in Nanning, Kwangsi. Canton, the Philippines, and other parts of the field are pleading for a physician and a small hospital where medical help can be given the people.

Evangelistic efforts are meeting with a fair degree of success. In 1918 the number of believers was 4,500; in 1924 it was more than 13,000. The membership of the Sabbath schools is more than 18,000, and many who have not joined the church are keeping the Sabbath, and are following on to know the Lord.

In many places the message enters by means of unforeseen agencies. The work began in Borneo through the visit to that island of a Chinese brother who volunteered to go there. He raised up a church, and then asked that a minister be sent to baptize the believers.

In the same way a Chinese convert opened the work in Siam, and prepared thirty-two converts there for baptism. One of the workers, a native of Celebes, was taken ill. He said he would like to go home to his father and mother and see if he could regain his health. He did so, and while he was recuperating, he talked the truth. Soon a letter came, stating that twenty-five had begun to keep the Sabbath. Many similar instances might be given. The whole East is ripe for the harvest. If men could be provided to follow up the openings, there is no limit to what could be accomplished.

The Australasian Union

The territory of the Australasian Union includes Australia, New Zealand, Tasmania, and practically all our denominational missions among the South Sea Islands.

The membership in 1924 was about 9,000, including a fair number of native believers in the various island groups. The island work is extending. A new field of labor — the Loyalty group, near New Caledonia — was entered in 1924.

More than a million dollars' worth of books were sold in the eight years from 1914 to 1921. In 1922 alone publications to the value of $222,000 were placed in the homes of the people.

The chief educational center is at Avondale, Cooranbong, New South Wales, where a college has been established. Educational institutions of growing importance are also found in New Zealand and West Australia. Schools for native workers have been established in the different island groups.

In connection with the college at Avondale, there has been built up a large and successful health food factory.

The New Zealand health food factory, at Christchurch, erected in 1921, was enlarged in 1923, and is running to its full capacity. At Wahroonga we have a large sanitarium, which is a training center for nurses.

South America

The South American Division, as organized in 1916, includes eight republics and the Falkland Islands, all lying south of the equator except portions of Brazil and Ecuador. The field is naturally divided into two language areas. Seven of the eight republics, with a population of 26,000,000, speak the Spanish language, while Portuguese is the prevailing language of Brazil with her 30,000,000. The four unions comprising the division are subdivided into six conferences and eighteen missions.

F. H. Westphal, our first ordained minister to South America, began his work in the Argentine Republic in 1894. F. W. Spies answered a call to Brazil in 1896, and all these years has labored as minister and executive. He is still doing aggressive work as president of the East Brazil Union. In 1901 J. W. Westphal went to the field. He settled in Argentina, and for years stood at the head of the entire field as president of the South American Union. He became the outstanding figure as administrator in the early development of our work there.

At the time of the reorganization of the field, in 1916, O. Montgomery was chosen vice-president. The plans and policies put into operation, beginning with this period, proved, under God, a blessing, bringing to our work financial strength and considerable increases in membership. When Elder Montgomery was called to be vice-president for North America in 1922, Charles Thompson took over the work in South America for a time, till failing health made it necessary for him to return to the United States. In 1924 P. E. Brodersen became vice-president of the General Conference for South America. W. H. Williams has served as secretary-treasurer and auditor of the division since 1916.

At the close of 1923 the number of organized churches was 148, and the total membership 12,505. Of this number 4,155 were gained during the first twenty years, and 8,350 during the last nine years. The membership gain in 1923 amounted to 1,501, which is the highest net increase in any year of our work in South America.

The two missionary magazines, *O Atalaia* (Portuguese) and *El Atalaya* (Spanish), have become a power in the field. Our Spanish magazine (30,000 circulation) is self-sustaining.

In 1908 a sanitarium was established in the province of Entre Rios, Argentina. Dr. G. B. Replogle joined the staff in 1909. Several classes of nurses have been graduated from the institution, and workers have been supplied for the Lake Titicaca Mission. Since Dr. Habenicht returned to the United States in 1923, due to failing health, Dr. Carlos Westphal has taken the superintendency of the institution. In the Inca Union we are operating seventeen dispensaries, besides a small hospital conducted by Dr. Theron Johnston in Juliaca, Peru.

Our five training schools, ever keeping before them the objective of winning souls, are developing our young people for service. The Brazil Training School, eight years old, graduated in 1922 its first class of eight bright young people, all of whom immediately entered the work. The River Plate Training School in 1923 graduated twelve from its academic course. These also were placed in active service.

During the school year (1923-24) there were enrolled in our training schools 536, and in our church and mission schools 4,588 students, or a total of 5,124.

Our first Indian mission was established by F. A. Stahl at Plateria, Bolivia, in 1911. He worked among them ten years, but was compelled to leave the high altitude, and E. H. Wilcox was chosen superintendent of the work in the Lake Titicaca Mission. In 1920 Orley Ford was chosen to pioneer the work in Ecuador, and Reid Shepard was called to open up the work among the Aymara Indians of Bolivia. The latter established a mission station at Rosario.

There are four points from which we are directing the Indian work. More than five thousand believers have been baptized, the greater number being from the Aymara tribe. In connection with the mission stations, seventeen medical dispensaries and seventy-five schools are being operated, with a combined enrolment of 3,929 students.

The Inter-American Division

The Inter-American Division was organized as a separate unit in 1922, E. E. Andross being elected vice-president of the

47

General Conference for the division. The territory extends from Rio Grande River along the northern boundary of Mexico to the northern boundary of Brazil and Ecuador in South America. It also reaches across the Caribbean Sea, and includes the West India Islands and the Bahamas.

The division includes three unions,— the Antillean, the Aztec, and the Caribbean. In these unions there are three organized conferences and eleven organized mission fields. The total number of organized churches is 211, and the membership 8,532. During 1923 there were 1,098 baptisms. The total offerings for church purposes amounted to $155,469.76.

In the division there are seven training schools, all industrial. Four are Spanish, two English, and one French. The West Caribbean Training School is conducting a Spanish department. The West Indian Training School in Jamaica is carrying its students through thirteen grades. This is the largest, and in some ways the best equipped, school in the field.

The publishing house at Cristobal, Canal Zone, is supplying our field with Spanish as well as English literature. The year 1923 was the best in its history, the total literature sales amounting to $156,425.40.

Our 342 Sabbath schools had 10,920 members in 1923. These schools are training centers for our entire church membership and the children. There is great love for the Sabbath school in this field. Some of the members hold a perfect attendance record for five years.

The Present Work in Africa

At present there are in the southern half of Africa, excluding Tanganyika and Kenya, seventy-nine Adventist church organizations, scattered from Cape Town to the heart of the great Belgian Congo. These churches are organized into twelve local conferences and mission fields, three union organizations, with another rapidly developing in the north, and a General Conference Division. The South African Union comprises the political union of South Africa, and the Bechuanaland Protectorate; the Zambesi Union Mission includes the two Rhodesias and Nyasaland; while the South Atlantic United Missions comprise the territories of Portuguese West Africa and (German) Southwest Africa. The Congo has its own union mission organization.

The membership of this division stands today at just over 5,000, although the total number of Sabbath keepers is 9,245. It is the policy of the field to require the native people who accept the truth to wait one or two years, and sometimes longer, before being baptized, in order that they may have opportunity to prove themselves; for this reason the number of Sabbath keepers always greatly exceeds the number of church members. There were 635 baptisms reported for the last quarter of 1923.

The fourth quarter's report of 1923 shows a total of 274 Sabbath schools in this field, with a membership of 12,058. The believers contributed more than $100,000 during 1923 in tithes and mission offerings, besides several thousand dollars for home missionary and church work. Of this amount, $10,654 was given by our native churches, and the rest by the European believers.

The mission offerings alone for the entire field in 1923 amounted to $44,355. This shows an increase over 1920 of $24,272. The European membership reached its goal of 60 cents a week for the first time in 1923. Thus the believers in South Africa have taken their place beside their brethren in other lands, sharing equally in the burdens and responsibilities of speeding the message on to the heathen world.

The literature sales now amount to about $50,000 annually. The publishing work has become one of the strongest factors in disseminating the truth throughout the entire field.

The institutions of the African Division consist of a sanitarium at Plumstead, Cape; a publishing house at Kenilworth; a training college at Ladysmith; five mission training schools, nine mission stations, and one medical mission. Several new missions are being established this year, and a number of medical dispensaries are being opened. Besides these, there are several self-supporting medical institutions, situated in some of the cities of South Africa, which have been doing good work for years, and exerting an influence in favor of the truth.

One thing to remember about the situation in Africa is that these poor, ignorant natives are pleading with us to let them come to our schools. They tell us they have heard rumors that God is with this people, and that we are teaching His Word and they feel that they must come and learn more. A worker in Northern Rhodesia writes:

" It is certainly hard for us to keep pace with the work. We have more openings than we can fill. . . . They [natives] build schoolhouses and homes for the teachers, and then come to the mission and say, ' We have the schoolhouses and the homes. You cannot deny us a teacher now.' And no less than twenty times in that one field during this year have we had to send them back and say, ' We are sorry, but we have no more money to pay teachers. You will have to go back and wait.' I know of places where they have been waiting for years, with the promise every year that perhaps by another year we could send them help."

W. A. SPICER
President of the General Conference 1922 to ————.

SEVENTH-DAY ADVENTIST CHURCH, TAKOMA PARK,
WASHINGTON, D. C.

CHAPTER XLII

The General Trend in North America

IN North America the general line of development in the last quarter of a century has been what might be expected from the history recorded in the earlier chapters of this book. After the great disappointment, the advent message, in the clearer light that grew out of that experience, was preached mainly in New England in the late forties. In 1852 the office of publication of the *Advent Review* was moved to Rochester, N. Y., and three years later it was taken farther west to Battle Creek, Mich., which continued to be the headquarters of the denomination for nearly fifty years.

It was in 1903, two years after the memorable General Conference of 1901, in which the denomination first began to lay its plans on a broader world basis, that the decision was made to transfer the headquarters to the capital of the nation. The move was indicative of the developments which have followed. While Battle Creek was the center, the work grew rapidly in the Mississippi Valley, and spread northward into Canada, westward to the Pacific Coast, and in the latter part of the century began to make encouraging progress in the South. During this half-century, the great bulk of the believers, old and new, were living in the United States; the money raised in the denomination was nearly all spent in this country; and the growth and development were largely here.

Nevertheless, during these years there was seed-sowing on a small scale also in other parts of the world. The printed page had entered many different countries, and General Conference operations in foreign lands had reached a stage in the middle nineties where the lack of adequate financial support created serious embarrassment. The interest in world evangelization had gone in advance of a world program of financial support.

At the General Conference of 1901 the proposition was first definitely advanced that the financial resources of the denomination should be pooled to give the advent message to the world. Before that time each local conference used the funds raised within its boundaries largely for its own work, barring a small percentage sent to the General Conference for the support of the central organization. After that meeting the conception gradually prevailed that the work is one the world over; that strong conferences should assist weak ones; and that believers in America shou d give freely for the support of the work in all parts of the woi ld. With the adoption of this plan, not only have the foreign mission offerings grown rapidly, but the regular tithe raised in the various conferences and unions for their local work has been shared with the General Conference for the support of the work in other lands.

Following such a program has necessarily involved some limitation as regards aggressive evangelistic efforts in the home field. But the taking over of the responsibility for a world effort has undoubtedly strengthened the *morale* of the home churches, and has made for the development of a finer type of Christian character.

The work in this country can be most easily understood if we regard America as the base for supplies of men and of means. The growth of our educational system, which has been recorded in other chapters of the book, is best understood in the light of the great demand for trained workers of all kinds. Our various sanitariums are likewise educational centers. The publishing houses are training men and women both within their walls and out in the field, and they have in their employment the largest number of trained workers in the denomination.

Moreover, our union and State conferences are continually training young evangelists and secretarial workers, as well as leaders
in all other lines of conference activity, in order that the most
promising of these may at the proper time enter the foreign
field.

On such a régime the work in this country will show a
higher degree of efficiency,— increased power to do the thing
expected of it,— rather than growth in numbers, and the latter
will be looked for in the work throughout the world. This is
in harmony with the facts. There has been a fair growth in
this country, as shown by the fact that while our membership
in 1901 was 61,916, in 1924 it was 106,941. But the membership
in other lands has in this same period increased from 16,272 to
123,891. Beyond this, the mission funds raised in America
during this same period increased from $162,206.80 in 1901
to $2,354,689.74 in 1924, thus showing that as a base for mis-
sion supplies the home churches have increased in efficiency at
a considerably higher rate than they have grown in members.

An encouraging feature of the work in North America is
the unanimity with which this world policy is being carried out.
Although all the General Conferences thus far, and most of
the General Conference Councils, have been held in the United
States, yet ever since 1901 by far the greater share of attention
at all these meetings has been devoted to world problems. In
fact, the time spent on North America has been devoted chiefly
to considering what it can do to further the work in foreign
fields.

In previous chapters we have told how the great question
of giving the message to the world occupied the energies of
the General Conferences from 1901 to 1922 inclusive. The same
thing has been true of the annual councils held between these
larger gatherings. Furthermore, this attention to the foreign
fields is not dependent on the number of delegates from those
fields. Some of the most important measures have been passed
when there have been present very few workers from countries
outside the United States.

This deep interest in the work overseas was a very marked
feature of the Fall Council held in Milwaukee in 1923, and
again at the Council the following year in Des Moines, Iowa.
At the Milwaukee meeting there was deep concern over the
financial conditions in Europe, and a desire to render such
effective assistance that the work should not suffer in that field
because of a lack of funds. At the meeting held a year later
the delegates from Europe reported a much more favorable out-

look, and yet the desire to plan for more aggressive work in that great field was in no way diminished. Perhaps the needs of the great Far Eastern Division made a still stronger appeal. Africa, South America, and the South Asiatic also received much serious consideration.

When Prof. Frederick Griggs and Dr. H. W. Miller expressed their conviction that they should devote themselves to the work in the Far East, it was an emphatic recognition of the needs of that great field. Professor Griggs, as head of one of our largest senior colleges, was already training workers for all fields. Dr. Miller was superintendent of one of our largest sanitariums, where his surgical skill was a very vital factor in the building up of the institution. It seemed almost impossible to spare these men from the positions of large responsibility that they already held; but the managing boards of the two institutions yielded to the call of the field as it came to these men, and the workers in the Far East rejoiced over the accession of two strong, experienced leaders.

There was another significant action taken at this Fall Council in Des Moines. It was strongly recommended that the institutions in this country limit their expenses in every possible way, getting along with present facilities, even at considerable inconvenience, in order that enterprises abroad might have needed support. Here, again, the principle prevailed that the home field should share as far as possible in the hardships and difficulties that must necessarily be met in foreign fields.

It was in line with the general policy outlined above that the North American Division began at once to devote special attention to the plans for paying off the debts on its institutions, especially academies and colleges. It was resolved also to follow in future a strict budget arrangement year by year, so that it will be impossible for debts to accumulate. This plan, in fact, is strongly advised for the institutions of the denomination throughout the world.

The closing word in this narrative cannot be otherwise than hopeful. From the earliest beginnings of the denomination there has been growth along all lines,— growth in conception of the work in its larger possibilities, and growth in actual numbers of those to whom the work is more precious than life itself. Moreover, in the last few years the rate of progress in most parts of the world, has been accelerated. While the greatness of the task yet to be done seems appalling, it is well to remember, after all, that the work to be done, and the agents brought into requisition to do it, are all in the hands of the great Master Workman. Adventists feel as Luther did at Worms, when he said in his prayer: " Lord, this is not my work, it is Thine; Thou Thyself must do it." It is right for the believers in this message to give their all to see it carried to the ends of the earth. Whole-hearted consecration of all one has and is,— this alone is Christianity. But having done this, which in a sense is our part, we may rest assured that God will not fail to do His part, for His Word declares that " He will finish the work, and cut it short in righteousness: because a short work will the Lord make upon the earth." There is nothing impossible with God.

HOW FAR FROM HOME?

How far from home? I asked, as on
    I bent my steps — the watchman spake:
" The long, dark night is almost gone,
    The morning soon will break.
Then weep no more, but speed thy flight,
    With Hope's bright star thy guiding ray,
Till thou shalt reach the realms of light,
    In everlasting day."

I asked the warrior on the field;
    This was his soul-inspiring song:
" With courage, bold, the sword I'll wield,
    The battle is not long.
Then weep no more, but well endure
    The conflict, till thy work is done;
For this we know, the prize is sure,
    When victory is won."

I asked again; earth, sea, and sun
    Seemed, with one voice, to make reply:
" Time's wasting sands are nearly run,
    Eternity is nigh.
Then weep no more — with warning tones,
    Portentous signs are thickening round,
The whole creation, waiting, groans,
    To hear the trumpet sound."

Not far from home! O blessed thought!
    The traveler's lonely heart to cheer;
Which oft a healing balm has brought,
    And dried the mourner's tear.
Then weep no more, since we shall meet
    Where weary footsteps never roam —
Our trials past, our joys complete,
    Safe in our Father's home.
                        — Annie R. Smith.

A Partial Bibliography

Armitage, Thomas : " A History of the Baptists," 1887.

Backhouse, Edward : " Early Church History to the Death of Constantine ; " edited and enlarged by Charles Tylor, 2d edition, 1885.

Bliss, Sylvester : " Memoir of William Miller," 1853.

Döllinger, John J. I. : " The First Age of Christianity and the Church," translated by N. H. Oxenham, 1906.

Fisher, George P. : " History of the Christian Church," 1913 ; " The Beginnings of Christianity, with a View of the State of the Roman World at the Birth of Christ," 1877.

Gibbon, Edward : " The Decline and Fall of the Roman Empire."

Haldane, Alexander : " Memoirs of the Lives of Robert and James A. Haldane," 1852.

Himes, J. V., Bliss. S., and Hale. A. : *The Advent Shield and Review*, Vol. I, 1844-45 ; *The Signs of the Times*, 1840- .

Hurst, John Fletcher : " The History of Methodism," 1902.

Johnson, Albert C. : " Advent Christian History : A Concise Narrative of the Origin and Progress, Doctrine and Work of This Body of Believers," 1918.

Leonard, Delavan L. : " A Hundred Years of Missions," 1895.

Litch, Josiah : " The Probability of the Second Advent of Christ About A. D. 1843." etc., 1838 ; " Prophetic Exposition, or a Connected View of the Testimony of the Prophets Concerning the Kingdom of God and the Time of Its Establishment," two volumes, 1842.

Loughborough, J. N. : " Rise and Progress of the Seventh-day Adventists," 1892 ; " The Great Second Advent Movement," 1905.

Miller, William : " Evidences from Scripture and History of the Second Coming of Christ About the Year 1843," issued at Troy, N. Y., in 1836 and at Boston in 1842.

Miller, Edward : " The History and Doctrines of Irvingism," two volumes, 1878.

Neander, Augustus : " General History of the Christian Religion and Church," translated from the German by Joseph Torry, 1861.

Newton, Isaac : " Observations upon the Prophecies of Daniel and the Apocalypse of St. John," edition of 1733.

Rogers, H. E. : Seventh-day Adventist Year Book, with historical summary, 1905.

Root, Jean Christie : " Edward Irving, Man, Preacher, Prophet," 1912.

Pierson, Arthur T. : " George Müller of Bristol, with an introduction by J. Wright," 1899.

Richards, George : " The Divine Origin of Prophecy Illustrated and Defended, being the Bampton Lectures for the year 1800.

Rutherford, Samuel : " Letters of, with a Sketch of His Life by A. A. Bonar," 1894.

Scholler, L. W. : " A Chapter of Church History from South Germany. Being Passages from the Life of Johann Evangelist George Lutz," translated from the German by W. Wallis.

Spicer, W. A. : " An Outline of Mission Fields," fourth edition, 1920 ; " Our Story of Missions." 1921.

Tefft, B. F. : " Methodism Successful and the Internal Causes of Its Success," 1860.

Wellcome. Isaac C. : " History of the Second Advent Message and Mission, Doctrine and People," 1874.

Wesley, John : " Notes on the New Testament," based on Bengel's " Gnomon," 1845.

White, Ellen G. : " Experience and Views," 1853 ; " How to Live," 1865 ; " Testimonies for the Church," Vols. I-IX.

White, James and Ellen G. : " Christian Temperance and Bible Hygiene," 1890.

White, James : *Present Truth*, Nos. 1-11, 1849-50 ; " The Early Life and Later Experience and Labors of Elder Joseph Bates," edited by James White, 1878 ; " Sketches of the Christian Life and Public Labors of William Miller," gathered from the memoir by Sylvester Bliss and others, 1875 ; " Life Sketches of James White and Ellen G. White," 1880 ; " Life Incidents in Connection with the Great Advent Movement as Illustrated by the Three Angels of Revelation XIV," 1868.

Wolff, Joseph. : " Researches and Missionary Labors Among the Jews, Mohammedans, and Other Sects," 1837.

Chronological Appendix

Representative Actions and Events in the History of the Advent Movement

1831 First Sunday in August, William Miller preached his first sermon on the coming of Christ.

1832 William Miller began a series of articles on the second advent, in the *Vermont Telegraph* of Brandon, Vt.

1833 March, Miller's first pamphlet published. September 14 he was granted a license to preach by the Baptist Church.

1836 Miller's course of sixteen lectures published in pamphlet form at Troy, N. Y.

1838 About the first of March, Josiah Litch, a Methodist minister of Lowell, Mass., embraced Miller's views, and began to proclaim them by voice and pen. His 48-page pamphlet, " The Midnight Cry," and his book of 204 pages, entitled, " The Probability of the Second Coming of Christ About A. D. 1843," came out this year.

1839 Early in December, Joshua V. Himes, of Boston, Mass., joined William Miller and Josiah Litch in the proclamation of the advent message.

1840 March 20, J. V. Himes began, in Boston, Mass., the publication of the *Signs of the Times*. The paper thus started was published for two years as a semimonthly, and then as a weekly.

March, William Miller gave his first course of lectures in Portland, Maine. They were attended by Ellen G. Harmon, later Mrs. E. G. White.

First " General Conference of Second Advent Believers " convened in the Chardon Street Chapel, in Boston, Mass., October 15, and continued two days.

1841 Second " General Conference of Advent Believers " held in Lowell, Mass., June 15-17.

Third " General Conference of Christians Expecting the Advent of the Lord," in Portland, Maine, Oct. 12, 1841.

Between that date and Feb. 8, 1842, seven similar conferences were held in the New England States.

1842 The *Signs of the Times* has not less than 50,000 readers.

More than 60,000 copies of various books and tracts have been issued from our establishment, and spread through the world in the four quarters of the globe and the islands of the sea. From three to four hundred ministers of the gospel are now engaged in giving the midnight cry.— *Signs of the Times, March 15.*

In the latter part of November, J. V. Himes began the publication, in New York City, of a daily paper entitled, *The Midnight Cry,* principally under the editorial supervision of N. Southard. Twenty-four numbers were published, and ten thousand copies of each number circulated.

During the summer, tent and camp meetings, with large attendance, held in Eastern Canada, Vermont, New Hampshire, Maine, New York, Massachusetts, and New Jersey.

James White attended the camp-meeting at Exeter, Maine, in October, and shortly thereafter went out to give the message.

December, Josiah Litch and A. Hale began public services in Philadelphia.

1843 Different ministers conducted meetings in the South and West, going as far as Richmond, Va., Washington, D. C., Pittsburg, Pa., and Cincinnati, Ohio. Papers devoted to the advent cause were published in Cincinnati, Philadelphia, and Washington; also in Eastern Canada.

James White ordained to the ministry by the Christian Church.

The Methodists, at an annual meeting held at Bath, Maine, passed resolutions condemning the advent teaching. Opposition on the part of the churches was becoming general.

1844 A second advent camp-meeting was held in the late summer at Exeter, N. H., following which the belief became general among the followers of William Miller that Christ would come Oct. 22, 1844.

Seventh-day Sabbath first brought to the attention of the Adventist people at Washington, N. H., by Mrs. Rachel D. Preston, a Seventh Day Baptist, from the State of New York.

From this place, several Adventist ministers received the Sabbath truth during 1844. One of these, T. M. Preble, put his convictions in writing.

1845 Preble's article on the Sabbath, dated Feb. 13, 1845, was written at East Wear, N. H., and was printed in the *Hope of Israel*, Portland, Maine, Feb. 28, 1845. It was rewritten by Elder Preble in March, 1845, and published in tract form. It was referred to by J. H. Waggoner, and briefly quoted by him in the *Review and Herald* of Dec. 21, 1869. Aug. 23, 1870, Preble's article as it appeared in the *Hope of Israel*, was printed in full in the *Review.*

Ellen G. Harmon given her first vision, on "The Travels of the Advent People to the Holy City."

Joseph Bates began keeping the Sabbath as a result of reading the article by T. M. Preble in the *Hope of Israel.*

1846 James White married to Ellen Gould Harmon, August 30.

Two-page leaflet by Mrs. E. G. White, entitled, "To the Remnant Scattered Abroad," published.

1848 First general meeting of Sabbath keepers, held at Rocky Hill, Conn., April 20, 21.

Mrs. E. G. White had vision concerning the beginning of the publishing work.

1849 First four numbers of *Present Truth* printed at Middletown, Conn., No. 1 dated July; Nos. 5 and 6 printed in Oswego, N. Y.

J. N. Andrews publicly took his stand for the truth in a meeting at Paris, Maine, September 14.

First number of the *Second Advent Review and Sabbath Herald*, printed in Paris, Maine, in November.

Death of William Miller, December 20. (Born Feb. 5, 1782.)

First Testimony for the Church, addressed " To Those Who Are Receiving the Seal of the Living God." Signed " E. G. White."

First hymn book used by the denomination published by James White. It contained fifty-three hymns, without tunes.

1850 Nos. 7 to 10 of *Present Truth* printed in Oswego, N. Y. No. 11 printed in Paris, Maine, in November.

1851 First number of second volume *Advent Review and Sabbath Herald*, dated August 5, printed at Saratoga Springs, N. Y.

Annie R. Smith took her stand for the truth, and entered the employ of the Review office at Saratoga Springs.

1852 First number of the *Advent Review and Sabbath Herald* published at Rochester, N. Y., bore date of May 6.

James White equipped the first printing office with money received in donations. Donations amounted to $655.84. The cost of equipment was $652.95. The first press bought was a Washington hand press.

First number of the *Youth's Instructor* appeared in August.

J. N. Loughborough kept his first Sabbath, October 2.

Uriah Smith observed his first Sabbath in December.

J. H. Waggoner accepted the message, and was ordained to the gospel ministry.

1853 Uriah Smith connected with the *Review and Herald*, May 3.

First subscription price put on publications was $1 for 26 numbers of the *Review*.

First regular Sabbath schools organized in Rochester and Buck's Bridge, N. Y.

1854 First tent-meeting conducted by J. N. Loughborough and M. E. Cornell at Battle Creek, Mich., June 10-12.

First sale of denominational publications at a tent-meeting in Rochester, Mich. A parcel containing one copy each of all tracts and pamphlets published, sold for 35 cents, price being fixed by J. N. Loughborough.

1855 Annie R. Smith died July 26.

Review office moved to Battle Creek, Mich. First number of *Review* printed there bore date of December 4.

1856 Name of S. N. Haskell first appeared in the *Review*, January 31.

1858 Bible class, conducted by J. N. Andrews, held in Battle Creek, Mich., in April. Its object was to learn what the Scriptures teach concerning the support of the ministry This effort resulted in the adoption of the plan known as " systematic benevolence," or the tithing principle.

1860 Name Seventh-day Adventist adopted for the denomination October 1.

On the same day a temporary organization, known as the Advent Review Publishing Association, was formed in Battle Creek, Mich.

1861 Seventh-day Adventist Publishing Association (now Review and Herald Publishing Association) incorporated May 1.

Churches first formally organized.

Michigan organized as the first State conference, October 5.

1862 Other conferences organized: Southern Iowa, March 16; Northern Iowa, May 10; Vermont, June 15; Illinois and Wisconsin, September 28; Minnesota, October 4; New York, October 25.

1863 General Conference organized at a meeting held in Battle Creek, Mich., May 20-23. Meeting was called by James White, J. N. Loughborough, and John Byington. There were twenty duly elected delegates, representing the work in six States.

John Byington elected first president of the General Conference May 21.

1864 August 29, Elder J. N. Andrews left Battle Creek for Washington, D. C., where he was successful in securing for Seventh-day Adventists in the army, recognition as being conscientiously opposed to taking human life even in war, and their assignment to noncombatant service in hospitals, etc.

1865 First health publication, " How to Live," published. Written and compiled by Mrs. E. G. White.

James White elected president of the General Conference, May 17.

1866 First denominational health journal published, bearing the name *Health Reformer*, August 1.

Health Reform Institute (Battle Creek Sanitarium) opened for patients September 5.

1867 J. N. Andrews elected president of the General Conference, May 14.

The Health Reform Institute incorporated, April 9.

1868 First California State gathering of Seventh-day Adventists held near Santa Rosa, April 10, 11.

James White again became president of the General Conference, May 12.

First general camp-meeting held at Wright, Mich., September 1-7.

First local tract and missionary society organized in South Lancaster, Mass., known as " The Vigilant Missionary Society."

1870 First conference tract and missionary society organized, November 6, called " Missionary and Tract Society of the New England Conference of Seventh-day Adventists."

1871 Tenth annual session of the General Conference convened in Battle Creek, Mich., December 29, with fourteen delegates present, representing twelve conferences and one mission.

George I. Butler succeeded James White as president.

1872 Joseph Bates died in Battle Creek, Mich., March 19, at the age of eighty. He was buried at Monterey, Mich.

First denominational school opened, June 3, at Battle Creek, Mich., G. H. Bell in charge.

1873 Eleventh session of the General Conference, Battle Creek, Mich., March 11. There were eighteen delegates representing thirteen conferences and one mission.

Total number of ministers, 51; licentiates, 83; churches, 239; membership, 5,875; systematic benevolence fund pledged to State conferences, $26,246.69.— *Review and Herald, March 18, 1873.*

1874 Seventh-day Adventist Educational Society incorporated March 11.

Main building of Battle Creek College erected.

First number of the *Signs of the Times* issued, Oakland, Calif., June 4.

James White again elected president of General Conference, August 10.

J. N. Andrews, our first foreign missionary, sailed from Boston, September 15.

General Conference Tract and Missionary Society organized.

1875 Main building of Battle Creek College dedicated January 4.

Seventh-day Adventist Publishing Association (now Pacific Press Publishing Association) incorporated at Oakland, Calif., April 1.

Missouri Conference organized June 2.

Kansas Conference organized September 10.

1877 North Pacific Conference organized October 25. (It embraced much of the territory now included in the North Pacific Union.)

First State Sabbath School Association organized in California.

J. G. Matteson sailed for Denmark, beginning his labors at Vejle, in Jutland.

1878 General Conference Sabbath School Association organized, and the first Sabbath school contributions given.

Battle Creek Tabernacle built.

St. Helena Sanitarium established.

1879 First local Young People's Society organized at Hazelton, Mich.

June 7, J. G. Matteson organized a church of thirty-eight members in Christiania, Norway.

A printing house was established in Christiania about the same time, and *Tidernes Tegn* (Signs of the Times) began to be issued.

Mrs. E. G. White wrote her first message regarding house-to-house work with our publications.

Tabernacle in Battle Creek, Mich., dedicated.

1880 First baptism of believers in England, at Southampton, February 8.

George I. Butler again president of General Conference, October 6.

1881 James White died at Battle Creek, Mich., August 6. (Born Aug. 4, 1821.)

1882 Healdsburg (Calif.) school opened April 11; chartered as a college July 29.

South Lancaster (Mass.) Academy opened April 19.

First subscription book, " Thoughts on Daniel and the Revelation," published by the Review and Herald, sold by George A. King, and purchased by D. W. Reavis.

1883 J. N. Andrews died at Basel, Switzerland, October 21. (Born in 1829.)

First Year Book of the denomination issued.

Total number of ministers, 165; licentiates, 135; churches, 680; membership, 17,436; tithes raised during the year, $96,418.62.— *From 1884 Year Book, p. 73.*

1884 First denominational training school for nurses opened at the Battle Creek Sanitarium.

Present Truth issued in England, M. C. Wilcox, editor.

1885 First party of workers for Australia (including S. N. Haskell, J. O. Corliss, and others) sailed from San Francisco.

R. F. Andrews began labor in Ireland.

Mrs. E. G. White and W. C. White visited the believers in Europe, arriving at Basel, Switzerland, in September.

1886 L. R. Conradi sent to Europe in January.

L. R. Conradi made his first visit to Russia. First Seventh-day Adventist church organized in the Crimea.

First number of the Australian *Bible Echo and Signs of the Times* issued in January.

Church organized in Melbourne, April 10.

1887 First European camp-meeting held at Moss, Norway, in June.

First missionaries (D. A. Robinson, C. L. Boyd, and others) sent to South Africa, reaching there in July.

Establishment of local or church schools recommended by the Educational Society.

A. La Rue went as a self-supporting missionary to China.

British Publishing House established at 451 Holloway Road, London, England.

1888 H. P. Holser sent to Europe.

B. L. Whitney died April 9, 1888. (Born Dec. 10, 1845.)

O. A. Olsen elected president of the General Conference, October 17.

1889 Message first reached South America through literature.

J. H. Waggoner died April 17.

National Religious Liberty Association organized July 21. The name was changed later to International Religious Liberty Association; and in 1901 was made a department of the General Conference.

1890 Maria L. Huntley died April 18. (Born in 1847.)

Missionary Ship " Pitcairn " launched in San Francisco Bay, July 28.

1891 Union College established at College View, Nebr.

Mrs. E. G. White and W. C. White, with a group of workers, landed in Australia in December.

1892 Walla Walla College established at Walla Walla, Wash.

1893 Portland (Oreg.) Sanitarium established.

College at Claremont, South Africa, opened February 1.

M. E. Cornell died November 2.

Number of ministers, 244; licentiates, 156; churches, 1,002; membership, 33,778; tithes, $302,310.19; offerings to missions, $75,296.59.— *From the 1894 Year Book, p. 65.*

1893-94 Canvassers pioneered the way in India.

1894 Miss Georgia Burrus reached Calcutta as our first missionary to India.

Missionaries sent to Matabeleland, South Africa, reached Bulawayo, July 4.

F. H. Westphal, our first minister to South America.

Union training school for the three Scandinavian countries opened at Frederikshavn, Denmark.

1895 D. A. Robinson began work in Calcutta, India.

Hamburg Publishing House established in Germany.

1896 Boulder (Colo.) Sanitarium established.

1897 G. A. Irwin elected president of the General Conference February 19.

Publishing House established at Buenos Aires, Argentina, South America.

Sanitarium established in Skodsborg, Denmark.

1898 First number of the *Oriental Watchman* issued in Calcutta; W. A. Spicer, editor.

1899 New England Sanitarium established at South Lancaster, Mass.; removed to Melrose, Mass., 1902.

1901 A. G. Daniells elected president of the General Conference, April 2.
Young People's work organized in connection with the Sabbath School Department.
Duncombe Hall Missionary College, our first British school, established in London, England.
Southern Publishing Association established at Nashville, Tenn.
J. N. Anderson, Mrs. Anderson, and Ida Thompson sailed for China.
H. P. Holser died September 11. (Born Oct. 5, 1856.)

1902 Buildings of the Battle Creek Sanitarium destroyed by fire, February 18.
Main building of the Review and Herald in Battle Creek destroyed by fire, December 30.
Battle Creek College moved to Berrien Springs, Mich.

1903 Uriah Smith died March 6. (Born May 2, 1832.)
A. La Rue died April 26, at Hongkong, China.
Dedication of the new building of the Battle Creek Sanitarium, May 30 to June 1, 1903.
Headquarters of the General Conference moved to Washington, D. C., August 10.
First number of the *Review* printed in Washington, August 20.
At the close of the year there were seventy-eight local conferences and two union missions directing the work. Ministers, 612; licentiates, 324; missionary licentiates, 662; churches, 2,120; membership, 69,072; Sabbath keepers, 77,554; tithes, $684,030.54; offerings to missions, $216,342.98.— *Review and Herald, Aug. 18, 1904.*

1904 September 21 date of the first issue of the *Signs of the Times* after the removal of the Pacific Press Publishing Association from Oakland to Mountain View, Calif.
Hinsdale Sanitarium established at Hinsdale, Ill.
Washington Training College established in Takoma Park, D. C.
Gland (Switzerland) Sanitarium established at Gland, on Lake Geneva.
Paradise Valley Sanitarium established at National City, Calif.

1905 General Conference offices moved from the city of Washington to Takoma Park, Washington, D. C., in February.
Loma Linda (Calif.) Sanitarium established.
Sanitarium established in Glendale, Calif.
Publishing House established in Brazil, South America.
Signs of the Times Publishing House established at Shanghai, China.

1906 Main building of the Pacific Press Publishing Company, Mountain View, Calif., destroyed by fire, July 20.

1907 Name adopted for the Missionary Volunteer Department at the first general Missionary Volunteer Convention, Mount Vernon, Ohio.
First Seventh-day Adventist church organized in Tokio, Japan, in June.
Washington Sanitarium dedicated June 12.

1908 Florida Sanitarium established at Orlando, Fla.
Publishing House established at Tokio, Japan.

1909 Pacific Union College established at St. Helena, Calif. (Post office now Angwin, Calif.)

48

1912 Stanborough Park Sanitarium established at Stanborough Park, Watford, Herts, England.

1913 Far Eastern Division of the General Conference organized.
Total number of workers, 5,248; churches, 3,589; members, 114,557; tithes, $1,771,989.60; home and foreign mission offerings, $1,094,737.80.

1915 O. A. Olsen died January 22, at Hinsdale, Ill. (Born July 28, 1845.)
Mrs. Ellen G. White died July 16, at St. Helena, Calif. (Born Nov. 26, 1827.)
H. R. Salisbury drowned December 30, en route to India on " Persia."

1916 A. C. Bourdeau died July 7.
South American Division of the General Conference organized.

1917 Treatment-rooms established at Shanghai, China.

1918 George I. Butler died July 25. (Born Nov. 12, 1834.)
R. C. Porter died July 29. (Born April 29, 1858.)

1919 Southern Asia Division of the General Conference organized. (India Union Mission since 1910.)
African Division of the General Conference organized.

1922 Tabernacle at Battle Creek destroyed by fire, January 7.
W. A. Spicer elected president of the General Conference, May 11.
S. N. Haskell died in California, October 9. (Born April 22, 1833.)
Inter-American Division of the General Conference organized.

1923 J. O. Corliss died in California, September 17. (Born Dec. 26, 1845.)
Total number of workers, 7,795; churches, 5,096; members, 221,874; tithe, $4,814,554.87; home and foreign mission offerings, $4,382,227.08.

1924 J. N. Loughborough died at the St. Helena Sanitarium, Calif., April 7. (Born Jan. 26, 1832.)

Index